The Encyclopedia of
VAMPIRES, WEREWOLVES,
and OTHER MONSTERS

The Encyclopedia of
VAMPIRES, WEREWOLVES,
and OTHER MONSTERS

Rosemary Ellen Guiley

FOREWORD BY
Jeanne Keyes Youngson,
President and Founder of the Vampire Empire

Facts On File, Inc.

Facts On File, Inc.
132 West 31st Street
New York NY 10001

Library of Congress Cataloging-in-Publication Data
Guiley, Rosemary.
The encyclopedia of vampires, werewolves, and other monsters / Rosemary Ellen Guiley.
p. cm.
Includes bibliographical references and index.
ISBN 0-8160-4684-0 (alk. paper)
1. Vampires—Encyclopedias. 2. Werewolves—Encyclopedias. 3. Monsters—Encyclopedias. I. Title.
BF1556.G86 2004
133.4'23—dc22   2003026592

Facts On File books are available at special discounts when purchased in bulk quantities for businesses, associations, institutions, or sales promotions. Please call our Special Sales Department in New York at (212) 967-8800 or (800) 322-8755.

You can find Facts On File on the World Wide Web at http://www.factsonfile.com

Printed in the United States of America

VB FOF 10 9 8 7 6 5 4 3 2

This book is printed on acid-free paper.

Photo on previous page: *A vampire bat looms above a wrought iron gate in Père-Lachaise Cemetery.* (Author's collection)

For David and Janet Hale

CONTENTS

FOREWORD

by Jeanne Keyes Youngson, Ph.D.
Founder of the Vampire Empire

Of all the creatures in our mythologies and demonologies, the vampire reigns as the most fascinating. Most people knowledgeable about vampires do not start out with the intention of becoming experts. The vampire does, however, have a way of getting into your bloodstream and staying there. At least that is what happened to me many years ago.

I did not just wake up one morning and decide to start the world's first Dracula fan club. It happened over a period of time—and it certainly has been an incredible journey.

This is how it happened: In the early 1960s, I was an animation filmmaker living in New York City with my husband, Robert Youngson, who had won two Oscars for his films *The World of Kids* and *This Mechanical Age*. We were movie mavens and went as often as time permitted. Those were the days of *Brides of Dracula, Horror of Dracula,* and *Dracula, Prince of Darkness,* which I was particularly drawn to, perhaps because I had loved Stoker's *Dracula* so much.

In 1965 I went on my first trip to Romania and learned firsthand about the Wallachian voivode, Vlad Tepes. The guide talked about this national hero nonstop and I, of course, remembered Harry Ludlam mentioning him in *A Biography of Dracula: The Life Story of Bram Stoker.* I suppose the combination of these factors was what started me thinking about starting a Dracula society—which I did as soon as I got back to New York. The original Count Dracula Fan Club was born on June 25, 1965, and, as it turned out, more people than I realized were as interested in the Prince of Darkness as I was.

Robert had a large office at 1 Fifth Avenue, and we had a lot of movie get-togethers where we showed films on his 16-mm projector. One of our regular guests was Edward Gorey, who later did the sets and costumes for John Badham's *Dracula,* starring Frank Langella. Gorey always came laden with gifts and balloons, sometimes with a bag of his latest books. Both Robert and I loved his wry humor and

wonderful stories about ballet. He was a real delight and a most appreciative audience for the movies Bob took such great care to choose.

The Count Dracula Fan Club was an immediate success, and word about the society spread like wildfire. We soon had a long mailing list for our newsletter and almost from the beginning I heard from people who asked all kinds of questions about vampires, wanted to tell me they thought they had become a vampire, or wanted to know how they *could* become one. Sometimes they wanted me to set them up with other blood-drinkers—as though the club was some sort of dating service. One woman wanted to marry a vampire and start her own dynasty! The letters still come in, many of them these days from prison inmates who are desperate for pen pals. And two men on death row inquired about becoming vampires so that they could live on as undeads following execution.

I started collecting Dracula, vampire, and horror memorabilia in 1965 and continued amassing a huge collection, which, I hoped, I could incorporate into a museum when the time was right (1990, as it turned out).

In 1974 Robert died suddenly and unexpectedly. Actor friends in London offered me their flat, and I jumped at the opportunity to live abroad. I had their apartment on Pall Mall for four years and later sublet a house in Cambridge, England, for four more years. I commuted between the United States and England during this time, which meant I could have two active club headquarters, one in the States and one in Britain—the best of all possible worlds.

One of the first things I did once I got to London was join the British Dracula Society, and in 1974 I accompanied them on their first trip to Romania. The journey was, in a way, a turning point in my life, when I realized that my society had far more potential than I had originally thought. Shortly thereafter I gave up filmmaking and turned my complete attention to running the Count Dracula Fan Club.

Through the years, I expanded the society, adding new divisions, which served several niche interests. I gave interviews, spoke at conferences, and fielded innumerable media requests. The public's appetite for vampires became as insatiable as the vampires' own blood lust. By 2000, it was obvious that the Count Dracula Fan Club had grown beyond Stoker's Count and far beyond being "just" a fan club. Vampires and Dracula had hit the big time in all respects and had become a potent force in entertainment, literature and the performing arts, and as pop icons. I renamed the society the *Vampire Empire* at the turn of this century, a title I thought more befitting our extensive modus operandi.

Along the way, I have had the privilege of traveling around the world, and I have met many terrific people, some of whom have become important parts of the Vampire Empire and the entire vampire field as well as close personal friends. One of these persons is Rosemary Ellen Guiley.

I met Rosemary in 1989, when she contacted me for her first book on vampires, *Vampires Among Us*. Having worked with many writers and reporters, I was most impressed with Rosemary's knowledge, professionalism, and thoroughness in research. *Vampires Among Us* became a must-read for vampire fans, and I have no doubt that this encyclopedia will be met with the same enthusiasm. Rosemary has compiled an encyclopedia of astonishing scope and depth, from little-known folklore to arts and entertainment, to role-playing in social cultures. Simply put, the book is fascinating and fun. No matter where you open it, you will find something amazing. It is also a substantial compendium of information, an indispensable and very accessible tool for anyone who undertakes research on vampires and werewolves, whether for academic study, for books and articles, or for novels and entertainment.

There is always something new to learn about the vampire and his cousin, the werewolf. *The Encyclopedia of Vampires, Werewolves, and Other Monsters* is a top pick, an important contribution to this ever-growing field.

ACKNOWLEDGMENTS

I am deeply grateful to Jeanne Keyes Youngson, my dear friend and the founder of the Vampire Empire (formerly the Count Dracula Fan Club), for her generous help in providing information and numerous pieces of art and for writing the foreword. Many hours were spent in the Vampire Empire archives and library. I met Jeannie in the late 1980s, when I started work on my first book on vampires, *Vampires Among Us.* Her contributions to the field and her knowledge are substantial.

I am also deeply grateful to my dear friend and longtime collaborator, Joanne P. Austin, for her considerable help on the *Buffy the Vampire Slayer,* Bram Stoker, and Anne Rice entries. Joanne also had a hand in my *Complete Vampire Companion,* long out of print now, from which some of the material in this encyclopedia has been adapted and updated.

Special thanks go to David and Janet Hale, friends from *Dark Shadows,* to whom this book is dedicated. When one of my cherished autographed, out-of-print, and scarce *Dark Shadows* books went missing at a conference, David and Janet set off on an international cyber-hunt to track down a replacement copy, finally landing one in Australia. And not only that, they arranged for the *Dark Shadows* stars to autograph it, making it nearly identical—and even better—than the one I lost. Thanks to Jim Pierson, director of the *Dark Shadows* Festival, for his help on making the arrangements.

I am indebted to the help, knowledge, and advice of numerous experts and scholars in the study of vampires, Dracula, Bram Stoker, and werewolves. Among them are Elizabeth Miller, arguably the foremost scholar on Stoker and *Dracula;* David J. Skal, film critic; Les Daniels, author and expert on horror and fantasy comics; Robert Eighteen-Bisang and Margaret L. Carter, literary experts and critics; and numerous others whose works were especially helpful, among them Clive Leatherdale, Harry Ludlam, J. Gordon Melton, Brad Steiger, and Martin V. Riccardo.

Once again I am pleased to include the fabulous art of my longtime friend and collaborator, Robert Michael Place, who contributed several images from his outstanding *Vampire Tarot.* Bob's art appears in several of my encyclopedias: *The Encyclopedia of Ghosts and Spirits; The Encyclopedia of Angels; The Encyclopedia of Saints,* and also *The Atlas of the Mysterious in North America, The Complete Vampire Companion,* and *The Mystical Tarot.* We collaborated on two Tarot sets, *The Alchemical Tarot* and *The Angels Tarot.*

I would also like to thank Linda S. Godfrey for her excellent drawing of the Beast of Bray Road and Bruce and Tina Haines for their photo of the impressive Mothman sculpture, provided courtesy of Rick Fisher of the Paranormal Society of Pennsylvania.

INTRODUCTION

by Rosemary Ellen Guiley, Ph.D.

Vampires do exist—an assertion that often raises eyebrows. That is because our impressions of vampires, and what we think we know about them, almost always derive solely from their portrayal in entertainment: brooding figures in sweeping capes with blood-dripping fangs; wealthy, magically empowered, and beautiful immortals, and so on. The real vampire is a much darker creature, a legitimate member of demonologies, folktales, myths, and superstitions around the world.

The vampire is the entity, force, or presence that brings illness, misfortune, death, and destruction. It is the demon parasite that threatens to suck health, vitality, and life away from its victims. It can be blamed for blight, pestilence, plague, stillbirth, sudden death, and wasting death. It is the embodiment of our darkest and most primeval fears, of the dark, the unknown, the grave, and the uncertainty of what, if anything, comes after death.

Vampires exist alongside countless other demonic entities credited with preying upon the living. They come in many guises, from the walking and ghostly dead to ugly abominations, but whatever their form, demonic vampires always elicit horror and revulsion.

Our intimate contact with vampires is as ancient as humanity. Vampires, or creatures like them, exist in every culture around the world; they are part of the dark hazards of life. Throughout history, people have developed ways to protect against such hazards and to conquer them whenever they threaten the stability of life. As societies have become more sophisticated, vampires and other supernatural entities have fallen into backwaters of superstition and have been dismissed to fictional realms. But humanity's darkest fears, especially of death, still exist, and so fascination with vampires persists. In fiction, the vampire has become increasingly attractive and alluring. Perhaps this is our attempt to face the dark head on and come to terms with it.

Like many people, my interest in vampires began with fiction and with reading the granddaddy of all vampire novels, *Dracula,* by Bram Stoker. Fiction led me naturally to films, and from there I explored vampires in folklore, mythology, demonology, psychology, and performing arts. As a metaphor for death, fear, evil, and alienation, the vampire has permeated virtually every part of society.

The European vampire cult was "discovered" nearly 300 years ago, and *Dracula* has been gripping audiences for more than 100 years. The field of vampire studies keeps expanding, with innumerable books, articles, and commentaries on the creatures published each year.

One cannot study vampires without examining their first cousins, the werewolves; vampire lore is intermingled with werewolf lore. Also involved are predatory shape-shifters and a host of demonic entities that, while not vampires per se, are vampiric in nature.

The bulk of this encyclopedia is devoted to vampires, followed by werewolves and then vampiric demons and shape-shifters. Special attention is given to folklore beliefs, practices, stories and anecdotes, and legends. A large body of folklore exists on vampires. They have many names and characteristics, and beliefs about them vary from one locale to another, even within small geographic areas. I also have included surveys and overviews of vampire studies and vampires in arts, entertainment, pop culture, and psychology, with individual entries on prominent people, cases, organizations, films, books, and so on. Fiction has created its own body of folklore, equally as fascinating as historical folklore.

I do not think we will ever tire of the vampire. An expert shape-shifter, the vampire constantly changes form to embody whatever contemporary society dreads the most. As soon as we think we have conquered it, it rises anew—like the reanimated dead of old—to haunt us in yet another form.

ENTRIES
A–Z

Abbott and Costello Meet Frankenstein (1948) American film in which the comedy team of Bud Abbott and Lou Costello contend with COUNT DRACULA, the Wolf Man, and Frankenstein.

BELA LUGOSI stars as Dracula, and LON CHANEY JR. plays his tortured werewolf role originated in *THE WOLF MAN* (1941). Glenn Strange plays Frankenstein.

The comedy plot concerns who will provide the brain for Frankenstein. Dracula tries to get Costello's brain because he is a simpleton. Dracula reasons that thus he will be able to control Frankenstein.

Abbott and Costello Meet Frankenstein was a hit and shored up the flagging careers of the comedy duo. But sequels, in which Abbott and Costello meet other monsters and villains—the Mummy, Dr. Jekyll and Mr. Hyde, the Invisible Man, and Captain Kidd—did not achieve the same success.

abchanchu Bolivian vampire. The *abchanchu* pretends to be a kindly old man who loses his way. His well-meaning, helpful victims are either stricken with a fatal disease or are sucked dry of their BLOOD while they are asleep.

Addams Family, The The American television sitcom based on the Charles Addams cartoons of the same name, about a family of eccentrics and monsters. *The Addams*

Family aired from 1964 to 1966 on the American Broadcasting Corporation (ABC).

The family features the vampiric Morticia Addams (Carolyn Jones) as the lady of a most strange household. Other members are Gomez Addams, her husband (John Astin); Uncle Fester (Jackie Coogan); Pugsley Addams, their son (Ken Weatherwax); Wednesday Addams, their daughter (Lisa Loring); Grandmama Addams (Blossom Rock); Lurch, their butler (Ted Cassidy); and the hairy Cousin Itt (Felix Silla, with Roger Arroyo playing the role in two episodes). In addition, there is Thing, an animated hand (played by Ted Cassidy) that lives in a box. Three different addresses are used for the family residence: 001 Cemetery Lane in Greenbriar, 001 Cemetery Lane in Woodlawn, and 001 North Cemetery Drive in Greenbrier. Their telephone number is Cemetery 13.

Plots concern the family's strange habits in the modern world. The series ran for 64 episodes.

In 1977 ABC attempted to revive the series with a made-for-television movie, *Halloween with the New Addams Family*, which reunited Astin, Jones, Coogan, Cassidy, Loring, and Weatherwax.

The characters appeared in two films, *The Addams Family* (1991) and *Addams Family Values* (1993). Both films were directed by Barry Sonnenfeld, and starred Raul Julia and Anjelica Huston in the lead roles.

The work of Charles Addams (1912–1988) first appeared in *The New Yorker* in 1932. His macabre style and

The cast of The Addams Family (Author's collection)

humor were popular throughout his career. The last of his cartoons was published in the magazine in 1989.

See also THE MUNSTERS.

FURTHER READING:
Glut, Donald. *The Dracula Book*. Metuchen, N.J.: The Scarecrow Press, 1975.

adlet   In Inuit lore, a race of DOGMEN created by the union of a large red dog and an Inuit woman. The woman bore ten offspring, five weredogs and five normal dogs. Revolted by them, she put them on rafts and set them adrift on the ocean. The dogs did not perish, but eventually reached Europe. The five dogs intermarried among the white Europeans. The ugly weredogs turned into flesh-eating monsters who took up habitats in the northern lands.

adze   In African lore, a vampiric entity who appears in the form of a firefly. The *adze* lives among tribal sorcerers of the Ewe in Ghana and southern Togo. If captured, it turns into a human and attacks its captors. If there is no BLOOD available, it drinks coconut water and palm oil. It especially likes the blood of beautiful children.

afrit   In Arabian lore, the vampiric spirit of a murdered man who seeks to avenge his death. The afrit rises up like smoke from the BLOOD of the victim. Like the European vampire, the afrit can be stopped by driving a nail into the bloodstained ground.

Akasha   See LESTAT DE LIONCOURT; *QUEEN OF THE DAMNED*.

al   In Armenian lore, a half-human, half-animal creature that especially likes to attack pregnant women. The *al* may have originated in the Babylonian lore of the *alu,* a malevolent spirit in the form of a black dog that causes diseases.

The *al* has one fiery EYE, IRON teeth, brass fingernails, the tusks of a wild boar, and long, snakelike hair. It possesses a pointed hat covered with bells that renders it invisible. The *al* likes to live in damp and dirty places, including homes and stables. It also frequents wet and sandy places along roads.

The *al* strangles pregnant women and their unborn children and pulls out their livers. It causes miscarriages and steals newborn infants up to seven months old.

The explanation for the *al*'s rage against women and infants is found in Christianized lore. God gave Adam an *al,* but the two were not compatible, for Adam was made of dust and the *al* was made of fire. God then created Eve as a substitute. This enraged the *al,* who dedicated itself to attacking women. (See LILITH.)

Another Christian story about the *al* tells that St. Peter once came upon a creature with iron teeth and tusks, sitting in a wet and sandy place along a road. The saint asked it to identify itself, and it gave its name and described its activities.

The best remedy against the *al* is iron: Keep numerous iron objects and utensils around; especially place them around the bed of a pregnant woman, or place an iron knife under her pillow. Prayers and charms also are effective for warding off attacks.

See also *TLAHUELPUCHI.*

FURTHER READING:
Mack, Carol K., and Dinah Mack. *A Field Guide to Demons, Fairies, Fallen Angels, and Other Subversive Spirits.* New York: Henry Holt/Owl Books, 1998.

ala   A Turkish term, borrowed by Serbs and Greeks, for an ECLIPSE vampire. The *ala* replaced the names of *VARCOLAC* and *VUKODLAK* as the sky creature who eats the sun and MOON. *Ale* (plural) assume human form and drink boiled milk, wine, and vodka like water. They bring storms that ruin crops.

According to a Serbian folktale, a peasant who lost all his money because his vineyard was plucked clean by an *ala* is told how to kill the vampire: he must wait under his pear tree with a shotgun loaded with pellets of lead, SILVER,

GOLD, and steel. The peasant replants his vineyard, which produces an abundant harvest. The *ala* comes to eat the grapes, and the sky becomes dark and menacing, with lightning, thunder, and hail. The peasant loads his shotgun and waits beneath the pear tree. Soon the *ala* arrives in the form of an eagle. The peasant shoots it and it falls to the ground; he kills it. The sky immediately clears. The peasant regains his wealth.

FURTHER READING:
Perkowski, Jan L. *The Darkling: A Treatise on Slavic Vampirism.* Columbus, Ohio: Slavica, 1989.

algul   Arabian vampire. Though the word *algul* means "horse leech," this demon lives in CEMETERIES and drinks the BLOOD of dead infants.
See also LILITH; *TLAHUELPUCHI.*

Alnwick Castle Vampire (12th c.)   English vampiric REVENANT account recorded by WILLIAM OF NEWBURGH in his history of England. The story was told to him by "a very devout old priest of high authority and most honorable reputation."

According to the priest, a depraved and dishonest Yorkshire man had lived a life of sin and crime. He escaped the law and went to Alnwick Castle, whose lord he knew. He settled there and continued his wicked ways. He married, but rumors circulated that his wife was unfaithful. To discover the truth, he told his wife that he was going away for several days. The first night, he hid himself on the roof above his bed in order catch his wife in the act of adultery. His wife was indeed cheating on him with a local youth. In shock, the man fell to the ground beside the bed. The youth escaped. The man rebuked his wife and threatened to punish her. But his injuries were so severe that he fell gravely ill. The priest visited the man and urged him to make his confession, but the man delayed doing so and then died impenitent.

Nonetheless, he was given a Christian burial. It was to no avail. Said William:

> For by the power of Satan in the dark hours he was wont to come forth from his tomb and to wander about all through the streets, prowling round the houses, whilst on every side the dogs were howling and yelping the whole night long. Throughout the whole district then every man locked and barred his door, nor did anyone between the hours of dusk and dawn fare to go out on any business whatsoever, so greatly did each one fear that he might haply meet this fellow monster and be attacked and most grievously harmed.

Wherever the dead man went, he left behind him an unbearable stench. The fetid and corrupt presence of the specter created a plague that affected every household in the town. People fled to other districts.

On a Palm Sunday, the priest called a council to decide on a course of action. But two young men who had lost their father to the plague decided to take matters into their own hands while the elders met. They set out to dig up the CORPSE and burn it.

The brothers found the body gorged and swollen, with a florid face and red, puffed cheeks. The shroud was dirty and torn. The conditions proved to them that the corpse was feeding off the BLOOD of his victims. They struck the corpse with a sharp spade. Fresh, warm blood gushed forth. They dragged the body out of town and burned it to ASHES on a pyre. They reported what they had done to the town elders, many of whom ran out to the fire to witness the destruction of the corpse. The air was cleansed and the plague stopped.

The term *vampire* was not used, as it had not yet entered the English language; however, the revenant exhibited the same characteristics attributed to vampires.

See also BUCKINGHAMSHIRE VAMPIRE; MELROSE ABBEY VAMPIRE.

FURTHER READING:
Glut, Donald. *True Vampires of History.* New York: HC Publishers, 1971.
McNally, Raymond T. *A Clutch of Vampires.* New York: Bell, 1984.

alp   In German lore, a vampiric, shape-shifting spirit associated with the nightmare, bogeyman, and INCUBUS. *Alps* can be demons or REVENANTS. Children are at risk of becoming *alps* if their mothers use horse collars to ease the difficulties of childbirth.

Alps can manifest as a butterfly vampire released by the breath of the *horerczy* demon, which sucks the life breath out of its victims. They also appear as cats, pigs, birds, and lecherous dogs. Even in animal form, the *alp* likes to wear a magical hat, which confers upon it invisibility and supernatural power.

The *alp* causes unpleasant dreams of both women and men, and also sexually molests both sexes. Oddly, it does not force itself on its victims, but enters through the victim's mouth as a mist or a snake. It also drinks BLOOD through the nipples of both men and women, and consumes the milk of women and cows. The *alp* assaults people with the EVIL EYE.

To protect against an *alp* attack, women should sleep with their shoes at the side of the bed and pointing toward the door.

***American Werewolf in London, An* (1981)**   Film directed by John Landis in which American youths are attacked by a werewolf while they vacation in England, and one of them is turned into a werewolf.

David Kessler (David Naughton) and his friend Jack Goodman (Griffin Dunne) are hitchhiking around England.

David Kessler (David Naughton) is horrified to turn into a werewolf in An American Werewolf in London. *(Author's collection)*

They are warned to stay away from the moors, especially on nights of the full MOON—which is precisely where they find themselves. Alone and away from the main road, they wander through the moonlit landscape. Suddenly they are attacked by what appears to be a ferocious wolf. Jack is mauled to death. David flees and then returns for his friend, finding him dead. The wolf attacks David. But before it can kill him, a band of hunters appears and shoots the wolf dead. Just before David passes out, he sees that the body of the wolf has been transformed into the body of a young man.

David awakens three weeks later in a hospital in London. The truth of the attack has been covered up: The "official" explanation given the medical staff in London is that the boys were attacked by an insane man. David's wounds were cleaned and dressed before he was sent to London.

David recovers and falls in love with the nurse, Alex Price (Jenny Agutter) who attends him. While still in the hospital, David begins having bizarre nightmares involving the werewolf. He has hallucinations of his dead friend, Jack, who tells him that since he did not die of his wounds,

he is cursed to become a werewolf, too. Jack is cursed to be in limbo, a kind of undead, until the new werewolf—David—is killed and the werewolf's bloodline is broken. Jack urges David to kill himself before he makes his first change at the full moon. David refuses to believe him.

After David is discharged, Alex takes him back to her flat. On the night of the full moon, David is alone in the flat and makes an excruciatingly painful change into a werewolf. He goes on a BLOOD rampage through London, brutally slaying six people. Jack, in increasingly advanced stages of decay, appears to him to continue urging him to commit SUICIDE. In his final appearance, Jack brings along the six newly dead victims, all of whom are doomed to the same undead limbo.

By this time, the London doctor who attended David is on to the truth, and he and Alex try to find David to save him. They are too late. David makes a second transformation into werewolf in a London porn theater. After a scene of mayhem in Picadilly Circus, police chase the werewolf into a dead end. Alex and the doctor arrive on the scene. Just as Alex proclaims her love for David, the police shoot him dead.

An American Werewolf in London was a commercial and cult success and led to AN AMERICAN WEREWOLF IN PARIS with a different cast in 1997. The special effects of David's transformation from human into wolf were dramatic for the state of the art at that time. Viewers see every part of the transformation, unlike earlier films in which most of the transformation had to be done off-camera. The film features some fictional werewolf lore concerning the victims who enter limbo until the werewolf's bloodline is severed.

Overall, the film suffers from schizophrenia: It is neither camp nor horror. There is too much silly humor for it to be horrifying, and not enough humor to be camp. Naughton gives a commendable performance, but he seems to try too hard to play a naive youth.

In a now macabre touch, the credits at the end of the film congratulate Prince Charles and Lady Diana Spencer on their wedding in the same year that the film was released.

American Werewolf in Paris, An (1997)   Film directed by Anthony Walker that uses some of the same plot elements as its predecessor, AN AMERICAN WEREWOLF IN LONDON (1981), but is more of a horror film.

In this version, three young men are traveling on their own: Andy (Tom Everett Scott), Brad (Vince Vieluf), and Chris (Phil Buckman). The trip is a "Daredevil Tour of Europe," with the three vying against one another to see who can perform the most dangerous stunt. Andy decides to bungee-jump off the Eiffel Tower. There he saves the life of a young woman, Serafine (Julie Delpy), who attempts to commit SUICIDE. Her secret is that she is a werewolf.

Andy falls in love with Serafine, but she remains elusive. One night Andy and Brad to go a Paris nightclub that, unbeknownst to them, is gathering place of WEREWOLVES. They are attacked. Brad is killed and Andy is wounded. As in *An American Werewolf in London*, Andy is doomed to become a werewolf, and Brad is consigned to limbo. Brad appears to Andy, as did Jack to David in the earlier film.

By 1997 special effects were more sophisticated, and Andy's transformation into a wolfish beast is slick and mesmerizing, making David Naughton's thrashings in the 1981 film look clumsy by comparison.

andandara   In the lore of the Azande of Africa, a race of malevolent wild CATS that have intercourse with human women, who then bear both human children and cats. The women suckle the cats. The *andandara* possess a killing look (see EVIL EYE), and the mere sight of them can cause death. It is extremely unlucky to hear their cries in the bush. Their presence brings misfortune.

Angel   A spin-off television show from BUFFY THE VAMPIRE SLAYER starring David Boreanaz as a tormented vampire with a soul.

Angel first aired on the WB network on October 5, 1999, and had its fifth season in 2004. From 1997 to 2001, *Buffy* also ran on the WB, allowing the writers to incorporate crossover appearances by the actors and parallel story lines. But when *Buffy* joined the UPN network in the fall of 2001, bad relations between the two networks ended the shows' cozy relationship until spring 2003.

Cast of Characters
By the beginning of season five in October 2003, David Boreanaz was the only remaining original cast member. As Angel, he runs Angel Investigations (AI), which helps locate and eradicate demons, VAMPIRES and other dark forces. His team includes Cordelia Chase, from *Buffy*, and Doyle, a half-man, half-demon who communicates with the Powers That Be (PTB) on Angel's behalf through intense visions. Besides Angel himself (see profile under *Buffy*), the major characters are as follows:

Cordelia (Charisma Carpenter): The former teen queen of Sunnydale High School, Cordelia now works for Angel and attempts to pursue her dream of an acting career (although her friends admit in private she's not very talented). Before Doyle dies fighting a devilish machine, he kisses Cordelia and psychically transfers his ability to have intense, painful visions to her. The pain eventually leads Cordelia to the dark side, and she becomes part demon. She has sex with Angel's son Connor, and they have a demon child, Jasmine.

Wesley Wyndham-Pryce (Alexis Denisof): Another character from *Buffy*, Wes has been thrown off the Watcher's Council and becomes a self-styled "rogue demon hunter," but he's better suited to helping Angel and Cordelia than taking off on his own. Eventually he joins Angel as a member of the law firm Wolfram & Hart.

Kate Lockley (Elisabeth Rohm): A detective in the Los Angeles Police Department, Kate is fascinated by Angel. His knowledge of evil forces and recognition of criminals past and present make him invaluable to her investigations. Rohm left the show in early 2001 to join the cast of *Law and Order* as the new assistant district attorney, Serena Southerlyn.

Charles Gunn (J. August Richards): A VAMPIRE HUNTER who originally led a gang of street kids, Gunn joins Angel's organization. The name Gunn represents the brothers Sean and James Gunn, friends of Joss Whedon's.

Lorne, the Host (Andy Hallet): The owner of a karaoke bar called the Caritas, Lorne performs psychic readings for Angel's gang. His full name is Krevlorneswath of the Deathwok Clan, and his home world is Pylea, a place where humans may be mistreated. Pylea can be reached only through a portal to another dimension. Lorne's face is green with small red horns protruding from his forehead.

Winifred (Fred) Burkle (Amy Acker): A new employ of Angel Investigations, Fred joins the cast in season two as a "demented" female physicist. Romantically, she pairs off with Gunn and Wesley.

Wolfram & Hart: An evil Los Angeles law firm that does everything in its power to stop Angel and his associates, until Lilah Morgan, the chief lawyer, dies. After that, Angel and company are invited to join the firm, which they do at the beginning of the fifth season.

Synopsis of the Episodes
During the first season, Angel tries to establish his new business and forget the heartbreak of leaving *Buffy*. Employing Doyle's visions, Angel hunts down vampires and demons, sometimes even helping the Los Angeles Police Department with an investigation. Cordelia decides to find another apartment and is delighted with the one-bedroom Doyle locates for her until the unhappy spirits of earlier residents haunt the place. In a vision Doyle sees The Scourge, a group of half-breed demons with Nazi-like tendencies. The Scourge have built a machine that kills any human within a quarter-mile, and Doyle volunteers to sacrifice himself to destroy the machine. Before he dies, Doyle kisses Cordelia, passing to her his ability to see the visions. Wesley joins AI after a brief stint as a rogue demon hunter. At the end of the season, Angel has been captured and forced to participate in battles with enslaved demons at a fight club.

Finally, while making a secret investigation of the law firm of Wolfram & Hart, Angel discovers a scroll that explains the prophecy of "the vampire with a soul" and includes the key word *shanshu*, which means either death or life. An evil demon steals the scroll and returns it to W&H as part of a ritual performed over a crate by an ancient warrior of the underworld called Vocah. The contents of the crate: Angel's vampire sire, Darla.

Season two begins with Gunn as a new investigator and the search of an abandoned Hollywood hotel, which takes them back to 1952. Angel complains of sleeping badly, unaware that Darla visits him every night. Angel finally sees Darla during the day and desperately tries to free her from Wolfram & Hart. Flashbacks take Angel to the day in 1609, when the Master sired Darla, a whore from the Virginia colony, and then she sired him. His memories show him the four friends—Angel, Spike, Darla, and Drusilla—who roamed together until the GYPSIES cursed Angel with a soul in 1898. Angel prevents Darla and Drusilla from destroying Los Angeles by burning them in a fire caused by a cigarette and gasoline.

Cordelia begins the third season enduring another very painful vision about violence to women. Meanwhile, Darla has returned, very pregnant, and searches for Angel, the father. She delivers a son, Connor, and surprises Angel with her tender love of the baby. Wolfram & Hart taint Angel's blood supply with traces of Connor's blood, goading Angel's hunger for the boy. Wesley tries to protect Connor but cannot keep Holtz the VAMPIRE HUNTER from taking the child with him into Hell. Angel tries black magic to bring Connor back but fails. Connor returns to Los Angeles from Hell at the end of the season, having zoomed through childhood. He is now an angry 17-year-old, bent on vengeance for Angel's past.

Angel and Cordelia remain missing for three months in season four, and Connor, who knows Angel's whereabouts, murders the only eyewitness to Angel's location so as to cover his tracks. Wesley is sleeping with Lilah Morgan of W&H. Angel reappears, but Cordelia is still missing. She has gone to a higher plane, where she becomes more demonlike, then returns, suffering from amnesia. Lorne casts a spell to return Cordelia's memory, but it erases all current information from the others' minds, taking them back to their high school days.

Cordelia's visions show the imminent arrival of the Beast, who intends to destroy the world. To do that, the Beast must slaughter five totems; the fifth is an AI client named Manny. Once the five have been destroyed, the sun disappears. In a vision, Cordelia learns that the Beast and Angelus were once a team, and Angel tells the others that in 1789 he helped the Beast kill some Nordic priestesses.

Angel and Cordelia make love, but that happy moment triggers the Gypsy curse, and Angel wakes up as Angelus, without a soul. His friends put his soul in a box and place it in a locked safe, but it later disappears. Faith breaks out of prison to help Angelus take on the Beast, stabbing it with its own weapon, and when the creature dies, the sunlight returns to Los Angeles. The friends believe the worst is over until Cordelia comes downstairs, pregnant with Connor's child. The delivery leaves Cordelia unconscious, and the gang does not understand that the full-grown woman standing next to her is her daughter, Jasmine—but never a child. Fred recognizes the real Jasmine behind her

beautiful face, which is now covered in maggots, and tries to shoot her. Angel realizes what a sham Jasmine is.

Angel and company encounter a monster that tells Angel that Jasmine was originally a god and worshiped, but now she lives in an oxygen-free dimension. Since as a vampire Angel doesn't breathe, he goes after Jasmine, finding a High Priest and a giant demon guarding her. Jasmine prepares to broadcast to the world the establishment of peace. Angel kills the priest and beheads the demon, while Connor finds Cordelia unconscious in a nearby church. They return to Los Angeles with Cordelia and the severed head, and when Angel brings out the head, Jasmine reveals her true nature. Several try to kill her, but it is her own father, Connor, who ends her life. The senior partners of Wolfram & Hart offer Angel and his gang the opportunity to work for the firm, and they accept. Connor, enraged that he has no chance of living with a happy family, goes berserk, killing innocent people at a mall.

The fifth season opens in Angel's new office at Wolfram & Hart, where he notices a strange envelope on his desk. When he opens it, an amulet falls out and begins spinning—until a screaming Spike appears. Spike's body had been destroyed and sent to Hell when Sunnydale collapsed into the Hellmouth, but his spirit was returned to the body against his will. Spike admits he is terrified of falling into Hell forever.

Later, Wesley is surprised to find his estranged father, Roger, at W&H. Roger steals an artifact from the vault and plans the vampire's enslavement. Another package arrives at W&H that allows Spike to regain his body, but the existence of two vampires with souls creates chaos in the world. Angel and Spike learn that drinking from the Cup of Perpetual Torment, which grants human life, is the only remedy, and they fight for this prize. Flashbacks reveal that Angel and Spike were once friends until they competed for Drusilla. Angel suffers intense fevers and hallucinations, fearing Spike will supplant him, and Spike is shown using wrist stakes to kill two vampires in an alley.

Noir Way Out

While *Angel* shares (but even more darkly) many of the same themes explored in *Buffy the Vampire Slayer*—the importance of a family group, no matter how unconventional; the bliss and agony of love; the ambiguity of good and evil within each individual—the central pursuit of each season is the journey to redemption, and what a difficult and dangerous path one must take to get there.

Angel Investigations employs misfits: Cordelia, a former teen bitch learning humility through constant rejection as she strives to succeed in acting; Wesley, an insecure but fairly pompous Watcher that grows into a sure leader; Doyle, a demon half-breed that dies to save Angel and the citizens of Los Angeles; and two vampires, Angel and Spike, tormented by the memories of their past crimes and burdened by the possession of souls. Even the secondary characters that come and go during the series learn the wisdom and rightness of sacrifice for the greater good.

The alternate Slayer named Faith, not known for remorse or compassion, finally acknowledges that her status does not ameliorate the cruelty of her actions and surrenders to the police, becoming the first Slayer to serve a prison sentence.

In her essay entitled "She Saved the World. A Lot," Roz Kaveney notes that, more than anyone else does, Angel craves redemption but sees no path to that end but through hard lessons. He suffers blinding guilt, cries out in anguish when true happiness turns him to evil, and cannot shake the flashbacks of his rebirth with Darla and the torture he inflicted on poor Drusilla before condemning her to immortality—and damnation. He desires Buffy but fears the consequences of that attraction. He loves his son, Connor, but fails as a father to protect him. "Angel suffers from the delusion that redemption is simply a matter of saving enough lives to pay off the karmic debt created during his years as Angelus, and staying humane while he does it," notes Kaveney. "He refuses any soft options—his redemption must be done the hard way." If Angel can continue to "fight the good fight," he may eventually be returned to full humanity.

FURTHER READING:
"Angel: Episode Guide." Seasons 1–5. TV Tome. URL: http://www.tvtome.com/tvtome/servlet/EpisodeGuideSummary. Downloaded on December 16, 2003.
Holder, Nancy, with Jeff Mariotte and Maryelizabeth Hart (eds.). Buffy the Vampire Slayer: The Watcher's Guide. Vol. 2. New York: Pocket Books, 2000.
Kaveney, Roz. "She Saved the World. A Lot." Reading the Vampire Slayer: An Unofficial Critical Companion to Buffy and Angel. Roz Kaveney, ed. London: Tauris Parke Paperbacks, 2002.

Angers Werewolf   See ROULET, JACQUES.

Anspach Werewolf (1685)   Strange German werewolf case with VAMPIRE overtones, in which a ravaging wolf was believed to be a returning dead person.

In 1685 a wolf terrorized Anspach (now Ansbach), Germany, killing women, children, and domestic animals. The townspeople believed the wolf to be the late burgomaster, a most detested man, who was returning to wreak havoc. A great hunt was mounted, and at last the wolf was chased into a well and killed.

The carcass of the wolf was then dressed up like the burgomaster in a flesh-colored suit, mask, wig, and beard. It was hung from a gibbet. Later, the carcass was put on display in a museum as a werewolf.

The belief of the townspeople that the burgomaster had returned from the dead to attack them made him a vampire of sorts, but in wolf form and not in his own form as the reanimated dead.

See also WEREWOLVES.

FURTHER READING:
Sidky, H. Witchcraft, Lycanthropy, Drugs and Disease: An Anthropological Study of the European Witch-Hunts. New York: Peter Lang, 1997.

The Ape Man (1934)   BELA LUGOSI plays a scientist experimenting with ways to give human beings the strength of apes. He injects another man (Wallace Beery) with a formula that shape-shifts (see SHAPE-SHIFTING) Beery into an ape. The Ape Man was directed by William Beaudine.

Armand   See RICE, ANNE.

arts and entertainment   Since its entry into Western media in the 18th century, when the "vampire cult" was reported in Europe, the VAMPIRE has played a key role in arts and entertainment. Initially a shocking monster and a disease- and death-spreading evil, the vampire has evolved into a sexual deviate, antihero, hero, romantic lead, comic lead—and even a stock character, as common as the person next door. WEREWOLVES, less popular, have followed a similar path.

Poetry and Literature
Although Western society's widespread familiarity with vampires dates only to the mid-18th century, vampiric characters have appeared in stories since ancient times, as dead lovers returning from the grave and demon lovers such as the SUCCUBUS and LAMIA. Vampirelike monsters appear in sagas such as *Gilgamesh, Beowulf,* and *Le Morte Darthur.* However, the vampire did not emerge as a distinct literary figure until after 1742, when JOHANN FLUCKINGER, an Austrian medical officer, wrote a report about vampire beliefs and practices in eastern Europe. Authors were quick to use vampirism as a literary device for exploring the themes of BLOOD, sex, and death in daring new ways. Heinrich August Ossenfelder's poem "The Vampire," which concerns the nocturnal visitation of a vampire lover, caused a scandal when it was published in 1748. Jacques Cazotte's novel *Le diable amoreux* (1772) is a charming fantasy about a soldier who conjures up a beautiful succubus named Biondetta. Casanova's *Icosameron* (1778) and some of the works of his contemporary, the marquis de Sade, describe the ecstasies of drinking human blood.

Berger's poem "Lenore" (1773), which tells of an undead lover, and Johann von Goethe's ballad "Die Braut von Korinth" (1797) are based on classical sources. "The Bride of Corinth" is an adaptation of Philostratus's story of "Apolloneus of Tyana" (ca. 225 C.E.), which tells how a young man was rescued from a lamia who planned to fatten him with pleasure before devouring his flesh. John Keats's "Lamia" and "La Belle Dame sans Merci" both bear Goethe's influence, while many of the works of Lord Byron, Percy

Bysshe Shelley, and other romantic poets reiterate the theme of "fatal men" and "femmes fatales" who attract and destroy those they love.

Wake Not the Dead (ca. 1800) is the first story in which the modern vampire can be recognized as such. It is usually attributed to the German fabulist Johann Ludwig von Tieck. *Wake Not the Dead* (or *The Bride of the Grave*) tells of a nobleman named Walter who becomes obsessed by the memory of his deceased wife, Brunhilda. He finds a necromancer who raises her from the grave and brings her back to life. At first he is ecstatic, but Brunhilda soon develops a thirst for human blood. After destroying his household and murdering the children whom he had fathered with his second wife, she turns on him. Walter overcomes her but ultimately pays a horrible price for disturbing the natural order.

The first contemporary vampire story in English was created by LORD BYRON and later plagiarized by his onetime companion, JOHN POLIDORI. Although history records the character of Polidori as dour and dull, filmmakers such as Ken Russell and films like *Haunted Summer* hint that his relationship with Byron deepened beyond friendship due mostly to their mutual enjoyment of narcotics such as laudanum. Byron, however, professed an intense dislike for Polidori. The story that became "THE VAMPYRE" was born on a night of oral storytelling that also birthed Mary Shelley's *Frankenstein*.

Polidori made notes of Byron's tale and published it anonymously in 1819 as "The Vampyre," about the cold, aristocratic but mesmerizing LORD RUTHVEN, loosely based on Byron himself, who vampirizes women of blood and men of their money. It was assumed that Byron was the author, prompting the poet to make an angry denial and then to create his own version, "Fragment of a Story," that was far less vampiric.

Byron could not prevent "The Vampyre" from becoming a sensation all over Europe, inspiring fiction, poetry, and drama. One critic noted that "the 'Broucolaca' (or vampire) has hitherto become a favorite in the English closet. But at Paris, he has been received with rapturous applause at almost all the spectacles, from the Odeon to the Porte St. Martin; all the presses of the Palais Royale have for the last two years been employed in celebrating, and describing, and speculating on him and his adventures. . . ."

Although Polidori's creation has few of the dramatic strengths and weaknesses now associated with the vampire, his story transformed the vampire from a moldering peasant wrapped in its burial shroud, to a foreign, sinister vampiric nobleman who interacts in genteel society. The character of Lord Ruthven shaped the pattern for the 19th-century male vampire as Byronic villain-hero, a hypnotically compelling creature possessed by satanic pride and/or secret sorrows. His nonsupernatural counterpart appears in heroes such as Heathcliff in Emily Brontë's *Wuthering Heights*—one of the books used as an inspirational source a century later in the soap opera DARK SHADOWS—and Mr. Rochester in Charlotte Brontë's *Jane Eyre*. The influence of Ruthven has continued on into the 21st century, touching BRAM STOKER's novel *DRACULA*, and ANNE RICE's vampiric elite.

In 1847 the serial *VARNEY THE VAMPIRE* was published in England, written anonymously by JAMES MALCOLM RYMER. Like "The Vampyre," *Varney* tells a tale of a rakish blue blood whose vampiric predations were described in ample purple prose. But unlike Lord Ruthven, Sir Francis Varney is tormented by his vampire state, and he is developed for the reader's sympathy. At the end, the disgusted Varney throws himself into the pit of an active volcano, Mount Vesuvius, to put a permanent end to himself.

Dracula. The cornerstone upon which all vampire characters now turn was laid in 1897 by Bram Stoker in his novel *Dracula*. COUNT DRACULA stands firmly in the Byronic tradition. There are hints of deeper sorrow and an alienation from the place and time in which he finds himself, but Stoker never allows the reader entry into the viewpoint of the vampire as he stalks his victims. Stoker researched the vampire legend and superstition, but his Dracula differs in important ways from the vampire of European folklore. In keeping with his folklore sources, Stoker gives Dracula animalistic features that hint of the WEREWOLF—bushy EYEBROWS, blunt-fingered, coarse hands, hairy palms, and foul breath. Then Stoker gives him more: mesmerizing, telepathic powers, lizardlike abilities, the ability to travel around the world as long as he has a box full of his native earth to sleep in, the ability to regenerate himself into youthfulness from blood (as opposed to merely sustaining his corpse in the grave), and so on.

Dracula's sexuality is not overtly described, largely due to Victorian mores. But when the heroine, Mina Harker, describes her inability to resist him as he drinks her blood, she implies rape rather than seduction. Stoker's VAMPIRE

A few of the many editions of Bram Stoker's Dracula *(Photo by R. E. Guiley. Courtesy Vampire Empire Archives)*

HUNTER, PROFESSOR ABRAHAM VAN HELSING, continually asserts that the vampire is evil, the emissary of Satan on Earth. He is the epitome of evil, and his actions are inevitably self-serving and cruel. Stoker probably would be appalled at the later image of Dracula, especially in film, as an alluring, romantic figure. Many of today's fictional vampires would be unrecognizable to Stoker as vampires.

Pulp fiction. The next classic vampire novel, Sydney Horler's *The Vampire*, was not published until 1935. But during the 1920s the continuing success of *Dracula* inspired many of the contributors to the new American pulp magazines to write stories about vampires. Although they were not always of the highest literary quality, these stories thrilled and entertained millions of readers. The first and most famous pulp magazine, *Weird Tales*, was published from 1923 until 1954. It presented such classic stories as "Four Wooden Stakes" by Victor Rowan (1925), "The Canal" by Everil Worrell (1927), "Revelations in Black" by Carl Jacobi (1933), "Doom of the House of Duryea" by Earl Peirce, Jr. (1936), "Yours Truly—Jack the Ripper" by Robert Bloch (1943), and "The Traveller" by Ray Bradbury (1943). Vampires also appeared in several of the most popular series in the magazine. C. L. Moore's Northwest Smith series includes some of the most memorable vampire stories in pulp fiction. In "Shambleau" (1933), Smith falls under the spell of a Medusa-like vampiress whose victims are held in her thrall by an irresistible but obscene pleasure. Many of Clark Ashton Smith's stories about Averoigne and Zothique contain exotic lamialike beings, while Seabury Quinn's occult detective, Jules de Grandin, confronts many different types of vampires.

Weird Tales's most famous contributor, H. P. Lovecraft, created the "Cthulhu Mythos" in which vampiric, extradimensional entities who once ruled the Earth attempt to return to power. Vampirism plays an explicit part in his stories "The Hound" (1924), "The Tomb" (1926), and "The Case of Charles Dexter Ward" (1941). Many of his students, including Robert Bloch, August W. Derleth, Robert E. Howard, and Frank Belknap Long contributed new stories to the Cthulhu Mythos, and his work has continued to inspire writers such as Ramsey J. Campbell, BRIAN LUMLEY, and Colin Wilson. *Horror Stories, Strange Tales*, and other magazines published some noteworthy vampire stories during the 1930s, but no other pulp magazine attracted the quality (or quantity) of stories that appeared in *Weird Tales*.

August Derleth and Donald Wandrei founded Arkham House in 1939 to promote the work of Lovecraft. They eventually published anthologies and collections by many of the above-mentioned writers; Lumley owes his break in publishing to Arkham House. In the 1970s Carcosa published four collections by contributors to *Weird Tales*. Manly Wade Wellman's *Worse Things Waiting* and Hugh B. Cave's *Murgunstrumm* reprint most of their vampire stories. The latter collection, which includes the title story, "The Purr of the Cat," and "Stragella," is illustrated by Lee Brown Coye.

Most of the vampire stories that appeared in the detective pulps are mysteries about bloodless corpses with two-mysterious-puncture-marks-in-their-necks. In contrast, the science-fiction magazines of this period contained a variety of original, rational explanations for vampirism. Most of these stories portray vampires as a separate species or treat vampirism as disease. Eric Frank Russell's novella *Sinister Barrier* (*Unknown*, 1939) is based on the Fortean theory that the human race serves as cattle for a superior race of beings (a theme later explored by SUZY MCKEE CHARNAS in her novel *Vampire Tapestry*). In A. E. Van Vogt's "Asylum" (*Astounding*, 1942) alien species at different stages of evolution fight for control of the solar system. Vampirism is portrayed as a (mis)step in our evolution toward godhood. This story was expanded as "The Proxy Intelligence" (*If*, 1968) and reworked as a novel in 1977. It also inspired Colin Wilson's novel *The Space Vampires*, which was filmed as *Lifeforce* in 1985.

During the 1950s, a new generation of fans was introduced to Dracula, Frankenstein, and the Wolfman when Universal's monster movies were revived for television. Their popularity inspired HAMMER FILMS to create a new series of vampire movies, ushering in an era of films that were then adapted into novels instead of vice versa. (See DRACULA FILMS.)

The world's first monster-movie magazine, *Famous Monsters of Filmland*, debuted in the late 1950s. It was edited by Forrest J. Ackerman, who contributed stories, articles, and puns under pseudonyms such as "Dr. Acula." "Forrey" is cast as the world's leading authority on vampires in David McDaniel's Man from U.N.C.L.E. novel, *The Vampire Affair* (1966), and Philip Jose Farmer's erotic underground classic, *The Image of the Beast* (1968). "4E" (as Ackerman is also known) created the comic-book character VAMPIRELLA and inspired many writers. (See COMICS.)

In the early 1960s, Simon Raven and Theodore Sturgeon created memorable, literate novels about human blood drinkers. Sturgeon's masterpiece, *Some of Your Blood* (1961), broke new ground by discussing the drinking of menstrual blood. Leslie H. Whitten's *Progeny of the Adder* (1965) is set in Washington, D.C., where a detective who is attempting to solve a series of murders fails to realize that they are the work of a vampire. In the latter part of the 1960s, Dan Ross began a series of novels that were based on the ABC television series DARK SHADOWS. *Barnabas Collins* (1968) tells how BARNABAS COLLINS became a vampire as the result of a curse and how he first arrived at Collinwood.

The copyright on *Dracula* expired in 1968, initiating a deluge of novels about Count Dracula. One of the earliest books, *The Adult Version of Dracula*, is an abridged pornographic adaptation of Stoker's opus. Other novels, such as Gail Kimberly's *Dracula Began* and Asa Drake's *Crimson Kisses* (which was written by C. Dean Andersson and Nina Romberg, 1981) explain how Dracula became a vampire. The events in Raymond Rudorff's *The Dracula Archives* (1971) take place before those narrated by Stoker, and link Dracula with VLAD TEPES and Countess ELIZABETH BATHÓRY.

Donald F. Glut's *Frankenstein Meets Dracula* (1977) is a continuation of both *Frankenstein* and *Dracula*. In John Shirley's bizarre offering *Dracula in Love* (1979), Dracula's son, who is an executive in San Francisco, is called upon by God (Lucifer/Bill/Marg), to help overcome Dracula and his followers in order to prepare the King of the Undead for a new incarnation.

Robert Lory's Dracula Horror series (1973–75) and Peter Tremayne's Dracula Unborn series (1978–80) place the count in the modern world. *The Dracula Tape* (1975), is the first book in FRED SABERHAGEN's Dracula series. It retells the story of Dracula from a unique, satiric point of view that still remains true to Stoker's creation. The much-maligned count provides alternative explanations for the most important events in Stoker's novel in an attempt to convince his audience that he has been unjustly portrayed as a monster by hordes of superstitious peasants and stake-wielding idiots.

Many subsequent books rework *Dracula* in original ways. In *Danse Macabre*, Stephen King says that his novel *'SALEM'S LOT* (1975) is "partially as a form of literary homage . . . So my novel bears an intentional similarity to Bram Stoker's *Dracula*." *'Salem's Lot* speculates on what might happen if a vampire descended on a small town in modern America. Another notable variation on this theme is the splatter-punk novel *The Light at the End* (1986) by John Skipp and Craig Spector, in which the vampires begin their conquest by taking over the subways of New York.

Although classic vampire novels such as Les Daniels's Don Sebastian de Villanueva series (1978–91), Robert R. McCammon's *They Thirst* (1981), and George R. R. Martin's *Fevre Dream* (1982) continued to appear on a regular basis, the writers of the 1970s tended to move away from the three V's of vampire, victim, and vampire hunter in order to concentrate on the vampire's motivations and emotions. This transition is evident in Robert Aickman's elegant novella *Pages from a Young Girl's Journal* (which debuted in *The Magazine of Fantasy & Science Fiction* in February 1973). A young girl who is vacationing in Europe is alienated from her family and the 19th-century in which she lives. As the story unfolds, it becomes evident that she is awaiting the coming of her vampire lover who will transform her into a member the undead elite.

The concept of vampirism as a desirable state was first brought to the attention of the public by Anne Rice's novel *INTERVIEW WITH THE VAMPIRE* (1976). The first novel in her Chronicles of the Vampire series captures the magic, romance, and sensuality of the vampire myth and shows the reader what it is like to *be* a vampire. The desire to be made a vampire became a dominant theme in vampire fiction that followed.

During the 1980s, many authors constructed elaborate explanations about the origin of the vampires and their powers. In Whitley Strieber's *THE HUNGER*, Miriam Blaylock is a member of a species of predators that has evolved separately from mankind. Jan Jenning's *Vampyr* provides many well thought-out explanations for vampires' strengths and weaknesses, while Garfield Reeves-Stevens's medical thriller, *Bloodshift,* portrays vampirism as the next step in human evolution. S. P. Somtow's haunting novel *Vampire Junction* revolves around Timmy Valentine, a 14-year-old vampire rock star who has emerged from the collective unconscious and can assume the form of people's deepest fears. In Brian Lumley's *Necroscope* (1986), Harry Keogh of the British Secret Service is a "necroscope" who can communicate with the dead. He and his Russian counterpart, Boris Dragosini, make contact with a vampire who has been buried in Romania and who lusts for freedom and revenge. When the Russians accidentally open an interdimensional portal, they discover the WAMPHRYI, an extraterrestrial race of vampires. NANCY A. COLLINS's *Sunglasses after Dark* (1989) populates the earth with "changelings"—vampires, werewolves etc.—who live and hunt among us. Her heroine, Sonja Blue, is a debutante, a prostitute, and a vampiress who is determined to destroy the vampire who created her.

Other popular fiction descendants of *Dracula* are POPPY Z. BRITE's *Lost Souls* (1992), which combines the power and horror of Stoker's *Dracula* with the desire to transcend the constraints of daily life, and Kim Newman's homage to vampiriana, *Anno Dracula* (1992), which plays with what might have happened had Dracula succeeded in taking over England.

Although most vampire literature embraces horror, it has transcended horror literature to become a genre unto itself. It is more and more difficult to classify vampire literature as "horror" per se, for an increasing number of vampire books fall into other genres or sub-genres, such as mystery and suspense, romance, fantasy, science fiction, action and adventure, westerns, and erotica.

Evolution of the vampire.   Drama and film adaptations of Stoker's novel softened Count Dracula and all vampires, and in turn have influenced fiction. The vampire's powers are sometimes seen not as a threat but as an asset, without worry about whether those powers come from the devil. More recently, fiction vampire protagonists have fallen into several primary lots:

Relentlessly evil.   Vampires continue to be primitive, evil creatures without conscience, such as in Stephen King's *'Salem's Lot* (1979), John Steakley's *Vampires* (1987), and Brian Lumley's Necroscope vampires.

Victims.   Vampires are hapless in their vampirism, such as in RICHARD MATHESON's *I AM LEGEND* (1954), which treats vampirism as a disease.

Romantic figures.   Vampires are wanderers who are romantic, seductive, and philosophical, such as in the Anne Rice books (see LESTAT DE LIONCOURT) and CHELSEA QUINN YARBRO's count, SAINT-GERMAIN. They are open citizens of the world, just another racial minority, such as in LAURELL K. HAMILTON's novels.

Do-gooders.   Vampires fight on the side of good, such as in the novels of Fred Saberhagen. Two novels by Lee Killough, *Blood Hunt* (1987) and *Blood Links* (1988), feature a police officer who, after his involuntary transformation into a vampire, uses his hypnotic talent and superhuman strength in his law enforcement duties. (The vampire-turned-cop also was the theme of television's FOREVER KNIGHT—see below).

Empathetic aliens. Vampires are the ultimate outsiders, a separate race that might as well be from another planet (a theme explored in science fiction and fantasy since the days of Lovecraft). Vampires feel superior to humans, but have empathy and even consideration for them, much as humans do for animals. In *Fevre Dream* (1982) by George R. R. Martin, Joshua, the vampire protagonist, belongs to an alien race living secretly among humans. Orphaned in childhood, Joshua grows up thinking himself an aberrant human being, possessed by an uncontrollable craving for blood at monthly intervals. By the time he rediscovers his own people, he has developed a sympathy for mortals that inspires him to spend his years searching for a blood substitute that will free his kind from the need to kill. Set in the Mississippi riverboat era, Joshua has perfected this potion and has gathered a band of followers who share his dream of living without the slaughter of human prey. Joshua befriends a steamboat captain, Abner Marsh, to whom he tells the story of his childhood and his quest. This self-disclosure is a daring innovation. Joshua says, "I have never told the truth to one of you before." Captain Marsh retorts, "To one of the cattle . . . Well, I never lissened to no vampire before, so we're even."

In P. N. Elrod's "Vampire Files" novels, the hero Jack's enemies are often brutal gangsters who inflict cruel deaths on their fellow men that are far more horrible than the attack of a peace-loving vampire who lives on cattle blood and takes an occasional sip from his very willing girlfriend. In *Blood Alone* (1990), the second book in Elaine Bergstrom's alien vampire series, noble, creative vampires, artists in stained glass, are contrasted with the human-perpetrated horrors of World War II. In *The Vampire Tapestry* by Suzy McKee Charnas, the vampire EDWARD WEYLAND seldom kills, except when driven to the act in self-defense. Most of his victims are none the worse for the small amount of blood he takes. In contrast to the destructive ambitions of human predators, Weyland says, "I wish only to satisfy my appetite in peace." Despite his consideration of humans, Weyland also considers them to be far inferior to himself, likening them to "livestock."

The theme of blood substitute has been used often in fiction as a way of relieving sympathetic vampire protagonists from the nasty business of feeding off humans.

ANNE RICE has compared her vampire subculture to the outsider gay subculture and has noted that her novels have a strong appeal for homosexual readers. Also, she made Lestat a rock musician, because they "are expected to be completely wild, completely unpredictable and completely themselves, and they are rewarded for that." The glorification of the outsider has strong intellectual, emotional, and sexual attraction.

Love interests. Vampires are lovers par excellence and romantic partners. In the mystery "Vampire Files" novels of P. N. Elrod, the vampire detective is a superb lover whose mistress tells him, "I really prefer it your way . . . When you do it this way, it just goes on and on." The implied contrast with the limitations of mortal men is obvious.

Vampires—and werewolves—are most popular as lovers in the romance genre, which has subgenres that blend paranormal, science fiction, and fantasy elements. Still, romance must be the central plot, and most paranormal/sci-fi/fantasy romances feature generous amounts of sex.

Linda Lael Miller's vampire Valerian, molded after Anne Rice's vampires, is both an Outsider and accessible lover. In *Time Without End* (1995), the story cuts back and forth across time. In the present (1995) Valerian is an eccentric Outsider, a stage magician in Las Vegas who captivates huge audiences with his show—which, unbeknownst to the mortal throngs, is accomplished with his real supernatural powers. He lives in an underground cave-like home and is, like Rice's Lestat, exceptionally wealthy. Valerian was a mortal in the 14th century; he was another Outsider, a peasant boy in love with a baron's daughter. The daughter dies tragically and Valerian, wandering in despair, is made a vampire by a former teacher. He spends the centuries looking for his lost soul mate, but whenever he finds her reincarnated, she mysteriously dies from some sort of curse. The curse is removed when Valerian finds the culprit is his younger brother, also made a vampire and secretly in love with the same baron's daughter. Ultimately, Valerian and his reincarnated love, a Las Vegas homicide detective named Daisy, find lasting happiness in their "mixed marriage." Thus, the vampire becomes just another minority figure with an odd lifestyle, but his supernatural, abilities, including time travel, make him an exotic lover. As he settles into married life, Valerian loses much of his aura of dangerousness.

CHRISTINE FEEHAN does a twist on the Beauty-and-the-Beast theme. In her best-selling Dark series novels, the vampire hunters and vampires are the Carpathians, a darker, more savage and predatory lot than Miller's Valerian and his kind. The male Carpathians can be transformed into better creatures only by their lifemates, whom they can find only among certain qualified mortal women.

SHERRILYN KENYON, creator of the best-selling Dark-Hunter vampire and Were-Hunter werewolf romances, features dangerous and sexy alpha heroes (strong and domineering), and weaves fantasy and classical mythology into her stories.

(See also the werewolf romances of SUSAN KRINARD.)

Eccentric minorities. More and more, vampires, along with werewolves, warlocks, demons, and other supernatural beings, have become "just the odd people next door," rather like Charles Addams's THE ADDAMS FAMILY and its imitator THE MUNSTERS. They populate a supernatural demimonde and mingle with mortals as friends, lovers, and enemies. CHARLAINE HARRIS's heroine Sookie Stackhouse goes from a dull life as a waitress to an exotic life with a vampire boyfriend, Bill, in *Dead Until Dark* (2001).

In Linda Lael Miller's *Tonight and Always* (1996), Kristina Holbrook is the 175-year-old progeny of the vampire Queen Maeve and Calder Holbrook, a mortal who opted to become a vampire. Her "uncle" is Valerian. Being only half-vampire, Kristina fortunately does not have to deal with the messy business of blood drinking, and she can go about in daylight. She has modest magical powers. When she falls in love with a mortal high school teacher, Max Kilcarragh, she agonizes over her inability to live as a mortal: to have children and to grow old. Oddly, Max does not do much other than raise an eyebrow when she informs him of her quasi-supernatural status, and her bizarre world of vampires, warlocks, magical powers, supernatural wolf pets (Daisy's), and so on. Luckily for Kristina, a genetic factor mutates her into a full human being, thus ridding her of vampire disadvantages as well as her mediocre magical powers. But Max inherits her eccentric "family."

When vampires are reduced to friends, lovers, and neighbors—and even rock stars and magicians—they lose some, or even all, of their outsider glamor and become ordinary. This version of the vampire raises the question: Can an "ordinary" vampire continue to inspire fear and terror?

Female vampires.   Most early vampire tales concerned "fatal men," but the Romantic poets inspired a profusion of stories about "femmes fatales." The female vampire of 19th-century fiction is patterned after the fatal woman of the Romantic sensibility, such as Keats's *Lamia* and *La Belle Dame Sans Merci.*

Theophile Gautier was the founder of the French decadence movement. His masterpiece, *La Morte Amoureuse* (1836), was first translated by Lafcadio Hearn as *Clarimonde.* It has been retranslated and reprinted as: *The Beautiful Vampire, Clarimonda, Clarimonde, Vampire and Harlot, The Dead Leman, The Dead Lover, The Dreamland Bride,* and *The Vampire.* The power of this tale lies in its dreamlike eroticism and ambiguity. Father Romuald is a pious young priest who is troubled by dreams of wild, erotic liaisons with a voluptuous courtesan named Clarimonde, whom he had met shortly before her death. These dreams take over his life, and he becomes weaker and weaker. When Romuald tells his superior about his dreams, he is told that he is under the spell of a succubus. They dig up Clarimonde's body and sprinkle it with holy WATER, whereupon it turns to dust. Clarimonde enters Romuald's dreams once more to berate him for betraying the love and happiness that she has given him. It is impossible to tell if Romuald was the victim of a succubus or if his dreams were a manifestation of his lust for his beautiful neighbor.

"CARMILLA" (1871), J. Sheridan Le Fanu's tale of a vampire countess by the same name, was a major force in vampire fiction. Carmilla is both evil predator and seductress, and seems desperate for her victim's love. She vampirizes young women in a lesbianlike fashion.

Other notable stories about female vampires include *The Last Lords of Gardonal* (1867) by William Gilbert, *A Mystery of the Campagna* (1887) by Anne Crawford (von Rabe), and *Ken's Mystery* by Julian Hawthorne (1888). Mary E. Braddon's *Good Lady Ducayne* (1896) is a variation on the life of the 16th-century Hungarian countess Elizabeth Bathóry, who murdered hundreds of young girls and bathed in their blood in an attempt to restore her youth and beauty. Lady Ducayne's physician injects her with blood he has drained from her unfortunate servants.

In more modern fiction, female vampires are, like their male counterparts, of varying types. In Whitley Strieber's THE HUNGER, Miriam Blaylock is cold and calculating. Queen Akasha, in Rice's QUEEN OF THE DAMNED, is ambitious, manipulative, powerful, and cunning—but still falls because of a male (the vampire Lestat).

More recent fiction has featured BadGirl/Tough Girl vampires who can fight, kick, and gun their way out of confrontations with evil males, yet are soft and sexy in the bedroom. In paranormal romances, Miller's female vampires, such as Queen Maeve, are formidable but femmes fatales. Such traits also have been given to female vampire hunters as well, such as Hamilton's Anita Blake.

Psychic vampirism.   Charles Wilkins Webber's *Spiritual Vampirism* (1853), is one of the first, if not the first, English-language novel to feature psychic vampirism (see PSYCHIC ATTACK). Like Sir Arthur Conan Doyle's novella THE PARASITE (1894), *Spiritual Vampirism* equates vampirism with hypnosis. Energy-draining vampires can be men or women but, unlike classic vampires, they can also be things. In addition, they can feed on various types of energy. In W. L. Alden's story of 1894, a student absorbs her teacher's talents and ideas. The ways in which these vampires obtain the energy that they need are limited only by the authors' imaginations. In J. Meade Faulkner's *The Lost Stradivarius* (1892), an undead sorcerer drains the energy of anyone who plays a certain violin. In H. J. Chaytor's novel *The Light of the Eye* (1897), a man's eyes draw the life force from his victims (see EYE).

Two important novels about energy-draining vampires were published in the 1890s. In James Maclaren Cobban's *Master of His Fate* (1890), Julius Courtney's friends deem him a brilliant and talented young man. However, he is older than he appears to be, for he has discovered a formula that allows him to renew his youth by absorbing energy from the people he touches. As the years pass, he needs to take more and more energy until his "donors" almost die. When Julius falls in love with his friend's sister, he declares himself unworthy of her and, finally, commits SUICIDE rather than risk harming her. Florence Marryat's *The Blood of the Vampire* (1897) is a rare book about an energy-draining femme fatale. Many of the people who befriend the young heiress, Harriet Brandt, sicken and die. The explanation is that just as some people are born to give of themselves and to nourish others, "Hally" is destined to take from and, ultimately, destroy the people she cares for.

F. Marion Crawford's "For the Blood Is the Life" (1911) first appeared in his collection *Uncanny Tales.* A Gypsy girl named Christina is murdered by thieves but returns to life as a vampire. Every night she courts a young man who had rejected her in life, draining his energy and drinking his blood. Finally, he digs up her body and drives a stake through her heart. Years later, her ghost can be seen hovering above her grave on moonlit nights. *The Transfer* (1912) by Algernon Blackwood builds to a unique confrontation between two types of energy-draining vampires—Mr. Frene, a psychic sponge who absorbs people's energy and ideas, and an arid patch of land known as the "Forbidden Corner." E. F. Benson wrote two popular tales about female vampires. In *The Room in the Tower* (1912), a spectral hag preys upon people who sleep in a certain room, while the vampiress in *Mrs. Amworth* (1923) appears to be a respectable, middle-aged woman who has recently arrived in a quiet English town. (See OLD HAG.)

Other early works, such as George Sylvester Viereck's *The House of the Vampire* (1907), Reginald Hodder's *The Vampire* (1913), DION FORTUNE's *The Demon Lover* (1927), and Hans Heinz Ewers's *Vampir* (1921), use vampirism as a metaphor.

Vampiric possession. Vampiric possession is an extreme form of psychic vampirism in which a being perpetuates its existence by taking over the body, mind, or soul of its host. In Guy de Maupassant's classic story "The Horla" (1886), the narrator becomes convinced that an invisible alien presence is attacking him in his sleep, and is taking over his body and his soul. The tension builds gradually as he degenerates and, when he finds that he can not destroy the Horla (or "stranger"), he commits SUICIDE.

Edgar Allan Poe's tales of obsession and necrophilia influenced many of the writers of his day. In two of his fantasies, femmes fatales cheat death by taking possession of another person's body. "Morella" (1835) features a woman who is wasting away from tuberculosis and who vows that she will not die. On her deathbed, she gives birth to a daughter who, to her husband's horror, grows to resemble her mother in face, form, and manner. The daughter remains unnamed until she is a young woman but, when her father baptizes her Morella, she responds, "I am here!" She falls down dead and is buried in her mother's grave—which is found to be empty. "Ligeia" (1838), another variation on this theme, tells of a dead woman who reanimates the corpse of her faithless husband's second wife.

Another, indirect form of vampiric possession occurs in some versions of the Faust legend, in which youth or immortality is purchased through periodic human sacrifices. For instance, W. Harrison Ainsworth's *Auriol* (1850) obtains an elixir of life in exchange for a human sacrifice that is made every 10 years. A similar compact is implied in *The Vampyre*, and Bram Stoker included the possibility that Dracula had made a deal with the devil when he called him a "sorcerer" and a "necromancer" who had studied at the SCHOLOMANCE. Smyth Upton's novel *The Last of the Vampires* (1845), and G. M. W. Reynolds's *Faust* (1847) contend that vampirism is a special form of magic in which the vampire obtains life, pleasure, and power by sacrificial means.

Vampire inspired. The term *pseudo-vampirism* may be applied to novels and stories that do not contain vampires, but revolve around some aspect of vampirism. This category includes mysteries in which a murder or murders appear to have been committed by a vampire but, ultimately, have a mundane solution; villains or femmes fatales who are characterized as "vampires"; and miscellaneous blood-drinking creatures. Clement Robbins's novel *The Vampires of New York* (ca. 1831) is one of the first detective stories with a pseudo-vampiric theme, while *Vampires* by Julien Gordon (1891) uses vampirism as a metaphor to describe the destructive relationship between a femme fatale and her suitor.

Vampires have served as metaphors for AIDS, colonialism, political repression and totalitarianism, terrorism, all manner of oppressions, and a host of psychic and other ills suffered by society.

Stage
Vampires are the subjects of more than 40 plays in English, French, and American drama, and are featured in more than 100 international stage productions, including opera and ballet.

The vampire character emerged in the 19th century during a time of changing social attitudes toward sex, women, eating, foreigners, disease, and death. Sex had to be camouflaged. The vampire provided the ideal camouflage because it could commit sexual violation without involving the genitals. The drinking of blood served as the sex act. As authors, playwrights, and producers discovered, vampires brought in money. Putting *vampire* in title of a production guaranteed an audience. The vampire enabled an exploitation of dark side of sexual fantasy while pretending to condemn it. Vampire dramas are emancipatory,

A selection of the many stage productions about Dracula (Photo by R. E. Guiley. Courtesy Vampire Empire Archives)

with the vampire serving not as an evil villain, but as a romantic antihero.

From 1820 numerous vampire plays were produced. Most of them originated in Paris—the home of the Grand Guignol, the theater of sex, violence, and blood—and were imported to England and America. Polidori's "The Vampyre" inspired Charles Nodier's novel *Lord Ruthven, ou les vampires* (1820), which was revised as a play entitled *The Vampire; or, The Bride of the Isles*. It was translated into several languages and toured Europe and North America for years. Stage adaptations of "The Vampyre" appeared on a regular basis until the middle of the century. The last noteworthy performance, Alexandre Dumas's play *Le Vampire*, opened at the Ambrigue-Comique in Paris in 1851. A masquerade and ballet, it was adapted into English and was retitled *The Phantom*. It also was satirized by Gilbert and Sullivan in the operetta *Ruddigore* in 1887.

Polidori's story also inspired Robert Southey's *Thalaba the Destroyer* (1823) and Ludvig Tieck's short story "Wake Not the Dead," which in turn inspired George Blink's play *The Vampire Bride* (1834). In 1828 the opera *Der Vampyr* by Heinrich Marschner opened in Leipzig and London.

Stoker probably had the stage in mind when he wrote *Dracula*, for his theater training is apparent in the manner in which the novel unfolds. Stoker organized a stage reading of his novel just months prior to its publication, and even held hopes that his employer, the illustrious actor Henry Irving, might play the count. Irving, however, reportedly was unimpressed by the reading, and a stage production never materialized during Stoker's lifetime.

HAMILTON DEANE, working with JOHN L. BALDERSTON, adapted *Dracula* for the stage in 1924, 12 years after Stoker died. Deane simplified the plot and transformed the count from a loathsome, evil creature into a tragic, romantic and well-dressed figure, more along the lines of Polidori's well-heeled Lord Ruthven. This reinvention of Dracula had a powerful impact on all subsequent stage productions of *Dracula* and especially films, forever changing the way audiences of all media regarded vampires. Florence Stoker, Bram's widow, did not like Deane's treatment, and commissioned another stage version from Charles Morrell, which starred Raymond Huntly as the count. But it was Deane's version that had the lasting international impact, and when it came to America in 1927, it helped to launch BELA LUGOSI in his American acting career.

Today *Dracula* seems tame by comparison to more modern offerings, but when it debuted in America it riveted audiences. Advertisements warned theater-goers ". . . that it would be wise for them to visit a specialist and have their hearts examined before subjecting them to the fearful thrills and shocks that *Dracula* holds in store for them."

Deane's play, with adaptations for the American stage by Balderston, was revived in the 1970s, with Frank Langella as a modern and very sensual count. There was little change in the original text; most of the innovations came in the form of new theater technology. Langella starred in John Badham's film version of *Dracula*, and so sensual is

Advertisement for a Philadelphia production of the Dracula *stage adaptation written by Hamilton Deane and John L. Balderston, starring Bela Lugosi (Courtesy Vampire Empire Archives)*

his portrayal of the count that it is difficult to think of him as an evil to be feared.

Like novelists, playwrights made innovative adaptations of *Dracula,* and also reached beyond Stoker's novel to create productions featuring other vampires and their victims and hunters. For example, Snoo Wilson's *Vampires* (1973) makes no reference to Dracula, but uses the vampire theme as a metaphor for oppression. Vampires as metaphor for a variety of human ailments of the psyche and soul became more popular in stage productions on into the 1980s. On the lighter side were satires like Charles Busch's *Vampire Lesbians of Sodom* (1985), which featured "vamps" in drag.

Vampires also have been the subject of musicals, operas, and ballet. For example, in the United States the Houston Ballet produced *Dracula* in 1997, choreographed by Ben Stevenson and featuring music by Franz Liszt. In Canada the Royal Winnipeg Ballet staged its own production of *Dracula,* truer to Stoker's novel than to the Houston production, with music by Gustav Mahler. The production was later adapted to film as *Dracula: Pages from a Virgin's Diary* (2002). And in the United Kingdom, the Northern Ballet Theatre toured with a production by Christopher Gable and Michael Pink, and original music by Philip Feeney.

Michael Kunze's musical *Dance of the Vampires*, based on the Roman Polanski film by the same title, was a smash hit in Germany and elsewhere in Europe. But when produced in New York City in 2002—starring superstar Michael Crawford as Count von Krolock—it was met with dismal reviews and box office failure, and closed within weeks. In 2003 rock star Elton John announced his plans to create a musical based on Rice's *Queen of the Damned*, about the vampire queen, Akasha.

Film and Television

Vampires were featured in the *fantasmagorie* (phantasmagoria) of Paris in the late 19th century. Since 1897 more than 600 vampire films have been produced, and Count Dracula has appeared in more than 130 of them—more than any other fictional character except Sherlock Holmes.

Films have generally looked to novels as sources for adaptation. Two dominant streams of vampire themes emerged early in filmmaking: the vampire as evil horror, and the vampire as romantic figure. Both are based largely on Stoker's *Dracula*, with other literary influences such as *Carmilla* and "The Vampyre." F. W. MURNAU's *NOSFERATU*, a silent film of 1922, was a plagiarism of *Dracula* and presented one of the most horrific vampires ever to appear on the screen (MAX SCHRECK as GRAF ORLOCK). Orlock is pure evil, and looks like a cross between a demon from hell and a walking cadaver. Nine years later, the official film adaptation of *Dracula* by TOD BROWNING, starring Lugosi, followed Hamilton Deane's model of the tragic and romantic figure. The Dracula films that followed have more or less portrayed a romantic figure, though CHRISTOPHER LEE's Dracula for HAMMER FILMS is cold and cunning. In 1994 *Interview With the Vampire*, based on Anne Rice's vampires, took vampire glamor to a new level in film. Numerous popular works of fiction have been adapted to film.

Predatory female vampires have been featured, most notably by INGRID PITT, and more recently by the singer Aaliyah as Queen Akasha in *Queen of the Damned*. Vampires have been satirized, such as in *Love At First Bite*, starring George Hamilton, and *Dracula, Dead and Loving It*, starring Leslie Nielsen.

Vampires provide excellent material for teen angst films, and offerings in that department have included THE LOST BOYS, starring Kiefer Sutherland and Jason Patric as alienated and vicious teenage gang vampires; and FRIGHT NIGHT starring William Ragsdale and Roddy McDowell, about a nice-boy teen who discovers the man next door is a vampire.

Numerous films follow the vampire-as-evil-monster theme. In these the vampires are outlaws who often are hideous, even demonic in appearance, and unrelenting gore and violence take place as they kill and are killed.

Among the films of this type are *Near Dark*, in which a scruffy band of modern vampires drive around in a Winnebago and slaughter people; *Vampires*, based on the John Steakley novel by the same title, in which professional vampire hunters rout vampires from their "nests" like colonies of vermin; *From Dusk Until Dawn*, starring George Clooney, in which demonic vampires masquerade as strippers in a cheap bar; and the *Subspecies* films, about a Vlad Tepes-like vampire.

On television the first made-for-television vampire program was a live performance of *Dracula*, starring John Carradine as the count, broadcast from New York City on November 23, 1956. Vampires then appeared in comic roles, in series such as *The Addams Family* and *The Munsters*, and in individual episodes of other comedy series. Vincent Price, who normally brings chills to a screen, played a vampire with a Lugosi accent for laughs in an episode of *F Troop* in 1966.

In 1966 Dan Curtis's *Dark Shadows* soap opera debuted on daytime television. It floundered until the vampire character, Barnabas Collins (JONATHAN FRID) was introduced in 1967. *Dark Shadows* went on to become one of the most popular and lasting series, still enduring despite its end in 1971.

Immediately after the end of *Dark Shadows*, Curtis produced a telemovie, KOLCHAK: THE NIGHT STALKER, directed by John Llewellyn Moxey and starring Darren McGavin as Carl Kolchak, a newspaper reporter who encounters a modern vampire, Janos Skorzeny (Barry Atwater). When Kolchak finds that no one will believe him about the vampire, he must take on the role of vampire hunter alone. The story was based on a novel by Jeff Rice, *The Kolchak Papers*, and was scripted by Richard Matheson. Aired on January 11, 1972, *The Night Stalker* was one of the highest-rated telemovies for its time, and led to a series by the same title, with McGavin continuing as Kolchak. Only one of the 20 episodes features a vampire: Catherine Rawlines is a vampire who masquerades as a prostitute, and leaves behind her dead clientele.

In 1973 Curtis produced and directed a sequel, *The Night Strangler*, scripted by Matheson. The story has a vampiric element but no vampire. A doctor discovers an elixir that is a macabre fountain of youth: It requires blood from a woman's brain, removed within 30 seconds of death.

Vampire-themed episodes appeared on shows such as Rod Serling's *The Twilight Zone* and *Night Gallery*; George Romero and Richard Rubenstein's *Tales from the Darkside* (which spawned *Monsters*); and Joel Silver and Roger Zemicks's *Tales from the Crypt*. These shows featured one-off episodes as complete stories.

Tales from the Crypt was based on the comics of the same title. The show benefited from being on cable, and thus not subject to the censorship rules of the networks. *Tales* featured high production values, big name stars, accomplished film directors, talented screenwriters, and state-of-the-art special effects. Three vampire and vampire/werewolf stories aired in four seasons. *The Reluctant*

"Vampire Lovers," from the Vampire Tarot *by Robert Michael Place*

Not all vampire shows were successful. *Forever Knight* struggled along for several seasons, and Dan Curtis's effort to revive *Dark Shadows* in 1991–92 with a new cast was quickly staked by lack of audience interest. (Another attempt at revival was announced in 2003 by the WB Network.) Another casualty of the early 1990s was *Dracula-The Series,* created by Universal Studios and billed as an "all-family weekly action-adventure" program. The show revolved around two teenage American brothers, Max and Chris Towsend, who are on a long trip to Europe with their mother. Interested in vampires, Max discovers that the local entrepreneur, Lucard (a sort of anagram of Dracula, but missing an *a*), is actually *the* Count Dracula, and he has a sinister plot to rule the world. The boys join their Uncle Gustav Helsing, a descendent of the Abraham Van Helsing family, to try to defeat Lucard.

The daytime soap PORT CHARLES on ABC had difficulty maintaining its audience once vampires and the supernatural were introduced. *Port Charles* started as an award-winning hospital drama in 1997, but switched to a vampire-slayer world à la BUFFY THE VAMPIRE SLAYER in 2001 in an effort to boost falling ratings. Ultimately the audience was ambivalent about the vampires, and the show was canceled in September 2003.

The Future of the Fictional Vampire

In the last 250 years, the vampire has covered considerable ground as a fictional character. It has become almost the opposite of its original nature, and it has played virtually every starring and supporting role there is to play. If the fictional vampire becomes integrated into society, a new villain will have to fill the vacuum. However, no other creature as yet has come close to the vampire in drawing power.

FURTHER READING:

Auerbach, Nina. *Our Vampires, Ourselves.* Chicago: The University of Chicago Press, 1995.

Carter, Margaret L., ed. *The Vampire in Literature: a critical bibliography.* Ann Arbor: UMI Research Press, 1989.

Carter, Margaret L. "From Hero to Villain." In *The Complete Vampire Companion.* Rosemary Ellen Guiley, with J. B. Macabre. New York: Macmillan, 1994.

Deane, Hamilton, and John L. Balderston. *Dracula: The Vampire Play.* Garden City, N.Y.: Nelson Doubleday, 1971.

Eighteen-Bisang, Robert. "Sinking Teeth Into the Literary Vampire," in *The Complete Vampire Companion* by Rosemary Ellen Guiley with J. B. Macabre. New York: Macmillan, 1994.

Frayling, Christopher. *Vampyres: Lord Byron to Count Dracula.* London: Faber and Faber, 1991.

Frost, Brian J. *The Monster With a Thousand Faces: Guises of the Vampire in Myth and Literature.* Bowling Green, Ohio: Bowling Green State University Popular Press, 1989.

Gladwell, Alicia, ed. *Blood and Roses: The Vampire in 19th Century Literature,* rev. ed. London: Creation Books, 1999.

Guiley, Rosemary Ellen, with J. B. Macabre. *The Complete Vampire Companion.* New York: Macmillan, 1994.

Vampire features a vampire who works the night shift as a guard in a blood bank, who is oddly queasy about blood. He falls in love, is discovered, does battle, and is killed, but he dies happy. *The Secret* concerns a boy who is adopted by a vampire family, the members of whom see him as a meal. But the vampires get a surprise when the boy turns out to be a werewolf. The third, *Werewolf Concerto,* is set in an old dark and isolated hotel. Guests are mysteriously killed off by both a vampire and a werewolf, who have a showdown over the bounty.

Frank Mancuso Jr.'s series *Friday the 13th, the Series,* about antique dealers who go around the world tracking down the cursed objects owned by a dead dealer who sold his soul to the devil, also featured vampires.

In 1989 rock star Rick Springfield starred in the tele-movie *Nick Knight,* about a vampire-turned-cop who seeks to amend his evil ways. The movie eventually led to the series FOREVER KNIGHT, starring Geraint Wyn Davies as Nick Knight.

Holte, James Craig, ed. *The Fantastic Vampire: Studies in the Children of the Night, Selected Essays from the Eighteenth International Conference on the Fantastic in the Arts.* Westport, Conn.: Greenwood Press, 2002.

Lennig, Arthur. *The Count: The Life and Films of Bela "Dracula" Lugosi.* New York: Putnam's, 1974.

Miller, Elizabeth. *Dracula.* New York: Parkstone Press, 2000.

Miller, Elizabeth, ed. *Dracula: The Shade and the Shadow.* Westcliff-on-Sea, Essex, England: Desert Island Books, 1998.

Senf, Carol A. *The Vampire in 19th Century English Literature.* Bowling Green, Ky.: Bowling Green State University Popular Press, 1988.

Silver, Alain, and James Ursini. *The Vampire Film: From Nosferatu to Interview with the Vampire,* 3d ed. New York: Limelight Editions, 1997.

Skal, David J. *Hollywood Gothic: The Tangled Web of Dracula from Novel to Stage to Screen.* New York: W. W. Norton & Company, 1990.

Stuart, Roxana. *Stage Blood: Vampires of the 19th-Century Stage.* Bowling Green, Ohio: Bowling Green State University Popular Press, 1994.

Twitchell, James B. *The Living Dead: A Study of the Vampire in Romantic Literature.* Durham, N.C.: Duke University Press, 1981.

Waller, Gregory A. *The Living and the Undead.* Urbana: University of Illinois Press, 1986.

asasabonsam (asanbosam) African VAMPIRES. In Ghana lore the *asasabonsam* have hooks instead of feet. They like to bite their victims on the thumb. They can be men, women, or children.

ashes In folklore, the ashes of the burned CORPSE or organs of a destroyed VAMPIRE have the power to heal the victims of vampires. The ashes are mixed in a drink and taken as a medicine.

An anecdotal account from the late 19th century in Romania tells about an old peasant woman from Amarasti who died and became a vampire. A few months after her death, the children of her eldest son died one by one. Then the children of her youngest son began to die. Suspecting that their mother had become a vampire, the sons dug up her body, cut it in two, and reburied her. Still the deaths of the children continued. The sons dug up the body a second time, and were astonished to find it whole and without any wounds. This time they carted the corpse deep into the forest and laid it under a tree. They disemboweled it and removed the heart. Fresh blood flowed from it. They cut the heart into four pieces and burnt them to ashes, which they saved. They burned the rest of the body to ashes and buried them.

The sons mixed the ashes of the heart into water and gave the potion to the remaining children to drink. This remedy destroyed the vampire and stopped the deaths.

In a similar Romanian case from the late 19th century, a crippled, unmarried man from Cusmir died. Soon thereafter, his relatives fell ill and some of them died. Several complained that one of their legs was withering. The association of an affliction of the leg pointed to the crippled man as a vampire, so the villagers dug him up on a SATURDAY night. They found him "RED as red" and curled into a corner of the grave. They cut him open, removed the heart and liver, and burned the organs to ashes. These were mixed with water and given to the ill relations, who included the dead man's sister. They all regained their health.

Another case from the Cusmir region tells of a family that fell ill and suffered several deaths. An old man who had been dead a long time was suspected of being the vampire. When disinterred, the corpse was found "sitting up like a Turk, and as red as red, just like fire." The vampire, "unclean and horrible," resisted attempts to take him out of the grave. The villagers quelled him by chopping at him with an axe, and finally got him out. They found, however, that they could not cut the body with a knife. They took the axe and a scythe, and cut out the heart and liver, and burned them. The mutilated corpse was reburied. The ashes were given to the sick to drink with water. All of the ill persons regained their health.

In some areas, the smoke of burning vampire organs is believed to protect against evil. Villagers passed through the smoke to acquire the protection.

In other Slavic lore, the consumption of the ashes of one's CAUL can prevent one from turning into a vampire after death.

In vampire cases in New England in the 18th and 19th centuries, several corpses were disinterred so that their organs could be burned and mixed into medicine for victims of consumption.

See also NEW ENGLAND VAMPIRES.

FURTHER READING:
Bell, Michael E. *Food for the Dead: On the Trail of New England's Vampires.* New York: Carroll & Graf Publishers, 2001.

Murgoci, Agnes. "The Vampire in Roumania," in *The Vampire: A Casebook,* Alan Dundes, ed. Madison: University of Wisconsin Press, 1998.

aspen The wood of Christ's cross, and thus in folklore a protection against all evil things. Aspen is a favored wood for STAKES for confining or destroying VAMPIRES. Branches of aspen laid on the graves of vampires and witches will prevent them from rising up at night to terrorize people.

asrapa In Indian lore, a BLOOD-sucking witch who attends Kali, the fierce human flesh-eating goddess from whom the *asrapa* draws its power. The *asrapa* roams naked in CEMETERIES, where it raises the dead to life and practices SHAPE-SHIFTING.

astral vampire   Spirit form of a VAMPIRE; also, a magically created vampire. In occult lore, the astral vampire is the spirit shape of a LIVING VAMPIRE, such as certain witches or sorcerers who have the ability to project themselves out of body to attack their victims at a distance.

Astral vampires—a type of THOUGHT-FORM—can be created through magical procedures for PSYCHIC ATTACK.

Vampire researcher VINCENT HILLYER theorized that an astral form also might be the "real" vampire in cases of the restless dead. Hillyer said the astral vampire, the spirit essence of the dead person, might be able to project itself out from the CORPSE, feed on the living, and then return to the corpse to sustain it. He developed a theory called the "hemolytic factor" to explain how an astral form can draw off the BLOOD of a living person. The theory rests on the process of hemolysis, which is the destruction of red corpuscles that occurs with the release of hemoglobin into surrounding fluids. Hemolysis is caused by hemolysin, a substance in the blood serum that causes destruction of the red corpuscles. This effect is sometimes produced when red corpuscles from a different blood group are injected into the blood.

According to the hemolytic factor theory, the vampire's astral body penetrates the victim's aura and physical body. The vampire, which is in great need of blood, has sparse red corpuscles and can be considered the "wrong blood group." Hemolysis occurs, and the vampire sucks up the red corpuscles released in the victim's blood. These are transported back to the grave and infused into the corpse.

See also VAMPIRE SORCERERS AND WITCHES.

FURTHER READING:
Fortune, Dion. *Psychic Self-Defence.* York Beach, Me.: Samuel Weiser, 1957. First published 1939.
Guiley, Rosemary Ellen. *Vampires Among Us.* New York: Pocket Books, 1991.

aswang manananggal   SHAPE-SHIFTING Philippine VISCERA SUCKER that flies about as a bodiless head with trailing entrails, feeding on human flesh, BLOOD, organs, and mucus, especially of fetuses and newborns. It has a long tongue that can suck a fetus out of a womb.

The *aswang manananggal* is accompanied by small birds who act as FAMILIARS and reconnaissance, locating prey. By day, the vampire is either a man or a woman who is likely to be a respected member of the community.

Pregnant women can protect themselves by wearing a necklace made of bullets on a string and by smearing coal dust on their abdomens.

ataru   VAMPIRE in Ashantiland lore. Like the ASASABONSAM, the *ataru* drinks BLOOD through its victims' thumbs.

Augustine, St.   See SHAPE-SHIFTING.

Auvergne Werewolf (1558)   Woman executed for being a WEREWOLF. The case of the Auvergne Werewolf took place in 1558 and was reported by the demonologist HENRI BOGUET in his book *Discours des Sorciers* (1602).

According to an account related to Boguet by a "reliable source," the events in the case unfolded in the following manner:

A gentleman asked a passing hunter to bring him some of his kill. The hunter was attacked in the woods by an enormous wolf. He tried to shoot it but could not wound it, and was forced to fight it with his hands. He was able to cut off one of its paws with his hunting knife. Howling, the wolf fled. The hunter took the paw to show to the gentleman, who lived near the place where the attack had occurred. When the hunter took it from his pocket, he was astonished to see that it had changed into a woman's hand with a ring on one finger. The gentleman recognized the ring as belonging to his wife. He went immediately into the kitchen, where he found his wife hiding her arm in her apron. He seized it and saw that she was missing one hand.

The wife confessed to transforming herself into a wolf in order to attend a SABBAT. She was burned alive at the stake in Ryon.

See also SHAPE-SHIFTING.

baital Indian VAMPIRE. The term *baital* succeeded the older term of VETALA. The *baital* is an evil, mischievous spirit that inhabits and reanimates CORPSES. Its form is half man, half BAT, and stands approximately four to five feet tall.

In the Hindu folktale *KING VIKRAM AND THE VAMPIRE*, the baital hangs upside down in a siras-tree (mimosa tree), for that is where the corpse he inhabits was placed. Its appearance is described thus:

> Its eyes, which were wide open, were of a greenish-brown, and never twinkled; its hair also was brown [a color associated with low-caste men, witches and fiends], and brown was its face—three several shades which, notwithstanding, approached one another in an unpleasant way, as in an over-dried coconut. Its body was thin and ribbed like a skeleton or a bamboo framework, and as it held onto a bough, like a flying fox, by the toe-tips, its drawn muscles stood out as if they were ropes of coir. Blood it appeared to have none, or there would have been a decided determination of that curious juice to the head; and as the Raja handled its skin, it felt icy cold and clammy as might a snake. The only sign of life was the whisking of a ragged little tail much resembling a goat's.

The *baital* has ironlike skin that makes it impervious to blows. He is wily and clever.

FURTHER READING:
Burton, Isabel, ed. *Captain Sir Richard F. Burton's King Vikram and the Vampire*. Rochester, Vt.: Park Street Press, 1992.

Balderston, John L. (1889–1954) American journalist and foreign correspondent, best known for his collaboration with actor HAMILTON DEANE on the American stage production of BRAM STOKER'S *DRACULA*. The New York production opened in 1927.

See also ARTS AND ENTERTAINMENT.

baobhan sith Vampiric Scottish fairies who appear as beautiful young women dressed in green. *Baobhan sith* is a Highland term for a banshee and usually is applied to dangerous and evil SUCCUBI. The *baobhan sith* dance with men until the men are exhausted, and then feed upon them. They can be killed with cold IRON.

The *baobhan sith* are especially fond of hunters and young men who are out after dark. One Scottish folktale tells of four young men who went hunting and spent the night in an empty shieling, a hut for the shelter of grazing sheep. To entertain themselves, they played mouth-music and danced. One of the men wished they had dancing partners. Immediately, four beautiful women appeared. Three danced with the men and the fourth stood by the music maker. The music maker suddenly noticed that drops of BLOOD were falling from his dancing friends. Terrified, he fled, pursued by the VAMPIRE. He hid himself among their horses, protected by the iron of their shoes. The vampire nonetheless kept circling him, but had to give up when dawn came. The hunter returned to the shieling and was horrified to find the bloodless bodies of his companions.

FURTHER READING:
Briggs, Katharine. *An Encyclopedia of Fairies*. New York: Pantheon Books, 1976.

Baring-Gould, Sabine (1834–1924)

Baring-Gould, Sabine (1834–1924)   English folklorist, archeologist, historian, parson, and novelist, best known for his work *The Book of Were-Wolves*, published in 1865. *The Book of Werewolves* was a source consulted by BRAM STOKER in his research for DRACULA (1897).

Sabine Baring-Gould was a prolific writer, authoring about 30 novels and 100 other books on various nonfiction subjects. Among his works is a 16-volume set on *Lives of the Saints*. He also was a collector of British folk songs, and he wrote one of the most popular Christian hymns, "Onward Christian Soldiers."

Baring-Gould's work on WEREWOLVES is the first comprehensive book on the subject to be published in English, and it remains a classic, authoritative source. The book was inspired by an incident he experienced as a young man while staying in the French countryside. Baring-Gould had gone to a Druidic cromlech, the Pierre labie at La Rondelle, near Champigni. It took longer to reach the cromlech than he anticipated—the hike was 10 miles from where he was staying—and he did not arrive until near sunset. He used the remaining sunlight to draw sketches. He then had to make the long trek home, complicated by an injury he had done to his leg while exploring the stones.

Baring-Gould walked to the nearby hamlet of Vienne, where he hoped he could hire a trap to take him the rest of the way. It was not as simple a matter as he expected. The villagers were horrified and tried to persuade him to stay the night. The priest at Vienne offered him lodging, but Baring-Gould declined, explaining that his family wished to depart early in the morning and so he had to return that night. The mayor told him that he could not travel back across the flats because of the danger of LOUPS-GAROUX.

The villagers discussed their options. One of them could accompany Baring-Gould, but would then face the treacherous journey back across the flats alone. Two could go, so that they would have each other on the return trip. The villagers were still afraid, however, for they said a werewolf as big as a calf and with glaring eyes had been seen in a buckwheat field recently one evening at sunset. They discussed at length the grave dangers of encountering the wolf-fiend.

Finally Baring-Gould said he would make the journey alone. He vowed that if he were attacked by the werewolf, he would crop the beast's ears and tail and send the trophies to the mayor. The villagers were relieved not to have to go with him.

Baring-Gould set out alone on the road across the desolate landscape, which was eerily illuminated by a sliver of new MOON. The landscape was spooky and meeting wolves actually was not out of the question. He armed himself with a stick in case an animal should attack. Nothing dangerous happened, but Baring-Gould's interest in werewolves was piqued, and he decided to investigate the subject.

He researched the legal records from the Middle Ages on court cases involving LYCANTHROPY, and also European folklore. His own conclusion was that lycanthropy was primarily a mental disorder rather than a supernatural phenomenon.

For *Dracula*, Stoker derived the name BERSICKER for his wolf from the BERSERKIR discussed in *The Book of Were-Wolves*. Baring-Gould's descriptions of werewolves also inspired Stoker's descriptions of COUNT DRACULA's wolfish appearance: his broad and squat fingers, hairy palms, sharp and pointed nails, sharp teeth that protrude over the lower lip, and heavy eyebrows that meet.

FURTHER READING:
Baring-Gould, Sabine. *The Book of Were-Wolves*. London: Smith, Elder & Co., 1865.
Frayling, Christopher. *Vampyres: Lord Byron to Count Dracula*. London: Faber and Faber, 1991.
Miller, Elizabeth. *Dracula: Sense and Nonsense*. Westcliff-on-Sea, England: Desert Island Books, 2000.

Bathóry, Elizabeth (1560–1614)

Bathóry, Elizabeth (1560–1614)   BLOOD-bathing noblewoman, called "the Blood Countess." It is not known if Elizabeth Bathóry actually drank blood, but she was obsessed with bathing in it. Her obsession might be considered a form of vampirism, especially considering the lives that were sacrificed for her habit.

Bathóry was born in 1560 in Ecsed, TRANSYLVANIA, to a noble family who dominated the region in the southeast of Hungary, in what is now Romania. She was a great beauty, but was an ill-tempered child. At age 14 she became pregnant by a peasant man and was sequestered until she gave birth. In 1575, at age 15, she was married to Count Ferencz Nadasdy, a wealthy man who was many years her senior. She went to live at Castle Savar, the count's family estate.

She was an accomplished hostess, but also sadistic to servants and peasants. The Magyar nobles had virtual free reign to do whatever they pleased, and the slightest whims and grossest of perversions had to be obeyed. Bathóry seemed to enjoy tormenting pretty girls. A cousin of her husband's was accused of stealing fruit, and in punishment Bathóry had her tied naked to a tree and smeared with honey to attract insects. Her husband also taught her to discipline servant girls by putting oiled paper between their toes and setting the paper afire. The girls' wild attempts to get rid of the paper was called "star-kicking," to the amusement of the nobles.

By age 25 Bathóry was terrified of losing her beauty, a fear that grew worse with each passing year. After her husband's sudden death—possibly of appendicitis—in 1604, she began to lead a twisted double life. She had already dabbled in sorcery, attending secret sacrifices of white horses and encouraging the company of a sorceress named Anna Darvulia who brought out her worst.

According to lore, Bathóry was introduced to the benefits of blood by accident. To punish a clumsy maid, she took a pair of scissors and struck the girl in the face, cutting her and causing blood to splash upon Bathóry's hand. Bathóry seemed to think the blood restored the youthful appearance of her skin (she was perhaps by now in middle age past menopause). Her sorceress concurred with her that bathing in virgin's blood would indeed help her to regain and retain her youth. Bathóry began bathing in blood as often as possible, performing it as a ritual at four in the morning, a mysterious time specified by Darvulia.

Serving girls were fattened up, tortured, bled, and killed. The victims were procured by two old women and an individual named Fitzko, who were Bathóry's accomplices. Bathóry had the girls tied up tightly so that their blood would spray out when they were cut with scissors or pricked with pins. She also had hot pokers stuck into their mouths, and when she was done bleeding them, she had them beaten to death with a whip. Bathóry also visited other abominations upon the hapless girls, such as ironing their feet with a hot iron, pouring cold water on them as they stood naked in the snow, and forcing them to eat the cooked flesh of other serving girls killed.

One of Bathóry's favorite activities was to sit beneath a cage full of servant girls that was hoisted up off the floor. The cage was lined with sharp spikes, and the girls were prodded into the spikes with burning irons. This way, Bathóry had her own blood shower. She reportedly forced her servant girls to lick the blood off her back.

And so the atrocities went. Young girls were lured to her with offers of fine jobs. Once inside, they were imprisoned, never to see the outside again.

By 1609 Darvulia was dead and Bathóry was convinced that the blood baths were no longer holding back the march of time. She consulted another sorceress, and was told that her victims should be virgins of nobility. Securing these victims was more difficult, but Bathóry used the ruse of offering them jobs as maids of honor. Still, there weren't enough noble young ladies to fill the blood bowls, and Bathóry's accomplices were forced to dress up peasant girls in fine clothing to pass them off as nobility.

Rumors about Bathóry, which had been circulating, finally could no longer be ignored. Perhaps it was of no official concern if only peasant girls were meeting their deaths, but the murders of gentry was another matter. One of Bathóry's cousins, Lord Palatine, Count George Thurzo, inspected her castle at Csejthe on December 30, 1610, accompanied by soldiers, the governor of the province, the village priest, and local gendarmes. The count was horrified to find the bodies of tortured girls, and living girls who'd been "milked" and were penned up like animals. The Lord Palatine immediately arrested Bathóry's accomplice servants, including her maid, Zsuzanna, and everyone else in the castle. Exhumations revealed the remains of more than 50 bodies. Bathóry's journals reportedly listed the names of more than 600 victims.

The accomplices were tried and convicted. One was beheaded and burnt, and two had their fingers torn off one by one with hot pincers, and then were burned alive.

Elizabeth Bathóry (Author's collection)

Bathóry was not arrested or tried, probably because of her nobility. Nonetheless, she was punished. Her cousin believed her to be insane, and had her walled up in her bedroom in her castle at Csejthe. Slits let in air, but very little light. Food was sent in through a slot. There she lived in isolation and misery until August 21, 1614, when she died suddenly.

FURTHER READING:
McNally, Raymond T. *Dracula Was a Woman: In Search of the Blood Countess of Transylvania.* New York: McGraw-Hill, 1983.

bat mass ritual   Ritual performed by Catholic Maya Indians in parts of Belize, to ward off VAMPIRE BAT bites. Many of the Indians raise hogs, which attract vampire bats. Whenever the level of biting of hogs—and humans—is deemed excessive, the Maya capture a bat (any kind) and perform a Mass over it. They pray over the bat, tell it their

Vampire bat (Author's collection)

problems, and ask it to ask the other bats to leave them and their livestock alone. The bat is then released back into the wild.

FURTHER READING:
Brown, David E. *Vampiro: the Vampire Bat in Fact and Fantasy.* Silver City, N.M.: High-Lonesome Books, 1994.

bats   One of the shape-shifted guises of VAMPIRES. Bats seldom appear in European vampire folklore; vampires are more commonly described as assuming the shapes of CATS, dogs, sheep, wolves, snakes, birds, and horses. The presence of bats increased in European vampire lore after Spanish conquistadores returned from the New World with stories of BLOOD-drinking VAMPIRE BATS.

BRAM STOKER has COUNT DRACULA shape-shift into the form of a huge bat in DRACULA (1897). However, bats make no appearance in the novel in the chapters set in TRANSYLVANIA—only in England after the count arrives there. Dracula's favored animal is the wolf.

In NOSFERATU (1922), the first (and unauthorized) film of *Dracula,* there are no bats, but plenty of RATS, who are commandeered by the vampire GRAF ORLOCK.

Bats have become a staple of vampire film and fiction as one of the guises of vampires.

See also SHAPE-SHIFTING.

FURTHER READING:
Miller, Elizabeth. *Dracula: Sense and Nonsense.* Westcliff-on-Sea, England: Desert Island Books, 2000.

Beast of Bray Road   Werewolf or were-animal creature seen in Wisconsin. A cluster of sightings from 1989 to 1992 ignited media interest. The sightings may be related to other, much earlier were-creature sightings elsewhere in Wisconsin and also in Michigan.

The Beast of Bray Road was so named because early known sightings and encounters were clustered around Bray Road, a one-mile stretch of isolated country road near

Elkhorn, in southeastern Wisconsin, a small town of 6,500 residents. Rumors and gossip circulated primarily among teenagers. The story received media attention when Linda Godfrey, a writer and cartoonist for a weekly newspaper called *The Week,* started collecting eyewitness testimonies and writing about them. Articles also appeared in *Strange* magazine. Sightings have been reported in a much wider geographical area, even as far away as Milwaukee.

Various descriptions of the Beast have been given, but common traits are its size and the fact that it stands, walks, and runs on hind legs, and also on all fours. Upright it is over six feet in height, even seven to eight feet. The figure is humanlike with clawed and hairy humanlike hands, and a wolfish or wolf head. It carries a revolting smell, and has sharp, canny, slanted and evil-looking eyes. It stares at people and smirks at them, giving them the feeling that it is intelligent and self-aware in a human way. Eyewitnesses say it is demonic and hellish.

The Beast is most often seen at night, but also has been seen during the day. It has menaced people and chased them, and has been seen kneeling by the road while apparently eating roadkill. No one to date has actually been physically harmed by the creature, although some eyewitnesses say they were certain the creature could have killed them had it chosen to do so.

One of the earliest encounters on record dates to 1936. Mark Schackelman was a night watchman at a Catholic convent, St. Colleta, near Jefferson, Wisconsin. He had two encounters with a bizarre creature resembling the Beast, both occurring around midnight. He spotted the creature atop a Native American burial mound, which it was clawing with its hands. The creature fled when Schackelman approached it.

But the second night, the creature—again found clawing at the top of the burial mound—stood up and faced Schackelman. The humanlike figure was over six feet tall and was covered with dark hair. It had a muzzle, prominent fangs, and pointed ears on the top of its head. It gave off a horrible smell, like "long-dead meat." The creature stared at him and made a guttural sound like "gadarrah" and growled. After an agonizing stare down in which Schackelman earnestly prayed to God for rescue, the creature turned and slowly walked away.

In 1989 a 24-year-old woman, Lorianne Endrizzi, got a good look at the Beast while driving on Bray Road at about 1:30 A.M. She saw what she thought was a person hunched over by the side of the road. Slowing to a crawl to look, she was startled to see that the figure was part human and part wolf. The face was long and snouty and the eyes glowed yellow. It had a wide chest, pointed ears, big fangs, and a covering of gray-brown hair. The limbs and appendages were humanlike: The hands looked like human hands with claws; the hairy calves were muscular. The creature's arms were jointed like a human's, and it was holding what appeared to be roadkill in upturned palms. The creature stared at her until she drove away. Later, Endrizzi found an illustration of a werewolf that closely resembled the Beast.

Linda Godfrey's concept and illustration of the indigenous dogman seems to represent the Beast of Bray Road best. (Courtesy Linda Godfrey)

Other sightings have yielded similar descriptions.

The Beast also has been described as bearlike, and ape-like and baboonlike, the latter giving rise to speculation about its relationship to Bigfoot (Sasquatch), and to legends about hairy "wild men" said to live in remote, wooded regions. According to Godfrey, the beast has striking similarities to the Dogman of Michigan (see DOGMEN), to the LOBIZON of South America, and to other WEREDOG creatures reported in diverse locations around the world. It may have a relationship to the European lore of large, spectral black dogs or "hellhounds," such as Black Shuck of England. Black dog lore migrated to America: For example, the Snarly Yow is a spectral hound that haunts parts of Maryland. In Chippewa lore, the Witchie Wolves are spirit dogs that guard the sacred graves of warriors. Native American burial mounds are associated with a host of paranormal phenomena, including haunting ghosts and spirits, strange lights and noises, and mysterious forms.

Other strange creature sightings similar to the Beast are of a were-deer, or a hairy biped that runs with deer.

Reports of strange lights in the sky—possible UFOs—and mutilated domestic dogs and cats have been reported in areas where the Beast has been seen, but there is no conclusive link among the phenomena.

Animals mistaken for supernatural creatures do not seem a likely explanation for the Beast. According to Godfrey, one explanation put forward has also been advanced for other mysterious creatures and for Bigfoot: It may be a remnant of prehistoric times, an indigenous dogman creature who somehow survives in remote areas.

FURTHER READING:

Godfrey, Linda S. *The Beast of Bray Road: Tailing Wisconsin's Werewolf.* Black Earth, Wisc.: Prairie Oak Press, 2003.

———. "The Bray Road Beast Update," *Strange* no. 11, Spring-Summer 1993, pp. 36–37+.

Sankey, Scarlett. "The Bray Road Beast: Wisconsin Werewolf Investigation." *Strange* No. 10, fall-winter 1992, pp. 19–21+.

Beast of Gevaudan (1764–1767)   Werewolf terror in the Gevaudan region of south-central France.

From July 1764 to June 1767, a pair of large and unusually colored man-eating wolves attacked and killed 60 to 100 people or more in Gevaudan, causing a wide-scale panic. Many feared the killings to be the work of a single wolf; others believed the creature to be a tiger or hyena, or the offspring of a tiger and lioness. Still others believed the Beast (La Bête) to be a werewolf.

A poster printed in 1764 described the unusual Beast:

Reddish brown with dark ridged stripe down the back. Resembles wolf/hyena but big as a donkey. Long gaping jaw, six claws, pointy upright ears and supple furry tail—mobile like a cat's and can knock you over. Cry: more like horse neighing than wolf howling.

The Beast of Gevaudan, 1765 (Author's collection)

MONTAGUE SUMMERS gave this description based on an article in *London Magazine* in 1765:

> For months this animal panic-struck the whole region of Languedoc, and is said to have devoured more than one hundred persons. Not merely solitary wayfarers were attacked by it, but even larger companies traveling in coaches and armed. Its teeth were most formidable. With its immense tail it could deal swinging blows. It vaulted to tremendous heights, and ran with supernatural speed. The stench of the brute was beyond description.

King Louis XV took a personal interest in the situation, for the panic could have political ramifications. The Gevaudan area was actually an independent state (it was not annexed to France until 1791) and was rife with tensions between the Huguenots and Jesuits. Huge bounties were posted for the killing of the Beast. Teams of professional wolf-hunters and dogs fanned into the forests. Several detachments of dragoons joined the hunt as well. At the height of the panic, more than 20,000 men joined the hunt in several parishes. More than 1,000 wolves reportedly were killed.

One of the more appalling means of trying to kill the Beast was an extensive use of poison, advocated by the king's chief wolf-catcher, M. Denneval. Dogs were fed high doses of poison, and their tainted carcasses were left out as bait for the Beast. Instead, the carcasses attracted and killed domestic dogs, farm animals, and other animals. The poisonings were finally ended when too many working dogs were lost among the peasants.

The Beast eluded all efforts. In one week in June 1765 alone, four people were killed and eaten: a woman, an eight-year-old child, a 15-year-old girl, and another person. Most victims were mutilated and torn to pieces; some remains were too small for burial. One girl was recognized only by her eyes.

The peasants became convinced that the Beast was a werewolf sorcerer, and would never be caught. One farmer claimed that he had seen it and had heard it speak.

The terror finally came to an end when the male wolf was killed on September 21, 1766, and the female of the pair was killed in June 1767.

The wolves may have been dog-wolf crosses. They were exceptionally large for wolves, and they had unusual colorations and markings.

The 2001 French film BROTHERHOOD OF THE WOLF is loosely based on the Beast of Gevaudan.

FURTHER READING:
Sidky, H. *Witchcraft, Lycanthropy, Drugs and Disease: An Anthropological Study of the European Witch-Hunts.* New York: Peter Lang, 1997.
Summers, Montague. *The Werewolf.* New York: Bell Publishing, 1966.

berserkir In Norse lore, men of superhuman powers who go about with bearskins or wolfskins over their armor, and who are capable of demonic rage. In folklore the *berserkir* ("men in a bear shirt") possess the ability to SHAPE-SHIFT into wolves, thus making them a type of werewolf.

Berserkir took advantage of feudal law in Norway. They roamed about the countryside challenging farmers to combat. According to law, if a man declined such a challenge, he had to forfeit his property to the challenger. If the farmer fought and was killed, the *berserkr* (singular) could seize his wealth. Thus, *berserkir* were widely feared in the countryside. They were known to invite themselves to local feasts, where they would slay anyone who displeased them, often by snapping the backbone or splitting open the skull.

The *berserkir* were valued as warriors, for they were reputed to be able to work themselves into frenzies of madness or demoniacal possession which gave them superhuman powers and insensibility to pain. SABINE BARING-GOULD gives this description in *The Book of Were-Wolves* (1865):

> No sword would wound them, no fire burn them, a club alone could destroy them, by breaking their bones, or crushing in their skulls. Their eyes glared as though a flame burned in the sockets, they ground their teeth, and frothed at the mouth; they gnawed at their shield rims, and are said to have sometimes bitten them through, and as they rushed into conflict they yelped as dogs or howled as wolves.

These rages were always followed by periods of extreme exhaustion.

Berserkir diminished as Christianity advanced through Europe. The characteristics of their frenzies, rages and superhuman strength are ascribed to werewolves. From their name comes the term *berserk,* for frenzied, uncontrolled behavior.

FURTHER READING:
Baring-Gould, Sabine. *The Book of Were-Wolves.* London: Smith, Elder & Co., 1865.

Bersicker In DRACULA (1897) by BRAM STOKER, the name of a Norwegian wolf that runs amok when he is recruited for an errand by COUNT DRACULA. Stoker's notes show that the source for the creature and his name was inspired by *The Book of Were-Wolves* by SABINE BARING-GOULD, which describes a "berserkr" (sic) as "a man possessed of superhuman powers, and subject to accesses [sic] of diabolical fury."

In the novel, an article attributed to the *Pall Mall Gazette,* dated Monday, September 18, relates the story of the wolf, which escaped from the Zoological Gardens in London (now the London Zoo, located in Regent's Park in north London).

According to the zoo keeper, Thomas Bilder, Bersicker is one of three gray wolves from Norway, which had arrived at the gardens four years earlier. Bilder describes Bersicker as "a nice well-behaved wolf, that never gave no trouble to talk of." He says that on the afternoon of September 17, the wolf went crazy and began tearing at its bars as if it wanted to get out. Nearby was the count: ". . . a tall thin chap, with a 'ook nose and a pointed beard, with a few white hairs runnin' through it. He had a 'ard, cold look and RED eyes, and I took sort of mislike to him, for it seemed as if it was 'im as they was hirritated at." Bilder noticed that the man wore white gloves, which, unbeknownst to him, hid the count's hairy palms and pointed nails.

The man suggested to Bilder that the wolves were upset, and he smiled with "a mouth full of white, sharp teeth." While they talked, the wolves settled down. Bilder stroked Bersicker's ears, and so did the stranger, saying he was used to wolves. When the man left, Bersicker watched him until he was out of sight, and then laid down in a corner.

When the MOON rose later, all the wolves began howling. Bersicker was discovered escaped, with the bars to his cage brent and broken. He reappeared the following day around noon, docile and calm, but with his head cut and full of broken glass, as though he had gone over a wall topped with a defense of broken bottles. He was locked up in his cage.

According to Stoker's notes, he originally intended to have a wolf captured and killed near the house of Dracula's victim, Lucy Westenra, whose health is failing as the vampire repeatedly drinks her BLOOD. Instead, Bersicker is sent by Dracula to breach the GARLIC defenses that PROFESSOR ABRAHAM VAN HELSING has put into place in the house to protect Lucy.

On the night of Bersicker's escape from the zoo, Lucy is frightened by flapping sounds at her window, and also the howling of what she takes to be a dog—though the howling is much fiercer and deeper than a dog's—in the shrubbery outside the house. She gets up and looks out the window, but sees only "a big BAT, which had evidently been buffeting its wings against the window." Lucy's mother comes into her room to keep her company while she sleeps. The flapping at the window comes again followed by a low howl in the shrubbery. Suddenly, the window explodes inward in a shower of glass "and in the aperture of the broken panes there was the head of a great, gaunt wolf."

Lucy's mother grabs Lucy's garland of garlic off her neck and falls over dead as if struck by lightning, hitting Lucy on the head and making her dizzy. The last things Lucy sees are specks that look like dust that blow in through the broken window—dust is one of Dracula's SHAPE-SHIFTED forms—and then she loses consciousness. Without the garlic, she has no protection against the VAMPIRE. She awakens later to hear dogs howling; she is weak and in pain, for Dracula has vampirized her yet again. Dracula, invisible, escapes through the dining room, flinging open and closing its door.

The episode with Bersicker demonstrates Dracula's affinity with wolves and his ability to command them.

FURTHER READING:
Leatherdale, Clive, ed. *Bram Stoker's Dracula Unearthed.* Weston-on-Sea, Essex, England: Desert Island Books, 1998.
Miller, Elizabeth. *Dracula: Sense and Nonsense.* Westcliff-on-Sea, England: Desert Island Books, 2000.
Stoker, Bram. *Dracula.* New York: Grosset & Dunlap, 1931.

Bertrand, Sergeant François (19th c.)   Frenchman whose delight in digging up and rending apart CORPSES likened him to one of the BERSERKIR.

In 1848 a mysterious series of grave desecrations took place in Paris, including at the prestigious Père-Lachaise CEMETERY. Graves were found opened and the corpses torn to pieces and left lying about. At first it was thought that animals were to blame, but then human footprints found at the scene told police that a person, probably deranged, was responsible. Watches were set up at Père-Lachaise, but no culprit was captured, and the desecrations soon ceased.

In March 1849 the perpetrator struck again at the cemetery of S. Parnasse, setting off a spring gun trap. Guards rushed to the scene in time to see a man in military garb leap over the cemetery wall and escape. He left behind a trail of BLOOD, indicating that he had been wounded by the spring gun. Police also found a bit of clothing torn from the man's military mantle.

Police went from barracks to barracks, searching for a man with gunshot wounds. They were able to find and arrest the culprit, a junior officer in the 1st Infantry regiment, by the name of Sergeant François Bertrand. He was hospitalized, and after he recovered from his wounds he was tried by court-martial. He made a complete confession.

Bertrand said he had entered the army at age 20, following his education at the theological seminary of Langres. He was known among his companions as a refined, gentle fellow, though prone to fits of depression.

In February 1847 a peculiar madness seized him. He was out in the countryside walking with a friend when they came upon a churchyard cemetery. The day before a woman had been buried, but the grave had not been completely filled in due to a rainstorm. As he looked at the grave and the sexton's pick and shovel lying beside it, he was overcome by an intense desire to dig up the corpse.

Bertrand made excuses and got rid of his friend. He sneaked back to the churchyard and exhumed the body. He testified:

> Soon I dragged the corpse out of the earth, and I began to hash it with the spade, without well knowing what I was about. A laborer saw me, and I laid myself flat on the ground till he was out of sight, and then I cast the body back into the grave. I then went away, bathed in a cold sweat, to a little grove, where I reposed for several hours, notwithstanding the cold rain that fell, in a condition of complete exhaustion. When I rose, my limbs were as if broken, and my head weak. The same prostration and sensation followed each attack.

> Two days after, I returned to the cemetery, and opened the grave with my hands. My hands bled, but I did not feel the pain; I tore the corpse to shreds, and I flung it back in the pit.

Bertrand suffered no more episodes until four months later, when his regiment was sent to Paris. One day he went walking through Père-Lachaise, and suddenly a violent urge to dig up a corpse and tear it up came upon him again. That night he returned to the cemetery and exhumed the corpse of a seven-year-old girl, tearing her in half. A few days later, he dug up a woman who had died in childbirth, and had been buried only 13 days earlier. On November 16, 1848, he dug up a 50-year-old woman, tore her to pieces, and rolled himself in the bits.

Bertrand gave numerous similar accounts of other desecrations he committed. At first these attacks came after he drank wine, but later they came upon him without noticeable cause. Bertrand dug up both men and women, but he mutilated only female corpses. Sometimes he hacked the corpses to pieces with a spade, and other times he tore them with his teeth and nails. He tore mouths open to the ears, opened stomachs, and pulled off limbs.

Bertrand said that during his hospital stay he had not felt any urges to continue his savage behavior, and he considered himself cured. The authorities evidently believed him, for he was given a light sentence of a year in prison.

The suddenness of his rage to rend corpses, followed by extreme exhaustion, is characteristic of *berserkir* behavior, and also of the medical symptoms found in LYCANTHROPY.

FURTHER READING:
Baring-Gould, Sabine. *The Book of Were-Wolves.* London: Smith, Elder & Co., 1865.

Berwick Vampire   See ALNWICK CASTLE VAMPIRE.

bewitchment   See EVIL EYE; VAMPIRE SORCERERS AND WITCHES.

bhuta   In Indian lore, malignant, flesh-eating spirits or demons, or spirits of the dead. If spirits of the dead, the bhuta are considered the restless souls of men who died untimely deaths, such as through SUICIDE, execution, or violence. Bhuta haunt forests and empty dwellings by day and night. They are flickering lights or misty apparitions that cast no shadows and hover above the ground. Thus they can be avoided by lying flat on the ground. In particular, they plague living persons who do not perform the proper funerary rights for the dead.

Like the European VAMPIRE, the bhuta are blamed for blighted crops, diseased livestock, natural and domestic calamities, accidents, illness, plagues, and insanity. They enter human bodies and make victims sicken and die.

The bhuta may be detected by its nasal twangs, its fear of burning turmeric, and its lack of a SHADOW. They never rest on the earth, so they may be avoided by lying on the ground.

See also GHOUL.

bisclaveret   Breton term for "werewolf." Bisclaveret is the name of the baron WEREWOLF in the medieval Breton fable *THE LAY OF THE WERE-WOLF.*

Blackman   In the lore of the Maya who live in the Chiapas highlands of southern Mexico, a winged, black demon renowned for insatiable sex and cannibalism. The Blackman may be related to local myths about a VAMPIRE BAT demon.

Descriptions of the Blackman vary; he is often described as having a lethal, six-foot-long penis capable of making his female victims go insane. The Blackman kidnaps women at night and carries them off to his cave, where he seduces or rapes her. The woman then cannot return to her village, and will be forever cursed with a bad smell. Her children will look like the Blackman.

The only way to destroy the Blackman is to impale him, burn him, or cook him.

See also TIN-TIN.

FURTHER READING:
Brown, David E. *Vampiro: the Vampire Bat in Fact and Fantasy.* Silver City, N.M.: High-Lonesome Books, 1994.

black stallion   In Slavic lore, a VAMPIRE detector. To find the grave of a vampire, a black stallion that has no spots or marks is led around graves. It will not step over the grave of a vampire.

See also WHITE HORSE.

black thorn   Wood deemed effective in slaying vampires. In the case of the LASTOVO ISLAND VAMPIRES, black thorn was considered to be the only wood capable of helping to destroy VAMPIRES. The supernatural power of black thorn, like other thorny woods, is believed to come from its association with Christ and the crown of thorns he wore in his Passion and crucifixion.

Lastovo Island VAMPIRE HUNTERS believed that if a thorn stake were set over the grave of a suspected vampire, it would prevent the devil that inhabited the CORPSE from emerging, and also would enable vampire hunters to thrash the devil with it.

Blacula (1972)   American film released by American International Pictures about an African-American vampire, Prince Maumuwalde, portrayed by William Marshall. William Crain directed the film.

In the 1780s Prince Maumuwalde is trying to bring an end of the slave trade. He enlists the help of COUNT DRACULA (Charles Macaulay). Dracula turns the prince into a VAMPIRE, entombs him, and curses him to become Blacula. The prince's wife, Luva, also attacked by Dracula, is left to die.

Blacula sleeps in his COFFIN in CASTLE DRACULA until 1965, when a California collector buys the castle's furnishings and has them shipped to Los Angeles. There Blacula revives and falls in love with Tina, who seems to be a reincarnation of Luva. Their love affair is doomed, however, when she is shot. Blacula attempts to save her by transforming her into a vampire, but she is staked by VAMPIRE HUNTERS who are after Blacula, and she dies. In despair, Blacula destroys himself by exposing himself to SUNLIGHT.

Scream, Blacula, Scream, a sequel to *Blacula,* was released in 1973. Blacula is resurrected into a society that alienates him. He wanders about in search of a way to end his vampire curse. He enlists a voodoo queen, Lisa, to help

Count Blacula (William Marshall) in Blacula *(Author's collection)*

him. Blacula falls in love with her. He nearly completes a voodoo ritual that will free him when police invade the house, and he is staked to death.

FURTHER READING:
Silver, Alain, and James Ursini. *The Vampire Film:* From Nosferatu *to* Interview with the Vampire, 3d ed. New York: Limelight Editions, 1997.

Blake, Anita   See HAMILTON, LAURELL K.

Blau (Blow) Vampire   See MYSLATA OF BLAU.

blood   Sustenance of VAMPIRES. The vampire takes blood, either literally or symbolically, thus robbing the living of life.

Because blood is the "river of life," carrying the vital energy of the cosmos through the body, human beings have throughout history conferred upon it great mystical and magical powers. Blood is soul, strength, and the rejuvenating force. Blood sacrifices, of humans and animals, are performed to unleash those powers and propitiate the gods with the greatest of all gifts. The blood of gods and monarchs, shed upon fields, ensures the fertility and abundance of crops. The drinking of the blood of one's enemies—a widespread and ancient practice—enables one to acquire the strength of the enemy.

The Koreans have an ancient belief that the blood of a faithful son serves as an elixir of life to the dying. According to this tradition, when a parent lay near death, a son cut himself, such as on the thigh, and used his blood to prepare a magic elixir.

The strongest oath is the blood oath, in which the parties mingle their blood. The blood oath is meant to be unbreakable and transcends all other duties and obligations. He who betrays it commits a grievous sin. Thus the vampire, by consuming the blood of a victim, wields not only the power of life and death, but magical power as well, and establishes a connection to the victim that is difficult to break.

Blood is a potent ingredient in magical charms and spells: A drop of a person's blood, used in a spell, can bring that person under one's power. In many cases, the blood of an evil person is believed to have the greatest magical power. For example, the blood of executed criminals is said to be a powerful protector against disease and bad luck, because of the energy of resentment and fury that is released upon execution. In East Prussian lore, the blood of executed criminals should be drunk for good luck. In Pomerania, a merchant who catches drops of the blood of a beheaded murderer on his handkerchief will be guaranteed an increase in business.

Similarly, the blood consumed by vampires, or the vampire's own blood, has great magical potency, according to Eastern European folklore beliefs. It is always dangerous,

but can be either a charm and a curse. When vampire CORPSES are disinterred and staked or cut up, the living must take care not to be sprayed by the corpse's blood, for they will either go mad instantly, or die instantly. Anecdotal accounts report that violated corpses often exploded with sprays of gases, blood, and decomposing flesh. These explosions were caused by the sudden release of the pressure inside the corpse caused by the buildup of gases. Thus, vampire corpses were carefully covered before mutilation, and most onlookers stood well away from the body. In Romanian lore, the staked vampire is believed to always send a geyser of blood high into the air. The blood, it is said, issues from a second heart that enables the vampire to stay alive beyond death.

In a normal death, blood coagulates quickly and thus would not spray from a corpse. However, in cases of a sudden end to the functions of the heart or central nervous system—such as a violent death—blood can reliquefy.

Contrary to the destructive power of the vampire's blood, it is also believed that the blood has great healing properties. Consequently, victims of vampires should either smear themselves with the vampire's blood or drink it, in order to secure release from the vampire's curse. The remedy often failed, however, according to accounts. In the early 18th century, the Serbian village of Medvegia suffered several vampire episodes, including the case of ARNOD PAOLE, who smeared himself with the blood of a suspected vampire, but died and became a vampire himself. During the same period, other persons in the village were falling victim to vampire attacks. One of these was a 20-year-old woman named STANA, who gave birth to a child who died immediately after being born. Stana herself then fell seriously ill. (In many folklore traditions, such events are blamed on vampiric birth demons and VISCERA SUCKERS.) She smeared herself with the blood of a vampire, but died, anyway, after a three-day illness. She, too, became a vampire. When her corpse was disinterred two months later, it was found to be undecayed, with a large quantity of "fresh" blood in the chest cavity. She was dispatched in the customary manner with a stake.

A variation of this blood remedy was reported in the MERCY BROWN vampire case in Rhode Island in the 19th century. Brown's ailing brother was given a medicine made with the ASHES of her burned heart and liver. The brother died despite the medicine.

In the folklore of the UPIR in Russia, the blood of the vampire is mixed with flour to make bread. When eaten, the bread is believed to protect a person against vampire attacks.

Blood Drinking Among Self-described "Vampires"
The purported magical properties of blood continue to be the primary element of appeal in modern-day fascination with the vampire. In some cases, obsessions with blood lead people to the vampire myth, to either become absorbed by it, or to want to become LIVING VAMPIRES who consume blood. Others want the association with blood

but do not wish to drink it themselves. The mere association with blood conjures up magic and power desired by want-to-be vampires.

Most people who experiment with blood drinking find that it makes them quite nauseated. In addition, there are other hazards of serious illness—such as hepatitis, mad cow disease, and HIV—and parasites that can be acquired from contaminated blood. Some blood drinkers screen their partners and participate in exchanges in which small amounts of blood from cuts and pricks are consumed. Some blood drinkers try drinking animal blood, including the watery blood from butchered meat; this also has illness hazards.

The metabolic disorders known as PORPHYRIA have been put forward as a cause of blood craving in some cases of living vampirism.

FURTHER READING:
Guiley, Rosemary Ellen, with J. B. Macabre. *The Complete Vampire Companion*. New York: Macmillan, 1994.
Guinn, Jeff, with Andy Grieser. *Something in the Blood: The Underground of Today's Vampires*. Arlington, Texas: Summit Publishing, 1996.

Blood Canticle (2003)   The final novel in ANNE RICE's Vampire Chronicles.

Blood Canticle is narrated by Rice's leading VAMPIRE, LESTAT DE LIONCOURT, for the first time since MEMNOCH THE DEVIL in 1995. The novel merges the streams of vampires and Mayfair witches in Rice's many novels, typing up loose ends with various story lines and characters.

The story opens at the end of *Blackwood Farm* (2002). Quinn Blackwood is free of his vampiric doppelganger. He and Lestat turn Blackwood's love, the witch Mona Mayfair, into a vampire. Lestat is obsessed with redemption and becoming a saint, a consequence of his experiences with Memnoch the Devil. This is an impossibility for him, though he desires it, nonetheless. He falls in love with Rowan Mayfair, a married woman, and is charmed by mortal life at Blackwood Farm. He learns about unconditional, pure love, and attempts to redeem himself in unselfish love concerning Rowan. In the end, he chooses to be neither good nor evil.

See also DOPPELSAUGER.

FURTHER READING:
"Q&A with Anne Rice About *Blood Canticle*." Available online. URL: http://www.randomhouse.com/features/annerice/interview03.html. Downloaded on December 21, 2003.
Rice, Anne. *Blood Canticle*. New York: Alfred A. Knopf, 2003.

"Blood Son" (1951)   Short story by horror master RICHARD MATHESON that captures the macabre outcome of obsession with VAMPIRES. "Blood Son" was first published in a small pulp magazine and then in 1957 in Matheson's collection, *The Shores of Space*.

Jules is a boy who wants to be a vampire. He was born strange, on a night when wind uprooted trees. People said he cackled and had three teeth and drew BLOOD when he suckled at his mother's breast. At two months of age he could walk, and he stared at the MOON.

By the time Jules enters school, he is precocious and commands a large vocabulary. He steals a copy of DRACULA from the library. He apparently drinks his own blood from his thumb. He calls himself "Jules Dracula" and says his ambition is to be a vampire when he grows up, and to drink the blood of girls after biting them with razor-sharp teeth. He is completely consumed with his obsession. People begin to avoid him.

At the zoo he finds a VAMPIRE BAT and names it COUNT DRACULA, talking to it every time he comes to visit. He plots with the bat to set it free so that they can go out and drink girls' blood together.

One night he steals the bat and takes it to an abandoned shack. He cuts his throat with a pen knife and lets the bat drink his blood. When his breathing becomes difficult, he rallies to his senses and flings the bat off of him. He tries to leave, but is too weak, and he falls to the ground. The bat returns. The next thing in Jules's dying awareness is a tall dark man whose eyes shine like rubies and who lifts him and says, "My son."

"Blood Son" is significant because it anticipates the fascination of some people, mostly youths, with the seemingly glamorous idea of becoming a vampire.

See also LIVING VAMPIRES.

FURTHER READING:
Daniels, Les. *Living in Fear: A History of Horror in the Mass Media*. New York: Charles Scribner's Sons, 1975.

bloodsucking witchcraft   See TLAHUELPUCHI; VAMPIRE SORCERERS AND WITCHES.

blue   In Greek lore, a color that repels VAMPIRES, as well as other evil entities. Blue paint applied around doorways and windows prevents vampires from entering a home.

Blue, Sonja   See COLLINS, NANCY A.

boanthropy   An oft-reported form of SHAPE-SHIFTING, in which human beings transform into cows.

Bodin, Jean (1529–1596)   French demonologist, ex-monk, and political theorist who aided the Inquisition against witchcraft and encouraged torture and punishment. Jean Bodin believed in the evil acts of witches, including SHAPE-SHIFTING into wolves and other beasts, and eating human flesh at SABBATS.

Bodin was born in Angers, France, in 1529. He served briefly as a Carmelite monk, but left the order to become a Roman law professor at the University of Toulouse. He distinguished himself in his studies of philosophy, law, classics, and economics, but his published political theory angered the king of France.

Bodin achieved his historical fame as an Inquisition judge and the author of *De la Demonomanie des Sorciers* (*The Demonomania of Witches*), published in 1580. The book was an immediate success and was reprinted frequently throughout Europe, serving as a guide to witch-hunters.

Bodin viewed witches less as heretics and more as vile and ugly social deviants. He claimed they entered into pacts with Satan, who gave them supernatural powers: bodily flying through the air to their sabbats with the help of magical OINTMENTS, copulating with INCUBUS and SUCCUBUS demons, casting evil spells, and turning themselves into ravaging WEREWOLVES. He was merciless in his advocacy of extreme torture to extract confessions, even from children and invalids. He forced children to testify against their parents. He thought witches should be made to suffer long and exquisitely for their sins. Being burned at the stake was too lenient because it brought death within a mere half an hour.

Bodin discusses famous werewolf cases in his book, such as GILLES GARNIER and the POLIGNY WEREWOLVES. He said that the reality of shape-shifting is supported by myth and also the writings of Sts. Thomas Aquinas and Augustine.

Bodin was opposed by skeptics. REGINALD SCOT was among those who leveled scorching criticism of him. Bodin's response was that the writings of his critics should be burned.

Ironically, all of Bodin's books on political theory were condemned by the Inquisition. Only *Demonomanie*, which served the purpose of the Church, was given approval.

Bodin died in Laon in 1596, a victim of the bubonic plague.

See also LIVONIA WEREWOLVES.

FURTHER READING:
Guiley, Rosemary Ellen. *The Encyclopedia of Witches and Witchcraft.* 2d ed. New York: Facts On File, 1999.
Scot, Reginald. *The Discoverie of Witchcraft.* Yorkshire, England: E. P. Publishing, 1973.
Summers, Montague. *The Werewolf.* New York: Bell Publishing, 1966.

Boguet, Henri (ca. 1550–1619)   Lawyer, demonologist, and chief judge at St. Claude in the France-Comte region of France. Henri Boguet sent many accused witches to their deaths. He wrote an authoritative text on witchcraft, *Discours des sorciers* (*Examen of Witches*). Although he believed in witches and devil pacts, he considered SHAPE-SHIFTING into wolves or any other creatures to be an illusion.

Like many of his fellow judges and witch-hunters, Boguet took a hard stand against what he considered to be a great danger of evil. By the time he wrote *Discours* in 1602, he had tried approximately 40 witches and had presumably sent all or most of their deaths. Some of the convicted were children; Boguet considered them to be beyond rehabilitation once under the influence of Satan. He ordered an eight-year-old boy to be tortured until he gave the names of accomplices; a mass witch hunt ensued.

Boguet believed in SABBATS and a wide range of evil acts committed by witches, but, unlike his contemporary JEAN BODIN, he refuted the popular superstition that witches could shape-shift into wolves. For such a transformation to take place, a man's soul would have to enter into the animal, and the devil would have to perform a miracle. Both were impossible, Boguet said.

However, he asserted that Satan could make witches *believe* they were transformed into wolves and incite them to maul and kill. Even if they only thought themselves to be wolves but committed no crimes, they still deserved to be executed for their intentions.

Discours des sorciers was lauded by Boguet's peers and became established as a leading handbook for witch-hunters. His family tried unsuccessfully to suppress its publication. Whether they were embarrassed by it or had sympathies for accused witches is not known.

FURTHER READING:
Monter, E. William. *Witchcraft in France and Switzerland.* New York: Cornell University, 1976.

Boreanaz, David   See ANGEL; BUFFY THE VAMPIRE SLAYER.

Borgo Pass   In BRAM STOKER's DRACULA, the location in TRANSYLVANIA's northern Carpathian Mountains of COUNT DRACULA's foreboding castle. The real Borgo Pass bears scant resemblance to the description given by Stoker, who in fact never visited Transylvania. The sharp alpine peaks he describes are more characteristic of Switzerland, a terrain he knew.

In the opening chapter of *Dracula*, Jonathan Harker is en route by carriage to the count's castle. It is May 3. The landscape Harker describes is thickly wooded with

... mighty slopes of forest up to the lofty steeps of the Carpathians themselves. Right and left of us they towered ... an endless perspective of jagged rock and pointed crags, til these themselves were lost in the distance, where the snowy peaks rose grandly. Here and there seemed mighty rifts in the mountains, through which, as the sun began to sink, we saw now and again the white gleam of falling water.

As the twilight thickens, the deep valleys fill with mist. At times, the slope is so steep that the horses must go slowly. The pass itself is a narrow slash in the towering

A cross guards a rural family cemetery plot in the Borgo Pass. (Author's collection)

mountains, and the coach rocks to and fro in an ominous, thunderous atmosphere.

At an appointed place, Harker is picked up by the count's calèche, drawn by four horses and driven by a mysterious man, who, unbeknownst to Harker, is actually the count himself. They continue through to the far side of Borgo Pass, where a tunnellike road crowded by "great frowning rocks" leads to the count's "vast ruined castle, from whose tall black windows came no ray of light, and whose broken battlements showed a jagged line against the moonlit sky." The castle is perched on the edge of a great precipice that drops at least 1,000 feet on three sides of the castle. The views from it are of jagged peaks, chasms, and gorges.

The real Borgo Pass is much tamer. It lies in northern Romania in approximately the middle of the 900-mile-long crescent of Carpathians, which extend from Romania into Ukraine, Poland, and Slovakia. Elevations of the peaks range from 3,000 to 8,000 feet. In the northern portion of the crescent, along the Polish-Slovakian border, the peaks are craggy, permanently snow-topped and spectacular—more like Stoker's description. Borgo Pass is nestled among smaller, more rolling peaks.

The road to Borgo Pass winds gently up to the crest, through heavy woods of fir and pine, and the pass itself opens onto rounded, wooded slopes and open fields with grazing sheep and haystacks. The horseshoe of the Carpathian Mountains makes an impressive display in the distance. The CASTLE DRACULA HOTEL, built like a small castle, is located at the top of the pass.

Modern scholars have attempted to identify the exact sources used by Stoker in his settings, but in all likelihood, he did what most fiction writers do: He used what he knew and added imagination to it. Without specific notes from Stoker himself, researchers are left to much speculation.

FURTHER READING:
Miller, Elizabeth. *Dracula: Sense & Nonsense*. Westcliff-on-Sea, England: Desert Island Books, 2000.
Stoker, Bram. *Dracula*. New York: Grosset & Dunlap, n.d.

bori   A vampiric spirit in West Africa lore. According to the Hausa, the *bori* lives in forested areas. It often appears in human form with hoofed feet or without a head. It can SHAPE-SHIFT into animal forms such as a python. The *bori* acts like a trickster as well, masquerading as a spouse or family member. Telltales signs of its true identity are a dreamy look and strange behavior, and footprints in ASHES that look like the claw prints of a rooster.

If properly placated with its favorite things, the *bori* will not harm people. It will even help people, and it likes to be called on for assistance. It will help in house-raising, healing, and other domestic activities. Learning its name will turn it into a slave. But if its name is spoken in vain, or if one is careless and causes the sparks of a fire to hit it, the *bori* becomes angry. It will kill the offender by slowly sucking off the life force so that the person dies of a wasting illness.

The attacks of a *bori* can be warded off with charms and prayers. IRON repels it so strongly that even saying the word *iron* is sometimes sufficient to banish it.

The Hausa believe that all illnesses are caused by a specific *bori*. Dances are held to placate all the spirits. Dancers enter a trancelike state in which each person speaks for a *bori*—a rite similar to the trance possession by *loa* in Vodoun.

In Australian lore, the *bori* is an invisible spirit who kills its victims by injecting them with fatal illnesses.

FURTHER READING:
Mack, Carol K., and Dinah Mack. *A Field Guide to Demons, Fairies, Fallen Angels, and Other Subversive Spirits*. New York: Henry Holt/Owl Books, 1998.

bottling vampires   In Bulgarian lore, an effective way to trap, contain, and destroy VAMPIRES. MONTAGUE SUMMERS gives this description of the procedure in *The Vampire: His Kith and Kin*:

> The sorcerer, armed with a picture of some saint, lies in ambush until he sees the Vampire pass, when he pursues him with his *Eikon* [icon]: the poor Obour [vampire] takes refuge on a tree or on the roof of a house, but his persecutor follows him up with the talisman, driving him away from all shelter, in the direction of a bottle specially prepared, in which is placed some of the vampire's favorite food. Having no other resource, he enters this prison, and is immediately fastened down with a cork, on the interior of which is a fragment of the *Eikon*. The bottle is then thrown into the fire, and the Vampire disappears forever.

FURTHER READING:
Summers, Montague. *The Vampire: His Kith and Kin*. New Hyde Park, N.Y.: University Books, 1960. First published 1928.

bouda   In the lore of Moroccan Berbers, were-hyenas. With the help of magical herb potions, certain men have the ability to shape-shift (see SHAPE-SHIFTING) into hyenas at night—especially after midnight—and resume their human form during the day. They have the ability to imitate human voices and can lure their enemies to their deaths.

boxenwolf   In the lore of the Schaumberg region of Germany, a WEREWOLF who is in league with the Devil. The boxenwolf dons a magical GIRDLE to achieve its transformation. In wolf form, it torments people. A boxenwolf can be forced to reveal its identity by holding a piece of steel over it.

brahmaparusha   Indian vampiric spirit similar to the BHUTA. The *bramaparusha* is a male demon wearing a wreath of intestines around his head, gnawing the flesh off a man's head and drinking BLOOD from a skull.

Bram Stoker's Dracula (1992)   Film adaptation of BRAM STOKER's novel *DRACULA* (1897) by director Francis Ford Coppola. *Bram Stoker's Dracula* takes liberties with Stoker's plot, but is the highest-grossing of all *Dracula* films. The screenplay was written by James V. Hart. The original title of the film was *Dracula: The Untold Story*.

Stars of the film are

- Gary Oldman as COUNT DRACULA
- Anthony Hopkins as PROFESSOR ABRAHAM VAN HELSING
- Keanu Reeves as Jonathan Harker
- Winona Ryder as Mina Harker
- Sadie Frost as Lucy Westenra
- Richard E. Grant as Dr. Jack Seward
- Cary Elwes as Arthur Holmwood
- Bill Campbell as Quincey Morris
- Tom Waits as R. M. RENFIELD

Coppola is a longtime fan of horror films. The first vampire movie he saw was *House of Dracula* (1945), starring John Carradine as Count Dracula/Baron Latoes. He considers the F. W. MURNAU adaptation, *NOSFERATU* (1922), to be "probably the greatest film made on the Dracula story," even though it does not closely follow Stoker's novel. (One reason for that is that *Nosferatu* was a plagiarism, and so changes in the plot and characters were made in an effort to subvert copyright.)

Coppola's intent was to be faithful to Stoker's novel. The film is faithful to Stoker's intent, but not to the letter. Stoker made no comparison between Dracula and VLAD TEPES; nor was *Dracula* a love story. Coppola's film uses the legend of Vlad Tepes as a frame to set the vampire story, and "love never dies" is an unspoken subtitle of the film.

Bram Stoker's Dracula opens in 1462, when Muslim Turks are sweeping into Europe. Dracula, "the Prince," wearing a wolf's helmet, fights bravely as a Christian and has thousands of the enemy impaled on stakes. But back at his castle, a Turkish arrow has brought a message of deceit to his bride, Elizabeth, saying that Dracula has been killed in battle. In anguish, she flings herself from the castle turret. Dracula arrives to find her broken body lying before an altar with a great CROSS. A priest informs Dracula that because she committed SUICIDE, her soul cannot be saved. Dracula, in grief and rage, renounces God, and swears that he will "arise from my own death to avenge hers with all the powers of darkness." Dracula impales the priest with the altar cross and fills the sacramental goblet with bloody holy WATER and drinks it, proclaiming, "'The blood is the life.' And it shall be mine!" Thus the vampire is born. Stone angels weep BLOOD tears.

Stoker opens his novel with Jonathan Harker, an English solicitor's clerk, journeying to CASTLE DRACULA in TRANSYLVANIA to bring real estate papers for the Count to sign. The enigmatic count talks a little of being part of a brave and noble line of warriors, but there are no direct parallels to Vlad. Dracula spends most of his time offstage in the novel, and the reader is never privy to his thoughts. When he vampirizes Lucy Westenra and then Mina Harker, there is no "lost love" romance—just predatory supernatural horror. In the film, Dracula finds Elizabeth in Mina. "I have crossed oceans of time to find you," he tells Mina.

The love story element—that one of the count's victims was his lost love from mortal life—also was featured in the 1974 telemovie *Dracula,* starring Jack Palance and written by RICHARD MATHESON and directed and produced by DAN CURTIS.

Coppola cast Gary Oldman as Count Dracula because he said Oldman could portray the passion he felt Dracula should express. When Harker comes to his castle, Dracula is an old man with a sweeping, blood-RED cape, a peculiar, upswept Kabuki hairdo (supposedly to emphasize Dracula's androgynous and universal qualities) and a SHADOW that moves independently of him. In Stoker's novel, the count is old and repulsively wolfish, and does not cast a shadow. In both novel and film, Dracula becomes progressively younger after arriving in England as he drinks the blood of his English victims.

Contemporary mores have made it possible to explicitly portray things that Stoker could only hint at. For example, the three vampire "brides" of Dracula in his Transylvanian castle are sensual and erotic in the novel, but do nothing explicit to Harker, not even pierce his flesh for blood. In the film, they actually rape him and have bloody mouths. Coppola's Lucy is more openly sexual, as is the count.

Coppola borrows a bit of symbolic drama from his film *The Godfather,* juxtaposing the holiness of the wedding of Jonathan and Mina against the unholiness of Dracula's final and killing assault on Lucy.

In TOD BROWNING's 1931 *Dracula* starring BELA LUGOSI, Browning—constricted by budget—changed the ending to have the VAMPIRE HUNTERS track and kill Dracula and his brides in his Carfax Abbey in London. Coppola's film follows part of the novel's ending. The vampire hunters pursue the fleeing count across Europe to his homeland. They overtake his GYPSY helpers, and Quincey Morris stabs Dracula with his bowie knife and Harker cuts his throat with his kukri knife. There the similarity to the novel ends. In Stoker's version, Dracula dies and crumbles instantly to dust. In Coppola's film, Dracula manages to escape into his castle and goes into the chapel, while Mina, still under his commanding spell, fends off the men with a rifle. She joins

Count Dracula (Gary Oldman) cuts an exotic figure in Bram Stoker's Dracula. (Author's collection)

him in the chapel and tries unsuccessfully to pull out Harker's embedded knife. She bids Dracula a tearful and loving farewell as he dies. She grips the knife and plunges it deeper into his heart. Dracula dies, in peace at last.

None of the scenes in *Bram Stoker's Dracula* was shot on location; all scenes were filmed on sound stages. The set for the BORGO PASS alone was the size of a football field, the largest in Hollywood. The final chase was conducted on an oval track.

FURTHER READING:

Coppola, Francis Ford, and James V. Hart. *Bram Stoker's Dracula: The Film and the Legend.* New York: Newmarket Press, 1992.

Silver, Alain, and James Ursini. *The Vampire Film: From Nosferatu to Interview with the Vampire.* 3d ed. New York: Limelight Editions, 1997.

Breslau Vampire (1591–1592)   Unnamed VAMPIRE who terrorized Breslau, Germany, after committing SUICIDE. The Breslau Vampire exhibited behavior associated with the OLD HAG syndrome.

On September 20, 1591, a well-to-do shoemaker stunned his family and the city by slitting his throat with a knife for no known reason. As suicides were a sin and a disgrace upon the family, his wife—who had just given birth—and her sisters sought to hide the cause of his death. They told others he had died of a stroke, and refused visitors. They quietly made funeral arrangements and hired an old woman to wash the CORPSE and completely tie up and cover the fatal wound. The widow and the old woman laid the corpse in the COFFIN. They finally allowed the priest to visit and view the body, but the wound was so well hidden that he detected nothing suspicious. On the third day after the suicide, the shoemaker's body was buried with a splendid funeral befitting the rich.

Despite the family's efforts, the secret of the suicide leaked out, and rumors began circulating about the city. At first, people refused to believe it, but the rumors grew so persistent that the city's council made inquiries. The shoemaker's family made up more lies. They said that he had fallen and injured himself on a sharp rock, and that a sharp awl had been found in his clothing. The rumors persisted, however, and the council considered what action to take. The widow's friends pleaded with her to prevent her husband's body from being exhumed or moved to unhallowed ground, or even worse, declared to be a sorcerer.

Meanwhile, a restless ghost looking like the shoemaker began appearing both day and night. It terrified people by making horrible noises, causing nightmares, and sexually assaulting them. (See OLD HAG.) The harassments increased, and finally the shoemaker's family went to the president of the court and said the man was being abused in his grave, and they desired to take the matter to the Kaiser.

The ghost now appeared at sundown every day, and no one in the city was free of it. According to an account in Prussian folklore:

> The ones most bothered were those who wanted to rest after heavy work; often it came to their bed, often it actually lay down in it and was like to smother the people. Indeed, it squeezed them so hard that—not without astonishment—people could see the marks left by its fingers, so that one could easily judge the so-called stroke. In this manner, the people, who were fearful in any case, became yet more fearful, so that they did not remain longer in their houses, but sought more secure places. Most of them, not secure in their bedchamber, stayed in the rooms, after bringing many others in, so that their fear was dispersed by the crowd. Nonetheless, although they all waked with burning lights, the ghost came anyway. Often everyone saw it, but often just a few, of whom it always harassed some.

After eight months of suffering the ghost, the council ordered the body to be publicly disinterred on April 18, 1592. The account continues:

> In the opened grave they found the body complete and undamaged by decay, but blown up like a drum, except that nothing was changed and the limbs all still hung together. They were—which was remarkable—not stiffened, like those of other dead people, but one could move them easily. On his feet the skin had peeled away, and another had grown, much purer and stronger than the first, and as almost all sorcerers are marked on an out-of-the-way place, so that one does not notice it easily, so did he have on his big toe a mole like a rose. No one knew the meaning of this. There was also no stench to be noticed, except that the cloths in which he was wrapped had a repulsive smell. The wound in his throat gaped open and was reddish and not changed in the slightest.

For several days the corpse was aired during the day and stored in a house at night. It was guarded around the clock. During the daytime, curious townsfolk came to view it. But the exhumation did nothing to abate the vampire attacks. The next remedy tried was the burial of the corpse under a gallows, but this only incited the vampire to increase the intensity of his assaults. The corpse seemed to get fuller in flesh.

Finally, the widow broke down and admitted that her husband had committed suicide, and said that the city officials could deal with him as they saw fit. According to MONTAGUE SUMMERS:

> Wherefore the seventh of *May* he was again digged up, and it was observable, that he was grown more sensibly fleshy since his last interment. To be short, they cut off the Head, Arms, and Legs of the Corps, and opening his Back, took out his Heart, which was as fresh and intire [sic] as in a Calf new kill'd. These, together with his Body, they put on a pile of wood, and burnt them to Ashes, which they carefully sweeping together, and putting into a Sack (that none might get them for wicked uses) poured them into the River, after which the *Spectrum* was never seen more.

The shoemaker's maid, who died after him, also returned and assaulted a fellow servant at night, laying on the woman so heavily that her eyes swelled. The spirit appeared also in the forms of a hen, CAT, and goat, and bedeviled others to the point where the maid's body was disinterred and burned. Her attacks ceased.

See also ASHES; BURNING.

FURTHER READING:
Barber, Paul. *Vampires, Burial and Death: Folklore and Reality.*
    New Haven, Conn.: Yale University Press, 1988.
Summers, Montague. *The Vampire in Europe.* New York: E. P.
    Dutton, 1929.

Brides of Dracula   See HAMMER FILMS.

Brite, Poppy Z. (1967–)   American horror novelist who writes about vampires as well as an occult underworld of other supernatural beings.

Poppy Z. Brite was born in New Orleans on May 25, 1967. After attending the University of North Carolina, she returned to live in her hometown. Prior to becoming a full-time writer she worked in an assortment of jobs, including exotic dancer, gourmet candy maker, cook, mouse caretaker, and artist's model.

Brite's first published works were short stories published in *The Horror Show* magazine (now defunct) between 1985 and 1990. Her first novel, *Lost Souls,* was published in 1992 by Asylum/Delacourte. The book was nominated for the Lambda Literary Award, and for the Best First Novel of 1992 by the Horror Writers of America.

Lost Souls features Nothing, the offspring of Zillah, a 100-year-old VAMPIRE, and another vampire with whom Zillah had a one-night stand. The alienated Nothing searches for his roots and meaning of his life. Among the other characters are Ghost, a psychic young man who is the son of a white witch and who sings the lead for the band Lost Souls; Christian, a New Orleans barkeeper who is a vampire; and Molochai and Twig, followers of Zillah. There are youths called "Deathers" who love Goth music and the vampire model of "dark beauty and fragile mortality."

Vampires also appear in *Wormwood* (1994), a collection of Brite's short stories. She has published stories in numerous anthologies, and is the editor of the critically acclaimed collections of horror stories, *Love in Vein* (1994) and *Love in Vein II* (1996).

Her novel *Exquisite Corpse* (1996) features a cannibalistic serial killer.

Brite lives in New Orleans with her husband, Christopher.

FURTHER READING:
Brite, Poppy Z. *Lost Souls.* New York: Asylum/Delacourte, 1992.

"Broken Promise, The"   Native American Indian folktale about a boy who becomes half wolf. The story goes that once upon a time, an Indian hunter grew weary of the wickedness and unkindness in his village, so he built a hut for his wife and three children out in a deep forest. For years they lived, isolated, and happy.

At long last the Indian knew he was dying. He told his wife she would soon follow him. He instructed his two older children never to abandon the youngest child, for he was weak. The children made their pledge.

After both their parents had died, the children remained together. But soon the oldest, now a young man, desired to return to his village. He resented the burden of his younger brother and wished to abandon him, but his sister argued against it.

Determined to have his way, the young man left and never returned. Eventually, the sister also grew weary of being burdened by her younger brother. One day she announced she was going off in search of the oldest brother. There was food in the hut, she said, and she would return soon.

But when she reached the village, she found her brother happily married. She herself was sought as a bride. She married and forgot about her younger brother.

Back in the hut, the boy ate all the food. Then he went out to forage for roots in order to stay alive. When winter came and there were no more roots, he hid in trees all night and during the day crept out to eat the leavings of the kills of wolves. Soon he sought their company. He would watch while the wolves ate their prey. The wolves shared their food with him.

One day in the spring, the eldest brother was fishing in his canoe in the great lake. He heard the voice of a child singing:

> My brother, my brother!
> I am becoming a wolf,
> I am becoming a wolf!

When the song was done, the boy's voice howled just as the wolves howl.

An Indian boy abandoned by his parents is befriended by wolves and transforms into a wolf. From The Yellow Fairy Book *(1894), edited by Andrew Lang*

Recognizing the voice of his brother, the young man called out for the lad to come to him. But the boy only continued his mournful song. Then he fled with the wolves, his skin grew heavier and heavier, and he vanished in the forest.

The young man went back to his village and told his sister, and they mourned their little brother and their broken promise until the end of their lives.

The story shares a prominent element found in werewolf stories: transformation into a wolf comes as the result of a curse. In this case, the curse is the broken promise and the abandonment of the elder siblings.

FURTHER READING:
Lang, Andrew, ed. *The Yellow Fairy Book*. New York: Dover Publications, 1966.

Brotherhood of the Wolf (*Le Pacte des Loups*)   French film directed by Christopher Gans and released in 2001, loosely based on the werewolf case of the BEAST OF GEVAUDAN, which panicked the entire region of south-central France from 1764 to 1767. *Brotherhood of the Wolf* was a major hit in France but was less enthusiastically received in America.

In France in 1765, Chevalier Grégoire de Fronsac, a young nobleman and naturalist (Samuel Le Bihan), and Mani, his Iroquois companion (Mark Dacascos), are hired by King Louis XV to hunt a bloodthirsty beast that has been killing women and children. Mani is skilled in martial-arts fighting, which is served up in ample amounts, and also has the ability to mystically commune with wolves. Fronsac becomes involved in a love triangle with a beautiful noblewoman, Marianne (Émilie Dequenne), and an equally beautiful prostitute, Sylvia (Monica Bellucci), who keeps secrets about political tensions and a grand conspiracy of church versus the king.

Fronsac suspects the Beast is really a human sorcerer, which proves to be the case. When it is finally revealed, the Beast is disappointing: it is merely an animal trussed up in armor.

broucolaca   See BURCULACAS.

Brown, James (ca. 19th century)   Alleged sailor VAMPIRE who was imprisoned in Washington, D.C. The account of "James Brown," the name given by the sailor, was reported in the *Brooklyn Daily Eagle* newspaper in 1892.

According to the story, the vampire incident took place in 1867. Brown, a Portuguese sailor, left on a fishing smack that sailed out of Boston. When two of the crew went missing, the captain searched the hold and found Brown sucking the BLOOD from the CORPSE of one of the men. The second man was also dead, and his corpse was bloodless.

Brown was convicted of murder and was sentenced to be hanged. However, President Andrew Johnson intervened and commuted the sentence to life in prison. Brown was jailed in Ohio, and in 1892 was transferred to the National Asylum in Washington, D.C.

FURTHER READING:
Fort, Charles. *The Complete Books of Charles Fort*. New York: Dover Publications, 1974.

Brown, Mercy Lea (1871–1892)   Most famous alleged VAMPIRE of America. News of the European vampire cult that leaked out to the West in the early 18th century swept on to infect the American colonies in New England, especially Connecticut and western Rhode Island. There, deaths due to highly virulent diseases such as tuberculosis, measles, and smallpox were blamed on vampirism, and bodies were exhumed and mutilated in the same fashion as had been done for centuries in the rural parts of the Balkans. The nature of infectious disease was not understood. Vampirism was an easy explanation, especially when people died of tuberculosis, a disease which literally wastes away the body.

The Mercy Brown vampire case of Rhode Island, which dates to the late 19th century, is the most famous of the vampire episodes. In the late 1800s, the George Brown family of Exeter, Rhode Island, was stricken with tuberculosis. Brown's wife, Mary, died, followed by their daughter, Olive. Four daughters and a son remained. Four years later, Edwin, the son, became ill with consumption. He and his bride left for Colorado, where Edwin sought treatment at mineral springs. During his absence, and about two years after Edwin had shown the first signs of lung trouble, daughter Mercy became sick and died on January 18, 1892. She was 19 years old. Edwin then returned to the home of his father-in-law, Willis Himes, where his condition worsened and he became critically ill.

It is possible that Brown was aware of the SARAH TILLINGHAST vampire case of 1796. According to an article in the *Providence Journal* on March 19, 1892, he was besieged by people who "expressed implicit faith in the old theory that by some unexplained and unreasonable way in some part of the deceased relative's body live flesh and blood might be found . . ." These friends and neighbors told Brown that the only way to save Edwin was to dig up the bodies of his wife and two daughters to determine if any of them still had hearts full of BLOOD, and to burn the heart (see BURNING) and feed Edwin the ASHES.

An article in the same newspaper on March 21, 1892, explained in detail the definition of vampires and the vampire cult, attributing its origins to the Slavic people of Russia, Poland, Bohemia, and other parts of Europe. The article went on:

> How the tradition got to Rhode Island and planted itself firmly here, cannot be said. It was in existence in Connecticut and Maine 50 and 100 years ago, and the people

of the South County say they got it from their ancestors, as far back in some cases as the beginning of the eighteenth century. The idea never seems to have been accepted in the northern part of the state, but every five or ten years it has cropped up in Coventry, West Greenwich, Exeter, Hopkinton, Richmond and the neighboring towns.

Brown himself had "no confidence in the old-time theory," but also received little help from the medical community. He finally acquiesced to pressure and agreed to dig up the bodies of Mary, Olive, and Mercy, in order to try to save his son.

The medical examiner, Dr. Harold Metcalf—who also did not believe in vampires—was on hand at Chestnut Hill Cemetery during the exhumations. The CORPSES of Mary and Olive were well decomposed. Mary was partially mummified and had no blood in her heart. Olive was only a skeleton with a thick growth of hair remaining. But the body of Mercy was judged by some to be in exceptionally good condition; however Metcalf said her state was natural and not exceptional. Witnesses who had been at her wake swore that her body had shifted in the COFFIN.

Brown instructed Dr. Metcalf to remove Mercy's heart and liver. Witnesses were astonished when clotted and decomposed blood dripped from the organs, which they took to be a sure sign of vampirism, even though Metcalf assured them it was not an unusual occurrence for a nine-week-old corpse. Brown took the organs to a rock and burned them. The ashes were saved. Dr. Metcalf told Edwin to take the ashes and mix a tiny amount in medicine he'd prescribed, and drink the mixture. Edwin allegedly followed the instructions, but died soon thereafter.

Over the years, the story has grown and become embellished. It has been claimed that six or seven girls in the Brown family died before Mercy was exhumed, and they all bore "the mark of the vampire" on their throats when they died (the vampire biting victims on the throat was popularized in fiction).

Mercy's grave continues to attract visitors. People report seeing a blue light or a glowing ball of light hovering over the grave, and other visitors claim they can hear a girl's voice whisper, "Please help me, let me out." It may be imagination, or the sighing of the wind—or perhaps the spirit of Mercy Brown still lies restless in her grave.

See also NEW ENGLAND VAMPIRES.

FURTHER READING:
Bell, Michael E. *Food for the Dead: On the Trail of New England's Vampires*. New York: Carroll & Graf Publishers, 2001.
Guiley, Rosemary Ellen, with J. B. Macabre. *The Complete Vampire Companion*. New York: Macmillan, 1994.
Rondina, Christopher. *Vampire Legends of Rhode Island*. North Attleborough, Mass.: Covered Bridge Press, 1997.

Browning, Tod (1880–1962)   Actor, screenwriter, and film director, best known for *Dracula* (1931), his adaptation of BRAM STOKER's novel by the same name, starring BELA LUGOSI as COUNT DRACULA. In the course of career, he directed 63 films and wrote for 28 films. Browning's early fascination with carnivals can be seen in his films with his characters who are misfits of all sorts.

Charles Albert "Tod" Browning was born on May 12, 1880 (some sources give 1882 as the year of birth), in Louisville, Kentucky. From childhood he was drawn to carnivals and the people who made their living in them. He made up his own backyard performances for friends and neighbors. In 1896 he left high school and ran away to join the Manhattan Fair and Carnival & Company. He adopted the name "Tod." His first job was as a barker. He was the star of a sideshow act called "The Living Corpse," in which he was "buried" for up to two days—but was sustained by a secret breathing apparatus—and then miraculously was "revived." By age 21, he had worked in just about every job in the sideshows, and also some of the vaudeville acts.

Browning's carnie interests eventually led him to New York City, where in 1913 he was performing in one-reel nickelodeon comedies with Charlie Murray, an ex-circus performer. Browning followed Murray to Hollywood, where he worked with director D. W. Griffith and advanced from acting to directing nickelodeons.

In 1915 he suffered an accident. Driving a car, he collided with a railway carriage. He was seriously injured and one of his two passengers, actor Elmer Booth, was killed. Hospitalized for about a year, Browning turned to scriptwriting. After his recovery, he went back to studio work, directing *Puppets* (1916), in which he used actors for harlequin puppets. In 1917 he directed his first full-length film, *Jim Bludso,* about a riverboat captain. In 1918 Irving Thalberg of Metro-Goldwyn-Mayer brought Browning together with LON CHANEY in *The Wicked Darling* (1919), the start of a long partnership between the director and actor. Browning directed Chaney in his only vampire role, LONDON AFTER MIDNIGHT (1927). In 1935 he remade the silent film as a sound film, MARK OF THE VAMPIRE, starring Lugosi and Carroll Borland.

Browning's first work with Lugosi was *The Thirteenth Chair* (1929), made as both a silent film and as a talkie. Lugosi was not his first pick for *Dracula.* He favored Chaney, but after Chaney died in 1930, Browning thought it would be best to feature an unknown European actor in the role. Lugosi lobbied heavily for the part and won it. *Dracula* suffered from budget constraints—for example, the movie ends in London, not TRANSYLVANIA, which kept sets to a minimum. The Spanish version of *Dracula* was shot on the same sets at night, and Universal executives preferred that to Browning's version. Nonetheless, audiences responded to the brooding presence of Lugosi, and Browning's *Dracula* became a big moneymaker, rescuing Universal from the brink of bankruptcy. It was Browning's most financially successful film.

Browning had to cope with serious personal problems. He had married his companion, Alice Houghton, in 1911, but she left him in the 1920s, when his problems with alcoholism increased. Browning also was blacklisted by several studios. His turning point came through Thalberg, who gave him the directing job for *The Unholy Three* (1925), about a dwarf jewel thief, a circus strongman, and a ventriloquist (Chaney) who poses as an old lady. The film was a huge success and established Browning as a top director. Alice returned.

Browning's last screen credit was *Miracles for Sale* (1939), after which he announced his retirement. He did some scenario work for MGM for several years, and then retired completely in 1942. Alice died in 1944.

In the late 1950s, Browning developed throat cancer—the same disease that killed Chaney—and had surgery on his tongue. He was found dead in the bathroom of friends on October 5, 1962, in Santa Monica, California.

After *Dracula*, Browning's best-known film is *Freaks* (1932), in which real circus freaks take revenge on a beautiful but treacherous woman. *Freaks* proved an embarrassment to MGM executives, who withdrew it from circulation, and in England the film was banned for 30 years. It achieved an underground cult status in the 1960s and debuted on American television in 1990.

FURTHER READING:
Skal, David J., and Elias Savada. *Dark Carnival: The Secret World of Tod Browning, Hollywood's Master of the Macabre.* New York: Anchor/Doubleday, 1995.

brujas (brujos)   Witches of Mexico, Mesoamerica, and Hispanic communities in North America, who are ascribed vampiric habits. The bruja, the woman, is more prevalent, and considered more powerful than her masculine counterpart, the brujo. The bruja is sought for folk remedies for physical illness, and spells and charms to remedy emotional, romantic, and social problems. In rural areas, the bruja is regarded more as sinister than helpful, and is blamed for the wounds of VAMPIRE BATS. The witch is believed to take the form of a bat and bite and suck out the BLOOD of her victims.

Brujas can be thwarted by covering up their entry points—cracks in a house or keyholes—and by sprinkling rice or wheat in front of the doorway. The bruja will be forced to stop and count all the grains, but will not be able to complete the job before dawn comes and takes away her powers.

See also SEEDS; VAMPIRE SORCERERS AND WITCHES.

bruxsa   In Portuguese lore, a VAMPIRE witch. The *bruxsa* prefers the BLOOD of infants and attacks them while they sleep in their cribs.

See also LILITH; *TLAHUELPUCHI*; VAMPIRE SORCERERS AND WITCHES.

Buckinghamshire Vampire (12th c.)   English VAMPIRE case recorded by WILLIAM OF NEWBURGH from an oral account related to him by Stephen, the archdeacon of the diocese of Buckinghamshire. The vampire was the restless ghost of a dead man who acted in a vampire-like way. He was not called a "vampire," for the term was not known in the English language until the 18th century.

The unnamed man died in 1192 in Buckinghamshire and was properly buried on the eve of Ascension Day. But the night after burial, the man left his grave and came to the wife, leaping upon her while she slept and nearly killing her with the press of his weight. (See OLD HAG.) He did the same the next night. On the third night, the wife gathered friends to keep vigil for her, and remained awake in order to repel her dead husband. When the vampire arrived, he was driven away by the shouts and cries of the wife and her friends. Instead, he attacked his brothers, who lived in the same town.

The brothers were, like the wife, forced to stay awake at night and make great noises in order to repel the vampire. As a result, the vampire began attacking other sleeping people, as well as animals who were resting. Soon every household was forced to have a member of the family stay awake all night to repel the specter. After a long period of harassing people and animals at night, he began appearing in daylight to the townspeople. He was visibly perceived by groups of people, and his evil presence was sensed by many more.

The townspeople appealed to Archdeacon Stephen for help. He convened a synod, and wrote a letter to St. Hugh, the bishop of Lincoln, asking what should be done to deal with the evil.

St. Hugh consulted priests and theologians, and learned to his astonishment that similar attacks had occurred elsewhere in England. Although he was told that no peace would be had until the CORPSE was dug up and burned (see BURNING), he rejected that as undesirable and unbecoming. Hugh wrote out an absolution and told the archdeacon to open the tomb and place it on the corpse's chest, then reseal the tomb. Hugh believed that no matter what the reason was that the vampire was wandering from the grave, the absolution would take care of the matter and set his soul to rest.

When the tomb was opened, the body was found to be incorrupt. The absolution was laid on his chest and the grave closed. The vampire never troubled anyone again.

FURTHER READING:
Glut, Donald. *True Vampires of History.* New York: HC Publishers, 1971.
McNally, Raymond T. *A Clutch of Vampires.* New York: Bell Publishing, 1984.

budas   In Abbyssinian lore, certain potters or ironworkers who have the power to shape-shift into WEREWOLVES and other ravenous beasts such as hyenas. *Budas* also have the malevolent power of the EVIL EYE. According to the lore, the *budas* were able to do their SHAPE-SHIFTING on one day of the year. They also wore peculiar earrings, which sometimes were found in the ears of trapped hyenas. Herodotus, a Greek historian of the fifth century B.C.E., said he did not believe the stories he heard about werewolf *budas*.

Buffy the Vampire Slayer   Extremely popular, two-time Emmy-winning television series created by Joss Whedon about the adventures of "the One Girl, the Chosen One of each generation," selected as the Slayer and responsible for ridding the world of VAMPIRES, DEMONS, and other forces of darkness. *Buffy the Vampire Slayer* aired from March 1997 to May 2003. The show's clever writing; inside allusions to past or future episodes, movies, and books; appealing cast; and the defeat of vampires much different from BRAM STOKER's Dracula or ANNE RICE's Lestat gave rise to worldwide fans, a host of Internet sites, merchandise, and even scholarly articles on Buffy's themes, symbolism, and universe: the "Buffyverse."

Unlike past VAMPIRE HUNTERS, Buffy Anne Summers does not fight evil alone but is supported by her friends Willow, Xander, and Oz, joined by others as the show progresses. Her Watcher, Giles, posing as a high school librarian, tutors her and the others in slayage, weaponry, self-defense, and recognition of monsters and demons. Angel, a vampire who was given a soul in a GYPSY curse and falls deeply in love with Buffy, helps the teens hunt demons and struggles with the memories of his horrific past. He leaves *BtVS* in the third season to form his own demon-hunting firm, Angel Investigations, and star in a spin-off, ANGEL. The first three seasons of *BtVS* take place in Sunnydale High School, which serves as a metaphor for Hell with its cliques of popular girls and jocks tormenting the geeks, while the final four years are set in Sunnydale University, a haven for mad professors, difficult roommates, and unfaithful lovers. Buffy overcomes most of these trials with cunning and a great fashion sense, but not always: Over the seven-year series she loses friends, family and, even her life—twice.

First the Movie
Before Academy Award– and Emmy-nominated creator Joss Whedon (*Toy Story, Alien: Resurrection*) took Buffy to series TV, there was *Buffy the Vampire Slayer* on the big screen in 1992, a predictable film in which Whedon introduces the Buffy concept: A beautiful, blond young woman, usually a victim in horror or slasher films, fights back. Kristy Swanson plays Buffy, a typical Southern California airhead interested only in boys, clothes, shopping, and cheerleading. But fate shows her a different path when the mysterious Merrick (Donald Sutherland) explains that she is the Slayer and begins teaching Buffy the fine art of vampire extermination. Her main adversary, Lothos (Rutger Hauer), is convincingly menacing but is not as exciting as Buffy's later TV nemeses. The best villain is Amilyn, played with camp humor by Paul Reubens, better known as Pee

Lothos (Rutger Hauer) menaces Buffy the Vampire Slayer (Kristy Swanson) in the film version of Buffy the Vampire Slayer. *(Author's collection)*

Wee Herman. Smaller parts are filled by young actors who command much meatier roles now, such as Ben Affleck, Hilary Swank, David Arquette, and Luke Perry.

Then the Television Series
Whedon did not feel the movie adequately explored the Buffy concept, whereas with television he had the creative freedom to expand plots, flesh out the characters, and play with the villains. None of the actors from the movie transferred to the TV show. Sarah Michelle Gellar became the new Buffy. She and her mother, Joyce (Kristine Sutherland), move from Los Angeles to the suburban town of Sunnydale, where Buffy might have an easier time at a smaller high school. Joyce doesn't know that Buffy has a different destiny:

> In every generation there is a chosen one.
> She alone will stand against the vampires,
> The demons and the forces of darkness.
> She is the Slayer.

Unfortunately for Buffy and Joyce, Sunnydale is a hotbed of demonic activity situated on a Hellmouth: a portal into the abyss. In medieval plays, a large skeleton of a whale's jaw often represented the Hellmouth, and demons would enter the stage from the orifice accompanied by smoke or fetid smells. Sunnydale's Hellmouth is under the high school.

The original pilot never aired. Unlike the eventual show, the pilot Buffy had brown hair and was ditzier. The school was called Berryman, and the friends' school hangout, the library, was enormous. Some of the plot elements, such as finding a dead student's body in a locker, were kept for the real first episode, "Welcome to the Hellmouth," which aired on March 10, 1997, on the WB network.

Some members of the cast of the television series Buffy the Vampire Slayer, *from left: David Boreanaz (Angel), Sarah Michelle Gellar (Buffy), Alyson Hannigan (Willow), Anthony Stewart Head (Giles), Charisma Carpenter (Cordelia), and, seated, Nicholas Brendon (Xander) (Author's collection)*

Synopsis of the First Season

Although *Buffy* started as a spring show for the WB, the quirky program about a girl whose destiny is to kill vampires immediately caught on. Buffy's tough stance was not the only appeal; viewers appreciated her ambivalence to "slayage," her desire to fit into high school, the establishment of close friends, and her attraction to edgy guys who had great sex appeal and maybe even a dark side, like the vampire Angel.

The story line for season one went as follows:

Episode one and two, "Welcome to the Hellmouth" and "The Harvest," aired in March 1997. Buffy arrives in Sunnydale only to discover that the small town sits atop a demon portal, and that the Master vampire will soon appear to take control. But with the help of Giles, her assigned Watcher and mentor, and the support of new friends Willow and Xander, Buffy dispatches her duties while trying to be a normal teenager facing the usual problems of homework, rules, and overly critical peers.

Buffy prepares to confront the Master, who plans to break out of his prison in the sewers through a ceremony called the Harvest. He fails. The remainder of season one deals with Buffy's attempts to attract a boyfriend, the exorcism of an evil hyena spirit from Xander, keeping Willow out of trouble on Internet chat rooms, saving the cheerleader Cordelia from the vengeance spirit of an ignored classmate, and fighting the vampire Master for control of the world. The friends call themselves the "Scooby Gang," a reference to the cartoon series "Scooby Doo, Where Are You?" In "Scooby," four friends—Daphne, Fred, Velma, and Shaggy—and the dog Scooby hunt the perpetrators of what appear to be supernatural crimes, just as the Scoobies (Buffy, Xander, Willow, and Giles) hunt evil forces. The vampire Angel also figures prominently in the first season, guiding Buffy or Giles in the ways of darkness and falling in love with Buffy.

However, can the Slayer fall in love with a vampire? Angel is really the cruel and sadistic Angelus, over 240 years old. He was made a vampire, or "sired," in 1753 by a female vamp named Darla, who was also his lover. Darla was a whore in Virginia before gaining immortality from the Master in 1609. A person cannot become a vampire by being the victim of feeding but must drink BLOOD from the vampire. Angel sired Drusilla, a former nun who appears in season two. Cursed by Gypsies in 1898, he regained a soul, but the curse also forced him to remember his atrocities.

In the last episode of season one, "Prophecy Girl," Buffy resolves to shoulder her responsibilities as Slayer and confront the Master. But she is not quite strong enough, and the Master feeds on her and leaves her to drown in a pool of WATER. Buffy actually dies briefly but is rescued by Xander and Angel. Since at the time of airing Whedon and his cast did not know if the WB wanted more of the show, this last episode of the first season had the finality of a complete story.

Synopses of Seasons Two and Three

Seasons two and three take place at Sunnydale High School, completing Buffy's early training. She returns from summer vacation following season one distant and depressed, especially when she learns that the vampires are still trying to resurrect the Master. She battles two students who have been killing teenage girls to use their body parts to create the perfect teen queen, and she overpowers an Incan spirit who resided in an ancient mummy. Vampires feed on a drunken Buffy at a fraternity party, she loses her powers while costumed as an 18th-century noblewoman

at a Halloween party, and the Scoobies uncover Giles's wild past, in which, known as the Ripper, he dabbled in the occult.

Two important new characters join Buffy in the second season: Spike and Drusilla. The vampire Spike, a hip, edgy personality with nearly white hair, comes to Sunnydale to restore the health of his ailing lover and sire, Drusilla. Spike's bloody past equals Angel's, and he boasts that he's already killed two Slayers. When Buffy dies in season one, the Watcher's Council in England—Giles's governing body—sends Kendra to be the next Slayer, but Drusilla kills Kendra by the end of the season.

The romance between Angel and Buffy dominates season two. Even though Angel is a vampire, Buffy senses a kindred spirit. They barely escape Spike and Drusilla's attempts to reassemble a demon called the Judge, whose body parts have been buried all over the world (much as Isis reassembled Osiris), and are unaware that Giles's new love interest, teacher Jenny Calendar, is actually Jenna Kalderash of the Romany clan that cursed Angel so many years before. While hiding from the Judge, Angel and Buffy make love—and that one moment of perfect happiness lifts the curse on Angel's soul, returning him to his vampire persona, Angelus. He cries out Buffy's name in extreme pain and becomes her adversary. At the end of the season, in episode 21 entitled "Becoming 2," Buffy realizes she has to stake Angel/Angelus in order to save him from descending into Hell with the demons Drusilla has called. She stabs Angel just as her friend Willow, a budding Wiccan, completes her spell, restoring Angel. Overcome with grief, Buffy leaves Sunnydale.

Buffy begins season three in Los Angeles, working as a waitress and trying to forget she ever was a Slayer. Since she has gone, the council appoints a new Slayer, Faith, who does not share Buffy's scruples about killing humans. Homesick, Buffy returns to Sunnydale. Various evil events, such as the mauling of a student by a WEREWOLF (possibly Oz, who has been turned by a bite from a relative), the affair of the band candy that resulted in her mother, Joyce, and Giles having sex twice on the hood of a police car, and the return of the Master, force Buffy to again accept her duty as the Slayer. Her very existence is wished away by Cordelia, however, who resolves to wreak vengeance on Xander for choosing Willow over her and blames everything on Buffy. Cordelia's plan is furthered by the demon Anyanka, patron saint of vengeance.

Meanwhile, Angel, who has returned to earth with his soul, remains tortured over his love for Buffy and its consequences. Knowing the risks, he refuses to escort her to the senior prom, an event Buffy had wanted to attend as a normal part of high school life. Anyanka reappears as Anya, no longer a vengeance demon, to warn the Scoobies that Faith, now completely without morals, has joined Mayor Richard Wilkins to facilitate his ascension into total evil. Faith has also poisoned Angel, and the only antidote is Faith's own blood. In the last two episodes of season three, "Graduation Day 1" and "Graduation Day 2," Buffy

Spike (James Wesley Marsters) on Buffy the Vampire Slayer
(Author's collection)

and Faith fight ferociously, but Faith manages to escape, albeit in a coma. To save Angel, Buffy offers herself, and he feeds reluctantly but hungrily.

Revived after a few hours in the hospital, Buffy joins her classmates at the graduation ceremony, where the mayor turns into a huge serpent and eats Principal Snyder. The entire student body has been enlisted to fight the snake, enabling Buffy to lure the enraged monster into the school library, packed with explosives. The school explodes, the snake dies, the ascension is averted, and the Scoobies reflect on their survival: not only the recent battle but high school itself. Angel says good-bye to Buffy and disappears into the smoke (and into his own spin-off show).

Synopsis of Season Four
Buffy begins season four trying to adjust to college life at Sunnydale University and balance her course work with her slayage. She detests her roommate, Kathy, sleeps with Parker Abrams but finds him indifferent, and copes with the return of Spike, accompanied by Cordelia's old friend Harmony, now a vampire. Oz, fighting his LYCANTHROPY (wolf behavior), escapes from his cage during a full MOON and encounters Veruca, another werewolf. She encourages him to embrace his wolfy self, and they sleep together until

Veruca tries to kill Willow. Oz kills Veruca instead and leaves Sunnydale and Willow.

Spike, meanwhile, has been captured by a group of secret commando dedicated to demon eradication called the Initiative, who operate underneath the university. The Initiative soldiers put a chip in Spike's head, rendering him helpless to hurt humans but able to fight demons. One of the Initiative, Riley Finn, falls in love with Buffy, but she is reluctant to reveal her true nature, and Riley also keeps his Initiative membership secret.

Episode 10, "Hush," was nominated for an Emmy award for best writing in a drama series. Creator Joss Whedon wrote and directed an innovative plot in which a group of fairy-tale demons called the Gentlemen (a scary skeletal group of men with macabre grins who float above the ground upright, followed by even uglier accomplices in unhooked straightjackets) invade Sunnydale and steal everyone's voices, then cut out their hearts. There is no spoken dialogue for most of the episode, only music, as the Scoobies and Giles frantically try to break the spell so Buffy's scream can dispatch the Gentlemen. Unbeknownst to the other, Buffy and Riley rendezvous in the old clock tower to fight the Gentlemen, and while they succeed, they realize that their secrets are out. Another significant event in "Hush": Tara (Amber Benson), a member of Willow's Wicca gathering, becomes Willow's friend and eventual lesbian lover—a breakthrough for TV.

Throughout the rest of season four, Buffy and Riley consolidate their relationship and spend a great deal of time in bed. Buffy's psychology professor, Maggie Walsh, is the secret head of the Initiative and has been giving Riley drugs to make him stronger. When he leaves the Initiative for Buffy, Walsh turns to Adam, her half-man, half-robot monster, to exact revenge, but he kills Walsh instead. Faith, meanwhile, has regained consciousness from her coma and uses a special device to switch bodies with Buffy. Once Buffy regains her body, she and Riley defeat Adam, but only after Spike defeats the Initiative, who were demons all along. Faith warns Buffy to "be home before Dawn," an allusion to the forthcoming mysterious appearance of Buffy's sister Dawn (Michelle Trachtenberg).

Synopsis of Season Five
COUNT DRACULA appears to the Slayer in episode one of the fifth season, materializing after she has "dusted" (dispatched to dust) a vampire. He flatters her by saying all vampires know her, and that she is beautiful and desirable. Dracula does not have the pinched nose and reptilian features that identify Sunnydale vampires, nor does he look like BELA LUGOSI. Instead, he more closely resembles the vampire LESTAT: youngish, long hair, and penetrating gaze. And unlike other vampires Buffy has met, Dracula has the ability to shape-shift: to become a BAT or dissolve into a mist. He can enter homes at will (ignoring the need for an invitation, a restriction on other vamps) and doesn't stay dead when staked. Dracula tempts Buffy to taste immortality after he feeds on her, and she considers it but refuses.

Illness and hospitals dominate the plot as Riley nearly dies from the drugs given him by Professor Walsh. Joyce, Buffy's mother, suffers from a brain tumor and requires surgery. Most puzzling is the appearance of Buffy's little sister, Dawn, who was unknown before. As the season develops, Buffy learns that a group of monks created Dawn from an energy called the "Key" then gave her a human form. The monks implanted familial memories in Buffy, Joyce, and Dawn, making it appear that Dawn was always in the family.

The Hell-Goddess Glory, who shares the body of Ben, a hospital intern, is the fifth season's Big Bad (as in Big Bad Evil). She is seeking the Key but does not know it is Dawn. Some of her efforts to locate the Key include a huge snake (Buffy chokes it); frequently changing bodies with Ben to confuse and perhaps trap the Key; and sending a group of Knights of Byzantium (reminiscent of the Knights Templar) to attack Buffy and kidnap Dawn. The Knights attack twice, confiding that Glory wants the Key so that she can return to Hell. But once the Key is activated, all the dimensions of earth become Hell. Although the Knights do kidnap Dawn, Glory becomes increasingly frustrated with her life on earth and possession of Ben's body. She and Ben fight in a bizarre body-switch back and forth, and Ben eventually gives Dawn to Glory to save himself.

Riley realizes that Buffy can never love him as deeply as he loves her. He begins consorting with female vamps and eventually leaves Sunnydale after Spike tells Buffy of Riley's late-night escapades. Spike, meanwhile, reveals his love for Buffy, even offering to kill Drusilla for her. Buffy does not reciprocate his affection, and in frustration Spike obtains a robot Buffy, dubbed the Buffybot, which substitutes for a while.

Joyce dies from an aneurysm toward season's end, and Dawn attempts a spell to bring her back but ultimately accepts her mother's death. Glory kidnaps Dawn to use her as the Key to unleash the apocalypse. The Scoobies prepare for battle, knowing some may not make it. Xander and Anya, who have had a rather lukewarm relationship, pledge to marry if they survive. The shocking ending: Once Buffy realizes that she and Dawn share the same blood, Buffy knows that she can give Dawn life by sacrificing hers. Her headstone reads:

> Buffy Anne Summers
> 1981–2001
> Devoted Sister
> Beloved Friend
> She Saved the World
> A Lot.

Synopses of Seasons Six and the Final Season Seven

Seasons six and seven were broadcast on the UPN network, part of Universal and Paramount Pictures. While the WB offered $1.6 million per episode, UPN offered to pay $2.3 million per episode for 44 episodes, or two seasons. The original cost to the WB had been $1 million per episode. *Buffy the Vampire Slayer* changed networks. This arrangement ended the plot and character sharing between *Buffy* and ANGEL, but those prohibitions fell by spring 2003, when Willow guest-starred on *Angel*.

Season six opens several months after Buffy's death. With no Slayer to watch, Giles—who loved Buffy as his daughter—plans to return to England. Willow, Anya, Tara, and Xander cast a spell to resurrect Buffy but are interrupted by demon bikers and leave without knowing whether the spell worked. The spell succeeds, but a very disoriented Buffy must dig herself out of her grave. She reverts to the Slayer to dust the bikers but yearns for the peace of Heaven, which she has left. The Buffybot, severely damaged by the bikers, informs Dawn of Buffy's resurrection. Buffy tries to take Joyce's place as homemaker and parent while remaining in school but is overwhelmed by demons, plumbing leaks, and Dawn's rebellious behavior.

Episode six, "Once More, With Feeling," features a strange force that compels the citizens of Sunnydale to reveal their innermost thoughts and feelings in song, and Buffy and the gang admit their failures and fears. Original score, songs, and lyrics were written by Joss Whedon, with music composition by Christophe Beck.

Willow continues magick (the real thing, not tricks) more vigorously, casting a spell to make Buffy forget Heaven but causing everyone else to have amnesia. Tara disapproves of Willow's growing addiction, and they break off their relationship. Spike pursues Buffy, this time successfully. Willow encounters a warlock who introduces her to some powerful magick, and she actually gets high casting the spells. Buffy takes a job as a fast-food worker to make ends meet in episode 11 but finds the customers dying from a "secret ingredient." The sponsors hated this story line.

Buffy turns 21 and receives a visit from her former lover, Riley Finn, and his wife, Sam. Their romance reminds Buffy that her relationship with Spike lacks something. Xander abandons Anya on their wedding day, afraid of turning into his father. Willow and Tara reunite, but Tara is accidentally shot and killed by Warren, creator of the Buffybot. Willow calls on Osiris to bring Tara back, but the spell fails. Consumed with anger, Willow vows to destroy the entire world. She is held back momentarily by a newly empowered Giles, who has returned from England, but her desire for vengeance is so great she nearly succeeds in her plans for Armageddon. Xander finally stops her.

Sunnydale High School reopens at the start of the seventh and final season, with Buffy hired as a new guidance counselor. Robin Wood is the new principal. Buffy contends with Dawn and her friends as well as bigger issues such as Willow's kidnapping by a demon, the raising of several undead and unwanted Baddies with the reconstruction of the high school, and the discovery of a student cult playing with the dark side. Invisible forces trash the Summers's home, depositing Joyce's body on the sofa. In episode six, "Conversations with Dead People," many of those who had passed, including Joyce, return to harass their loved ones. These spirits are not ghosts but demons representing the First Evil.

The Scoobies become suspicious of Spike's possible role in some recent murders and hold him captive in Buffy's home until they investigate. Strange, hooded figures called Bringers trash the Summers's house and take Spike to Sunnydale High, where they try to raise an old vampire. While helping clean up Buffy's house, Giles reveals that the First Evil is killing off Slayers so that the Hellmouth can open. Many of the new Slayers, or Potentials, are on their way to Buffy's home. Buffy confronts a particularly powerful vampire, a Turok-Han, barely defeating him and saving the Slayers. Buffy searches for Spike, who has endured excruciating torture. Buffy and Spike train the remaining Slayers and Potentials for the final battle. Principal Wood tells Buffy that his mother was a Slayer in New York—and that Spike killed her.

Meanwhile, Faith returns yet again to guide the Potentials, resulting in animosity between Faith and Buffy. Spike refuses to let Buffy concede her influence to Faith, and he and Buffy learn that a man named Caleb is living at a nearby vineyard as leader of the Bringers. Caleb and his minions battle Buffy and the Potentials, but finally confront Xander as "the one who sees things," blinding him in one eye. Buffy returns the next day to fight Caleb, and although he strikes at her again and again she is unhurt. Buffy discovers a hidden room containing a large weapon called a Scythe, and Faith and the Potentials search the sewers for more weapons, but find a ticking bomb instead. Caleb is furious that Buffy so easily pulls the ancient Scythe out of its stone (like Excalibur). The bomb explodes, leaving Faith unconscious and some of the Potentials dead.

Unsure of the Scythe's history and power, Buffy finds an old woman at a tomb who explains that the Scythe was created to destroy the last pure demon. Caleb arrives and snaps the old woman's neck then attacks Buffy, overpowering her. Angel, who has returned from Los Angeles in the night, knocks Caleb to the ground and then steps back to let Buffy finish the job. Buffy guts Caleb, leaving him for dead, then kisses Angel passionately. Spike watches them, heartbroken.

Caleb rises one more time, and Buffy slices him in half, starting with his genitals. She turns to Angel, but he jealously senses Spike's smell on her. The First Evil appears and tells Buffy that it is everywhere and will never die, and that the Slayer will always fight alone. Buffy realizes that she need not be a solitary killer and asks Willow to cast a spell that divides the Scythe's power equally among all the Potential Slayers. The remaining Scoobies and the new Slayers enter the Hellmouth and engage in a huge battle. The powers of an amulet prevent Spike from fighting, and he begins to burn inside. A beam of pure SUNLIGHT shoots outward from his soul, instantly dusting the powerful Turok-Han vampires. Most of Sunnydale has been swallowed by the Hellmouth, but the remaining citizens flee on a bus. Spike and Buffy embrace, then Spike enters Hell while Buffy runs for the bus, smiling with the knowledge she is no longer the One but one of many. The epic story closes, leaving the fans—as always—to debate how well the closing was done.

Themes and Appeal

What was it that made *Buffy the Vampire Slayer* a good, possibly great, television show, appealing not only to teen audiences but to older fans as well? Comments on over 750,000 Web sites and opinions expressed in scholarly essays and panel discussions, university seminars and dinner party conversations, say the show was clever, humorous, well-written, edgy, cool, hip, and different from other books or programs on vampires.

While the appeal may have been its trendiness, the themes explored by Buffy and the Scoobies were timeless: the fight of good versus evil and the ambiguity of that conflict; the metaphor of high school as Hell (not much has changed at high school—there are still the same patterns of behavior); the security of family and the bonds of friendship; the realization that life's pleasures are priceless; the nature of love, female empowerment, and the right to do things "her way"; and the need for sacrifice to gain redemption.

Sarah Michelle Gellar was not comfortable with descriptions of *Buffy* as feminist programming, saying, "Feminism has sort of a negative connotation. It makes you think of women who don't shave their legs." Yet Buffy was empowered and made no excuses for being a young woman who would assume the role of Slayer and perform daily acts of necessary violence for the common good. Neither did she apologize for a fairly active sex life with several partners over seven seasons. At least two of her partners were practicing vampires. In other words, Buffy "kicked ass," a most favorable character trait. According to Rhonda V. Wilcox, in her essay "Who Died and Made Her the Boss?: Patterns of Mortality in *Buffy*," her affair with Angel is not a match made in Heaven. They come from separate worlds, they often hurt each other yet risk their lives for each other, but their relationship is based first on friendship and transcendent love, not a one-night stand. And coincidentally, the lovers (nearly all of them, not just Buffy and Angel), practice safe sex.

Buffy's ability to exact violent retribution against the forces of evil does not mean she is indiscriminate. To her, even vampires and demons are not necessarily entirely evil, and deserve respect and perhaps love if they express guilt over their past actions and seek redemption. Essayist Mimi Marinucci notes that Buffy extends such consideration first to Angel and later to Spike. On the other hand, humans do not necessarily get a break for their humanity if they are evil, like Mayor Wilkins. Buffy argues with the Slayer Faith when Faith tries to convince her that as Slayers she and Buffy are better and therefore above the rules: "People need us to survive. In the balance, nobody's gonna cry over some random bystander who got caught in the crossfire." When Buffy protests, Faith replies, "Well, that's your loss."

Sarah Michelle Gellar (Author's collection)

important as the lines characters speak. . . . [and] provides a common 'language' for characters and fans."

Dechert says that *Buffy* uses popular music in three primary ways: first as a contributor of mood to various scenes, providing a backdrop, and secondly as a way to establish the identities of characters. The third use is to reinforce the "communal identity" between the music of *Buffy* and the show's fans. Whereas most shows feature a "card" of the band—its album cover and a five-second promotional spot of the song at the end of the show—*Buffy* chooses simply to incorporate the music. Knowing the songs and bands allows fans to be insiders. Artists are encouraged to submit their own material for consideration, so little-known musicians get the chance to shine. Such an approach fits right in with *Buffy*'s main theme: accepting those who are different, who don't quite fit in—yet.

However, what defines *Buffy* for many viewers is its sense of humor. According to Steve Wilson in his essay "Laugh, Spawn of Hell, Laugh," without the jokes the show "would be little more than your average teen melodrama action horror hybrid. And a silly one at that." The writers employ slapstick, puns, satire, inside jokes and allusions, dry wit, sight gags, and irony to lighten the plot without relying too much on any one comedic form. Wilson maintains *Buffy* has mastered its own brand of comedy: really weird dialogue.

Wilson continues: "Without . . . levity, the rhythm of emotion, suspense and action would lose its potency." Shakespeare understood the importance of comic relief. "A little ho-ho and ha-ha and even the most credulous viewer is looking past the fright masks," notes Wilson, "not quite suspending disbelief, but willing to be entertained, moved, perhaps edified and, above all, to refrain from dwelling too long on the absurdity inherent in watching a show about a vampire slayer with the dubious name of Buffy."

Fan Interaction

As noted earlier, there are over 750,000 Web sites devoted to the Slayer, offering fans the latest on the episodes, the plots, the characters, the bios of the actors, access to *Buffy* merchandise and the opportunity to submit fan fictions, also known as "slash fiction." Slash stories present fantasies about two or more of the characters having a relationship who might not otherwise have been together, signified by a name, then a slash mark, then the other name. They are not horror/slasher tales in the traditional sense.

The Characters

The list of characters for *Buffy the Vampire Slayer* expanded over the seven seasons to include brief appearances by demons and vampires, lovers and other friends, but the main roles were as follows:

Buffy Anne Summers: the Chosen One of her generation, the Slayer, a teenage girl from Southern California selected to rid the world of vampires and demons. Meanwhile Buffy makes close friends to counterbalance

Buffy's ethos can be distilled into seven precepts, according to Richard Greene and Wayne Yuen in their essay entitled "Morality on Television: The Case of *Buffy the Vampire Slayer.*" To summarize, Buffy believes that harm should not come to those who pose no threat to humans, or no immediate threat at all. And unless there is an urgent matter, take fairness into account, controlling only those that do harm. Nevertheless, if the benefits of a good opportunity outweigh the risks of a situation, attempt the good.

Buffy's independence from the strictures of an earlier age is evidenced in her decision to share her burden of slayage with her friends so that together they were stronger than she alone. And if traditional methods fail, don't give up: Try a rocket launcher instead.

One of the most pervasive influences on the show is the music that appears in the episodes, either as featured pieces or background. In the essay "My Boyfriend's in the Band!: *Buffy* and the Rhetoric of Music," S. Renee Dechert notes that, "music is at the heart of the Scooby Gang . . . it functions as a form of rhetorical discourse every bit as the angst of high school. She has superhuman strength and heals faster than regular humans. Her fashion sense is impeccable, usually featuring leather pants. Her parents are divorced—Mom's name is Joyce and Dad is Hank. She is an only child until season five when Dawn enters the family as her younger sister. Buffy's birthday is January 19, 1981.

Rupert Giles: a Watcher, the Slayer's trainer and mentor, disguised as the librarian at Sunnydale High School. Giles is English and attended Oxford University but left before graduation to dabble in the black arts and spend much of his time prowling about the British Museum. In his younger, wilder days he was known as Ripper. Because he loves Buffy like a daughter, the governing Watcher's Council feels his judgment could be compromised and fires him. He stays in Sunnydale anyway, only returning to England at the beginning of season six. Fortunately, Giles returns to Sunnydale late in season six to confront the vengeful Willow and play a role in the final apocalypse of season seven.

Xander (Alexander) Harris: One of Buffy's first friends at Sunnydale High School. Although scared of Buffy's powers and her encounters with demons and monsters, Xander joins the Scooby Gang and remains a loyal ally and soldier. He is unique among the friends in that he possesses no supernatural powers at all. He dates Willow and Cordelia and nearly marries Anya in season six, although he's always loved Buffy.

Willow Rosenberg: Another original member of the Scooby Gang. Willow embraces Wicca and becomes a powerful witch, casting spells to resurrect Buffy after death and nearly destroying the entire world in season six. She has a crush on Xander at first, then falls in love with Oz. In season four she meets Tara McLay, also a witch, with whom she has an intense lesbian relationship.

Angel: The vampire with a soul who loves Buffy and helps the Scoobies in their fight against evil. Angel's real name was Liam, a form of William. He was born in 1727 and died in 1753, at which time he was "sired," or made a vampire, by Darla, who became his lover. After his conversion, Angel returned to his home to murder his family. His sister, astounded at his rise from the dead, proclaimed him an angel—hence the name. As a vampire, Angel—or Angelus as he was notoriously known—performed some of the worst atrocities in recorded history. He sired Drusilla, a Victorian-era psychic and nun, in 1860, but not before he drove her insane. In 1898 Gypsies cursed him, giving him a soul and the ability to remember all his horrible crimes. Angel reverts to his vampire persona only on occasion, otherwise appearing normal, but he must feed on blood. Angel loves Buffy deeply, but when they make love—thereby giving Angel a moment of bliss—the curse is lifted and Angelus reappears. Angel leaves

Buffy and starts his own business in Los Angeles as well as his own show. Contrary to fictional vampire lore, Angel has a son, Connor, by his old flame, Darla.

Spike: also a vampire with a soul deeply in love with Buffy. He has almost white hair and dresses very coolly in black and leather, resembling British rocker Billy Idol. His real name is also William, and he wrote Victorian poetry. After he was sired by Drusilla, he tried to save his dying mother—the only family member he loved—by vamping her. But she turned on him, trying to seduce him, and he had to stake her. Like Angelus, Spike has had quite a past, although its memories do not torment him. He has killed two Slayers, one of whom was Sunnydale High School principal Robin Wood's mother; she died in 1977 on a New York City subway. Buffy goes hot and cold on Spike, attracted by his dangerousness and repelled by his past. In season five, Spike casually mentions that for a little crunch he crumbles Weetabix cereal into his cup of blood.

Oz (Daniel) Osbourne: One of the Scooby Gang by the second season, Oz became a werewolf after being bitten by his nephew Jordy (in another source Jordy is identified as Oz's cousin). He performs at The Bronze with his band, Dingoes Ate My Baby, making him quite cool. He loves Willow but betrays her by sleeping with Veruca, another werewolf who encourages him to give in to his wolf side. Oz leaves Sunnydale and a heartbroken Willow. He returns later to find that Willow has chosen Tara, and this time he leaves for good.

Cordelia Chase: Originally a bitchy cheerleading queen at Sunnydale High, Cordelia eventually becomes a Scooby. Her high school followers, including future vampire Harmony, were known as the Cordettes. Xander falls for her early on. Cordelia moves to Los Angeles to help Angel at Angel Investigations and pursue her dream of an acting career. She's not very talented, but she does inherit the ability to have blinding visions that foretell events and evil forces. She has a daughter, Jasmine, by Angel's son, Connor.

Cast Biographies

Sarah Michelle Gellar (Buffy): Born on April 14, 1977, in New York City. Gellar is five feet, three inches tall and married actor Freddie Prinze Jr. in September 2002. She was discovered by a casting agent at age four while eating in a fast-food restaurant. Not long afterward Gellar made her first film, *An Invasion of Privacy.* McDonald's named Gellar as a defendant in the fast-food giant's suit against Burger King, in which little Gellar had to mention McDonald's unfavorably. In her early 20s, Gellar became the spokeswoman for Maybelline cosmetics. Movie credits include: *Scream 2, I Know What You Did Last Summer, Cruel Intentions, Simply Irresistible,* and *Scooby Doo.*

Nicholas Brendon (Xander): Born Nicholas Brendon Schulz on April 12, 1971, in Los Angeles. Brendon has a twin brother, Kelly Donovan Schulz, and during the summers Brendon often grows a goatee so that people can tell him from Kelly. He is married to Tressa di Figlia, whom he met on the set of *Piñata*. Shy and a stutterer, Brendon pursued acting to help overcome his speech disorder. He also worked odd jobs, in and out of show business, trying to catch a break. He had bit parts on several soap operas and did commercials, finally getting some experience as associate producer of *Dave's World*. His big movie appearance was playing Starcat (a play on Moondoggie in *Gidget*) in *Psycho Beach Party*; he also appeared in *Children of the Corn 3*.

Anthony Stewart Head (Giles): Born on February 24, 1954, in the Camden neighborhood of London. Besides his role in *Buffy*, he's known for appearing in Nescafe (UK) and Taster's Choice (US) ads, borrowing coffee from beautiful neighbors and perhaps staying to play? Head has had starring roles in *Manchild, Jonathan Creek*, and *VR.5*, and has appeared as a guest star in numerous series and television shows, both in the United States and Great Britain.

Alyson Hannigan (Willow): Born on March 24, 1974, in Washington, D.C. Hannigan is five feet, six inches tall and is married to actor Alexis Denisof, who plays Wesley on *Angel*. She began her acting career in Atlanta, also at age four, doing commercials for McDonald's, Nabisco Oreo cookies, and Six Flags amusement parks. Television work included *Picket Fences, Roseanne, Touched by an Angel* and *The Torkelsons*. Movie credits include *American Pie, My Stepmother is an Alien, Boys and Girls*, and *Beyond City Limits*.

James Marsters (Spike): Born James Wesley Marsters on August 20, 1982, in Greenville, California. Marsters is five feet, 11 inches tall and has a scar on his left eyebrow as a result of a mugging in the Queens borough of New York City. He is the front man for a band called Ghost of the Robot, which released its first album, *Mad Brilliant*, in February 2003. Marsters has a huge fan following in the sci-fi/fantasy community with hundreds of Web sites devoted to him alone. He performed in live theater in New York, Chicago, and Seattle, and appeared in the movie *House on Haunted Hill*.

Seth Green (Oz): Born Seth Gesshel Green on February 8, 1974, in Philadelphia. His parents, Herbert and Barbara Green, already had a daughter, Kaela. Green began acting at age six when he appeared in a summer camp performance of *Hello, Dolly!* He followed that debut with appearances in various commercials, one of which was with Sarah Michelle Gellar when she was four. Television credits include *The X-Files, The Wonder Years, Beverly Hills 90210, Evening Shade*, and *seaQuest DSV*. Green has an extensive movie résumé, with parts in *Hotel New Hampshire, Radio Days, My Stepmother is an Alien* with Alyson Hannigan, *Pump Up the Volume, Stonebrook, Idle Hands, Enemy of the State, Can't Hardly Wait*, and a part in the original *Buffy* movie that ended up being cut. Besides his role as Oz in *Buffy the Vampire Slayer*, Green is well known for being Dr. Evil's son in the Austin Powers movies.

David Boreanaz (Angel): Born David Patrick Boreanaz on May 16, 1971, in Buffalo, New York. Boreanaz is six feet, one inch tall and is married to Jaime Bergman. They have a son, Jaden Rayne, born on May 1, 2002. Boreanaz was previously married to Ingrid Quinn. He is the son of Philadelphia weatherman Dave Roberts, has two sisters, and was discovered by an agent while out walking his dog. Boreanaz has appeared in several commercials, including a "Got Milk?" ad in 2000. *People* named him one of the "50 Most Beautiful People" in 1999.

Charisma Carpenter (Cordelia): Born on July 23, 1970, in Las Vegas, Carpenter also uses her married surname of Hardy. She is five feet, seven and one-half inches tall and married Damien Hardy on October 5, 2002. Their son, Donovan Charles Hardy, was born on March 24, 2003. Carpenter notes that her mother named her after an inexpensive perfume. Her credits include the starring role of Ashley Green on *Malibu Shores* and appearances on *Miss Match, Strange Frequency, Hey, Arnold, Boy Meets World, Baywatch*, and *Celebrity Undercover*. Movies include *See Jane Date, The Groomsmen*, and *Josh Kirby, Time Warrior*.

FURTHER READING:

Antulov, Dragan. "All-Reviews.com Movie/Video Review: 'Buffy the Vampire Slayer'." URL: http://www.all-reviews.com/videos-4/buffy-vampire-slayer.htm. Downloaded on December 11, 2003.

Britannia Film Archives. URL: http://www.britannia.org/film/filmography.php?Name=Gellar. Downloaded on December 11, 2003.

Buffy the Vampire Slayer: Episode Guide. Seasons 1–7. TV Tome. URL: http://www.tvtome.com/tvtome/servlet/EpisodeGuideSummary. Downloaded on December 16, 2003.

Dechert, S. Renee. "My Boyfriend's in the Band!: *Buffy* and the Rhetoric of Music." *Fighting the Forces: What's at Stake in* Buffy the Vampire Slayer. Rhonda V. Wilcox and David Lavery, eds. Lanham, Md.: Rowman & Littlefield, 2002.

Greene, Richard, and Wayne Yuen. "Morality on Television: The Case of *Buffy the Vampire Slayer*." Buffy the Vampire Slayer *and Philosophy: Fear and Trembling in Sunnydale*. James B. South, ed. Chicago: Open Court Publishing, 2003.

Holder, Nancy, with Jeff Mariotte and Maryelizabeth Hart, eds. *Buffy the Vampire Slayer: The Watcher's Guide*, vol. 2. New York: Pocket Books, 2000.

Larbalestier, Justine. "A *Buffy* Confession." *Seven Seasons of Buffy: Science Fiction and Fantasy Writers Discuss Their Favorite Television Show.* Glenn Yeffeth, ed. Dallas: Benbella Books, 2003.

Marinucci, Mimi. "Feminism and the Ethics of Violence: Why Buffy Kicks Ass." Buffy the Vampire Slayer *and Philosophy: Fear and Trembling in Sunnydale.* James B. South, ed. Chicago: Open Court Publishing, 2003.

Postrel, Virginia. "Why *Buffy* Kicked Ass: The Deep Meaning of TV's Favorite Vampire Slayer." URL: http://reason.com/0308/cr.vp.why.shtml. Downloaded on December 11, 2003.

Wilcox, Rhonda V. "Who Died and Made Her the Boss?: Patterns of Mortality in *Buffy.*" *Fighting the Forces: What's at Stake in* Buffy the Vampire Slayer. Rhonda V. Wilcox and David Lavery, eds. Lanham, Md.: Rowman & Littlefield, 2002.

Wilson, Steve. "Laugh, Spawn of Hell, Laugh." *Reading the Vampire Slayer: An Unofficial Critical Companion to* Buffy *and* Angel. Roz Kaveney, ed. London: Tauris Parke Paperbacks, 2002.

Bunnicula   Vampire rabbit created in a humorous children's book by James and Deborah Howe. Bunnicula is black and white and has fanglike teeth and strange markings on his back that look like a cape. He sleeps from sunup to sundown, and raids the refrigerator at midnight for food. He drains vegetables white, leaving them with two small fang marks.

Bunnicula made his debut in 1979 in *Bunnicula: A Rabbit-Tale of Mystery.* The story is told by Harold, a dog who belongs to Mr. And Mrs. X (Monroe) and their sons Toby, eight, and Pete, 10. Bunnicula is part of the household, as is a CAT named Chester.

The rabbit is found by the boys at a movie theater showing a Dracula film. They want to name him Dracula, then decide on Bunnicula.

The dog and cat become aware of Bunnicula's oddities, and the cat Chester makes a garlic pendant and fends off Bunnicula from raiding the refrigerator. The rabbit begins to starve. The family takes the animals to a veterinarian. Bunnicula is given liquid carrot juice, a diet he remains on which replaces his need to vampirize vegetables. The overwrought cat is sent to see a cat psychiatrist.

FURTHER READING:
Howe, Deborah, and James Howe. *Bunnicula: A Rabbit-Tale of Mystery.* New York: Atheneum, 1979.

burculacas   Greek VAMPIRE. The BLOOD-drinking *burculacas* is made of slime and excrement, and is blamed for spreading plague.

Burgot, Pierre   See POLIGNY WEREWOLVES.

burial customs   Numerous customs exist for the treatment, handling, and burial of CORPSES to prevent them from becoming VAMPIRES or REVENANTS. An unburied corpse or an improperly buried corpse is at risk. Among the most common practices are

Ritual cleansing of the body and household. Washing the corpse with soap, WATER, and sometimes wine purifies it to protect it against takeover by a demon. In parts of Greece, folklore holds, that at the moment of death, Charos, the angel of death, slashes the throat of the person, releasing the soul out through the mouth, an act that symbolically bathes the corpse and the entire household in BLOOD. The dead person's clothes must be changed and taken out of the house, and all members of the household must change their clothes as well. An older custom calls for washing down the room in which the death occurred, and then whitewashing it later.

Weighing down the corpse's eyelids with coins. The money serves as payment for the transport of the soul to the afterworld. Once there, the soul can not return to the world of the living.

Tying the mouth closed. According to lore, the soul escapes from the mouth at death. A lingering soul might return to the body to subsist as a vampire. Tying the mouth will prevent it from leaving the grave.

Stuffing the mouth with GARLIC, GOLD coins, CROSSES, or dirt. Garlic wards off vampires. Stuffing the mouth thus prevents vampirism as well as stops any vampire soul from leaving the corpse. It also prevents the corpse from chewing on itself, a sure sign of vampirism.

In China, jade is used to fill a corpse's mouth to keep the soul from becoming restless, while elsewhere in the world plant fibers and wool are used.

Covering the MIRRORS in the house upon death. According to widespread lore, mirrors are soul-stealers. If a corpse is seen in a mirror, then the soul will have no rest, and thus is at risk to return as a vampire.

Stopping the clocks in the dead person's house upon death. This puts the corpse into a suspended, protected state until its safety is attained by burial. The corpse has some measure of protection from invasion by demonic forces.

Putting a lighted candle near or on the corpse or in its hands. Souls get lost in the dark, so a lighted candle will prevent the soul from wandering away and becoming a vampire. Instead, the light will help the soul get to heaven. In Greek lore, the most important candle is the *isou* ("equal"), made soon after death and placed in the corpse's navel. The *isou* provides light to the soul for the 40 days that it remains connected to the earth.

Keeping a vigil over the corpse. Watching a corpse until burial prevents such unlucky occurrences as animals stepping over it or under it, which doom the corpse to vampirism. In fact, nothing at all should pass over a corpse, and people must take care not to hand things to each other over the body when preparing it for burial. (See CATS.)

Painting a cross in tar on the door of the deceased's house. Tar remedies abound in magical lore for stopping all manner of evil entities from crossing a threshold. The time between death and burial is a dangerous one, when the corpse is vulnerable to contamination by evil. The cross shape reflects the influence of Christianity.

Removing the corpse from the house with great care. A corpse should never be taken out through the front door, which enables the revenant to return to plague the living. The proper removal varies. In some cases, corpses are removed feet first, or through the back door, or out a window or a hole in a wall cut especially for the purpose; in other cases, they are taken out head first. (See *DOPPELSAUGER; NELAPSI.*)

Traveling to the grave in a certain direction. The coffin should be taken "with the sun," that is, in an east-to-west direction, to its grave. Otherwise both the dead and the living will be ill-omened.

Pinning the burial garments. Shrouds and clothing should never touch the face of a corpse, lest the corpse eat them for sustenance and thus be able to leave the grave. Pinning the burial garments to the COFFIN will help to keep the corpse in its grave.

According to a 19th-century case in Lower Sorbia (a region in Germany), two daughters in a family died. Someone remembered that the burial cloth that covered the face of the first daughter's corpse was left in the coffin by mistake. She was exhumed, and the cloth was removed so that no more relatives would die.

Burying the corpse facedown. This will prevent the vampire from finding its way to the surface. It also protects the living who must bury the corpse, as well as those who have to dig it up later, if necessary. The gaze of a vampire is considered fatal (see *ERETICA; EYE*), so turning the corpse facedown prevents its baleful glance from falling upon the living.

Burying the corpse at a CROSSROADS, boundary, or remote location. The vampire is trapped by the unhallowed ground of a crossroads and cannot wander among the living. Boundaries provide the least offensive neutral zone for unwanted corpses. The easiest prevention of vampirism is to bury the body as far away from the village as possible.

Staking or mutilating the corpse. The physical vehicle of a vampire can be ruined by driving STAKES through the shoulders, back, heart, belly, or head; decapitating it; cutting out the heart; or cutting off the limbs. Other measures are slitting the soles of the feet, the tendons behind the knees, or the palms of the hands, or inserting nails into the feet.

Wrapping the corpse in a net. Superstition holds that a vampire will be forced to untie all the KNOTS before being able to leave the grave. According to German lore, the vampire can untie the knots only at the rate of one per year.

Tying body parts together. Binding the feet, knees, or hands together imprisons the vampire in the grave.

Weighing down the corpse, coffin, or grave with stones. Stones prevent the vampire from escaping the grave. The tombstone not only serves as a record of the dead, but also helps to hold the dead in their graves.

Filling the coffin with SAND or SEEDS. The vampire will be forced to collect all the grains of sand or all the seeds—or eat all the seeds—one at a time and one per year before being able to leave the grave. Favored seeds are poppy (which has a narcotic effect and might be intended to put the corpse to sleep), mustard, linen, and carrot. Millet and oats also serve the same purpose.

Placing food in the coffin. A well-fed corpse will not feel the need to leave as a vampire and suck the blood of the living. This practice ties in with ancient and universal beliefs that the soul requires food, water, and money to make its journey to the next world.

Placing an object on the corpse, especially its midsection. Sharp objects such as needles, skewers, spikes, thorns, daggers, nails, and sickles, as well as tin plates and crucifixes buried with corpses will prevent vampirism. Metal objects may be heated first. In Romanian lore, the sickle is placed around the neck, so that if the vampire tries to rise from the grave it will decapitate itself. Sickles also are imbedded in hearts, believed to be the seat of the soul.

Driving stakes into the grave. In Romanian lore, three stakes driven into the grave of a suspected vampire will automatically impale and kill it if it tries to leave the grave.

BURNING the body and scattering the ASHES. The most certain way to prevent vampirism is to annihilate the revenant's physical vehicle altogether. Cremation, however, was not always easy in earlier times—corpses are difficult to burn unless a fire is exceptionally hot.

A contradictory superstition holds that one should save the ashes of a cremated vampire, for they hold the power to cure terrible illness, and should be fed to the sick. (See BROWN, MERCY.)

Performing a supplemental burial. A custom among some Serbs called for disinterring a corpse three years after death for a ritual cleansing of bones. Clean bones ensured that a soul will rest in peace and not attack the living. In Greece, the color of the bones is important: White indicates a soul at peace, but dark bones reveal the presence of sin, which requires intercessory prayers.

FURTHER READING:
Barber, Paul. *Vampires, Burial and Death: Folklore and Reality.* New Haven, Conn.: Yale University Press, 1988.
Dundes, Alan, ed. *The Vampire: A Casebook.* Madison: University of Wisconsin Press, 1998.
Perkowski, Jan L. *The Darkling: A Treatise on Slavic Vampirism.* Columbus, Ohio: Slavica Publishers, 1989.

burning   In vampire lore, the burning of a CORPSE to ASHES is considered the best way to destroy a vampire. Piercing a corpse with a STAKE, or mutilating it, will prevent it from leaving its grave; however, some stubborn vampires continue their attacks after such measures are taken, and can be stopped only by being burned.

In WEREWOLF lore, the burning of a were-animal's skin prevents a person from ever SHAPE-SHIFTING into animal form again, or either destroys the creature altogether. The skin is laid aside or hung up whenever the person is in human form, and thus it can be seized.

A story in Armenian folklore tells about a man who sees a wolf dash past him, carrying a child. He sets off in pursuit and soon finds the child's hands and feet. The man finds a cave, in which lies a wolf-skin. He throws the skin into a fire. Immediately a woman appears, howling in rage. She tries to rescue the skin from the flames, but he stops her from doing so. As soon as the skin is burned up, the woman werewolf vanishes in the smoke.

See also BURIAL CUSTOMS.

FURTHER READING:
Baring-Gould, Sabine. *The Book of Werewolves.* London: Smith, Elder & Co., 1865.

butterfly   In Slavic lore, a shape assumed by the soul when it leaves the body, either during sleep or at death. The soul can also appear in the form of a moth, fly, or a bird. When the CORPSE of a VAMPIRE is impaled, witnesses watch anxiously for the appearance of a butterfly or moth around the grave, which indicates the vampire is attempting to escape its destruction. If a butterfly is seen, every attempt is made to capture it. The butterfly is thrown onto a bonfire, which completely destroys the vampire. If the butterfly escapes, the vampire will wreak vengeance on the village for seven years.

See also DEATH'S HEAD MOTH; LIVING VAMPIRE.

FURTHER READING:
Krauss, Frederich S. "South Slavic Countermeasures Against Vampires," in *The Vampire: A Casebook,* Alan Dundes, ed. Madison: University of Wisconsin Press, 1998.

Byron, Lord George   See "FRAGMENT OF A STORY"; POLIDORI, JOHN; *THE VAMPYRE.*

Caine, Hall   See HOMMY-BEG.

callicantzaros   Greek VAMPIRE. The *callicantzaros* lives in the underworld for most of the year, and emerges only from December 25 to January 7 to attack victims with its exceptionally long and sharp talons.

Calmet, Dom Augustin(e) (b. 1672)   Benedictine scholar who wrote skeptically about VAMPIRES. Dom Augustin Calmet was born on February 26, 1672 at Mesnil-la-Horgne in Lorraine, France. In 1688 he joined the Benedictine order at Saint Mansuy Abbey in Toril, and was ordained in 1696. Calmet devoted most of his life to studying the Bible and presiding over an academy at the abbey of Moyen-Moutier. During his life, he was one of the best-known biblical scholars of his time.

News of the vampire cult in Eastern Europe intrigued Calmet, and he began collecting information on it. In 1746 he published a two-volume work, *Traite sur les Apparitions des Esprits, et sur les Vampires, ou les Revenans de Hongrie, de Moravie, etc.,* concerning the vampire cult largely in Hungary, Moravia, and Silesia. The work was an instant best seller and was published in three editions in three years. In 1759 it was translated into English. The English edition was republished in 1850 under the title *The Phantom World,* edited by Reverend Henry Christmas.

Calmet approached the subject with an open-mindedness that earned him criticism from skeptics. Still, he found vampires a mystery, and sought to find the answers to that mystery. Questions that obsessed him the most concerned whether vampires were really dead, and how they managed to exit and reenter their graves. If vampires were dead, and not persons buried alive who somehow found their way out of their graves, then humanity was forced to consider what power reanimated the CORPSES, Calmet said. If demons were responsible, they could not do so on their own power, but only with the permission of God. Therefore, God was responsible for unleashing vampires upon the living, but why he did so remained a mystery, Calmet said.

"We must then keep silence on this article, since it has not pleased God to reveal to us either the extent of the demon's power, or the way in which these things can be done," Calmet wrote. "There is very much the appearance of illusion; and even if some of the reality were mixed up with it, we may easily console ourselves for our ignorance in that respect, since there are so many natural things which take place within us and around us, of which the cause and manner are unknown to us."

As for the matter of how the vampire exits and reenters his grave, Calmet gave consideration to a prevailing belief that demons dematerialized the physical corpse and turned it into spirit, which enabled the vampire to pass through matter. He rejected this notion, commenting that ". . . we cannot even conceive that an earthly body, material and gross, can be reduced to that state of subtilty and spiritualization without destroying the configuration of its parts and spoiling the economy of its structure; which would be contrary to the intention of the demon, and render this body incapable of appearing, showing itself, acting and speaking, and, in short, of being cut to pieces and burned, as it commonly seen and practiced in Loravia, Poland, and Silesia." Calmet concluded that it was impossible for the vampire to leave the grave. "No one has ever replied to this difficulty, and never will," he wrote. "To say that the demon subtilizes and spiritualizes the bodies of vampires, is a thing asserted without proof or likelihood."

Calmet also was troubled about the incorruption of the vampire corpse. The incorrupt condition was, in the eyes of his Church, a state enjoyed by deceased saints—a testament by God to the degree of their sanctity. He recognized that the Eastern Church viewed incorruptibility differently, asserting that sinners and the excommunicated would not enjoy dissolution into the earth, but would become vampires. If all excommunicated did not decay, he wrote, then "all the Greeks towards the Latins, and the Latins towards the Greeks, would be undecayed, which is not the case. That proof then is very frivolous, and nothing can be concluded from it. I mistrust, a great deal, all those stories which are related to prove this pretended incorruptibility of excommunicated persons. If well examined, many of them would doubtless be found to be false."

Ultimately, Calmet found himself forced to reject the notion of vampires on intellectual grounds. He could not reconcile the claims about the vampire with the teachings of the Western Church. He could not transcend the limits of those teachings, or the limits of the prevailing thought of the time that vampires, like other supernatural entities, had to exist in, and behave according to, the literal terms of the physical world.

FURTHER READING:
Calmet, Dom Augustin. *The Phantom World: Concerning Apparitions and Vampires*. Ware, England: Wordsworth Editions in association with The Folklore Society, 2001.

cannibalism See BERTRAND, SERGEANT FRANÇOIS; LYCANTHROPY; LYCAON; SHAPE-SHIFTING; WEREWOLF.

Captain Kronos—Vampire Hunter See HAMMER FILMS.

"Carmilla" (1872) VAMPIRE short story by J. (Joseph) Sheridan Le Fanu. "Carmilla" concerns a lesbian relationship between a young woman, Laura, who lives in a castle in Austria, and a stranger, Carmilla, who comes to stay for three months. Carmilla is secretly a vampire, having once been the Countess Mircalla Karnstein who died 150 years previously. The vampire is unmasked and destroyed.

"Carmilla" is one of the most important works of vampire fiction for its long-reaching influence on subsequent fiction and films. Le Fanu was inspired by Samuel Taylor Coleridge's poem fragment "Christabel" (1816). His elegant presentation of "Carmilla" concentrates on the erotic relationship between a vampire and her prey. Carmilla the vampire is completely at home in her homosexuality. She takes her BLOOD sustenance not from strangers, but from the object of her adoration, forming a tight bond that is both physical and psychical.

"Carmilla" is narrated by the principal victim, Laura, a beautiful and lonely 19-year-old girl. She tells the story 10 years later, at age 29. Laura begins the story by relating an incident that took place when she was about six years old. One night she awoke to find herself alone in her bedroom; the nursery maid and nurse were absent. Laura whimpered in fear. Suddenly, a pretty female face materialized by the bed, and Laura saw a young woman kneeling beside her with her hands beneath the covers. The woman caressed her and lay down beside her on the bed. Soothed, Laura fell asleep. She was awakened abruptly when she felt a sensation like two needles stabbing deep into her breast. She cried out. The young woman disappeared, seemingly beneath the bed. The nursery maid later assured Laura that it was she who bent over her, and the rest was a bad dream. But soon a priest came to pray with Laura.

The story jumps to when Laura is 19. She lives with her father and servants; her mother had died when she was an infant. Laura is out walking with her father one day when they witness a coach accident that injures a girl. The girl's mother is distraught and says she must not delay her journey while her daughter recovers, and she asks directions to the nearest village. At Laura's prodding, the father invites the mother to leave her daughter with them. The mother says she will return in three months. She informs the father that during her stay, the girl will not speak of her family, where she came from, or the purpose of their journey. Unbeknownst to father and Laura, a haglike old woman dressed in black remains inside the coach, watching secretly from the window.

Carmilla is given a room in the castle. When she receives Laura as a visitor, Laura is astonished to recognize her as the young woman who appeared in her bedroom 12 years earlier. Carmilla says she recognizes Laura as well. She says she had a strange dream in which she found herself in a strange nursery, and she hid beneath the bed. She woke up back in her own bed.

Carmilla soon enchants Laura despite her odd habits. She sleeps until late in the day, declines food (though on occasion drinks hot chocolate or wine), has an aversion to religious objects, and so on. She seems to tire easily and be frail, but then suddenly rebounds in a blush of health and vigor. Laura's initial fear of her pretty visitor is overcome by a sensual attraction. Carmilla visits Laura every night and caresses and kisses her with professions of love until she falls asleep.

Meanwhile, young girls in the surrounding area are dying of a mysterious wasting-away illness. They all tell

Carmilla (Annette Vadim), a reincarnation of the vampire Countess Carmilla, rises from her grave in Roger Vadim's Blood *and* Roses, *based on Le Fanu's story "Carmilla."* (Author's collection)

the same or similar stories, of being attacked by a "ghost" that bites them. The local people blame the deaths on an epidemic.

A hunchback entertainer and juggler visits the castle and sells Laura and Carmilla charms that he says will keep away the *oupire* that is "going like the wolf . . . through these woods." The charms are oblong bits of vellum with cabalistic symbols inscribed on them. Laura drops hers into a vase in the drawing room.

One night Laura has a nightmarish dream that begins "a very strange agony." The description of it is reminiscent of OLD HAG attacks. She feels both asleep and awake. She sees at the foot of her bed a sooty-black animal like a monstrous CAT, about four to five feet long. It has a sinister feel, and it paces back and forth like a restless beast in a cage. Laura is paralyzed and cannot cry out, even though she is terrified. As the beast paces, the room becomes darker, until Laura can see only the eyes of the creature:

I felt it spring lightly on the bed. The two broad eyes approached my face, and suddenly I felt a stinging pain as if two large needles darted, an inch or two apart, deep into

my breast. I waked with a scream. The room was lighted by the candle that burnt there all through the night, and I saw a female figure standing at the foot of the bed, a little to the right side. It was in a dark loose dress, and its hair was down and covered its shoulders. A block of stone could not have been more still. There was not the slightest stir of respiration. As I stared at it, the figure appeared to have changed its place, and was now nearer the door; then close to it, the door opened, and it passed out.

At first Laura thinks Carmilla has played a trick on her, but she is horrified to find her bedroom door locked from the inside, as she had left it when she retired for the night. She spends the rest of the night cowering beneath her covers in fear.

Carmilla professes to have had bad dreams, too, about a dark figure in her room. She urges Laura to retrieve her charm. Laura pins it to her pillow and then experiences languid sleep every night. In the mornings she awakens tired and full of melancholy, with thoughts of slipping into death. Her health declines. Carmilla tells her she thinks the charm has been fumigated with a drug and is an antidote against malaria. Laura has dreams of being kissed by warm lips, of having her throat lovingly stroked by a female presence, and of feelings of strangulation.

Laura then has a dream in which her dead mother gives her a clear warning that her life is in danger:

> One night, instead of the voice I was accustomed to hear in the dark, I heard one, sweet and tender, and at the same time terrible, which said, "Your mother warns you to beware of the assassin." At the same time a light unexpectedly sprang up, and I saw Carmilla, standing, near the foot of my bed, in her white night-dress, bathed, from her chin to her feet, in one great stain of blood.

Thinking she has dreamed of Carmilla being murdered, Laura leaps up and gets servants to open the door of Carmilla's bedroom. But the young woman is gone. She reappears in her bedroom the next morning, and professes to have been out sleep-walking.

Dr. Spielsberg is summoned to attend to Laura, and he recognizes the signs of vampirism. Laura's father takes her and two others, including a Bulgarian general who is a visiting friend, to Karnstein. Along the way, the general relates how his daughter was seduced and murdered by a vampire, Millarca, who also proved to be Countess Mircalla, who had died 150 years earlier. The description and details match Carmilla—in fact, Millarca and Carmilla are anagrams of her original name.

At Karnstein they find the castle in ruins and the village deserted. A woodsman explains that the village was ravaged by vampires, who have been dispatched. However, an admirer of Millarca concealed her tomb many years ago.

With the help of a baron, they find the tomb. They witness Carmilla enter it. The general attacks her, but she turns fiendish in appearance, fights him off, and disappears.

The following day they open the countess's grave and find Carmilla in the COFFIN, her eyes open and seemingly in perfect health. The coffin is virtually flooded with blood:

> The body, therefore, in accordance with the ancient practice, was raised, and a sharp stake driven through the heart of the vampire, who uttered a piercing shriek at the moment, in all respects such as might escape from a living person in the last egony. Then the head was struck off, and a torrent of blood flowed from the severed neck. The body and head were next placed on a pile of wood, and reduced to ashes, which were thrown upon the river and borne away, and that territory has never since been plagued by the visits of a vampire.

In concluding her story, Laura relates bits of vampire folklore. She says it is not known how they manage to escape their graves without disturbing the earth. One sign of a vampire is its iron grip, which leaves a mortal hand or limb numb.

Le Fanu was probably acquainted with the vampire reports that had circulated from Europe since the early 18th century (see JOHANN FLUCKINGER). His description of the destruction of the vampire bears a resemblance to the

account of the destruction of JOHANNES CUNTIUS. The vampire as old family aristocrat appears in fiction with which he probably was familiar as well, such as JOHN POLIDORI'S *THE VAMPYRE* and JAMES MALCOLM RYMER'S *VARNEY THE VAMPIRE*.

BRAM STOKER also probably was familiar with all of these, including "Carmilla."

"Carmilla" has been adapted into films, among them *Blood and Roses* (1960), directed by Roger Vadim and starring Mel Ferrer as Leopoldo del Karlnstein and Annette Vadim as Carmilla—not the actual countess but a reincarnation of her; *The Vampire Lovers* (1970), HAMMER FILMS production, directed by Roy Ward Baker, and starring INGRID PITT as Carmilla and PETER CUSHING as the General; *Lust for a Vampire* (1971), a Hammer production, directed by Jimmy Sangster and starring Barbara Jefford as Carmilla; and *Twins of Evil* (1971), a Hammer film directed by John Hough and featuring Peter Cushing in the supporting role of Gustav Weil, and starring Katya Keith as Countess Mircalla. *THE HUNGER* (1983), based on the Whitley Streiber novel by the same name, features a Carmilla-like Miriam Blaylock (Catherine Deneuve), whose love interest is Sarah (Susan Sarandon), the scientist who studies her.

FURTHER READING:
Auerbach, Nina. *Our Vampires, Ourselves.* Chicago: University of Chicago Press, 1995.
Gladwell, Alicia, ed. *Blood and Roses: The Vampire in 19th Century Literature,* rev. ed. Creation Books, 1999.
Miller, Elizabeth. *Dracula: Sense and Nonsense.* Westcliff-on-Sea, England: Desert Island Books, 2000.
Senf, Carol A. *The Vampire in 19th Century English Literature.* Bowling Green, Ky.: Bowling Green State University Popular Press, 1988.

Carpathians   See FEEHAN, CHRISTINE.

Castle Argeş   See CASTLE POENARI.

Castle Bran   Restored castle in TRANSYLVANIA, Romania, sometimes erroneously associated with the fictional CASTLE DRACULA, perhaps because its appearance evokes the atmosphere of BRAM STOKER's novel.

Castle Bran, located near Brasov, was built in 1382 to defend Bran Pass in the Carpathian Mountains. Popular legend holds that it was built by Basarab, the first prince of Wallachia; other lore credits it to the Teutonic knight Deitrich earlier in the 13th century. However, the first document concerning Castle Bran is an act issued by King Ludovic I d'Anjou on November 19, 1377, authorizing the people of Brasov to build the castle.

Castle Bran was an important trading post in the Middle Ages. It was never occupied by VLAD TEPES, though it is likely that he sought refuge there for a few nights during his flight from the Turks in 1462.

The well-preserved Castle Bran is often mistaken for "Dracula's castle." (Photo by R. E. Guiley)

On December 1, 1920, Brasov donated the castle to Queen Marie of Great Romania, in gratitude for her work in unifying the country in 1918. Queen Marie undertook a restoration of the castle in a seven-year project that transformed it into a glorious summer residence. Researchers RAYMOND T. MCNALLY and RADU R. FLORESCU offered the sheer speculation that Queen Marie—who was the granddaughter of England's Queen Victoria—chose Castle Bran as her summer residence because of its similarity to Stoker's fictional castle. "The analogies between Stoker's description of Castle Dracula and the real Castle Bran are simply too close to be coincidental," the authors state in their 1972 best seller, *In Search of Dracula.* "Moreover, like Stoker, Queen Marie had a great love and understanding of Romanian folklore, which is so richly invested in the supernatural."

Queen Marie willed the castle to her daughter, Princess Ileana. In 1948 the royal family was expelled from Romania by Communist rule. The castle became state property; it was abandoned and allowed to deteriorate. In 1956 it was opened as a museum. No major renovation was undertaken until the fall of the Nicolae Ceauşescu regime in 1989. Restoration was completed in 1993.

Today the castle stands in fine condition and is one of Romania's major tourist attractions. It has multilevel battlements, winding staircases, spooky corridors, several inner courtyards, an underground passageway, a tall water tower, a Gothic chapel, and stern-looking German furnishings.

FURTHER READING:

McNally, Raymond T., and Radu Florescu. *In Search of Dracula: a true history of Dracula and vampire legends.* Greenwich, Conn.: New York Graphic Society, 1972.

Castle Dracula   The Transylvanian abode of COUNT DRACULA in BRAM STOKER's novel, *DRACULA* (1897).

Stoker places Castle Dracula in the BORGO PASS in the Carpathian Mountains of TRANSYLVANIA. In the opening chapter, legal clerk Jonathan Harker is traveling to the castle to meet with the count concerning his purchase of property in London. His midnight coach ride through the pass is eerie, accented by howling wolves and a baleful MOON. His first glimpse of the castle comes when moonlight illumines it as a "vast ruined castle, from whose tall black windows came no ray of light, and whose broken battlements showed a jagged line against the moonlit sky."

The door to the castle is gigantic and massive, and is obviously very old. The walls are "frowning" and the windows are dark. After Dracula welcomes Harker in, the clerk sees a great winding staircase and a long passage. Their footsteps ring on the stone floor. "Long, quivering shadows" are cast by the light from the count's lamp.

To his relief, Harker's suite in the castle is well lit by a warm fire, and has a table prepared for supper. His bedroom is octagonal-shaped. After he has slept and is rested, Harker explores a bit of the castle. He notices there are no MIRRORS. He finds a large library well stocked with books, especially a large collection on England. Dracula finds him there, and says he may access the library whenever he wishes, and can go wherever else in the castle he wishes except where doors are locked.

Harker soon discovers that the gloomy castle is more a prison. The count comes and goes at strange hours, stays up all night, and never takes a meal with Harker. In one room, Harker finds a magnificent view to the south and observes that the castle is perched on the edge of a terrible precipice that drops at least a thousand feet. He finds more and more doors that are locked—and no exits from the castle itself. He seems to be alone in the castle, for there is no evidence of servants. He catches the count himself making the bed for him and laying out his food.

After a week passes, Dracula warns Harker not to fall asleep anywhere in the castle except his own bedchamber. The castle, he says, "is old, and has many memories, and there are bad dreams for those who sleep unwisely."

After supper Harker goes alone to the room with the magnificent view and looks out a tall, deep, stone-mullioned window. The landscape is bathed in soft moonlight. Harker is filled with fear and foreboding as to what will become of him. As he looks out the window, a window below his opens and the count emerges. Harker is stunned to see him crawl facedown the sheer wall:

> I saw the fingers and toes grasp the corners of the stone, worn clear of the mortar by the stress of years, and by thus using every projection and inequality, move downwards with considerable speed, just as a lizard moves along a wall.

Three night later, Harker sees the count exit the castle again in the same fashion. Panicked, he goes about the castle trying the locked doors, looking for a way out. At the top of a stairway in a wing of the castle different from the one his room is in, he finds a room that seems to be locked, but the door gives under pressure. Its view shows that the castle is built on the corner of a great rock, with sheer precipices on three sides. After writing in his diary, Harker gets sleepy and, against the warnings of the count, pulls out a dusty couch and falls asleep.

In a nightmarish experience, he is assaulted by three VAMPIRE women who materialize in the room. The attack is interrupted by the count, who is furious with them, and sends them away with a sack containing a small child.

Harker awakens in his own bed. He returns to the mysterious room, but he finds it is now locked from the inside, and it has been shut so forcibly that the wooden jamb is splintered.

Harker knows he must escape the castle and appeals to Szgany peasants who are working outside, but his efforts are foiled. One day he manages the death-defying feat of clinging to the outside of the castle walls, and is able to scoot along a ledge of stones from his window to the count's room. The window is unlocked. Inside he finds a dusty, barely furnished room. An unlocked door opens to a circular staircase that descends to a dark, tunnel-like passage "through which came a deathly, sickly odor, the odor of old earth newly turned." Harker opens a heavy door and finds himself in an old, ruined chapel that had evidently been used as a graveyard. There is no other exit from the chapel save through the tunnel and staircase to the count's room. A great heap of gold coins of various nationalities are in the room.

Harker observes that the newly dug earth has been placed in 50 great wooden boxes. He goes through them all and makes the horrible discovery of the count lying in one of them, in a weird deathlike sleep, with BLOOD oozing from his mouth. Shocked, Harker flees, and crawls back to his own room via the outside castle wall ledge.

Two months after his arrival at the castle, Harker sees the count crawl down the castle wall dressed in Harker's own clothing, and Harker fears for his own life. That night Dracula announces that Harker is to leave in the morning in Dracula's coach. Harker doesn't believe him and asks to leave that night. Dracula obliges, taking him to the heavy main entrance. He effortlessly opens the massive door, which strangely does not seem to be locked. A ferocious howling of wolves rises, and Harker agrees to wait until morning.

The boxes of earth leave the castle—and Harker knows the count is in one of them. He is left alone in the castle with the vampire women. He decides he will take some of the gold and somehow scale down the wall of the castle in order to escape. His escape takes place offstage in the novel; he next surfaces in a Budapest hospital, where he has been ill for six weeks with "violent brain fever." The castle is left behind, and the action of *Dracula* shifts to England.

Though Stoker never visited Romania, *Dracula* enthusiasts have sought to identify a real castle with the fictional one. Castle Csjethe, CASTLE BRAN, and CASTLE POENARI have been put forward, but based on no real evidence.

Researchers also have put forward the ruins of Slain's Castle near Cruden Bay, Scotland, as the model that inspired the description of Castle Dracula. The manor house—not a fortress—sits near rugged cliffs. Cruden Bay was visited often by Stoker while he was working on *Dracula*. Stoker's surviving notes give no specific information concerning his inspirations on the count's Transylvanian abode. He undoubtedly saw plenty of castles in his native Ireland, and encountered plenty of them in the fiction that he read. As Dracula scholar ELIZABETH MILLER notes, "Or, he could have just made it up!"

FURTHER READING:
Haining, Peter, and Peter Tremayne. *The Undead: The Legend of Bram Stoker and Dracula.* London: Constable, 1997.
Miller, Elizabeth. *Dracula: Sense & Nonsense.* Westcliff-on-Sea, England: Desert Island Books, 2000.
Stoker, Bram. *Dracula.* New York: Grosset & Dunlap, n.d.

Castle Dracula Hotel   Tourist castle-style hotel located at the summit of BORGO PASS in the Carpathian Mountains of TRANSYLVANIA, Romania. Built in 1983, the hotel attempts to re-create for enterprising and imaginative tourists the abode of BRAM STOKER's COUNT DRACULA.

Guests can arrange a visit to the hotel's crypt, accessed by a narrow, dark stairwell. The walls have holes that enable hidden staff persons to reach out grab at people as they go along, much like a house of horrors in an amusement park. The crypt is a small room colorfully painted with scenes from Stoker's novel, and a wooden COFFIN. A staff person hides in the coffin, and at an appropriate moment when the lights mysteriously go out, jumps out and escapes.

Castle Poenari   Castle in the foothills of the Carpathian Mountains, overlooking the Argeş River near Poenari, Romania, about 20 miles from Curtea de Argeş, the former capital of Wallachia. Once used by VLAD TEPES, the castle now is in ruins. In 1969 it was identified as the "real" CASTLE DRACULA by researchers RAYMOND T. MCNALLY and RADU R. FLORESCU.

Castle History
Castle Poenari dates to the 14th century and probably was built by Basarab princes; some historians say it was built in the 12th century by a Teutonic knight. Prince Basarab I (1310–1352) used it in his struggle against Hungarian rulers. It was taken over by Wallachians. Another castle faced it on the opposite side of the river, known as Castle Argeş.

By the time Vlad Tepes assumed power in 1456, both castles were in ruins due to damage from assaults by Turks and Tartars. Despite its small size—about 100 feet by 120 feet—Vlad appreciated the strategic location of Castle Argeş, which granted an excellent view of the River Argeş, the narrow river gorge, and the surrounding countryside. Around 1459 he decided to rebuild it, with a novel plan to exact revenge on some of his enemies, the elite boyars. The boyar partisans of Vladislav II, Vlad's father, had murdered the father and buried Vlad's brother, Mircea, alive and face-down—the latter of which was a prevention against Mircea becoming a vampire.

Vlad invited the boyars and their families to a lavish Easter feast at his castle in Tirgoviste. He seized the old boyars and their wives and had them impaled on STAKES. Those who were younger and in good health—men, women, and children—were marched immediately to the castle, where they were set to work, passing stones, bricks, and building materials from hand to hand in a giant human chain from the village of Poenari to the castle. Some were set to work making bricks. A description from an old Wallachian chronicle follows:

> So when Easter came, while all the citizens were feasting and the young ones were dancing, he surrounded them and captured them. All those who were old he impaled, and strung them all around the city; as for the young ones together with their wives and children, he had them taken just as they were, dressed for Easter, to Poenari, where they were put to work until their clothes were all torn and they were left naked.

When reconstruction was completed, the castle had three towers and walls thick enough to withstand cannon fire. A secret staircase reportedly existed to give quick escape, if necessary, through a tunnel in the mountain that led to the riverbank far below. No physical evidence of such a staircase or tunnel has ever been found, however.

In 1462 the Turks attacked the castle, and Vlad escaped unharmed. According to lore, his wife, left behind to face the wrath of the Turks, threw herself over the castle walls and into the river gorge.

After Vlad's death in 1476, the castle was used by others, but eventually was abandoned and allowed to sink into disrepair. Earthquakes in 1913 and 1940 severely damaged the castle. By the time Florescu and McNally wrote about it as "Castle Dracula" in 1972, the castle's remains were little more than piles of deteriorated stone. A partial reconstruction was undertaken in the 1970s by the Romanian government to allow tourist access to the ruins. The castle can be reached by a walk up the slope and then a climb up 1,531 wooden steps. It is a popular tourist attraction.

McNally and Florescu Discover "Castle Dracula"
In the 1960s historians McNally and Florescu, along with a team of other experts, set out to research the historical roots of BRAM STOKER's novel, *DRACULA*. If Vlad Tepes had been the historical Dracula, what was his castle? They identified Castle Poenari as the "real" Castle Dracula, even though CASTLE BRAN seemed—at least in appearance—a much likelier candidate for the real castle behind Stoker's fictional version. Stoker never visited Romania, however, so it is unlikely that either Bran or Poenari served as an inspirational model.

Vincent Hillyer's Night in the Ruins
In 1977 vampire researcher VINCENT HILLYER received permission to spend a night alone in the castle ruins, despite the dangers of roaming bears and wolves. Hillyer took with him a blanket roll, lantern, and bag containing dinner. He also wore a CROSS, which he concealed because of religious prohibitions of the then-Communist regime. In an interview for *Vampires Among Us*, Hillyer described his night:

> It took me about an hour and a half to climb the steps. When I got to the top, it was just about sunset. The wind had come up, and it was a cold, biting wind, even though

Wooden steps lead to the ruins of Castle Poenari. (Photo by R. E. Guiley)

it was the month of July. My leather jacket was soaked through from the perspiration of all that climbing, and I felt quite a chill.

The first thing I did when I went inside was to check the different rooms and the little narrow stairs going upstairs to orient myself so I wouldn't walk around in the darkness and go in the wrong place or fall somewhere.

When the sun did set, I sat down in the what would have been the main hallway. The roof was all broken in this old castle, so it was exposed to the night sky and the elements. I set out these provisions that I'd brought for dinner—a smoked ham, a sharp white cheese, bread, some fresh vine-ripened tomatoes, and a bottle of vintage red wine. After that long climb, I was hungry and the food tasted wonderful. I'd noticed all these little pebbles on the

floor around me. Suddenly all these little "pebbles" started jumping around and moving! I held up my lantern, and saw that they were fat, scaly, shiny beetles and ugly, hairy *huge* spiders. They were crawling all over, coming up my pant leg. They looked ferocious. The beetles were varying sizes, anywhere from the size of a 10-cent piece up to the size of a 25-cent piece. The spiders were of myriad sizes and shapes. They all so seemed to move so fast in my direction. I frantically brushed them off, and got rid of them by setting out some of my food for them. And they were *ravenous*. Really greedy! They crawled all over the food, eating.

I moved further down the hallway to avoid being overrun by them and to await the approaching night. I could hear the chirping of birds and bats. Soon I heard the wolves begin to howl, and that was delightful, because then it really set the scene. Here we have a film in the making: the wolves are starting to howl as night descends and darkness covers everything.

I reminded myself what the Romanian officials told me about the bears and wolves coming into the castle at night on some occasions. Neither of which are known to be overly friendly to visitors. So I determined that if they came, I would go up a little narrow stairway to this room at the top of the tower. It was a small opening and I could block with some of the loose stones lying around. Or I could stand there and shout—you know, scare the animals a little bit if they began to act unfriendly.

This little room was the room that Dracula's first wife had jumped from when she committed suicide. She jumped from the balcony down to the Argeș River below. There is one spot where the natives say her blood still colors the Argeș River. In actuality, the red color to the water probably comes from the red sandstone in the area.

But that night, when I looked down, I could see the moonlight reflecting on the Argeș River below, and I thought this must be the very room that she had jumped from when the castle was surrounded by the Turkish troops. And she, rather than be captured alive, killed herself. And Dracula himself escaped through a secret tunnel. The cad didn't take her with him.

Then I heard these noises downstairs. I thought, oh, boy, I wonder if the animals have come in. I peeked down the stairs but I didn't see anything. It was a little hazardous to try to sleep in this upstairs room, so I went back down the hall and put out my blanket and went to sleep. I was so tired, and I wasn't afraid to sleep. I fell into a heavy, uncomfortable sleep and had this strange dream that I was riding in a horse-drawn carriage that was rushing pell-mell up a winding mountain pass with precipitous cliffs. I seemed to be pursuing someone. The carriage shot around a sharp corner and came suddenly upon a Gypsy woman who was beating a fallen horse. The horse was dead, and its eyes stared blankly at the heavens. I was angered at the Gypsy's cruelty, and I shouted at her that I would never invite her into my house.

I came awake with an ominous sense of a presence, like somebody, or something, was watching me. Then I noticed this pain at my collarbone and rubbed it. I was shocked to see little drops of blood on my finger. I immediately thought, nobody is going to believe this, I spent the night in Dracula's castle, and got puncture wounds! But I didn't have time to think about the wounds because of this overpowering feeling that I was not alone, that somebody was watching me. And it was a feeling that was so strong that it made me turn and look down the end of the hallway. I had to decide whether to go down and investigate or stay there safely under the blanket and forget the whole thing.

I decided to investigate. I walked down the end of the hall half expecting to meet Dracula himself. I saw these watery, glassy eyes in the darkness. But it was an old wolf.

The ruins of Castle Poenari in Romania (Photo by R. E. Guiley)

I assumed it was old because it had a gray muzzle and backed off fast and ran down the mountainside.

As the wolf retreated, I noticed a powerful odor of rotting flowers spreading through the chamber. I was puzzled because I had observed earlier that there were no flowers around the ruins at all. I knew I wasn't going back to sleep, and I was chilled to the bone from the wind blowing through the place. It was near sunrise, and I decided to leave, even though it was still dark. But I felt in a bit of a jocose mood, so I went back upstairs on the balcony and I waved my lantern and howled, like a Transylvanian miscreant. Way off in the distance I could see the fire of a Gypsy camp, and I thought my voice just might carry—at least they could see this lamp swinging back and forth.

Then I started back down. Even though the sun rose, the light still didn't penetrate the thick forest, and I had to make my way through the darkness with my lantern. I panicked when I heard twigs break behind me, and I knew I was being followed. I thought maybe this time a wolf wouldn't be frightened off so easily. I began to walk faster, but whatever it was behind me was coming up fast. Below me I saw a light—a flashlight perhaps—and I shouted. There was a shrill whistle and I heard a thundering of paws behind me. I thought I surely would be attacked, but the paws raced past me. They were two hunting dogs, evidently answering their master's signal.

Once I reached the valley, I had to walk several miles before I came upon a power station with a telephone. I called the Posada Inn, where my guide and driver were staying. The driver came to pick me up. When I walked into the Posada Inn, Mrs. Velescu and the mayor of Curtea were startled at my appearance. I had a cold sweat. I went to lift my arms, and I just felt so rotten, so nauseated. I must have looked great just coming in from Dracula's castle—pallid, about ready to faint and with a bloody neck. They took me right away to the Curtea de Arges hospital. Mrs. Velescu didn't believe that I had been bitten. She was startled when the doctor told her I had puncture wounds.

The doctor seemed divided between whether he should be concerned or amused at my predicament, having been bitten at Dracula's castle. He kept saying, "No, no, it wasn't Dracula, it wasn't Dracula, it was a spider." It must have been a very big spider, because there was about a half an inch between the two wounds. He gave me an antitoxin shot, but I was sick with nausea, fever and malaise for about 24 hours. The bite healed in a few days.

Hillyer maintained that he was then permanently sensitive to sunlight and burned easily. He developed keratoses, a pre-cancerous condition of the skin.

He related his experience to experts, among them Professor Corneliu Barbulescu of the Romanic Folkloric Institute in Bucharest, Florescu, McNally, Dr. Devandra Varma—a vampirologist from India—and several psychical researchers in Southern California. From them, Hillyer pieced together theories about what had happened to him at Dracula's Castle. The castle itself may be a sort of psychic magnet for evil because of its bloody history and the huge number of CORPSES buried on the mountaintop. The dream of not inviting the Gypsy woman in could relate to the superstition that the vampire cannot enter a house unless it first has been invited in. The smell of rotting flowers might have signaled the presence of malevolent forces. Smells are common in hauntings and possession cases; the worse the smell, the more negative the presence.

FURTHER READING:
Guiley, Rosemary Ellen. *Vampires Among Us*. New York: Pocket Books, 1991.
Hillyer, Vincent. *Vampires*. Los Banos, Calif.: Loose Change Publications, 1988.
McNally, Raymond T., and Radu Florescu. *In Search of Dracula: a true history of Dracula and vampire legends*. Greenwich, Conn.: New York Graphic Society, 1972.
———. *Dracula: A Biography of Vlad the Impaler 1431–1476*. New York: Hawthorn Books, 1973.

catacano   Cretan vampire. The *catacano* mysteriously laughs for no known reason.

cats   In vampire folklore, the animals most likely to doom a CORPSE to vampirism. Folklore beliefs hold that vampirism will result if an animal jumps over a corpse before it can be buried. Dogs, donkeys, birds, horses, and cats are cited most frequently, and cats top the list, especially in Greek lore.

Widespread folk beliefs hold that cats are intrinsically evil. They are both domestic and unsocialized, and thus it is difficult to control their behavior. In Greek lore the phrase "the cats will eat him" refers to the unhappy fate that awaits someone after death.

caul   The inner fetal membrane of amniotic fluid, which at birth sometimes still covers the body, or especially the head. In folklore, persons "born with the caul" are reputed to have special supernatural powers, either good or evil.

In Greek lore and among the KASHUBS, a child born with a caul is immediately identified as a VAMPIRE, and precautionary measures must be taken. In Kashub tradition, the caul is dried and reduced to ASHES. The ashes are fed to the child when he reaches age seven, as an antidote to vampirism.

In Romanian lore, the caul of a newborn must be broken immediately. If the infant swallows it, he is doomed to be an evil vampire, and will cast the EVIL EYE all of his life and eat his relations after he dies. To avert this fate, the midwife should clean the baby and take it outdoors, calling out, "Hear, everyone, a wolf is born onto the earth. It is not a wolf that will eat people, but a wolf that will work and bring luck." This ritual transmutes the evil power of the vampire into good, and makes the vampire child lucky.

Others born with the caul are believed to be blessed with good fortune, to have the power to see evil spirits, and to battle them and neutralize their evil spells. Their powers and roles are similar to the DHAMPIR and SABBATARIANS.

The *benandanti* ("good walkers"), a pagan agrarian cult of northern Italy, were persons born with the caul who went out in their astral bodies on the "Ember Days" (the solstices and equinoxes) to battle witches and wizards. The *benandanti* SHAPE-SHIFTED into the forms of butterflies, mice, cats and hares. If they triumphed over the witches, the crops would be abundant. If they lost, the crops would be poor. The *benandanti* often saved their cauls, dried them and wore them about their necks as amulets.

Elsewhere cauls were carefully preserved and kept as amulets. Midwives sold them as charms, especially to sailors who considered them protection against drowning at sea.

FURTHER READING:
Guiley, Rosemary Ellen. *The Encyclopedia of Witches and Witchcraft.* 2d ed. New York: Facts On File, 1999.
Murgoci, Agnes. "The Vampire in Roumania," in *The Vampire: A Casebook*, Alan Dundes, ed. Madison: University of Wisconsin Press, 1998.
Perkowski, Jan. L. *The Vampire of the Slavs.* Cambridge, Mass.: Slavica Publishers, 1976.

cemeteries   The traditional dwelling places of VAMPIRES. Local traditions govern the proper burial of CORPSES so that evil influences will not turn them into vampires or restless REVENANTS who attack the living.

All cemeteries are sacred grounds. The word *cemetery* is derived from the Greek for "sleeping chamber." It was applied to the catacombs of the dead in Rome, then to the consecrated grounds of a church, and then to any place where the dead are buried.

SUICIDE victims, criminals, and stillborn children traditionally are not buried in hallowed ground, or else are buried on the north side of a cemetery, the side associated with dark forces.

Graves in many cemeteries traditionally are dug east to west and the bodies are placed in the grave so that the feet face east. It is universally considered unlucky to step over a grave. If an animal jumps over a grave, it is often a sign that the corpse will become a vampire. Remedial measures must be taken instantly.

It is considered unlucky to disturb a grave, unless one is hunting for vampires, which requires the exhumation and examination of corpses, and, if necessary, the mutilation or destruction of the bodies if found in a vampire condition.

Gravesites may be scattered with GARLIC or SEEDS, which have antivampire properties, or may be pierced by wooden STAKES or IRON nails as a prevention against vampires escaping into the realm of the living.

GHOULS frequent cemeteries looking for victims.
See also BURIAL CUSTOMS; COFFINS.

Châlons Werewolf (1598)   French WEREWOLF trial. The Châlons Werewolf was a Sweeney Todd–like tailor who was executed by burning in Paris on December 14, 1598. MONTAGUE SUMMERS described the case in *The Werewolf*:

> This wretch was wont to decoy children of both sexes into his shop, and having abused them he would slice their throats and then powder and dress their bodies, jointing them as a butcher cuts up meat. In the twilight, under the shape of a wolf, he roamed the woods to leap out at stray passers-by and tear their throats to shreds. Barrels of bleaching bones were found concealed in his cellars as well as other foul and hideous things. He died (it is said) unrepentant and blaspheming.

Summers reports that the details of the case were so gruesome that the court ordered the documents to be burned.

FURTHER READING:
Summers, Montague. *The Werewolf.* New York: Bell Publishing, 1966.

Spooky cemeteries are a vampire's haven. (Courtesy Vampire Empire Archives)

Chaney, Lon (1883–1930)   Silent film star best known for his roles as the grotesque vampire in LONDON AFTER MID-NIGHT (1927), as the hunchback in *The Hunchback of Notre Dame* (1923) and the phantom in *The Phantom of the Opera* (1925). Lon Chaney was called "the man with a thousand faces" for his ability to play diverse characters, often tragic and dark in nature.

Chaney was born Alonso Chaney on April 1, 1883, to parents who were deaf. Having to communicate with them by body language perhaps contributed to his later ability to project on the screen with great intensity.

Lon Chaney as The Man With the Beaver Hat "vampire" in London After Midnight *(Author's collection)*

When Chaney was 10, his mother became incapacitated with rheumatism, and he quit school to care for her and the family. His father worked as a barber.

Chaney launched his stage career in 1901, and by 1913 he had landed his first silent film role in *Poor Jake's Demise.* For the next 10 years he worked exclusively for Universal Pictures, making more than 100 films. He also worked later for MGM. From 1913 to 1930, he played 150 different roles.

Chaney began working with director TOD BROWNING in 1921 in *Outside the Law.* Browning admired him greatly, and the two did 10 films together, including *London After Midnight,* Chaney's only vampire role and the last film he did with Browning.

Chaney made his first and only talking picture—and the last film of his life—in 1930 in *The Unholy Three,* in which he did five different voices as a ventriloquist. He developed cancer and underwent radiation treatments, which made him anemic. After a series of bronchial hemorrhages, Chaney died on August 26, 1930, two months after the release of the film. BELA LUGOSI, who was enjoying a success in the stage version of DRACULA, was one of his pallbearers.

Chaney went to great lengths to achieve special effects via his appearance, even to the point of inducing pain and jeopardizing his health. In his vampire role—the "Man with the Beaver Hat" in *London after Midnight*—he inserted fish hooks in his cheeks to help him maintain the corpse-like, gaping leer that showed his full rows of saw teeth. He tightened circles of fine wire around his eyes to make them protrude. It was said that he used chemicals to dilate the pupils of his eyes.

For his role as a legless cripple in *The Penalty* (1920), Chaney strapped up his legs into painful positions in a harness behind him with his feet up against his thighs. He put his knees into leather stumps. Circulation problems caused a breakage of blood vessels. For the deformed Quasimodo in *The Hunchback of Notre Dame,* he wore a 50-pound hump and harness on his back, and twisted his body.

Chaney's death deeply affected Browning, who looked for replacements of him in Lugosi and Lionel Barrymore, but never found another actor whom he liked as well. Chaney was Browning's pick for the count in his 1931 film *Dracula,* and Universal Pictures went so far as to leak word that they would make the film with Chaney in the lead role before the studio got the film rights for the book. Chaney reportedly even had his makeup as the count planned. But his terminal illness prevented him from undertaking the project, and a contract was never signed. The role went to Lugosi and made him famous.

FURTHER READING:

Anderson, Robert G. *Faces, Forms, Films: The Artistry of Lon Chaney.* Cranbury, N.J.: A. S. Barnes, 1971.

Lon Chaney Web site. URL: http://www.lonchaney.com/lc5/jrpages/lcjrbiok.html. Downloaded on December 10, 2003.

Riley, Philip J. *London After Midnight.* New York: Cornwall Books, 1985.

Skal, David J., and Elias Savada. *Dark Carnival: The Secret World of Tod Browning, Hollywood's Master of the Macabre.* New York: Anchor/Doubleday, 1995.

Chaney, Lon, Jr. (1906–1973)   Actor renowned for his horror roles as monsters and supernatural creatures. Lon Chaney Jr. is best known for his portrayal of Lawrence Talbot the werewolf in THE WOLF MAN (1941).

Chaney Jr. was born Creighton Tull Chaney on October 6, 1906, in Oklahoma City. He was nearly stillborn after a difficult delivery, but was revived by his father, who rushed him outside and immersed him in cold lake water.

Chaney Jr. followed in the footsteps of his famous father, Lon Chaney, and his silent screen star mother, Cleva Creighton-Chaney. At age six months, he was a prop in one of his father's stage acts. His childhood was marked by traveling vaudeville tours.

After his father's death in 1931, he entered film acting under his given name of Creighton Chaney. He had bit roles as extras and a stunt man, and took acting lessons. He used several names, including his own. He soon found that Hollywood was more receptive to him as the son of Lon Chaney, and he began using Lon Chaney Jr. professionally.

Chaney Jr. got his first major acting break for a role in the stage production of *Of Mice and Men,* which led to his role in the film version.

Universal Pictures signed him to play the werewolf in *The Wolf Man.* The movie launched him on a career of horror roles, and made him the leading horror box office draw for the studio, eclipsing BELA LUGOSI.

Like his father, Chaney Jr. went to painful lengths for some of his roles. For *The Wolf Man,* he endured being strapped into a chair with his chin in a brace for the makeup changes required to film his transformation. A small alteration in makeup was done and then was shot. The process was repeated over and over to accomplish the on-screen change from man to beast. The tedious process consumed four hours. The first transformation shows only his feet changing from human legs to hairy paws. The second and last transformation shows his face as he dies, and the wolf head returns to human form.

Chaney Jr. reprised his role in *The Wolf Man* in four other films: FRANKENSTEIN MEETS THE WOLF MAN (1943); *House of Frankenstein* (1944); *House of Dracula* (1945); and ABBOTT AND COSTELLO MEET FRANKENSTEIN (1948). He played COUNT DRACULA in *Son of Dracula* (1943).

Chaney Jr.'s career includes more than 150 film credits, 60 television appearances, and numerous stage appearances. He died of a heart attack on July 12, 1973, in San Clemente, California, after years of poor health. Per his request, his body was donated to medical research.

FURTHER READING:
Lon Chaney Web site. URL: http://www.lonchaney.com/lc5/ jrpages/lcjrbiok.html. Downloaded on December 10, 2003.

Lon Chaney Jr. as Larry Talbot the werewolf in The Wolf Man. *(Author's collection)*

Charnas, Suzy McKee   American novelist of horror, science fiction, and fantasy fiction and creator of the existential and scholarly vampire EDWARD WEYLAND. Suzy McKee Charnas has also written nonfiction, drama, and musicals.

Charnas was born and raised in New York City. Her parents were commercial artists, and Charnas trained to be an artist, too. She wrote and drew her own comics at age six.

In Barnard College, she took a joint major in economic history, because she wanted the knowledge to create convincing societies for her fantastic stories. After college she joined the Peace Corps and served in Nigeria.

Charnas's first fictional work was published in 1974: *Walk to the End of the World,* a novel about Amazon nomads who live without men. A sequel, *Motherlines,* was published in 1978.

Her science fiction career was well established by the time she became interested in vampires. Charnas was at work on her third novel and was suffering from writer's block, and so set it aside. She happened to read a magazine article on the search for artificial BLOOD for medical use. Soon thereafter, she attended a revival of the stage version of DRACULA, starring Frank Langella, who also starred in the John Badham film version of the novel. Both article and play sparked the inspiration for her first vampire work, *The Vampire Tapestry*, published in 1980, which introduced Weyland. The novel began as short stories.

In *The Vampire Tapestry*, Weyland is not human, but is a member of an ancient race of predators that hibernates for long periods and arises from their graves to assume new identities in keeping with social and technological changes. An anthropologist in the modern world, he cannot remember his origins as a vampire. His first antagonist is Katje de Groot, a Boer widow from South Africa, living in the United States, and an excellent hunter of game. For Charnas, the significance of South Africa represented the racism of blood.

Unicorn Tapestry (1980) in which Weyland enters therapy and has an erotic encounter with his therapist, Floria Landauer, won the Science Fiction Writers of America Nebula Award for Best Novella. The novella became part three of the *Tapestry*.

Throughout the novel, Weyland experiences different relationships with humans and then must decide whether or not to continue with his life among people. On a more subtle level, *The Vampire Tapestry* is concerned with the relationship between a predator and its prey. When the vampire sheds the skin of its former identity, it also forgets the friends that is has left behind and pain and suffering that it has caused during its previous incarnations.

Other of Charnas's novels about vampires as central characters are

The Ruby Tear (1997): Written under the pen name of Rebecca Brand, the romantic horror story concerns an actress whose role in a play about Central Europe causes her to tangle with a vampire, Baron Ivo con Cragga.

Music of the Night (2001): This e-book consists of mythic monster stories about a vampire, a werewolf, and a witch, as well as the Phantom of the Opera and his soprano wife.

Charnas also has written a stage play, *Vampire Dreams*, a two-act play based on *Unicorn Tapestry*. The play was first staged in San Francisco at the Magic Theater in 1990.

Charnas has published numerous other short stories and works of fiction. Her nonfiction tribute to her father, *My Father's Ghost: The Return on My Old Man and other Second Chances*, was published in 2002.

FURTHER READING:
Carter, Margaret L. "From Villain to Hero," in *The Complete Vampire Companion* by Rosemary Ellen Guiley with J. B. Macabre. New York: Macmillan, 1994.
Suzy McKee Charnas Web site. URL: http://suzymckeecharnas. com. Downloaded on December 18, 2003.

Chase, Richard (1950–1980) Convicted "vampire murderer." Richard Chase, of Sacramento, California, went on a killing spree in the 1970s because he believed his own BLOOD supply was disappearing from his veins. Unlike other famous vampiric killers of record, Chase said he derived no satisfaction or sexual pleasure from drinking the blood of his victims. Rather, he seemed to believe that it was their lot to sacrifice their own life force so that his could be replenished.

Born on May 23, 1950, Chase had a normal early childhood. He was a good student in elementary school, joined the Cub Scouts, and performed well in athletics. By adolescence, however, he showed signs of what psychiatrists later would term chronic paranoid schizophrenia.

At about the time Chase was entering his teens, his parents fell into in a terrible pattern of fighting. His father, an Englishman, acted rather sternly toward his son. Chase's mother, who was German, suspected her husband of infidelity. In arguments, Chase heard his mother accuse his father of trying to poison her. During this time of increasing domestic turmoil and unhappiness, Chase began experimenting with drugs, perhaps in an effort to escape. He drank alcohol, smoked marijuana, and took LSD. His grades at school dropped.

Chase began to fantasize that someone was out to poison him. Once after he ate some breakfast cereal, he became convinced that some unknown person had mixed syphilis in it in a deliberate attempt to poison him. He then came to believe that the real culprit was his mother, who was poisoning him slowly by adding laundry detergent to his food. He could not pinpoint why or exactly when his mother turned against him. He was certain she had, because he could feel the walls of his blood vessels thickening, thus preventing his blood from flowing through his heart. Further evidence was his sense of growing weakness, including spells of light-headedness that he feared would lead to fainting and even coma. If he did not take action, he believed, his blood would clot in his body and he would die. His pulmonary artery was not moving his blood around, he believed.

By the time Chase entered high school, he also was living in fear of a gang of "Germans" at his school. No one else seemed to be aware of them, or any of their names, but Chase knew they existed, and they were out to get him. Their vendetta stemmed from something Chase had discovered his parents had never told him, that he was part Jewish. Some of these "Germans," he believed, became powerful drug dealers and coerced his mother to poison him with laundry soap.

Chase escaped his imagined persecutors when he turned 17 in 1967 and left home to live with friends while he attended American River College in Sacramento. He returned home in 1972—the same year his parents' marriage broke up—thinking that the influence of the "Germans" was over. To his horror, he came to believe he was wrong. He got into a fight and was struck repeatedly on the head, leaving minor injuries. Sometime afterward he thought he heard a telephone caller inform him that the Mafia was out to get him in addition to the Nazis. Chase believed that both groups had pressured his mother into resuming slipping doses of laundry soap into his food. He felt weak and sick. On a number of occasions, certain that his heart was indeed failing from the poison, he called the fire department first aid rescue team. They were unable to help him to his satisfaction. To prevent more poison from entering his system, he often refused to eat anything besides milk from previously unopened cartons.

On December 1, 1973, Chase believed that his pulmonary artery had been "stolen" and his blood had stopped flowing inside his body. It never seemed to occur to him that death would be immediate under such circumstances. Wild-eyed, he raced to an emergency room in Sacramento, where he informed the staff that he was suffering from cessation of blood flow, blocked intestines and an abdomen that was turned to stone. He was admitted as a psychiatric patient, but checked out against medical advice when he realized his claims were not taken seriously.

Chase became frantic about his failing body. He was certain that his heart stopped completely on several occasions. He developed a phobia about dirt and tried desperately to purify his body by taking three or four baths a night. During his bathing, he believed he received telepathic messages from his mother and sister. He also tried to purify his body with doses of vitamin C. Ingesting tablets was insufficient, and he had to absorb it directly through his skin. Every day he wrapped several oranges in a turban and tied it to his scalp, wearing his lumpy headdress out in public. He failed to feel better.

In yet another effort to save himself, Chase turned to studying anatomy. He arrived at the conclusion that the only thing that would counteract the laundry soap and save him from slow death was to get blood plasma. He visited doctors and patiently explained his self-diagnosis, but none would give him any blood plasma. Apparently, he thought, they resented the fact that he could diagnose himself, and so they refused to cooperate. Without plasma, Chase was forced to try the next best alternative in his eyes: fresh animal blood.

Chase left his family home at age 25 and moved to a house in North Sacramento, where he could satisfy his need for blood without interference. He bought rabbits and killed them. He drank their blood and ate them—usually raw, sometimes cooked. Once he bought a rabbit from a German woman and shot it dead. After consuming its blood and flesh, he became convinced that she had poisoned the animal. "I got sick," he recalled to doctors later. "I was poisoned like battery acid. I almost died."

In April 1976 Chase sought help at two health care institutions in Sacramento, a hospital and a healthcare center. He was seen by a psychiatrist at the hospital and was discharged after two days. He immediately checked into the healthcare center, where he was treated with antipsychotic medication and was kept under observation.

In May 1976 Chase was transferred to a sanitarium. Despite his treatment with antipsychotic and tranquilizing drugs, and the ministrations of mental health professionals, he was not to be dissuaded from the belief that more blood was the only thing that could save his life. In a grotesque imitation of R. M. RENFIELD in BRAM STOKER's novel DRACULA, Chase was observed by the staff strolling about the grounds pouncing on birds. He bit off their heads and sucked out their blood.

Chase was released into the care of his family on September 29, 1976. The family pets began mysteriously disappearing. His mother witnessed him play with a family cat, kill it, and smear its blood on his neck. He tied more oranges to his head to try to absorb vitamin C.

Unable to get along at home, Chase moved out and took an apartment of his own before the end of the year. He began mixing his own remedies of raw animal meat, putting bits of liver, heart, and other organs in a blender with cola added for sweetness.

In August 1977 Chase was found on the Pyramid Lake Indian Reservation near Sacramento by police officers from the Bureau of Indian Affairs. He was naked with dried blood smeared all over his chest, arms, and legs. He was in possession of 30-30-caliber and .22-caliber rifles. In his truck were clothing, shoes, and rags soaked in blood, and a bucket containing a fresh animal liver—probably from a dead cow found on the reservation. Charges were not pressed, and Chase was urged to get psychiatric help.

By this time Chase felt that psychiatrists were not going to help him get the blood he desperately needed. He bought dogs, killed them, and ate them raw. One day he became enraged by the thought that his neighbors had deliberately poisoned one of the dogs he had eaten with battery acid. Outraged, he purchased a handgun on December 29, 1977, and went driving around looking for someone to shoot. His unfortunate victim was a 51-year-old man, Edward Griffin, who was unloading groceries from his car when Chase drove by. A bullet from Chase's gun killed him instantly. Chase escaped, and the crime initially was blamed upon vandals.

Less than a month later, Chase decided animal blood would no longer suffice, and he would have to have human blood. His first attempt netted him nothing. On January 23, 1978, he forced his way through a rear window of the home of the Robert Edwards family, all of whom were out. They returned home and surprised him; he fled without attacking any of them. They found human feces in the middle of one of the children's beds, and urine in the baby's crib. It appeared as though Chase had been preparing to steal a few small items.

Later the same day, Chase walked about the streets and stopped at the last house on a block. He knocked on the door, and a 22-year-old married woman, Teresa Lynn Wallin, answered. He had never seen her before. He shot and killed her and dragged her body into her bedroom. He mutilated the body with his hunting knife, and then found a glass in which to catch her blood, which he drank. He later said that he had felt starved at the time: "starved for being a Jew and poisoned, and I just wanted to kill her." He returned to his apartment and spent a quiet evening watching television. He seemed unconcerned about the body he left behind, which was so mutilated that even the police and coroner were shocked.

Wallin's blood failed to make Chase feel better. A few days later, on January 27, he went on his last rampage. He murdered three people in one house, and drank the blood of the female victim after mutilating her body. His sixth and final victim was an infant from the same house. He took the infant home in his car, shot it, drank some of its blood, and threw the body in the trash. Then he went to sleep. His own description of the event, given later, was detached and seemed devoid of emotion: "I saw a guy go into the house and the door was left open; so I just walked in after him. He was a German guy. . . . There were three people standing there, and I shot them. Guess they were all Germans. And then I . . . [went to] that lady. I took her clothes off and cut out her stomach and drank her blood."

The Sacramento police arrived at Chase's apartment on January 28, having been alerted by area residents who had seen him near the homes of the victims. He surrendered quietly. The police searched the premises and found a container full of human organs in the kitchen.

Chase was charged with six counts of murder on February 28, 1978. During his psychiatric examination, Chase stated that he understood the charges but thought they were unfair. He said that an angiogram and an X-ray of his blood vessels, would demonstrate that his head was a "mess" and would present evidence for reason of insanity by poisoning. His lawyer, Chase said, should present a "medical defense" based on "an admission to poisoning me by my parents, being jumped and hit in the head by a couple of gang musicians," as well as negligence on the part of the hospital.

In subsequent interviews, including sessions with other doctors, Chase said he didn't remember the killings, and that meant they could have been done by someone else. Later, he said he believed he did do the killings, even though they were blanked from his memory. He also asked to be transferred from jail to a state hospital, because he believed there were "Germans" in the kitchen who were trying to poison him. He became convinced that he had contracted a venereal disease from the jail food. His heart had gotten turned around inside his body, he said, and caustic acid was destroying his stomach.

Chase was declared sane and was convicted of first-degree murder. He was sent to Atascadero, a prison for the criminally insane, for psychiatric treatment. He then was transferred to San Quentin. There he hid his tranquilizers until he accumulated enough to take his own life. He died on December 27, 1980, at age 30.

FURTHER READING:
Guiley, Rosemary Ellen, with J. B. Macabre. *The Complete Vampire Companion*. New York: Macmillan, 1994.
London, Sondra. *True Vampires: Blood-Sucking Killers Past and Present*. Los Angeles: Feval House, 2004.

Christmas Day   In Greek lore, children born on Christmas Day will become VAMPIRES, as punishment that their mothers conceived on the same day as the Blessed Virgin Mary.

chupacabra   A vampiric entity prominent in the folklore of Puerto Rico and Central and South America, and which also has been reported in the United States and Europe. *Chupacabra* means "goatsucker."

The *chupacabra* sucks the BLOOD from farm and domestic animals, killing them.

Numerous face-to-face encounters with the *chupacabra* have been reported, and the deaths of many farm and domestic animals have been attributed to it. Eyewitness descriptions vary in some details, but the general description of the *chupacabra* is as follows:

It has a humanoid form that stands erect on powerful, animal hind legs. It has short and scrawny forelimbs that end in hands with three claws. It is covered with fur, has membranes that give it the effect of BAT wings, and has glowing, elongated RED eyes. Multicolored spines are along its back, and constantly change color. It is reported to run and jump with supernormal speed and power, and to either fly, glide, or levitate into the air. It emits terrible screams.

Animals attacked by *chupacabras* have puncture marks on their bodies, usually on the neck, forehead, legs, and genitals. In some Mexican cases, animals have twin puncture marks. Some of the cuts are described as clean and precise, more like surgical cuts than teeth marks. In some cases the animal's genitals have been removed, or the liver or brains have been taken out of the head. Slime is found around the carcasses.

While the creature seems to prefer animals, attacks on humans have been reported. In 1996 a *chupacabra* attack on a human was reported in Mexico. The victim, a woman, was clawed on the back. The wounds resembled burn marks. A Costa Rican woman reported that a creature with large wings and a small face and eyes grabbed her by her dress and attempted to carry her off, but she escaped.

One explanation put forward is that the *chupacabra* is a real creature that survived the age of dinosaurs. No remains are ever found, however, and the creature acts in a more supernatural fashion.

Chupacabra killings have been reported all over the United States. A wave of attacks on domestic pets, goats, chickens, geese, and ducks have been reported in Sweetwater, Florida, near Miami, and have been blamed on *chupacabras*. Though eyewitnesses claimed to see the creature, others blamed the attacks on a large dog. A cast of a print found in the area resembled that of a dog, but had what appeared to be human or ape nails rather than claws.

Some *chupacabra* attacks have been linked to UFO sightings, especially since the 1970s, as well as to waves of mysterious, unexplained animal mutilations and deaths reported in the United States and elsewhere.

See also CHUPA-CHUPA; EXTRATERRESTRIALS; MOTHMAN.

FURTHER READING:
Corrales, Scott. *Chupacabras and Other Mysteries*. Murfreesboro, Tenn.: Greenleaf Publications, 1997.

Downes, Jonathan and Richard Freeman. "Shug Monkeys and Werewolves: The Search for Dog-Headed Men," in *Fortean Studies* vol. 5, Steve Moore, ed. London: John Brown Publishing, 1998.

chupa-chupa "VAMPIRE UFO" or "vampire in the sky." *Chupa-chupas* are named after the CHUPACABRA "goat-sucker" entity that attacks animals and drains them of BLOOD. The *chupa-chupa* is associated with RED UFO lights that burn and injure people, leaving them weak and sometimes anemic, as though their BLOOD has been drained. Some victims have died, according to reports.

Chupa-chupas have been reported in South America, as well as in Central America and Puerto Rico. The attacks have come in waves since the 1970s, about the same time that reports of the *chupacabra* increased. *Chupa-chupa* and *chupacabra* attacks often coincide.

From July 1977 to November 1978, a wave of deadly UFO sightings and encounters around Colares, Brazil, killed people and at least one animal—a dog—and left others seriously ill. In all, about 40 people, most of them adults, received medical treatment for injuries. Most of the victims were struck by mysterious beams of red light that severely burned their chests. Blood tests showed the victims to have abnormally low levels of hemoglobin. Some of the victims did not die directly from the burns, but suffered a wasting away over a period of months, and then died. Some people in the area believed that the aliens in the UFOs had come specifically to suck the blood or energy from people.

One victim, a woman, described how she was sleeping in a hammock in her house one night when she was awakened by a green light shining in her window. The beam turned to red. She saw that it came from what appeared to be a pistol wielded by something that looked like a man wearing a diving suit. She could see it only from the chest up; it had very small eyes. It pointed the pistol at her chest and shined a hot red beam on her three times. She felt as though she were being stuck by a needle, and she became thirsty. Though she was terrified and screamed, she felt paralyzed and could not move—a characteristic also seen in OLD HAG attacks. She felt as if the beam took blood out of her. The beam left three pinpoint scars in a triangle just above her right breast.

The woman's screams awakened her cousin, who came to her aid. The mystery creature disappeared. The victim was taken to the hospital and treated. For weeks, she suffered a headache and fever and general malaise.

A doctor who treated victims of the UFO attacks observed that they had small puncture wounds on their arms. She thought they had had blood taken. The wounds were not similar to the bites of VAMPIRE BATS.

A pregnant woman suffered bruising from the UFO beams, and then miscarried. A barking dog was struck by a beam, and suffered a wasting away until it died about three weeks later.

In *Confrontations* (1990), ufologist Jacques Vallée describes other cases of *chupa-chupas* that affected three towns in Brazil in the early 1980s: Parnama, São Luis, and Belém. The bodies of some of the victims reportedly looked as though they had had the blood sucked out of them. The victims were either out hunting and fishing at night, or sleeping in hammocks at home. The ones who were attacked while sleeping reported that they awakened to feel hit by a heavy weight on their chest that immobilized them.

Two hunters, Ribamar Ferreira and Abel Boro, said they were struck by a *chupa* light. According to Vallée:

> It was so bright that it turned night into day . . . Abel screamed as the object—looking in this case like a giant spinning tire truck with lights on it—surrounded his body with a glittering glow. Ferreira ran to Abel's house and returned with his family: they found Abel Boro dead, his body white "as if drained of blood."

Vallée observes that it is natural for CORPSES to look whitish gray because hemoglobin begins to break down after death. However, this does not explain the abnormally low hemoglobin found in dozens of victims who were not killed immediately by *chupas*. Vallée reports of a woman who, like the one described above, was struck in the chest by a beam of red light that left two puncture marks on her left breast. The woman had a decrease in red blood cells, and suffered dizziness, headaches, weakness, and numbness. She deteriorated, fell into a coma, and died.

Vallée also cites other lethal UFOs, many involving attacks by beams of light, after which the victims wasted away to death. In 1946 a man in Brazil was struck by a UFO beam of light while returning from a fishing trip. His flesh began to fall off his bones, and he died six hours later. His body rapidly decomposed. In 1954 UFO beams reportedly burned to death an entire village and their livestock in Nairobi, Africa, one night. In 1969 a man near Anolaima, Colombia, was irradiated by a UFO. He became seriously ill and blue spots appeared all over his skin. He died within a few days.

Some of the *chupa* victims survived, but never recovered. They continue to suffer chronic physical complaints of weakness, dizziness, and headaches. Some suffer mentally with fear and paranoia.

Vampire UFO attacks remain a mystery. Some ufologists believe that they are caused by weapon-wielding aliens. Vallée has drawn some comparisons to the fairylike beings found in local folklore traditions. Another possibility is that *chupa-chupas* represent a modern version, a mutation, of the vampire myth.

See also EXTRATERRESTRIALS.

FURTHER READING:
Corrales, Scott. *Chupacabras and Other Mysteries*. Murfreesboro, Tenn.: Greenleaf Publications, 1997.
Guiley, Rosemary Ellen. "Vampires from Outer Space: An Exploration of Common Ground Shared by Vampires and

Extraterrestrials Concerning Death and Immortality." Paper presented at the "Communication with the Beyond" colloquium in Sinaia, Romania, May 10–12, 2002, sponsored by the Transylvanian Society of Dracula, Bucharest; International Society for the Study of Ghosts and Apparitions, New York; and Ghost Club, London.

Pratt, Bob. *UFO Danger Zone: Terror and Death in Brazil— Where Next?* Madison, Wisc.: Horus House Press, 1996.
Vallée, Jacques. *Confrontations: A Scientist's Search for Alien Contact.* New York: Ballantine Books, 1990.

churail   In Indian lore, a female VAMPIRE. The *churail* is a woman who dies ritually unclean or pregnant during the Dewali Festival. She has a horrible appearance: a black tongue, needlelike teeth, thick and slimy lips, dirty and unkempt hair, and long, pendulous breasts. In some descriptions she is white in front and black in back.

The *churail* attacks its relatives first. It can be stopped or prevented by burying the CORPSE facedown. A ball of wool or twine placed in the grave will keep the vampire occupied and prevent it from leaving.

See also BURIAL CUSTOMS.

civateteo   In Mexican lore, a VAMPIRE witch. The *civateteo* is the evil spirit of a noblewoman who died in childbirth and returns to take revenge upon other children, attacking them and causing infantile paralysis and death. The *civateteo* hold SABBATS at CROSSROADS.

See also VAMPIRE SORCERERS AND WITCHES.

clinical vampirism   Pathological conditions in which a person experiences a compulsion to drink BLOOD. Clinical vampirism is not the same as consensual blood-drinking practiced by LIVING VAMPIRES or "vampyres."

In the psychiatric literature since the 19th century, the term *vampirism* has been used to cover a range of activities often related to lust murders:

- autovampirism, the drinking of one's own blood
- vampirism, the drinking of the blood of other living beings
- necrophagia, eating the flesh of CORPSES
- necrophilia, sexual excitement and contact with corpses
- necrosadism, the abuse of corpses
- cannibalism

Clinical vampirism also is called "Renfield's syndrome," a term coined by clinical psychologist Richard Noll after the character R. M. RENFIELD in BRAM STOKER's novel *DRACULA* (1897), who believes he must subsist on blood in order to survive. In Renfield's syndrome, a person believes he must consume blood in order to live. Compulsion to drink blood defines the syndrome.

Noll outlines the following characteristics of Renfield's syndrome:

- A pivotal event occurs that initiates the syndrome. Usually this event happens in childhood. The taste of blood (such as from an accident or a beating) is enjoyable and exciting. After puberty sexual excitement is associated with the taste of blood.
- There is a progression of the condition. First comes autovampirism, or the drinking of one's own blood, followed by the drinking of blood of insects and animals, and then true vampirism, the drinking of the blood of other people. The individual may attempt to procure or steal blood from blood banks and hospitals. Consensual blood drinking usually involves sex. Lust murders may involve forced sex and blood drinking.
- The compulsion to drink blood almost always has strong sexual associations.
- Blood takes on a mystical power.

Clinical vampirism varies in frequency and intensity. Some individuals may experience occasional episodes of compulsion to drink blood, while other cases become part of paranoia, schizophrenia, and possible violent and aggressive behavior toward others.

FURTHER READING:

Noll, Richard. *Vampires, Werewolves and Demons: Twentieth Century Reports in the Psychiatric Literature.* New York: Brunner/Mazel, 1992.
Ramsland, Katherine. *The Science of Vampires.* New York: Berkeley Boulevard Books, 2002.

cock   Symbol of light and goodness and thus the enemy of all evil spirits, ghosts, and VAMPIRES. The cock has a long association with sun deities, which gives it a power to banish evil. It heralds the dawn, which brings an end to the powers of infernal night creatures such as vampires. One widely held superstition says that on Judgment Day all cocks will set up an enormous crowing, even the IRON ones on church spires, and the cacophany will awaken both the living and the dead. The crowing of a cock is used in many vampire movies as a signal that the vampire is about to be rendered harmless, and risks destruction under the rays of the sun.

In parts of Europe, folklore holds that black cocks are servants of the devil. In the lore of some GYPSIES, vampires fear black cocks; keeping one inside a house will deter a vampire from entering.

coffin   Burial container to protect a CORPSE. The coffin symbolizes separation of the dead from the living. Various practices exist for ensuring that ghosts and VAMPIRES do not escape their coffins and return to harass the living.

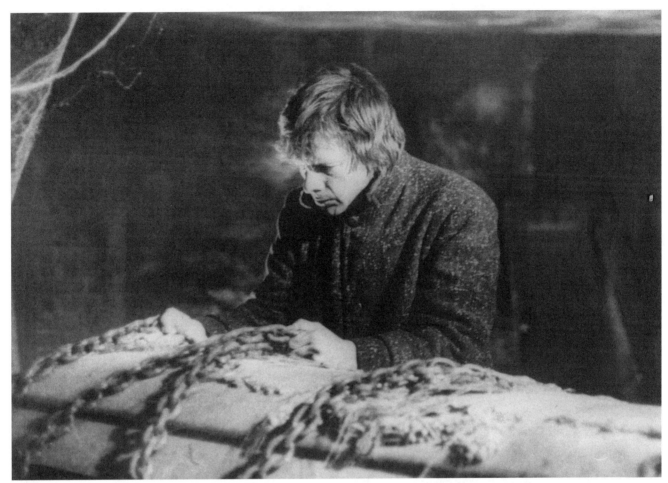

Willy Loomis (John Karlen) finds the chained coffin that imprisons the vampire Barnabas Collins in Dark Shadows. *(Author's collection)*

Coffins can be filled with sand, SEEDS, or grains, which vampires must count particle by particle before being able to leave. Heavy stones placed upon coffins before being covered with earth also will keep restless spirits in their proper place. (See BURIAL CUSTOMS.)

A widely held superstition holds that no item of clothing belonging to a living person should be placed in a coffin with the dead. To do so effectively vampirizes away the life of the living, for as the clothing rots, so will the living decline toward death.

A modern anecdote collected in 1977 by Harry A. Senn in *Were-Wolf and Vampire in Romania* (1982), tells of a novel use of a coffin by a vampire:

> A dead man who was killed by stabbing, and who had been buried would come back each night to look for his wife and daughter. Then he'd get back in his coffin, the lid would close, and off he'd go, like an automobile. Back into the grave. The neighbors told him his family had moved away and he stopped coming back.

No folklore tradition exists that vampires must sleep in coffins containing their native earth. In BRAM STOKER's 1897 novel, *DRACULA*, the count sleeps in an earth-filled coffin in his castle, and transports 50 boxes of Transylvanian earth to England. In WHITBY, ENGLAND, he takes refuge in the grave of a SUICIDE.

FURTHER READING:
Dundes, Alan, ed. *The Vampire: A Casebook*. Madison: University of Wisconsin Press, 1998.
Senn, Harry A. *Were-Wolf and Vampire in Romania*. Bluder, Colo.: East European Quarterly, 1982.

Collins, Barnabas   VAMPIRE character the popular daytime serial *DARK SHADOWS*, which aired from 1966 to 1971. The 175-year-old Barnabas Collins was played by JONATHAN FRID.

More than 200 episodes of the show had been done before Barnabas was introduced, in hopes of boosting sagging ratings. According to the story line, Barnabas lies trapped in his COFFIN on the estate of Collinwood, the estate of the wealthy Collins family of Collinsport, a fictional seaport town in New England. Willie Loomis (John

Barnabas Collins (Jonathan Frid) with his cape and walking stick on Dark Shadows *(Author's collection)*

Karlen), a drifter who becomes employed as a handyman by the Collinses, is bent on finding the lost jewels of the family when he discovers the mausoleum containing Barnabas's chained sarcophagus. He unwittingly opens it, thus freeing the vampire. Barnabas then appears at Collinwood, the gloomy New England mansion owned by the Collins family, and introduces himself as an English cousin, a descendant of the Barnabas Collins whose portrait decorates the foyer. He is attracted to Maggie Evans (Kathryn Leigh Scott), who resembles his lost love, Josette Duprés, and he attacks her to try to make her a vampire so that she can be with him. Dr. Julia Hoffman (Grayson Hall) discovers his secret and falls in love with him. She attempts to find a cure for him.

Barnabas's trademarks are his black cloak and wolf-headed SILVER cane, the latter perhaps a borrowed touch from *THE WOLF MAN* (1941). Like COUNT DRACULA, he SHAPE-SHIFTS into a BAT, has supernormal strength, can be invisible, can appear and disappear at will, and can mesmerize others and bend them to his will. Frid, a Shakespearean-trained actor, played Barnabas as a sensitive, tragic figure rather than the purely evil figure of Count Dracula.

Barnabas's entire background was not revealed immediately in the show. His past, or "backstory," is this: In the late 18th century, he was the son of Joshua Collins and nephew of Jeremiah Collins, the present Collinses' patriarch. His fiancée was Josette DuPrés (Kathryn Leigh Scott), the daughter of André Duprés, a wealthy plantation owner from Martinique. Josette, her father, and her maid, Angelique Bouchard (Lara Parker), came to stay at the Collins mansion. Angelique was a witch, and she was attracted to Barnabas. She tried to win him away from Josette, but he refused her. Furious, Angelique used witchcraft to make Josette marry Jeremiah. Enraged, Barnabas killed him in a duel. Angelique then tricked Barnabas into marrying her. He discovered her witchcraft and shot her. Angelique thought she was dying and cursed Barnabas: "I set a curse on you, Barnabas Collins. You will never rest. And you will never be able to love. Whoever loves you will die. That is my curse, and you will live with it through all eternity." A VAMPIRE BAT flew out of a closet and bit Barnabas, killing him and turning him into a vampire. Barnabas then tried to make Josette a vampire, but before he could succeed, Angelique's ghost lured her to Widow's Hill and forced her to jump to her death. Joshua Collins learned what his son had become, and chained him in a coffin in the family mausoleum.

As the series evolved, Barnabas becomes less and less predatory. He is cured of his vampire curse and then is cursed again. However, he kills less and less as the show went on. He becomes committed to good.

Barnabas time travels to explore his past and also to help others, such as Chris Jennings (Roger Davis), who is cursed to be a werewolf; Barnabas sets out to find the reason why, and the cure. In 1897 he encounters the brooding QUENTIN COLLINS (DAVID SELBY), who is the source of the curse. Back in the present, Barnabas learns that he is the pawn of a greater power, collectively known as the Leviathans, who are plotting to bring a devil baby into the world to take it over. Barnabas must do their bidding.

Throughout the series, Barnabas is aided by Julia, who knows his secret and who loves him. He has only friendly affection for her, and she eventually comes to terms with the status of their relationship. He searches ardently for his long-lost love, Josette. At times this endless love story is dropped, and Barnabas falls in love with other women, such as Roxanne Drew (Donna Wandrey), a reanimated CORPSE whom he turns into a vampire. Angelique is a nearly constant nemesis throughout the years, though at times she becomes a reluctant ally of Barnabas in order to defeat a larger evil. In the next-to-last time sequence set in 1840, Barnabas realizes he has loved Angelique all along—but she is killed by a righteous witch-hunting reverend, Lamar Trask (Jerry Lacy).

As Barnabas became less vampiric, his powers waned. The story line of his search for a cure of his vampire curse was dropped without resolution. In the final sequence at the end of the series, he and Julia go into parallel time to 1841, where Barnabas is only a memory. Frid plays Bramwell Collins, son of Barnabas, and he is not a vampire.

FURTHER READING:

Scott, Kathryn Leigh. *35th Anniversary Dark Shadows Memories.* Los Angeles: Pomegranate Press, 2001.

Scott, Kathryn Leigh, and Jim Pierson, eds. *Dark Shadows Almanac Millennium Edition.* Los Angeles: Pomegranate Press, 2000.

———. *Dark Shadows Almanac: 30th Anniversary Tribute.* Los Angeles: Pomegranate Press, 1995.

Scott, Kathryn Leigh, ed. *The Dark Shadows Companion 25th Anniversary Collection.* Los Angeles: Pomegranate Press, 1990.

Collins, Nancy A. (1952–) American horror novelist and creator of Sonja Blue, a VAMPIRE who is also a VAMPIRE HUNTER. Nancy A. Collins also writes for COMICS.

Collins was born in rural Arkansas and grew up there. In 1982 she moved to New Orleans. She lived in Louisiana for 10 years.

As a teenager, she became interested in vampires and created the character of Sonja Blue. By the 1980s she had developed a script for a comic book featuring Blue. Unable to find an artist, she wrote short stories featuring Blue. In 1989 Blue became the central character in Collins's first novel, *Sunglasses After Dark.* Blue is a not-so-nice girl who dedicates herself to hunting vampires in revenge for being made one herself. Her hidden, vampire nature is called The Other.

In the beginning of *Sunglasses,* Blue is imprisoned in an insane asylum as a dangerous person. She breaks out, hunts vampires, and faces off with the main villain, a tele-evangelist.

Sunglasses After Dark received the Horror Writers of America's Bram Stoker Award for First Novel. The success of the novel and the popularity of Blue led to a continuation of the character in subsequent novels and short stories. The novels are

- *In the Blood* (1992): Sonja's creator, Morgan, seeks to create a race of vampires that is immune to SILVER bullets. Some of the action revolves around a haunted house called the "Ghost Trap."
- *Wild Blood* (1993): Blue deals with Vargr, members of a band who are also WEREWOLVES and who have lost their power, and coyotero, shape-shifters who still have their power.

- *Paint It Black* (1995): Sonja confronts both Morgan and The Other.
- *A Dozen Black Roses* (1996): Set in Deadtown, the capital of vampires—the Kindred of the World of Darkness—the action concerns a rivalry for power between two vampires. Blue sets out to try to destroy all the vampires.
- *Darkest Heart* (2002): Sonja is targeted by a vampire hunter, Jack Estes, and an evil ancient vampire.

Other novels are *Tempter* (1990), *Nameless Sins* (1994), *Walking Wolf* (1995), *Fantastic Four: To Free Atlantis* (1995), and *Angels on Fire* (2004). Collins has edited collections of horror stories: *Dark Love* (1995), *Forbidden Acts* (1995), and *Gahan Wilson's Haunted House* (1996).

Sunglasses After Dark became a comic, and the attention Collins received led to her being hired by DC Comics' Vertigo imprint to write for *Swamp Thing.* She also created *Dhampire,* about a half-human, half-vampire named Nicholas Gaunt, who is obsessed with sadistic and suicidal impulses. He must come to terms with his nature. Only the first graphic novel was published, *Dhampire: Stillborn,* in 1996. Collins's editor died and the project was shelved.

Other comics credits are *2099 Unlimited* number 9 and 10 (1995), *Jason vs. Leatherface* (1995–96), *Verotika* numbers 3, 4, 5, and 7 (1995–97), *The Legend of the Fallen Angel* (1996), *The Big Book of Losers* (1997), *Aliens Special* (1997), and *Predator: Hell Come A-Walkin'* (number 1 and 2, 1998).

In her works, Collins has looked at vampirism as both a sociological disorder and a disease. To some extent, her vampire society is modeled after insect society: The masses act collectively as supporting workers for the few who run things. Vampires become bored during the course of their immortality and engage in power games to amuse themselves. Biting and killing a victim infuses it with vampire DNA, and if the CORPSE is not damaged, it will revive as a vampire. Damaged corpses become brain-damaged or zombielike vampires. The kings of vampires have evolved so they no longer need BLOOD to survive (like Akasha in QUEEN OF THE DAMNED), but instead vampirize negative psychic energy (see PSYCHIC ATTACK).

Collins has won the British Fantasy Society's Icarus Award. She was nominated for the Campbell Award in 1989 and 1990 and the comics industry's Eisner Award in 1992. She is founder of the International Horror Critics Guild.

FURTHER READING:

Collins, Nancy A. *A Dozen Black Roses.* Atlanta: White Wolf, 1997.

———. *Midnight Blue: The Sonja Blue Collection.* Atlanta: White Wolf, 1995.

———. *Sunglasses After Dark.* New York: New American Library, 1994.

"Dried Blood and Ink Presents: Nancy A. Collins." Available online. URL: http://www.vampn.com/NAC.html. Downloaded on December 21, 2003.

"Nancy Collins House of Blues." Available online. URL: http://www.vampn.com/Collins/html. Downloaded on December 21, 2003.

"Nancy Collins: Hardheaded Horror with a Southern Accent." Available online. URL:http://www.lby3.com/comic/archive/collins.html. Downloaded on December 21, 2003.

Collins, Quentin   Character in the gothic soap DARK SHADOWS (1966–71) plagued by the curse of being a werewolf. Quentin Collins was introduced to the series in 1968 and was played by DAVID SELBY. The character became the series' romantic lead and made a star of Selby.

In the present time, Chris Jennings (Don Briscoe) is the twin of Tom Jennings (also played by Briscoe), a handyman at the Collins estate of Collinwood in Collinsport, a seaport village in New England. Tom becomes a vampire after being attacked by the witch, Angelique Bouchard (Lara Parker). Chris is afflicted with the werewolf curse,

Quentin Collins (David Selby) on the set of Dark Shadows (Author's collection)

and sends his young sister, Amy (Denise Nickerson), to live at Collinwood for her safety. Amy plays with David Collins (David Henesy), the son of Roger Collins (Louis Edmonds), the family head. The children discover a mysterious disconnected telephone, through which the voice of the ghost of Quentin speaks to them and attempts to possess David. The ghost forces everyone to leave Collinwood and then lures them back. BARNABAS COLLINS, the family's secret vampire, uses a ritual with I-Ching wands to go back in time to try to learn about Quentin, and also discover the source of Chris's curse and its cure.

In 1897 Barnabas finds that Quentin is the troubled and angry younger brother of Edward Collins (Louis Edmonds), the head of Collinwood. The black sheep of the family, Quentin has flouted his family by marrying a GYPSY girl, Jenny (Marie Wallace), who dies. Blaming him for her death, Magda Rakosi (Grayson Hall), Jenny's sister, curses him to be a werewolf. Quentin lives at Collinwood, brooding with his terrible secret that turns him into a murderous beast every full MOON. (Werewolf scenes are played by a stuntman in costume, Alex Stevens.) Quentin drinks heavily and spends long hours alone in his room, playing the same mournful song on his phonograph over and over ("Quentin's Song" became a popular hit as a result).

Despite his social problems, Quentin is irresistible to women. Beth Chavez (Terry Crawford), a servant at Collinwood, falls in love with him. He romances Charity Trask (Nancy Barrett), the daughter of Reverend Trask (Jerry Lacy), who also becomes possessed by the spirit of murdered Pansy Faye (Barrett), a Cockney dance hall girl brought home by estranged Collins brother Carl (John Karlen).

The developing plot spreads to an evil sorcerer, Count Petofi (Thayer David) and a magical Gypsy hand that empowers whoever owns it with supernatural abilities. Petofi empowers a failing painter, Charles Delaware Tate (Roger Davis), so that whatever he paints comes into being. Tate paints a beautiful girl, Amanda Harris (Donna McKechnie), who comes to life. Quentin falls in love with her over all the others and vies with Charles for her affections. Tate also paints a portrait of Quentin that holds the power of his werewolf curse. Whoever owns the painting can determine the fate of Quentin.

When Barnabas arrives from the future, he brings with him a Collins family album. The book falls into Petofi's hands. When he sees that Quentin Collins is somehow alive 70 years into the future, he magically switches minds with Quentin and attempts to time travel himself, where he believes he will be powerful beyond his wildest imagination.

Ultimately, Petofi fails and is killed by a zombielike creature raised from the dead. Tate's studio goes up in flames, and with it, presumably, Quentin's portrait.

When Quentin next appears, he is in the present—1969—as Grant Douglas, the reincarnation of Quentin, who has no memory of his former identity. His supernatural love, Amanda, is now known as actress Olivia Corey (still played by McKechnie). She has been searching for

Quentin, but her time on earth is running out. She strikes a deal with Mr. Death that if she can get Grant to remember himself as Quentin, she will be allowed to live. Grant recovers his past-life memories, but too late, and Amanda/Olivia is taken away by Death.

In the subsequent story lines, Quentin Collins is always Quentin Collins: not the original Quentin, but different family members who bear the same name. Quentin's final appearance is in episode, 1,230, 15 episodes before the end of the series. In that story line the characters are in parallel time in 1847, and Quentin is a Collins son trying to hold the family together despite a curse.

FURTHER READING:
Scott, Kathryn Leigh. *35th Anniversary Dark Shadows Memories*. Los Angeles: Pomegranate Press, 2001.
Scott, Kathryn Leigh, and Jim Pierson, eds. *Dark Shadows Almanac Millennium Edition*. Los Angeles: Pomegranate Press, 2000.
———. *Dark Shadows Almanac: 30th Anniversary Tribute*. Los Angeles: Pomegranate Press, 1995.
Scott, Kathryn Leigh, ed. *The Dark Shadows Companion 25th Anniversary Collection*. Los Angeles: Pomegranate Press, 1990.

comics   Comic books were the first entertainment medium to portray VAMPIRES as complex characters instead of just evil monsters.

Comic books began as vehicles for reprinting newspaper comic strips, but came into their own when original material was created for them. In 1935 *New Fun Comics* (later called *More Fun Comics*) debuted, published by National Periodical Publications, with the concept of recurring characters in an anthology format. Soon after followed *Action Comics* (which introduced Superman in 1938) and *Detective Comics* (which introduced Batman in 1939), thus inaugurating the idea of the costumed superhero. Both Superman and Batman quickly acquired their own titles. The publishing company adopted the name DC (from *Detective Comics*), and a new form of entertainment was born.

The Golden Age
Superheroes required villains who also possessed extraordinary powers, and vampires were among those who answered the call. In what might be considered the first significant appearance of the undead in comics, Batman battled vampires in his fifth appearance (*Detective Comics* 31, September 1939) and finished them off in the following issue. According to Batman's creator, Bob Kane, one of the influences on the development of his hero was the TOD BROWNING 1931 film version of *DRACULA*, starring BELA LUGOSI. The untitled 20-page story, written by Gardner Fox and drawn by Kane, may have been intended as a tribute to BRAM STOKER's character, but Kane's early art is more functional than atmospheric, and Fox's story takes so

many twists and turns that it's possible he didn't decide on the vampire gimmick until well into the second part of the story.

At first the villain appears to be merely a hypnotist, who casts his spell on Batman's fiancée, Julie Madison (soon dropped from the series). Julie is lured into a cruise to Europe, where the menace is revealed as "the arch-criminal known as The Monk." He sends an ape to attack Julie in Paris, tries to drop Batman into a snake pit, then flees for Hungary, uttering threats about WEREWOLVES. In the second half of the story, Batman takes Julie along with him to Hungary, where she is bitten in the throat by The Monk's slinky female companion, Dala. Eventually, both couples end up at The Monk's castle "in the lost mountains of Cathala by the turbulent River Dess." By now the evildoers have definitely been established as vampires, but nonetheless The Monk transforms himself into a wolf briefly, as Kane had seen Lugosi do. Batman trails the vampires to their COFFINS and shoots them with SILVER bullets, more characteristic of a fictional solution to werewolves than vampires.

Batman's battle with The Monk and his mate is heavy with gimmicks as if to compensate for its static technique. Individuals like Kane and Fox grew in sophistication along with the medium, and before long their work improved. Batman changed, too. Reportedly, the editors at DC were not happy with a hero who killed people (even the undead), and Batman was forbidden to engage in such grim behavior for decades to come. Only in more recent years have writers returned to the vengeful figure of 1939, and in the intervening decades there would be much concern about the content of comic books.

Another major hero of the golden age of comics to encounter a vampire was Captain America. Created in 1941 by Joe Simon and Jack Kirby, Captain America was dressed in a costume based on the flag. He immediately became a best seller, and the most popular character produced by Timely Comics, the company that would later be known as Marvel Comics. A product of World War II, this superhero specialized in battling Axis antagonists, and the comics in which he appeared were noted for unusual page layout, exaggerated action poses, and grotesque villains.

In the 1942 story "The Vampire Strikes," Captain America and his kid assistant, Bucky, took on a crazed Japanese scientist, Dr. Togu, who had "delved into the realm of black pseudoscience," and created a formula that could transform him into a vampire. Ugly enough without chemical assistance, Togu after downing his drug became a humanoid monster with leathery wings, huge pointed ears, and fangs several inches long. This nontraditional image of the vampire would gain wide exposure four decades later in such makeup-heavy movies as *Fright Night* (1985). Nothing dismayed Captain America, however, and he greeted the fiend with breezy remarks like, "I think you're a vampire and I'm gonna play rough," or, "Good grief! It seems to be our vampire friend again!" Artist Al Avison's view of the vampire, juxtaposed with the hero's wisecracks, gives the story a surprisingly modern touch despite its dated plot and racial attitudes.

The vampire stories featuring classic characters like Batman and Captain America were only the tip of the iceberg. Innumerable comic book heroes battled the undead during the medium's early days, but these were not exactly horror comics as they are known presently. The stories that came closest were magical in origin. Many comic book anthologies featured stories about magicians; perhaps the most successful was Ibis the Invincible, who made his debut in the first issue of the anthology *Whiz Comics* (February 1940) from Fawcett Publications. Two years later, Ibis got his own comic book, and since his foes were almost invariably supernatural, it can be argued that its appearance marks the genre's official inauguration. In its concluding story, the resurrected Egyptian prince battles the ancient Mayan bad god, Zoltil, in a tale with clear vampiric overtones.

Post–World War II
At the end of World War II, public interest superheroes waned, and a new era dawned in which overall sales rose to new heights as publishers tried every conceivable genre, from humor to crime, from western to romance. In this environment, experiments with horror became increasingly commonplace. Artist Dick Briefer mixed humor with horror beginning with the first issue of *Frankenstein* in 1945, depicting the monster, which he had previously portrayed seriously, as a lovable dimwit whose nose had been inadvertently placed in the middle of his forehead. A forerunner of the 1964 television series THE MUNSTERS, Briefer's comic book featured a variety of genial GHOULS. In the 11th issue, actor "Boris Karload" meets the monsters and is frightened into retiring after an affectionate female vampire plants a harmless kiss on his neck. Considerably less innocent was the lurid "jungle" genre, often no more than an excuse to show scantily clad people engaging in acts of nasty mayhem. In Fox Feature's *Rulah, Jungle Goddess* 17 (August 1948), the title character, clad in what looked like a giraffe-skin bikini, battled the Wolf Doctor. The writer seems to be confusing werewolves and vampires, as most of the tribe of werewolves on view here are women who are not noticeably furry, drink BLOOD, and must be killed with wooden STAKES through their hearts. Rulah spends most of the tale's 10 pages shoving spears bloodily into their torsos while offering helpful remarks like, "Sorry, but you were a doomed creature of evil." Comics like these, along with comparably gruesome offerings in such titles as *Crime Does Not Pay*, were beginning to make the whole medium of comics controversial, especially since it was widely (if not completely accurately) believed to appeal only to children.

In January 1947 Avon Periodicals published one issue of a comic book called *Eerie*, then promptly forgot about it. Yet *Eerie* is sometimes cited as the first horror comic, despite such predecessors as *Ibis the Invincible* or *Frankenstein*. *Eerie* did introduce the format that would characterize the genre during its heyday: a collection of short terror tales with no recurring characters. *Eerie* was revived in 1951, when horror

comics were finally taking the country by storm. Its 12th issue included a 25-page adaptation of Stoker's *Dracula*.

The first regularly published horror anthology was American Comics Group's *Adventures into the Unknown* (fall, 1948). *Adventures into the Unknown*, which lasted for 168 issues over 19 years, may have been a pioneer as far as format was concerned, but the contents were traditional, with stiff drawing and rigid writing. Vampire stories were commonplace, but so were their plots: Boy Meet Girl, Girl Meets Vampire, Boy Saves Girl. The only personal characteristic the vampires seemed to display was a fondness for evening wear.

In April 1950 *Tales from the Crypt* and its companions, *The Vault of Horror* and *The Haunt of Fear,* debuted and created a lasting sensation. The firm that produced them was named EC, and its publisher was William M. Gaines.

Gaines had two unique qualifications for presiding over the creation of what proved to be the classic line of horror comics: He was a lifelong horror fan, and he had inherited a comic book company. His father, M. C. Gaines (who is credited with inventing the comic book as a commercial commodity) had been a major force in the pioneering DC Comics, and then left to start Educational Comics. This was not successful, and when Bill took over he turned it into Entertaining Comics. He dropped high-minded magazines like *Picture Stories from American History* and went with the current trend toward crime comics, but before long horror stories were appearing in their back pages. Gaines plotted these with his editor, Al Feldstein, who when wrote the scripts. They turned the crime comics into *The Vault of Horror, The Haunt of Fear,* and *Tales from the Crypt* (which was called *The Crypt of Terror* for its first three issues).

In lieu of continuing characters, EC provided three hosts to introduce the stories: the Crypt Keeper, the Vault Keeper, and the Old Witch. Based on the narrators of radio horror shows such as *Inner Sanctum* and *The Witch's Tale,* the hosts specialized in graveyard humor and monstrous puns, thus creating a certain aesthetic distance between the reader and visual displays more gruesome than anything seen previously in the mass media. A typical EC story might show a murderer who ends up the victim of gruesome supernatural revenge. In one notorious instance, the parts of a dismembered killer's body were used for baseball equipment. Most of these short narratives were constructed like jokes, with a grim punch line at the end. The writing was unusually literate, and artists were encouraged to develop their own techniques rather than conform to a house style. The result created a sensation.

EC did not neglect vampires, nor did the dozens and dozens of imitators that followed. During the early 1950s, when novels and films with supernatural themes were in a state of hibernation, the boom in horror comics kept vampires in the public eye.

EC's first vampire story, entitled simply "Vampire," appeared in the second issue of *Haunt of Fear* (July 1950). It concerns an isolated Louisiana community where a young doctor concludes that mysterious deaths must be the work of a vampire. His suspicions center on a wealthy neighbor, a dignified gentleman who wears a tuxedo and resides in a neglected mansion with his invalid daughter. When the hero finds two wounds on her neck, he concludes that her father is one of the undead and kills him with a stake. In a twist for an ending, the demure young daughter suddenly admits that she was the vampire and sinks her fangs into the hero. In its modest way, "Vampire" is EC's manifesto on the subject. The most common theme was that anybody might be a bloodsucker, and tales frequently climaxed with an apparently innocent party suddenly lunging for a throat. In this early effort, readers were expected to believe what the hero did: People who wore tuxedos were fiends in human form. In EC's pages, vampires were democratized.

Some EC vampires had roles in show business. Johnny Craig, who had drawn "Vampire," soon became the company's only artist to regularly write his own stories, and in his best work involving the undead he depicted them as entertainers—an occupation that would be taken up two decades later by ANNE RICE's most famous vampire, LESTAT, the rock musician. Craig drew in a clean, elegant style, and his characters looked as if they belonged in the era's advertisements; the contrast between their appearance and their activities was dramatically effective. In "One Last Fling" (*Vault*, October 1951), Harry and Olga are performers who have a knife-throwing act. Olga is bitten while they tour Europe, and after her death returns as a vampire. Harry, who still loves her, is delighted to have her back again and arranges to protect her as they travel across America in their trailer, leaving corpses in every city where they put on their act. Eventually, the strain begins to tell on Harry, and the marriage disintegrates. He demands that she control her addiction and locks her in by sealing their door with a CROSS. Olga can't help herself and drinks Harry's blood while he sleeps. "I just took . . . a little!" she says. In despair, her husband solves their problem in a professional manner. On stage, dying from lack of blood, he announces a show-business first and dispatches his wife with a well-flung stake. What makes the story remarkable is not the gimmick, but rather the emphasis on personalities. It would be years before novelists would follow the lead and begin to treat vampires as complex characters instead of sinister stereotypes.

Craig's sweetest, sickest vampire love story was "Two of a Kind" (*Vault of Horror*, August 1952). An actor and an actress, both stage stars reeking of glamor, fall in love and run off for a ski weekend. "Sounds like a lot of goofy mush, eh?" leers the Vault-Keeper. "Well, don't be impatient! The good part is just beginning!" It turns out that he's a ghoul and she's a vampire, and they end up snowbound in an isolated cabin. Trapped, starving, but committed to the concept that love is as strong as death, they romantically refrain from destroying each other. Instead, she secretly drinks her own blood while he furtively devours his own flesh, and neither survives.

Bill Gaines and Al Feldstein, who wrote almost all the EC horror stories except Craig's, were not so sentimental about relationships. In their typical stories, marriage was little more than a motive for murder. In "Bats in My Belfry," illustrated by Jack Davis (*Tales from the Crypt*, June 1951), an actor becomes unemployable when he loses his hearing, and is nagged by his mercenary wife into seeking treatment from a quack. He is cured by a transplant from a bat's "auditory system," but side effects transform him into a vampire. He makes a nice adjustment, however, putting the bite on his wife and her lover, then retiring to a COFFIN and a new career as a supernatural menace. Employment remained a problem for many EC vampires, however; they weren't aristocrats with ancestral castles, and many of them had to scramble for survival.

Jack Davis, the most prolific of EC's horror artists, was an especially appropriate choice for tales about the undead on the job. A fast worker who used a slightly cartoonish style in even his grimmest work, Davis made a specialty of rumpled, seedy, slack-jawed characters. He eventually became one of the country's most popular illustrators, his work appearing in magazines from *Time* to *TV Guide*. In 1951 he produced EC's funniest and funkiest vampire yarn, "The Reluctant Vampire" (*Vault of Horror*, August 1951). The premise is that a vampire has taken a job as a night watchman in a blood bank. This idea had been around for years (*The New Yorker's* macabre cartoonist, Charles Addams, reported that people were constantly suggesting it to him), but EC picked it up and used it. Mr. Drink, a pathetic derelict, sleeps by day in the trash-filled basement of an abandoned building, and maintains his existence by pilfering supplies from the office. His modest aspirations are achieved, but only until it is announced that the blood bank may close because its quota for donations has not been met. In desperation and disgust, Drink takes to the street for the first time in years, forced to kill and then contribute the blood so he won't lose his job. He works so hard that his boss wins a medal "for patriotic and unselfish effort," but Drink's deeds are discovered and the medal goes to him—pinned to his chest with a STAKE.

Another Jack Davis offering, about a moonlighting taxi driver who consumes his passengers, was entitled "Fare Tonight, Followed by Increasing Clottiness . . ." (*Tales from the Crypt*, June 1953). In tales like this one, which expended most of their energy inventing something new for a vampire to do, the trademarked EC violence was notably restrained. The shock lay not in gruesome visuals but in increasingly outrageous variations on a theme.

The apotheosis of EC's audacity may have been achieved in "A Little Stranger" (*Haunt of Fear*, July 1952). It was drawn by Graham Ingels, the third in EC's triumvirate of top horror artists, who often signed his work "Ghastly." A master at delineating shadowy decay, Ingels used ink to suggest the essence of putrescence, often in a Gothic setting like the one in this tale. In old Bavaria a male werewolf and a female vampire fall in love, but angry villagers see to it that he is shot with a SILVER bullet while she is transfixed by the traditional shaft. The lovers rise from their graves and are wed amid a throng of rotting corpses. Months later, the dead gather once more, this time to celebrate a birth. The vampire lies in her coffin, a baby cradled in her arms, and that infant is the narrator of the story—the Old Witch herself. In this unexpected bit of metafiction, the vampire has become the mother of the very comic book in which she and her daughter appear.

EC used the werewolf-and-vampire combination with surprising frequency, usually in stories with a jack-in-the-box structure characterized by the climactic revelation that the least likely person was a vampire. In Craig's "Werewolf Concerto" (*Vault*, December 1950), a hotel is haunted by a werewolf, and suspicion falls on a glamorous guest. Actually, the manager is the guilty party, but in the end he is killed by the woman, who, although not what she seemed to be, is nonetheless definitely a vampire. In "The Secret," written by Carl Wessler and drawn by George Evans (*Haunt*, March 1954), an orphan is adopted by parents who have undead designs on his blood, but he turns out to have lycanthropic tendencies and ends up eating them instead. Readers are left to wonder which monster was actually tougher (the element of surprise seemed crucial), but by then EC had bigger problems: "The Secret" was one of the stories that publisher William Gaines was summoned to defend before the U.S. Senate Subcommittee to Investigate Juvenile Delinquency.

Suppression of Horror
By 1954 EC's success had inspired a host of inferior imitators, and dozens of different horror comics were on sale each month. Comic book circulation was at an all-time high; close to 70 million copies of issues of all types (not just horror) were published monthly. It was almost inevitable that someone would declare the medium a menace. A New York psychiatrist, Dr. Fredric Wertham, declared in his book *Seduction of the Innocent* (1954) that the lurid images in comic books were corrupting the youth of the nation, causing everything from mental illness to juvenile delinquency. Wertham spearheaded a successful campaign, working up the public to the point where humble newsprint pamphlets became the subject of congressional consideration. The hearings included such enigmatic exchanges as this one between Gaines and subcommittee investigator Herbert Hannoch, who asked the publisher, "Do you know any place where there are such things?"

"As vampires?" asked Gaines.

"Yes."

"No sir," answered Gaines. "This is just fantasy."

Ultimately, the government did nothing about comic books, but the industry did. Unnerved by Wertham, the Senate, and the public, publishers capitulated to an attack on a mass medium that set the pattern for many more to come but remains the most devastating to date. A self-censorship body, the Comics Code Authority, was established by leading comic book companies to regulate content and placate an unduly inflamed nation. Restraints included a ban on almost all horror themes, including "vampires and vampirism." Despite these efforts if not because of them, comics went into a slump that lasted for years. Most publishers went out of business. EC survived and finally flourished by turning its humor comic book, *Mad*, into a black-and-white magazine that was not subject to the Comics Code. The horror comics, however, were dead.

Most of the horror comics that had flourished between 1950 and 1955 were blatant attempts to cash in on EC's success, and thus not much of a loss. One was *Mysterious Adventures*, published by Story Comics. In April 1953 EC's *Tales from the Crypt* presented "Midnight Mess," in which artist Joe Orlando depicted an entire town full of vampires. An innocent traveler, dropping into a restaurant for a late meal, is marked for death when he inadvertently reveals himself as an interloper by failing to digest such dishes as "french-fried scabs." This bit of sick humor, which became EC's most renowned vampire tale when it appeared as a segment of the 1973 movie *The Vault of Horror,* was also popular with the editors of *Mysterious Adventures*. They condensed it to four pages, retitled it "Ghost Town," and printed it in their February 1954 issue. Rival publishers didn't always sink to plagiarism, however, and occasionally came up with a cute idea in the EC vein. In the first issue of Farrell Comics' *Strange Fantasy* (August 1953), anonymous creators had a nice gimmick for the story "Nightmare Merchant": Wearing a black uniform and driving a black van, a "milkman" for the undead makes nightly deliveries of bottled blood to selected customers on his route. The dark inversion of a wholesome ritual makes the story sound far better than it is, however; the art is stiff and the plot makes so many pointless turns that its impact is lost. Only EC had the knack for introducing modern twists into an ancient theme.

A traditional approach was likely to be even less rewarding. "Partners in Blood," a story from Superior Comics' *Journey into Fear* (March 1952), seems almost wholly dependent on Hollywood clichés. A professor and his niece visit a European castle, complete with a hunchbacked caretaker. The owner is the beautiful Baroness von Erich. The professor discovers she is a vampire through time-tested means like family records and mysterious portraits, and on the story's last page he hammers a stake into her. The writer attempts an EC-style surprise: The professor's niece has been recruited to the ranks of the undead. Lest villainy triumph, at the last moment the new vampire and the hunchback accidentally fall off the castle's battlements to their apparent deaths, complete with cries of "Aggggggg . . ." and "Eeeeeee!"

A look at the competition only shows how much EC gave to the undead. Bill Gaines and company defined the horror comic and the vampire's place in it. They used vampirism as a metaphor for everything from addiction to a dead-end job, and also presented the condition as a desirable opportunity to fight injustice, to create a viable subculture, or even to experience undying love. The three EC horror comics published 31 vampire stories and changed this legendary figure from an abstract embodiment of evil into a complex, contemporary figure. It would take other media decades to catch up.

The Horror Renaissance
The suppression of the horror comics could not completely banish the vampire. EC's contribution to popular culture was gradually validated by film adaptations, a television series, and countless reprints, but the undead came crawling back even faster. By 1957 the United States was caught up in a new horror boom that has continued to the present. A package of horror films, including entries in the classic Dracula series from Universal Pictures, was released to television and attracted huge audiences. (See DRACULA FILMS.) At the same time, small studios such as American-International and England's HAMMER FILMS began producing new movies with traditional supernatural themes. Within a year the United States was enjoying a widespread "monster" fad. In 1958 a magazine called *Famous Monsters of Filmland* debuted, published by James Warren and edited by Forrest J. Ackerman. *Famous Monsters* was a celebration of fright films geared to a juvenile audience; its success encouraged other magazines of the same ilk, including Warren's own *Monster World*. With its first issue in 1964, *Monster World* introduced film adaptations in comic book form, a format that would prove very successful.

In 1964 Warren Publications released the premiere issue of *Creepy*, an event that marked the return of the horror comic after a decade spent in an unmarked grave. *Creepy* used a format similar to *Famous Monsters* and *Mad*, larger than a traditional comic book and printed in black-and-white. Technically, it was a magazine for a mature audience and thus not under the jurisdiction of the Comics Code. Nonetheless, it might have had trouble getting distribution if not for the fact that no one any longer believed the once-compelling contention that comics were capable of corrupting the nation.

With its first issue, edited by Russ Jones, *Creepy* presented two vampire tales, both written by Archie Goodwin. A dedicated EC fan, Goodwin became editor with *Creepy*'s fourth issue and wrote nearly all the stories during its most fruitful period. However, it was the artists who most firmly established *Creepy* as a direct descendent of *Tales from the Crypt*. The cover of the first issue was drawn by Jack Davis, who also designed a host named Uncle Creepy. Davis was only one of the EC alumni to come on board, and their artwork was shown to good advantage by large, clear, monochrome reproductions that emphasized detail.

Many of the handsome if horrific images in *Creepy* involved vampires; the undead appeared in two of the first issue's seven stories. "Pursuit of the Vampire," illustrated by Angelo Torres, concerns a visitor to an Austrian village who helpfully rids the region of bloodsuckers, but is ultimately revealed to be a werewolf who wants exclusive grazing privileges for himself. In "Vampires Fly at Dusk," the new bride of a Sicilian count finds evidence that someone in their villa is drinking blood. Convinced that her husband is guilty, she draws back a window's velvet curtains to destroy him with SUNLIGHT. She dies instead, an amnesiac whose mind blotted out memories of her own transgressions. With these two tales, writer Goodwin demonstrated his facility with gimmick stories and also with a more psychological approach; and he showed a fondness for period pieces that was enhanced by Reed Crandall's drawing for "Vampires Fly at Dusk." Crandall, who had worked at EC and soon became a mainstay for *Creepy*, had developed an elegant style based on fine line work that suggested Victorian engravings.

Vampires began appearing in almost every issue, and so did former EC artists: Joe Orlando, George Evans, Al Williamson, John Severin, and Wallace Wood. Johnny Craig made a comeback, initially working under the alias "Jay Taycee," and contributed a piece about a maritime vampire, "Midnight Sail," for the 10th issue. Other artists of equal talent arrived, including Steve Ditko, Alex Toth, Neal Adams, and Gene Colan. Although contributors came and went, overall they represented an impressive collection of talent. Younger artists such as Berni Wrightson and Richard Corben would later make their mark as well. A few opportunities were missed, however. A long adaptation of J. Sheridan Le Fanu's vampire classic "CARMILLA," in the 19th issue, was faithful to the author but was weakened by mediocre artwork.

Warren Publications followed *Creepy* with an identical twin called *Eerie*. Using the same approach and the same contributors, it flourished as well, and was joined in 1969 by VAMPIRELLA, the first regularly scheduled comic magazine to include vampires in its title.

In the 1930s it was discovered that Stoker had failed to properly register *Dracula* for copyright in the United States, making his work available there in the public domain. *Dracula* appeared in many forms, including comics. In 1966 Ballantine Books published a 150-page adaptation of Stoker's novel in paperback form. The script by comic book veterans Otto Binder and Johnny Craig (under the alias Craig Tennis) was an unusually accurate version of a book frequently subject to change, but the artwork by Alden McWilliams, although capable, was lacking in panache. Another version, more condensed at 55 pages, was published in 1973 by Pendulum Press. The art by Nestor Redondo was effectively atmospheric, but perhaps the most remarkable aspect of this version was that it was conceived and marketed as an educational tool for use in schoolrooms. Part of the Now Age Illustrated Series, this *Dracula* was intended to encourage students to develop reading skills—a marked turnaround from the days when horror comics were condemned as a menace to American youth. The supervisor of Now Age, Vince Fago, had been one of the first editors at Marvel Comics, and it was Marvel that would bring vampires back into the mainstream of color comic books.

In 1971 Marvel took on the Comics Code. Stan Lee, Marvel's editor-in-chief, was determined to do a story in which the popular hero Spider-Man could warn readers about the dangers of drug addiction, but this was a topic strictly forbidden by the code. Convinced that the code was outdated and that he was working in a good cause, Lee went ahead with the story and the sky did not fall. In fact it was widely praised, and as a result the Comics Code was revised and modernized. The new guidelines permitted the use of such "traditional" horror figures as vampires, and although the ruling was not exactly a license to splatter the page with gore, the undead were unleashed. Almost immediately, Spider-Man ran into a menace called Morbius, the Living Vampire, whose condition was the result of a scientific experiment gone awry. Marvel's big move, however, came with its creation of THE TOMB OF DRACULA in 1972. *Tomb* quickly rose to the top of the horror comics, reigning until 1979.

In the 1980s dramatic changes occurred in the comic book industry. Once available on virtually every newsstand in the country, comics had gradually become a specialty item with customers including collectors and connoisseurs as well as kids. Comic book shops by the thousands sprang up all over the country and soon accounted for a substantial majority of sales. These changes did not necessarily mean a reduction in the impact of the medium; in fact, certain popular heroes continued to set sales records. Yet publishing programs became more focused, and a number of new "independent" companies were started to share at least a small portion of the market with giants such as Marvel and DC. Theoretically, the independents provided a forum for individualistic projects that were not geared toward huge sales, but in practice economic considerations encouraged comics that were spin-offs from popular films or books. As a result, creativity was not at a premium. Not all of the independents survived. For example, despite its publication of Anne Rice works, Innovation Publishing went out of business.

FRIGHT NIGHT, a Columbia film about a teenager battling a vampire, proved to be quite successful on its release in 1985, and a sequel was being prepared for 1989 when Now Comics introduced its *Fright Night* comic book in 1988. *To Die For* inspired a one-issue adaptation from Blackthorne Publishing; its only distinguishing characteristic was its production in 3-D, complete with red-and-blue glasses. When the soap opera DARK SHADOWS (1966–1971) made a prime-time television comeback in 1991, a comic book from Innovation Publishing was close behind (there had also been a comic book spin-off of the original series, from Gold Key). Innovation Publishing also capitalized on today's most popular vampire fiction by producing versions of Anne Rice's best-selling novels, INTERVIEW WITH THE VAMPIRE, THE VAMPIRE LESTAT, and QUEEN OF THE DAMNED. In her own interviews, Rice has expressed some doubt about the degree to which the comics capture the mood of her work, but they are handsomely produced, employing full color paintings instead of line drawings.

Some of the Warren and EC lines were reprinted, while other publishers produced endless variations on the theme of Dracula. Warp Graphics published *Blood of the Innocent*

(Dracula vs. Jack the Ripper); Malibu Graphics released *Scarlet in Gaslight* (Dracula vs. Sherlock Holmes) and *Ghosts of Dracula* (Dracula vs. Houdini). Warp Graphics produced *Blood of Dracula*, which in turn produced four separate spin-offs: *Dracula in Hell*, *Death Dreams of Dracula*, *The Vampiric Jihad*, and even *Big Bad Blood of Dracula*. Malibu created *Dracula: The Suicide Club*, mixing Stoker's character into a story by Robert Louis Stevenson.

Marvel revived its old *Tomb of Dracula* for at least a four-issue limited series, complete with the writer/artist team of Marv Wolfman and Gene Colan. DC teamed Batman with Dracula in a book-length graphic novel, *Red Rain*, written by Doug Moench and illustrated by Kelly Jones. With Batman once again battling the undead just as he did in the earliest days of the medium, the story of vampires in comic books came full circle.

Bad Girls and Vampire Erotica

The 1990s saw the emergence of the "Bad Girls" and vampire erotica trends, featuring tough, bad-girl sexy heroines, including vampires—a reflection of trends in popular vampire fiction as well. Artist Wendy Snow-Lang's *Night Children*, about contemporary vampires, emphasized sexuality more than gore and was aimed at an adult audience. The independent Chaos! Comics created the vampire bad girls Purgatori and Chastity. Purgatori debuted in March 1995 in an issue of *Lady Death*. According to her story, she is a demonic vampire who in mortal life was a slave girl named Sakkara in ancient Egypt. She was taken into the harem of the lesbian queen of Egypt. The queen intended to marry the male ruler of a neighboring country for political purposes. He demanded that she kill all of her lovers. Sakkara managed to survive the slaughter, and she escaped. She met Kath, a vampire, who turned her into Purgatori, so named because of her association with fallen angels. Purgatori has reddish skin, batlike wings, big fangs, and two horns.

Purgatori appears at the queen's wedding and wreaks her revenge, creating several vampires among the guests, who are destined to be her dedicated enemies. Brazen, she goes on to summon Lucifer himself, and has the chutzpah to bite him. Enraged, he banishes her to Necropolis, the city of the dead, where she encounters Lady Death. Lady Death spurns her and sends her away to be a wandering vampire. Purgatori was joined in 1996 by Chastity Marks, a teenage punk rock roadie who had been made into a vampire in London.

Brainstorm Comics created Luxora in its *Vampirerotica*. Other bad girls of note are Sonja Blue, introduced in the NANCY A. COLLINS novel, *Sunglasses After Dark* (Verotik); Donna Mia, a SUCCUBUS in *Dark Fantasies: Lady Vampire* (Blackout); and Taboo in *Backlash* (Image).

Other vampire comics from this period include *Wetworks*, from Image, which pits commandos against werewolves and the Blood Queen's Vampire Nation, and *Vigil*, starring a female vampire detective created by Arvin Laudermilk, debuting in 1992.

FURTHER READING:
Daniels, Les. "It Seems to Be Our Vampire Friend Again: The Undead in Comic Books," in *The Complete Vampire Companion* by Rosemary Ellen Guiley with J. B. Macabre. New York: Macmillan, 1994.

Connecticut Vampires   See NEW ENGLAND VAMPIRES.

corpses   In VAMPIRE lore, corpses exhibit telltale signs of vampirism. However, these sign are due mostly to natural decomposition and variations, which were not known in earlier times.

In vampire scares in Eastern Europe, almost any sign of decomposition might be greeted as a sign of vampirism, as in this account from 18th-century Wallachia (now part of Romania):

> We opened the coffin, and, to be sure, with most of the dead, one saw that a foaming, evil-smelling, brown-black ichor welled out of their mouths and noses, with the one more, with the other less. And what kind of joy did this cause among the people? They all cried, "Those are vampires, those are vampires!"

Signs of Vampire Corpses
Conditions of corpses often taken as proof of vampirism are

Bloating. A puffy corpse reveals that a vampire is sating itself full on the BLOOD of the living. Bloating actually is caused by a buildup of gases, mostly methane, in the tissue and cavities.

Oozing blood. Trickles of blood from the body orifices, especially the mouth and nose, are signs of a vampire. Since it was believed that corpses could not bleed, the blood therefore had to have come from the living—thus bolstering the notion that vampires suck blood. However, blood inside a corpse coagulates and can sometimes reliquefy, especially if death was sudden. The gases of decomposition are capable of forcing the corpse's own blood up through the mouth and nose. If the body was buried facedown—a common preventative measure against postmortem vampirism—then the body's blood would naturally follow gravity to the mouth and nose. (See BURIAL CUSTOMS.)

Bright blood. A vampire exudes fresh-looking, bright RED blood. Actually, a corpse's blood darkens as the oxygen in the blood is consumed. But some postmortem conditions, such as low temperatures, can prevent all the oxygen from being used up, thus giving the blood a brighter red color.

Ruddiness of skin. Immediately after death, flesh assumes a bluish gray color and gums become pale. Thus, when weeks-old corpses are disinterred and found to be pink and red in complexion, as though in the blush of health, it is a sign of vampirism. However, ruddiness is a natural phase of decomposition, caused by the pooling of the body's own blood in capillaries.

Flaccid limbs. Burial in earlier times usually was swift, especially if the dead were victims of plague or other illness. Consequently, bodies were interred while still stiff from rigor mortis. But rigor mortis is only a stage, followed by flaccidity once again. If a flaccid corpse was handled—as it often was later by investigators—it might appear to move of its own accord, when actually it was being shifted by gravity.

Warm to the touch. Corpses that feel warm seem still alive. However, heat can be generated by decomposition, and it is possible that the temperature of a corpse may actually—albeit temporarily—increase.

Erection. If male corpses exhibit an erection, it is taken as proof of vampirism, for vampires are known to be sexually insatiable. In fact, normal decomposition bloats corpses and can inflate the penis.

Movement in the COFFIN. Corpses naturally shift due to the expanding gases of decomposition. Some modern researchers have suggested that premature burial accounted for the shift in positions found in disinterred bodies—victims awoke in their graves and attempted to claw their way out. This may account for a small number of vampire cases, but the most likely explanation is natural postmortem decay.

Incorruption. Disinterred bodies found not decomposed—or not decomposed enough according to local opinion—are vampires, for the soul cannot be free so long as the body is not decomposed. A trapped soul is unhappy and as a result seeks to avenge itself on the living as a vampire. However, rates of decomposition vary significantly due to a number of factors, such as the means of death, the health of the victim at the time of death, the season (cold slows the process), and the presence of insects, microorganisms, air, and moisture. Some vampire accounts tell of bodies found with few obvious physical signs of decomposition, yet giving off a tremendous stench—the most obvious olfactory sign of a normal decomposition process.

"New" skin and nail growth. A vampire corpse has new growth of skin and nails, thus proving an unnatural life beyond death. This new growth is found beneath skin and nails that had sloughed off. The sloughing off is really a normal phase of decomposition, and merely exposes raw areas of skin and nail beds beneath that appear to be fresh.

Chewed shrouds and limbs. According to lore, the undead chew on their shrouds or on their own limbs. In Slavic lore, vampires whose teeth are like steel can gnaw through anything. As vampires eat their hands and feet, the living relatives and neighbors sicken and die. The vampires then go forth to attack cattle and babies, and other living next of kin.

Natural explanations can be found for chewed shrouds and limbs, however. A "chewed" shroud may have been nothing more than a bit of the cloth clinging to the mouth. "Chewed" limbs were merely partially decomposed.

Noises. When staked, vampire corpses often make noises in protests—even shrieks according to the story of ARNOD PAOLE, an ex-soldier from Serbia who died after falling off a haywagon in the early 1700s. Noises thought to be shrieks and groans most likely were gases forced by the pressure of staking to make noises as they passed the glottis, the slitlike opening between the windpipe and pharynx. (See VRESKET.)

Destruction of Vampire Corpses
Once identified, a vampire corpse should be mutilated it so that its spirit cannot wander the earth. Mutilation practices are a form of sympathetic magic in the belief that what is done to the body also is done to the spirit. Corpses are slashed, staked, and cut up. This is an unpleasant task, for corpses that are filled with decomposing gases will gush forth the most foul contents when violated. Numerous accounts exist of onlookers becoming violently ill or losing consciousness when blasted with the stench of gases, decaying matter, and rotting blood.

In Slavic lore, the best ways to contain and destroy vampires are

Driving an ASPEN STAKE **through the corpse's heart with a shovel.** Aspen is considered the best wood for killing vampires. Other good woods are ashwood, hawthorne, maple, BLACK THORN, or white thorn. Spades, thorns, sharp pieces of IRON, nails, or needles also are effective. The head, belly or navel, and back are good targets as well as the heart. According to lore, the impalement pins the soul to the corpse and prohibits it from further wanderings.

As an extra precaution, it is advisable to wash the staked corpse with boiling wine, scorch it with a hot iron, or fill the coffin with GARLIC or poppy SEEDS.

Stories of European vampires tell of staked corpses resisting destruction and turning their stakes into their own weapons of destruction. In a case from 1647 an Istrian vampire near Laibach was staked with a sharp thorn cudgel. He pulled it out of his body and flung it back at his would-be assassins. MYSLATA OF BLAU reportedly used his stake to fend off dogs.

Decapitating the corpse with a shovel belonging to either a gravedigger or a sexton. A gravedigger's shovel possesses a certain supernatural potency from its association with the dead. A sexton's shovel possesses the holy power of God. The corpse is covered with a cloth to avoid sprays of the vampire's blood. Anyone unlucky enough to be hit by a vampire's blood will either go

mad or die instantly. The severed head should be stuffed with garlic, coins, or stones, and then placed under the corpse's arm, at its buttocks, or at its feet. The mutilated corpse may be reburied, but with extra dirt between the head and the torso. It is better to rebury the pieces at a CROSSROADS or distant location. In some cases, the head and body are reburied in separate locations or are thrown into a river.

Burning the body. When staking or other remedies fail to stop a vampire, the body is burned as a final solution. In some parts of Europe, both staking and burning were done. Among Slavs around the Black Sea, all corpses once were burned as a prevention against vampirism.

Cremation proved difficult in earlier times, when a bonfire was the chief means of burning. Bodies do not burn well due to their high water content; nor do they burn on the sides they lie on because of a lack of sufficient oxygen for combustion. Village bonfires did not reach the 1,600-degree Fahrenheit temperature necessary to burn a single adult body to ash, in about 45 minutes. As a result, the village hangmen usually were left with the task of chopping the partially burned bodies into bits that were small enough to burn more easily. Sometimes a hangman had to labor away for an entire day to dispatch a single vampire. In some cases, it was a preferred alternative to burn only body parts, especially the heart or the head. Destroying either part would put an end to the REVENANT. The failure of bodies to burn well only reinforced the conviction of the reality of vampires.

A hazard of burning—and perhaps why it is a measure of last resort—is that the buildup of the gases in a decomposing corpse can cause flames to shoot out of its mouth and orifices.

See also MYSLATA OF BLAU; LEWIN WITCH.

FURTHER READING:
Barber, Paul. *Vampires, Burial and Death: Folklore and Reality.* New Haven, Conn.: Yale University Press, 1988.
Dundes, Alan, ed. *The Vampire: A Casebook.* Madison: University of Wisconsin Press, 1998.

Corwin Family Vampire   See WOODSTOCK VAMPIRE.

Count Dracula   VAMPIRE character created by BRAM STOKER in his novel *DRACULA* (1897), and the most famous fictional vampire of all. Count Dracula's name has become synonymous with vampires.

At some point in his work on the novel, Stoker named his vampire "Count Wampyr." But in 1892 his notes show the name Count Dracula. Stoker found the name in *An Account of the Principalities of Wallachia and Moldavia* (1820) by William Wilkinson, which he read while staying in WHITBY, ENGLAND. The 15th-century Wallachian voivode

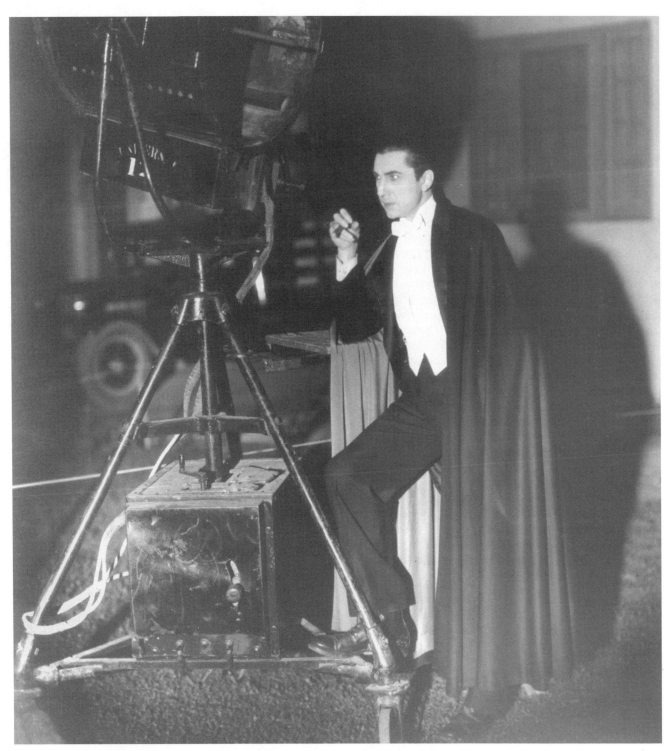

Bela Lugosi in his Count Dracula finery on the set of Universal Pictures (Courtesy Vampire Empire Archives)

(prince) VLAD TEPES was known as "Dracula" for "son of the devil." Stoker liked the name and its meaning, and so he lifted it for his vampire. He did not base the count on Vlad, except to describe Dracula as being descended from a line of fierce warrior noblemen. Nor did he base Dracula on ELIZABETH BATHÓRY, as some researchers have suggested.

Count Dracula is mysterious and unknowable. He spends little time onstage in the novel, adding to the aura of mystery around him. Unlike the modern vampires created by ANNE RICE and other authors, Count Dracula does not concern himself with morality. He is a fiend and a monster. If he agonizes over issues about good and evil and the morality of his actions, the reader is not privy to it in *Dracula*. His first-person voice explaining his thoughts and motives is never heard. All that is known about Count Dracula comes through the perceptions and experiences of others. *Dracula* is told via the letters and diaries of the principal characters.

Appearance, Characteristics, and Powers

Stoker relied on other fiction models and his imagination for his description of Count Dracula. The limited folklore accounts of vampires that were available in English discussed primarily the conditions of disinterred CORPSES, going into detail about the ruddiness of complexions, flaccidity of limbs, growth of hair and nails, and so forth.

Count Dracula followed well-known fictional vampires such as LORD RUTHVEN, Carmilla and VARNEY THE VAMPIRE, all of whom come from aristocratic stock and possess a sensual allure that draws others to them. Ruthven is rakishly seductive; Carmilla is beautiful and seductive; Varney manages to prey upon young women while being "hideous" in appearance. While the count's preying upon young women has sexual overtones, the figure of the count himself is unappealing. After his arrival in England, his countenance becomes more youthful, and his hair darkens—but he is still unattractive.

Stoker also was inspired by Transylvanian folklore he gleaned from an article, "Transylvania Superstitions" (1885) by Mme. EMILY DE LASZOWSKI GERARD, which describes the evil NOSFERATU or vampire, as well as a secret devil's academy called the SCHOLOMANCE, where apprentices learn all the demonic arts and magical skills.

The reader first encounters the count through the eyes of Jonathan Harker, a young English solicitor's clerk who has been sent to the count's castle in TRANSYLVANIA to finalize a real estate purchase—Carfax Abbey in London. Harker's first glimpse of the count comes late at night upon his arrival at the castle:

> Within, stood a tall old man, clean shaven save for a long white moustache, and clad in black from head to foot, without a single speck of color about him anywhere.

When the count grasps his hand, Harker notices he has an exceedingly strong grip, so strong it makes Harker wince. Dracula's flesh is so cold it seems more like the flesh of a dead man than a living one. After Harker arrives at the castle, is settled and he dines, he has his first opportunity to really study the count, and finds him to be "of a very marked physiognomy":

> His face was a strong—a very strong—aquiline, with high bridge of the thin nose and peculiarly arched nostrils; with lofty domed forehead, and hair growing scantily around the temples, but profusely elsewhere. His eyebrows were very massive, almost meeting over the nose, and with bushy hair that seemed to curl in its own profusion. The mouth, as far as I could see under the heavy moustache, was fixed and rather cruel-looking, with

peculiarly sharp white teeth: these protruded over the lips, whose remarkable ruddiness showed astonishing vitality in a man of his years. For the rest, his ears were pale and at the tops extremely pointed; the chin was broad and strong, and the cheeks firm though thin. The general effect was one of extraordinary pallor.

Harker also notices the Count's hands:

> . . . they were rather coarse—broad, with squat fingers. Strange to say, there were hairs in the center of the palm. The nails were long and fine, and cut to a sharp point.

The elements of this physique are wolfish; one of Stoker's sources was SABINE BARING-GOULD's *The Book of Werewolves* (1865).

As his stay at the castle becomes more of an imprisonment, Harker observes other horrors about his host. He never eats food. He is about only during the hours of darkness. He casts no reflection in MIRRORS. He is drawn to BLOOD. He has the ability to crawl lizardlike down the sheer face of the outer castle wall. He commands three women who attempt to vampirize Harker. He materializes in specks of swirling dust that glitter in the moonlight. He commands wolves.

Harker's greatest shock comes when he finds the count lying in a box of earth down in the castle's chapter, and knows the horrible truth about him:

> There lay the Count, but looking as if his youth had been half renewed, for the white hair and moustache were changed to dark iron-grey; the cheeks were fuller, and the white skin seemed ruby-red underneath; the mouth was redder than ever, for on the lips were gouts of fresh blood, which trickled from the corners of the mouth and ran over the chin and neck. Even the deep, burning eyes seemed set amongst swollen flesh, for the lids and pouches underneath were bloated. It seemed as if the whole awful creature were simply gorged with blood; he lay like a filthy leech, exhausted with his repletion.

Thoroughly revolted, Harker can barely bring himself to touch the count and search for a key that will enable him to escape the castle. As he does so, the count seems to make a mocking smile at him that nearly drives Harker mad. Harker is appalled at the thought that he is helping the count come to England, where undoubtedly he will attack others to satisfy his bloodlust. He is seized with an overwhelming desire to destroy Dracula, "to rid the world of such a monster." He grabs a shovel and lifts it high to strike at the "hateful face." But just as he does so, Dracula's head turns and his eyes, "with all their blaze of basilisk horror," paralyze Harker. The shovel turns in his hand, and all he succeeds in doing is making a deep gash in the count's forehead. As the lid to the box falls, the last glimpse Harker has is of "the bloated face, bloodstained and fixed with a grin of malice which would have held its own in nethermost hell."

Thus the inhuman monster, the unspeakable evil, is unleashed upon England, a symbol of the civilized world.

When the count arrives in England, he leaps off his ship in the form of a wolf. After he ensconces himself and his vampire women in the abbey, he mesmerizes and takes over the unfortunate insane R. M. RENFIELD in Dr. John Seward's asylum, turning him into a mindless slave. He preys upon 19-year-old Lucy Westenra, coming to her bedroom in window in the form of a BAT. He is a cunning predator, able to slip through cracks and under doorways as a mist, and make himself invisible to others. He can hypnotize others and send them telepathic commands. As he preys upon others, their blood rejuvenates him. His hair darkens, and his appearance becomes more youthful, but is still hard and sinister. He can be out in daylight, though SUNLIGHT weakens him, and he cannot SHAPE-SHIFT then. He casts no SHADOW. His RED, demonic eyes haunt others. (See EYE.)

About two-thirds of the way through the novel, PROFESSOR ABRAHAM VAN HELSING, the vampire expert, delivers a long monologue on Dracula and the powers of vampires. Dracula's family was great and noble, he says, and in life the count was fearless and intelligent—a statesman, soldier, and alchemist. But some members of the family served the devil, and Dracula himself attended the Scholomance and learned every dark art possible. Dracula "is known everywhere that men have been. In old Greece, in old Rome: he flourished in Germany all over, in France, in India, even in the Chersonese [Malaysian region]; and in China, so far from us in all ways, there even is he, and the peoples fear him at this day," Van Helsing says.

The count has all the powers of vampires, which Van Helsing calls the *nosferatu*:

> The *nosferatu* do not die like the bee when he sting once. He is only stronger; and being stronger, have yet more power to work evil. This vampire which is amongst us is of himself so strong in person as twenty men; he is of cunning more than mortal, for his cunning can be the growth of ages, he have still the aids of necromancy, which is, as his etymology imply, the divination of the dead, and all the dead that he can come nigh to are for him at command; he is bright, and more than brute: he is devil in callous, and the heart of him is not; he can, within limitations, appear at will when, and where, and in any of the forms that are to him; he can, within his range, direct the elements: the storm, the fog, the thunder; he can command all the meaner things: the rat, the owl, and the bat—the moth, and the fox, and the wolf; he can grow and become small; and he can at times vanish and come unknown.

Dracula shows no remorse for his horrifying predations. Like an animal, he must kill in order to survive. But to the cast of principal characters, he is an abomination that must be destroyed. Mina Harker, who is vampirized herself and is in danger of becoming like Lucy, is the sole character to express sympathy for Dracula as a lost soul.

In the end, Dracula meets a violent end. The others, now VAMPIRE HUNTERS, pursue him as he goes back to his natural land in Transylvania. They catch up with a band of GYPSIES who are carrying his box of earth, just as dusk is

An early cover of Bram Stoker's Dracula *showing Count Dracula crawling down the wall of his castle* (Courtesy Vampire Empire Archives)

approaching. Inside, the count is deathly pale and waxenlike, with his red eyes glaring open. As the sun sinks, a triumphant look comes over him. But Jonathan Harker slashes his throat with a knife, and his cohort Quincey Morris plunges a bowie knife into his heart. In the drawing of a breath, the count crumbles to dust and vanishes.

Romanticizing the Count

The job of romanticizing Dracula was left to HAMILTON DEANE, the son of a friend of Stoker's. Working with JOHN L. BALDERSTON, Deane adapted *Dracula* for the stage. They presented Count Dracula as a suave, sophisticated gentleman in evening dress, including a black opera cape. The cape became a standard part of the count's wardrobe in numerous portrayals that followed, and a staple of popular vampire lore. Deane simplified the novel, and in the end Dracula is staked, not stabbed.

TOD BROWNING's 1931 movie *Dracula* was adapted more from Deane's stage play than from the novel, and when the magnetic BELA LUGOSI appeared as the sophisticated count, women the world over swooned for him. Lugosi's Hungarian accent and measured English also became incorporated into portrayals of the count. Draculas to come had to speak slowly and in a heavy foreign accent. Browning's Dracula is staked at the end, too.

The sophisticated image of Dracula was reinforced by other leading Draculas such as CHRISTOPHER LEE, Louis Jourdan, and Frank Langella, sweeping about in their grand capes. Lee especially revised the stiff image of Dracula established by Deane and Lugosi, portraying a high-action, violent, and crafty villain in the HAMMER FILMS productions involving the count.

The only film of note to portray Dracula more as Stoker envisioned him was NOSFERATU, made in 1922 as a silent film starring MAX SCHRECK and remade in 1979 starring Klaus Kinski. *Nosferatu* features a monster even more horrid and repulsive than Count Dracula—an ugly, ratlike vampire with long, pointed nails and two front teeth that are long and sharp and better suited for biting than canine teeth. The vampire GRAF ORLOCK becomes the first vampire to die by SUNLIGHT, thereby creating another institution in popular lore. Orlock simply fades into nothingness when he is hit by sunlight. Film and fiction vampires since who are not staked are struck by sunlight and die dramatically, by bursting into flames and incinerating.

Over time, Dracula's appearance and demeanor have become a caricature: a white-faced, fanged, red-lipped man with a widow's peak, slicked-back black hair, and high-collared black cape. This cartoonish "Dracula" has graced almost every commercial product imaginable. Dracula has been parodied in comedies and by characters such as "Count Duckula."

Symbolic Meanings of Count Dracula

Dracula can be read as a horror story about the primordial battle between good and evil or interpreted in terms of sexual repression, alienation, and the decline of Victorian England. Count Dracula has been analyzed extensively from perspectives of Victorian mores, Freudian psychology, Jungian psychology, and the feminist movement. He is seen as a symbol of humanity's greatest fears: fear of death, fear of the grave, fear of the dark, fear of the demonic, fear of all things—and people—strange and alien. He is the Outsider. He is a symbol of alienation itself, the sense of isolation and alienation that are part of industrialized society.

Most often the count is interpreted in terms of sexual desire. Dracula represents unleashed desire and eroticism, the consequences of wantonness, the lure of the forbidden.

Count Dracula has been played in films and portrayed in novels many times; artists search for new twists and nuances. His story line is changed. His countenance is more often alluring than repulsive. Vampire characters inspired by Count Dracula have acquired more soul and have more depth and dimension than the count. Rice's vampires, for example, put themselves through psychoanalysis on the page. Yet the glamorous vampire has not sounded the death knell of vampires or of the count. No matter how great the popularity of other vampires, Count Dracula remains the definitive human bloodsucker. No other character has eclipsed him, not even LESTAT DE LIONCOURT. There is always yet another tale that can be told of the most famous monster of all.

FURTHER READING:

Auerbach, Nina. *Our Vampires, Ourselves.* Chicago: University of Chicago Press, 1995.

Carter, Margaret L., ed. *The Vampire in Literature: a critical bibliography.* Ann Arbor: UMI Research Press, 1989.

Frost, Brian J. *The Monster with a Thousand Faces: Guises of the Vampire in Myth and Literature.* Bowling Green, Ohio: Bowling Green State University Popular Press, 1989.

Holte, James Craig, ed. *The Fantastic Vampire: Studies in the Children of the Night, Selected Essays from the Eighteenth International Conference on the Fantastic in the Arts.* Westport, Conn.: Greenwood Press, 2002.

Leatherdale, Clive, ed. *Bram Stoker's Dracula Unearthed.* Weston-on-Sea, Essex, England: Desert Island Books, 1998.

Senf, Carol A. *The Vampire in 19th Century English Literature.* Bowling Green, Ky.: Bowling Green State University Popular Press, 1988.

Stoker, Bram. *Dracula.* New York: Grosset & Dunlap, 1931.

Count Dracula Fan Club   Organization founded in 1965 by JEANNE KEYES YOUNGSON. In 2000 the club was renamed the VAMPIRE EMPIRE.

Count Yorga (1970)   Campy cult film about a COUNT DRACULA–type VAMPIRE, written and directed by Bob Kelljan.

The opening of the film explains the previous arrival of the Bulgarian Count Yorga (ROBERT QUARRY) to Los Angeles, in his wooden crate on a cargo ship. He moves into an old mansion high in the hills with his manservant, Brudah (Edward Walsh), who had collected the crate. He becomes a medium.

A neighbor, Donna (Donna Anderson), asks Yorga to hold a seance to contact her dead mother (Julie Conners), a friend of the count's. The seance, at Donna's home, is attended by several people, including her boyfriend, Michael (Michael Macready), and friends Paul (Michael Murphy) and Erica (Judith Lang). When the seance gets scary, Donna faints. The count carries her to a couch, but he hypnotizes her to do his bidding from then on.

After the seance, Paul and Erica take the count home, but their van becomes stuck in mud outside his mansion. Wolves begin to howl. They divert themselves by having sex and falling asleep. Erica is awakened by noises outside, and when she pulls back the curtains of the van, she is startled to see the snarling face of Yorga. Paul leaps outside to do battle, but the count knocks him out and then bites Erica on the neck.

Later Erica cannot remember how she got the wounds on her neck, but she feels exhausted. She goes to Doctor

Count Yorga (Robert Quarry) pursues a victim in The Return of Count Yorga. *(Author's collection)*

Hayes (Roger Perry), who is mystified by the wounds and prescribes steak for anemia.

Meanwhile, the boyfriends Paul and Michael suspect Yorga of having a sinister influence over their girlfriends. They find Erica eating a CAT and summon the doctor. Paul transfuses his BLOOD into Erica. But Hayes refuses to believe that Yorga is a vampire.

Back at his mansion, Yorga is holding court with two vampire women, one of whom is Donna's mother. He abducts Erica. Paul attempts to rescue her, but meets a violent death at the hands of Brudah.

The count summons Donna. Michael and Hayes—who now is convinced that Yorga is a vampire—break furniture to make STAKES and CROSSES and go to the mansion. Fights ensue. The vampire women rip up Hayes and he dies. Michael stabs Brudah in the stomach and kills him. He confronts the count with his stake and cross, but the vampire shoves Donna's mother into the stake and escapes.

Michael pursues him and manages to stake him. The count dies in a crumble of dust. Michael and Donna are attacked by the vampire women, now including Erica. Michael manages to lock them in the cellar. In a final twist, Michael is killed by Donna, who has become a vampire herself.

Count Yorga became an instant hit and enduring cult classic, launching Quarry to fame as a horror film star. Made for a mere $64,000, it grossed several million dollars for the studio, American International Pictures.

A sequel, *The Return of Count Yorga,* was released by American International in 1971, with Kelljan as director. Yorga, played again by Quarry, is resurrected from his fatality without explanation. He is attracted to Cynthia Nelson (Mariette Hartley) and offers her eternal life. She rejects him. He sends a horde of female vampires to ravage her family. Cynthia's fiancé, David (Roger Perry), fatally stabs Yorga in the heart. However, Yorga had turned him into a vampire, and he turns on Cynthia and bites her in the neck.

Plans for a third Count Yorga film were dropped when the studio shifted its attention to producing and promoting *BLACULA.*

Coventry Street Vampire (1922)   VAMPIRE scare in London. On the night of the full MOON in April 1922, an enormous black BAT-like creature with a six-foot wingspan was reported flying around West Drayton Church in London. Several people said they witnessed it dive down into the CEMETERY and prowl about the tombs. Two policemen gave it chase, causing it to emit a blood-curdling screech and fly away. An old man opined that the creature was the spirit of a vampire who, in the 1890s, had murdered a woman by drinking her BLOOD.

Later, on April 16th around 6 A.M., a man walking down Coventry Street in London's West End felt himself seized by an invisible presence and bitten on the neck. He felt as though his blood were being sucked out, and he fell unconscious. When he awakened in Charing Cross Hospital, doctors said he appeared to have been stabbed with a thin tube.

Two and a half hours later, a second unconscious man was brought to the same hospital; he was bleeding heavily from the neck. When he regained consciousness, he also told of being attacked by an invisible presence while walking down Coventry Street. Later in the evening, a third victim with the same story and wounds was admitted to the hospital. All three said they'd been stabbed at exactly the same spot.

Rumors of a vampire on the loose circulated; the police had no apparent leads. Another rumor circulated that the police had hired a VAMPIRE HUNTER, who had tracked the creature down and taken it to Highgate Cemetery, where he drove a STAKE through its heart. That rumor apparently originated in a Covent Garden pub.

It is not known whether the mystery of the Coventry Street Vampire was ever solved, but the attacks apparently stopped.

See also HIGHGATE VAMPIRE; MOTHMAN.

FURTHER READING:
Slemen, Thomas. *Strange But True: Mysterious and Bizarre People*. New York: Barnes & Noble, 1998.

cremation   See BURIAL CUSTOMS; CORPSES.

Cressi Werewolves (1604)   French WEREWOLF case involving five accused sorcerers in the village of Cressi near Lausanne.

Arrested and put on trial in 1604, the accused confessed to sorcery, SHAPE-SHIFTING, and witchcraft. They said they changed themselves into wolves and attended SABBATS. They kidnapped a boy and took him to one of their infernal gatherings, where they killed him, drank his BLOOD, and offered him to the devil. They hacked his body into pieces, boiled them, and ate them. They used the fat for their magical OINTMENTS.

The five were condemned to death and were burned to ASHES.

FURTHER READING:
Summers, Montague. *The Werewolf*. New York: Bell Publishing, 1966.

Croglin Grange Vampire   VAMPIRE attack recorded in Victorian England. The story of the Croglin Grange Vampire is set in Cumberland, now part of Cumbria. A vivid account of the incident was recorded by Dr. Augustus Hare, a clergyman of good repute who lived in a rectory in Devonshire, in his autobiographical book, *Memorials of a Quiet Life* (1871). Though there are plausible elements to the story, it has not been historically verified. There is no record of a "Croglin Grange," but there is a Croglin Low Hall.

Hare, an author of numerous European guidebooks, claimed to have had at least one encounter with a ghost himself. Shortly after being installed at his rectory, he entered his study one day to find an old woman seated in the armchair by the fire. The woman appeared to be real, but Hare knew that was impossible—there was no such woman in or near the rectory. He shrugged, chalked it up to indigestion, and sat down on her in the chair. She promptly vanished. The next day he encountered her again in a passage and boldly rushed up against her. Again she vanished. After a third encounter, Hare had to find out who this mysterious woman was. He wrote to his sister and asked her to check with two spinsters who were sisters of the clergyman who had preceded him at the rectory. Upon hearing about Hare's encounters, the spinsters were distressed. The ghost was their mother, they said, and she had appeared to them frequently during their stay at the rectory. They had hoped that upon their departure the old lady would be at rest.

Hare heard other stories of family ghosts. When a man named Captain Fisher related to him the chilling story of the Croglin Grange vampire, Hare recorded it as it was told. The story he heard may already have been expanded for the benefit of entertainment, but as a folktale, it may have some basis in fact. Here is Hare's rendition of the story:

> Fisher may sound a very plebeian name, but this family is of very ancient lineage, and for many hundreds of years they have possessed a very curious place in Cumberland, which bears the weird name of Croglin Grange. The great characteristic of the house is that never at any period of its very long existence has it been more than one story high, but it has a terrace from which large grounds sweep away towards the church in the hollow, and a fine distant view.
>
> When, in lapse of years, the Fishers outgrew Croglin Grange in family and fortune, they were wise enough not to destroy the long-standing characteristic of the place by adding another story to the house, but they went away to the south, to reside at Thorncombe near Guildford, and they let Croglin Grange.
>
> They were extremely fortunate in their tenants, two brothers and a sister. They heard their praises from all quarters. To their poorer neighbors they were all that is

most kind and beneficent, and their neighbors of a higher class spoke of them as a most welcome addition to the little society of the neighbourhood. On their parts the tenants were greatly delighted with their new residence. The arrangement of the house, which would have been a trial to many, was not so to them. In every respect Croglin Grange was exactly suited to them.

The winter was spent most happily by the new inmates of Croglin Grange, who shared in all the little social pleasures of the district, and made themselves very popular. In the following summer, there was one day which was dreadfully, annihilatingly hot. The brothers lay under the trees with their books, for it was too hot for any active occupation. The sister sat in the verandah and worked, or tried to work, for, in the intense sultriness of that summer day, work was next to impossible. They dined early, and after dinner they still sat out in the verandah, enjoying the cool air which came with evening, and they watched the sun set, and the moon rise over the belt of trees which separated the grounds from the churchyard, seeing it mount the heavens till the whole lawn was bathed in silver light, across which the long shadows from the shrubbery fell as if embossed, so vivid and distinct were they.

When they separated for the night, all retiring to their rooms on the ground-floor (for, as I said, there was no upstairs in that house), the sister felt that the heat was still so great that she could not sleep, and having fastened her window, she did not close the shutters—in that very quiet place it was not necessary—and, propped against the pillows, she still watched the wonderful, the marvelous beauty of that summer night.

Gradually she became aware of two lights, two lights which flickered in and out in the belt of trees which separated the lawn from the churchyard, and as her gaze became fixed upon them, she saw them emerge, fixed in a dark substance, a definite ghastly *something,* which seemed every moment to become nearer, increasing in size and substance as it approached. Every now and then it was lost for a moment in the long shadows which stretched across the lawn from the trees, and then it emerged larger than ever, and still coming on—on. As she watched it, the most uncontrollable horror seized her. She longed to get away, but the door was close to the window and the door was locked on the inside, and while she was unlocking it she must be for an instant nearer to *it.* She longed to scream, but her voice seemed paralyzed, her tongue glued to the roof of her mouth.

Suddenly—she could never explain why afterwards—the terrible object seemed to turn to one side, seemed to be going round the house, not to be coming to her at all, and immediately she jumped out of bed and rushed to the door, but as she was unlocking it she heard scratch, scratch, scratch upon the window, and saw a hideous brown face with flaming eyes glaring in at her. She rushed back to the bed, but the creature continued to scratch, scratch, scratch upon the window. She felt a sort of mental comfort in the knowledge that the window was securely fastened on the inside. Suddenly the scratching sound ceased, and a kind of pecking sound took its place. Then, in her agony, she became aware that the creature was unpicking the lead! The noise continued, and a diamond pane of glass fell into the room. Then a long bony finger of the creature came in and turned the handle of the window, and the window opened, and the creature came in; and it came across the room, and her terror was so great that she could not scream, and it came up to the bed, and it twisted its long, bony fingers into her hair, and it dragged her head over the side of the bed and—it bit her violently in the throat.

As it bit her, her voice was released, and she screamed with all her might and main. Her brothers rushed out of their rooms, but the door was locked on the inside. A moment was lost while they got a poker and broke it open. Then the creature had already escaped through the window, and the sister, bleeding violently from a wound in the throat, was lying unconscious over the side of the bed. One brother pursued the creature, which fled before him through the moonlight with gigantic strides, and eventually seemed to disappear over the wall into the churchyard. Then he rejoined his brother by his sister's bedside. She was dreadfully hurt, and her wound was a very definite one, but she was of strong disposition, not either given to romance or superstition, and when she came to herself she said, "What has happened is most extraordinary and I am very much hurt. It seems inexplicable, but of course there is an explanation, and we must wait for it. It will turn out that a lunatic has escaped from some asylum and found his way here." The wound healed, but the doctor who was sent for to her would not believe she could bear so terrible a shock so easily, and insisted that she must have change, mental and physical; so her brothers took her to Switzerland.

Being a sensible girl, when she went abroad, she threw herself at once into the interests of the country she was in. She dried plants, she made sketches, she went up mountains, and, as autumn came on, she was the person who urged that they should return to Croglin Grange. "We have taken it," she said, "for seven years, and we have only been there one; and we shall always find it difficult to let a house which is only one story high, so we had better return there; lunatics do not escape every day." As she urged it, her brothers wished nothing better, and the family returned to Cumberland. From there being no upstairs in the house, it was impossible to make any great change in their arrangements. The sister occupied the same room, but it is unnecessary to say she always closed her shutters, which, however, as in many old houses, always left one top pane of the window uncovered. The brothers moved, and occupied a room together exactly opposite that of their sister, and they always kept loaded pistols in their room.

The winter passed most peacefully and happily. In the following March, the sister was suddenly awakened by a sound she remembered only too well—scratch, scratch, scratch upon the window, and, looking up, she saw, climbed to the topmost pane of the window, the same hideous brown shrivelled face, with glaring eyes, looking in at her. This time she screamed as loud as she could. Her brothers rushed out of their room with pistols, and out the front door. The creature was already scudding away across the lawn. One of the brothers fired and hit it in the leg, but still with the other leg it continued to make way, scrambled over the wall into the churchyard, and seemed to disappear into a vault which belonged to a family long extinct.

The next day the brothers summoned all the tenants of Croglin Grange, and in their presence the vault was opened. A horrible scene revealed itself. The vault was full of coffins; they had been broken open, and their contents, horribly mangled and distorted, were scattered over the floor. One coffin alone remained intact. Of that the lid had been lifted, but still lay loose upon the coffin. They raised it, and there, brown, withered, shrivelled, mummified, but quite entire, was the same hideous figure which had looked in at the windows of Croglin Grange, with the marks of a recent pistol-shot in the leg; and they did the only thing that can lay a vampire—they burnt it.

The story of the "old vampire" remains alive in Cumbrian lore. Croglin Low Hall still exists, part of an ancient countryside that was settled long before the Romans arrived in Britain. The churchyard is about one mile away. It has no tomb as described in the story; the tomb may have been an embellishment.

FURTHER READING:
Guiley, Rosemary Ellen. *Vampires Among Us.* New York: Pocket Books, 1991.

cross   One of the oldest amulets against evil, predating Christianity by many centuries. The cross has been associated with sun deities and the heavens, and in ancient times may have represented divine protection and prosperity. In

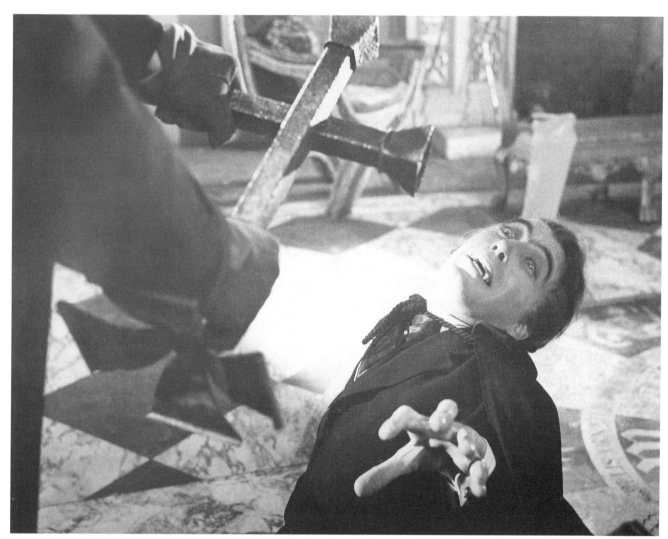

Professor Abraham Van Helsing (Peter Cushing) uses candlesticks to make a cross against Count Dracula (Christopher Lee) in Horror of Dracula. *(Author's collection)*

Christianity, it symbolizes the crucified Christ and the power of his body and sacrificed BLOOD, and thus everything that is good and divine.

The cross or the sign of the cross is considered to be one of the most potent protections against evil. It is employed to exorcize demons and devils, ward off INCUBI and SUCCUBI, prevent bewitchment of man and beast, protect crops from being blasted by witches, and force vampires to flee. During the Middle Ages, inquisitors often wore crosses or made the sign of a cross while in the presence of accused witches in order to ward off any evil spells they might cast. People crossed themselves routinely before the smallest task, just in case an evil presence was near.

To prevent vampires from leaving their graves, GOLD crosses are placed in the corpse's mouth or laid on the body in the COFFIN. (See BURIAL CUSTOMS; *DOPPELSAUGER*.)

In Slavic lore, vampires leave their graves at night and rock to and fro upon wayside crosses, wailing continually.

The cross is prominent in vampire literature, film, and pop culture; no competent VAMPIRE HUNTER would be without it. One of the most memorable scenes in vampire film is COUNT DRACULA shrinking from a large cross held up by PROFESSOR ABRAHAM VAN HELSING.

Not all fictional vampires obey folklore, however. To introduce plot twists, writers such as ANNE RICE have created formidable and powerful vampires who are not affected by crosses or any holy objects, which makes them more dangerous and difficult to defeat.

In the first chapter of BRAM STOKER's *DRACULA*, Jonathan Harker travels in the BORGO PASS to the count's castle, and sees many cross shrines along the roadside. These shrines still exist, and are sometimes decorated with a crucified Christ or with angels. In the local lore they are considered protection for the area.

crossroads   The intersection of roads and pathways are dark and dangerous places, according to widespread and ancient superstitions. Crossroads are unhallowed ground; haunted by vampires, demons, the devil, witches, fairies, ghosts, and a host of supernatural creatures, such as trolls and spectral hounds. Spirits who like to lead travelers astray, like the Will-O'-Wisp, also haunt crossroads.

Crossroads especially are no place to be after midnight, when VAMPIRES rise from their graves. According to some superstitions, they take their shrouds with them and station themselves at crossroads, looking for victims. In Romanian lore, LIVING VAMPIRES—people who are destined to become vampires after death—send their souls out of their bodies at night to wander at crossroads with reanimated CORPSES.

Crossroads also play roles in various funeral and BURIAL CUSTOMS designed to keep the dead from returning to harass or attack the living. An old Welsh custom calls for corpses to be laid down at every crossroads and prayed over as they are carried from house to graveyard, in order to protect the corpse from the evil spirits and to prevent the return of the dead. In the lore of parts of Germany, the return of the dead is prevented by smashing the pottery of the deceased at a crossroads.

In many locales, victims of murder and SUICIDES traditionally were buried at crossroads. Suicides, who committed the sin of taking their own lives, were not allowed to be buried in the consecrated ground of churchyard CEMETERIES. Some murder victims were taken to crossroads because it was feared their spirits would be troubled and restless and would return to the living to take revenge. Burial at a crossroads would keep them in place.

Superstitions are often contradictory from place to place, and so it is with the supernatural nature of crossroads. As mentioned earlier, vampires are believed to stalk their victims at crossroads, their place of power. Conversely, crossroads are said to neutralize malevolent beings and render them powerless. According to Eastern European lore, vampires become confused at crossroads and lose their prey.

According to Romanian lore, vampires wander at crossroads. Brave persons can obtain whatever they desire by going to a crossroads with a black CAT and performing a ritual. The black cat, which represents the soul of the devil, is boiled in a pot of water over a fire. Devils will appear and ask for the boiling of the cat to stop. One must not speak until the chief of all devils appears and promises whatever one desires. One can exchange the cat for the granting of this desire.

In the lore of some GYPSIES, when a vampire first appears and is "felt" by someone, it must be ordered—perhaps by a family member—to go to the village crossroads: "Go, O Demonic Power, the soul of the vampire, to the crossroads, so that the wolves may tear you to pieces, there is no place for you here among our Christian souls!" This banishes the vampire, who leaves behind only a little puddle of a jellylike substance.

FURTHER READING:

Murgoci, Agnes. "The Vampire in Roumania," in *The Vampire: A Casebook,* Alan Dundes, ed. Madison: University of Wisconsin Press, 1998.

Vukanovic, Professor T. P. "The Vampire," in *The Vampire of the Slavs* by Jan L. Perkowski. Cambridge, Mass.: Slavica Publishers, 1976.

Crowley, Aleister (1875–1947)   Controversial and highly skilled English magician. Aleister Crowley is considered by many to be the greatest magician of his time. He reportedly could will bad things to happen to people, and could command terrifying demons. A rival occultist, SAMUEL LIDDELL MACGREGOR MATHERS, engaged him in a battle of PSYCHIC VAMPIRISM and lost. (See PSYCHIC ATTACK.)

Crowley liked to think of himself as a writer and poet, while many of his contemporaries, including the authors BRAM STOKER, Bulwer-Lytton, and W. B. Yeats were in awe of his magical prowess. Yeats loathed the man but often commented on Crowley's magnetic character, while occult scholars Kenneth Grant and Israel Regardie (who was for a time Crowley's personal secretary) have hinted that the magician often practiced some form of psychic vampirism, drawing body magnetism or life energy from those around them.

Crowley's writings also hint that he drew sexual energies from young male and female prostitutes and that he also sacrificed a black CAT during a Paris magical working in order to drink its BLOOD. The incident may well be true, but Crowley was a supreme joker, and it should be viewed in much the same way as the story that LORD BYRON drank cat's blood from the pallet of an upturned skull.

Crowley was born in 1875 in Warwickshire, England. His father was a brewer and a preacher of Plymouthism, the beliefs of the Plymouth Brethren, a strict sect founded in 1830 that considered itself the only true Christian order. As a child, Crowley participated in the preaching with his parents, then rebelled against it. His behavior inspired his mother to call him "the Beast" after the Antichrist, a title he embraced later in life. Crowley demonstrated an early interest in occultism and came to believe he had been Ankh-f-n-Khonsu, an Egyptian priest of the XXVIth dynasty. He discovered he was excited by descriptions of torture and blood and liked to fantasize about being degraded by a Scarlet Woman who was both wicked and independent. He developed a massive ego that yearned for fame.

Crowley entered Trinity College at Cambridge, where he wrote poetry and pursued his private occult studies. He wrote in his first published book of poems that God and Satan had fought for his soul, and God had won—but he wondered which of the two was God.

On November 18, 1898, Crowley joined the London chapter of the Hermetic Order of the Golden Dawn, which was the First or Outer Order of the Great White Brotherhood. He discovered he had a natural aptitude for magic and rose quickly through the hierarchy. However, he clashed with Mathers, one of the founders of the Golden Dawn and his sponsor for membership, and was at odds with other members as well. He enraged his fellow members by publishing the secret rituals of the Golden Dawn. Crowley formally declared that he should be at the head of the Golden Dawn, and declared war against Mathers. The order expelled him and Mathers, which prompted Mathers to initiate PSYCHIC ATTACK on Crowley. Crowley claimed that Mathers magically killed most of his bloodhounds and made his servants ill. A strange plague of horned beetles seemed to come out of nowhere, infesting Crowley's house and property. A workman on his property inexplicably went berserk and started attacking Crowley's wife. Mathers also attacked him with a magically created psychic vampire.

A superior magician, Crowley turned the tables and sent the horrible creature back to assault Mathers, who never got rid of it for the rest of his life. Crowley also sent on the attack "Beelzebub and his forty-nine survivors," a horde of hideous demons. One was green-bronze with slobbery lips, and another was like a large, red, spongy jel-lyfish. Mathers's health was ruined. After he died in 1918, his widow blamed his deteriorated health on Crowley's vampire.

Crowley traveled widely. He became involved with the Ordo Templi Orientis, a German occult order that practices sex magic. In 1903 he married Rose Kelly, who bore him one child. Rose began to receive communications from the astral plane, and in 1904 told Crowley that he was to receive an extremely important message. It came from Aiwass, a spirit and Crowley's Holy Guardian Angel, or True Self. Crowley also later identified Aiwass as a magical current of solar-phallic energy worshiped by the Sumerians as Shaitan, a "devil-god," and by the Egyptians as Set. On three consecutive days in April 1904, from noon until one P.M., Aiwass manifested as a voice and dictated to Crowley *The Book of the Law,* the most significant work of his magical career. It contains the Law of Thelema: "Do what thou wilt shall be the whole of the law." Though some have interpreted it to mean doing as one pleases, it means that one must do what one must and nothing else. Admirers of Crowley say the Law of Thelema distinguishes him as one of the greatest magicians of history.

Crowley kept with him a series of Scarlet Women, followers who participated in his magical rites. The best known of these was Leah Hirsig, the "Ape of Thoth," who indulged with him in drinking, drugs, and sexual magic and who could sometimes contact Aiwass. Crowley's fascination with blood, torture, and sexual degradation were well known to his contemporaries. He sharpened his teeth so that he could give blood-drawing "Serpent Kisses" to his Scarlet Women. He apparently made several attempts with various Scarlet Women to beget a "magical child," none of which was successful. He later fictionalized these efforts in his novel, *Moonchild,* published in 1929, the same year he married his second wife, Maria Ferrari de Miramar, in Leipzig.

Crowley was said to have at least one encounter with a human vampire, a living person of flesh and blood. The account is given by one of Crowley's early biographers, J. F. C. Fuller, and is quoted by Crowley in his own autobiography. In that account, the person in question is referred to as "Mrs. M." Crowley was warned that she was "a vampiress and sorceress," and he was asked to help free a woman who was caught in her clutches. Crowley himself admits this story is told rather "floridly," but he still presents it as a true experience.

On the day Crowley met Mrs. M, he was at one point alone in a room with her. He was sitting near the fireplace and gazing at a bronze head of the novelist Balzac. A "strange dreamy feeling" came over him, and he looked up to see Mrs. M bending over him, the soft erotic touch of her fingertips having just glided over his hand. However, she was not the middle-aged woman he had just been speaking to. She had transformed into "a young woman of bewitching beauty."

Crowley calmly rose from his seat, talking to her in a way that would imitate small talk. She sensed now that by engaging him in this way she had entered into a life-and-death struggle; her efforts were "no longer for the blood of another victim." Recognizing that Crowley was a true match for her, she appeared to be even more beautiful and irresistible than before as she approached him.

With catlike agility, she sprang toward him with the clear intention of giving him a fatal kiss. Crowley stopped her, held her away from him, and then "smote the sorceress with her own current evil." With that, he could see a light, blue-green in color, appearing around her head. What had been an exquisitely beautiful young woman rapidly turned into a wrinkled, decrepit old woman, cursing as she left the room.

Crowley's later years were plagued with poor health, heroin addiction, and financial trouble. He kept himself afloat by publishing his writings, both nonfiction and fiction. In 1945 he moved to a boardinghouse in Hastings, where he lived the last two years of his life, a dissipated shadow of his former vigorous self. During these last years, he met Gerald B. Gardner, an English Witch, and shared some ritual material with Gardner. Crowley died in 1947 in Hastings.

Crowley referred to himself in some of his writings as "the Master Therion" and "Frater Perdurabo." He spelled "magic" as "magick" to "distinguish the science of the Magi from all its counterfeits."

FURTHER READING:
Gilbert, John. "The Vampire Poets," in *The Complete Vampire Companion* by Rosemary Ellen Guiley with J. B. Macabre. New York: Macmillan, 1994.
Riccardo, Martin V. "Living Vampires, Magic and Psychic Attack," in *The Complete Vampire Companion* by Rosemary Ellen Guiley with J. B. Macabre. New York: Macmillan, 1994.
Symonds, John and Kenneth Grant, eds. *The Confessions of Aleister Crowley, an Autobiography.* London: Routledge & Kegan Paul, 1979.

Cuntius, Johannes (Pentsch Vampire)   Silesian vampire who behaved like a poltergeist and INCUBUS. The case was recorded by Henry More in *An Antidote Against Atheism* (1653).

Johannes Cuntius was an alderman who, at age 60, was kicked in the groin by one of his horses. He fell ill. Upon his deathbed, he proclaimed that his sins were too grievous to be pardoned by God, and that he had made a pact with the devil. When he died, his eldest son observed a black CAT run to his body and violently scratch his face. A great tempest arose and did not subside until he was buried. Friends of Cuntius prevailed in persuading the local church to bury him on the right side of the altar, an exceptionally hallowed spot.

Cuntius was dead only one or two days when rumors circulated around the village that an incubus in his form was forcing itself upon women. Sexual molestations continued after burial, as well as poltergeistlike disturbances. Trampling noises resounded throughout his house at night, so severe that the entire house shook. Objects were flung about. Sleeping persons were beaten. Dogs barked all over town. Strange footprints, unknown to man or beast, appeared around the house.

The list of more disturbances was long. The Cuntius specter demanded conjugal rights with his widow and molested other women. It strangled old men, galloped around the house like a horse, wrestled with people, vomited fire, spotted the church's altar cloth with BLOOD, bashed the heads of dogs against the ground, turned milk into blood, drank up supplies of milk, sucked cows dry, threw goats about, devoured chickens, and pulled up fence posts. Terrible smells and the sensation of foul, icy breath permeated the Cuntius house.

Signs of vampirism were visible around the grave: Mouse-size HOLES were found going all the way down to the COFFIN. If they were filled, they reappeared. The villagers at last had the body of Cuntius dug up. According to MONTAGUE SUMMERS in *The Vampire in Europe:*

His Skin was tender and florid, his Joynts not at all stiff, but limber and moveable, and a staff being put into his hand, he grasped it with His fingers very fast; his eyes also of themselves would be one time open, and another time shut; they opened a vein in his Leg, and the blood sprang out as fresh as in the living; his Nose was entire and full, not sharp, as in those that are ghastly sick, or quite dead: and yet *Cuntius* his body had lien [sic] in the grave from *Feb.* 8 to *July* 20 which is almost half a year. . . .

His body, when it was brought to the fire, proved as unwilling to be burnt, as before to be drawn; so that the Executioner was fain with hooks to pull him out, and cut him into pieces to make him burn. Which, while he did, the blood was found so pure and spiritous, that it spurted into his face as he cut him; but at last, not without the expense of two hundred and fifteen great billets, all was turned into ashes. Which they carefully sweeping up together . . . and casting them into the River, the *Spectre* never more appeared.

FURTHER READING:
Barber, Paul. *Vampires, Burial and Death: Folklore and Reality.* New Haven, Conn.: Yale University Press, 1988.
Summers, Montague. *The Vampire in Europe.* New York: E. P. Dutton, 1929.

Curse of the Werewolf   See HAMMER FILMS.

Curtis, Dan (1928–)   American writer, director, and producer, and creator of DARK SHADOWS, the first gothic soap opera.

Dan Curtis was born on August 12, 1928, in Bridgeport, Connecticut. He entered the entertainment industry as a sales executive for NBC and MCA and created and produced two golf shows.

In 1966 he created and produced *Dark Shadows*, inspired by a dream he had in 1965. He introduced numerous supernatural elements—vampires, werewolves, witches, ghosts, time travel, and more—which made the series an enduring gothic classic. The original series ended in 1971. Curtis tried to recreate it in 1991–92, but the show did not succeed. Curtis produced and directed two *Dark Shadows* films based on the original show and cast: *House of Dark Shadows* (1970) and *Night of Dark Shadows* (1971).

Curtis also created and produced KOLCHAK: THE NIGHT STALKER, based on a script by RICHARD MATHESON, and the 1973 made-for-television movie *Dracula*, starring Jack Palance, also written by Matheson. (See DRACULA FILMS.) Other horror credits are *Burnt Offerings*, starring Bette Davis, Oliver Reed, and Karen Black; *The Turn of the Screw*, starring Lynn Redgrave; *Trilogy of Terror*, starring Karen Black; *Dead of Night*, starring Ed Begley Jr., Patrick Macnee, and Joan Hackett; and *The Strange Case of Dr. Jekyll & Mr. Hyde*, starring Jack Palance.

Curtis was executive producer, director, and cowriter of the critically acclaimed miniseries *The Winds of War* (1983) and its sequel, *War and Remembrance* (1988–89), based on the works of Herman Wouk. He produced and directed *Intruders*, a 1991 television miniseries about EXTRATERRESTRIALS and alien contact, based on the nonfiction book by Budd Hopkins, *Intruders: The Incredible Visitations at Copley Woods* (1987).

FURTHER READING:

Scott, Kathryn Leigh. *35th Anniversary Dark Shadows Memories*. Los Angeles: Pomegranate Press, 2001.

Scott, Kathryn Leigh, and Jim Pierson, eds. *Dark Shadows Almanac Millennium Edition*. Los Angeles: Pomegranate Press, 2000.

———. *Dark Shadows Almanac: 30th Anniversary Tribute*. Los Angeles: Pomegranate Press, 1995.

Scott, Kathryn Leigh, ed. *The Dark Shadows Companion 25th Anniversary Collection*. Los Angeles: Pomegranate Press, 1990.

Cushing, Peter (1913–1994)   English actor known for his horror and fantasy roles, especially that of PROFESSOR ABRAHAM VAN HELSING, the VAMPIRE HUNTER in BRAM STOKER'S *DRACULA*. Peter Cushing played numerous other roles in 91 films, including some of the greatest horror film classics. He also performed on television, stage, and radio. Throughout his career, Cushing was called a gentleman and "the gentle man of horror."

Cushing was born on May 26, 1913, in Kenley, Surrey. From early childhood, he aspired to be an actor. His first job was as an assistant stage manager in Sussex. He made his debut as an actor onstage in 1935 in Worthington, in a

Abraham Van Helsing (Peter Cushing) is the vampire hunter in Horror of Dracula. *(Author's collection)*

production of *The Middle Watch*. His first film role came in 1941 in the Hollywood movie *Vigil in the Night*.

After World War II, he took both stage and film roles. In 1948 he played Osric in *Hamlet*, starring Laurence Olivier in the title role. The film also featured CHRISTOPHER LEE as a spear-thrower who had a one-word part. It was the first time the two future horror stars were in the same film, but they did not meet, and would not for another nine years.

Cushing's career break came in 1957, when he starred at Victor Frankenstein in the HAMMER FILMS production *The*

Curse of Frankenstein. Christopher Lee starred as the monster. The success of that film, plus the burgeoning horror film market, propelled both Cushing and Lee into stardom.

Cushing and Lee became immediate friends. In his autobiography *Tall, Dark and Gruesome* (1977), Lee said of Cushing:

> Our very first encounter began with me storming into his dressing-room and announcing in petulant tones, "I haven't got any lines!" He looked up, his mouth twitched, and he said drily, "You're lucky. I've read the script." It was a typical wry comment. I soon found Peter was the great perfectionist, who learnt not only his own lines but everybody else's as well. He had a gentle humour which made it quite impossible for anybody to be pompous in his company.

In 1958 Cushing and Lee starred in another Hammer classic, *Dracula* (titled *Horror of Dracula* in the U.S. market), a remake of Stoker's novel. As COUNT DRACULA, Lee established himself as the reigning film vampire, and Cushing became the quintessential vampire hunter in the character of Van Helsing. The two worked together in films off and on for the next 20 years, but they did not share every Hammer Dracula or vampire film. Cushing also worked for Amicus, a rival of Hammer.

Cushing reprised the role of Van Helsing in Hammer's *The Brides of Dracula* (1960). Lee is not in it; in fact, the character of Count Dracula is offstage for the entire film. Cushing had more permutations of Van Helsing. In *Dracula A.D. 1972* (1972), he is a descendant of the original Van Helsing battling Lee as the immortal count. The latter film shows the emotional and physical toll taken by the death of Cushing's beloved wife, Helen Beck, a few months prior to shooting. The role of his daughter was rewritten as his granddaughter to compensate.

Cushing plays a descendant again in *Count Dracula and His Vampire Brides* (1973). He is the original Van Helsing again—and for the last time—in *The Legend of the Seven Golden Vampires* (*The Seven Brothers Meet Dracula*) in 1974, a film that mixes the horror and martial arts genres.

His other major vampire film roles are:

- *The Blood Beast Terror* (a.k.a. *Blood Beast from Hell, The Deathshead Vampire,* and *The Vampire-Beast Craves Blood*) in 1967
- a supporting part in *The Vampire Lovers* (1970), an adaptation of "CARMILLA"
- *Incense for the Damned* (1970)
- a supporting part in *Bloodsuckers* (1971)

- a starring role opposite Lee in *The Satanic Rites of Dracula* (1974)
- a starring role in *Tender Dracula* (*The Big Scare*) in 1974, a French comedy in which he portrays an actor playing Dracula

In all, Cushing and Lee shared 22 film credits, not all of them horror. Cushing starred with Lee in *The House that Dripped Blood* (1971), an anthology; *Nothing but the Night* (1972), a film produced by Lee's own production company, Charlemagne; and *The Creeping Flesh* (1973).

Cushing also starred with John Hurt in a film about GHOULS, *The Ghoul* (1975), and in a werewolf film, *Legend of the Werewolf* (1975). He appeared with Boris Karloff (*The Mummy*) and Vincent Price (*Dr. Phibes Rises Again*).

Cushing was originally hired to play the role of Obi Wan Ben Kenobi in *Star Wars* (1977), but the part went to Alec Guinness and Cushing took a supporting role as a villain.

The House of Long Shadows (1982) marked Cushing's last appearance with Lee, as well as with Vincent Price and John Carradine. His final commercial film was a supporting role in *Biggles—Adventures in Time* (1986), a science fiction film aimed at children. He also appeared in a documentary on Hammer Films.

In his spare time, Cushing enjoyed painting. He was knighted in 1989. He wrote two autobiographies, *Peter Cushing: An Autobiography* (1986) and *Past Forgetting: Memoirs of the Hammer Years* (1988). He contributed to books and anthologies on Sherlock Holmes, hunting, comedy, horror and other topics, and also drew illustrations for books. *The Bois Saga* (1994) is a fantasy story he wrote and illustrated.

Cushing died on August 11, 1994.

FURTHER READING:
Cushing, Peter. *An Autobiography and Past Forgetting.* Midnight Marquee Press, 1999.
Del Vecchio, Deborah. *Peter Cushing: The Gentle Man of Horror and His 91 Films.* Jefferson, N.C.: McFarland & Co., 1992.
Lee, Christopher. *Tall, Dark and Gruesome: An Autobiography.* London: W. H. Allen, 1977. Rev. ed. London: Victor Gollancz, 1997.
Miller, Mark A., and Peter Cushing and Christopher Lee. *Christopher Lee and Peter Cushing and Horror Cinema: A Filmography of Their 22 Collaborations.* Jefferson, N.C.: McFarland & Co., 1994.

cyanthropy   See KUANTHROPY.

dachnavar In Armenian lore, VAMPIRES who suck BLOOD through the toes of their victims.

danag VAMPIRE in Filipino lore. The *danag* is not dangerous until it tastes its first BLOOD.

Dark-Hunters See KENYON, SHERRILYN.

Dark Shadows The first gothic soap opera, created by director and producer DAN CURTIS, best known for its VAMPIRE character BARNABAS COLLINS, played by JONATHAN FRID. During its run of 1,225 episodes from 1996 to 1971, *Dark Shadows* featured nearly every major gothic, horror, and fantasy plot element and theme: ghosts, vampires, WEREWOLVES, a character like Dr. Jekyll and Mr. Hyde, a character like Frankenstein's monster, curses, possession, reincarnation, Satanic cults and a devil's baby, madness, witches and witchcraft trials, black magic, zombielike CORPSES, time travel, and parallel time. *Dark Shadows* stands as a unique creation; nothing like it had ever before appeared on television, and nothing since has been able to duplicate it, re-create it, or surpass it—not even Curtis's own attempt to reprise it in 1991.

Dark Shadows was born in a dream Curtis had one night in 1965 of a beautiful young woman riding on a train, headed for a brooding mansion. The dream was vivid and left a strong impression upon him when he awakened. The result was a story line about the wealthy Collins family, living in gloomy mansion called Collinwood, the focal point of a New England seaport town called Collinsport. Elizabeth Collins Stoddard (Joan Bennett), the family matriarch, hires a young woman, Victoria Winters (Alexandra Moltke) as governess for 10-year-old David Collins (David Hennesy), the son of Elizabeth's brother, Roger (Louis Edmonds) and his estranged wife, Laura (Diana Millay). Roger Collins objects and does not want the young woman. She comes anyway. Winters, an orphan, travels by train from New York City to her new home (thus becoming Curtis's young woman on the dream train). She hopes to learn something about her past in Collinsport. On the same train is Burke Devlin (Mitchell Ryan and then Anthony George), a private detective who is investigating the Collins family.

Strange and gothic things happen at Collinwood. The story line also was based on an earlier work, a teleplay titled *The House,* by the series' story creator and writer, Art Wallace. *The House* is about a reclusive woman whose husband has been missing for years. That woman became Elizabeth Collins Stoddard.

Curtis found the model for his brooding mansion in Newport, Rhode Island: the privately owned Carey mansion, known as Seaview Terrace Estate, built in 1928 and patterned after a Renaissance French chateau. The 65-room mansion sits on seven acres near the edge of the Atlantic Ocean, and the site served as the exterior in the opening credits. Crashing waves on the dark and rocky

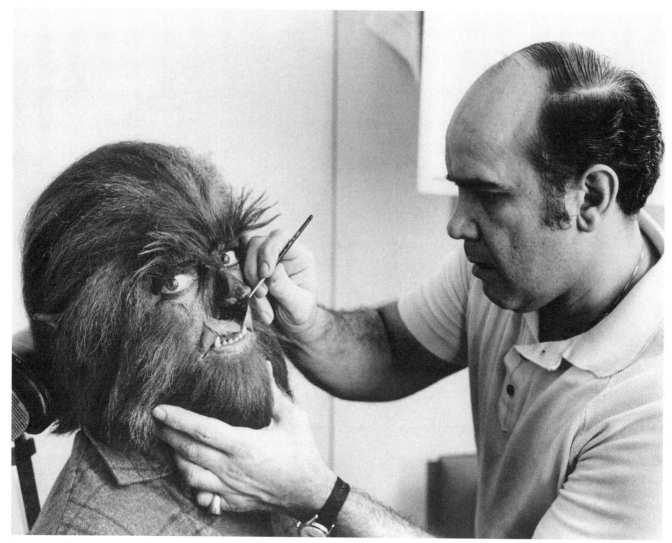

Stuntman Alex Stevens gets his werewolf makeup applied for an episode of Dark Shadows. *(Author's collection)*

coastline adjacent to Seaview Terrace added to the gothic atmosphere. (The mansion is now rented to Salve Regina University as a men's dormitory.)

The first name of the series was *The House on Storm Cliff*, followed by *Shadows on the Wall*. Under its final name, *Dark Shadows*, the series debuted on June 27, 1966, running 30 minutes five days a week.

Initially, the show was a modest success but then struggled for viewership. There were few supernatural elements in the beginning. The plot revolved around Winters and her search for her past. There were the usual soap elements of blackmail, revenge, and kidnapping, with a few ghosts and an immortal phoenix (Millay) tossed into the mix. As ratings sank and threatened the show's survival, Curtis got the idea to add a vampire to the cast. A drifter, Willie Loomis (John Karlen) comes to Collinwood and is employed to look after the grounds. He is fascinated by a portrait of Barnabas Collins, a family ancestor. He searches for family jewels that have been long missing, and acci-

dentally discovers a mausoleum on the grounds that contains three stone sarcophagi. He opens one that is chained, and the 175-year-old vampire is released from his prison. Jonathan Frid debuted in April 1967, introducing himself as Barnabas, a Collins cousin from England and a "descendant" of the Barnabas in the portrait. Elizabeth welcomes him into the family, and he is given the Old House on the estate grounds for his residence. (Exterior shots for the Old House were done on the grounds of the historical Lyndhurst mansion near Tarrytown, New York.)

With the addition of the vampire, the story line became permanently supernatural in nature. Ratings soared. Dr. Julia Hoffman (Grayson Hall) was introduced soon after Barnabas. Posing as a historian, she arrives at Collinwood. She discovers Barnabas's secret and offers to help find a cure for him. The cure is a plotline that runs through much of the series. Barnabas is temporarily cured first by Dr. Erik Lang (Addison Powell). Hoffman, who falls in love with Barnabas, also is temporarily successful, enabling Barnabas to subsist without BLOOD and to go about in SUNLIGHT. She becomes Barnabas's staunch ally, following him through all the time travels. Frid played Barnabas more as a tragic hero than a villain, and viewers loved him.

Barnabas's past is explored when Winters, at a seance, is transported beck to the year 1795. There Barnabas is a normal man in love with Josette DuPrés (Kathryn Leigh Scott). The jealous witch Angelique (Lara Parker) destroys the relationship and curses Barnabas to be a vampire. Josette commits suicide. Winters is condemned as a witch, but just before she is about to be hanged, she returns to present time.

Moltke left the show in 1968; in the story line, Barnabas returns to the past to 1795–96 to save her from hanging, and she stays in the past to be with Peter Bradford (Roger Davis), her love interest.

In 1968 the character of QUENTIN COLLINS (DAVID SELBY) was introduced in present time as a ghost. Chris Jennings (Don Briscoe) is cursed as a werewolf. Barnabas travels back in time to try to learn the origin of the curse and how to break it. In 1897 he finds the origin in Quentin, who has been cursed by the Gypsy Magda Rakosi (Grayson Hall). Handsome and brooding, Quentin quickly became a hit with viewers, rivaling Barnabas in popularity. The 1897 sequence is considered by many fans to be the peak of the show. The audience of *Dark Shadows* was at a peak during the sequence's run in 1968–69, with 18 million-plus viewers tuning in every week.

Writers moved the characters around in different time lines, sending them into the past and the future. A core cast played in all the time lines, with other characters being introduced for more limited roles. Other time sequences were 1840, 1949, 1692, and 1995. Time travel was accomplished by magical rituals with I-Ching wands or a mysterious staircase in the mansion. There also were parallel time sequences, made possible by an equally mysterious room in the mansion that served as an erratic time portal to 1970, 1841, and 1680. The different time lines provided an excellent way to recycle cast members, as they could be killed off in one time line and reincarnated in another.

Other principal characters are (with some of their identities)

- Nancy Barrett (Carolyn Collins Stoddard/Pansy Faye)
- Chris Pennock (Jeb Hawkes/Cyrus Longworth)
- Thayer David (Professor Timothy Stokes/Ben Stokes/ Eliot Stokes)
- Humberto Allen Astredo (Nicholas Blair/Evan Handley)
- James Storm (Gerard Stiles/Ivan Miller)

Kate Jackson, who went on to fame in *Charlie's Angels*, made her television debut on *Dark Shadows* in 1970 and appeared in 70 episodes as Daphne Harridge. (Her *Charlie's Angels* costar, Jaclyn Smith, was offered the role of Victoria Winters when Moltke departed in 1968, but she declined.)

Dark Shadows set several firsts:

- first color soap for ABC-TV
- first soap to attract a large young audience
- first soap to use special effects
- first daily network soap to go into syndication
- first series purchased by the new Sci-Fi Channel in 1992

Throughout the series, Curtis gave dreams prominence. They are a means to know the future and to know the truth about someone or a situation. Dreams are also used to control and manipulate others, and to plant thoughts in the heads of others. Gerard Stiles, who controls people through their dreams, says in one episode, "I like dreams. You find out so much about yourself."

The vampire fangs worn by Barnabas and other vampires on the show prevented the actors from being able to speak. If the actors had to speak before biting their victims,

Advertisement for House of Dark Shadows *(Author's collection)*

the camera had to cut away in order to give the actors time to insert the fangs.

The series came to an end on April 2, 1971. In the final sequence, a parallel time travel to 1841, Barnabas is not present, but Frid plays the character of Bramwell Collins, the son of Barnabas, who is down-on-his-luck and completely mortal. The story line, a derivative of Emily Brontë's *Wuthering Heights* and Shirley Jackson's *The Lottery,* involves a curse on the Collins household: Every generation a member of the family must spend a night in a dreaded room. The experience usually kills them or renders them permanently insane. The curse is ended, and all the ghosts are laid to rest. Bramwell and Catherine Harridge Collins (Lara Parker) marry and take over as the heads of Collinwood.

Curtis produced two *Dark Shadows* films, *House of Dark Shadows* (1970) and *Night of Dark Shadows* (1971), featuring principal cast members. Curtis planned a third *Dark Shadows* film, but it was never made.

In 1991 *Dark Shadows* was resurrected on network television on NBC with an all-new cast, starring Ben Cross as Barnabas, Jean Simmons as Elizabeth Collins Stoddard, Roy Thinnes as Roger Collins, Barbara Steele as Julia Hoffman, Joanna Going as Victoria Winters, Barbara Blackburn as Carolyn Stoddard, Lysette Anthony as Angelique, and Jim Fyfe as Willie Loomis. The reprise used many of the original plot elements. The show failed to capture an audience and lasted only part of a season, from January 13 to March 22, 1991.

In 2003, the WB Network planned to revive *Dark Shadows* with an all-new cast but rejected the pilot.

Meanwhile, the original series enjoyed international airings and long-running syndication, fueled by fan conventions. Among the spin-offs in addition to the two films were comics, three novels, a syndicated newspaper comic strip that ran from 1971 to 1972, and an off-off-Broadway play in New York City produced by the Dance Theater Workshop.

Dark Shadows has numerous flaws. Some story lines were not well developed and had inconsistencies, or made leaps in development without explanation, or had elements in them drop without resolution. In one early story line, "The Creation of Adam and Eve" (episodes 486–626), Barnabas and Julia bring to life Adam (Robert Rodan), a Frankenstein-monsterlike man made of assorted human body parts and Barnabas's life force. A partner Eve (Marie Wallace) is created. Adams kills Eve. At one point, Adam is sent into a closet to hide. He never comes out; the whole story line is dropped.

One of the endearing traits of *Dark Shadows* that has always delighted fans is the inclusion of gaffs and bloopers in the aired shows. Viewers occasionally see such things as props that fall apart, stairways that go into nowhere, distracting flies, production crew members on the sides, and microphones and their shadows peeking into the frames. Nearly every member of the cast suffered from forgotten or blown lines from time to time, even calling characters by the wrong name. Through it all, the cast never missed a beat but continued on. The scenes were not reshot because editing was much more expensive and time consuming than in the present, and would have been prohibitive on *Dark Shadows*'s lean budget. Curtis also never expected the show to survive to reruns, let alone international syndication. The bloopers have long since entered the lore of the show and even have been catalogued and chronicled by fan publications.

The Carey Mansion (Seaview Terrace) in Newport, Rhode Island, served as the exterior model for Collinwood. (Photo by R. E. Guiley)

Only one episode of the show is completely lost. The video masters of a handful of episodes have been lost, but exist in kinescopes (a black-and-white taping of the show on a television screen). The lone missing episode, number 1,219, a parallel time show that aired on February 25, 1971, has been reconstructed in a similar fashion as the reconstruction of the lost LONDON AFTER MIDNIGHT: still frames from surrounding episodes are used to illustrate the original audio recording of the script.

Although there were 1,225 episodes, the final show is numbered 1,245. ABC counted days when the show did not air due to preempting.

Dark Shadows had a significant influence on the appearance of vampire characters in film, television programs, drama, fiction, and other media. A notable influence was the love story between Barnabas and Josette, and the music box Barnabas gave to Josette which is passed on down through the years to reincarnations of Josette. These elements were used in Curtis's 1974 television movie, *Dracula*, starring Jack Palance, and they also appeared in Francis Ford Coppola's BRAM STOKER'S DRACULA in 1992. (See DRACULA FILMS.)

In the 1970 parallel time sequence, Desmond Collins (John Karlen), a failing writer suffering from severe writer's block, imprisons Barnabas to force him to submit to an interview for Desmond's book idea, *The Life and Death of Barnabas Collins*. ANNE RICE had already written the first version of her short story INTERVIEW WITH THE VAMPIRE in 1969—though it was not published in any form until 1976, when it appeared in novel length.

Besides *Wuthering Heights* and *The Lottery*, other literary works that inspired some of the story lines are

- *Jane Eyre* by Charlotte Brontë
- *The Crucible* by Arthur Miller
- *The Cask of Amontillado, The Premature Burial, The Pit & the Pendulum,* and *The Tell-Tale Heart* by Edgar Allan Poe
- *The Dream Deceivers* (unknown)
- *Frankenstein* by Mary Shelley
- *The Turn of the Screw* by Henry James
- *Nicholas Nickelby* by Charles Dickens
- *The Monkey's Paw* by Guy de Maupaussant
- *The Picture of Dorian Gray* by Oscar Wilde
- "The Cthulhu Mythos" by H. P. Lovecraft
- *Rebecca* by Daphne du Maurier
- *The Strange Case of Dr. Jekyll and Mr. Hyde* by Robert Louis Stevenson

House of Dark Shadows

House of Dark Shadows (1970) adapts the television series' story lines, but in its end Barnabas and other key characters are killed. Roger Collins (Edmonds) lives at the Collinwood estate with his son, David (Henesy), his sister Elizabeth Stoddard Collins (Bennett), and her daughter Carolyn (Barrett). Willie Loomis (Karlen), a handyman, tells the governess, Maggie Evans (Scott), that he has discovered something about the family's missing ancestral

Barnabas Collins (Ben Cross) dines on a victim in Dan Curtis's remake of Dark Shadows. *(Author's collection)*

jewels. In the family cemetery, Willie finds a secret vault with a chained coffin inside. He opens it. Immediately that night, two people have mysterious wounds.

Barnabas appears, introducing himself as a cousin from England. He is allowed to move into the dilapidated Old House on the estate grounds. He attacks Carolyn, who becomes infatuated with him. She resembles his long-lost love, Josette. When Carolyn threatens to reveal Barnabas's secret, he kills her, and she becomes a vampire. Dr. Julia Hoffman (Hall) and Professor Eliot Stokes (Thayer David)—a character reminiscent of PROFESSOR ABRAHAM VAN HELSING—get on the vampire track. Carolyn attempts to attack David, but she is staked by Stokes.

Julia offers to try to cure Barnabas; she falls in love with him. He agrees to the experiments, desiring to marry Maggie, the governess. Jealous, Julia gives Barnabas an overdose of serum, causing him to age to his 175 years. He kills Julia, attacks Maggie, and goes on the run. Eliot and Roger pursue. Barnabas turns Eliot into a vampire, who in turn attacks others. Jeff Clark (Roger Davis) shoots Eliot, and then finds Roger dead. Barnabas hypnotizes Maggie, who prepares for their wedding. In the melee to stop the ceremony, Jeff tries to shoot Barnabas with a crossbow but hits Willie instead. Fatally injured, Willie manages to plunge a wooden arrow into Barnabas's back. The vampire dies, and Maggie is saved.

Night of Dark Shadows

Night of Dark Shadows (1971) picks up where *House* ends and introduces a new story line, though a less dynamic one than the first film. The atmosphere of the film is dark, and the plot is slow to unfold.

Quentin Collins (Selby) and his wife Tracy (Kate Jackson) come to live in Collinwood, which Quentin has inherited as the last remaining Collins family member.

They meet the housekeeper, Carlotta Drake (Grayson Hall), and her cousin, Gerard Stiles (James Storm), the caretaker. They are joined by husband-and-wife friends, Alex and Claire Jenkins (Karlen and Barrett), who move into a cottage on the property.

Quentin soon has strange visions, dreams, and flashbacks. He sees a woman hanging from a tree on the property, and Quentin is possessed by a malevolent ghost. He has flashbacks of a man who looks like him—Charles Collins (Selby)—dressed in period clothing and riding a horse, trampling a man, Reverend Strack (Thayer David) to death. He has another flashback of attending the funeral of the man.

At the suggestion of Carlotta, Quentin, a painter, goes into the tower to do his painting. There he has another flashback vision of Charles Collins making love to a beautiful woman, Angelique (Lara Parker). In the vision, Angelique's husband, Gabriel (Christopher Pennock), storms in with Reverend Strack and others and takes the couple away. That night Quentin, unable to sleep, goes up to the tower, where he meets and is entranced by the ghost of Angelique. Gerard appears and attacks Quentin, who tries to kill him. Angelique vanishes, and Tracy appears and stops Quentin, who comes out of his trance.

Carlotta then reveals the dark secret: Quentin is the reincarnation of Charles, and she is the reincarnation of Sarah Castle, the daughter of the housekeeper of Collinwood more than 150 years ago. Charles—also a painter—had an affair with Angelique, the wife of his brother, Gabriel. The punishment was death by hanging for Angelique, and Charles was walled up alive. Angelique haunts Collinwood and wants the ghost of Charles to possess Quentin so that she can be with him again.

Alex is attacked by Angelique but is rescued by Claire. Angelique entrances Tracy. Quentin attacks her, believing her to be Gabriel's jealous wife, Laura, and tries to drown her in the pool house. Alex saves her. Confronted by Alex, Quentin denies what is happening to him.

Gerard tries to kill Alex, Claire, and Tracy. He abducts Tracy, who kills him by pushing him off a railroad bridge. Realizing that Carlotta is fueling the ghost of Angelique, the two couples go to confront her, but she commits SUICIDE by throwing herself from the tower.

Quentin decides to sell Collinwood. But before he can leave, he is completely possessed by Charles, who, with Angelique, have been able to reincarnate in the flesh. The film ends with Quentin intending to kill Tracy. A postscript says that Alex and Claire have died in a mysterious car crash, and their new novel, *The Ghost at Corinth Bend,* will soon be made into a film.

FURTHER READING:
Scott, Kathryn Leigh. *35th Anniversary Dark Shadows Memories.* Los Angeles: Pomegranate Press, 2001.
Scott, Kathryn Leigh, and Jim Pierson, eds. *Dark Shadows Almanac Millennium Edition.* Los Angeles: Pomegranate Press, 2000.
———. *Dark Shadows Almanac: 30th Anniversary Tribute.* Los Angeles: Pomegranate Press, 1995.
Scott, Kathryn Leigh, ed. *The Dark Shadows Companion 25th Anniversary Collection.* Los Angeles: Pomegranate Press, 1990.

Darvell, Augustus   See "FRAGMENT OF A STORY."

Deane, Hamilton (1891–1958)   Actor most noted for his adaptation of BRAM STOKER's novel *DRACULA* for the stage.

Hamilton Deane was born in Ireland. His father, Colonel Deane, was a friend of Stoker's father, Abraham Stoker. Hamilton Deane was an aspiring actor who worked as a bank clerk. He debuted in 1899 with the Henry Irving Vacation Company, a touring company of the Lyceum Theater. Bram Stoker was Deane's manager.

In the early 1920s Deane formed his own repertory company, the Hamilton Deane Company, and produced

Hamilton Deane (Courtesy Vampire Empire Archives)

and acted in plays in the provinces of Britain. Deane wanted to produce DRACULA, but was unsuccessful in interesting any playwright to adapt it for the stage. He was convinced to write the adaptation himself by Dora May Patrick, his leading lady, who became his wife.

Deane said that a severe cold fortuitously forced him to bed. To pass the time, he became immersed in writing his adaptation. He secured reluctant permission from Florence Stoker, Bram's widow, who didn't like his adaptation, but needed the money from sale of the drama rights. Deane completed the script over the next four weeks.

Deane's adaptation of *Dracula* opened in London at the Little Theatre on February 14, 1927, with Patrick playing the role of Mina Harker. Nurses with brandy were on hand to minister to the fainthearted.

The play ran for 391 performances and for more than three years in the provinces. Deane sometimes played the role of PROFESSOR ABRAHAM VAN HELSING. The play returned to London's West End in 1939.

In October 1927 the production was taken to New York, where collaborator JOHN L. BALDERSTON shared billing with Deane. The American production opened at the Fulton Theatre on October 5.

See also ARTS AND ENTERTAINMENT.

FURTHER READING:
Deane, Hamilton, and John L. Balderston. *Dracula: The Vampire Play.* Garden City, N.Y.: Nelson Doubleday, 1971.
Glut, Donald. *True Vampires of History.* New York: HC Publishers, 1971.

dearg-diulai In Irish lore, one of the un-dead, a vampiric entity who usually takes the shape of a beautiful woman and preys upon the life BLOOD of others. *Dearg-diulai* means "red blood sucker." The *dearg-diulai* especially likes to haunt lonely places where she can waylay unwary travelers.

A legend exists of a *dearg-diulai* in Waterford who lures men with sexual enticements and then sucks their blood. In Antrim, there is a legend of a female *dearg-diulai* who cannot find peace as a CORPSE until she finds another female to take her place. In County Kerry, a *dearg-diulai* once haunted a stretch of road. A drunken man encountered her, but instead of fleeing he blessed her and prayed for her, and she was released from purgatory and her fate as a *dearg-diulai*.

The legend of a male *dearg-diulai* comes from County Derry. In Slaghtaverty, there once was a local chieftain, Abhartach, who was cruel and evil. His suffering people engaged a nearby chieftain, Cathan, to get rid of him, and he did. Abhartach was buried standing in his grave, according to Celtic tradition. But the next day he rose up out of his grave and drank the blood of others in order to sustain his corpse. Cathan killed him again and he was reburied—but he again reappeared as a blood-drinker. Cathan consulted a Druid. The third time, he killed Abhar-

tach with a sword made of yew, a wood whose magical properties quells all evil things. Abhartach was buried with his head facing downward (see BURIAL CUSTOMS). His grave was weighted down with a great stone and covered with twigs of rowan (mountain ash), which, like yew, repells evil. Abhartach was seen no more.

FURTHER READING:
Haining, Peter, and Peter Tremayne. *The Undead: The Legend of Bram Stoker and Dracula.* London: Constable, 1997.

death's-head moth In the lore of parts of Romania, the souls of VAMPIRES are incarnated in death's-head moths. If such a moth is captured and impaled to a wall with a pin, the vampire will be unable to fly about.

See also BUTTERFLY.

Devil's Manor, The First VAMPIRE film. *The Devil's Manor,* also known as *The Haunted Castle* and *The Manor of the Devil,* is a three-minute silent film released in 1896 in France (as *Le Manoir du Diable*) by Louis and Auguste Lumière, the inventors of the first practical motion picture projector, and Georges Méliès, a magician, mime, and showman. At three minutes and 195 feet in length, the film was three times longer than other films of the day.

The Devil's Manor is set in a gothic castle and features the devil as a VAMPIRE BAT. The bat flies in a window, circles around in the air, and materializes as Mephistopheles, the devil, who is performed by Méliès. Mephistopheles conjures a cauldron, which produces a parade of beautiful girls, witches, skeletons, and demons. A cavalier arrives and thrusts a crucifix at the devil, who disappears in smoke.

See also ARTS AND ENTERTAINMENT.

dhampir In Slavic lore, the male son produced by the union of a widow and her dead VAMPIRE husband. Such a child can only be male. The *dhampir* is a magician who has the special ability to see and destroy all vampires of the world, and among many GYPSIES is the chief vampire slayer. The *dhampir* is the "devil's partner," and protects people from all manner of evil. He is both greatly feared and greatly respected.

According to tradition, the *dhampir* is summoned to a village when a vampire is suspected of causing problems and deaths. His expenses are paid, and he usually receives a generous honorarium as well. The fee—which may be money, food, clothing, or livestock—is paid by the family of the vampire, or by the family of the vampire's victims.

When the *dhampir* arrives, he makes a show of detecting and hunting down the vampire, who is invisible to others, but not to him. He claims that the air stinks. He takes off his shirt and looks through the sleeve like a telescope. He is given a gun for shooting the vampire. He may order all the cattle to be taken to stand near or in flowing WATER, which protects them against the vampire while he works. He is stern, and others must follow his orders and are not allowed to speak during the hunt and destruction of the vampire.

The *dhampir* may employ ruses to lure the vampire into a trap. Since vampires like to strangle cattle, the *dhampir* may ring a cow bell and hide to ambush the vampire when it appears.

Prior to destroying the vampire in a ceremony, the *dhampir* is searched for hidden objects to prevent falsification of evidence. He is required to give a general description of the vampire, such as a human or a specific animal. He may even identify the vampire as a Serb, a Turk, and so forth, in keeping with the politics of the village. He shoots the gun into the air and declares the vampire killed, or he simply states that the vampire has been destroyed. In some areas, it is traditional for him to pour a bucket of water on the spot where the vampire falls.

The hunt and kill may take more than one night. If so, the villagers must keep their silence and follow the *dhampir's* instructions until the job is done. If for any reason the *dhampir* cannot destroy the vampire, he has the power to send it far away merely by ordering it to go to a certain place. It is preferable to destroy the vampire rather than sending it away.

In some lore, *dhampires* (plural) pass on their magical skills to their own sons; their ability is inherited as a family trade, but it cannot be taught to outsiders.

Dhampires can enable others to see vampires by taking off their shirts and letting them look through the sleeves.

Dhampires have been reported in modern times in rural areas.

See also MULLO.

FURTHER READING:
Vukanovic, Professor T. P. "The Vampire," in *The Vampire of the Slavs* by Jan L. Perkowski. Cambridge, Mass.: Slavica Publishers, 1976.

diarrhea-causing vampires   See LASTOVO ISLAND VAMPIRES.

djadadjii   In Bulgarian lore, VAMPIRE HUNTERS. The *djadadjii* lure VAMPIRES into bottles with the help of icons of Jesus or the Virgin Mary, then toss the imprisoned vampires into a fire to destroy them.

See also BURNING; *KRVOPIJAC*.

dodo   In West African lore, a SHAPE-SHIFTING, cannibalistic spirit, sometimes regarded as the spirit of a dead man that returns to attack the living. According to the Hausa, the *dodo* haunts forests, where it lies in wait for human victims. It can take any animal shape, but favors snakes and those with especially keen senses of smell. Sometimes the *dodo* appears as a giant whose body is covered with long hair.

The best way to escape a *dodo* is to cross running WATER; the *dodo* will not be able to follow.

dogmen   Legendary creatures with canine or wolf heads and anthropoid bodies capable of walking and running upright. Unlike WEREDOGS, or shape-shifters, dogmen seem to be hybrids. Dogmen are reported around the world. In lore they have been considered a type of debased human being.

The Cynocephali, or Dog-heads, were well known in classical times, and were among the most feared of monstrous races. In some descriptions, they were fire-breathing cannibals with enormous teeth.

A race of raw-meat-eating dog-headed men said to live in India was described as early as the fourth century B.C.E. Ctesias of Cnidus, the court physician to Artaxerxes of Persia and a philosopher, historian, and writer, wrote of them. Ctesias's works were extensively quoted by Pliny the Elder in the first century C.E. in his work *Historia Naturalis*. Ctesias called the mutants the Dog-Headed Men of the Northern Hills:

> In the hills there are men who have a dog's head, and whose clothes are the skins of wild beasts. They have no language; they bark like dogs and so make themselves understood to one another. Their teeth are longer than those of dogs; their nails are like those of animals, but longer and more curved. They are black and very honest, like the rest of the Indians, with whom they trade; they understand the Indian language, but they cannot reply except by barking and making signs with their hands and fingers like deaf-mutes. The Indians call them Calystrians in their language, which means dog-headed. They live on raw meat. Their population may reach 129,000.

The explorer Marco Polo also described a race of dog-headed men on the island of "Angaman," thought to be one of the Andaman Islands.

Ctesias's writings have long been dismissed by scientists, who point out that he never went to India himself and knew of it only by hearsay and second-hand reports. His "dog-men" may have been monkeys, or a race of hairy pygmies called the Vedduh from Ceylon. As for Polo, he also is dismissed as probably having been influenced by Ctesias.

In Egyptian lore, Queen Hatshepsut sent sailors to the "land of Punt" (part of Somalia), where they found dog-headed men who were fierce warriors.

References to dog-headed men appear in Christianity. The Theodore Psalter in the British Library features an illustration of Jesus preaching to dog-headed men—perhaps a symbol of the heathen. An apocryphal work, *Contendings of the Apostles*, tells of Andrew and Bartholomew preaching to a giant cannibal named Abominable, who has a doglike head and bestial body features. The legendary St. Christopher was described in the eighth century as being "one of the Dog-heads," who ate human flesh.

In North America, the Dogmen of Michigan are said to haunt northern Michigan. The legend dates to the late 19th century, when loggers were said to encounter a strange, large black dog that reared up on its hind legs.

Folklore accounts recorded since then tell of sightings of a creature with a dog's head and a man's body. "Dogmen" were said to break into houses and buildings, leaving claw and teeth marks on doors, and to attack people and animals, some of whom supposedly died of fright. A creature with a man's body and dog's head was encountered swimming in Claybank Lake near Manistee, where fishermen had to fight it off to keep it out of their boat.

See BEAST OF BRAY ROAD; WEREWOLF.

FURTHER READING:
Downes, Jonathan, and Richard Freeman. "Shug Monkeys and Werewolves: The Search for Dog-Headed Men," in *Fortean Studies* vol. 5, Steve Moore, ed. London: John Brown Publishing, 1998.
Godfrey, Linda S. *The Beast of Bray Road: Tailing Wisconsin's Werewolf.* Black Earth, Wisc.: Prairie Oak Press, 2003.
Heuvelmans, Bernard. *On the Track of Unknown Animals.* London: Kegan Paul, 1995.

Doppelsauger (*Dubbelsuger*)

VAMPIRE of the Slavs of the Hannover region of Germany. *Doppelsauger* means "doublesucker," and refers to persons who are weaned twice. Their fate is to become a vampire after death. In the grave, their lips remain undecayed, and they absorb the fleshy part of their own breast. As a result, their living relatives become vampirized of their vitality through a sympathetic connection.

To prevent a *Doppelsauger* from leaving its grave, a GOLD coin or gold CROSS is stuck between the teeth of the CORPSE, or a half-moon-shaped board is placed under the chin in order to separate the head and chest. The burial garments must not touch the lips. When the corpse is removed from the house, the front doorsill is raised and the COFFIN and funeral entourage pass out beneath it; the sill is then tightly replaced. According to lore, the only way a *Doppelsauger* can get back into its house is to return the same way it left. The moving of the sill prevents it from doing so.

Nonetheless, *Doppelsaugers* still can escape their graves. If a family member loses weight rapidly and becomes sickly, then other relatives must go to the cemetery in the middle of the night and exhume the *Doppelsauger* and knock off the back of its neck with a spade. If it is a genuine *Doppelsauger,* it will let out a loud cry.

FURTHER READING:
Perkowski, Jan L. *The Darkling: A Treatise on Slavic Vampirism.* Columbus, Ohio: Slavica Publishers, 1989.

Doyle, Sir Arthur Conan   See *THE PARASITE.*

Dracula (1897)

Novel by BRAM STOKER featuring the most famous fictional vampire of all, COUNT DRACULA. *Dracula* was a modest success for Stoker, but after his death in 1912 the novel went on to inspire a huge and enduring body of literature, film, art, drama and other performing arts, scholarly study, and popular interest in the subject of vampires.

Dracula has been dissected over and over since the 1960s. The first biography of Stoker, written by Harry Ludlam, was published in 1962, lifting Stoker himself out of obscurity. In 1972 the first of several works purporting to link the fictional Dracula with the historical figure of VLAD TEPES was published by the team of RAYMOND T. MCNALLY and RADU R. FLORESCU: *In Search of Dracula: a true history of Dracula and vampire legends.* In 1977 a fortuitous discovery was made by McNally and Florescu—the research notes and working papers of Stoker. The two had gone to the Rosenbach Museum in Philadelphia to see an original woodcut of Vlad. There they were offered a look at the papers, which had vanished from scholarly sight in 1913, when Stoker's widow, Florence, had sold them at auction at Sotheby's in London. The papers had been acquired by the Rosenbach Museum in 1970.

In 1977 Stoker's original finished manuscript of *Dracula,* also missing for decades, surfaced in Pennsylvania and was acquired by a private collector in California.

With the discovery of Stoker's notes on *Dracula,* including his outlines—now publicly accessible to researchers—a new flood of scholarly and popular commentary on *Dracula* was unleashed, increasing around the 100th anniversary of publication of the novel in 1997. The desire to know *precisely* where Stoker derived every minute comment on vampires, the places on which he based his settings, and the people on which he based his characters has driven some commentators to the thinnest of speculations. Stoker's notes revealed a great deal of what went into *Dracula,* but they are not comprehensive. It is not known how much of his working papers may even be missing, as Stoker was wont to jot down ideas on scraps of paper. Many of his pages are not numbered or dated, which invites more speculation as to the order of ideas for the novel, or the order in which he read his sources. Some of his handwriting is illegible. The old Watergate question, "What did he know and when did he know it?" can be rephrased for Stoker, "What was he thinking, when did he think it, and what made him think it?" The questions have been asked repeatedly about the evolution of the world's most famous vampire novel. There are few certain answers.

Many commentators seem to lose sight of the fact that *Dracula* is a work of fiction. Every writer of fiction draws upon research of real places, people, history, lore, and so forth, but mixes in generous amounts of imagination. Fact and fiction are blended together. Trying to separate fact from fiction in *Dracula* has proved to be an uncertain undertaking. There has been a tendency among commentators to assume that Stoker's use of someone's name for a character meant that the character was "modeled" on that person, or that the real person somehow had been influential to the novel.

These and other pitfalls are demonstrated in *Dracula: Sense and Nonsense* (2000) by ELIZABETH MILLER, which discusses many of the errors and speculations that are reiterated in books about Stoker, *Dracula,* and vampires. Much speculation get repeated as facts, thus entering a twilight of "truths" about Stoker and *Dracula.* Stepping through the *Dracula* literature is like walking through a minefield.

The Genesis and Development of Dracula

Stoker's notes do not reveal the exact inspiration for his vampire novel, but they do show that he began work on *Dracula* in March 1890. In the summer of that year, Stoker visited WHITBY, ENGLAND, for a holiday, and later used the village as the setting for three chapters in *Dracula.* His research in Whitby also led him to the discovery of the name "Dracula," which he adopted as the name for his vampire. (At some point—it is not known when—he had the name as "Count Wampyr.") He also found bits of Wallachian lore and history that he later incorporated into his novel. (See VLAD TEPES.)

In 1893 he took the first of several vacations to Cruden Bay, a fishing village on the northeast coast of Scotland. How much work was done on the novel there is not known; some researches have asserted that he completed it there in 1896. Florence Stoker later wrote in what was probably an embellished recollection of Cruden Bay:

> When he was at work on *Dracula* we were all frightened of him. It was up on a lonely part of the east coast of Scotland, and he seemed to get obsessed by the spirit of the thing. There he would sit for hours, like a great bat, perched on the rocks of the shore or wander alone up and down the sandhills, thinking it out.

Stoker was thorough in his research. His notes show that he consulted at least 32 sources for information about geography, history, and folklore. He originally set his story in Styria, Austria, but moved it to TRANSYLVANIA.

Of the misconceptions about the origins of the novel, these are some of the most common:

- *Dracula was inspired by a bad dream following a dinner of dressed crab.* Stoker did tell this, but it seems to have been more of a joke than fact. His notes do not support it.
- *Stoker did extensive research at the British Museum.* There is no evidence to back this up. Stoker did do extensive research, including at the Whitby library. More likely, an extrapolation has been made from the novel. In the opening scene, Jonathan Harker relates that he went to the British Museum to learn as much

as he could about Transylvania before setting out on his journey to meet with the count.
- *Stoker traveled to Transylvania.* Stoker never went farther east than Vienna. His descriptions of Transylvania are derived from some of his sources and his writer's imagination.
- *Stoker learned about vampires from Hungarian scholar Arminius Vambery.* Stoker did meet with the man. Vambery never wrote on vampires or was known as an expert on the subject. He was, however, knowledgeable about Eastern European folklore. Stoker used his name for a character in the novel.
- *Count Dracula is based on Vlad Tepes.* Stoker borrowed only part of his name, Dracula. Vlad was a voivode of Wallachia, not Transylvania.

Like any novelist, Stoker embellished on his research. He uses the term *un-dead* as a synonym for vampires, which is not found in lore. He borrows the erroneous term NOSFERATU from one of his sources as another term for vampires.

Stoker's vampires must sleep in their native earth no matter where they are. This evidently was Stoker's invention, for it appears nowhere in recorded folklore. In folklore accounts, vampires reside in their graves and always return to them after they have been out on their prowls. Stoker's count keeps boxes of earth in his chapel crypt for his resting places. When he moves to England, he must transport the boxes, too. Stoker's vampires do not sleep in COFFINS—that was a later invention by others.

Another invention concerns MIRRORS: Stoker's vampires cast no reflection in them. There is quite a bit of folklore about mirrors and the dead, such as turning mirrors in a house when someone dies so that they do not see themselves, which dooms them to become a restless ghost. However, there is nothing in vampire folklore about vampires casting no reflections in mirrors. This invention may have served to illustrate Dracula's soullessness, that he is no longer completely human. At the least, it is a good theatrical device, one that translated well to the stage and screen.

Stoker says the vampire cannot cast a SHADOW. Vampire folklore does discuss shadows, but the inability of a vampire to cast a shadow is an invention of Stoker's. This is another device with theatrical assets, used to great effect in films. Stoker's vampires cannot cross running WATER except at slack or flood tides—another invention. Folklore holds that witches and evil spirits cannot cross running water, but vampire lore does not feature this disadvantage.

For story structure, Stoker used the style of author Wilkie Collins: telling the tale in the first-person from the mouths of several characters. This method worked well to give the different perspectives of the principal characters and their views on Count Dracula. But the reader is never privy to the viewpoint of the count himself.

Dracula went through numerous changes as Stoker worked on it right up to submission, judging from his handwritten changes and corrections to the typewritten manuscript he submitted to his publisher. While he was working on it, he also wrote and published two other novels, *The Watter's Mou'* and *Shoulder of Shasta,* both of which came out in 1895.

When Stoker turned his vampire manuscript in, it bore the handwritten title *The Un-Dead.* Somewhere between submission and publication the title was changed to the name of his vampire, Dracula. Whether it was Stoker's idea or the idea of his editor is not known. But contemporary critics generally agree that the change was fortuitous, for *Dracula* captures the attention and imagination far more strongly than *The Un-Dead. Dracula* is the only one of Stoker's books to bear the principal character's name as the title.

Dracula was published in May 1897. Critical reviews were mixed, but many saw it as the best and the most horrible of English horror fiction. Stoker's mother, Charlotte, found the book to be his finest work, though it was not a great financial success. Nonetheless, it stayed in print and was in its ninth printing at the time of his death in 1912.

Prior to the book publication, Stoker staged a single performance of *Dracula* at the Lyceum Theater in May 1897. The dramatization fell between a reading and a full-scale production.

Principal Characters
In addition to Count Dracula, the central characters are

- *Jonathan Harker:* Solicitor's clerk in London who is sent to Transylvania with contracts finalizing Count Dracula's purchase of Carfax Abbey in London
- *Mina Harker:* A schoolmistress and fiancée and then wife of Jonathan, who falls under the spell of Dracula
- *Lucy Westenra:* Nineteen-year-old friend of Mina's. Beautiful, desirable, and flirtatious, with multiple suitors. Vampirized to death by Count Dracula
- *Dr. John Seward:* The director of an insane asylum outside London next door to Carfax Abbey, a partially ruined place. A failed suitor of Lucy
- *R. M. RENFIELD:* Lunatic at Seward's asylum who is turned into a slave by Dracula
- *Arthur Holmwood:* Suitor of Lucy who wins her hand and becomes her fiancé. After his father dies partway through the novel, he becomes Lord Godalming
- *PROFESSOR ABRAHAM VAN HELSING:* Friend of Dr. Seward's who lives in Amsterdam and is summoned by Seward to help with the mysterious illness of Lucy. Knowledgeable about vampires and the occult, he becomes the chief vampire hunter
- *Quincey Morris:* Texan who is among the failed suitors of Lucy

Synopsis
Dracula opens with Jonathan Harker traveling to the count's castle, bearing contracts for the count's purchase of Carfax Abbey, a ruined place, in London. Harker finds the count to be odd but hospitable—however, he soon finds himself a prisoner in the castle. Horrible things happen: He is nearly vampirized by three female vampires, and he learns the awful truth about the count's true nature. Harker realizes Dracula intends to vampirize and kill him. He tries to kill Dracula and fails. He manages to escape, and he next appears in a Budapest hospital, ill with "brain fever."

Meanwhile, Lucy Westenra has had three marriage proposals in one day, from John Seward, Quincey Morris, and Arthur Holmwood. She accepts Holmwood's proposal. Seward is somewhat preoccupied with one of his patients, an insect-eating lunatic, R. M. Renfield. Lucy and Mina meet for a holiday in Whitby. Mina is worried because she has not heard from Jonathan in a month.

While the young women are in Whitby, the count comes to England aboard the ship *Demeter,* bringing 50 boxes of earth with him. Along the way he has killed the entire crew. The derelict ship crashes into the harbor at Whitby, and Dracula jumps off in the form of a wolf. The dead captain is tied to the wheel with a crucifix. The ship's log reveals something monstrous stalked the crew.

Lucy is restless at night and sleepwalks. One night Mina awakens to find her gone, and goes out looking for her. She sees her in the ruins of the abbey on the opposite cliff at Whitby, with a figure bending over her. Mina dashes to the abbey and sees a long, dark form, white face and RED eyes. The figure vanishes. The women do not know that Dracula has found a new victim.

A mysterious BAT comes at night, and Lucy mutters in her sleep about "red eyes." She sleepwalks. Her health declines. Renfield exhibits strange and more excitable behavior. He manages to get out, and he is found on the grounds of Carfax. He rants about "Master."

Mina receives a letter from the hospital about Jonathan and departs for Europe to meet him. He gives her his diary, which tells his ordeal. She does not read it but puts it away.

Lucy's health declines to the point where Holmwood appeals to Seward for help. Lucy notes that at night there is a strange flapping or scratching at her bedroom window. Seward sees something is obviously wrong with her, and she seems to have lost BLOOD. He communicates with his friend Professor Abraham Van Helsing, who knows about "obscure diseases."

Van Helsing is concerned. Lucy's condition deteriorates drastically, and Van Helsing orders a blood transfusion. Seward volunteers, but Holmwood arrives and gives his blood, which restores some color to Lucy. The effect does not last, and she worsens with each passing night. Seward gives blood.

Van Helsing places wreaths of GARLIC around Lucy's room and around her neck. He latches the windows and rubs the sashes with the bulbs. He explains only that they are "medicinal." Seward is mystified and speculates on whether or not the flowers are to keep out an evil spirit. Van Helsing, cryptic, says maybe so.

During the night, Lucy's mother removes the garlic because of the stuffiness in the room. Lucy's condition worsens. Van Helsing is upset. For the first time he makes

Count Dracula, observed by Jonathan Harker, crawls down the wall of his castle. From the cover of the Constable edition of Dracula, *1897.* (Author's collection)

remarks about fighting "the devil." The garlic is restored, and at night Lucy hears an "angry flapping" at her window.

Her window is broken by BERSICKER, a wolf at the London Zoo that Dracula commands. The invisible count comes in on the heels of the wolf, kills Lucy's mother, who is keeping her company in her room, and vampirizes Lucy.

Mina and Jonathan return to England and settle in Exeter. Lucy dies, her teeth now fanglike. Van Helsing warns she is not at peace—the worst is yet to come. Lucy and her mother are buried together. Jonathan is unnerved when he spies the count—now looking very youthful—in London.

Lucy, now a vampire, rises from her tomb at night and attacks children, who call her the "bloofer lady," probably meaning "beautiful lady." Van Helsing visits the Harkers and reads Jonathan's diary of his experiences in Transylvania.

Van Helsing hints more as to the cause of Lucy's death, telling Seward about VAMPIRE BATS. He takes Seward to Lucy's tomb at night, where they find her coffin empty. Seward sees a white figure flitting among the trees, carrying a small child. The figure disappears, and they rescue the child.

The two men return to Lucy's tomb in the day. They find her in her coffin, her skin in the bloom of life, as though she were only sleeping. Van Helsing explains that she was bitten by the vampire while she was in the trance of sleepwalking, and in trance she died and become an undead herself. He proposes to cut off her head and stuff her mouth with garlic.

Arthur—who is now Lord Godalming after the death of his father—angrily refuses this desecration. Van Helsing takes him, Seward, and Morris to the tombs at night. He seals its door with a crumbled Eucharist in the crevices. Soon a figure approaches—it is Lucy with another child. She looks demonic and unholy. When she sees Arthur, she implores him to join her. Van Helsing repels her with a crucifix. Denied entry into her tomb, she flies into a fury. Van Helsing removes some of the wafer, and she slips through the cracks into the tomb.

Broken, Arthur agrees that Lucy must be stopped. Van Helsing tells the men more about vampires. The men return to the tomb the next day. Arthur takes a hammer and drives a STAKE through the heart of Lucy while the others offer a prayer for the dead. Lucy is freed of the vampire's curse.

The Harkers put together information for Van Helsing on the count's move to England and the derelict ship at Whitby. Jonathan's journal is shared. They realize Renfield is under the vampire's influence. The group—the Harkers, Morris, Godalming, Seward, and Van Helsing—assembles at the asylum and takes up residence in the living quarters. The professor delivers a long speech on the existence and powers of vampires, and how Dracula, when he was alive, studied at the devil's school, the SCHOLOMANCE.

The men go to Carfax Abbey, where they find only 29 boxes of earth left. While they are there, Dracula attacks Mina in her sleep. He steals in as a mist. She weakens. The others discover that the count is moving his boxes to other locations in the London area—Picadilly, Bermondsey, and Mile End. Jonathan notices Mina's pallor.

Renfield is found in his room in a pool of blood, seriously beaten and injured. He is dying, but he rallies enough to relate that Dracula came to him and offered him all the blood life he wanted in exchange for worshiping him. Renfield was shown a vision of thousands of RATS that would replace the insects Dracula has sent him for sustenance. Renfield fell down and worshiped him. But the next day he received no rats, not even flies, which made him angry. Then he saw Mina and became angry that the count was taking her blood. When Dracula returned that night, Renfield attempted to attack the mist. He was fatally beaten. (Renfield evidently dies, but offstage.)

The men rush to the Harkers' room at the asylum, where they find Jonathan unconscious and Mina in the grip of the count. He is forcing her to drink blood trickling from a wound in his chest. Dracula throws her aside and attacks the men, but Van Helsing pulls out a Eucharist, which sends the vampire into a cower. He vanishes in a vapor.

Mina is horrified when she rouses, crying, "Unclean, unclean!" Van Helsing secures her room against further attack and touches a Eucharist to her forehead. It burns the flesh. The men go to ruin Dracula's boxes in all his locations by placing sacred wafers in them.

A furious count confronts them all at Seward's asylum. Harker tries to slash him with a knife, but he only cuts the vampire's coat, and money and GOLD fall out. Seward repells him with a crucifix and holy wafer. The vampire grabs some of the money and throws himself through a glass window. He turns and vows revenge. He has already claimed their women and will make more vampires to be his jackals when he wants to feed.

They are uncertain what to do next, but Mina comes up with the solution. At her suggestion, Van Helsing hypnotizes her. She has a sympathetic connection now to Dracula, and she is able to relate that he is aboard a ship. Dracula has taken his last earth box and fled back to Transylvania. While Mina becomes more vampirelike in appearance, the men organize themselves for pursuit of Dracula. They all depart for Transylvania. Via hypnosis, Mina relays information on the count's changing locations.

The count's three vampire women materialize and try to attack Mina, but she is protected within a holy circle cast by Van Helsing. The women call to her as a sister to join them.

The pursuers reach Dracula's castle. Van Helsing finds the tombs of the vampire women and resists their beauty and allure even as they lie in their boxes. He stakes them and cuts off their heads as they shriek. Dracula's tomb is empty, and Van Helsing ruins it with a holy water. Upon leaving, he seals the entrances to the castle so that Dracula will be unable to enter it.

Morris, Seward, and Harker chase down a band of GYPSIES who are transporting Dracula in his last box of earth. It is nearly sunset and snow is falling. They fight, and Morris is seriously wounded by a knife. The Gypsies are overcome, and the men tear open the box. For a moment, it appears the count is going to be victorious, for he sees the setting sun. But Harker slashes his throat with a kukri knife, and Morris plunges his bowie knife into the vampire's heart. Dracula instantly crumbles to dust and vanishes. The Gypsies flee. Morris dies.

Seven years later, the Harkers return to Transylvania to revisit the scene. They have a son whom they have named Quincey, who was born on the same day of the month that Morris died. Seward and Godalming have gotten married. The curse is over.

Dracula *Incarnations*

Dracula received mixed reviews upon its publication, but it stayed in print. The novel might have fallen into obscurity with Stoker and the rest of his works if it had not been adapted for the stage and film. Stoker was well aware of his novel's dramatic potential, and his years of training in the theater working for Henry Irving undoubtedly influenced the structure of the book. Stoker created an abridged version of the novel, *Dracula: Or the Un-Dead,* cut and pasted from printer's proofs, which was read onstage at the Lyceum on May 18, 1897. Stoker's official reason for doing so was to protect his copyright. But he harbored the desire that Irving would play Dracula in a full stage production, and the reading may really have been for Irving's benefit.

Irving had played the devil Mephistopheles in *Faust* for five years, and Stoker envisioned him as the vampire count. The reading of Stoker's adaptation lasted for five hours. Irving is said to have thought it "dreadful."

HAMILTON DEANE's stage production in 1924 substantially romanticized Count Dracula, giving him fine clothing—and a red-lined black cape—and lessening his demonic, wolfish characteristics. Dracula becomes a suave fellow who gets himself involved with the other characters by feigning an interest in Mina's "anemia." The high collar of the cape now so familiar as part of Dracula's wardrobe actually had a stage function, to hide the back of the actor's head as he slipped through doors and panels and left others holding an empty cape. For the American stage, Deane's version was rewritten to make it less stiff. BELA LUGOSI took the role for the Broadway production, and then was chosen for TOD BROWNING's 1931 film adaptation of the movie. Florence Stoker also commissioned Charles Morrell to write another adaptation; it included some of Stoker's long monologues verbatim.

From Stoker's own adaptation to 1994, there were 11 major stage adaptations of *Dracula,* plus countless more comedy and amateur productions.

Browning's film adaptation, *Dracula,* was a huge success for Universal Pictures and made a star out of Lugosi. But the monster Dracula reached his film peak in the HAMMER FILMS productions starring CHRISTOPHER LEE as the aristocratic count.

Dracula has inspired numerous adaptations of the novel and also vampires by other names for radio, film, and television. The role of Dracula has attracted major stars, among them Vincent Price, Frank Langella, Louis Jourdan, Jack Palance, and Gary Oldman. Dracula has been reinvented in characters such as *BLACULA* (1972) and *COUNT YORGA* (1970) and has been parodied, such as in *Dracula: Dead and Loving It* (1995), Mel Brooks's production starring Leslie Nielsen.

In fiction, Dracula has continued on as a character in numerous novels, adapting himself to changing times and the modern world, and even engaging in introspection. Dracula is the root inspiration of many vampire characters in various genres: horror, fantasy, science fiction, and even romance. Dracula is in comics, such as THE TOMB OF DRACULA and *Ghost of Dracula,* and in musicals, dance productions, ballet and opera, as well as commercials, advertising, and greeting cards.

Dracula is of ongoing interest to scholars of literature, the performing arts, folklore, and pop culture, and is the subject of commentaries, analyses, and critiques. Of particular interest is the sexuality expressed in *Dracula:* the overt sexuality of women, in the vampire brides and Lucy; the sexuality of vampirism itself and the eroticism of blood; and the homoerotic undercurrents, in Dracula's claiming of Jonathan Harker and the vampire brides' invitation to Mina. It is also significant that Dracula is brought down in the end largely through the intervention of a woman, Mina, through her own inspiration and determination. Mina emerges from her ordeal significantly strengthened and possessing an independence that cannot be diminished or controlled by men despite her return to a traditional domestic life with Jonathan as wife and mother.

FURTHER READING:

Auerbach, Nina. *Our Vampires, Ourselves.* Chicago: University of Chicago Press, 1995.

Auerbach, Nina, and David J. Skal, eds. *Dracula.* New York: W. W. Norton Co., 1997.

Glut, Donald. *The Dracula Book.* Metuchen, N.J.: The Scarecrow Press, 1975.

Leatherdale, Clive, ed. *Bram Stoker's Dracula Unearthed.* Weston-on-Sea, Essex, England: Desert Island Books, 1998.

Miller, Elizabeth. *Reflections on Dracula: Ten Essays.* White Rock, B.C.: Transylvania Press, 1997.

Miller, Elizabeth, ed. *Dracula: The Shade and the Shadow.* Westcliff-on-Sea, Essex, England: Desert Island Books, 1998.

Miller, Elizabeth. *Dracula: Sense & Nonsense.* Westcliff-on-Sea, England: Desert Island Books, 2000.

Skal, David J. *Hollywood Gothic: The Tangled Web of* Dracula *from Novel to Stage to Screen.* New York: W. W. Norton, 1990.

Stoker, Bram. *Dracula.* New York: Grosset & Dunlap, 1931.

Dracula, Prince of Darkness   See HAMMER FILMS.

Dracula A.D. 1972   See HAMMER FILMS.

Dracula films   Of the nearly 700 VAMPIRE films that have been made, the character COUNT DRACULA has appeared more than 130 times, more than any fictional character except Sherlock Holmes. The story of Dracula has undergone numerous changes and interpretations, just as he has in fiction.

The first official *Dracula* film adapted from the 1897 novel by BRAM STOKER was the Universal Pictures production released in 1931, directed by TOD BROWNING and starring BELA LUGOSI. After her husband's death in 1912, Florence Stoker was not quick to license even stage productions, but guarded her rights to *Dracula* in an effort to maximize her profits. Stoker's modest estate had left her in "genteel poverty," and she was determined to make the most of her copyrights. *Dracula* was the only one of Stoker's books that was earning much income.

Florence licensed stage rights to HAMILTON DEANE, but was unhappy with his production that debuted in 1924. She commissioned Charles Morrell to do another version. She turned down F. W. MURNAU for film rights, but the German director went ahead with a plagiarism, *NOSFERATU*, in 1922 that resulted in years of legal wrangling.

Universal Pictures opened negotiations to acquire the film rights, but Florence's asking price of $50,000 was more than they wanted to pay. Even before a deal was finalized, the studio leaked its intentions to cast the film. Browning favored LON CHANEY, and there was talk of the versatile actor taking on two roles, as he did in *LONDON AFTER MIDNIGHT* (1927), those of Dracula and his chief opponent, PROFESSOR ABRAHAM VAN HELSING. But Chaney died of throat cancer in 1930. Browning then favored bringing in an unknown European actor. However, the studio leaked word that well-known German actor Conrad Veidt would play the role of the count. But Veidt lost his champion in Hollywood when director Paul Leni died, and Veidt soon returned to Germany. Lugosi, who had done well with the role of Dracula in the Broadway stage production, desperately wanted the film role, and lobbied heavily for it. Among other actors who were considered were Chester Morris, Paul Muni, and John Wray. Lugosi interceded with Florence and succeeded in convincing her to lower her asking price to $40,000—provided he got the leading role.

Lugosi got the part but did not accomplish a financial coup for himself. He settled for a work-for-hire contract of $3,500—$500 per week for seven weeks of shooting—which even then was a paltry sum. The highest-paid actor was David Manners, who plays Jonathan Harker; he received $2,000 per week. The role of Van Helsing went to Edward Van Sloan, who had been in the Broadway production. Other principal cast members were Helen Chandler in the role of Mina Harker; Francis Dade as Lucy Westenra; Herbert Bunston as Dr. John Seward; and Dwight Frye in his scene-stealing performance as the lunatic R. M. RENFIELD.

Lugosi's poor command of English meant that he had to learn his lines phonetically. In addition, he decided that his performance would be aided if he stayed in character as much as possible, and so he refrained from speaking to others backstage. His demeanor was mistaken for haughtiness by some of the cast and crew.

Universal was in financial trouble when it undertook *Dracula,* and the budget for the film was tight. Sets had to be kept to a minimum. Browning did not show much creative challenge in making the film, which is static and flat for long stretches, and makes little or poor use of special effects that were available at the time. He was able to keep the production $14,000 under budget, but the film suffers artistically. Browning's *Dracula* follows the Deane stage production more closely than most of the film remakes of *Dracula* that followed.

The film made a significant change in the opening of the story, which was copied in some sequels. Renfield, not Harker, is the one who goes to the count's castle with the real estate papers. This shift in story line was done ostensibly to better explain Renfield's relationship with the count, which is never satisfactorily explained in the novel. Renfield accompanies Dracula on the journey to England via ship. His horrific experiences lead to his insanity. Browning himself did the voice-over for the WHITBY harbormaster who goes aboard the derelict ship, *Vesta,* (*Demeter* in the novel) that crashes into the harbor. Renfield is found cackling below decks, and the harbor master says, "Why he's mad—look at his eyes—the man's gone crazy."

Once Dracula arrives in England, he doesn't leave. Stoker set the end in TRANSYLVANIA, but in the film, Dracula meets his demise at Carfax Abbey in London. In the end, the count is staked, not stabbed. Incredibly, the end of the monster is done off-camera, and viewers are cheated out of seeing Dracula die.

Browning added the odd touch of armadillos scurrying about the count's castle in Transylvania, even though the creatures are not native to Europe. He had used armadillos in *London After Midnight*—they are not native to England, either—and evidently thought their appearance added to the macabre atmosphere.

There were significant alterations in the roles of the two principal female characters, Mina Harker and Lucy Westenra. In the novel, Mina evolves from a subordinate Victorian teacher and wife to a strong and assertive woman who brings about the downfall of the count. In the film, her role was rewritten to make her weaker, more passive and more dependent on men. The entire subplot of discovering and destroying Lucy once she has become a vampire was dropped partway through the film.

In all his appearances in the film, Lugosi as the count is dressed to the nines in formal evening wear, an invention of the stage production. There are no fangs, Lugosi consented to wearing a hairpiece that gave him a pronounced widow's peak, but he insisted on doing his own makeup.

A Spanish version of *Dracula* was shot simultaneously at night, using the same sets, under the direction of Paul Kohner and starring Carlos Villarias as the count and Lupita Tovar as Mina. It is considered to be a much better production than Browning's, and even Universal executives favored it.

Despite its cinematic shortcomings, Browning's film had its world premiere in New York on February 13, 1931, before an eager audience. More than 50,000 tickets were sold in the first 48 hours. As it opened in major cities around the United States, some theaters had to offer round-the-clock screenings to accommodate demand.

Dracula earned $700,000 in its first domestic release and $1.2 million worldwide, making it Universal's only profitable movie during the Depression, and the most financially successful film of Browning's career. Though the film launched Lugosi into stardom, it did not help the actor financially; a year after the film's release, he declared bankruptcy. Lugosi would never be able to command a major star's salary.

Dracula was released to television in 1957.

A sequel, *Dracula's Daughter,* was released by Universal in 1936, directed by Lambert Hillyer. The film had its genesis in 1933, when Florence Stoker sold film rights to "DRACULA'S GUEST," one of Bram's short stories, to David O. Selznick. Selznick intended to adapt it as *Dracula's Daughter,* and he hired JOHN L. BALDERSTON to write a treatment. Selznick failed to sell it to MGM, and ultimately it went to

Count Dracula (Frank Langella) in front of Castle Dracula in John Badham's Dracula *(Author's collection)*

Universal. It was then discovered that Stoker had failed to register *Dracula* properly for copyright in the United States, which meant that *Dracula* was in the public domain in that country. Universal made *Dracula's Daughter,* but it was an entirely different story, using a different screenplay by Garrett Fort. The film presents the vampire as a victim of evil—through a curse or a disease—a theme that would become more prominent in vampire film and fiction in the years to come.

Countess Maria Zaleska/Countess Dracula (Gloria Holden), Dracula's daughter, is, like her father, a mesmerizing killer. She uses a ring to hypnotize her prey. She considers herself "normal" save for a hereditary disease that forces her to subsist on BLOOD. She tries to distract herself in painting, and then tries to purge the curse by stealing

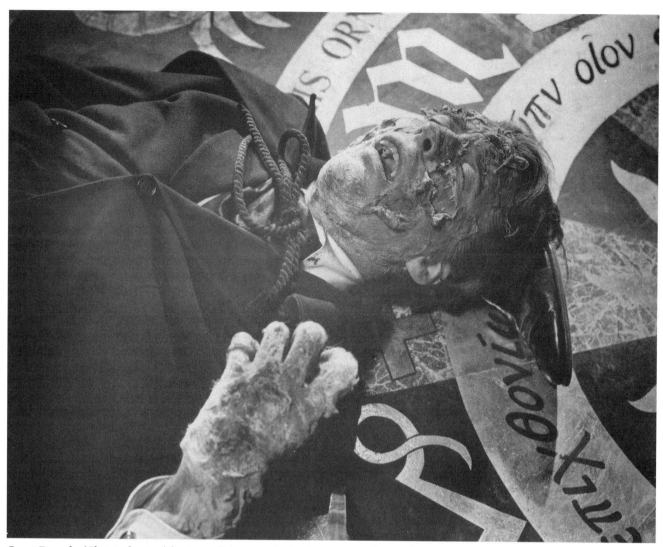

Count Dracula (Christopher Lee) begins to disintegrate in death in Horror of Dracula *(Author's collection)*

and burning Dracula's body in a rite of exorcism, but it fails to work. She seeks psychiatric help.

After *Dracula's Daughter* came *Son of Dracula* (1943), another Universal Pictures production, directed by Robert Siodmak. *Son of Dracula* takes up existential questions concerning vampirism—but not by the Dracula figure. LON CHANEY JR. is Count Alucard (an anagram that would be used frequently). Alucard's coffin rises up out of swamp water, and the count himself materializes out of mist that seeps from the lid. He also can take the form of a bat. Alucard vampirizes the owner of a plantation, which passes to his daughter, Katherine Caldwell (Louise Albritton). Katherine wants to become undead and immortal, and so she dumps her lover, Frank Stanley (Robert Paige) and marries Alucard. Stanley attempts to murder Alucard by shooting him, but the bullet passes through him (his form being insubstantial) and strikes Katherine instead, killing her. Stanley is jailed for murder. Katherine visits him, and

poses the existential question, "Frank, isn't eternity together better than a few years of ordinary life?"

Stanley breaks out of jail and destroys both vampires. He burns Alucard's coffin and exposes the vampire to SUN-LIGHT. He sets Katherine on fire in an upper room of her house as she sleeps in her coffin bed.

In the 1940s and 1950s the figure of Count Dracula remained largely a creature without a conscience, to be hunted down and destroyed by civilized society. Universal Pictures portrayed Dracula as a sympathetic figure who is not entirely evil in *House of Dracula* (1945), a multiple monster film featuring John Carradine as Dracula, Chaney Jr. as Lawrence Talbot, the werewolf (from THE WOLF MAN), and Glenn Strange as Frankenstein's monster. Carradine's Dracula is a monster with a heart—he saves lives as well as takes them. Like LORD RUTHVEN in JOHN POLIDORI'S THE VAMPYRE (1819), he can be revived by the light of the MOON.

Dracula appears in some monster comedies, such as *ABBOTT AND COSTELLO MEET FRANKENSTEIN* (1948). Female vampires were portrayed largely as seductive SUCCUBI, both heterosexual and homosexual, or as youth-obsessed maniacs.

In the late 1950s HAMMER FILMS ushered in a new era of vampire films in which Dracula (usually played by CHRISTOPHER LEE) is evil, cunning, and dynamic—but not remorseful or given to introspection. Filmed in color, the Hammer horror films offered audiences plenty of realistic blood, lush atmospheric settings, and ample heaving bosoms.

In Mexico, a cycle of vampire films were based on Count-like figures: Count Duval in *The Vampire* (1956), Count Swobota in *World of the Vampires* (1960), and Nostradamus in *Curse of Nostradamus* (1960), *Blood of Nostradamus* (1960), and other films. In the Nostradamus films, the vampire introduces himself under a pseudonym, Erickson, in the first film, and seeks a "revindication" of the prophecies of the original Nostradamus, who was the vampire's father.

Hammer's reign ended in the mid-1970s, but a revival of interest in vampires continued to inspire the production of films.

The 1974 made-for-television *Dracula* features Jack Palance as a sympathetic count. The film was directed by Dan Curtis, creator and producer of *DARK SHADOWS*, and was written by RICHARD MATHESON, whose 1954 classic novel, *I AM LEGEND*, presents vampirism as a disease. The Curtis/Matheson *Dracula* is both faithful to Stoker's novel and yet innovative at the same time. Harker is restored to his role as solicitor's clerk who journeys to Transylvania. Curtis strengthens the association between Dracula and VLAD TEPES. This Dracula bears emotional wounds, longing for the woman he loved in mortal life, and attempting to reclaim her in his vampirism of Lucy. When Dracula discovers that Lucy has been destroyed, the viewer cannot help but feel sorry for him in his anguish. Dracula dies by spear by Van Helsing and by exposure to SUNLIGHT, but his CORPSE does not disintegrate. In death he is linked once again to Vlad via a portrait of the voivode.

The British Broadcasting Corporation produced a three-part *Count Dracula* in 1978 for television, starring Louis Jourdan as the count. Jourdan is sexy, sensual, mysterious, and powerful, but does not attempt to arouse sympathy.

John Badham's *Dracula* (1979) stars Frank Langella, who, like Lugosi, was successful playing Dracula onstage. The story is changed and trimmed, bypassing Harker's entire trip to Transylvania and opening with the arrival of the count's ship in England—but to Tintagel in Cornwall, not Whitby. The characters are changed: Lucy is Dr. Seward's daughter who is engaged to Jonathan Harker; Mina is Van Helsing's daughter and Dracula's first victim. Langella is erotic and sensual, and even kind; he carries an aura of sadness about him. In the end he is burned to a crisp by sunlight, but Lucy is not cured. Despite plenty of mood and atmosphere and a stellar cast—other big stars are Kate Nelligan as Lucy, Laurence Olivier as Van Helsing,

and Donald Pleasance as John Seward—the movie failed to ignite audiences.

The next major *Dracula* production was Francis Ford Coppola's opulent *BRAM STOKER'S DRACULA* (1992), starring Gary Oldman as Dracula, Anthony Hopkins as Van Helsing, Keanu Reeves as Harker, and Winona Ryder as Mina. Despite the title, the film is not completely faithful to the novel. Reviews were mixed, but Coppola's version remains the highest-grossing *Dracula* production.

Dracula-inspired films have portrayed various facets of the count: monster, lover, philosopher, warrior, hero. *INTERVIEW WITH THE VAMPIRE* (1994), based on the novel of the same title by ANNE RICE, portrays a new breed of vampire that has captured popular fancy: glamorous, immortal, exotic, powerful—but tortured and introspective. LESTAT DE LIONCOURT, Rice's principal vampire, engages in debates about good and evil, and ponders the nature of his being, creation, and existence. So soul-baring is he that his blood-drinking—the very thing that makes him a vampire—becomes at times a secondary consideration.

Female vampire characters have not fared as well in film as male vampires. In Stoker's novel, the female vampires are brides or concubines, pale shadows under the complete dominance of the count. Lucy, as the only other female vampire, becomes a despised predator of children. As mentioned earlier, female vampires in films have tended to be portrayed in highly sexual roles. Rice's female vampires fare somewhat better in her novels, but the only female vampire of hers to get top film billing—Akasha, the queen of vampires (*QUEEN OF THE DAMNED*, starring Aaliyah)—still is easily dispatched by a male, and comes off as a cardboard character.

FURTHER READING:
Silver, Alain, and James Ursini. *The Vampire Film: From Nosferatu to Interview with the Vampire*. 3d ed. New York: Limelight Editions, 1997.
Skal, David J. and Elias Savada. *Dark Carnival: The Secret World of Tod Browning, Hollywood's Master of the Macabre*. New York: Anchor/Doubleday, 1995.
Skal, David J. *Hollywood Gothic: The Tangled Web of Dracula from Novel to Stage to Screen*. New York: W. W. Norton, 1990.
Stuart, Roxana. *Stage Blood: Vampires of the 19th Century Stage*. Bowling Green, Ohio: Bowling Green State University Popular Press, 1994.
Waller, Gregory A. *The Living and the Undead*. Urbana: University of Illinois Press, 1986.

Dracula Has Risen from the Grave   See HAMMER FILMS.

Dracula Museum   The world's first museum devoted to VAMPIRES, founded in 1990 in New York City by JEANNE KEYES YOUNGSON, founder of the COUNT DRACULA FAN CLUB (later renamed the VAMPIRE EMPIRE).

The Dracula Museum housed thousands of objects in the largest assemblage in North America of materials relating to COUNT DRACULA, vampires, BRAM STOKER, WERE-WOLVES, Frankenstein, the Phantom of the Opera, and other horror characters. The collections included toys, games, recordings, comics, books, art work, stamps, jewelry, and numerous other objects. Exhibitions were available to be seen by private appointment; there were occasional open houses. In its nine years in New York City, more than 6,000 persons visited the museum.

In 1999 the Dracula Museum was sold to the Raimund Theater organization and was moved to Vienna, Austria, to be displayed as an added attraction to the Roman Polanski stage musical, *Dance of the Vampires*. It was then moved into storage.

The Vampire Empire retained most of the Bram Stoker items and a small number of pieces from the collections.

"Dracula's Guest" (1914)   Short story by BRAM STOKER published posthumously by his widow, Florence Stoker, in a collection of Stoker's stories. Despite its title, COUNT DRACULA never makes a direct appearance in the story.

The story involves an anonymous narrator who has a frightening experience with a wolf during a snowstorm on Walpurgisnacht, the night of April 30–May 1, a time when the forces of evil are said to be active in the world.

The narrator, who has been staying at the Quatre Saisons Hotel, is setting out on a journey to Munich. He is admonished by the mâitre d'hôtel to complete the trip by nightfall because a snowstorm is brewing, and because "you know what night it is." The nervous coach driver says it is Walpurgisnacht. Even the horses seem nervous. As they go along, wolves howl. They stop at a CROSSROADS, and the horses act upset—the driver, in his limited English, conveys that SUICIDES are traditionally buried in such locations.

Along the way, the narrator sees a road that winds down into a valley. The road looks intriguing, and he asks the coach driver to take it. The driver resists. He says the road leads to the ruins of a village where no one has lived for hundreds of years. Numerous vampires had been unearthed, and the villagers had fled for their lives. The driver's reluctance and fear irritate the narrator, and he tells the man to depart, and he will walk. As the coach leaves, the horses go mad and bolt.

The narrator sets out down the road. He is completely isolated without sight of any house or person. Snow begins to fall, and soon the crude road is covered. The narrator realizes he has strayed from it. He takes shelter in a copse of cypress and yew trees; both woods offer protection against evil, according to folklore.

After the snowstorm passes, the narrator realizes he is among the ruins of a village. While dogs or wolves howl in the distance, he finds a tomb that reads in German "Countess Dolingen of Gratz in Styria sought and found in death, 1801." A great IRON spike has been driven through the

marble. On the back of the tomb "the dead travel fast" has been engraved in Russian. For the first time, the narrator feels frightened.

A terrible hailstorm erupts, and he takes shelter in the tomb. Amid flashes of brilliant lightning, he sees "a beautiful woman, with rounded cheeks and red lips, seemingly sleeping on a bier." A flash of lightning seems to strike the iron spike, and she rises up in agony, lapped in flames, screaming.

The narrator loses consciousness, then awakens to find a gigantic wolf with flaming eyes lying on top of him, licking his throat. The man is paralyzed. But suddenly a group of armed men—soldiers—arrive and shoot at the wolf, which flees. Some of the men go in pursuit, and some attend to the narrator.

It is determined that the narrator's throat has not been pierced. The soldiers take him back to the Quatre Saisons Hotel.

The next day the narrator learns from the maitre d'hotel that the maitre d' had known he was lost, and had sent out the soldiers to search for him. First, a telegram had arrived at the hotel from "the Boyar," whose guest the narrator is, and second, the coach driver had appeared with the remains of his coach, telling of the narrator's decision to take the road on foot alone.

The telegram reads:

> Be careful of my guest—his safety is most precious to me. Should aught happen to him, or if he be missed, spare nothing to find him and ensure his safety. He is English and therefore adventurous. There are often dangers from snow and wolves and night. Lose not a moment if you suspect harm to him. I answer your zeal with my fortune.—Dracula.

The story ends with the narrator having a vague unease, yet grateful for his "mysterious protection."

In her preface to *Dracula's Guest and Other Weird Tales*, Florence Stoker said that "Dracula's Guest" was a chapter cut out of the novel *Dracula* (1897) "owing to the novel's length." Scholars have questioned that assertion ever since publication.

The narrator is assumed to be Jonathan Harker, though he is never identified in the story. Stoker's notes for *Dracula* that he made in 1890 mention Harker's start for Munich, his stay at the Quatre Saisons Hotel, his visit to the Dead House and "adventure snowstorm and wolf." But experts note that the narrator is much different from Harker—bolder—and the story is not written in the diary style that characterizes *Dracula*.

Whether Stoker wrote the material originally as part of his novel and then excised it, or whether he wrote it as a story in its own right, probably will never be known. One possibility put forward is that Stoker removed it because it was too similar to J. Sheridan Le Fanu's story "CARMILLA" (1872), about a 150-year-old vampire countess from Styria, whose village was ruined by vampires and was deserted.

FURTHER READING:

Leatherdale, Clive. *Dracula: The Novel and the Legend*. Welling-borough, Northamptonshire, England: The Aquarian Press, 1985.

Frayling, Christopher. *Vampyres: Lord Byron to Count Dracula*. London: Faber and Faber, 1991.

Miller, Elizabeth. *Dracula: Sense and Nonsense*. Westcliff-on-Sea, England: Desert Island Books, 2000.

Dracula Society   Organization founded in 1973 in England by Bernard Davies and Bruce Wightman.

The Dracula Society, based in London, is devoted to the film, literature, myth, folklore, and other aspects of VAMPIRES, WEREWOLVES, monsters, and other creatures of the gothic genre. BRAM STOKER and his novel DRACULA (1897) are the primary, but not the only, focus of members, whose numbers have averaged about 100 internationally since founding. The society has a crest and a motto, "Credo Quia Impossibile," which means "I believe because it is impossible." The motto is intended to express the society's open-minded approach. Members receive a quarterly newsletter, *Voices From the Vaults*. The society does not engage in any psychical or scientific research.

The society holds meetings and film screenings, sponsors field trips to places of interest, such as Romania, and hosts an annual Bram Stoker birthday anniversary banquet as close as possible to Stoker's actual birth date of November 8. In 2003 the society hosted its 30th anniversary conference, the first-ever conference for the organization, in Rochester, Kent.

The society maintains a small archive that includes the complete papers of HAMILTON DEANE, coauthor of the stage version of *Dracula*, and a cloak worn by CHRISTOPHER LEE in his film portrayals of Dracula. The cloak is draped over an empty chair at the Stoker banquet every year, the seat reserved for "the Count."

Annual awards for notable contributions to the field are given at the banquet. The Hamilton Deane Award, not given necessarily annually, goes to the best dramatic presentation in the gothic genre for the previous year. Lee was the recipient in 2000 for his portrayals of Flay in *Gormenghast* and M. R. James in *Ghost Stories at Christmas*.

The Children of the Night Award is given annually for the best piece of literature in the gothic genre, fiction or nonfiction. Dracula scholar ELIZABETH MILLER won the award in 2000 for *Dracula: Sense and Nonsense*.

Honorary life members of the Society are

- Ken Barr, artist
- Richard Dalby, editor
- Bernard Davies, cofounder
- RADU R. FLORESCU, author
- Clive Leatherdale, author and publisher
- Nicolae Padararu, founding member of the TRANSYLVANIAN SOCIETY OF DRACULA

One of the Dracula capes worn by Christopher Lee is always present on an empty chair designated for "the Count" at the annual Bram Stoker's birthday banquet celebrated by the Dracula Society. (Photo by R. E. Guiley)

- Harry Ludlam, author and biographer of Stoker
- Monica Wightman, founding member and former spouse of cofounder Bruce Wightman
- JEANNE K. YOUNGSON, president and founder of the VAMPIRE EMPIRE

FURTHER READING:

Dracula Society Web Site. URL: http://www.draculasociety.org.uk. Downloaded on December 1, 2003.

Dracula theme park   A Disneyland-style horror-theme entertainment park based on COUNT DRACULA and VAMPIRES, planned for Romania. Construction was scheduled to begin in 2004 at Snagov Lake, the reputed burial site of VLAD TEPES, the "historical" Dracula.

The controversial park was on and off for several years as various private, government, and political factions warred over its location and even whether or not there should be a Dracula park at all. Plans to build the park on the outskirts of Sigishoara, the 13th-century town where Vlad Tepes supposedly was born, and of great importance as a medieval historic site, were finally killed in October 2003 by an international consortium of the UNESCO World Heritage Committee, the cultural arm of the United Nations, and other activists. Opponents argued that the park would destroy the fragile environment around Sigishoara, a World Heritage Site that includes Saxon villages.

Snagov Lake is not in TRANSYLVANIA, but is about 40 miles north of Bucharest, the capital of Romania.

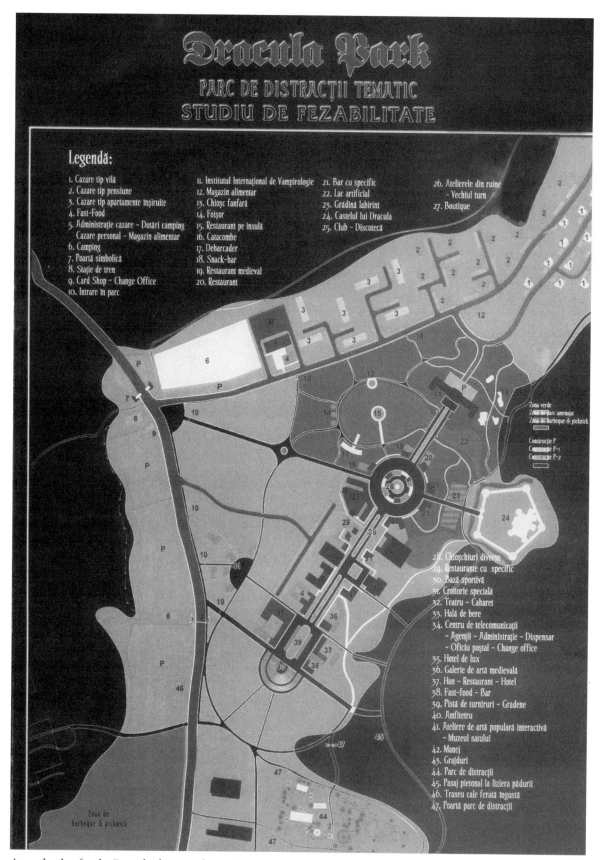

An early plan for the Dracula theme park in Romania, part of a prospectus to attract investors (Courtesy John Turner)

The estimated cost of the park is $30 million. The park is projected to attract about 1 million visitors a year by its fourth year of operation.

FURTHER READING:
"Update on the Dracula Park." Dracula's Homepage Web site. URL: http://www.ucs.mun.ca/~emiller/DrLand.htm. Downloaded on January 7, 2004.

dream sending In sorcery and witchcraft, a means of influencing, attacking and even killing a person via a FAMILIAR or were-animal dispatched to invade the person's dreams. Dream sending is a widely held belief about witches and sorcerers, and magical practices for it have existed since ancient times. Dream sending is based on the also widely held belief that dreams are real experiences, not imaginary.

The Egyptians and Greeks had dream-sending rituals for causing a person to be influenced to a certain course of action in accordance to instructions given in a dream. Egyptian magicians also summoned the dead to appear in the dreams of others. The dead were considered to have great power, and thus could enforce a spell or curse. A magician might send the spirit of a dead person to haunt the dreams of an enemy.

Among the Azande of Africa, bad dreams are considered to be actual experiences of witchcraft. A sleeping witch has the power to send the soul of his witchcraft to a sleeping victim and eat the soul of his flesh. Dreams of being chased or attacked by animals or were-animals, such as human-headed beasts or animal-headed humans, are certain signs of nocturnal dream sending attacks. Supernatural animals such as the *wangu*, a rainbow snake, or the *moma ime*, a water-leopard, are especially feared in dreams. Dream attacks can cause wasting illness, death, and misfortune, and can only be countered by seeking the help of an oracle.

In *Witchcraft, Oracles and Magic Among the Azande* (1976), E. E. Evans-Pritchard gives this example of a dream-sent attack reported by a young man:

> I slept soundly and dreams came to me and I dreamt a dream. A man came in the guise of an elephant and began to attack me. The elephant stood outside my hut and put its trunk through the side of the roof and hauled me outside.
>
> The bottom part of its body was like a man, and its head was the head of an elephant. It had hair like grass on its head, so that its head resembled the head of an aged man.

The dreamer was able to evade the attacker by climbing a tree, and then awakening before the beast could harm him in the dream. Had he been physically harmed in the dream, he would have felt certain to be harmed physically in waking life.

Dreams also can be sent by spirits and supernatural beings as a means of communication and conferring power. The actual dream messenger may appear in the form of an animal significant to the dreamer. In Iroquois lore, to refuse the wishes of a supernatural that have been sent in a dream is to court disaster.

Dreams and dream sending appear in vampire fiction. In DRACULA (1897) by BRAM STOKER, vampire attacks are conveyed through nightmares. In CASTLE DRACULA, Jonathan Harker experiences a "nightmare" in which he is attacked by three vampire women, the "brides" of COUNT DRACULA. He goes into a forbidden room one night and lies down on a couch:

> I suppose I must have fallen asleep; I hope so, but I fear, for all that followed was startling real—so real that now sitting here in the broad, full sunlight of the morning, I cannot in the least believe that it was all sleep.

Harker becomes aware of three young women standing before him in the moonlight:

> I thought at the time that I must be dreaming when I saw them, for, though the moonlight was behind them, they threw no shadow on the floor.

The women have piercing eyes, voluptuous RED lips, and brilliant sharp white teeth. One of them fastens her teeth on his neck, but before she can pierce his flesh, the count appears and angrily sends them away.

When Dracula begins his attacks on Lucy Westenra in London, she has disturbing dreams of red eyes and flapping sounds at her bedroom window. If Lucy had existed in a tribal society, she would have tried to escape from the eyes or send them away, and thus would have prevented actual physical attack.

The gothic soap opera DARK SHADOWS gave dreams prominence as a means of supernatural experience. Dreams were sent by magically empowered characters such as Gerard Stiles (James Storm) to influence people.

See also SABBATS; SHAPE-SHIFTING; VAMPIRE SORCERERS AND WITCHES.

FURTHER READING:
Child, Alice B., and Irvin L. Child. *Religion and Magic in the Life of Traditional Peoples.* Englewood Cliffs, N.J.: Prentice-Hall, 1993.
Evans-Pritchard, E. E. *Witchcraft, Oracles and Magic Among the Azande.* Oxford, U.K.: Oxford University Press, 1976.
Guiley, Rosemary Ellen. *Dreamwork for the Soul: A Spiritual Guide to Dream Interpretation.* New York: Berkley Books, 1998.
Parrinder, Geoffrey. *Witchcraft European & African.* London: Faber and Faber, 1958.
Wallace, Anthony F. C. "Dreams and the Wishes of the Soul: A Type of Psychoanalytic Theory Among the Seventeenth Century Iroquois," in *Magic, Witchcraft, and Curing,* John Middleton, ed. Austin: University of Texas Press, 1967.

Drunken Boy   In Japanese lore, an ogre demon who dresses in RED and likes to gorge himself on BLOOD. The Drunken Boy's favorite victims are women. He is attended by other ogre demons.

In lore the Drunken Boy is quelled by the medieval hero Raiko, who, in disguise, manages to enter the ogre's lair. The Drunken Boy and his ogre followers are drinking blood from their female victims. Raiko reveals himself and battles the ogres. He decapitates the Drunken Boy, but the ogre fights on for a time. Raiko eventually triumphs. He takes the trophy head back to Miyako, the imperial capital (Kyoto), as well as the female captives.

duppy   See JUMBY.

eclipses See VARCOLAC.

eigi einhamr A pagan cult of were-animals in Nordic and Icelandic lore. *Eigi einhamr* means "not of one skin." The *eigi einhamr* were men who had the ability to transform themselves into animals and take on the form (*hamr*), powers, and characteristics of those creatures. The transformed and empowered man was called *hamrammr*.

The SHAPE-SHIFTING could be accomplished by donning the skin of the animal. The human body was left in a cataleptic trance while the spirit of the man entered the animal form. Another means of transformation was through magical incantation. The original form of the man remained the same, but those who saw him were bewitched to perceive the form of an animal.

The *eigi einhamr* retained his human intellect while an animal. If changed into a wolf, he went on a "wolf-ride" ravaging animals, humans, and property.

See also BERSERKIR; WEREWOLF.

FURTHER READING:
Baring-Gould, Sabine. *The Book of Werewolves*. London: Smith, Elder, 1865.

ekimmu In Babylonian and Assyrian demonology, the restless spirit of the dead that is denied entry to the underworld, and so is doomed to prowl the earth. *Ekimmu* means "that which is snatched away." One became an *ekimmu* by dying a violent or unsavory death, such as by murder, in battle, drowning, or succumbing to exposure in the desert, which left the CORPSE unburied. An *ekimmu* also is created due to lack of burial, improper burial, and lack of proper attention by the living, especially concerning the leaving of food and liquids intended to sustain the spirit on its journey to the underworld.

The *ekimmu* vampirizes humans not by preying on their BLOOD or flesh, but by entering their households at night and causing misfortune and destruction, behavior also attributed to vampires. In some cases, the *ekimmu* can cause the deaths of all people in a household.

The *ekimmu* is invisible and can easily take possession of humans. Merely looking at an impure corpse can result in being haunted by an *ekimmu*. Once attached to the living, it is extremely difficult to exorcize.

The *ekimmu* can be destroyed with wooden weapons.

empusa Greek demonic vampire spirit. *Empusa* is usually translated into English as "vampire," though it is a demon that takes over a CORPSE and is not the walking dead.

The *empusa* has no shape of its own, but appears as a foul phantom in a myriad of guises, sometimes in the form of an alluring young woman. It enters the body of its human prey to consume its flesh and drink its BLOOD.

A story about an *empusa* appears in *The Life of Apollonius of Tyana* by Philostratus, a Greek biography of the philosopher and wonderworker who lived in the first century. Apollonius was credited with great feats of magic and the ability to summon spirits and see the future. Philostratus's work is unreliable, for it draws upon the probably fictional memoirs of one of Apollonius's disciples, Damis.

The story centers on a 25-year-old man of Lycia, Menippus, who is smart and exceptionally handsome and well built. One day as he walks along the road to Cenchreae, he is met by an apparition—an *empusa*—in the guise of a Phoenician woman. He falls under her spell and falls in love with her, not realizing what she really is. They make plans to marry.

Apollonius is skeptical of her. He attends the wedding and is introduced to her by Menippus. The woman acknowledges she is the owner of all the GOLD and SILVER trappings in the house, and is the mistress of all the servants. Apollonius tells Menippus that his bride is really a vampire—one of the LAMIAE or hobgoblins—who is devoted to the delights of Aphrodite and loves to devour the flesh and blood of their victims. Menippus's bride is offended at this and orders Apollonius to leave, but he has broken her spell, and all the gold, silver, and servants disappeared.

The woman weeps and begs Apollonius not to force her to confess her true identity, but he does. She admits she was fattening up Menippus for a kill, and that she loves to dine on young and beautiful bodies because their blood is pure and strong. Thus was Menippus saved from a gruesome fate.

FURTHER READING:
McNally, Raymond T. *A Clutch of Vampires*. New York: Bell Publishing, 1984.
Philostratus. *The Life of Apollonius of Tyana*. F. C. Conybeare, trans. London: Heinemann, 1912.

erestun   In Russian lore, a VAMPIRE that is a variant of the ERETIK. The *erestun* is an ordinary person who while dying or after death has his body invaded by an evil, living sorcerer (heretic). The favored victims are villains, robbers, and the depraved. The transformed sorcerer becomes a vampire that stalks first the family of the dead person and then others, and devours them.

The *erestun* is destroyed by whipping him to death with a whip used for heavily loaded horses. To prevent him from reanimating in the grave, a STAKE made of ASPEN is driven through his back between the shoulders.

In the lore of Olonec, the *erestun* is a living vampire who maintains the outward appearance of a good peasant, but carries on his vampiric activity among the people in secret.

See also VAMPIRE SORCERERS AND WITCHES.

eretica   In Russian lore, a vampire that is a variant of the ERETIK, and which has associations with witches. The *eretic y* (plural) are women who sell their souls to the devil while alive. After death they return as VAMPIRES, roaming about and turning people away from Christianity. They have the power of the EVIL EYE, and one eye can act on its own as a vampire.

The *eretic y* walk about only in the spring and the fall. In daytime they appear as ugly old women in rags. In the evening they gather in "heathen" ravines (similar to the SABBATS alleged of European witches). At night they enter the sunken graves of the impious and sleep in their COFFINS. If they do not enter a grave, they go down the chimney of the village bathhouse and noisily splash around, and jump and dance to the accompaniment of the devil. An *eretica* will someday give birth to the Antichrist.

If a living person sees an *eretica* or falls into a sunken grave up to his belt, he will soon die.

The EYE of the *eretica* is powerful and can act on its own as a vampire and send the evil eye, causing victims to waste away and die. A folktale from Temirev tells about a peasant's daughter who dies. Her father plies the girl's godfather with food and drink and asks him to dig her grave. Drunk, the godfather agrees. He goes to the cemetery, finds a sunken grave, and descends into it to dig. He hits a coffin, and then suddenly sees the eye of an *eretica*. He jumps out and runs home without looking back. But the *eretica* is already there waiting for him, looking at him with the same evil eye. The man runs to the yard and then the manger, but the *eretica* is ahead of him, and he sees her lying in the manger, laughing at him demonically. From that time on, the godfather wastes away. The peasants hold church services for him and have him sprinkled with holy WATER, but the efforts are to no avail, and he dies.

FURTHER READING:
Oinas, Felix J. *Essays on Russian Folklore and Mythology*. Columbus, Ohio: Slavica Publishers, 1984.

eretik (eretnik)   In Russian lore, a type of cannibalistic VAMPIRE associated with heretics. The heretics—the Old Believers or non-Christians—were associated with sorcery, and sorcerers were believed to become vampires after death. The term *eretik* became a substitute for the much older Russian term for vampires, UPIR.

The *eretik* is a dead person who leaves its grave and attacks people to eat them. When disinterred, it is found lying on its stomach. It is dispatched by being staked through the back with ASPEN, or by being burned to ASHES.

See also ERESTUN; ERETICA; KOLDUN; VAMPIRE SORCERERS AND WITCHES.

evil eye   The ability to cause illness, misfortune, calamity, and a wasting death by malevolent, lingering, or envious looks. LIVING VAMPIRES, such as certain VAMPIRE SORCERERS AND WITCHES who have the power to drain away the life force, are believed capable of withering any living thing—and even damaging inanimate objects—with their look. Vampires who return from the grave may have the ability to kill with a glance. (See *ERETICA; NELAPSI.*)

The evil eye exists in lore around the world, dating to ancient times. The oldest recorded reference to it appears in the cuneiform texts of the Sumerians, Babylonians, and Assyrians, about 3000 B.C.E.

There are two kinds of evil eye, involuntary and deliberate. Most cases of evil eye are believed to occur involuntarily; the person casting it doesn't mean to do it and probably isn't even aware of it. For example, a jealous or envious look from a friend or a stranger upon possessions, one's appearance, or one's children can cast the evil eye. People who have odd-looking eyes are believed to be the agents of the evil eye.

Malevolent evil eye is called "overlooking," and is a form of witchcraft that can be vampirizing in many ways by causing misfortune or catastrophe: illness, poverty, injury, loss of love, even death. In the Middle Ages, witches were said to give anyone who crossed them the evil eye, and to use it to bewitch judges from convicting them.

Remedies against the evil eye include SPITTLE, making certain horned signs with the hands, wearing various amulets, and seeking the services of a person skilled in the magical arts. Phallic-shaped objects are considered powerful counters to the evil eye.

One Scottish folk remedy gives the following prescription:

Without speaking, take a clay or wooden vessel to a ford or bridge over which the living and the dead have passed. With cupped hands, lift water into the vessel three times below the ford or bridge and three times above it. Invoke the Trinity, place a silver coin in the vessel and take it back to the victim. Carry the vessel three times around the fire or chimney, going clockwise in the direction the sun travels in the sky. Sprinkle the water over the "eye-smitten" victim or give it to him to drink. Pour what is left onto a rock or throw it behind the hearthstone.

FURTHER READING:
Elworthy, Frederick Thomas. *The Evil Eye: An Account of This Ancient and Widespread Superstition.* New York: OBC, Inc., 1989.
Radford, E., and M. A. Radford. *Encyclopedia of Superstitions.* Edited and revised by Christina Hole. London: Book Club Associates, 1974.

extraterrestrials From the perspective of VAMPIRE folklore, a type of modern vampire. Many reported descriptions of encounters with extraterrestrials involve phenomena and characteristics described in vampire accounts centuries old. ETs as modern versions of vampires may explain some, but not all, encounters with ETs.

Arguments have been made that earth has been visited by space aliens throughout its history, but the modern age of UFO sightings and encounters began in the late 1940s. Reports of ETs have included a wide range of descriptions, many of them resembling beings from fairy lore. Encounters have been both benign and unpleasant. By the 1960s many ET encounters had become increasingly sinister in nature. Since then, contactees have reported missing time, fear, attack, and terrifying abductions. In kidnappings, victims are paralyzed and taken aboard spacecraft, where they are vampirized by sexual and physical assault. While benevolent ETs are still reported, the ET encounter is more feared than welcomed.

Dominant characteristics of abducting ETs parallel those of the vampire, as follows:

- They usually strike at night while the victims are asleep.
- They can be invisible.
- They have supernatural powers over human and animals.
- They have SHAPE-SHIFTING power.
- They create poltergeistlike disturbances.
- They cause nightmares.
- They paralyze their victims while they attack.
- They subject their victims to sexual assault.
- They leave their victims weak, disoriented, bruised, and exhausted.

ETs also have been compared to fairies. Both fairies and ETs come from otherworldly places where time passes much differently than it does among humans, and both are intensely interested in human babies, since their own are weak and sickly.

ETs have been compared to angels as well. Like angels, some ETs say they are on missions to help humanity; their appearances are shining and elegant.

While the ET is not a fairy, vampire, or angel per se, it does embody characteristics among all three. Thus, it can be hypothesized that ETs are a modern expression of humanity's mythological experiences. The ET, like the vampire, comes to steal away life. Outer space, like the grave, symbolizes the feared unknown.

Other phenomena associated with ETs are vampiric in nature. Mysterious animal mutilations and deaths also have been blamed on vampiric ETs. Since the 1970s UFOs have been linked to mysterious animal mutilations around the world. These mutilations often happen in waves. Cows, sheep, dogs, horses, and other animals have been found exsanguinated, with tongues, eyes, and vital organs removed with surgical precision. Predators and humans are not always satisfactory explanations. The wounds left on the carcasses sometimes show signs of intense heat, as though lasers were used. UFO sightings and ET encounters often are reported in the areas where mutilated animals are found.

The evidence of intense heat is similar to the burning heat experienced by *CHUPA-CHUPA* victims. The *chupa-chupas* are "vampires in the sky," UFO encounters in which victims reportedly are attacked by beams of RED light that leave them sick and feeling as though they are drained of BLOOD. Some victims have died. Some of *chupa-chupa* cases are questionable, but others are credible and an enigma.

See also *CHUPACABRA*; MOTHMAN.

FURTHER READING:

Guiley, Rosemary Ellen. "ET Dreaming," *FATE*, September 2003, pp. 8–11+.

Guiley, Rosemary Ellen. "Vampires from Outer Space: An Exploration of Common Ground Shared by Vampires and Extraterrestrials Concerning Death and Immortality." Paper presented at the "Communication with the Beyond" colloquium in Sinaia, Romania, May 10–12, 2002, sponsored by the Transylvanian Society of Dracula, Bucharest; International Society for the Study of Ghosts and Apparitions, New York; and Ghost Club, London.

Vallee, Jacques. *Passport to Magonia: From Folklore to Flying Saucers.* Chicago: Henry Regnery, 1969.

eye   In Russian and German lore, the eye of the dead has the power to draw the living into the grave; thus the eyes are closed at the time of death. In the lore of some GYPSIES, the eye—along with other parts of the body—can act as a VAMPIRE on its own. The Russian *ERETICA* vampire possesses such a vampiric eye, which causes the living to waste away to death.

See also EVIL EYE; KASHUBS.

eyebrows   Widespread folklore beliefs hold that persons whose eyebrows meet are associated with deceit, ill temper, witchcraft, vampires, and werewolves. Meeting eyebrows especially is a sign of being a VAMPIRE in Greece, and of being a WEREWOLF in Iceland, Denmark, and Germany.

In general, meeting eyebrows are associated with bad luck, immorality, premature death, and violent temper (perhaps because they give the face a dark and brooding appearance).

familiars A spirit that takes on the shape of animals and serves a sorcerer or witch. The familiar is found in magical traditions around the world. It assists in the performance of spellcasting and is sent out on magical errands. It serves only the person to whom it is bonded. It may receive its sustenance in the sorcerer's BLOOD.

During the European witch hunts of the Middle Ages and Renaissance, witches were said to have one or more familiars, usually dogs, cats, toads, birds, and mice. The familiars were believed to be gifts of the devil, and were dispatched by witches to bewitch people and animals into sickness and death. Lore held that the familiars were nourished by sucking the blood of the witch through the thumb, fingers, or breasts. Unusual markings on the body were called "witches' marks" and indicated where the familiars sucked the blood.

See also *TLAHUELPUCHI*; VAMPIRE SORCERERS AND WITCHES.

FURTHER READING:
Guiley, Rosemary Ellen. *The Encyclopedia of Witches and Witchcraft.* 2d ed. New York: Facts On File, 1999.

Feast of Trimalchio Story from the *Satyricon* involving a WEREWOLF by the first-century Roman writer Petronius. The Feast of Trimalchio is a classic werewolf tale that features deeply rooted staples of werewolf lore, such as the transformation by ritual beneath the light of the MOON, the savage attack of animals, and the sympathetic wound that reveals the werewolf's identity.

The story is related by Niceros, a freedman, at a banquet of his friend, Trimalchio. Niceros tells that while he was still a slave he fell in love with Melissa, the wife of an innkeeper. When her husband died, he plotted how to court her. The opportunity arose when his master went out of town. That night, with the moon shining "bright as midday," Niceros set off to visit Melissa. He persuaded a young soldier who was staying in his master's house to accompany him. Along the way they passed a CEMETERY, and the soldier stopped to relieve himself. Niceros sat down to wait and amused himself singing songs and counting stars.

> After a while I looked round to see what my companion was up to, and ecod! my heart jumped into my very mouth. He had taken off all his clothes and laid them in a heap by the road's edge. I tell you I was as dumped as a dead man, for I saw him piss in a circle all around his clothes, and then hey presto! he turned into a wolf.

The wolf rushed howling into the woods. Niceros bent to pick up the soldier's clothing, but the garments had all turned to stone. Upset and "half-dead with fear," Niceros hurried on to the home of his mistress.

> There I tottered in looking like a ghost; every second I thought I was going to breathe my last; my eyes were set and staring; the sweat was pouring down my form in streams; it was all I could do to gather my wits.

Melissa was annoyed that Niceros had not arrived earlier to help fend off a large wolf that had attacked their cattle and sheep. The wolf managed to escape, but not before it was wounded in the neck by a spear cast by one of the hired help. Niceros immediately suspected his acquaintance, but said nothing.

In the morning, Niceros returned home, passing by the cemetery. The stone clothes were gone, but the ground was covered with a "horrid pool" of BLOOD. At home he found the soldier lying in his bed with a heavily bleeding gash in his neck. He was being tended by a doctor.

Realizing for certain that the man was a werewolf, Niceros vowed that he would never eat with him again. Thus ends the tale.

Though fiction, the Feast of Trimalchio was often cited by demonologists of the Inquisition as an example of how werewolves transformed and behaved.

FURTHER READING:
Summers, Montague. *The Werewolf.* New York: Bell Publishing, 1966.

Feehan, Christine   Best-selling American author of romantic fantasy novels featuring the Carpathians, a race of VAMPIRE HUNTERS and VAMPIRES. Christine Feehan began writing fiction at an early age. She has created several series and has written other fictional works as well. Her most popular series is the Dark Series, launched in 1999 with *Dark Prince.* Feehan has been nominated for and has won numerous awards, including the 2003 Career Achievement Award.

The Dark Series features the Carpathians, an ancient race of predatory, savage, and immortal humans with supernatural powers. The males, who are powerful vampire hunters, require a lifemate—a sort of soulmate—in order to live a fully functioning life. Without a lifemate, they cannot feel emotions or see colors. They live lonely, solitary lives until they at last "meet the sun," that is, become destroyed by SUNLIGHT, or they turn into bestial vampires. Over the centuries, the number of Carpathian women has decreased and the males have been forced to wander the earth in search of a lifemate. They must search among mortal women for candidates, whom they transform into Carpathians. Only certain mortal women are suitable: they must be psychic, and they must be strong enough physically, mentally, and emotionally to survive the dangerous transformation.

The Dark Series books feature different Carpathian males and their quests for lifemates. Titles are

Dark Prince (1999): The world of the Carpathians is introduced. Prince Mikhail Dubrinksy finds his salvation, his lifemate Raven.

Dark Desire (1999): Carpathian Jacques is suspected of being a vampire by human vampire hunters. They cap-

The cover of one of Christine Feehan's Dark Series of vampire novels. (Courtesy Christine Feehan)

ture him, torture him, and bury him alive. He lives in his grave for seven years, sustained by a mental contact with Shea O'Halloran, an American surgeon. Led by her dreams, she goes to the Carpathian Mountains and finds Jaques, who wants her for his lifemate.

Dark Gold (2000): In San Francisco, Alexandria Houton becomes embroiled in a love relationship with the Carpathian Aiden Savage, the twin of Julian Savage. Aiden seeks to transform her into his lifemate.

Dark Magic (2000): Gregori impatiently waits to be united with Savannah, his lifemate and the daughter of Prince Mikhail and Raven. He has given her five years after turning 18, but she runs off to New Orleans and becomes a famous magician. He must convince her to bind to him.

Dark Challenge (2000): Julian Savage has failed to find his lifemate and is about to self-destruct in the sun when he is tasked to warn a singer that she is being stalked. He meets Desari and realizes she is his lifemate.

Dark Fire (2001): Darius (Desari's brother) meets Rusti Trine, also called "Tempest," who is the new auto mechanic for his traveling troupe the Dark Troubadours. He sees her as his lifemate and must capture her heart.

Dark Legend (2002): Gabriel hunts for his twin, Lucien, who has turned vampire. In Paris he meets his lifemate, the enchanting Francesca Del Ponce, a healer.

Dark Guardian (2002): Jaxon Montgomery is a police officer who shuns relationship because her crazy stepfather, Tyler Drake, has sworn to kill anyone who gets close to her. When Jaxon is shot on duty, she is rescued by Lucian Dratrazanoff, who transforms her into a Carpathian to be his lifemate. They hunt vampires together and fend off Drake.

Dark Symphony (2003): Byron Justanico is a "good" vampire who is a vampire hunter for the Carpathians. He feeds only to sustain himself. In Italy, he becomes enchanted with Antonietta Scarlatti, a blind, orphaned concert pianist who is an heiress to a great fortune. She is psychic, and she is to be his lifemate. Justanico uncovers a plot to poison her and some of her relatives.

Dark Melody (2003): Dayan, a guitar player and singer in the Dark Troubadours, finds his lifemate in Corinne Wentworth, a telepathic widow. The murderer of her husband is stalking Corinne and her sister-in-law, Lisa. To complicate matters, Corinne has a weak heart that may jeopardize her ability to transform into a Carpathian.

Dark Destiny (2004): As a child, Destiny was captured by a vampire. Now she is grown. Nicolae hunts the world for her, hoping the Prince of the Carpathians can help her. He finds in her his lifemate. They must battle a conspiracy of vampires.

Two "Dark" stories are in anthologies: "Dark Dream" in *After Twilight* (2001), and "Dark Descent" in *The Only One* (2003). *Dark Melody* was made into a film for video and DVD release.

Other series created by Feehan are the Leopard Series, the Ghost Walkers, and the Drake Sisters.

FURTHER READING:
Christine Feehan website. URL: http://www.christinefeehan.com. Downloaded on January 4, 2004.
Feehan, Christine. *Dark Destiny*. New York: Jove, 2004.
———. *Dark Melody*. New York: Dorchester Publishing, 2003.
———. *Dark Symphony*. New York: Jove, 2003.
———. *Dark Guardian*. New York: Dorchester Publishing, 2002.
———. *Dark Legend*. New York: Dorchester Publishing, 2002.
———. *Dark Fire*. New York: Dorchester Publishing, 2001.
———. *Dark Challenge*. New York: Dorchester Publishing, 2000.
———. *Dark Magic*. New York: Dorchester Publishing, 2000.
———. *Dark Gold*. New York: Dorchester Publishing, 2000.
———. *Dark Desire*. New York: Dorchester Publishing, 1999.
———. *Dark Magic*. New York: Dorchester Publishing, 2000.
———. *Dark Prince*. New York: Dorchester Publishing, 1999.

finding vampires   Means for identifying unknown VAMPIRES. In some cases the identity of a vampire may be known to its victims or others who can identify characteristics and appearances. If the identity is not known, certain procedures can be followed to locate the right grave. In southern Europe, the search is best done on a SATURDAY, because that is the only day of the week that vampires are obliged to lie in their graves. Professional VAMPIRE HUNTERS such as the *DHAMPIR* may be employed. Various ways of finding and identifying vampires are

Footprints. Ash or salt scattered about graves will reveal the imprint of the vampire's feet.

Horse sense. Find a WHITE HORSE and lead it around the graves. Horses are sensitive to spirits and the supernatural; thus, the horse will refuse to step over the grave of a vampire. The best equine candidates for the job are ones that have never stumbled. Ideally, a virgin boy should ride the horse. The purity in both boy and horse will recoil in horror in the presence of the evil of the vampire.

Blue light. A vampire's grave may give itself away by the presence of an eerie, bluish flame at night. In European folklore, the BLUE glow is the soul.

Grave oddities. Other telltale signs are graves that have HOLES in them, graves that are sunken (see ERETICA), and graves that have crooked CROSSES or tombstones. All of these indicate that a vampire is dwelling underneath. In Greek lore, a vampire grave has a hole about the size of two cupped hands, located in the area of the head or chest. Those who are brave enough to look into the hole will see the vampire's gleaming eyes.

Random digging. Without obvious signs, vampire hunters are forced to randomly dig up graves and examine CORPSES.

FURTHER READING:
Barber, Paul. *Vampires, Burial and Death: Folklore and Reality.* New Haven, Conn.: Yale University Press, 1988.
Dundes, Alan, ed. *The Vampire: A Casebook.* Madison: University of Wisconsin Press, 1998.
Perkowski, Jan L. *The Darkling: A Treatise on Slavic Vampirism.* Columbus, Ohio: Slavica Publishers, 1989.

fishing net   Means to hold VAMPIRES in their graves. Fishing net placed over a CORPSE in its COFFIN will prevent the vampire from escaping.

See also PNIEWO VAMPIRE.

Florescu, Radu R. (1925–)   Romanian scholar best known for his partnership with RAYMOND T. MCNALLY in researching VLAD TEPES. Radu R. Florescu traces his family lineage to Vintila Florescu, a contemporary of Vlad Tepes. Vintila supported Vlad's brother, Radu the Handsome, who succeeded the throne upon the death of Vlad in the 15th century.

Florescu holds degrees from Oxford University and Indiana University. He joined Boston University as a professor of history. There he met McNally, who was interested in finding any historical basis for BRAM STOKER's novel, *DRACULA* (1897). In the 1960s Florescu and McNally went to Romania and teamed with Romanian historians Constantin Giurescu and Matai Cazacu, and genealogist George Florescu, the uncle of Radu Florescu. The team identified CASTLE POENARI as the most likely CASTLE DRACULA.

Florescu and McNally published their findings in 1972 in the best-selling book *In Search of Dracula,* followed in 1973 by *Dracula: A Biography of Vlad the Impaler, 1431–1476.* Both books emphasized slim historical connections between Vlad Tepes and the fictional COUNT DRACULA.

Florescu and McNally coauthored other books: *The Essential "Dracula": A Completely Illustrated and Annotated Edition of Bram Stoker's Classic Novel* (1979); *Dracula, Prince of Many Faces: His Life and Times* (1989); and *In Search of Dr. Jekyll and Mr. Hyde* (2000). Both championed the ability of Romanian scholars to work with their professional colleagues in the West; this was not possible until the fall of the Ceauşescu dictatorship in the later 1980s.

Florescu also independently wrote *In Search of Frankenstein: Exploring the Myths Behind Shelley's Monster* (1997), as well as several books on Romanian and Eastern European history, culture, and folklore.

FURTHER READING:

Florescu, Radu R. *In Search of Frankenstein: Exploring the Myths Behind Shelley's Monster.* Boston: New York Graphic Society, 1975.

McNally, Raymond T. *Dracula Was a Woman: In Search of the Blood Countess of Transylvania.* New York: McGraw-Hill, 1983.

McNally, Raymond T., and Radu Florescu. *In Search of Dracula: a true history of Dracula and vampire legends.* Greenwich, Conn.: New York Graphic Society, 1972.

———. *Dracula: A Biography of Vlad the Impaler 1431–1476.* New York: Hawthorn Books, 1973.

Fluckinger, Johann (18th c.)   Austrian army surgeon who documented VAMPIRE cases in Serbia. Johann Fluck-

inger's work led to the spread of the term *vampire* into the English language.

Fluckinger was stationed in Belgrade, Serbia (occupied by the Austrians), and was sent with several other medical officers to investigate reports of vampirism in the area around Medvegia. Their report, published by Fluckinger on January 7, 1732, created a sensation in Europe. The report stated that the undead really existed and were spreading throughout the German-speaking world. It was quickly translated into other languages, including French and English.

The report prompted other researchers to rush to investigate the vampire phenomenon, among them DOM AUGUSTIN CALMET, a Benedictine abbot from France, whose own voluminous work appeared in 1749 in French and 1759 in English.

See also ARNOD PAOLE.

fly   See BUTTERFLY; LIVING VAMPIRE.

foot licker   See *PALIS.*

footprints   In WEREWOLF lore, drinking WATER that collects in the footprints of wolves, especially those left in clay, will give a person the power to become a werewolf.

Forever Knight   Canadian television show about a modern-day VAMPIRE who works as a police detective in Toronto.

Forever Knight originated in 1989 as *Nick Knight,* a made-for-television movie with rock star Rick Springfield in the lead role. Plagued by guilt over his sins as a vampire, Knight becomes a policeman to try to redeem himself. He seeks a cure with the help of Natalie Lambert, a coroner who knows his secret—a story angle similar to the relationship between BARNABAS COLLINS and Dr. Julia Hoffman in *DARK SHADOWS.*

The movie aired on the Columbia Broadcasting System (CBS) network but did not garner sufficient ratings for a spin-off television series. CBS tried again in 1992 by revamping the movie into a two-hour series pilot renamed *Forever Knight* and starring Geraint Wyn Davies. The pilot launched the series the same year.

In the series, Knight, who became a vampire in the 13th century, works as a homicide detective for the Toronto police force on the night shift. His goal is to regain his mortality. In his work he is aided by the police department's pathologist, Natalie Lambert (Catherine Disher), who find him attractive. He confides his dark secret to her. She helps to cover for him when he cannot be out in the daytime. One of her official explanations is that he suffers from a severe allergy to SUNLIGHT. Knight is also aided by his partner, Tracey Vetter (Lisa Ryder), a policewoman

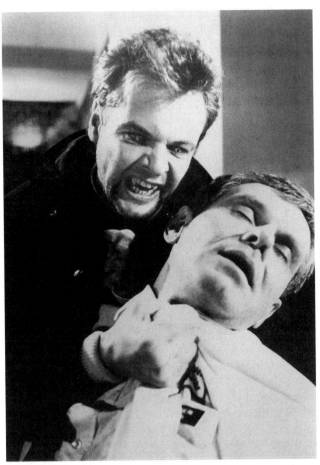

Nick Knight (Geraint Wyn Davies) throttles a victim in Forever Knight. (Author's collection)

who believes everything should be done strictly according to regulations.

Knight turns away from the community of vampires, which angers them, including LaCroix (Nigel Bennett), his master, who made him a vampire in Paris in 1228. Knight investigates some vampirelike murders and discovers they are the work of LaCroix, who is now his archenemy. Another Adversary is Vachon (Ben Bass), a 16th-century vampire who is frozen in youth.

The show moves back and forth in time, showing Knight's past vampire life as well as his cop life. Despite his desire to be part of the human community, Knight must still consume BLOOD to survive.

From the beginning, *Forever Knight* suffered from low budget and change, with major cast changes after the first season. CBS cancelled the series from its late-night lineup when it acquired David Letterman's *Late show*. TriStar revived *Forever Knight* in syndication, and the show resumed in late 1993.

For a brief period, three different versions of the show were filmed for different audiences. One version was made for the markets in Europe, Canada, and Australia, and a separate and shorter version was made for the American market. A third version, intended for Europe, was racier, with nudity; only a few of these were filmed.

The series continued to suffer cast changes and lack of interest from network buyers. Despite heroic efforts by fans, the show could not be saved from cancellation after three seasons.

In the final episode, Natalie succeeds in initiating a sexual encounter with Knight, but the vampire loses control and kills her. He is killed by being staked by LaCroix. Other major characters also are killed off.

FURTHER READING:
"Forever Knight." Available online. URL: http://www.loftworks.com/FK/Show_Info/premise.html. Downloaded on December 27, 2003.

Fortune, Dion (1891–1946)   English occultist and expert on PSYCHIC ATTACK. Dion Fortune was her pen name taken from a magical motto; she was born Violet Mary Firth. Fortune exhibited mediumistic abilities by her teens.

Fortune became an expert on psychic attack through her own experience, which she described in her book *Psychic Self-Defence* (1930). She had her first encounter with psychic attack as a naive young woman of 20. She took a job working for a woman who had extensive occult knowledge learned during a residency in India. The woman controlled her staff with techniques of mind power, and a number of her employees suffered mysterious breakdowns. Fortune herself became the object of mind manipulation when her boss wanted her to give testimony in a lawsuit. The testimony contradicted Fortune's direct knowledge of the events surrounding the suit, and she resisted. But after spending time in the presence of her boss, whose intense gaze helped direct her what to say, Fortune became so dazed and exhausted that she was forced to retire to bed, where she slept for 15 straight hours. During a second session with her boss, she found herself agreeing to baseless charges. This session also was followed by extreme exhaustion and dead sleep.

When Fortune decided to terminate her employment, her boss used the same technique to try to break her will. "You are incompetent, and you know it. You have no self-confidence and you have got to admit it," the woman said. Fortune denied this. Her boss pressured her for four hours. "I entered her room at ten o'clock, and I left it at two," Fortune wrote years later. "She must have said these two phrases several hundreds of times. I entered it a strong and healthy girl. I left it a mental and physical wreck and was ill for three years."

Fortune's experience caused her to research occultism to determine what had happened to her, and how she could have defended herself against it. "My body was like an electric battery that had been completely discharged," she wrote. "It took a long time to charge up again, and every time it was used before charging was completed, it ran down again rapidly. For a long time I had no reserves of energy, and after the least exertion would fall into a dead sleep at any hour of the day."

Her research led her to conclude that damage had been sustained by her etheric double, a nonphysical replica of the body that is attached to it and helps channel the universal life force to it. It is part of the aura, or invisible energy field, said to surround the body. Some psychics say they can see the aura and etheric body, and say that symptoms of illness and disease are evident in the etheric body, manifesting there before they do in the physical. Fortune believed that the damage to her etheric double, caused by this woman, created a leak in her life force. Thus, she suffered profound exhaustion and mental fatigue.

Magical Initiation

Fortune's turnaround came in 1919, when she took initiation into an occult order, the Alpha and Omega Lodge of the Stella Matutina. She crafted her pen name from the magical motto of the order, *Deo Non Fortuna* ("By God, not chance"). The Stella Matutina was an outer order of the renowned Hermetic Order of the Golden Dawn, the greatest, albeit short-lived, Western magical order in modern times. The Golden Dawn boasted such occult luminaries as SAMUEL LIDDELL MACGREGOR MATHERS, ALEISTER CROWLEY, William Butler Yeats, Arthur Edward Waite, and Israel Regardie. Mathers and Crowley had a falling out and waged psychic warfare against each other.

Fortune had a great talent for the magical arts. She witnessed bizarre phenomena and participated in psychic feuds, fending off psychic attacks in the name of the Masters of the Great White Lodge. As she wrote later, she "kept the occult vigil when one dare not sleep while the sun is below the horizon; and hung on desperately, matching my staying-power against the attack until the moon-tides changed and the force of the onslaught blew itself out." She worked in psychiatric care, and attributed many of the symptoms in cases she saw to psychic attacks.

Fortune did not get along with the wife of Mathers, one of the founders of the Golden Dawn, and believed Mrs. Mathers sent psychic attacks at her. In 1924 Fortune departed Stella Matutina and founded her own order, the Community (later Society) of the Inner Light. Initially, the order was part of the Golden Dawn, but later separated from it.

Fortune wrote a number of fiction and nonfiction books about the occult. *Psychic Self-Defence* is still considered the definitive work on psychic attack and psychic vampirism.

Fortune was married to a Dr. Evans. She died in January 1946. The Society of the Inner Light is based in London and continues to offers teachings in the Western occultism.

Fortune's Werewolf

Once Fortune materialized a THOUGHT-FORM WEREWOLF, the product of her resentful thoughts about revenge against someone who had done her harm. She accidentally discovered how to create an elemental thought-form by concentrating the highly charged negative thoughts with appropriate magical invocations as she drifted into the borderland phase of sleep. On this one occasion, she was seized with thoughts of going berserk (see BERSERKIR), and then felt a curious drawing-out sensation from her solar plexus. A large ectoplasmic wolf materialized on the bed beside her. Fortune was horrified, but knew through her magical experience that she could control the thing with her own will as long as she did not panic; otherwise, it would gain the upper hand on her. It snarled at her and bared its teeth, but she boldly poked it and shoved it to the floor. There it changed from a fierce wolf into a meek dog. It then disappeared through a gap in the northern corner of the room (north is associated with dark forces in magic and the supernatural). Fortune learned the next morning that another member of her household had disturbing nightmares of wolves that night and had awakened to see the eyes of a wild animal in the corner of her room.

Fortune was told by her magical teacher that the elemental werewolf was a protruding part of herself, and she must reabsorb it into herself at all costs. If she did not, it would gain strength on its own and would sever the psychic umbilical cord that attached it to her solar plexus.

At the first dusk, Fortune summoned the werewolf, which reentered the room through the same northern corner through which it had departed. It looked like an Alsatian and seemed pleasant and smelled doggy. Fortune could see the etheric umbilical cord that connected it to her. She concentrated her will and began to draw the life out of the thought-form through the cord, as though she were sucking on a giant straw. As the wolf form began to fade, Fortune was seized with violent impulses to go berserk. She was able to resist them. The wolf form dissipated into a shapeless gray mist, which she also drew up the cord into herself. There were no more materializations of the werewolf.

FURTHER READING:
Fortune, Dion. *Psychic Self-Defence.* York Beach, Me.: Samuel Weiser, 1957. First published 1939.
Richardson, Alan. *Priestess: The Life and Magic of Dion Fortune.* Wellingborough, England: Aquarian Press, 1987.

fox fairy   See HULI JING.

"Fragment of a Story"   Short story written by LORD BYRON in response to JOHN POLIDORI's story, THE VAMPYRE.

Byron created the original story during an evening of storytelling in 1816 in his rented maison at Lake Geneva, Switzerland. He was in the company of his physician and traveling companion, John Polidori, poet Percy Bysshe Shelley and his soon-to-be wife, Mary Wollstonecraft, and Mary's half sister, Claire Clairmont. Polidori borrowed Byron's idea to write "The Vampyre," published in 1819 and attributed to Byron.

Furious at the success of the story, and complaining he detested VAMPIRES, Byron was forced to write his own version, much shorter than Polidori's novella, and without the lurid vampiric details and violence that Polidori had added to the tale. "Fragment" was published as an appendix to Byron's poem *Mazeppa*. It has an unsatisfying end.

The first-person narrator of the story is an unnamed man. He tells how he befriends a man named Augustus Darvell, who comes from a family of considerable fortune and lineage. Darvell is enigmatic and remote, but is not the sinister, deceitful womanizer portrayed by the vampire antihero, LORD RUTHVEN, in Polidori's story. He suffers from some unknown and "cureless disquiet" that puzzles the narrator.

The narrator convinces Darvell to join him in travels abroad. They go to the south of Europe and then to the East. In Turkey, events take a turn for the worst. Darvell—normally a man in robust health—begins wasting away and experiences increasing difficulty sleeping. En route to Ephesus, they are forced to stop at a Turkish CEMETERY so that Darvell can rest.

Darvell announces that his life is near its end and he has come here to die. He has a final request, which the narrator agrees to fulfill. Darvell gives him a ring inscribed with Arabic characters. He says that on the ninth of the month—any month—precisely at noon, the narrator is to fling the ring into the SALT springs that run into the Bay of Eleusis, and the following day at noon he must go to the ruins of the temple of Ceres and wait one hour. Darvell gives no reason for these instructions, but says the reason will become known when the instructions are followed. The narrator notes that this very day is the ninth.

While they are speaking, a stork alights nearby with a writhing snake in its mouth. The stork does not eat the snake, but seems to watch the men. This unnerves the narrator for reasons unknown to him. Darvell says he must be buried at the exact spot where the bird is perched.

As soon as the stork flies away, Darvell falls dead. His face turns nearly black. The narrator and their servants bury him. The story ends there with the line, "Between astonishment and grief, I was tearless."

Byron professed a great distaste for vampires. There are dark hints about the true nature of Darvell, but no overt vampiric signs or behavior.

See also ARTS AND ENTERTAINMENT.

FURTHER READING:
Frayling, Christopher. *Vampyres: Lord Byron to Count Dracula.* London: Faber and Faber, 1991.

Frankenstein Meets the Wolf Man (1943)

A sequel to Universal Pictures' highly successful WEREWOLF film, THE WOLF MAN (1941), starring LON CHANEY JR. and BELA LUGOSI.

In *The Wolf Man*, Chaney Jr. plays Larry Talbot, who becomes a werewolf after being bitten by one in the forest near his family castle in Wales. Talbot dies, clubbed to death by his own father who does not realize the wolf monster is his own son.

Death has never been an obstacle to scriptwriters of film and television shows, and the popularity of *The Wolf Man* led Universal Pictures to simply restore Talbot to life without explanation.

In *Frankenstein Meets the Wolf Man,* Talbot is suffering under the curse of the werewolf and hates his monthly bloodlusts under the spell of the full MOON. He appeals for help to Maleva, an old GYPSY woman, who, in *The Wolf Man,* was mother to the werewolf (Lugosi) who infected Talbot by biting him. Once again the role of Maleva is played by Maria Ouspenskaya. Maleva tells Talbot that the only person who can help him is Dr. Frankenstein. The two of them set out for Europe to find the doctor.

When they arrive in the village of Vasaria, they learn that Frankenstein and his Monster were destroyed in a fire set by the villagers. When the villagers discover Talbot is a werewolf, they pursue him as well.

Talbot flees to the ruins of Frankenstein's laboratory, where he discovers that the Monster (Lugosi) is not dead after all, but is frozen. He revives the creature. Later—after his transformation back into a man—he meets Frankenstein's daughter (Ilona Massey). She agrees to furnish him with her father's research notes, but only after the notes are used to destroy the Monster.

Meanwhile, the Monster escapes during a full moon, and Talbot, now a werewolf, engages him in a ferocious battle. The villagers blow up a nearby dam to send floodwaters racing down to destroy the ruined laboratory and both monsters.

Frid, Jonathan (1924?–)

Canadian actor best known for his portrayal of the vampire BARNABAS COLLINS in the daytime soap series *DARK SHADOWS*.

Jonathan Frid was born on December 2, 1924 (some sources say 1927) in Hamilton, Ontario. Attracted to the theater, he began acting in prep school and studied acting at McMasters University. School was interrupted during World War II, when Frid served in the Royal Canadian Navy. After the war, he returned to McMasters and became the head of the drama society. He graduated in 1948.

In 1949 he went to London, where he studied at the Royal Academy of Dramatic Arts. After two years he went back to Canada and acted with repertory companies and on radio and television. He moved to the United States in 1954 and earned a master's degree in directing in 1957. He intended to become a drama professor, but continued acting in productions around the country.

Frid was in New York City in 1967 when he was offered the role of Barnabas Collins. Originally, the role was supposed to last only a few weeks to provide a ratings boost to the show. Frid never auditioned for the role and admitted later that he did not particularly want it. But he took it, and Barnabas was immediately so popular that the show—

Barnabas Collins (Jonathan Frid) bares his fangs in Dark Shadows. *(Author's collection)*

his own production company, Clunes Associates, with partner Mary O'Leary, to perform three touring readers' theater productions for small audiences: "Jonathan Frid's Fools and Friends," "Jonathan Frid's Fridiculousness," and "Jonathan Frid's Shakespearean Odyssey." Frid toured from 1988 to 1994, during which he also toured with the Broadway revival of *Arsenic and Old Lace*.

In 1994 Frid returned to Canada and retired from public life, though he continued to develop short programs derived from his one-man shows. His retirement proved to be semi-retirement, and he has occasionally appeared in productions in Canada and the United States.

FURTHER READING:
Jonathan Frid Web site. URL: http://jonathanfrid.com. Downloaded on January 3, 2004.

***Fright Night* (1985)**   Humorous VAMPIRE film directed by Tom Holland and released by Columbia, in which a mysterious man who is secretly a vampire moves into a suburban neighborhood and is noticed by the boy next door.

Jerry Dandrige (Chris Sarandon) and his companion Billy Cole (Jonathan Stark) move in to the empty house next door to Charley Brewster (William Ragsdale), a teen who lives with his single mother. Charley is attempting unsuccessfully to seduce his girlfriend, Amy (Amanda Bearse), in his bedroom when he notices Cole moving what appears to be a COFFIN into the house under the cover of darkness. Later, he notices that Dandridge has odd habits—he is seen only at night—and he thinks he sees Dandridge attack someone. No one—not even Amy—believes Charley.

When finally Charley knows for certain that Dandridge is a vampire, he seeks out the help of the only VAMPIRE HUNTER he knows, Peter Vincent (Roddy McDowall), who is really only an actor playing a "Vampire Slayer" as the host of a late-night television horror show, *Fright Night*. Vincent turns Charley down, but agrees when Charley offers him money.

Meanwhile, Dandridge turns Charley's friend Evil Ed (Stephen Geoffreys) into a vampire. He goes after Amy to attempt to seduce her. A key scene takes place at a disco, where Dandridge dances with an increasingly mesmerized Amy. As she dances, her appearance changes from innocent teen girl to a sexually mature and aggressive young woman. The scene underscores the erotic and sexually liberating component of vampirism that has been present in vampire literature and entertainment since the 19th century.

When Vincent realizes he is dealing with a real vampire, he becomes frightened and abandons Charley, admitting he is only an actor, not a real vampire slayer. Later, he comes back to the rescue. He and Charley go to Dandridge's coffin to stake him, but the vampire awakens and attacks Vincent, rendering him helpless. Charley rips the curtains from the window, letting in fatal SUNLIGHT. Dandridge is destroyed, and Amy is saved.

and Frid—went on for another four years. Frid appeared in 594 of the 1,225 episodes. Throughout the series, Frid remained uncomfortable with memorizing lines every day. He said this discomfort helped to create the character.

Frid acted in stage productions during *Dark Shadows*, and he also appeared in the first *Dark Shadows* film, *House of Dark Shadows* (1970), in which he is killed at the end.

After *Dark Shadows* ended in April 1971, Frid pursued a variety of acting roles on stage, television, and film, and to do seminars, readings, and theater workshop productions. He appeared at *Dark Shadows* fan conventions, where he read poetry and short stories. In 1986 he formed

Fright Night was novelized by John Skipp and Craig Spector in 1985 and was issued as a COMIC by Now Comics in 1988.

Fright Night Part 2, released in 1988, reprises the roles of Ragsdale as Charley and McDowall as Vincent. Charley has been sent to a psychiatrist to disabuse him of the notion that vampires are real. Just when he is willing to agree, another vampire, Regine (Julie Cameron), moves in next door, and it seems the same thing is going to happen again. Regine is Dandridge's sister, and she has come to avenge his death.

Regine replaces Vincent as show host. He denounces her as a real vampire and is institutionalized in a mental hospi-tal. Regine kidnaps Charley, planning to turn him into a vampire. Charley's girlfriend, Alex (Traci Lin), frees Vincent, and the two rescue Charley. Vincent succeeds in destroying Regine by using a MIRROR to reflect sunlight on her.

Fright Night Part 2 was directed by Tommy Lee Wallace and was released by Tri Star/Vista.

FURTHER READING:

Silver, Alain, and James Ursini. *The Vampire Film: From* Nosferatu *to* Interview with the Vampire. 3d ed. New York: Limelight Editions, 1997.

Skipp, John, and Craig Spector. *Fright Night*. New York: TOR Books, 1985.

Charlie Brewster (William Ragsdale) and his girlfriend, Alexandra Goode (Traci Lin), hold vampires at bay with a cross in Fright Night Part 2. *(Author's collection)*

games Board, role-playing, and computer entertainment with VAMPIRE and WEREWOLF themes have been increasingly popular since the 1960s. Initially, games were spin-offs of novels and films, but the huge popularity of role-playing games has led to spin-off novels from the games, often written by leading horror and fantasy authors.

Vampire Games

The popular gothic soap opera DARK SHADOWS inspired one of the first vampire board games in the 1960s. The BARNABAS COLLINS "Dark Shadows" Game featured a challenge to assemble a skeleton, with the winner being able to wear a pair of Barnabas-style fangs. Board games that followed in the 1970s and 1980s featured vampire hunting, and even vampire murder mysteries. *BRAM STOKER'S DRACULA* (1992), Francis Ford Coppola's film, inspired a spin-off game that featured characters from Stoker's novel (and the film) who try to rescue Mina harker from COUNT DRACULA. It also inspired a computer game and a role-playing game.

Role-playing games were dominant by the 1990s, thanks to the success of the magic-and-fantasy Dungeons and Dragons, which had featured vampires and werewolves in Ravenloft, set on an island. Board games suddenly looked tame by comparison. In 1991 White Wolf, Inc. introduced Vampire: The Masquerade, created by Mark Reign-Hagen, which quickly established itself as the reigning vampire role-playing game.

Role-playing games establish a complete fantasy world, with a history, players, and rules of engagement. In The Masquerade, the history traces to the biblical character of Cain, cursed for killing his brother, Abel. According to the game, the curse is a thirst for BLOOD and eternal life to pursue the thirst, and thus the race of vampires—the Kindred—was born. Vampires created more vampires, but with each succeeding generation, the powers became weaker. Vampires lived in the open, not necessarily proclaiming themselves but not hiding either.

In 1435 events took a radical turn. The Inquisition turned on vampires as well as witches, and threatened them with extinction. In 1486 a global convocation of vampires organized the Camarilla, a secret, underground network, and established The Masquerade. All vampires were to live in secret, and make every effort to convince mortals that vampires were either all destroyed, or had never existed in the first place.

The Masquerade features clans of vampires, each with its own history, alliances, and characteristics. The clans are

- Brujah: "Rabble," rebels with a biker flair
- Gangrel: "Outlanders," nomad warriors
- Malkavian: "Lunatics," intelligent but unpredictable maniacs
- Nosferatu: "Sewer Rats," deformed monsters but good survivors
- Toreador: "Degenerates," impassioned artists

- Tremere: "Warlocks," ambitious and skilled in intrigue
- Ventrue: "Blue Bloods," social aristocrats
- Lasombra: "Keepers," murderous and manipulative
- Tzimisce: "Fiends," the elite intelligentsia and scientists

The Camarilla clans are opposed by The Sabbat, a huge, barbaric sect that considers vampires to be superior to mortals, and believes in aggressive conquest.

Independent or unallied clans are

- Assamites: "Assassins," predatory Middle Easterners
- The Followers of Set: "Serpents," shadowy, into drugs, sex, money, and power
- Giovanni: "Necromancers," materialists after wealth and power
- Ravnos: "Deceivers," thieves, liars, and wanderers

In addition, there are social distinctions, or social castes:

- Caitiff: degenerates, often clanless, who feed off the weak and dying
- Childe: immature, still under the dominance of their Sire or creator
- Neonate: freshly minted, full-fledged vampires
- Anarch: rebels against society who have achieved some status and respect
- Ancilla: young, but proven to the Elders
- Elder: power holders who are between 200 and 1,000 years old
- Methuselah: vampires 1,000 to 2,000 years old who retreat in a sort of melancholy
- Antediluvian: the oldest and most powerful vampires of all

Princes rule over large metropolitan areas. There are supporting supernatural characters, such as witches, warlocks, and werewolves, who are called "lupines."

Players in The Masquerade create characters and then interact with other players in games that are created by a gamemaster or storyteller. The gamemaster evaluates their performances. Initially, the game was played with dice; in 1993 hand signals enabled it to be played more dynamically and in constant character.

The Masquerade, as well as other vampire role-playing games, have an international community of players.

Werewolf Games

Werewolf games have not achieved the popularity of vampire games, but nonetheless have dedicated followings. White Wolf created Werewolf: The Apocalypse, structured similarly to The Masquerade, though with a simpler world. The setting is the World of Darkness, a grim version of earth that is in danger of being plunged into The Apocalypse by the evil Wyrm. The werewolves, or Garou, are dedicated to protecting Gaia, or Mother Earth, from the machinations of the Wyrm.

There are three breeds of Garou:

- Hominids, those born and raised as humans
- Lupus, those born and raised as wolves
- Metis, those who are deformed half-breeds, the product of forbidden unions of two Garou

The three breeds live in 13 main tribes:

- Black Furies: females of Greek origin who defend the wilderness
- Bone Gnawers: jackal-like urban street dwellers, hated by other Garou
- Children of Gaia: peacemakers
- Fianna: Celtic bards and singers
- Get of Fenris: warriors and warmongers
- Glass Walkers: urban financiers and technocrats
- Red Talons: all-lupus, hominid-haters
- Shadow Lords: ambitious conquerors
- Silent Striders: nomadic ones believed to have psychic powers
- Silver Fangs: equivalent of royalty
- Stargazers: martial arts experts
- Uktena: magical experts, very secretive
- Wendigo: warrior descendants of Native Americans

Like other role-playing games, players in The Apocalypse create characters and then engage in situations set by a gamemaster.

gander   In Romanian lore, a VAMPIRE detector. A gander will not walk over the grave of a vampire. The gander is not as favored as a BLACK STALLION or WHITE HORSE in locating vampire graves.

See also FINDING VAMPIRES.

Gandillon Werewolves (1598)   A French family of WEREWOLVES. The bizarre case of the Gandillon family involved a sister, her brother, and two of his children who ravaged the Jura area in wolf forms.

The case unfolded with Pernette Gandillon, a poor girl who ran about on all fours in the belief that she was a wolf. One day while in her wolf madness, she came upon a boy and girl, siblings, who were out gathering wild strawberries. A BLOOD rage came upon Pernette, and she attacked the girl. The girl's four-year-old brother successfully fended Pernette off with a knife. Pernette turned on the boy and dealt him a fatal slash to his neck. The girl identified Pernette as the attacker. Enraged peasants seized Pernette and tore her to pieces.

Soon thereafter, Pernette's brother, Pierre, was accused of witchcraft. He was said to kidnap children and take them to witches' SABBATS, to make damaging hail, and to transform himself into a wolf. The transformation was made possible by an OINTMENT he had received from the devil. On one occasion, Pierre changed into a hare, but usually he was a wolf, with long, shaggy gray hair.

Pierre readily acknowledged that these charges were true. Furthermore, while in the form of a wolf, he had killed and eaten animals and humans. When he wanted to resume his human form, he rolled in dewy grass.

Pierre's son, Georges, confessed that he too had used the ointment to become a wolf. Once he had killed and eaten two goats. During his adventures as a wolf, his human body would lie in a cataleptic state for hours in his bed. Once this state had lasted for three hours, during which he went off to a witches' sabbat.

Both Pierre and Georges had terrible scars upon their faces, arms, and legs, the result of dog bites they had received while in the form of wolves.

Pierre's daughter, Antoinette, confessed that she had sold her soul to the devil, who had appeared to her in the form of a black cat. She made hail and attended sabbats.

In prison, Pierre and Georges behaved like raving maniacs, running about their cells on all fours and howling. They did not change shape into wolves, because, it was believed, they did not have their magical ointments with them.

All three—Pierre, Georges, and Antoinette—were convicted, hanged, and burned.

See also LYCANTHROPY.

FURTHER READING:
Baring-Gould, Sabine. *The Book of Werewolves*. London: Smith, Elder & Co., 1865.
Otten, Charlotte F., ed. *A Lycanthropy Reader: Werewolves in Western Culture*. New York: Dorset Press, 1989.

garlic   A species of the onion universally regarded as a significant protection against evil supernatural entities, such as witches, DEMONS, VAMPIRES, and the EVIL EYE. Garlands of garlic worn around the neck or hung in a house will prevent the entry or attack of vampires and demonic spirits. Garlic is stuffed in the mouths of CORPSES, rubbed on corpses, and strewn about COFFINS and gravesites to prevent vampires from leaving their graves.

Garlic should be rubbed around doors, windows, and chimneys to keep vampires away and prevent them from attacking. Windows should be anointed with garlic in the form of a CROSS. Livestock should be rubbed with garlic.

In European lore, the charm "here's garlic in your eyes" is said to ward off the evil eye.In China, children can be protected against vampires by wetting their foreheads with garlic. In Philippine lore, one rubs the armpits with garlic.

In Romanian lore, failure to eat garlic identifies one as a LIVING VAMPIRE.

Garnier, Gilles (1873)   French WEREWOLF. Gilles Garnier, also known as "the hermit of St. Bonnot," was an ugly

Wreaths of garlic for sale in a farmer's market in Budapest, Hungary (Photo by R. E. Guiley)

recluse shunned by others. He lived with his wife, Apolline, in an inaccessible, turf-roofed, and rudely constructed hovel near Amanges, France.

In autumn 1873 a werewolf was said to have carried off several small children in the area of Dole. The court parliament at Dole issued a proclamation authorizing the peasants to hunt the creature down.

Initially, Garnier was not a suspect, despite his odd appearance and manner. He had bushy EYEBROWS that met, a pale face with livid complexion, a long gray beard, and a stooping walk. He seldom spoke to others.

On November 8, 1873, a girl was attacked by a wolf. Her screams attracted some of the peasants. When they reached her, they saw a ferocious wolf and the wounded girl trying to defend herself. The appearance of the peasants frightened off the wolf, who ran into the forest. Several peasants said they thought they had recognized the features of the hermit in the creature.

A few days later, on November 14, a 10-year-old boy went missing. Garnier was arrested and put on trial. Both he and his wife confessed to his being a werewolf, and their testimony was corroborated by witnesses.

Garnier confessed to taking the form of a wolf and attacking and slaying a number of children. On the last day of Michelmas, he attacked and killed a 12-year-old girl. He carted her body into the woods, stripped off her clothing, and gnawed her arms and legs. He thought the flesh so tasty that he took some of it home to his wife for her enjoyment.

Eight days later, he seized another girl but did not kill her, for he was surprised by three persons, and he fled. But soon he attacked a 10-year-old boy and strangled him to death. He ate the arms and legs, tearing one leg completely off with his fangs, and also ate most of the boy's belly.

Garnier's next victim was a boy of 12 or 13, whom he seized and killed. He intended to take the body into the woods to eat, but once again the appearance of peasants frightened him off. Those men testified at Garnier's trial that they had seen him in human form and not a wolf form.

Garnier was convicted and sentenced to be dragged to the place of public execution, where he was burned alive.

See also SHAPE-SHIFTING.

FURTHER READING:
Baring-Gould, Sabine. *The Book of Werewolves*. London: Smith, Elder & Co., 1865.
Otten, Charlotte F., ed. *A Lycanthropy Reader: Werewolves in Western Culture*. New York: Dorset Press, 1989.

Gellar, Sarah Michelle   See *ANGEL*; *BUFFY THE VAMPIRE SLAYER*.

Gerard, Emily de Laszkowski   Englishwoman whose article on little-known lore and superstitions of TRANSYLVANIA was used by BRAM STOKER in his research for *DRACULA* (1897).

Emily de Laszkowski Gerard was married to a military man in the Austro-Hungarian forces and spent 16 years in Austria. In 1883 her husband was appointed to the command of the cavalry brigade in Transylvania, composed of two hussar regiments in Hermanstadt and Kronstadt. The couple spent two years in the "Land Beyond the Forest," which is the meaning of "Transylvania."

For Gerard, Transylvania was an exotic place, a mysterious land isolated almost islandlike from the Western world, stuck in a past time and steeped in superstition and odd customs. Her book about her experiences and observations, *The Land Beyond the Forest*, was published in England in two volumes in 1888. She also wrote several articles, including "Transylvania Superstitions," for English periodicals.

Gerard said that she felt like Robinson Crusoe when she left Transylvania. She had become attached to the place, but also was glad to return to the outer world. She wrote:

> Situated by nature within a formidable rampart of snow-tipped mountains, and shielded by heavy curtains of shrouding forests against the noise and turmoil of the outer world, the very name of Transylvania tells us that it was formerly regarded as something apart, something out of reach, whose existence even for a time was enveloped in mystery. In olden times these gloomy forest-gorges were tenanted only by the solitary bear or packs of famished wolves, while the mistrustful lynx looked down from the giddy heights, and the chamois leaped unchecked from rock to rock. The people who lived westward of this mountain rampart, knowing little or nothing of the country on the other side, designated it as Transylvania or the land beyond the forest, just as we sometimes talk of the "land beyond the clouds . . .
>
>   . . . [T]he old-world charm still lingers around and about for many things. It is floating everywhere and anywhere—in the forests and on the mountains, in medieval churches and ruined watch-towers, in mysterious caverns and in ancient gold-mines, in the songs of the people and the legends they tell.

Gerard wrote that she attempted to "seize the general color and atmosphere of the land." She discusses history, terrain, clothing, food, superstitions, and customs concerning marriage, death and burial, other superstitions, and the lore of VAMPIRES and WEREWOLVES.

FURTHER READING:
Gerard, Emily de Laszkowski. *The Land Beyond the Forest: Facts, Figures and Fancies from Transylvania*. Edinburgh and London: William Blackwood and Sons, 1888.

ghoul   A demon who feeds on the flesh of human beings, especially travelers, children, or CORPSES stolen out of graves. Ghoulish entities are universal. They are prominent in Arabic lore; the name comes from the Arabic terms *ghul* (masculine) and *ghula* (feminine).

Ghouls are nocturnal creatures with long nails who inhabit graveyards, ruins, and other lonely places. Sometimes they are described as dead humans who sleep for long periods in secret graves, then awake, rise, and feast on both the living and the dead.

Ghouls also personify the unknown terrors held by the desert and may be compared to the LAMIAE and LILITH night terror and childbirth demons.

In Arabic lore, the most feared type of ghoul has the ability to appear as a normal, flesh-and-blood woman. Such a creature marries an unsuspecting man, who becomes her prey. The following Arabic folktale set in 15th-century Baghdad is about such a ghoul, and blends ghoul and vampire characteristics:

An aged and wealthy merchant had an only son, Abul-Hassan, whom he wished to marry to the daughter of another merchant. This daughter was wealthy but ugly. When Abul-Hassan was shown a portrait of the girl, he was so repulsed that he asked his father to postpone the wedding so that he would have time to reconcile himself to his fate. His father agreed.

Meanwhile, Abul-Hassan fell in love with the beautiful daughter of a sage, Nadilla, and begged his father to allow him to marry her. Abul-Hassan was so persistent that at last his father acquiesced. The wedding was lavish.

Abul-Hassan might have been quite happy, had he not noticed a peculiarity about his bride. She never ate supper, and each night, as soon as she thought him to be asleep, she rose up out of bed and left, not returning until dawn.

One night Abul-Hassan feigned sleep and followed his wife. She went into a CEMETERY and entered a tomb. Abul-Hassan stepped inside after her and came upon a revolting sight. A party of ghouls was feasting on the flesh of decomposing corpses. One of the ghouls was Nadilla. Abul-Hassan managed to avoid detection and at the earliest opportunity fled back to his home.

The next evening at supper, Nadilla as usual refused to eat. Abul-Hassan confronted her with what he had seen inside the tomb. Nadilla had no reply, but took to their bed. At midnight she rose and attacked her husband with her long nails and teeth. She tore his throat and opened a vein, attempting to suck his BLOOD. Abul-Hassan killed her with a single blow. She was buried the following day.

Three days later, Nadilla reappeared a midnight and attacked her husband again, attempting to suck his blood. Abul-Hassan escaped. The next day he went to her tomb, took out her body, burned it to ASHES, and cast the ashes in the Tigris River. Thus the vampiric ghoul was destroyed.

See also BERTRAND, SERGEANT; O'DONNELL, ELLIOTT; *VETALA.*

FURTHER READING:
Baring-Gould, Sabine. *The Book of Werewolves.* London: Smith, Elder & Co., 1865.

Giles, Rupert   See *ANGEL; BUFFY THE VAMPIRE SLAYER.*

Gilles de Laval (15th c.)   French nobleman accused of murdering and mutilating children. The case of Gilles de Laval, also known as Gilles de Rais and the Maréchal (Marshal) de Retz, shocked his contemporaries. Gilles became associated with the story of Bluebeard. The case is associated with LYCANTHROPY, perhaps because of the bestial nature of the maréchal's crimes, and with vampirism because of his delight in BLOOD.

Gilles de Laval was the oldest son of Guy de Laval, a leading noble of Brittany, France. Gilles inherited his father's estate when he was 20 years of age, and he increased his fortunes by marrying Catharine de Thouars in 1420. Gilles distinguished himself in military service to King Charles VII and participated with Joan of Arc in the battle for Orléans.

Gilles's maternal grandmother died in 1432, and his inheritance from her so increased his wealth that he quit the service of the king. He spent huge sums of money. Within two years much of his fortune was gone, and he sold and ceded some of his lands.

Gilles spent much of his time at one of his residences, the moated Castle of Machecoul. A great deal of mystery surrounded his life there. Gilles was said to be pious and attend Mass three times a day and to be passionate about ecclesiastical music. Tradition holds that an astrologer once told him that he would come into the hands of an abbé in the future, and he took this to mean that he would become a monk.

From time to time, the drawbridge to his castle was lowered, and servants distributed money and food to the poor. Stories began to circulate that the children who went to beg for alms were asked to come to the kitchen of the castle and were never seen again.

In 1440 the people accused Gilles of murdering children and sacrificing them to the devil. At first the duke of Brittany ignored the matter, but under mounting pressure he agreed to have Gilles arrested. Gilles surrendered willingly and was taken to court in Nantes. All of his servants fled but two, his chamberlain, Henriet, and Pontou, both of whom remained loyal to him.

An investigation against Gilles was opened in September of that year, with instructions from the duke to make the case as weak as possible. It proved to be anything but weak.

Tearful parents came forward to make depositions that their children were last seen going toward or into the castle. Some said their children had been kidnapped by the maréchal's henchmen while they were in the woods or tending sheep. They said their children had been murdered and their bodies burned.

The testimonies were compelling, and the investigators reported them to the duke of Brittany. While he reluctantly pondered what action to take, he received a bizarre letter from the imprisoned Gilles confessing to the crimes. Gilles desired to repent and spend the rest of his life in a Carmelite monastery. His goods and wealth should be given to the poor. He signed the letter "Friar Gilles, Carmelite in intention."

The duke was urged to proceed with a trial, and he agreed to do so. Gilles's estranged wife, from whom he had been long separated, attempted to intercede with both the duke and the king to get a pardon for him. She failed.

The trial against Gilles began in October 1440. By then, he exhibited obvious signs of mental instability. He assumed himself to be a Carmelite novice and dressed in white. He spent much of his time in prayer and singing litanies. He expressed great piety. But when he appeared in court, he was dressed up in white military regalia with heavy gold chains and the collars of knightly orders. He audaciously wore a belt of ermine, a fur only the highest lords were allowed to wear.

Gilles told the court that he would endow several churches in Nantes. He asked them to expedite his case so that he could fully consecrate himself to God. He seemed to think that his declaration of piety absolved him of all responsibility for his crimes and of the need to be punished for them.

The court charged Gilles with murdering more than 200 children and burning their bodies to ASHES. It was recommended that he be punished and his lands and goods confiscated. Shocked, Gilles then denied the charges, claiming them to be false.

Henriet confessed to participating in the crimes. He said that upon orders of Gilles he had helped to remove the mutilated CORPSES of children from the dungeon of Castle Chantonce, owned by Gilles and ceded to the duke of Brittany. The corpses were transported to Machecoul, where they were burned. Many of the 36 bodies had no heads.

Henriet then began to procure children for his master. He painted a horrifying picture. The children were murdered in one particular room of Castle Machecoul. Henriet and other servants tortured the children and then stabbed them in the jugular vein so that their blood gushed over Gilles in a shower in which he bathed. When the children were dead, the maréchal would collapse in remorse and grief, wailing, weeping, and praying on his bed. While the servants washed the floor and the corpses burned in the great fireplace, Gilles recited litanies and prayers. He inhaled the fumes of the burning bodies as though it were incense in a church. The ashes were flung out a window into the moat.

Henriet said he knew of dozens of children disposed of in this unspeakable manner. He was able to provide sufficient details to corroborate the identities of some of the missing children reported in the depositions of parents. He further testified that Gilles had murdered and burned children at the Hôtel de la Suze in Nantes, where he sometimes stayed. Dozens of charred bodies had been stashed in a hayloft at Castle Marchecoul.

The story was so horrific and incredible that some of the court officials refused to believe it. Henriet insisted it was the truth and stated that Gilles took greater pleasure in hacking off the head of a child than in giving a banquet. According to the record of his testimony, he claimed:

> Sometimes he [Gilles] would seat himself on the breast of a little one, and with a knife sever the head from the body

at a single blow; sometimes he cut the throat half through very gently, that the child might languish, and he would wash his hands and his beard in its blood. Sometimes he had all the limbs chopped off at once from the trunk; at other times he ordered us to hang the infants till they were nearly dead, and then take them down and cut their throats. I remember having brought to him three little girls who were asking charity at the castle gates. He bade me cut their throats while he looked on. Andre Bricket [a servant] found another little girl crying on the steps of the house at Vannes because she had lost her mother. He brought the little thing—it was but a babe—in his arms to my lord, and it was killed before him. Pontou and I had to make away with the body. We threw it down a privy in one of the towers, but the corpse caught on a nail in the outer wall, so that it would be visible to all who passed. Pontou was let down by a rope, and he disengaged it with great difficulty.

Henriet said that Gilles had become inspired to commit such grisly murders by learning the stories of the caesars of the Roman Empire, whose similar deeds of torturing and killing children for pleasure were recorded by the historians Tacitus and Suetonius.

Pontou initially defended his master to the court, but when threatened with torture on the rack, he substantiated everything said by Henriet.

When Gilles was next brought before the court on October 24, he was still under the illusion that he would be allowed to retire to a monastery to repent his sins. He was stunned when told the king would not intercede for him, and that Henriet and Pontou had made full confessions.

Gilles broke down and confessed. He said he had cut throats, chopped off heads with cleavers, smashed skulls with hammers, hacked off limbs, torn open bodies to examine entrails and hearts, strangled, and caused slow deaths. He had committed these atrocities for eight years and had taken "incomparable delight" in them. The urge to do so had come over him—no doubt from the devil, he said—when he had read the Roman histories of the caesars in books he had found at Castle Chantonce. He decided to imitate and surpass them, and had begun his crimes the same night.

Gilles said initially he kept the killings secret, but gradually took in several confidants, including his cousin and several servants. He confessed to approximately 800 murders, 120 of which had been committed in a single year alone.

Because of Gilles's claims of involvement of the devil, and therefore witchcraft, he was turned over to a church court. His new trial lasted only a few hours. He attempted to bribe the court by promising all his lands and goods to the church in exchange for retirement to the Carmelite monastery at Nantes. He was refused. The court sentenced Gilles, Henriet, and Pontou to death.

The men were executed on October 26 by hanging and burning. Gilles delivered a sermon on the gallows. He urged people to resist the temptations of the devil and said there was no sin so great that God would not pardon it.

Gilles's body was cut down before the fire could consume it by six Carmelites and six white-robed women who appeared bearing a COFFIN. They placed the body in the coffin and took it away to the monastery, thus fulfilling the wishes of the maréchal. It was rumored that one of the women was Gilles's wife. The bodies of the two servants were burned to ashes, and the ashes were thrown to the wind.

See also BATHÓRY, ELIZABETH.

FURTHER READING:
Baring-Gould, Sabine. *The Book of Werewolves*. London: Smith, Elder & Co., 1865.
Michelet, Jules. *Satanism and Witchcraft*. Secaucus, N.J.: Citadel Press, 1939.

girdle   A magical belt that enables a person to become a WEREWOLF, or transform into other animal shapes. In werewolf lore, the girdle is usually bestowed by the devil in return for a pledge of allegiance and service to him.

Confessed werewolves said that their girdles were made either of wolf pelts or of human skin. Other magical girdles used by witches were made of the skin of the animal into which the wearer transformed. If made of human skin, it had to come from a murderer or criminal who was broken on the wheel of torture. The girdle was the width of three fingers.

Demonologists said that this infernal girdle mocked the girdles worn by the Augustinian order of saints, and by St. Monica, who was given a black belt by the Blessed Virgin Mary.

In his book *Restitution of Decayed Intelligence* (1605), historian Richard Verstegan wrote of werewolves and girdles:

> . . . werewolves are certain sorcerers, who having anointed their bodies, with an ointment which they make by the instinct of the devil; and putting on a certain enchanted girdle, do not only to the view of others seem as wolves, but to their own thinking have both the shape and nature of wolves, so long as they wear the said girdle. And they do dispose themselves as very wolves, in worrying and killing, the most human creatures.

See also SHAPE-SHIFTING; STUBB, PETER.

FURTHER READING:
Sidky, H. *Witchcraft, Lycanthropy, Drugs and Disease: An Anthropological Study of the European Witch-Hunts*. New York: Peter Lang, 1997.
Summers, Montague. *The Werewolf*. New York: Bell Publishing, 1966.

Girl and the Vampire, The   Slavic folktale prominent in Romanian VAMPIRE lore, which has several variations. According to the story, once in a village a girl and a youth were in love, but their parents did not know. The youth asked the girl's family for permission to marry, but they rejected him because he was poor. In despair, he hanged himself and became a vampire (see SUICIDE).

Being a vampire, he was able to come and visit the girl at night and make love to her, but she did not want anything to do with an evil spirit. She consulted a wise woman, who told her to fix a needle attached to a large ball of thread to the back of the vampire's coat. When he left, she should follow him to see where he went. The girl did so, and found that the vampire went into a grave in the churchyard CEMETERY.

The next night, she went back to the churchyard and saw the vampire come out of his grave, open another grave, and eat the heart of the dead man in it. Then he set out for the village to come to her.

When he met her, he asked her where she had been and what she had seen. She answered she had been nowhere and had seen nothing. The vampire warned her that if she did not tell the truth, her father would die. She refused, and two days later, her father died. The vampire did not come to her again for some time after his burial.

The next time he came to her at night, he again questioned her about what where she had been and what she had seen on that previous night. She declined, and he said her mother would die. She refused, and two days later her mother died and was buried.

Some time later, the vampire came again to her at night. This time, he told her she herself would die if she did not answer his questions truthfully. She refused, and the vampire left.

The girl called together her relatives and informed them she would die soon. She gave them instructions provided by the wise woman. They were not to take her CORPSE out of the house through the door or window, but through a hole they would knock in the wall. They were not to travel on the road, but go straight across the field to a hollow in the forest trees, and make her grave there. She then died, and the relatives followed the instructions.

Some time later, a beautiful flower bloomed on the grave of the girl. The son of the emperor was attracted to it and had it taken home. At night the flower turned into a beautiful maiden, who went to the sleeping son. One night she awakened him with a kiss. Opening his eyes, he fell in love with her. They were married and were very happy—except for one thing: The wife would never go out of the house because she was afraid of the vampire.

One day her husband took her to church, and along the way at a corner was the vampire. The girl rushed into the church with the vampire in pursuit. She hid behind a holy picture. Just as the vampire was about to grab her, the picture fell on his head and he disappeared in smoke. The girl and her husband lived happily ever after.

See also MARUSIA.

FURTHER READING:
Murgoci, Agnes. "The Vampire in Roumania," in *The Vampire: A Casebook*, Alan Dundes, ed. Madison: University of Wisconsin Press, 1998.

Glamis Castle   The oldest inhabited castle in Scotland, reportedly haunted by a monster, a VAMPIRE, and ghosts.

Glamis Castle was built in the 14th century as the home of the lords of Glamis, who, according to legend, were drinking, gambling spendthrifts who lost their family fortune. By the mid-17th century, the castle was in ruins. It was inherited by Patrick Lyons, who rebuilt the castle and rehabilitated the family, for which he was made the earl of Strathmore. But in the 18th century, the family's fortunes declined again.

According to lore, in the early 1800s the first son of the 11th earl of Strathmore was born a hideously deformed, egg-shaped monster with no neck, tiny arms and legs, and a large, hairy torso. The Monster of Glamis, as he became known, was the true heir to the family estate. To everyone's horror, the monster did not die but remained strong and hearty. The estate was unlawfully passed on to the second son. In successive generations, each earl of Strathmore was shown the creature and became psychologically disturbed as a result. The monster reportedly died sometime between 1921 or 1941. The marriage in the early 1880s of Claude George Bowes-Lyon, 14th earl of Strathmore, and Nina Cavendish-Bentnick, grandparents of Queen Elizabeth II, later raised the specter of introducing the blood of the Monster of Glamis into the royal bloodline, a fear that came to nothing. The Monster of Glamis exists only in lore; no records have ever been found to substantiate it.

Glamis Castle's vampire is said to be a woman servant who was caught sucking the BLOOD of a victim. Legend has it that she was walled up alive in a secret chamber, where she continues to sleep the sleep of the undead, until someone finds her and she is loosed once again.

Numerous ghosts, said to be former earls or unknown ladies and servants, haunt the castle and grounds.

FURTHER READING:
Guiley, Rosemary Ellen. *The Encyclopedia of Ghosts and Spirits.* 2d ed. New York: Facts On File, 2000.

gold   Metal used as a PROTECTION AGAINST VAMPIRES, though less frequently than SILVER. Gold is associated with the sun, goodness, light, divinity, and purity, and thus is an antidote to evil. Gold coins or CROSSES placed on a CORPSE will prevent it from leaving its grave as a vampire.

See also DOPPELSAUGER.

Graf Orlock (Orlac, Orloc, Orlok)   VAMPIRE in the F. W. MURNAU silent film, NOSFERATU (1922). Graf Orlock is the counterpart to BRAM STOKER's COUNT DRACULA, and is played by MAX SCHRECK. However, unlike Dracula, who can pass in normal society, Graf Orlock is a true horror.

Orlock looks like a walking cadaver just risen from the grave: He is emaciated, withered, nearly hairless, with oddly hanging arms and strange, dead eyes. He is stiff and halting in movement. He becomes increasingly alien and monstrous as the film progresses: His ears become more pointed, his fingers become elongated with pointed nails, and he develops long front teeth, so that he looks like a giant, loathsome RAT. He casts a SHADOW, unlike Dracula, but has control over animals, as does Dracula, and favors rats.

Orlock is a predator who springs from the deepest collective fears of humanity, one that can never fit within society. He acts in a primitive way, beyond reason. He is death itself. In his book *Hollywood Gothic* (1990), film critic David J. Skal comments:

In one famous scene aboard the doomed ship, the vampire springs from his rat-filled coffin like an obscene jack-in-the-box, an image simultaneously suggesting erection, pestilence, and death.

In 1979 Klaus Kinski starred as the vampire in a remake of *Nosferatu* directed by Werner Herzog. Kinski's vampire has pale skin, a hairless head, dark encircled eyes, ratlike fangs, and sharp fingernails, but he does not evoke the revulsion and horror elicited by Schreck.

FURTHER READING:
Skal, David J. *Hollywood Gothic: The Tangled Web of Dracula from Novel to Stage to Screen.* New York: W. W. Norton & Company, 1990.

Grando, Giure (d. 1672)   Alleged VAMPIRE. In 1672 Giure Grando died near Laibach, Istria. The dead man was seen immediately after his burial sitting behind the door in his house. Thereafter, he appeared repeatedly at night to have sexual relations with his widow. He also ran up and down the village streets, knocking on doors, whereupon someone inside died. His distressed widow appealed to the village mayor for help, and he found several brave men to open Grando's grave. An account, written by Baron Jan Vajkart Valsovar in 1689, continues:

In it they found Giure Grando intact. His face was very red. He laughed at them and opened his mouth. At first [the mayor's] companions fled, but soon they came back again and set about driving a sharpened hawthorn stake through the belly of the corpse, which recoiled at each blow. Then the priest exorcised the spirit with a crucifix, "Behold you vampire (strigon), here is Jesus Christ who has delivered us from hell and has died for us; and you, vampire (strigon) can have no rest, etc." At these words tears flowed from the corpse's eye. Finally they cut off the dead man's head with one blow, at which he let out a cry like a living person and the grave was filled with fresh blood.

FURTHER READING:
Leatherdale, Clive. *The Origins of Dracula.* London: William Kimber, 1987.

grave plants and vines   See SPAULDING FAMILY VAMPIRES.

Grenier, Jean   Thirteen-year-old WEREWOLF of Landes in southern France. The case of Jean Grenier became one of the most famous and most-discussed episodes of LYCAN-THROPY in Europe. It began one spring afternoon with two girl shepherds. They came upon an odd-looking boy who was sitting on a log. His long RED hair was thick and matted, and he had an olive complexion. He was emaciated, but his eyes were bright and fierce and he had prominent canine teeth that protruded over his lower lip when his mouth was closed. His hands were excessively large and powerful-looking. His fingernails were black and pointed like the talons of a bird. His clothing was in tatters. He was given to bursts of maniacal laughter.

He introduced himself as Jean Grenier, the son of a priest, and he demanded to know which of the girls was prettier, for he would marry that one. He said he looked the way he did because sometimes he wore a wolf-skin. The wolf-skin had been given to him by a man named Pierre Labourant, who wore an IRON chain about his neck, which he gnawed, and who lived in a hellish place of gloom and fire.

Grenier said that Labourant wrapped the wolf-skin cape around him every Monday, Friday, and Sunday, and for about an hour at dusk every other day. This transformed Grenier into a werewolf. He told the girls:

I have killed dogs and drunk their blood; but little girls taste better, their flesh is tender and sweet, their blood rich and warm. I have eaten many a maiden, as I have been on my raids together with my nine companions. I am a werewolf! Ah, ha! If the sun were to set I would soon fall on one of you and make a meal of you!

The girls fled.

Meanwhile, a 13-year-old girl, Marguerite Poirier, who lived near the village of St. Antoine de Pizon, was well acquainted with Grenier, for she tended sheep with him. He often frightened her with his wild and gruesome stories of being a werewolf and killing and eating dogs and girls. He claimed to have eaten many girls, whose flesh he preferred to dogs, and he described two incidents to Poirier: One girl he nearly devoured, and threw the remainder of her CORPSE to a wolf that arrived; the second girl he bit to death, lapped up her BLOOD and ate every bit of her except for her arms and shoulders.

One day Poirier had an experience that terrified her so much that she abandoned her flock and ran home. She was tending the sheep alone when she was suddenly attacked by a wild beast that tore her clothing with its fangs. She beat it off with her shepherd's staff. It sat up on its hind legs like a begging dog, and gave her a look of utter rage. It resembled a wolf but was not a wolf: It was shorter and stouter, with a stumpy tail, small head, and red hair.

The villagers were alarmed at this report, for several little girls had gone missing. Poirier's account and her descriptions of Grenier and his stories caused an investigation to be mounted. Grenier was arrested.

It was revealed that he was not the son of a priest, but was the son of a poor laborer in the same village as Poirier. Three months earlier, he had left home and did odd work and begged. He had taken several jobs tending sheep, but had been dismissed for neglecting his work.

Grenier willingly told the court about his werewolf escapades. He said that when he had been 11 years old, a neighbor had taken him deep into the woods and introduced him to Monsieur de la Forest, a black man who signed him with his nail and gave Grenier and his neighbor an OINTMENT and a wolf-skin. From then on, Grenier had run about as a werewolf.

He admitted attacking Poirier, intending to kill her, but she fended him off. He said he had killed only one dog, a white one, and had drunk its blood. He had wounded another dog, but was chased off by its owner. He described killing several children:

- an infant he dragged from its cradle and devoured and shared with a wolf
- a girl shepherd he tore with his teeth and nails, and ate
- a child by a stone bridge he assaulted

Grenier said that he went out hunting for children when commanded to do so by the Lord of the Forest, who was his master. When so ordered, he rubbed the ointment on his body and left his clothes in a thicket. He preferred to go out in the daytime when the MOON was waning, but sometimes went out as a wolf at night. The Lord of the Forest had forbidden him to bite the thumbnail of his left hand, and to always keep it in sight when he was in wolf form. This nail was longer and thicker than his other nails.

According to Grenier, his own father also had a wolf-skin and ran with him on one occasion when he killed and ate a girl who was tending geese in the village of Grilland. His stepmother left because once she had seen him vomit the paws of a dog and fingers of a child.

Many of the details given by Grenier in his testimony matched details of known attacks and wounds. However, the only witness who corroborated his assertion that he transformed himself into a wolf was Poirier.

When confronted with his father, Grenier wavered but then stuck to his story. There was no other evidence against the father, who was dismissed by the court.

The president of the court opined that Grenier was merely a feeble-brained imbecile who had hallucinations, and that he was not under any influence of the devil. The court sentenced Grenier to life imprisonment at a monastery at Bordeaux, where he was to receive religious instruction.

At the monastery, Grenier ran about on all fours and ate bloody and raw offal. Seven years into his confinement he was visited by the noted demonologist Pierre Delancre. By then, both his appearance and his mind had greatly deteriorated. He told his complete story to Delancre, and insisted that the Lord of the Forest had visited him twice at the monastery but he had driven him off with a CROSS.

Soon after Delancre's visit, Grenier died, at age 20.

See also SHAPE-SHIFTING.

FURTHER READING:
Baring-Gould, Sabine. *The Book of Werewolves.* London: Smith, Elder & Co., 1865.
Otten, Charlotte F., ed. *A Lycanthropy Reader: Werewolves in Western Culture.* New York: Dorset Press, 1989.

Guazzo, Francesco-Maria (ca. 17th c.)   Italian monk, scholar, and demonologist considered by his peers to be an authority on witchcraft and LYCANTHROPY. The exact dates and the details of Francesco Maria Guazzo's life are not known; he was active in the late 16th and early 17th centuries. MONTAGUE SUMMERS thought that he may have died circa 1640.

Guazzo was a member of the Brethren of St. Ambrose ad Nemus and St. Bartholomew, a local order in Milan. He was inclined toward the prevailing superstitions about witches and their collusion with the devil. At the time, much of Italy, especially the northern provinces, were rife with reports of SABBATS and diabolical activities. In 1595 the archbishop of Milan asked Guazzo to define, discuss, and classify witches and witchcraft.

In 1605 Guazzo was summoned to Cleves to aid and advise the prosecution of a witch accused of bewitching a witch-hunter, the Serene Duke John William. The accused was a 90-year-old man who was made to confess that he had used charms and "evil runes" to curse the duke with a wasting sickness and frenzy. Condemned to die by burning at the stake, the convicted witch stabbed himself fatally in the throat while in prison—or so it was said. Some believed the devil himself had done the deed.

Guazzo spent the next three years composing and compiling *Compendium Maleficarum (Handbook of Witches).* He reviewed the works of 322 other writers and relied especially upon NICHOLAS RÉMY, an ardent believer in the witch superstitions and in the SHAPE-SHIFTING of humans into wolves.

Compendium was published in 1608 and became a leading guide for witch-hunters. Guazzo discusses lycanthropy at length. He agreed with most demonologists that transformations into wolves and other animals were illusions:

> No one can doubt but that all the arts and metamorphoses by which witches change men into beasts are deceptive illusions and opposed to all nature. I add that anyone who holds the contrary opinion is in danger of Anathema; and in this I am supported by the opinion of S. Augustine, and also by logical reasoning. For a human soul cannot inform the body of a beast . . .

However, Guazzo could not ignore the deeply entrenched popular superstitions that the SHAPE-SHIFTING actually did take place and could be proved by the sympathetic wounds exhibited by people that they had received while in their witnessed animal forms. He proposed that such transformations were not entirely illusions:

> For the devil . . . deceives our senses in various ways. Sometimes he substitutes another body, while the witches themselves are absent or hidden somewhere in a secret place, and himself assumes the body of a wolf formed from the air and wrapped around him, and does those actions which men think are done by the wretched absent witch who is asleep.

Or, the devil might construct an even more elaborate deception:

> Sometimes, in accordance with his pact, he surrounds a witch with an aerial effigy of a beast, each part of which fits onto the correspondent part of the witch's body, head to head, mouth to mouth, belly to belly, foot to foot, and arm to arm; but this only happens when they use certain ointments and words . . .

In either case, should the wolf be wounded, the devil would inflict a corresponding wound on the body of the absent witch—thus producing the sympathetic wound evidence.

Compendium is Guazzo's best-known work; he also wrote two other books, including a biography of a fellow monk. His order declined and was dissolved in 1645.

FURTHER READING:
Guazzo, Francesco-Maria. *Compendium Maleficarum.* Secaucus, N.J.: University Books, 1974.

Gypsies   Nomadic, dark-complected people who probably emerged out of northern India and spread throughout Europe, then the British Isles, and eventually America. Some Eastern European beliefs about VAMPIRES have been influenced by Gypsies.

Gypsy tradition has little in the way of its own religious beliefs but is steeped in magic and superstition. Gypsies have various beliefs about the dead and the afterlife. Generally, they view the world of the dead as nothing more than the grave itself. Consequently, the cult of the dead imposes special burdens upon the living and has special terrors as well—especially the threat of vampirism.

Little is known about the origins of the Gypsies (more properly called the Roma. They were in Crete as early as 1322. The first record of them in continental Europe is in Germany in 1417. It is likely that they arrived much earlier, perhaps as early as the 10th century by some estimates; reasons for their migrations are not known. They came as Christian penitents and claimed to be exiles from a land called "Little Egypt." Europeans called them "Egyptians," which became corrupted as "Gypsies." Their language, Romany, is related to Sanskrit, and many of their customs are similar to Hindu customs. They brought Indian beliefs about gods and the dead to the Balkans, and in turn absorbed the local pagan and Christian superstitions and beliefs, disseminating them to others as they traveled.

A Turkish legend explains the Gypsies' lack of a specific religious credo: When religions were given to the peoples of the earth a long time ago, each wrote them down to preserve them. Rather than write in books or on wood or metal, the Gypsies recorded their religion on a cabbage. A donkey came along and ate the cabbage.

The Gypsy universe is populated with various deities and spirits. Del is both God and "everything which is above"—the sky, heavens, and heavenly bodies. Pharaun is a god said to once be a great pharaoh in the Gypsies' long-lost "Little Egypt." Beng is the Devil, the source of all evil. He is ugly and reptilian in appearance, and has the power to shape-shift (see SHAPE-SHIFTING). The cult of Bibi concerns worship of a lamia-like birth demon goddess who strangles *gorgio*, or non-Gypsy, children by infecting them with cholera, tuberculosis, and typhoid fever (see LAMIAE). The Gypsies consider fire divine, with the ability to heal, protect, preserve health, and punish evil. Among Serbo-Albanian Gypsies, Dispater, the god of death, is the abstraction of all WEREWOLVES.

Gypsies have a strong fear of death and the dead, and numerous taboos govern the way they deal with the dead and dying. All of a dead person's possessions, including his animals, are considered polluted and will haunt the living unless they are destroyed or buried with him. This practice has lessened since the 19th century, due to economic factors and the fact that Gypsies are not so nomadic as in previous times. In addition, there are taboos upon a dead person's favorite foods and pastimes. The living also make regular trips to gravesites to whisper messages to the dead through cracks in the earth, and to offer presents and feasts of food and drink intended for the dead to share with the living.

A great fear exists that the dead, trapped forever in their graveworld, are angry at being dead, and will return as vampires, or MULLOS, to avenge their deaths. This view is characteristic of primitive concepts that death itself is unnatural—that there is no logical reason why life, with all its pleasures, should ever end. Death, then, must be caused by evil. The dead, who come under the influence of evil, are likely to become restless and vampiric. A vampire is the ultimate occult evil.

Beliefs about Vampire Origins and Characteristics
The Gypsies have various beliefs for how vampires come into being, among them:

- A CORPSE is jumped over by a snake, dog, hen, ox, or ram.
- A person's wishes were not satisfied during life.
- A person who while living was a bandit or impure and sinful person.
- A dead person's SHADOW pours fire from its mouth.
- A person had slow-healing wounds in life.
- Only men become vampires, especially if they harmed others in life or did not ask forgiveness for their sins. They rise as a ghost and then take on human form

outside the grave. They look horrible, with hair reaching to the ground and bodies like filmy mist.
- A man who has been a great lover of women becomes one of the most dangerous of vampires.
- Corpses swell before burial.

Corpses are considered highly dangerous to the living until they have completely decayed. The most dangerous corpses are those of persons who died unnaturally, by violence or suicide or sudden accident; who were evil or ill-tempered in life; and who are stillborn or died right after being born. In the cases of infants, it is believed that they continue to grow in the grave until they reach either their eighth year or adulthood, when they become restless and want to leave their graveworld. Bodies destined to become vampires turn black prior to burial.

A *mullo* is feared with the greatest horror. The *mullo* is full of hatred, and seeks revenge against: those who caused his death; persons who kept his possessions instead of destroying them; and persons who failed to observe the proper burial and graveside respect. *Mullos* are sexually insatiable and will attack anyone of either sex. It is dangerous to speak of them to others. While having sex with a vampire, it is permissible only to scream.

If married, a male vampire visits his wife for sex on the seventh night after burial. If he was single, he seeks out any young and pretty woman, or divorcées and widows.

A Gypsy mother and vampire father can procreate a child, called a *vampijerovic*, or "little vampire." The child is born posthumously. If it is a boy it is called *vampir*, if a girl, *vampiresa*. These children have the power to see and kill vampires (see DHAMPIR).

Gypsies have different beliefs concerning the appearance of the *mullo*. Some regard it as having the same form as when it was buried; the corpse remains undecayed. The *mullo* rises at midnight to strangle people and animals, and fill itself up with blood. Some Slavic and German Gypsies believe the blood-filled vampire has no use for bones, and leaves them behind in the grave. In other cases, vampires have monstrous appearances: ragged hair that touches the ground; flaming yellow hair; skin the color of congealed blood; tusklike fangs; missing middle fingers on both hands; animal feet.

Still others believe that the vampire always is invisible and will reveal itself only to its victims. The vampire can be seen by looking under one's own arms, under the arms of a witch, or by performing certain magical charms, though to do so invites the risk of illness and death.

The *mullo* also can shapeshift to a wolf, dog, or CAT; Swedish Gypsies believe it can take the form of a bird or horse.

Gypsy lore also holds that certain parts of the body, especially the EYE, can become vampires on their own. Certain animals, vegetables, and even tools can become vampires. The most likely animal candidates are snakes, dogs, cats, horses, lambs and sheep, oxen, and chickens. The most evil are snakes, horses, and lambs. Any animal can become a vampire under certain conditions, especially if it jumps over a human corpse prior to burial, or if another animal jumps over the animal's own corpse. Large fur-bearing animals are not hunted by some Gypsies out of fear that they will return as avenging vampires. Apparitions of vampires can take on white animal forms. They have supernatural powers and cannot be caught or killed by guns.

Vegetable vampires—all kinds of pumpkins and watermelons—are more annoying than dangerous. Pumpkins and watermelons kept longer than 10 days, or kept after Christmas, will show traces of blood on them, and will go about on their own shaking and noisily disturbing people and animals. Some vegetable vampires go about at night harming people, though not seriously.

Tool vampires are similar. Wooden knots for yokes and wooden rods for binding wheat sheaves will become vampires if left undone for more than three years, and will make disturbances on their own much like poltergeists.

Protection Against Vampires

Preventative measures against vampires are similar to those practiced by others. Fences of IRON—an amulet against evil—are constructed around graves in order to keep the *mullo* from escaping. Corpses are pierced with a steel needle through the heart before burial, or are buried with bits of steel or iron in the mouth, ears, and nose, near the head and between the fingers. The heels of shoes are removed to prevent walking, or HAWTHORN is placed in a sock or driven through the legs.

Other precautions include placing a saw, file, or small axe in the COFFIN; these are removed when the body is placed in it. If the deceased was ill prior to death, a nail is driven into the spot where he had lain and died.

A custom among Orthodox Gypsies in southern Yugoslavia and Albania is for mourning relatives to pour wine or brandy in one glass, place bread and salt in a second glass, and pour water in a third glass. The glasses are placed in a baking tin along with a few grains of wheat, and left at the spot where the deceased had lain ill and died. If the glasses are found emptied a little the next morning, the deceased will not become a vampire. The procedure is followed for three nights in a row. The contents are then poured over the grave.

Gypsies also seek to appease a vampire god by leaving out rice balls and bowls of milk or animal blood. The names of the dead, which are believed to have magical power, are used in oaths and invocations to ward off their return. Homes can be protected with fishing nets—vampires must stop to count every knot before entering—or a sprinkling of thorns or the posting of rosaries, CROSSES, and pieces of wood feared by vampires. One of the most unique charms against vampires is to live in a home with a twin brother and sister who were born on SATURDAY, and who will wear their underwear inside out. Just to see them will send a vampire screaming. (See SABBATARIANS.) Saturday is a magical day in folklore, bestowing upon people the ability to see ghosts and spirits. Saturday is the one day that vampires must rest in their graves.

Witches and Werewolves

In lore in Hungary, the Balkans, Russia, and Poland, Gypsy witches enhance their own health by sucking the blood of men who are born during the waxing of the MOON. In Hungary and the Balkans, these victims are called *panikotordimako*, which means "water-casks." When vampirized, the men turn into a kind of werewolf called a RUVANUSH, a Romany term for "wolf-man." According to MONTAGUE SUMMERS:

They are characterized by a pale sunken countenance, hollow mournful eyes, swollen lips, and flabby inert arms. They are parched by a burning thirst, and soon can only utter bestial sounds, for the most part howling like wolves, and many at night are transformed into fierce wolves. Being larger and stronger than the natural wolf, these creatures become "wolf-kings," and their subjects must supply them with the finest meat. At dawn they recover the human shape, but they can eat nothing save raw flesh and they lap blood.

A female witch can become a *ruvanush* as well.

FURTHER READING:
Summers, Montague. *The Werewolf.* New York: Bell Publishing, 1966.
Trigg, Elwood B. *Gypsy Demons & Divinities.* Secaucus, N.J.: Citadel Press, 1973.
Vukanovic, T. P. "The Vampire," in *The Vampire of the Slavs* by Jan L. Perkowski. Cambridge, Mass.: Slavica Publishers, 1976.

Haarman, Fritz (1879–1925) The "Vampire Butcher" of Hanover, Germany. Fritz Haarman was born in Germany on October 24, 1879, to a stern household. He particularly disliked his authoritarian father. Haarman was a poor student, and joined the military, where he fared better. After the service, he returned home to Hanover, where he was accused of molesting children, and was placed in a mental institution. He escaped and attempted to resume living with his father, but the two fought physically.

Haarman then took up a violent, crime-ridden life on the streets. He spent much time in jail. After release in 1918, he found a job as a butcher, and then as a police informant. He molested boys. His modus operandi was to wake up boys sleeping at the Hanover railway station and demand to see their ticket. If they had none, he would offer them a place to stay for the night. The boys mysteriously "disappeared" after that.

In 1919 Haarman met Hans Grans, a 24-year-old male prostitute, whom he recruited as a lover and as an accomplice to his sex and murder schemes. They selected their victims based upon Grans's taste for their clothes. In killing the boys, Haarman would bite into their throat at the jugular vein and drink their BLOOD.

Haarman and Grans went about their grisly business until 1924, when police discovered human remains in the Leine River and along the mud banks. At about the same time, Haarman was jailed on indecency charges. While he sat in jail, police searched his rented room and found bloodstains. The blood was determined to be human,

which set police off on a more careful search outside. They found the remains of 22 corpses.

The evidence, however, was circumstantial, and no charges could be brought against Haarman, until a mother of one missing boy identified a scrap of clothing worn by her son, which was traced to Haarman. Questioned by police, he confessed to murder and named Grans as accomplice.

All the victims were between the ages of 12 and 18. Grans would often select the victims. Haarman would take them to his meat shop, where he also kept his room. He would feed them a generous meal, lavish praise upon them for their beauty, and then turn into a VAMPIRE killer, sexually assaulting them and inflicting a fatal bite upon their necks. (If Haarman failed to kill the victims, Grans would beat him.) Grans got some of the victims' clothes, and the rest were sold through Haarman's butcher shop. It appears that some of the victims were sold as meat and sausages as well. A third man, Charles, who was a butcher as well, assisted Haarman in grinding and cutting up the bodies. After one such episode, an unwitting shop patron helped Haarman with the making of the human sausages in the kitchen, which they both cooked and ate on the spot.

In court, Haarman claimed that he was sane, but that when he committed the murders, he was always in a trance and not aware of what he was doing. The court rejected that argument, based upon Haarman's quite specific description of the manner in which he would have to bite the victims in order to kill them.

Haarman was accused of 24 murders. Some estimated that his actual number of victims was much higher, to 50. Haarman himself opined that he had killed "30 or 40" boys. Haarman was judged to be sane and was executed by beheading in 1925. He asked that his tombstone read, "Here lies Mass-Murderer Haarman," and that Grans should lay a wreath on his grave every year on his birthday.

Charles disappeared, and Grans was sentenced to life in prison.

FURTHER READING:
Glut, Donald. *True Vampires of History*. New York: HC Publishers, 1971.
Guiley, Rosemary Ellen, with J. B. Macabre. *The Complete Vampire Companion*. New York: Macmillan, 1994.

Haigh, John George (1901–1949)   Vampire murderer. Born in England in 1910, John George Haigh was raised in a strict Pilgrim Brethren family. He seemed to have a normal childhood and remained affectionate toward his parents throughout his life. He was intelligent and made friends easily. He was briefly married at age 25, and he expressed no further interest in sex after it ended. In the following 10 years he served three prison sentences for dishonesty and fraud.

During his childhood from about the age of six, Haigh enjoyed BLOOD and would wound himself so that he could suck his own blood. He was also fascinated by the Holy Communion and the Crucifixion. He frequently dreamed about railway accidents with injured and bleeding people. These symptoms went into remission until 1944, when at age 35, blood dripped into his mouth from an accidental head wound. He began again having dreams about blood. In a typical dream he would watch a forest of crucifixes become trees dripping with blood, which he would drink, and then awake with the desire for blood. The dreams tended to follow a weekly cycle of increasing intensity from Monday through Friday.

With a growing compulsion for blood, Haigh rented a storeroom and bought some drums of acid. In the next five years he killed nine of his acquaintances by shooting or clubbing. He plugged their wounds and then cut their necks, drawing out of cupful of blood, which he drank. Afterward, he said, he felt "relieved." He dissolved the bodies of his victims in the acid.

Haigh was arrested, tried, and convicted. It is possible that he made up the blood-drinking in order to appear insane. However, he did describe disturbing dreams prior to each killing:

> Before each of my killings, I had a series of dreams, I saw a forest of crucifixes that changed into green trees dripping with blood . . . which I drank, and once more I awakened with a desire that demanded fulfillment.

Haigh was executed by hanging in London in 1949.

FURTHER READING:
Glut, Donald. *True Vampires of History*. New York: HC Publishers, 1971.
Noll, Richard. *Vampires, Werewolves and Demons*. New York: Bruno-Mazel, 1992.

Hamilton, Laurell K. (1963–)   American author of VAMPIRE novels and creator of Anita Blake, a VAMPIRE HUNTER and reanimator.

Laurell K. Hamilton was born in Heber Springs, Arkansas. Soon she, her mother, and grandmother, Laura Gentry, moved to the hamlet of Sims, Indiana, where Hamilton grew up.

Hamilton credits her interest in the occult to her grandmother, a good storyteller of spooky tales. By age 12, Hamilton knew she wanted to be a writer and wrote her first short story. She was particularly attracted to heroic fantasy and vampires. She also was influenced by the horror films produced by HAMMER FILMS.

She attended Marion College, a Christian school that is now Indiana Wesleyan University. She enrolled in the writing program, but was expelled from it by a professor who believed her writing would have a corrupting influence. She enrolled in the biology program, but never gave up on writing.

Hamilton's first published novel was *Nightseer* (1992), in which she creates an alternate reality of witches, sorcerers, and magic. The heroine is Keleios Nightseer, a noble half-elf who is a prophet and master enchanter. She battles evil sorcerers and demonic entities led by a witch who murdered her mother.

She conceived the idea of a strong heroine who would raise zombies from the dead. That heroine, Anita Blake, originated in short stories, and was moved to novels in *Guilty Pleasures* (1993). Blake works for Animators, Inc., raising the dead, and she also is a licensed vampire hunter in Missouri. She is tough in talk and action and can engage in ferocious fights, but she is ultra-feminine and sexy. In Blake's world, vampires, werewolves, shape-shifters (see SHAPE-SHIFTING), and occult practitioners live in open society with legislated civil rights. The supernatural creatures are organized around the world into councils and political groups. They carry on lives just as do mortals, working, marrying, and having children. Blake is licensed to kill, but only those officially designated. Blake's primary opponent is Jean-Claude, a 400-year-old vampire who is Master Vampire of the City, but he is destined to become her lover.

Hamilton does not shy away from sex and violence, and Blake has been called "an x-rated BUFFY THE VAMPIRE SLAYER." The novels are written with the dialogue of hard-boiled detective novels and a touch of humor.

Anita Blake captured a following, and more novels in the series followed:

- *The Laughing Corpse* (1994): Blake declines an offer to raise a 300-year-old zombie from the dead, but someone else does, and the zombie goes on a killing spree. Blake battles the voodoo priestess who is controlling the zombie.

- *Circus of the Damned* (1995): Blake meets the handsome alpha WEREWOLF Richard. She battles a rogue master vampire, Alejandro, who seeks to make her his human servant.
- *The Lunatic Café* (1996): Blake falls in love with Richard. She must solve some gruesome murders, find some missing werewolves, and prevent the bounty hunter Edward from killing Richard and Jean-Claude.
- *Bloody Bones* (1996): Blake is sent to Branson, Missouri, to raise some old zombies from their graves to settle a land dispute. She unexpectedly encounters a killer vampire and must summon Jean-Claude for help.
- *The Killing Dance* (1997): Enemies put a $500,000 bounty on Blake's head and she is hunted by professional killers. Blake struggles to find out who is trying to kill her. Jean-Claude and Richard are rivals for her affections, and Richard also faces the leadership rivalry of Marcus, another alpha werewolf.
- *Burnt Offerings* (1998): Blake tracks a psychic arsonist who is torching vampires. In addition, she is serving as protector of a pack of wereleopards whose leader she killed in an earlier book, and is policing the werewolf pack run by Richard, her ex-boyfriend. She comes to the defense of Jean-Claude when he is threatened by the Vampire Council, the ruling body of all vampires, who consider him dangerous. Richard comes to their aid.
- *Blue Moon* (1998): Blake's ex-fiancé, Richard, goes to Tennessee to study trolls and is arrested and jailed on rape charges. He calls Blake for help. She is opposed by the local vampires and werewolves.
- *Obsidian Butterfly* (2000): Blake assists bounty hunter Edward ("Death") in tracking monsters in New Mexico who are skinning, mutilating, and dismembering their victims. She seeks the help of Itzpapalotl ("Obsidian Butterfly"), an Aztec vampire goddess who is the Master Vampire of Albuquerque.
- *Narcissus in Chains* (2001): The title comes from a dominant/submissive leather bar by the same name. Blake is wounded in a battle in the bar while trying to protect wereleopards, and her wounds start turning her into a werewolf. The wereleopards are abducted, and Blake must find out who is behind it. She also struggles with trying to choose between Richard and Jean-Claude as lovers.
- *Cerulean Sins* (2003): Blake attempts to regain a "normal" life after breaking up with her werewolf lover, Richard. She turns to Micah, king of the wereleopards, and Jean-Claude. Jean-Claude must deal with Bella Morte, the originating vampire of his clan, who demands he turn over a vampire, Asher. Blake defies her by taking Asher as her lover. She investigates a series of brutal killings that lead her to

Laurell K. Hamilton (Photo by Roy Zipstein. Courtesy Berkley Books)

Cerulean Sins, an organization that deals in erotic videos and is run by vampires.

The Blake series is open-ended. Hamilton created a second series, for which she planned seven to 11 books, about Meredith (Merry) Gentry, an American-born fairy princess and private investigator. The first three books in that series are *Kiss of Shadows* (2000), *Caress of Twilight* (2002) and *Seduced by Moonlight* (2004).

Hamilton lives in St. Louis County, Missouri, with her husband, Gary, and daughter.

FURTHER READING:

Hamilton, Laurell K. *Bloody Bones*. New York: Ace Books, 1996.

———. *Blue Moon*. New York: Ace Books, 1998.

———. *Burnt Offerings*. New York: Ace Books, 1998.

———. *Cerulean Sins*. New York: Berkley Books, 2003.

———. *Circus of the Damned*. New York: Ace Books, 1995.

———. *Guilty Pleasures*. New York: Ace Books, 1993.

———. *The Killing Dance*. New York: Ace Books, 1997.

———. *The Laughing Corpse*. New York: Ace Books, 1994.

———. *The Lunatic Café*. New York: Ace Books, 1996.

———. *Narcissus in Chains.* New York: Berkley Books, 2001.
———. *Obsidian Butterfly.* New York: Berkley Books, 2000.
Laurell K. Hamilton Web site: URL: http://www.laurelhamilton.org. Downloaded on December 20, 2003.
Pulse, "An Interview with Laurell K. Hamilton 12/31/2001." Available online. URL: http://www.twoheadedcat.com/Interviews/lkhamilton.htm. Downloaded on December 22, 2003.
Ricker, Jeffrey and Alex Graves, "Tales from the Landing." Available online. URL: http://www.playbackstl.com/Current/Archive/hamilton1.htm. Downloaded on December 22, 2003.

Hammer Films   English film studio that became synonymous with horror films, especially its productions involving COUNT DRACULA and Frankenstein. Hammer Films boosted to fame such actors and actresses as CHRISTOPHER LEE, PETER CUSHING, and INGRID PITT.

Hammer Films grew out of a partnership between Will Hinds (known as "Will Hammer"), a film producer with his own company called Hammer Films, founded in 1934, and Enrique Carreras, the owner of a chain of London-based cinemas. Hinds and Carreras joined forces in 1935. From 1935 to 1937, Hammer Films made five films, including *The Mystery of the Mary Celeste,* which starred BELA LUGOSI. In 1937 Hammer Films went bankrupt. In 1947 Carreras and Hinds reorganized it as Hammer Productions, Ltd. Its four principals included Hinds and his son Anthony, and Carreras and his son James. In addition, James Carreras and William Hinds formed Hammer Films in 1947. Michael Carreras, another son of Enrique, also joined Hammer Films, and became a successful scriptwriter.

The studio began making films immediately, enjoying success in the postwar years. By 1952–54, the studio was making eight to nine films a year. In the mid-1950s it produced hits in the science fiction genre, *The Quartermass Xperiment* (1955), *X the Unknown* (1956), and *Quartermass II* (1957). The studio entered the horror market with the purchase of Universal Pictures' film rights to *Dracula* and *Frankenstein.*

The Curse of Frankenstein was released in 1957. Directed by Terence Fisher ("the father of British horror film"), it starred Lee as the monster and Cushing as Victor Frankenstein. The film delivered realistic shock violence and was a huge hit. It earned £6 million at the box office and had cost only £200,000 to produce.

Hammer executives turned their attention to *Dracula.* The figure of Count Dracula and the story line were in need of updates to appeal to an audience who wanted action, gore, and sex rather than long speeches and insinuations of sex and BLOOD.

Hammer Films provided audiences with spectacular scenes. Count Dracula and other vampires die in novel ways, and are resurrected from death in even more novel ways. Tried-and-true formulas of death-resurrection-revenge, mixed with liberal amounts of sex and seduction, worked time and time again. In the Hammer films, there is no final end to vampires, and especially to Dracula, the King of All Vampires.

Hammer reigned as the top horror studio for nearly two decades. By the time it produced its final Dracula film, *The Legend of the Seven Golden Vampires,* it was in financial trouble. Its final film altogether was *The Lady Vanishes,* a remake of the 1938 Alfred Hitchcock classic. The film garnered good reviews, but it was not enough to pull the studio out of difficulty.

In 1975 Hammer Films went bankrupt. In 1980 it was purchased by Ray Skeggs and Brian Lawrence, the respective former company accountant and secretary, and company director and business manager. Hammer was restructured and produced a 13-episode television series, *Hammer House of Horror.* By 1982, Skeggs and Lawrence had repurchased all remaining outstanding Hammer Films stock. In 1983 they began production on 13 made-for-television films under the banner of *Hammer House of Mystery and Suspense.* Skeggs bought out Lawrence in 1985. In 1993 he joined forces with Warner Bros. to remake *The Quartermass Xperiment* and to produce a 44-part series, *Haunted House of Hammer.* In the same year he announced that Hammer would not make any Draculas or Frankensteins, which were "old Hammer."

The following are the original Hammer Films' horror classics of note:

Dracula Films
Horror of Dracula (1958), *directed by Terence Fisher.*   For Hammers's entry into vampire films, Jimmy Sangster, the writer of *The Curse of Frankenstein,* revamped BRAM STOKER's novel. Sangster made substantial changes in the characters and story, some to accommodate the low budget. He set the entire story in an unnamed place in Central Europe to minimize sets and props. Thus, the Hammer Dracula never goes to England, but terrorizes Europeans.

Christopher Lee, the tall, regal, and relatively unknown actor who had done well as the monster in the Frankenstein film, was hired to play the role of Dracula. He was outfitted all in black with a sweeping black cloak; a wig of thick, dark and gray-streaked hair with a pronounced widow's peak; a set of false fangs; and RED contact lenses to give his eyes a demonic look. The fangs were not problematic for Lee, but the contact lenses were uncomfortable and made it difficult for him to see.

According to Sangster's plot, PROFESSOR ABRAHAM VAN HELSING (Peter Cushing) sends Jonathan Harker (John Van Eysen) to Dracula's castle to investigate the count for possible involvement in a rash of vampire incidents. Harker goes under the pretext of indexing the count's journals and books. The first person Harker meets at the castle is a beautiful woman in white (Valerie Gaunt), who says she is Dracula's prisoner and begs him to help her escape. They are interrupted by the entrance of the imperious count, and the woman flees. Dracula is taken with Harker's picture of his fiancée, Lucy Holmwood (Carol Marsh). When Dracula leaves, Harker deduces he is a vampire and must be destroyed.

Alone in the library, Harker is attacked by the woman, who is a vampire. She bites him on the neck and draws blood. Dracula suddenly appears and attacks her in a rage. Harker faints. When he awakens, he vows to destroy Dracula. He finds the crypt and stakes the woman, who shrivels into an old woman. But the sun has set, and Dracula's COFFIN is empty. Dracula turns Harker into a vampire.

Van Helsing comes to the castle in search of Harker. He arrives just as Harker's coffin is being taken away. When he finds the vampire, Van Helsing stakes him. (Harker's decomposition was deleted by British censors.)

Dracula claims Lucy as a replacement for his lost mistress. Lucy dies and stalks children as a vampire. Van Helsing and Arthur Holmwood (Michael Gough) stake her. Dracula next attacks Mina (Melissa Stribling), and kidnaps her. Van Helsing and Holmwood chase them to CASTLE DRACULA, arriving just as the count is attempting to bury Mina. While Holmwood rescues her, Van Helsing takes on Dracula in the final battle.

The fight between them is highly charged, with Dracula exhibiting his superhuman strength and hurling the VAMPIRE HUNTER about. Van Helsing manages to open the heavy red draperies, and SUNLIGHT disintegrates Dracula's foot. Screaming, the vampire tries to pull away, but Van Helsing makes a CROSS of two candlesticks and forces him to remain in the light. Dracula decays and crumbles to dust, which is blown away by a breeze. (British censors allowed only part of the decomposition to be shown.)

Horror of Dracula (released as *Dracula* in Britain) established Lee as a major star. It was an audience-pleaser that became an instant classic in horror film lore, and it influenced Dracula and vampire movies to come. There were a few gaffes that brought complaints from some fans, such as the SHADOW cast by Dracula when he appears at the head of the stairs.

Dracula's costume was a point of contention during filming. In his autobiography, *Tall, Dark and Gruesome* (1977), Lee describes how he prevailed to tone down the formal attire that had been introduced in the stage versions and 1931 *Dracula*:

> My sticking point came when the suggestion was mooted of evening dress with an Order, which struck me as unlikely in a castle in the middle of Transylvania. Stylization is all very well, but if it goes over the top you're left with camp. In the end I was allowed to wear a black suit with cravat and pearl tiepin. We held out against ruby tie pins and cufflinks, and scarlet lining to the cloak, until the sequel.

Brides of Dracula *(1960) directed by Terence Fisher.* The success of *Horror of Dracula* was almost undone by the sequel, also written by Sangster. Having dispatched Count Dracula, the studio left him dead. Despite the title of the

Poster advertising the Italian release of Dracula, Prince of Darkness, *starring Christopher Lee* (Author's collection)

sequel, Dracula makes no appearance. The plot concerns the evil vampires he created, who still live on.

The central character in *Brides of Dracula* is the blond Baron Meinster (David Peel), a sinister vampire who can shape-shift (see SHAPE-SHIFTING) into a giant BAT with his own human face. (Leslie Nielsen gives a hilarious parody of this in Mel Brooks's 1995 comedy, *Dracula: Dead and Loving It.*)

Marianne Danielle (Yvonne Montlaur), a schoolteacher, must travel across TRANSYLVANIA to her new job at the Badstein Girls' Academy. She stays at the chateau of the Baroness Meinster (Martita Hunt). She meets the handsome baron, the baroness's son, who is supposedly suffering from a mental disorder. Marianne discovers he is kept chained like a prisoner. She releases him, and he drinks his mother's blood, turning her into a vampire. He escapes and begins attacking others.

Marianne flees but is caught by the baron. She is rescued by Abraham Van Helsing (Cushing), who is doggedly pursuing vampires created by Count Dracula. The baron escapes, but Van Helsing dispatches some of his victims with STAKES. He also stakes the baroness.

The baron attacks the girls' academy and turns students into his brides. He holes up in a deserted windmill. Van Helsing confronts him there, but the vampires attack him and the baron bites him. Van Helsing purifies the wound with a hot metal bar and a Eucharist.

Meinster kidnaps Marianne and brings her to the windmill. Van Helsing overcomes him with holy WATER, and the baron, in agony, kicks over a brazier. The windmill goes up in flames. Van Helsing and Marianne escape, and the baron flees. In what is probably the most novel approach to destruction of vampires, Van Helsing leaps upon a vane of the windmill, turning it in the moonlight so that it casts the shadow of a giant cross upon the vampire. Screaming, the vampire dies.

Despite the absence of Lee as Count Dracula, *Brides of Dracula* was very profitable. Hammer was on its way to becoming the reigning studio of vampires and horror. But Lee would never again have as much presence on the screen of the Hammer films as he did in *Horror of Dracula*.

Dracula, Prince of Darkness *(1965), directed by Terence Fisher.* By the time the third Dracula film was undertaken, Lee was a high-priced actor. To keep costs low, the studio gave him only brief scenes and no dialogue at all.

Dracula, Prince of Darkness opens with the end of *Horror of Dracula* and the demise of the count, and then jumps to the present plot. Two English couples—Charles Kent (Francis Matthews), his wife, Diana (Suzan Farmer), his brother Alan (Charles Tingwell) and Alan's wife, Helen (Barbara Shelley)—are traveling through the Carpathian Mountains. At an inn, a monk (Andrew Keir) warns them to stay away from Castle Dracula in Carlsbad. The warning piques their curiosity and they set out for the castle. But partway their coach driver refused to go any farther and makes them get out at an abandoned house. Soon a horse-drawn carriage with no driver arrives, and they get in. Of course, it takes them to the castle.

They find dinner has been laid out for four people. They are greeted by Klove the butler (Philip Latham), who tells them his master is dead. The couples dine and retire to their bedrooms, considering themselves to be quite lucky. But Alan hears noises coming from the cellar in the night, and when he investigates, he is killed by the butler.

Klove hauls his body to an open coffin containing the dust of the dead Dracula. He hoists the CORPSE over the coffin. Alan's blood falls on the dust, which swirls around until it reconstitutes Dracula (Lee). The monster is resurrected.

Dracula turns Helen into a vampire. Charles and Diana escape and return to the inn. The monk Sandor assumes the role of vampire expert and hunter. Helen arrives and attacks Diana, but Sandor stakes Helen through the heart. Diana is led to the count by a monastery servant (Thorley Walters) whom Dracula controls. The vampire escapes with his prey, making off in a coach driven by Klove.

Charles and Sandor give chase. Charles shoots Klove as the coach reaches the ice-covered moat of Dracula's castle, and the coach overturns. Charles and Dracula fight on the ice. Sandor fires enough bullets into the ice to open it. Dracula sinks into the frigid waters, trapped by the ice, and Charles and Sandor escape.

Dracula, Prince of Darkness underwent so many rewrites that Sangster changed his name to a pseudonym in the credits: John Sansom.

Dracula Has Risen from the Grave *(1968), directed by Freddie Francis.* Lee returns to a small but speaking role, and his heretofore all-black cape is changed to black with a red lining. Lee also wears a duplicate of the ring worn by Lugosi in *Dracula* (1931).

In the opening of *Dracula Has Risen from the Grave*, the body of a girl who has been killed by a vampire is found in a village church. No one will attend services there. The monsignor (Rupert Davies) and his assistant priest (Ewan Hooper) go to up the mountain to Castle Dracula to perform an exorcism that will release the church from its taint. But along the way the priest's courage fails, and the monsignor leaves him behind. The monsignor does his rites and places a large cross on the castle door. Immediately, a terrible lightning and thunder storm erupts. The priest, alone, panics and falls down the mountain slope, coming to a stop along a frozen stream. There he makes a horrible discovery—the frozen body of Count Dracula. Blood from the priest's wounds falls into the vampire's mouth and revives him. Dracula vampirizes the priest, turning him into a slave.

When he discovers the cross on his door, Dracula vows revenge against the monsignor via the monsignor's niece, Maria (Veronica Carlson). Paul (Barry Andrews), an atheist, is Maria's love interest. Dracula manages to bite Maria and is driven off by her crucifix-wielding uncle. The priest fatally wounds the monsignor. As he dies, he manages to tell Paul how to kill vampires.

Using the monsignor's crucifix to break Dracula's spell, the priest takes Paul to the vampire's coffin. Just as the sun sets, Paul drives a huge stake into the vampire. However, as an atheist, he cannot say prayers that are required to finalize Dracula's demise. Dracula yanks out the stake, escapes, kidnaps Maria, and takes off in a hearse.

At the castle, Dracula forces Maria to remove the cross, which falls down the mountainside. Paul arrives, and he and the vampire engage in a huge struggle. Paul trips Dracula and he plummets down the mountain to be impaled on the cross. He writhes, crying tears of blood, and then dies in a crumble to dust.

Hammer's four Dracula films had now surpassed their Frankenstein films in profits, and studio executives laid plans to release one Dracula film a year.

Taste the Blood of Dracula *(1969), directed by Peter Sasdy.* The powdered blood of Dracula from his demise on the cross has been saved by a merchant. The blood and other of the count's relics—his cape and ring—are purchased by Lord Courtley (Ralph Bates), a disciple of Dracula's, and three no-good cohorts: William Hargood (Goeffrey Keen), Jonathan Secker (John Carson), and Samuel Paxton (Peter

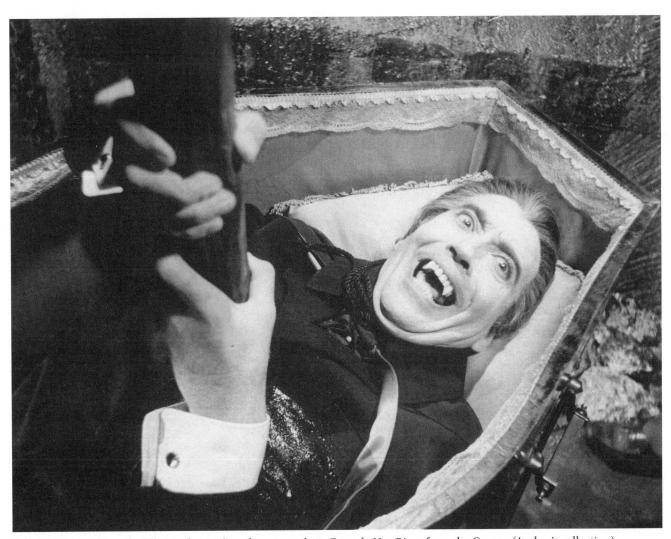

A gloating Count Dracula (Christopher Lee) yanks out a stake in Dracula Has Risen from the Grave. *(Author's collection)*

Sallis). The men conduct a ritual in which they each take a chalice with some of the powdered blood, and Courtley mixes in some of his own blood. When the two bloods meet, the powdered blood begins to bubble. Courtley drinks his blood brew, but the others do not. They kill Courtley and flee, Courtley's corpse is enveloped by a cocoon from which emerges the resurrected Count Dracula (Lee).

Once again the count is bent on revenge, and he goes after the children of the three killers. He hypnotizes Alice Hargood (Linda Hayden) and forces her to kill her father by slashing his throat with a shovel. He turns Lucy Paxton (Isla Blair) into a vampire; she and Alice kill her father with a stake through the heart. Lucy bites Jeremy Secker (Martin Jarvis), and Jeremy then stabs his father to death.

His revenge complete, Dracula tries to kill Lucy and attacks her in the abandoned church where he has hidden his coffin. She and Paul Paxton (Anthony Corlan) fend him off with crucifixes, which they use to prevent him from escaping. Forces of good return to the church, over-coming Dracula as he attempts to escape. He falls from high over the altar and dies, decomposing to dust.

Lee was not pleased with the script and announced that *Taste the Blood of Dracula* would be his final Dracula film. Hammer announced they were grooming Bates for the role as Count. But Lee and the studio patched their relationship, and Lee continued on as Dracula.

Scars of Dracula *(1970), directed by Roy Ward Baker. Scars of Dracula gave Lee a bigger role and used elements from Stoker's* Dracula.

Dracula (Lee) is reborn once again when a VAMPIRE BAT, a devoted disciple of the count, drops its own blood on his dust remains. Dracula returns to his castle in Kleinenburg, Transylvania. The villagers are unhappy to see him and vow to destroy him, this time for good. A group of angry men storm the castle and set it ablaze. But when they return to their homes, they are horrified to find their families have been murdered by the disciple bat. Neither Dracula nor the castle have been destroyed.

Meanwhile, the rakish Paul Carlson (Christopher Matthews) gets caught with the burgomaster's daughter and is forced to flee; he winds up at Castle Dracula. Invited to stay, he is entertained by the beautiful Tania (Anoushka Hempel). But when the count finds him in bed with his mistress, he stabs her to death and imprisons Paul.

Paul's brother Simon (Dennis Waterman) and his girlfriend, Sarah (Jenny Hanley), come to the castle in search of Paul. They too are invited to stay. Fortunately, Sarah's crucifix keeps the count at bay. Dracula's derelict servant, Klove (Patrick Troughton) falls in love with her and helps the couple escape. As punishment, Dracula scars his back with a hot sword.

Simon leaves Sarah with the village priest and goes back to kill Dracula. Alas, Paul has been killed. Just as Simon is about to stake the vampire in his coffin, he is hypnotized by the count through shut eyes. Simon passes out. Dracula dispatches his killer bat to destroy the priest and drive Sarah back to the castle, which the bat does.

Before Dracula can make Sarah a vampire, Klove appears and tries to stab him. Dracula hurls him to the valley below. Simon appears and throws a pike into Dracula. The vampire pulls it out and is about to impale Simon upon it when a fortuitous lightning bolt strikes the pike, and the vampire bursts into flames and plummets off the castle.

Dracula A.D. 1972 *(1972), directed by Alan Gibson.*   Hammer's attempt to bring Dracula into modern times marked a low point in its Dracula series, despite its reunion of Lee and Cushing. The count is in the midst of swinging London.

Dracula A.D. 1972 opens with Dracula (Lee) and Abraham Van Helsing (Cushing) fighting aboard a runaway coach in the 19th century. Dracula is impaled by a broken spoke on the wheel. Van Helsing dies soon thereafter. At Van Helsing's funeral, a minion of Dracula's buries some of the count's ashes in the same CEMETERY.

Flash forward to 1972. Johnny Alucard (Christopher Neame), a descendant of the count assembles a group for a Black Mass on the anniversary of Van Helsing's death, in the cemetery where he is buried. Among the group is Jessica Van Helsing (Stephanie Beacham), granddaughter of the current Dr. Van Helsing (also played by Cushing). Johnny, who has obtained the powdered blood of Dracula, mixes his blood in the powder and pours it over their sacrificial woman (Caroline Munro). Restored, Dracula leaps up out of the graveyard and swears revenge against the Van Helsings.

Dracula obliges Johnny's request to become a vampire, and then he begins stalking Jessica. Dr. Van Helsing destroys Johnny in the vampire's apartment by turning on running WATER when they struggle and Johnny falls into his bathtub.

Van Helsing then confronts Dracula in the ruins of a church. He stabs Dracula in the heart, but the count pulls out the knife. Just as Dracula is about to overpower Van Helsing, he falls backward into the original Van Helsing's

grave—and into a trap of sharp wooden stakes. He dies and crumbles to dust.

The Satanic Rites of Dracula *(1973), directed by Alan Gibson.*   The last of Hammer's Dracula films to star Lee—and Lee and Cushing together—began life with the improbable title of *Dracula Is Dead . . . and Well and Living in London.* The title was changed during production.

Van Helsing (Cushing) is sent by authorities to the home of a high government official who is participating in a Black Mass. In the old mansion, Van Helsing finds a basement full of vampire girls, and his own daughter Jessica (Joanna Lumley) on the altar as the sacrificial victim of Dracula (Lee). After dispatching some of the female vampires, Van Helsing takes on the count. Dracula dies when the mansion goes up in flames.

After filming *Satanic Rites,* Lee declared he was at last finished with the character of Dracula and would play him no more.

The Legend of the Seven Golden Vampires *(1974), directed by Richard Blackburn.*   In the early 1800s a Chinese emissary awakens an Asian-looking Dracula (John Forbes-Robertson). The count goes to China, where he establishes a vampire cult. Lawrence Van Helsing (Cushing) goes to China on a lecture tour. There he encounters Dracula, and dispatches him after a lot of martial arts fighting.

Other Vampire-Related Films

The Vampire Lovers *(1970), directed by Roy Ward Baker.* *The Vampire Lovers* features lesbian sex scenes and graphic violence. Based on J. Sheridan Le Fanu's "CARMILLA," the film stars Ingrid Pitt as the vampire Carmilla of Karnstein. Carmilla returns to her native castle and enters society. She vampirizes Laura (Pippa Steele), the governess (Kate O'Mara), and Emma Morton (Madeleine Smith). Vampire hunters prevent Carmilla from killing Emma, and chase the vampire to a chapel where the general (Peter Cushing) stakes her in her coffin.

Countess Dracula *(1971), directed by Peter Sasdy.*   Starring Ingrid Pitt as Countess Elisabeth Nadasdy, the movie is based on the story of ELIZABETH BATHÓRY. The countess is not a vampire, however, but merely a deranged human who becomes younger after bathing in the blood of young women. The film opens with the countess as an old and wrinkled woman. She accidentally discovers the rejuvenating power of blood and goes on a killing spree. Captain Dobi (Nigel Green) becomes her lover.

Vampire Circus *(1971), directed by Robert Young.*   In Serbia in 1810, Count Mitterhouse (Robert Taylor) is a vampire who is revived after languishing for about 100 years. He vows revenge on the town that destroyed him. The hit squad he recruits is a band of circus performers who set up their tents on the outskirts of town. They all start murdering the most prominent citizens. When others discover what is going on, they band together and kill the circus vampires. Count Mitterhouse is dispatched by being staked and decapitated.

Lust for a Vampire (1971), directed by Jimmy Sangster. Inspired by the success of The Vampire Lovers, Lust for a Vampire again features graphic violence and sex. Carmilla (Yutte Stenguard) and her husband, Count Karnstein (Mike Raven), are in their graves when they are roused by a sacrificial victim who has been killed on top of the graves. Carmilla vampirizes men this time. When the villagers discover her secret, they set a fire that kills her and the Karnstein family. The count survives.

Twins of Evil (1972), directed by John Hough.   "Carmilla" provides inspiration for this story of evil twins Mary and Freida Gelhorn, played by real twins Mary and Madeleine Collinson. Count Karnstein sets the twins loose to avenge the killings of the Karnstein family in Lust for a Vampire.

The rampant vampirism attracts Gustav Weil (Cushing), a zealous and puritanical—but flawed—vampire hunter. Weil, the count, and the vampires manage to kill one another, along with one of the twins.

Captain Kronos—Vampire Hunter (1972), directed by Brian Clemens.   Horst Janson is Captain Kronos, a cowboy-like, horse-riding vampire hunter who rides about dispatching fanged villains. The film is dry and static compared to the bloody rock-and-roll of Hammer's style in other films, and it did poorly at the box office.

Werewolves

Hammer did not embrace WEREWOLVES as much as vampires and other monsters. Most notable is:

The Curse of the Werewolf (1961), directed by Terence Fisher.   Michael Carreras wrote the script for this film, loosely basing it upon the novel The Werewolf of Paris (1933) by

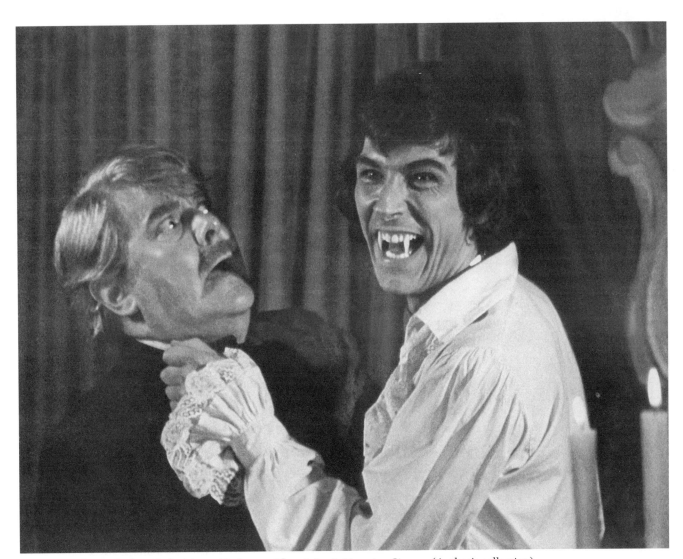

Count Mitterhouse (Robert Taylor) bares his fangs with a victim in Vampire Circus. (Author's collection)

Guy Endore, which in turn is based on the true story of SARGEANT FRANÇOIS BERTRAND, who mutilated and ate corpses in France.

In 18th-century Spain, Leon the werewolf (Oliver Reed) inherits his awful destiny through the misfortunes of his mother (Yvonne Romain), a mute serving girl in the court of the marques of Santa Vera (Anthony Dawson). Soon after the marques marries, he attempts to seduce the serving girl, who resists him. He punishes her by throwing her into the dungeon, where she wastes away for years. A mad beggar (Richard Wordsworth) who is thrown into the dungeon rapes and impregnates her; he dies after his attack. The girl escapes the dungeon. She kills the evil marques. Feeling sorry for her, a professor, Don Alfredo Cortello (Clifford Evans) takes her in. On Christmas she dies giving birth to a son, Leon. According to superstition, Leon is destined to become a werewolf, because to be born on the day of the Lord's birth is an affront to heaven.

By age six, the young Leon (Justin Walters) is attacking sheep. He is plagued with nightmares of drinking blood and running with wolves. The professor is told by the village priest that he is possessed by an evil spirit whose animal nature is brought out by vice and greed, especially at the full MOON. Love can reverse the evil.

Thus tempered, Leon grows up not knowing he is a werewolf. He leaves home and goes to work in a vineyard, where he falls in love with the manager's daughter, Christina (Catherine Fuller).

But a drunken night in a bordello brings out the werewolf demon in him, and Leon goes berserk. He kills two people, including a friend, and flees into the woods. Don Alfredo finds him the next day in his own bed. Leon returns to the vineyard. Christina's love prevents him from changing into a werewolf again on the following night.

Leon is arrested for multiple murders he has committed. He is jailed. When the moon becomes full, he goes into a werewolf fury and escapes, fleeing across the rooftops of the town. He is finally killed by a SILVER bullet made from a crucifix, and fired at him by his adopted father.

FURTHER READING:
"The Curse of the Werewolf," *Hammer Horror Collector's Special*, p. 26.
"Dracula Has Risen from the Grave," *Hammer Horror #6*, pp. 21–32.
"Dracula Prince of Darkness," *Hammer Horror #2*, pp. 21–33.
Dudley, Keith. "Who Were Hammer?" *Hammer Horror #1*, pp. 48–50, and *Hammer Horror #2*, pp. 45–50.
Glut, Donald. *The Dracula Book*. Metuchen, N.J.: The Scarecrow Press, Inc. 1975.
Hearn, Marcus. "The House of Horror," *Hammer Horror Collector's Special*, p. 5.
Lee, Christopher. *Tall, Dark and Gruesome: An Autobiography.* London: W. H. Allen, 1977. Rev. ed. London: Victor Gollancz, 1997.
Marrero, Robert. *Horrors of Hammer.* Key West, Florida: RGM Productions, 1984.

hamrammr   Old Icelandic name for WEREWOLF. *Hamrammr* refers to one who is able to change his shape.

hannya   A Japanese VAMPIRElike entity. The *hannya* is a demon-possessed woman who eats children and drinks their BLOOD.

hantpare   An Asian VAMPIRE. The *hantpare* attaches itself to running sores and sucks BLOOD through them.

hantu langsuir (hantu langsuyar)   In Malaysian lore, the spirit of a woman who dies in childbirth and becomes a demon that subsists on the BLOOD, milk, and entrails of newborns, nursing mothers and pregnant women. The *hantu langsuir* drains its victim's blood through a hole at the base of its neck. It sometimes shape-shifts into the form of an owl.

See also LILITH; SHAPE-SHIFTING.

hantu laut   In Malaysian lore, vampiric and cannibalistic spirits who attack fishermen and sailors. *Hantu laut* means "sea spirits." The *hantu laut* either feast on flesh or vampirize the *semangat*, the soul or vital essence of the living.

hantu penanggalan   Malaysian VISCERA SUCKER, usually female, that flies about as a bodiless head with trailing entrails. Like other child birth demons, the *hantu penanggalan* preys upon pregnant women and newborns, sucking their BLOOD and eating their viscera.

See also LILITH; *TLAHUELPUCHI.*

Harker, Jonathan, and Mina Harker   See DRACULA.

Harris, Charlaine (1951–)   Mystery writer and creator of the "Southern Vampire" series of novels featuring telepathic heroine Sookie Stackhouse. Charlaine Harris's books are popular for their light humor and engaging characters.

Harris was born in 1951 in the Mississippi Delta region and grew up there. She attended Rhodes College in Memphis, Tennessee. From an early age she had an interest in mysteries, science fiction, and the paranormal.

Her first novel, *Sweet and Deadly*, a mystery, was published in 1981. After a second stand-alone mystery novel, *A Secret Rage*, was published in 1984, Harris decided to create a series with her character Aurora Teagarden. Her second series features Lily Bard, and is set in Shakespeare, Arkansas.

Her third series takes a different turn with the adventure/romance/mystery novels involving VAMPIRES, WERE-

"Rural America finally has a vampire story to call its own." —Tanya Huff

A Southern Vampire Novel

DEAD UNTIL DARK

Maybe having a vampire for a boyfriend isn't such a bright idea....

Charlaine Harris

Charlaine Harris's novel Dead Until Dark *introduces Sookie Stackhouse.* (Courtesy Berkley Books)

WOLVES, and other supernatural creatures. The heroine, Sookie Stackhouse, is a human with telepathic abilities. She takes a boyfriend who turns out to be a vampire, and becomes increasingly immersed in a supernatural world. Her telepathic abilities do not work on vampires.

- *Dead Until Dark* (Ace 2001): Sookie Stackhouse is a waitress in Bon Temps, Louisiana, a small town. She has telepathic abilities. She meets Bill, a vampire, who becomes her boyfriend. The invention of synthetic blood makes it possible for vampires to come out of the COFFIN, and they now desire to live openly in society.
- *Living Dead in Dallas* (Ace 2002): Sookie goes to Dallas to use her telepathic skills to search for a missing vampire. She continues her affair with Bill. Meanwhile, back home there is a mysterious beast loose, murder, and some strange orgies taking place.
- *Club Dead* (Ace 2003): The book takes its title from a nightclub for the supernatural crowd known as Club

Dead. Stackhouse's vampire boyfriend, Bill, is kidnapped by his ex-girlfriend, vampire Lorena. A werewolf attempts to abduct Stackhouse and fails. She goes to Jackson, Mississippi, to look for Bill. Along the way she meets an attractive werewolf, Alcide, and enlists his help. Elvis is now a vampire.

Harris lives in Arkansas, where she has served as president of the Arkansas Mystery Writers Alliance.

FURTHER READING:
"Charlaine Harris: Putting the Bite on Cozy Mysteries." Available online. URL: http://www.crescentblues.com/4/int_charlaine_harris.shtml. Downloaded on December 27, 2003.
Charlaine Harris Web site. URL: http://www.charlaineharris.com. Downloaded on December 29, 2003.

Harris, Rachel (d. 1793)   American VAMPIRE case reported in the 18th century. In 1790 Captain Isaac Burton, a naval officer of Manchester, Vermont, married Rachel Harris, the stepdaughter of Esquire Powel and the daughter of his second wife. Shortly after their wedding, Rachel contracted tuberculosis and died in about a year's time.

Burton then married Hulda Powel, a daughter of Esquire Powel by his first wife. Shortly after they were wed, Hulda also contracted tuberculosis. As she lay near death, friends of the family became convinced that a "Demon Vampire" was sucking the BLOOD of Hulda, and that the vital organs of Rachel should be disinterred, burned, and consumed by Hulda, which would cure her of her fatal affliction. Burton organized a ceremony at the cemetery when Rachel Harris was buried in February 1793. There, before an excited crowd of an estimated 500 to 1,000 onlookers, Rachel's remains were exhumed. What was left of her heart, liver, and lungs was removed, taken to a blacksmith's forge, and burned. A sacrifice to the "Demon Vampire" was performed at an altar.

The measures failed to help Hulda Powel, who died on September 6, 1793.

If the reports of the size of the crowd are accurate, then most of Manchester would have turned out to witness the exhumation.

Some versions of the story attribute the deaths of the Harris wives to witchcraft rather than vampirism.

See also NEW ENGLAND VAMPIRES.

FURTHER READING:
Bell, Michael E. *Food for the Dead: On the Trail of New England's Vampires.* New York: Carroll & Graf, 2001.

hawthorn   A favored wood for staking vampires. Hawthorn—as well as other thorny woods—is considered effective against all evil spirits because of its association with Christ and his crown of thorns.

In his book *Traveling Through Serbia* (1827), Serbian author Joakim Vujic relates how hawthorn was used to destroy an exhumed VAMPIRE in a village near Novi Pazar. The priest, named Stavra, forced open the vampire's clenched teeth with a sharp hawthorn stick. He took a twig of hawthorn and placed in between the jaws. He poured three drops of holy WATER into the mouth. An old man named Petko took the sharpened hawthorn stick and struck the vampire once on the chest. BLOOD poured out of its mouth. The vampire was considered destroyed.

In another anecdotal account from Serbia, a dead man reportedly became a vampire, in accordance with local belief that a CORPSE could become possessed by an evil spirit in the 40 days after death. The corpse was exhumed. A priest read from the Book of Thunder: "Come out, O cursed soul, come out. I curse you three hundred and seventy times; go, O cursed demon, to the abyss." A fire was lit around the corpse. The body was pierced with several hawthorn STAKES, and boughs of hawthorn were waved over it to prevent the evil spirit from flying out and escaping. The body was reburied, and the vampire was laid permanently to rest.

In Serbian lore, a secondary meaning of hawthorn is BUTTERFLY, which is one of the forms assumed by vampires.

In the lore of Orthodox GYPSIES in southern Yugoslavia and Albania, a sprig of hawthorn is placed in the stocking of a corpse prior to burial to prevent it from becoming a vampire. If an animal jumps over the body before it is interred, a hawthorn stake is driven into the leg. (See BURIAL CUSTOMS.) Hawthorn also is driven into a hole in the grave, so that the vampire will prick itself as it attempts to leave, and be rendered harmless.

Hawthorn placed on a windowsill will prevent a vampire from entering a house.

Tossing hawthorn or thorns on a grave is an ancient custom to prevent the dead from wandering; it was not limited to suspected vampires, but applied to anyone who might avenge himself on the living.

See also GRANDO, GIURE; PROTECTION AGAINST VAMPIRES.

FURTHER READING:
Vukanovic, T. P. "The Vampire," in *The Vampire of the Slavs* by Jan L. Perkowski. Cambridge, Mass.: Slavica Publishers, 1976.

Head, Anthony Stewart   See *BUFFY THE VAMPIRE SLAYER*.

Hebrides Werewolf   Case of a phantom WEREWOLF in the Hebrides Islands off Scotland, similar in characteristics of the MERIONETHSHIRE WEREWOLF of Wales, in which an angry ghostly werewolf comes looking for its bones.

The incident occurred in the early 20th century to Andrew Warren and his grandfather, an elder of the local church. Interested in natural history and geology, the grandfather would often go out into the countryside, looking for interesting specimen. One day while poking around in a dried up tarn, he found some odd bones and brought them home and showed them to Warren. They appeared to be the bones of a human skeleton with a wolflike head.

One evening the boy was alone at home while the adults were at church. He heard a noise at the back of the house, but could find no signs of an intruder. The bones were laid out on the kitchen table. Suddenly, there was a loud rapping of knuckles on the window. Looking up, Warren saw a dark face, at first indistinct, and then becoming clearer. It was a large wolf head atop a human neck. Shocked, Warren's immediate thought was that it was some bizarre illusion caused by reflections of the setting sun in the glass. But the face did not go away. Warren took in its details: It has slightly distended jaws; lips curled in a snarl that showed sharp, white teeth; pointed ears; and green eyes. The werewolf raised a humanlike hand that had long, curved nails.

Fearing that it was about to smash through the glass, Warren ran out of the kitchen, locking the door behind him. He stayed in the hallway until the family came home. By then, the werewolf had gone. The next day, Warren and his grandfather returned the bones to the tarn. The werewolf was never seen again.

FURTHER READING:
Downes, Jonathan, and Richard Freeman. "Shug Monkeys and Werewolves: The Search for Dog-Headed Men," in *Fortean Studies* vol. 5, Steve Moore, ed. London: John Brown Publishing, 1998.
McEwan, Graham. *Mystery Animals of Britain and Ireland.* London: Hale, 1986.

Hexham Heads   A case of a demonic, phantom WEREWOLF that appeared in conjunction with the discovery of some strange stone skulls in England. The Hexham Heads case occurred in 1972 in Hexham, Northumberland.

In February 1972, 11-year-old Colin Robson was weeding his family's garden when he dug up a carved stone head. He and his brother dug more and found a second stone head. Both were slightly smaller than tennis balls and were very heavy. One appeared to be that of a man, and the other seemed like one of a female witch. The boys took the stone skulls into the house.

Strange poltergeistlike things began to happen, both in the Robson household and the Dodd household next door. The heads would be found turned around, seemingly of their own accord. Objects would be found broken. The bed of one of the Robson daughters was found covered with shards of glass.

In the Dodd household, a "werewolf" was seen in the middle of the night in the bedroom of the husband and wife. The half-man, half-beast ran down the stairs on its hind legs and went out the front door.

The heads were acquired by an expert on Celtic culture, Dr. Anne Ross, who lived in Southampton, and who knew nothing about the apparition or disturbances. Ross thought the heads to be common religious ritual objects about 1,800 years old. She already had several similar ones in her collection—but the new ones proved to be problematic.

One night Ross suffered troubled sleep and awoke feeling very cold and frightened. (See OLD HAG.) She looked toward her door and saw a black figure, half-man and half-beast, about six feet tall. Its upper part was wolf and the lower part human. The whole body was covered with black fur. Upon being seen, the figure disappeared, and Ross heard it running on padded feet down the stairs. She felt compelled to pursue it and saw it disappear toward the back of her house.

The figure was seen one afternoon by her teenage daughter. Arriving home from school to an empty house, the girl opened the front door and saw the werewolf on the stairs. It vaulted over the banister, landed in the hall, and took off for the back of the house. Like her mother, the girl felt oddly compelled to pursue it, despite her terror, and saw it disappear in the doorway of the music room where the hall ended.

The Ross family encountered the werewolf several more times. It was usually seen on the stairs, and it would always jump over the banister and run down the hall, disappearing. Sometimes the sound of its padded steps could be heard, though nothing was seen. Ross felt the house became permeated with a definite presence of evil, and visitors remarked on this as well.

A most unusual turn to the case occurred when a man stepped forward and claimed to be the maker of the heads. Desmond Craigie had lived in the house occupied by the Robsons. He said he had made the heads as toys for his two daughters in 1956, and they had been lost in the garden.

No explanation was ever found for the strange werewolf manifestations.

FURTHER READING:
Downes, Jonathan and Richard Freeman. "Shug Monkeys and Werewolves: The Search for Dog-Headed Men," in *Fortean Studies* vol. 5, Steve Moore, ed. London: John Brown Publishing, 1998.
McEwan, Graham. *Mystery Animals of Britain and Ireland.* London: Hale, 1986.

Highgate Vampire   Episodes of alleged vampire activity reported in Highgate Cemetery in north London. The case reached a peak in the media in the early 1970s, but reports of vampire activity continued for years.

Consecrated in 1839, Highgate Cemetery is famous for its Victorian crypts and tombs, which lend it a spooky atmosphere. Rumors of ghosts and dark figures moving about the CEMETERY at night are a permanent part of its history.

The Highgate Vampire case began around 1967 with reports of a phantom figure seen gliding about the older, western side of the cemetery at dusk. Dead animals, mostly foxes and other nocturnal creatures, began to appear in nearby Waterlow Park and the cemetery. The animals reportedly were lacerated around the throat and drained of blood. In February 1970, the local press speculated on the presence of a vampire, and suddenly the "Highgate Vampire" was a sensation.

A mass vampire hunt by self-proclaimed VAMPIRE HUNTERS was organized for the night of Friday, March 13, 1970. Hundreds of vampire hunters invaded the cemetery, armed with wooden STAKES, GARLIC, and CROSSES. No vampire was found, but the cemetery suffered vandalism and theft damages amounting to £9,000 to £10,000. The vandals left behind graffiti and the exhumed remains of a female CORPSE, and stole lead from COFFINS.

As lurid stories fueled more interests, vampire hunters and the curious continued to enter the cemetery at night. In 1974, a group of vampire hunters claimed they had found the vampire and had destroyed it, but others disputed this.

In October 1975, the Friends of Highgate Cemetery was formed to protect the interests of Highgate Cemetery as a national monument and historical burial ground, to represent the interests of grave owners, to secure public access to the grounds and to sponsor conservation of the cemetery. To discourage occult activity and vandalism, the cemetery was closed at night and access was severely restricted.

From 1977 to 1980, mysterious animal deaths were reported in the areas near Highgate Cemetery. The bodies of pets and various small wild animals were found with wounds in their throats. It was speculated that dogs or wild animals were the culprits, but the "vampire theory" also stayed in circulation.

FURTHER READING:
Guiley, Rosemary Ellen. *Vampires Among Us.* New York: Pocket Books, 1991.
Slemen, Thomas. *Strange But True: Mysterious and Bizarre People.* New York: Barnes & Noble Books, 1998.

Hillyer, Vincent (1930–2000)   American adventurer and author. Vincent Hillyer was best known for his account of his night spent in CASTLE POENARI in Romania, which he recounted in his book *Vampires* (1988).

Hillyer was born in 1930, the son of a wealthy almond farmer known as the King of Almonds. Hillyer studied fine arts and literature at the University of California. While in college, he met the noted psychical researcher Dr. Hereward Carrington and assisted him in some of his experiments on mental telepathy and psychokinesis. He demonstrated what he called "average" psychic abilities.

One of his college friends was Prince Mahmoud, the brother of Shah Mohammed Reza Pahlevi of Iran. The prince invited the 25-year-old Hillyer to spend a summer with him in Iran at the palace. Hillyer accepted, and there he met the shah's youngest sister, Princess Fatemah Fahlave.

Within a year, in 1950, Hillyer and the princess married, in a civil ceremony in Citavecchia, Italy. The marriage made Hillyer the first American to wed royalty since Wallace Simpson.

The shah and his household were enraged, however, and the shah disowned his sister and stripped her of her royal rights. Hillyer managed to make amends and agreed to a Muslim wedding. The ceremony took place in a Paris mosque, with Rita Hayworth serving as matron of honor.

Hillyer and his wife lived in Beverly Hills, where he established the Magic Carpet Travel Company, and also lived in Europe and in the royal household in Iran. Hillyer led an exotic lifestyle, exploring the jungles of Borneo, working as an actor in Rome, owning an airline and export agencies in Teheran and Beverly Hills, and keeping an apartment at the Ritz-Carlton Hotel in Paris.

In 1969 he and the princess divorced. Hillyer married an Italian actress, Milly Vitale. After the end of that marriage, he settled in Los Banos, California, which served as home for the remainder of his life. Hillyer was fascinated by the paranormal and continued to participate in psychical experiments and conduct investigations of haunted places.

Hillyer's interest in VAMPIRES began when, as a youth, he saw BELA LUGOSI in *DRACULA* (1931) and *MARK OF THE VAMPIRE* (1935). He read vampire comics. In college, Hereward Carrington had related to him various vampire incidents, which increased his interest in vampires.

Hillyer said that superstitious villagers in Iran sometimes thought him to be a vampire because of his RED hair and BLUE eyes. He had numerous encounters with the paranormal. In an interview for *Vampires Among Us*, he recounted:

We were living in a very old palace in Teheran called Sahab Garanieh Palace . . . It was an edifice about 300 years old. One of the 18th-century shahs, Nasr-i-Din, had lived in there and reputedly still haunted this palace. We lived in the upper floor in one wing. It was too difficult to try to heat the whole palace—we only had small fireplaces in each room. We had nine servants, and they were all deathly afraid to go down to the subterranean rooms below where the old shah had maintained a favorite chamber. There once was a pool there, the ruins of which were still in the room. The old shah would sit on a big cushion there with his dozens of wives and concubines around him.

Even though our servants didn't want to go downstairs, there were times when they *had* to go down to find things that had been stored. I decided I would take them down myself and show them that there was nothing to be afraid of. One windy evening, we all got candles and lighted them, and went down. Of course I did want to dispel their fears, but I was half hoping at the same time that maybe there really *was* something that they should be fearful of. There I was, leading this group of very timorous people, and from nowhere a sudden shift of wind came up and blew out all the candles. I heard a commotion behind me, and by the time I got my candle lit, I was alone. The servants had taken off and run back upstairs.

The wind was eerie and was making strange sounds in these lower chambers. I always wondered about that wind and the way and moment it came up. None of these servants would ever go back down there again. Nothing I could do could convince them to go. Maybe the old shah *was* haunting the place.

He gave another story about the local beliefs in the supernatural:

Out in the villages there were beliefs that some people could change into spirits. They didn't necessarily call them vampires, they called them *djinn* or *afrit*. The villagers were very superstitious. I went to a village up north one time, in the province of Mazanderan at the Caspian Sea, and I sat having tea on a large carpet near a stream with the chief. Through an interpreter he told me about a man in the village that used to go out hunting tiger armed only with an axe. People don't realize that northern Iran is all jungle, filled with tigers and wild pig. The tigers are the large Persian tiger, second in size only to the Bengal tiger of India.

The chief said that one day the hunter went out and followed a tiger. Unbeknownst to him, a second tiger was following *him*. He never came back. The people believed that he had been turned into a weretiger.

Once I made a trip on horseback with some of the Shah's brothers, and we went through a village called Kelardasht in the Alborz Mountains. It was late afternoon, and the people were all standing in the little dirt streets. As we passed by, the men turned away and the women put part of their veils up higher over their eyes. I wondered what happened—"did I forget to shower this morning?"—because everyone was shunning me. I asked one of the guides with us, and he said, "You have blue eyes, and the people here believe that blue eyes belong only to a demon. They are afraid of you, and they're afraid you can transform yourself into some type of a creature and drink their blood." That night, when I went out walking through the streets, even the dogs ran off. I felt safer than I would on the streets of New York—nobody came near me! It gave me a funny feeling.

Then I met a very interesting Englishman who came to Iran on an exchange program to teach English at some of the schools there. He had brilliant red hair, red mustache and beard. Turned out he was an English witch. I thought that was interesting, in light of the superstition that people with red hair are witches. One evening he talked to me about various incantations and spells that he used, and said that the same methods were used in Iran, such as tying knots in a string, or sending orange seeds in a letter.

Fatemeh told me that the Queen Mother . . . would send her servants out every morning to check her front doorstep to make sure there were no black roosters slain and put there to curse her. A lot of this sort of witchcraft and magic goes on in Iran.

Around 1974 Hillyer met RAYMOND T. MCNALLY and RADU R. FLORESCU, who had recently identified CASTLE POE-

NARI as "CASTLE DRACULA." Hillyer went to Romania in 1977 to spend a night alone in the castle ruins.

In Bucharest, he met with the deputy minister of tourism, H. E. Stefan Enache, who tried to dissuade him from staying alone in the castle during the night. It was too dangerous, Enache said, but not because of vampires—a superstition not officially tolerated by the Communist regime in power at the time—but because the ruins offered no protection against the bears and wolves who roamed about at night. Just prior to Hillyer's arrival, a German hiker walking in the Arges Valley near the castle had been torn to pieces by a bear. Furthermore, local laws prohibited Hillyer from carrying a weapon with him.

Hillyer would not be swayed, and so Enache dispatched him with a guide, Michaela Velescu. Velescu took him on a week-long trip through TRANSYLVANIA, culminating in their arrival at the foot of the Carpathian ridge where the ruined castle sits. There, Hillyer was left by his guide to spend the night in the ruins.

He was inspected by a wolf, but otherwise experienced no nocturnal threat. While he slept, he received a large, painful bite on his collarbone that made him ill; a local doctor identified it as the bite of a spider. Hillyer said that ever afterward, he was more sensitive to SUNLIGHT. He developed pre-cancerous skin lesions.

Hillyer participated in vampire-related research and forums around the world. JEANNE KEYES YOUNGSON named him a vice president of the COUNT DRACULA FAN CLUB. He also served as board member of the American Chapter of the TRANSYLVANIAN SOCIETY OF DRACULA.

Hillyer did not believe in reanimated CORPSES, but said that vampires could indeed exist in an astral, or spirit form. He developed a theory called the "hemolytic factor" to explain how an ASTRAL VAMPIRE could draw off the blood of a living person by penetrating a victim's aura and physical body. He also believed that living persons can turn themselves into psychic vampires through occult practices and rituals.

Hillyer died in 2000 of complications of cancer.

See also VAMPIRE DAY.

FURTHER READING:
Guiley, Rosemary Ellen. *Vampires Among Us*. New York: Pocket Books, 1991.
Hillen, John Sean. *Digging for Dracula*. Dublin: Dracula Transylvania Club, 1997.
Hillyer, Vincent. *Vampires*. Los Banos, Calif.: Loose Change Publications, 1988.

Hoffman, Kuno   VAMPIRE grave robber and murderer of Germany, called the "Vampire of Nuremberg." At age 41, Kuno Hoffman, a deaf-mute laborer, was arrested in 1973 and charged with murder and attempted murder. He also exhibited a obsession with CORPSES.

Hoffman would read the obituaries in the newspaper and then break into the graves. He stabbed the corpses with knives and sliced them with razors. He drank their BLOOD, convinced it would make him "good-looking and strong." Sometimes he cut of the heads of the corpses or cut out their hearts. He shot and wounded a night watchman while trying to break into a mortuary.

Hoffman was alleged to desecrate at least 35 corpses in this manner. He was caught after murdering a man and woman in a lover's lane and drinking the blood from their wounds. He declared that the blood of the living was much tastier than the blood of the dead.

Two court-appointed psychiatrists disagreed on Hoffman's mental stability. He was convicted and sentenced to life in prison.

FURTHER READING:
Perkowski, Jan. L. *The Vampire of the Slavs*. Cambridge, Mass.: Slavica Publishers, 1976.

holes   In European lore, VAMPIRES exit and reenter their graves by holes in the ground. One way to find a vampire is to look for a grave that has a serpent-sized hole on it or near it.

A Bulgarian custom calls for placing bowls of human excrement or poison by the hole to deter the vampire from leaving. According to lore, the vampire will eat the excrement instead of desiring the BLOOD of the living.

In Romanian lore, a hole is made on the stomach of a CORPSE in order to prevent it from becoming a *STRIGOI*.

holy water   See WATER.

Hommy-Beg   The dedication to the novel *DRACULA* (1897) by BRAM STOKER. Stoker's full dedication reads "To My Dear Friend Hommy-Beg." Hommy-Beg is Manx for "little Tommy," and was the childhood nickname of Stoker's friend Hall Caine, given to Caine by his grandmother.

Six years Stoker's junior, Caine, born on the Isle of Man, was a talented and successful author in his own right, but never achieved the long-lasting fame of Stoker. He remained a good friend of Stoker's throughout his life, and was the only other person outside of Henry Irving with whom Stoker formed a close relationship. Stoker compared his appearance to that of Shakespeare.

Caine shared Stoker's interest in the supernatural and occult. His patron was the pre-Raphaelite painter Gabriel Rossetti, and Caine lived with him when he was a young man.

In 1893 Caine dedicated *Capt'n Davy's Honeymoon* to Stoker, citing him first among his friends. Stoker reciprocated in 1897 with his dedication in *Dracula*.

Horerczy   German DEMON. The *Horerczy* releases BUTTERFLIES from its mouth, which are really breath-sucking VAMPIRES called *ALPS*.

Horror of Dracula   See HAMMER FILMS.

House of Dark Shadows   See *DARK SHADOWS.*

Howling, The   Series of films featuring WEREWOLVES. The first *Howling* deputed in 1981, directed by Joe Dante, an associate of Roger Corman, and loosely based on the novel by the same name by Gary Brandner.

A coven of werewolves in Los Angeles is committing a string of grisly murders. A Los Angeles news anchor (Dee Wallace) investigates and discovers the werewolves. She is captured by them, but manages to escape and burn out their lair. However, she has been turned into a werewolf, and makes the change during one of her newscasts.

Director Dante winked at fans by naming some of the characters after directors of well-known horror films, and by including in-jokes for the horror cognoscenti.

Six more *Howling* films were produced through 1995:

- *The Howling II—Your Sister Is A Werewolf* (1995): In a sequel of sorts to the first *Howling,* a psychic investigator goes to TRANSYLVANIA on the trail of werewolves, and finds the Queen of the Werewolves herself. CHRISTOPHER LEE has a supporting role. Directed by Philipe Mora.
- *The Howling III—The Marsupials* (1987): A weird tribe of werewolves with kangaroolike pouches for carrying their young live in Australia. Directed by Philipe Mora.
- *The Howling IV—The Original Nightmare* (1988): A woman suffers terrible nightmares of werewolves, so her husband takes her on holiday to Drago, a seemingly charming village. Unfortunately for them, everyone in the entire village is a werewolf. Directed by John Hough of HAMMER FILMS fame.
- *The Howling V—The Rebirth* (1989): In 15th-century Budapest, a family cursed to become werewolves commits mass SUICIDE to end the curse, and their castle is abandoned. An infant survives, however, and centuries later the curse is still active. Directed by Neal Sundstrom.
- *The Howling VI—The Freaks* (1991): The proprietor of a carnival freak show, Harker's World of Wonders—and who is a vampire—kidnaps a wandering werewolf and puts him on display with the other freaks. Local townspeople get angry and storm the carnival. The werewolf kills the vampire and escapes. Directed by Hope Perello.
- *The Howling VII—The New Moon Rising* (1995): Werewolf murders are being committed in Pioneertown in Yucca Valley, California. The werewolf hunters are a policeman, a priest, and an Australian wanderer, the latter of whom is really the werewolf. Directed by Clive Hunter.

FURTHER READING:
Steiger, Brad. *The Werewolf Book: The Encyclopedia of Shape-Shifting Beings.* Detroit: Visible Ink Press/Gale Research, 1999.

huli jing (fox fairy)   In Chinese lore, the malevolent spirit of the returning dead who vampirizes victims sexually. The *huli jing* rises from its grave and shape-shifts (see SHAPE-SHIFTING) into a seductive woman, scholar, or old man. It seduces victims and sucks off the victims' life force during orgasm. When the victim falls ill with consumption, the *huli jing* leaves it for another victim. Female *huli jing* especially like scholars for their virtuousness.

The *huli jing* has other powers and abilities that make it one of the most feared of all spirits in Chinese lore. It can shape-shift into dead people, haunt places, and terrify the living. It can take on the appearance of living people. It can transport people through the air and enable them to pass through walls and closed windows. The *huli jing* is invisible during the day but can often be seen at night, especially lurking on the rooftops of homes. The power of the *huli jing* resides in its tail.

The *huli jing* is responsible for a form of possession that reduces a person to insanity. If madness affects generations of a family, it means an ancestor once injured a *huli jing.* (See *KITSUNE.*)

The *huli jing* is so feared that it is treated with great respect; above all, great care must be taken never to harm one. However, if one cuts off the tail, it will leave a home and never return. If a female *huli jing* can be given enough wine to become drunk, it will revert to its true form and will vanish.

One remedy against the *huli jing* is similar to that found in European and American folklore, especially in cases where victims contracted consumption. Paper charms (written prayers) are burned and the ASHES are mixed in tea and drunk. (See NEW ENGLAND VAMPIRES.)

FURTHER READING:
Mack, Carol K., and Dinah Mack. *A Field Guide to Demons, Fairies, Fallen Angels, and Other Subversive Spirits.* New York: Henry Holt/Owl Books, 1998.

Hunger, The (1983)   VAMPIRE novel by horror novelist Whitley Strieber, made into a film starring David Bowie and Catherine Deneuve as the vampires, and directed by Tony Scott.

The central character of *The Hunger* is Miriam Blaylock, an ancient vampire whose origins are not known, but her vampirism seems to be a disease of the BLOOD. She is part of a species that has developed separately from humans. She is old by the time of Christ. Blaylock does not bite her victims, but uses an ankh-shaped knife to slice open their arteries. As she drinks from them, she telepathically shares their emotions, which heightens the erotic elements of the experience for both her and her victims. She needs to eat only once a week, and she can go about in SUNLIGHT. She cares about her victims, who always die, and she preserves their bodies in boxes and totes them about the world with her.

One of five children, Blaylock loses all her siblings in the late 18th century in Swabia: Her brother dies during the trip there, and her three sisters are ambushed by VAMPIRE HUNTERS, making her the last of her kind. She escapes to England, where she meets David and makes him her vampire companion. By the modern times in which the novel is set, the pair are living in New York City, where they are loners who seldom meet other vampires. Lonely, Blaylock views her human victims as the equivalent of pets that give their love to her in their dying.

Though Blaylock never ages, David begins to deteriorate. Blaylock seeks help from a medical doctor, Sarah Roberts. Secretly, she plans to make Roberts a vampire companion if the doctor is unable to save David.

Roberts's efforts fail and David dies. Blaylock inters him in one of her boxes, and he joins her macabre collection of preserved CORPSES. She seduces Roberts. Roberts turns on her, and the two women fight. Blaylock wins.

In the film, Deneuve plays Miriam Blaylock and Bowie plays her dying lover, John. The doctor's name is Sarah; she is played by Susan Sarandon. Sarah is turned into a vampire by Blaylock. In the end, Sarah wins the confrontation with Blaylock, destroying her.

FURTHER READING:
Strieber, Whitley. *The Hunger.* New York: William Morrow, 1981.

I Am Legend (1954) VAMPIRE novel by RICHARD MATHE-SON, considered a classic in contemporary vampire literature and in the horror genre. *I Am Legend* is the first contemporary novel to present vampires as the victims of illness and not as creatures of evil, and it influenced many vampire novels in subsequent years.

I Am Legend was the third novel of prolific author Matheson and originally was published in the science fiction genre. Subsequently, it has been called one of the greatest horror novels and one of the most influential vampire novels.

The hero is Robert Neville, who becomes the last human on an earth that is taken over by vampires. Vampirism is a bacteria-caused plague spread through BLOOD infection. The plague has decimated the population of the world. Those who aren't killed by it becomes vampires. Cities are in ruins as the plague of vampirism infects more and more people.

Neville seems to be immune to the plague, but this soon becomes more of a curse than a blessing, as he becomes the Outsider. He spends his nights barricaded against the vampires, who are after his blood. During the day, he becomes a brutal VAMPIRE HUNTER, killing vampires one by one in gory fashion. He must deal with his own loneliness, and also the increasingly sophisticated society being created by the vampires who now dominate the planet and are creating a new world, mutating into a new species. Alone with his hoard of frozen food and his stock of classical music, Neville has no creature comfort from either man or beast. He coaxes in a stray dog, but it soon

dies. Ruth, a widow who appears, turns out to be in the employ of the vampires.

Neville also spends time searching libraries and archives for scientific information on plagues, bacteria, and the blood, hoping he will find something that will lead to an antidote against the vampire plague. It is a more and more a futile battle, as impossible as trying to stop the tide.

As the shift takes place from human to vampire, the novel considers the question, what is "normal"? When vampires prevail, are they the normal ones and Neville the alien who should be destroyed? What if vampirism is a normal course of evolution?

I Am Legend inspired horror novelist Stephen King and horror film director George Romero. It was filmed in 1964 as *The Last Man on Earth* starring Vincent Price, and in 1971 as *The Omega Man* starring Charleton Heston. In the latter film, the vampirism element is nearly absent, but has been replaced by a mutating plague.

FURTHER READING:
Matheson, Richard. *I Am Legend.* New York: TOR Books, 1997.

identification of vampires See CORPSES; *DHAMPIR*; FINDING VAMPIRES.

ikiryoh In Japanese folklore, a spirit that is born of evil thoughts and feelings harbored by a person. The *ikiryoh,* energized by hatred, becomes powerful enough to leave its source and enter and possess the object of the person's hatred. Once inside, it kills the victim in a VAMPIRE-like fashion by slowly draining the person's energy. The *ikiryoh* is extremely difficult to exorcize. Rites to drive it away include the reading of Buddhist sutras.

See also DION FORTUNE; THOUGHT-FORM.

incubus   A male demon who sexually assaults women. The incubus and his female counterpart, the SUCCUBUS, visit women and men in their sleep and seduce them. In VAMPIRE lore, vampires are sexually insatiable and behave like incubi and succubi. A man who became a vampire after death was often expected to return to his wife or others seeking sexual favors. During the witch hysteria in Europe, incubi were believed to be instruments of the devil, tormenting people for the sole purpose of degrading their souls and perverting them to more vices.

Incubi have the ability to impregnate women. In demonology lore, they do not possess their own semen, but collect it from men in nocturnal emissions, masturbation, or in coitus while masquerading as succubi. The demons have the power to preserve semen and use it later on one of their victims. Similarly, vampires were believed to have the capability of impregnating women. In some cases of VAMPIRE FRAUD, in which living men masqueraded as dead vampire husbands in order to carry out love affairs, any resulting children were passed off as the offspring of the "vampire husband."

See also CUNTIUS, JOHANNES; *MULLO*; SCOT, REGINALD.

FURTHER READING:
Guiley, Rosemary Ellen. *The Encyclopedia of Witches and Witchcraft.* 2d ed. New York: Facts On File, 1999.

incus   A Vietnamese VAMPIRE. The *incus* sucks out its victims' BLOOD through an antennae that grows out of its nose.

International Society for the Study of Ghosts and Apparitions   See VAMPIRE EMPIRE.

Interview with the Vampire   Ground-breaking first novel by ANNE RICE that launched her Vampire Chronicles series and influenced the portrayal of VAMPIRES in other fiction, film, and entertainment media.

Interview with the Vampire began as a 30-page short story Rice wrote in 1969. The inspiration came one day when she wondered what it would be like to interview a vampire. As she started to write, Rice found herself taking the vampire's point of view as he told his story to a reporter.

The story was not published. After the Rices' daughter, Michele, died of leukemia in 1972 at age five, Rice began to write again as a way to heal her grief. She revised and expanded the story into a book, adding the character of LESTAT DE LIONCOURT and a host of other vampires.

The main character, Louis, comes from southern Louisiana and New Orleans. In 1791, while grieving over the death of his brother, Louis is made a reluctant vampire by the vampire Lestat. Yet Louis is no COUNT DRACULA; instead, he—like Lestat—is an androgynous character, smooth and white-skinned, who succumbs to the desire for immortality yet finds it hard to bear. Unlike traditional vampires, Rice's immortals are beautiful, do not live in graves, do not avoid GARLIC, and can see their reflections in MIRRORS. According to Rice, in Catholic theology, the inability so see one's reflection means the soul is in hell, and she did not want her vampires to have any better assurance of a God than mortals.

Louis suffers tremendous guilt over his now-evil nature. In an interview with a reporter, he explains how he dealt with being a vampire, how he finally surrendered to his BLOOD thirst by attacking a five-year-old girl, and how his mentor, Lestat, saved her by making her a vampire as well. Young Claudia resembled Michele, Rice's daughter who died of leukemia in 1972 at age five. The Rices had even once called Michele Claudia. In the first manuscript, Claudia joins a band of children terrorizing Paris, but lives forever—in other words, giving Michele immortality. Lestat was inspired by Stan Rice.

Louis and Claudia do not like Lestat and resent him for making them vampires. Claudia sets their house on fire and the two abandon him, thinking they have killed him. They go to Central Europe in search of other vampires who can tell them about their origins and roots. In Central Europe they find only vampire creatures, rather subhuman, who feed mindlessly. Disgusted, they go to Paris, where they meet the vampire coven run by the beautiful Armand, which operates the decadent Theater of the Vampires.

Louis falls in love with Armand. He creates a vampire for Claudia, Madeleine. Lestat tracks them down and informs the vampire coven of Claudia's treachery. The coven destroys Claudia and Madeleine, and Louis retaliates by burning down their underground lair.

Louis rejects both Lestat and Armand and winds up alone in San Francisco, telling his story to the reporter. The journalist asks to be made a vampire.

Like Rice's novels that followed, *Interview with the Vampire* deals with lengthy philosophical and theological conversations and anguished introspections on the part of vampire protagonists as they struggle with the evil of their nature as blood predators.

Initially, publishers rejected the manuscript. It was sold to Alfred A. Knopf in 1974 for a $12,000 advance, about $8,000 more than the average advance of the times for a first novel. *Interview* was published in 1976 to mixed reviews, but it gained a following that eventually propelled Rice to best-sellerdom. *Interview with the Vampire* is the second-highest-selling vampire novel, bested only by BRAM STOKER's, *DRACULA*.

Film rights to *Interview with the Vampire* passed through the hands of three studios—Paramount, Lorimar and, Warner Bros.—before landing at Geffen Pictures. In 1994 the film version of the novel was released. It stars Tom Cruise as Lestat, Brad Pitt as Louis, Kirsten Dunst as Claudia, and Antonio Banderas as Armand. Initially, Rice did not approve of Cruise as the choice for Lestat and thought a better actor for the role was Rutger Hauer, who starred as the vampire in the film version of BUFFY THE VAMPIRE SLAYER. But after seeing a preview of the film, Rice changed her mind and publicly supported it.

FURTHER READING:
Rice, Anne. *Interview with the Vampire.* New York: Alfred A. Knopf, 1976.

iron   In folklore, iron—like SILVER—is protection against evil, including VAMPIRES, witches, and evil spirits, and also against FAIRIES. Iron repels the *djinn,* the demonic children of LILITH and the devil, and vampiric childbirth demons. Iron scissors or small implements are placed at beds to ward off attacks by vampiric entities that drain off the life force of the living.

Iron objects placed in COFFINS and grave sites, and iron nails driven into coffins and graves will prevent vampires and restless ghosts from leaving their graves to attack the living. A Romanian tradition calls for stabbing iron forks into the heart, eyes, and breast of a vampire and reburying the CORPSE facedown. In Bulgarian tradition, a RED-hot iron is driven through the heart.

According to Romanian lore, if a dead man who is a vampire has a brother who was born on the same day of the year or in the same month, a danger exists that the dead vampire will turn his brother into a vampire. This can be prevented by a procedure called "taking out the iron." An iron chain, such as one used to hang a pot over the fire, or used in bullock carts, is wrapped around both brothers. The ends are solemnly closed and opened three times while a priest reads a religious service. When the ends are opened the third time, the living brother is freed from the danger of becoming a vampire.

FURTHER READING:
Murgoci, Agnes. "The Vampire in Roumania," in *The Vampire: A Casebook,* Alan Dundes, ed. Madison: University of Wisconsin Press, 1998.

iron-fingered demon   In Cherokee lore, a vampiric demon who causes consumption. According to a version of the legend recorded in North Carolina in 1892, in times before the arrival of the white settlers, a demon with an IRON finger lived in a cave. The demon fed on human lungs and livers, which he accomplished by impersonating absent members of a household. In his guise, he would enter unchallenged into a household at night and select his victim. The demon, who had soft fingers, fondled the head and hair of the victim, lulling him into sleep. Then he used his iron finger to pierce the victim's side and painlessly remove the lungs and liver. The wound healed immediately without leaving a mark.

The victim would awaken without knowing anything was amiss. But over time, his health would decline, and he would waste away and die.

See also NEW ENGLAND VAMPIRES.

FURTHER READING:
Bell, Michael E. *Food for the Dead: On the Trail of New England's Vampires.* New York: Carroll & Graf, 2001.

Jack My Hedgehog Were-hedgehog in a fairy tale, record by the Grimm Brothers, by the same name. The story of Jack my Hedgehog, a half-man, half-hedgehog creature, has elements similar to the lore of WEREWOLVES.

The story goes that a farmer lived in great comfort, but he was unhappy because he had no children. Other farmers chided him for being childless. On one occasion he became angry and exclaimed, "I must and will have a child of some sort or kind, even should it be a hedgehog!"

The farmer's wife soon became pregnant, and she gave birth to a boy who was male on the bottom and a prickly hedgehog on the top—the result of being cursed by the farmer's oath. They named him Jack my Hedgehog and gave him a bed of straw behind the stove, and there he slept for eight years. He was a cheerful fellow, always happy and in a good mood.

One day Jack my Hedgehog asked his father for bagpipes, and for a COCK to be shod. He promised he would ride off and trouble his father no more. The father gladly obliged, for he wished to be rid of his strange son. Jack my Hedgehog departed astride his cock, followed by a large number of pigs and asses. Jack my Hedgehog took the herd into the forest and flew his cock up into a tree. There he sat and played his bagpipes. Over time, his herds grew in size.

One day a king lost his way in the forest and was drawn to Jack my Hedgehog's music. The boy agreed to tell him the way home if the king would promise to give him the first thing he encountered on his return. The king agreed and wrote out his promise.

But when the king arrived home, he was first met by his beautiful daughter. He decided he would not give her to Jack my Hedgehog, and figured that the creature could not read, and so the promise was void. The daughter was delighted.

Meanwhile, another king lost his way in the forest, and Jack my Hedgehog struck the same bargain with him. He, too, was met by his beautiful daughter when he arrived home. But this king resolved to honor his promise and give her to Jack my Hedgehog.

Jack's herds grew so large that he drove them back to his home village and let the people slaughter whatever they needed. He asked his father—who was not pleased to see him—to have another cock shod.

Jack my Hedgehog then set out for the first kingdom. He confronted the king, who reluctantly agreed to let his daughter go with him. But when the couple departed, Jack my Hedgehog tore off all the princess's clothing and stuck her with his prickles as punishment for their treachery. He sent her home in shame.

Jack my Hedgehog went to the second kingdom, where the king greeted him warmly and willingly gave over his daughter in betrothal. Jack my Hedgehog asked for the king's men to watch him when he went to sleep. When he took off his skin prior to retiring, they were to throw it on the fire and stay until it was completely burned.

The king's men did so. As soon as the skin was completely consumed by the flames, Jack my Hedgehog was freed of his cursed enchantment. He turned into a whole

Jack My Hedgehog is half-boy, half-hedgehog. From The Green Fairy Book, *1892, edited by Andrew Lang*

man, albeit a severely burned one. After treatment by the king's physicians, he was a remarkably handsome young man. Jack my Hedgehog and the princess were married, and he inherited the kingdom.

Years later, Jack my Hedgehog and his wife went to visit his father. The old man did not recognize him and insisted he had no son, save for a strange creature who was half-human and half-hedgehog. Jack my Hedgehog told his story. The father rejoiced and went to live with them in their kingdom.

The were-animal form as a result of a curse is common to many stories about werewolves. In werewolf lore, the werewolves take off their animals skins at night when they sleep. If the skins are burned in a fire, they cannot change back into their wolf forms.

FURTHER READING:
Lang, Andrew, ed. *The Green Fairy Book*. New York: Dover, 1965.

jaracaca   In Brazilian lore, a snake-shaped VAMPIRE. The *jaracaca* attacks nursing mothers and sucks the milk from their breasts, meanwhile lodging its tail in the mouths of the infants.

Jewett City Vampires   See NEW ENGLAND VAMPIRES; RAY FAMILY VAMPIRES.

jumby   In Caribbean lore, a term applied generally to spirits, but usually in reference to ghosts of the dead. Many *jumbies* are malevolent in nature, and some are vampiric. Another name for *jumby* is *duppy*.

juniper   In the lore of some Slavic GYPSIES, a protection against VAMPIRES. A sprig of juniper kept in a home will prevent a vampire from entering and causing harm to the occupants. A juniper STAKE thrust through the navel of a vampire CORPSE will contain or destroy it.

kalagkalag In Philippine lore, the restless dead who leave their graves to attack their living relatives by sending them sickness of unknown origin.

kappa In Japanese lore, a horrible water imp who likes to drink human BLOOD and eat entrails. The *kappa* is named after the river god Kappa, whom it serves as a messenger.

The *kappa* resembles a monkey. It is about the height of a 10-year-old boy and has webbed hands and feet, a monkey face, a long beaklike nose, and a tortoise shell on its back. On top of its head is a bowl-like indentation that contains a clear, jellylike substance, which is the source of the *kappa's* power. Short black hair rings the indentation.

The *kappa* lives in swampy areas, ponds, lakes, and rivers, where it taunts its victims—men, women, and children—into treacherous or deep waters so that they drown. It also attacks animals. After the victims are dead, the *kappa* enters the bodies through the anus, drinks their blood, and sucks out their entrails. It is especially fond of livers. Sometimes it will devour some of the flesh.

The *kappa* offers a supernatural explanation for a phenomenon of drowning: a bulging anus.

Folklore stories about the *kappa* tell of it losing an arm in an attack. It goes after its arm and promises people favors in exchange for the limb. It promises not to attack the local people anymore, or it teaches someone how to heal.

Kappa-like beings have been reported in UFO and EXTRATERRESTRIAL encounters in South America. The creatures are described as about two to three feet tall and covered with reptilian scales. They have webbed and clawed hands and feet, skulllike heads, pointed ears, and slits for noses and mouths. They have not taken blood directly, but seem to vampirize eyewitnesses of energy and leave them feeling weak, anemic, and faint, similar to the effects experienced in *CHUPA-CHUPA* attacks.

See also VISCERA SUCKERS.

FURTHER READING:
Mack, Carol K., and Dinah Mack. *A Field Guide to Demons, Fairies, Fallen Angels, and Other Subversive Spirits.* New York: Henry Holt/Owl Books, 1998.
Picasso, Fabio. "Infrequent Types of South American Humanoids." *Strange* No. 8, Fall 1991, pp. 21–23+.

Kashubs Devout Christian sect of Slavs in North America, residing mostly in Ontario, Canada, with an active VAMPIRE cult existing into modern times. Though Christian, the Kashubs retain pre-Christian pagan practices. They are bicultural and bilingual, speaking English and Kashubian. They imported their demonology from Europe.

Kashubian vampire beliefs have been researched by Jan L. Perkowski, a professor of Slavic languages and literature. Perkowski's initial interest in vampires was established when he visited a Kashubian farm family in 1968 to ask questions about their customs and beliefs, including vampires. The wife, a middle-aged woman whose upper incisors were missing, acknowledged matter-of-factly that she was a vampire.

Vampire Beliefs

The Kashubian vampire relieves social anxiety concerning birth anomalies, unexplained deaths, and protection against evil in general. The Kashubs recognize two types of vampires: the VJESCI and the OPJI. Both can be identified at birth. The *vjesci* is born with the CAUL on the head, and the *opji* has one or more teeth already showing. The *vjesci* can lead a normal life if certain measures are taken immediately. The caul is dried and reduced to ASHES, and then fed to the child at age seven. At death, special measures must be taken again to ensure that he does not rise up out of the grave. If these measures are not taken, the vampire will eat his burial garments, rise at midnight, leave his grave, and suck the BLOOD of his family and relatives, causing them to sicken and die. He will ring the church bell, and all who hear the bell with die. The only action that can put a stop to the dying is to dig up the vampire's CORPSE and cut its head off.

The *opji,* more dangerous, cannot be prevented during life from becoming a vampire after death and must be dealt with accordingly once buried. (See BURIAL CUSTOMS.)

By some accounts, both *vjesci* and *opji* look and live normally, but other accounts describe them as excitable and restless, and having blood-red faces. The Kashubs have an expression for anger and excitability: "as red as a vampire." Vampires refuse to take the Eucharist at their death and refuse a priest. After they die, they become cold more slowly than other corpses. The face remains RED, the limbs do not stiffen, and spots of blood appear on the face or beneath the fingernails.

If the vampires are active after death, they must be exhumed at midnight. They are found sitting up in their COFFINS with open EYES, naked to the waist because they have eaten part of their burial clothing. They move their heads and may make unintelligible sounds. Remedies taken against them include a long nail driven into the forehead, or, preferably, decapitation with the head being placed between the feet. When the head is cut off, a dark stream of blood flows forth. This blood should be collected and given to those who have fallen ill to mix in their drink. It will enable them to recover. (See BROWN, MERCY.)

It is much better if post-burial measures do not have to be taken at all. Dying people, and especially vampires, should be given the Eucharist. Earth from under the threshold of the vampire's house is placed in the coffin to prevent him from returning to his former abode. The sign of the CROSS is made on his mouth, and a crucifix from a rosary or a coin is placed beneath his tongue for him to suck, so that he will not eat his shroud. A brick beneath the chin will make the vampire break his teeth on it. Miniature poplar crosses and netting (see KNOTS) or quantities of sand or poppy SEEDS are placed in the coffin. The corpse is laid facedown so that he will descend lower and lower into the earth instead of finding his way back to the surface.

A vampiric SUCCUBUS entity prominent in Kashubian lore is the MWERE.

FURTHER READING:
Perkowski, Jan. L. *The Vampire of the Slavs.* Cambridge, Mass.: Slavica Publishers, 1976.

kathakano   Cretan VAMPIRE. The *kathakano* can be killed only by decapitating it and boiling the head in vinegar.

Kempe, Ursula (d. 1582)

Kempe, Ursula (d. 1582)   English witch brought to trial and executed for harming others. Her CORPSE was staked like a VAMPIRE.

Ursula Kempe was accused of crime in a witch hysteria that swept through St. Osyth in a remote coastal area of Essex, England, in 1582. Fourteen women were indicted. The first to be accused of malevolent witchcraft was Kempe of St. Osyth, a poor woman who made a meager living by midwifery, harlotry, and "unwitching," or removing bad spells that people believed had been cast against them. Kempe had a falling-out with a woman named Grace Thurlowe and threatened her with lameness. Soon, Thurlowe was severely crippled with arthritis.

Thurlowe complained to the county session judge, Bryan Darcy, who started an investigation against Kempe. Her illegitimate eight-year-old son, Thomas, was forced to confess to incredible stories about his mother, among them that she had four FAMILIARS who sucked blood from Kempe's arm at night. In addition, a man claimed Kempe had bewitched his wife to death.

Kempe denied these stories, but Darcy tricked her by falsely promising her leniency if she confessed. Fearful for her life, Kempe confessed to having familiars and consorting with other St. Osyth witches, whom she named. These accused women in turn named others, hoping for mercy from the court. They falsified evidence against one another.

The women were charged with crimes of bewitching animals, bewitching brewing, baking, and butter churning, striking people with wasting sickness, and bewitching people to death. Not all went to trial. Of those who did, four of them pleaded not guilty and were acquitted. Four others pleaded not guilty, but were convicted and then reprieved. One who was charged with bewitchment through the EVIL EYE was sentenced to a year in prison. Two—including Kempe—were convicted and hanged. Kempe was charged with bewitching three people to death between 1580 and 1582. She confessed to the crimes.

In the mid-20th century, the remains of Kempe were exhumed by occultist Cecil Williamson and placed on display in an open elm COFFIN lined with purple satin in Williamson's Museum of Witchcraft. The exhumation was televised. Williamson discovered that Kempe's body had been driven through with IRON spikes, suggesting that people had feared she would return from the grave to haunt or vampirize them. Williamson sold the museum in 1996 to Graham King and others, who moved it to Boscastle, Cornwall. Williamson kept Kempe's remains for his personal collection. After his death in 2000, the remains went to King.

FURTHER READING:
Guiley, Rosemary Ellen. *The Encyclopedia of Witches and Witchcraft.* 2d ed. New York: Checkmark Books/Facts On File, 1999.

Kenyon, Sherrilyn (1965–)   Best-selling American author of science fiction and fantasy romance novels about VAMPIRES, VAMPIRE HUNTERS, WEREWOLVES, and werewolf hunters. Sherrilyn Kenyon also had authored stories and novels in numerous other genres and subgenres, as well as nonfiction titles. She also writes historical romances under the pseudonym Kinley MacGregor, the maiden name of her great-grandmother. As Sherrilyn Kenyon, she created the Dark-Hunters (vampire hunters), and Were-Hunters series.

Kenyon, a fan of horror, science fiction, and fantasy in childhood, published her first fantasy short story at age 14. She earned a degree in history and became a full professor of history and also kept writing, for magazines, television, and radio. She also became a professional Web site designer.

In the mid-1980s, Kenyon was writing for a small press science fiction/fantasy magazine, *Cutting Edge.* The genesis of her Dark-Hunter series was born during that time, when she was asked to create a long-running serial in order to increase sales. She took characters she had created in different worlds and brought them together in a single series. But 17 years elapsed before the Dark-Hunters emerged in novels.

During the 1990s, Kenyon wrote paranormal and historical romances. Her first science fiction romance novel, *Born of the Night,* was published in 1996.

Dark-Hunters

The Dark-Hunters are sensuous, sexy "bad boys" who are "immortal and immoral." Kenyon's novels have been described as a cross between BUFFY THE VAMPIRE SLAYER and the television series *Sex and the City.* Dark-Hunters have no souls, so that they do not betray themselves to their vampire prey, the Daimons.

Fantasy Lover, about a Greek general cursed to be a love slave, was published in 2002, and became the basis from which the Dark-Hunter series evolved. Kenyon attributes some of the success of the Dark-Hunter novels to her interactive Web site.

Dark-Hunter novels are

Night Pleasures (2002): Kyrian of Thrace, introduced in *Fantasy Lover,* is a Dark-Hunter who has traded his soul in order to seek vengeance upon his wife. Unable to kill her, he lives in a shadowland, hunting down the vampires who prey upon humans. He falls in love with Amanda Deveraux, sister of the Gypsy Selena from *Fantasy Lover.* Amanda is an accountant who is unaware of her own powers.

Night Embrace (2003): In New Orleans, Dark-Hunter Talon of Morrigantes faces off with his revenge-bent enemy, Calamus, who also has targeted Sunshine Run-

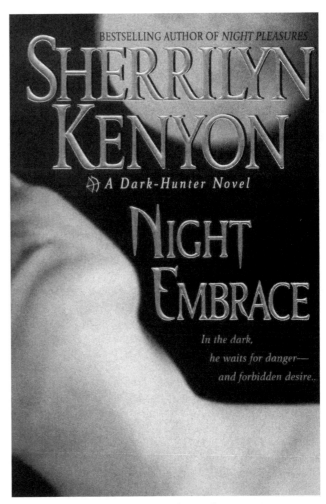

A book in Sherrilyn Kenyon's popular Dark-Hunter series (Courtesy Sherrilyn Kenyon)

ningwolf. Talon discovers that Sunshine is his reincarnated lover from ancient Greek times.

Dance with the Devil (2003): Zarek, the nastiest of all Dark-Hunters, is still bitter about his former mortal life as a Greco-Roman slave. He has been exiled to Alaska for 900 years. Astrid, a sister to the three Fates, sets challenges out to see if Zarek can redeem himself. She is protected by Sasha, a werewolf.

Kiss of the Night (2004): An ancient curse has rendered Wulf Tryggvason, a Viking warrior, completely forgettable: once he leaves a room, no one remembers him. He is astonished when he meets Cassandra Peters, who can remember him once she shares exotic dreams with him. But she is the last of her bloodline, doomed to die in a year, and she must have a child before she expires in order for her race to continue.

Were-Hunters

The Were-Hunters trace their origins to KING LYCAON of Arcadia, who unknowingly married a woman not entirely human and a member of the accursed Apollite race doomed to die at 27. Lycaon and his queen had two sons. Lycaon decided to use magic to prolong the lives of his boys, so he mingled the Apollite blood with that of animals, birds, and dragons. He perfected a new race from humans, dragons, and wolves and turned his sons into this new race. They acquired animal strength, supernatural and magical powers, and the ability to live at least 10 times longer than mortals.

Angry at this abomination, the Fates ordered Lycaon to kill his sons, but he refused. The Fates declared that Lycaon's sons would hate one another and fight for their entire lives. Thus two races were destined for eternal struggle: the Arcadians, who have human hearts, and the were-animals, the Katagaria, who have animal hearts. Both have the ability to shape-shift at puberty, when they acquire their magical powers. They are excellent warriors and can be ruthless and cold-blooded. The Arcadians are the Were-Hunters, the spiritual brethren of the Dark-Hunters, and also the Dream-Hunters, another series created by Kenyon.

The first Were-Hunter story was introduced in an anthology, *Tapestry,* in 2002. In the novel *Night Play* (2004), Bride McTierney is an independent woman put off by men because of past unhappy experiences. Still, she yearns to meet the right one. Meanwhile, Val Kattalakis is a Were-Hunter being hunted himself by his enemies. The Fates decree that Bride is to be his mate. If he cannot with her over in three weeks, he will be neutered.

Another Were-Hunter story is "At the Stroke of Midnight" in the anthology *Stroke of Midnight* (2004).

A prolific writer, Kenyon had, as of 2004, at least 20 more novels planned in various stages of development. She lives in Nashville, Tennessee, with her husband and three sons.

FURTHER READING:
Sherrylin Kenyon/Kinley MacGregor Web site. URL: http://www.kinleymacgregor.com. Downloaded on January 4, 2004.
Kenyon, Sherrilyn. *Born of the Night.* New York: Pinnacle, 1996.
———. *Fantasy Lover.* New York: St. Martin's Press, 2002.
———. *Night Pleasures.* New York: St. Martin's Press, 2002.
———. *Night Embrace.* New York: St. Martin's Press, 2003.
———. *Dance with the Devil.* New York: St. Martin's Press, 2003.
———. *Kiss of the Night.* New York: St. Martin's Press, 2004.
———. *Night Play.* New York: St. Martin's Press, 2004.
Ward, Jean Marie. "Sherrilyn Kenyon: Coloring Outside Traditional Romance Lines." Available online. URL: http://www.crescentblues.com/6_8issue/int_kenyon.shtml. Downloaded on January 4, 2004.

keres   In Greek lore, fearsome spirits of the dead who, like VAMPIRES, afflict the living with disease and illness. *Keres* escape from the *pithoi,* the jars once traditionally used to contain the bodies of the dead. They devote themselves to pestering the living. They also carry off CORPSES of the dead.

Keres are exorcized by ritual and incantation. Sticky tar painted on door frames catches them and prevents them from entering a dwelling.

kiangshi   In Chinese lore, a CORPSE that becomes a VAMPIRE demon. *Kiangshi* means "corpse specter."

In Chinese lore (as well as Slavic lore), a human being has two souls, one good and one evil. If an unburied corpse is exposed to the rays of either the sun or the MOON, the evil soul will be strengthened and will not depart from the body, but will go forth at night to seek human BLOOD for sustenance.

A folktale tells about a *kiangshi* that vampirizes a man from Wukiang. Liu N. N., a low-level literary graduate, goes home on holiday to sweep out the tombs of his ancestors. He does this and prepares to return to his post. He instructs his wife to cook him a meal early in the morning and wake him. She does so, fixing some rice and vegetables. But when she calls him, he does not answer. She finds him in his room, dead and headless, but without a trace of blood.

The terrified wife tells her neighbors, but they suspect her of adultery and murder, and report her to the magistrate. The magistrate opens an inquest and has the corpse put into a COFFIN. He arrests the wife and lets her languish in prison for months.

One day one of the wife's neighbors stumbles upon a neglected grave with the coffin visible and the lid slightly raised. He suspects thieves and summons other villagers. They raise the lid and discover a corpse with the features of a living person and its body covered with white hair. Between its arms it holds a head, which the villagers recognize as Liu. They report their discovery to the magistrate.

Coroners order the head to be taken away, but no one can pry it from the grip of the *kiangshi.* Finally, the arms of the corpse are chopped off in order to free the head. Fresh blood gushed out of the wounds—but Liu's head has been drained of every drop of blood by the *kiangshi.* The corpse is burned, and the wife is released from jail.

FURTHER READING:
McNally, Raymond T. *A Clutch of Vampires.* New York: Bell Publishing, 1984.

killing vampires   See CORPSES; VAMPIRE HUNTERS.

King Lycaon   See LYCAON.

King Vikram and the Vampire   A collection of Hindu folktales about the adventures of a great raja, King Vikram, and a BAITAL, or VAMPIRE. The tales first appeared in Sanskrit as the *Baital-Pachisi (Twenty-five Tales of a Baital)*; they established the literary foundations of the *Arabian Nights* tales, inspired Apuleius's *Golden Ass*, and influenced the development of the chivalric tale in medieval Europe.

King Vikram and the Vampire was translated into various languages. It was translated into English by Sir Richard F. Burton and was published in 1870. Burton also translated the *1001 Arabian Nights,* the *Kama Sutra,* and other texts.

The tales are set "some nineteen centuries ago." King Vikram (short for Vikramaditya) is a semi-historical figure, a King Arthur of the East. He leaves his throne for a time and wanders with his son, Sharma Dhwaj, in search of truth. During his adventures, a giant warns him that a certain *jogi* (yogi) is plotting to kill the raja. The *jogi* has murdered the son of an oilman, whose body he has hung upside down in a siras-tree (mimosa tree). He has also murdered his own son.

Vikram returns to his throne and resumes his duties as judge, dispensing justice. He punishes his enemies. One day a wealthy young merchant begins paying him daily calls, bringing him gifts of precious jewels. The king asks him what he desires. The young man says he is not a merchant, but is really a devotee and *jogi,* and he lives down by the river Godavari in a *smashana,* a CEMETERY where bodies are burned. It is his wish that the raja and his son come to him one day and do his bidding. The raja agrees, though he dislikes the idea of going to the cemetery.

When Vikram and his son arrived at the ill-omened spot, they find a horrible scene:

> There was an outer circle of hideous bestial forms; tigers were roaring, and elephants were trumpeting; wolves, whose foul hairy coats blazed with sparks of bluish phosphoric light, were devouring the remnants of human bodies; foxes, jackals, and hyenas were disputing over their prey; while bears were chewing on the livers of children. The space within was peopled with a multitude of fiends. There were the subtle bodies of men that had escaped their grosser frames prowling about the charnel ground, where their corpses had been reduced to ashes, or hovering in the air, waiting till the new bodies which they were to animate were made ready for their reception. The spirits of those that had been foully slain wandered about with gashed limbs; and skeletons, whose moldy bones were held together by bits of blackened sinew, followed them as the murderer does his victim. Malignant witches with shriveled skins, horrid eyes and distorted forms, crawled and crouched over the earth; while specters and goblins now stood motionless, and tall as lofty palm trees; then, as if in fits, leaped, danced and tumbled before their evocator. The air was filled with shrill and strident cries, with the fitful moaning of the storm-wind, with the hoarse gurgling of the swollen river, from whose banks the earth-slip thundered in its fall.

In the midst of this sits the *jogi,* now ugly and disheveled, his face painted with ASHES from cremated CORPSES. He plays upon a human skull with two bones, making a weird drumming. The 'ogi tells him that about four miles away there is another cemetery where bodies are burned. A body is hanging on a mimosa tree there. The *jogi's* request is that Vikram and his son fetch the body back to the *jogi.*

The task proves to be more difficult than the raja and his son anticipated. They find the body inhabited and transformed by an ugly *baital.* It takes many blows to bring it down from its tree and subdue it. It wails, shrieks, gnashes its teeth, and laughs and cackles. Vikram realizes the *baital* has taken over the corpse of the oilman's son.

The *baital* finally surrenders of his own accord. The *baital* informs the king that he is "of a loquacious disposition," and to fill the hour that it will take to travel to the *jogi,* he will entertain the king with "sprightly tales and profitable reflections." He will ask the king questions at the end of every tale. The *baital* strikes an agreement that if the king gives false, ignorant, or erroneous answers to the questions, the *baital* will go free and will be able to return to his beloved tree. But if the king remains silent, has no answer, or humbly admits his ignorance, the *baital* will go willingly to the *jogi.*

In his translation, Burton included 11 of what he judged to be the best of the *baital's* tales. They deal with Indian customs, manners, and religious, and magical practices. At the end of each tale, the *baital* poses questions that are like riddles.

At last both Vikram and his son are stumped for answers to the *baital's* questions and wisely remain silent. The *baital* tells him the *jogi* is plotting against the king to avenge a wrong done to his father by Vikram. The *jogi* killed the oilman's son because he threatened to interfere with his plans. The body was hung in the tree as a trap to Vikram. He whispers the *jogi's* plans.

Vikram and his son return to the hideous cemetery and deliver the corpse to the *jogi,* who is quite pleased. The form of the corpse has changed back into the oilman's son. The *jogi* requests that Vikram and Dharma Dhwaj pay a devotion to Smashana-Kali, the Kali (eight-armed goddess of destruction) of the cemetery. He leads them to a giant statue of the goddess. His secret plan is to have the statue fall on the king, crushing him. But Vikram outwits him and cuts off his head with a blow of his sword. Dharma Dhwaj pulls his father out of the way just as the giant statue of Kali comes crashing down.

The god Indra appears and grants Vikram a boon. The king asks for his history to become famous throughout the world. Thus, according to tradition, all storytellers invoke Vikram when spinning their tales.

FURTHER READING:
Burton, Isabel, ed. *Captain Sir Richard F. Burton's King Vikram and The Vampire.* Rochester, Vt.: Park Street Press, 1992.

Kisilova Vampire   See PLOGOJOWITZ, PETER.

kitsune   In Japanese lore, a wild fox demon that often appears in the form of a beautiful maiden, who vampirizes her victims sexually. The *kitsune* appears in many Japanese folktales. It originated in the lore of China, where it is described as a lewd creature.

To accomplish its SHAPE-SHIFTING, the *kitsune* flicks its fire-shooting tail once, puts on a human skull, turns around, and bows to the Big Dipper constellation. If the skull remains in place and does not fall, the transformation is successful.

Fox maidens hide in forested areas and use human voices to lure victims and cast spells over them. They also frequent eating and drinking establishments and prey upon people who eat and drink too much. If they eat and drink too much themselves, they vanish without harming the victim. In addition to sexually ravaging victims, the fox maidens love to cut women's hair and shave men's heads as pranks.

According to lore, whenever it rains when the sun is shining brightly, a fox maiden bride is going through the woods in a procession to the home of her groom. Marsh lights are fireballs breathed by the foxes or created by their fire-shooting tails; or the lights are the torches carried by the foxes who lead a wedding procession.

In the mountainous areas of Japan where *kitsune* lore is strong, annual rites traditionally are held to ward off *kitsune* troubles. Processions of people take straw foxes and dolls to a mountain outside of the village, where they are buried.

Kitsune-tsuki is a form of possession in which a person—usually a woman—taken over by a wild fox spirit exhibits cravings for certain food, insomnia, restlessness, and aberrant behavior. The person becomes a proxy for the fox as a messenger of Inari, the god of rice. The possessed person especially wants to eat RED beans and rice.

The possessing spirit enters the body either through the breast or under the fingernails. It resides on the left side of the body or in the stomach. The victim hears the fox spirit speak inside her head; when she talks out loud, the fox spirit takes on a different voice.

Kitsune-tsuki has been recorded in Japan since the 12th century. The possession originated in China (see *HULI JING*). Some cases of *kitsuni-tsuki* are believed to be revenge for a family's former offenses against the *huli jing*.

FURTHER READING:
Mack, Carol K., and Dinah Mack. *A Field Guide to Demons, Fairies, Fallen Angels, and Other Subversive Spirits.* New York: Henry Holt/Owl Books, 1998.

Kolchak: The Night Stalker   American made-for-television movie and television series about a newspaper reporter who investigates cases involving the supernatural, including VAMPIRES and WEREWOLVES.

Kolchak: The Night Stalker originated as a TV movie in 1972, airing on ABC. Created and produced by DAN CURTIS, the movie was based on *The Kolchak Papers,* a novel by Jeff Rice, and was scripted by horror writer RICHARD MATHESON, author of *I AM LEGEND* (1956).

Karl Kolchak (Darren McGavin) is a hard-nosed Chicago newspaperman whose world gets turned upside down when he discovers a vampire, Janos Skorzeny (Barry Atwater). No one believes him, and he must confront the vampire himself.

The success of the movie led to the television series, which debuted in 1974 on ABC. In the 20 episodes of the series, Kolchak confronts a vampire (a woman who masquerades as a prostitute and commits serial murders), a werewolf, EXTRATERRESTRIALS, and other bizarre creatures. Kolchak is constantly cofounded in his attempts to prove their existence. His camera film and notes are always somehow lost or destroyed. His boss and peers dismiss his claims of the supernatural.

koldun   In Russian lore, a sorcerer who becomes an ERETIK after death and roams about villages at night capturing people and eating them. The *koldun* is destroyed by having his CORPSE exhumed and burned on a bonfire, or by piercing the back of the corpse with an ASPEN stake, which pins the *koldun* into the grave.

See also VAMPIRE SORCERERS AND WITCHES.

kosci   A Croatian term for VAMPIRES. A male vampire is a *koscima* and a female vampire a *kosicama*. In the case of the diarrhea- and illness-causing LASTOVO ISLAND VAMPIRES in the early 18th century, a villager of Lastovo testified in an official investigation that *kosci* "designate the dead who have revived and who, residing in their graves, especially people who drowned during their lives, kill and destroy people and all too frequently go to their homes and have sexual intercourse with their wives when they are men, as they did before death." Another villager said that vampires are created by spirits returning to their bodies, or by the entry into the bodies of evil beings.

Another villager testified that *kosci* "would enter houses at night, and they would chew on people's hearts, because they feed on the hearts and innards of the living and drink their blood, above all of those with whom they had had a quarrel . . . Vampires must be stabbed with pointed objects, decapitated, struck in the knees with an axe or sword."

BLACK THORN STAKES are the only wood powerful enough for impaling *kosci*.

FURTHER READING:
Perkowski, Jan L. *The Darkling: A Treatise on Slavic Vampirism.* Columbus, Ohio: Slavica Publishers, 1989.

kozlak (kuzlak)   In Dalmatian lore, a poltergeist VAMPIRE. The *kozlak* likes to enter homes at night and torment sleeping persons and annoy housewives by throwing around their pots and pans. If it goes to a farm, it likes to pull the wagon around noisily.

If a CORPSE is feared to become a *kozlak,* a preventative measure calls for not sweeping out the room where the death occurred for several days. Despite this practice, the remedy seldom works, and another measure must be taken.

A troublesome *kozlak* must be dealt with by a priest. The priest must go to the *kozlak's* grave and say prayers and summon the vampire. When it appears, the priest must run it through with a thorn that has been grown high on a mountain, in a place from which the sea cannot be seen. The *kozlak* will not return to plague the living.

krasyy In Thai and Laotian demonology, old women who shape-shift (see SHAPE-SHIFTING) into VISCERA SUCK-ERS and fly about on moonless nights. The *krasyy* particularly like infants, but will feast on human excrement as a substitute.

Krinard, Susan American author of WEREWOLF and VAM-PIRE paranormal romance novels and other fantasy, futuristic, and paranormal romances.

A science fiction and fantasy fan from childhood, Susan Krinard intended to become a cover artist for works in her favorite genres. She earned a bachelor of fine arts degree from the California College of Arts and Crafts. She took a portfolio of her art to New York publishers, but none commissioned her. A turning point came in her mid-30s, when a published author friend read a "fanfic" story Krinard had written, based on the television series *The Beauty and the Beast.* The friend suggested she try her hand at writing romance novels. Krinard has written contemporary and historical paranormal romances that blend fantasy and science fiction, not all of which feature werewolves or vampires.

Krinard's first romance was *Prince of Wolves* (1994), a paranormal contemporary featuring werewolves and set in the Canadian Rocky Mountains. Protagonist Joelle Randall comes to the Rockies to search for the site where her parents were killed in a plane crash. Her guide is Luke Gevaudan, who is secretly a werewolf.

The werewolf novels that followed are not a series, but do track the stories of characters featured among them, as well as introducing new werewolf characters.

Other werewolf novels are

Prince of Shadows (1996): In Minnesota and Canada in contemporary times, Alex Warrington, a wolf researcher, finds a black wolf that has been poisoned and saves it from death. The wolf actually is werewolf Kieran Holt, who has lost his memory about his past.

Touch of the Wolf (1999): In Victorian England, Braden Forster, the blind Earl of Greyburn, heads a clan of powerful werewolves and is trying to keep the bloodline pure. But his brother Quentin and sister Rowena do not help him much. Cassidy Holt, a wild

American girl who is half mortal and half werewolf, arrives in England and claims Braden's heart.

Once a Wolf (2000): In the American West, Rowena Forster struggles to reject her werewolf heritage and becomes engaged to a powerful financier, the mortal Cole McLean. Her heart gets stolen by one of McLean's enemies, a werewolf desperado called "El Lobo," Tomas Alejandro Randall, who kidnaps her.

Secret of the Wolf (2001): In the California Napa Valley in contemporary times, Johanna Schell, a hypnotist, and her father have founded Def Hafen for the mentally challenged. Johanna takes in an unconscious stranger, Quentin Forster, suffering from amnesia about his werewolf heritage.

To Catch a Wolf (2003): In contemporary Denver, wheelchair-bound Athena Morgan has entered high society thanks to her brother's wealth and her philanthropy. When she hires French's Fantastic Family Circus to entertain orphans, she gets more than she bargained for. A player in one of the sideshows is Morgan Holt, an ex-con convicted of killing his father, and a werewolf.

Krinard's vampire novel is *Prince of Dreams* (1995), set in modern San Francisco. Psychologist Diana Ransom's young cousin disappears, and Ransom suspects the brooding but magnetic Nicholas Gale, secretly a vampire.

Her novel *The Forest Lord* (2002), set in Regency England, features a SHAPE-SHIFTING faerie who becomes involved with a mortal woman, Eden Fleming.

FURTHER READING:
Housley, Susan. "Enchanting Words: An Interview with Susan Krinard." Available online. URL: http://www.myshelf.com/beneaththecovers/01/krinard.htm. Downloaded on January 4, 2004.
Krinard, Susan. *To Catch a Wolf.* New York: Berkley, 2003.
———. *The Forest Lord.* New York: Berkley, 2002.
———. *Secret of the Wolf.* New York: Berkley, 2001.
———. *Once a Wolf.* New York: Bantam, 2000.
———. *Touch of the Wolf.* New York: Bantam, 1999.
———. *Prince of Shadows.* New York: Bantam, 1996.
———. *Prince of Dreams.* New York: Bantam, 1995.
———. *Prince of Wolves.* New York: Bantam, 1994.
Sheridan, Barbara. "Meet Susan Krinard." Available online. URL: http://www.paranormalromance.writerspace.com/SusanKrinard.htm. Downloaded on January 4, 2004.
"Susan Krinard." Available online. URL: http://www.writerspage.com/authors/krinards.htm. Downloaded on January 4, 2004.

krsnik In Slavic lore, the enemy of the KUDLAK, a VAM-PIRE who may be either living or dead. *Krsnik* comes from the root *krst,* which means "CROSS," and implies baptism. Thus, the *krsnik* has strong Christian associations. The *krsnik* is white, as opposed to the *kudlak,* who is black.

The *krsnik* interferes with the attacks of the *kudlak* and engages the vampire in ferocious fighting. In combat, the *krsnik* always wins.

See also VAMPIRE HUNTERS.

krvopijac (krvoijac; obour)   Bulgarian VAMPIRE. The *krvopijac* stays in the grave for 40 days after death, acquiring its supernatural power. It has only one nostril and a pointed tongue. It can be immobilized by placing ROSES around its grave. It can be destroyed by a magician who forces it into a bottle and throws it on a bonfire.

See also DJADADJII.

kuanthropy (cyanthropy)   A variant of LYCANTHROPY, in which human beings shape-shift into dogs.

See also SHAPE-SHIFTING; WEREDOGS.

kubikajiri   In Japanese folklore, a head-eating ghost that lurks about graveyards late at night searching for its own lost head. The *kubikajiri* eats the heads of both the living and the dead. It announces its presence with the smell of fresh BLOOD. To see it means one will likely to lose his own head.

See also GHOUL.

kudlak   Slavic VAMPIRE active during both life and after death, reported in Czechoslovakia and Istria. The term *kudlak* probably is a shortened version of VUKODLAK.

The *kudlak* assumes the shape of an animal, most frequently an ox, horse, or pig, but also a dog, horse, bull, or bear. It strikes in the middle of the night. It attacks people to frighten or kill them, and also renders land barren and infertile. The *kudlak* has an opposite, the KRSNIK, which strives to protect people against the vampire.

In some areas, lore holds that every tribe has one *kudlak*, and also its opponent, the *krsnik*. The *kudlak* is black and plots to make its attacks at midnight. It can be thwarted by the *krsnik,* and the two may engage in wild battles. A *kudlak* can be a living person who is under the influence of evil spirits. They may be able to rid themselves of the spirits by confessing their sins. They are most troublesome and dangerous after they die. If a suspected *kudlak* dies, the tendons below his knees are severed when he is buried, to prevent his wandering and attacking. If a dead *kudlak* causes trouble, his CORPSE is exhumed and staked with HAWTHORN.

See also BURIAL CUSTOMS.

FURTHER READING:
Perkowski, Jan L. *The Darkling: A Treatise on Slavic Vampirism.* Columbus, Ohio: Slavica Publishers, 1989.

lamiae A class of monstrous female childbirth demons, named after Lamme, a destroyer deity in Babylonian and Assyrian lore, and Lamia, a goddess who was the mistress of Zeus. Hera, the wife of Zeus, was so enraged by the liaison that she killed the offspring that resulted from the union. In revenge, Lamia swore to kill the children of others. Lamiae became female demons with deformed lower limbs (often depicted as snakes) who preyed upon newborns, drinking their BLOOD and consuming their flesh. In Hebrew lore, lamiae are represented by LILITH, Adam's first wife, who was punished for leaving her husband.

See also TLAHUELPUCHI.

lampir In Bosnian lore, a VAMPIRE comparable to the VUKODLAK. The *lampir* has associations with wolf's hair and thus with WEREWOLVES. Like other vampires, it is blamed for deaths due to highly contagious and deadly diseases.

A *lampir* case recorded in 1906 in a village near Vlasenitza concerned a young man who died of typhus. Soon thereafter, his wife fell ill with the same disease. She told others that her husband had become a *lampir,* and was returning at night to suck her BLOOD. The fear-stricken neighbors petitioned the village authorities for permission to dig up the *lampir's* body and burn it. Permission was denied, and the villagers panicked. Fifteen deaths were blamed on the *lampir,* who reportedly was seen and heard by many people in the village.

FURTHER READING:
Perkowski, Jan L. *The Darkling: A Treatise on Slavic Vampirism.* Columbus, Ohio: Slavica Publishers, 1989.

larvae In Roman lore, evil spirits that harm and frighten the living. Larvae usually are associated with lemures, the evil spirits of the dead.

See also LEMURES.

Lastovo Island Vampires (1737–1738) Cases of diarrhea-causing VAMPIRES on the Croatian island of Lastovo off the coast of Dubrovnik. The VAMPIRE HUNTERS were brought to court on charges of grave and CORPSE desecration. Beliefs in vampires ran strong on the island, and a ban by the archbishop and councillor on opening graves to hunt for vampires was not entirely successful in quashing the beliefs.

In 1737 and 1738 residents of Lastovo were summoned to the archbishop's court in Dubrovnik to be questioned in an inquest about the grave and corpse desecrations. The residents testified that on various occasions over many years, vampires (KOSCI) had been sought whenever plague or illness had occurred, including a recent malady involving severe diarrhea that resulted in many deaths. Many residents believed that the victims of vampires then became vampires as well.

Some of the islanders banded together to search out the graves of the plague-causing culprits and STAKE them with

BLACK THORN. The vampire hunters sometimes were accompanied by a priest, whose presence was believed to be necessary in order to complete the killings. Not all of the islanders participated in the hunts; nor did they all believe in the vampire "superstitions."

The first grave opened was that of a man who had died of drowning a year earlier—a death that according to lore meant a devil would inhabit the corpse—but his corpse had been reduced to a skeleton, and thus he was not a vampire. Three more graves were opened but revealed no vampires. As they closed the graves, the vampire hunters shouted out pleas for forgiveness from God and the dead.

Other graves were desecrated in the attempts to find vampires. Corpses believed to be in a vampire condition were mutilated, dismembered, and chopped up with stakes, pruning knives, stilettoes, and axes. Sometimes positive identification was made of vampire corpses by the peculiar sounds they made, called VRESKET, as well as dog and donkey noises heard at night.

One of the villagers called to testify in the inquest was a 63-year-old priest, Dom Marin Pavlovic. He recalled different instances over the course of years that demonstrated the locals' clinging to vampire superstitions. Pavlovic said that 50 years earlier another priest had attempted to convince him of the existence of vampires by telling him that he and several men had opened the grave of a suspected vampire, and the vampire leaped out and fled. The priest fired a small rifle at the vampire, and the *kosac* (singular) went back into his grave. Pavlovic also said that 17 years earlier another plague had swept the island, and residents went about digging up graves in search of the vampires believed to be responsible. He accidentally came upon a group that had opened the grave of a priest and were tearing at his vestments with hooks. Pavlovic cursed them, but they insisted the dead priest was a vampire, for his BLOOD had flowed freely when they stabbed him.

At the conclusion of the inquest, 17 residents of Lastovo were found guilty of grave desecration. They offered no defense and threw themselves on the mercy of the archbishop of Dubrovnik.

The sentence meted out by the archbishop called for all 17 to wear a stone about the neck and visit three churches, hear holy Mass, and call out for God's mercy and forgiveness for their crimes. Some of the defendants were required to perform this sentence for two to four consecutive years. One defendant was required to also beg loudly for forgiveness of the people. The defendants were threatened with anathema if they failed to obey the sentence.

FURTHER READING:
Perkowski, Jan L. *The Darkling: A Treatise on Slavic Vampirism.* Columbus, Ohio: Slavica Publishers, 1989.

Lay of the Were-wolf, The Breton fable recorded by Marie de France, probably in the latter part of the 12th century. Marie de France, a native of the Île-de-France,

The werewolf of Bisclaveret, cornered by hunting dogs, appeals to the king for mercy. (Author's collection)

lived for a time in England. She recorded traditional Breton fables, or *lais*, in rhyming poetry of about 1,000 lines. *Lais* were sung by troubadours.

The Lay of the Were-wolf tells the story of BISCLAVERET ("werewolf"), a Breton baron. The baron was greatly favored by the king and was happily married to a beautiful woman. But every week the baron mysteriously disappeared for three days; his wife did not know where he went or what he did during his absence. This behavior began to prey upon her mind, and one day she begged him to tell her his secret. The baron resisted, but as she cried and pleaded he at last gave in.

He told her that he became a *bisclaveret*. "I hide myself in the depths of the forest, live on wild animals and roots, and go unclad as any beast in the field," he said.

Horrified, the wife wanted to know where he hid his clothing while he was in wolf's form. The baron refused to tell her, for if anyone should see him shedding his garments, or if he should lose them, then he would be doomed to remain a werewolf until he recovered them.

Again the wife cried and begged to know where he kept his clothes, insisting that he should tell her if he trusted her and loved her. So the baron revealed his hiding place.

However, the wife was now filled with fear and revulsion of her husband, and she plotted against him. She summoned a knight who had long been in love with her, and when the baron next disappeared, she directed the knight to the clothing and told him to take it away. The knight did this, and the baron did not come home. His subjects searched diligently for him, but he could not be found. His wife married the knight.

Some months later, the king was out hunting near the baron's castle, and his hounds began chasing a wolf. Unknown to them, it was Bisclaveret, and he led them on a chase for many hours. Just as the hounds were about to seize him, he turned with a humanlike gesture of despair and placed his paws together in supplication. The king was so moved that he ordered the unusual wolf to be taken alive to his palace.

Back at court, Bisclaveret became the king's companion, acting like a loving and gentle dog. He slept in the king's room and was constantly at his side. Everyone loved him.

One day the king held high court and summoned all his lords. When the knight who had married Bisclaveret's wife appeared, the wolf flew at him in great fury and would have killed him had not the astonished king intervened. Later, at the king's hunting lodge, the former wife of the baron came to offer the king a present. When Bisclaveret saw her, he attacked her and mutilated her face. The king would have reluctantly destroyed the wolf, but one of his advisers suggested that an evil must have been done to the animal to make it behave in such a ferocious manner.

Under questioning, the wife admitted what she had done and said she believed the wolf to be her former husband. The king ordered the knight to bring forth the baron's clothing. The knight complied, and the garments were laid out before the wolf, but the animal ignored them. The same adviser told the king that Bisclaveret must hide his shame and make his transformation in secret.

The wolf was placed in a chamber with the clothing. When the king and two lords visited it, they found the wolf gone and the baron sleeping peacefully in the bed. Awakened, the baron told the king about his adventures as Bisclaveret.

The king restored to him all that had been taken from him by the knight, and bestowed upon him even more gifts and wealth. The king banished from his realm the knight and the baron's wife.

FURTHER READING:
Spence, Lewis. *Legends and Romances of Brittany.* Mineola, N.Y.: Dover, 1997.

lead   In Indian lore, an effective amulet that will protect against demonic beings who roam about on nights of the full MOON.

See also IRON; SILVER.

Lee, Christopher (1922–)   English actor most famous for his portrayals of COUNT DRACULA, a role he performed in seven films. At six-foot-four, Christopher Lee cuts an imposing figure as a VAMPIRE, but his height was a constant drawback in his film career, eliminating him from many romantic leads.

Lee was born in London on May 27, 1922. He was schooled in Switzerland, then entered Wellington College in England. In 1939 his family's bankruptcy and domestic troubles led to his going to Paris to live with an American friend. After death of his father, Lee volunteered for the Royal Air Force. He was sent to Africa, where he served with the Rhodesian police and worked in intelligence. He became a flight lieutenant.

Following World War II, Lee was introduced to Filippo del Giudice, the head of Two Cities Films with the Rank Organization. Through Giudice, he obtained his first film role in 1947, in director Terence Young's *Corridors of Mirrors.* This was followed by a one-word part in Young's *One Night with You,* and then a bit part in *Hamlet* directed by Laurence Olivier. Lee attended the Charm School at Highbury to learn more acting skills.

Despite the disadvantage of his height, he landed roles onstage in London's West End, and he also worked on television. Lee met Boris Karloff, whom he admired greatly but

Count Dracula (Christopher Lee) meets his doom in the ice in Dracula, Prince of Darkness. *(Author's collection)*

Count Dracula (Christopher Lee) goes for a bite in Dracula A.D. 1972. (Author's collection)

had no aspirations to emulate as a master of horror. That changed, however, when HAMMER FILMS purchased the rights to remake some of Universal Pictures' classic horror films. In 1957 Lee appeared as the monster in *The Curse of Frankenstein*, a remake of the 1931 Universal version, *Frankenstein*, starring Karloff. Another star in *Curse* was PETER CUSHING; it was the first movie that Lee and Cushing made together; they were friends immediately.

The Curse of Frankenstein received negative reviews— one critic said Lee looked like a "road accident"—but it was a great commercial success and launched Lee on his career of horror. He next played the villainous Marquis des St. Evremonde in *A Tale of Two Cities,* a role originated by Basil Rathbone. Then Hammer Films cast Lee as Count Dracula in *Dracula* (1958), released in the United States as *Horror of Dracula.* Hammer's film reinterprets BRAM STOKER's novel. The success of this film made Lee a true star and cemented him permanently in the horror genre.

To prepare for the role, Lee read the Stoker novel twice, but did not view Universal Pictures' 1931 *Dracula* starring BELA LUGOSI; he did not want to be influenced by Lugosi's performance. From his reading of the novel, Lee saw Dracula as

> . . . a vampire not at all like me in physical character, but there were aspects of him with which I could readily iden- tify—his extraordinary stillness, punctuated by bouts of

manic energy with feats of strength belying his appear- ance; his power complex; the quality of being done for but undead; and by no means least the fact that he was an embarrassing member of a great and noble family.

Lee said he tried to convey nobleness; superhuman strength; an erotic element; irresistibility; hypnotic power; poignancy; "the loneliness of evil;" and sadness and resig- nation in his portrayal of the count. He disliked having to cringe in front of a crucifix. He wore contact lenses to give him blood-red eyes, which made him weep copiously and impaired his vision so that he crashed into people and objects on the set.

Fans loved the movie and loved Lee as the count. With his fame rising, Lee starred with Karloff in *Doctor of the Seven Dials,* which later was renamed *Corridors of Blood.* Shooting was interrupted so that Lee and Cushing could go to America for the premiere of *Horror of Dracula.* The actors celebrated birthdays on the Empire State Building. Univer- sal Pictures threw a party. A giant poster of Lee as the count, holding a girl victim, was displayed in Times Square. The midnight premiere screening was a huge success.

Horror grossed $25 million and pulled Universal Pic- tures free of bankruptcy. Its profit/cost ratio was the highest of any British picture ever made to date. Lee was paid £750.

Lee's next film role for Hammer was as Kharis in *The Mummy* (1960). He also made vampire films in Italy.

Lee was in Stockholm when he met 19-year-old Henri- ette von Rosen on a blind date. The relationship deepened, and she accepted Lee's proposal of marriage. Her aristo- cratic father, however, objected to his daughter marrying a mere actor, and asked the couple to wait a year. Lee soon decided that their two worlds were not compatible, and he broke the engagement.

Friends introduced him to Birgit (Gitte) Kroencke, a Danishwoman; they were married on March 17, 1961, in London. They moved to Switzerland for a tax haven and took up residence on the northern shore of Lake Geneva. Their daughter, Christina, was born there. Her feet were turned at right angles, and though the problem was cor- rected, she needed ongoing medical help, and so the family returned to London.

Lee starred in *The Devil Rides Out,* based on the Dennis Wheatley novel of the same title, and he turned down the lead in *The Story of O.* As Dr. Neuhardt in *The Oblong Box,* he became friends with Vincent Price. In *Scream and Scream Again,* he appeared with Price and Cushing; it was the only movie three of them made together.

Despite his other successes, Lee was most identified as Dracula. However, he felt that the quality of the vampire films decreased over time. In his autobiography, he said:

> It was aesthetically depressing to see the films step by step deteriorate, chiefly because after the verve and dash of their first decade, Hammer became complacent and care- less, backed unimaginative scripts and tawdry produc- tions in the casual view that they had a captive audience who would take anything.

Lee felt that the first three Dracula movies—*Dracula* [*Horror of Dracula*] (1958); *Dracula, Prince of Darkness* (1965); and *Dracula Has Risen from the Grave* (1968)—were all good, even though he had no lines at all in the second movie. *Taste the Blood of Dracula* (1970) marked a turning point. *Count Dracula* (1971) was an improvement, in which the count starts as an old man who gets younger as he drinks more BLOOD. *Scars of Dracula* (1970) was "truly feeble" with an unhealthy-looking vampire, said Lee. "It was a story with Dracula popped in . . . I was a pantomime figure. Everything was over the top, especially the giant BAT whose electrically motored wings flapped with slow deliberation as if it were doing morning exercises." Lee thought it was less effective to show the actual bite of Dracula's fangs rather than the results of his bite.

After the limp *Dracula A.D. 1972* (1972) and *The Satanic Rites of Dracula* (1973), Lee decided to forgo playing Dracula unless it met certain specifications: good parody, or a film that stayed true to Stoker's novel as much as possible. *Satanic Rites*, in which Dracula is a corporate executive who plots how to conquer the world via germ warfare, was originally given the improbable title *Dracula Is Dead and Well and Living in London*. Lee described it as "unintentional parody . . . Dracula was a mixture of Dr. No and Howard Hughes, and spoke with a false Russian accent." The movie was retitled *Count Dracula and His Vampire Brides* for the U.S. market.

In 1970 Lee agreed to star in a Spanish Film, *El Conde Dracula*, which was true to the novel at least in its beginning, and portrayed a very Stokeresque vampire. Lee's final performance as Dracula was in 1976 in *Dracula père et fils* (*Dracula father and son*), a French comedy.

Lee considered his best acting performance to be the dual character Dr. Charles Marlowe and Blake in *I, Monster*, though the movie itself was a "catastrophe" because it was done in 3-D. The best-scripted film he was in was *The Wicker Man*, in which he played Lord Summerisle, the head of a pagan community. The high point of his career was working under director Billy Wilder in *The Private Life of Sherlock Holmes* (1970), a movie in which he had a supporting role. Wilder, Lee said, was a "a driving perfectionist" who had enormous capacity to "cut actors off at the ankles with some devastating comment."

He played the villain in the James Bond movie *The Man with the Golden Gun* (1974), and went on to appear in numerous other films. His career regret was that he didn't do more singing, as he had a good baritone voice.

Lee was 50 years old before he saw Lugosi's 1931 screen performance as Dracula; it was the very first time Lee saw any other actor portray the count. He didn't like the film and felt "absolutely shattered" by it: Lugosi seemed like a stiff puppet; his smile was not in the least sinister; and Lugosi rising up out of his coffin was not scary. He said:

> I don't think the film comes off. There are aspects of it, for instance, that I considered ridiculous. There were so many mistakes. Renfield's being on the ship is all wrong;

and all that business with cobwebs in Dracula's castle is amateurish . . . not even a dissolve through . . . And Dracula is played too "nice" at the beginning. Practically no menace in the character . . . though the women are superbly done.

At age 50 Lee also decided to "Draculate" no more, but to seek other roles.

Other films of note are *Airport 77* (1977), *Gremlins 2* (1990), and *The Lord of the Rings* trilogy (2001–03), in which he plays the wizard Saruman.

Lee has performed in more than 100 films.

FURTHER READING:
Lee, Christopher. *Lord of Misrule: The Autobiography of Christopher Lee*. London: Orion Books, 2003.
Lee, Christopher. *Tall, Dark and Gruesome: An Autobiography*. London: W. H. Allen, 1977. Rev. ed. London: Victor Gollancz, 1997.
Wolf, Leonard. *A Dream of Dracula: In Search of the Living Dead*. Boston: Little, Brown, 1972.

Le Fanu, Joseph Sheridan   See "CARMILLA."

Legend of the Seven Golden Vampires, The   See HAMMER FILMS.

lemures   In Roman lore, the restless ghosts of people who died without a surviving family; also, ghosts evil in nature who are associated with LARVAE.

The Romans considered it a curse to die without surviving issue. One also becomes a lemure by suffering premature death, drowning, or dying by murder, violence, or execution. Lemures leave their graves to attack the living. To prevent this, Romans burned black beans around the tomb as the body was interred. If a lemure succeeded in escaping its grave, it was exorcized by banging on drums.

Leopard Men   African cult of were-leopards, active in Guinea and Senegal for centuries until about the 1960s, when authorities attempted to crack down on its members.

Leopard Men practice magical rites that enable them to acquire the strength and characteristics of leopards. Reminiscent of WEREWOLF lore, they don the skins of leopards as a way of facilitating the transformation. They carry razor-sharp, clawlike tools in their hands, and crawl around the bush imitating leopards. Leopard Men were reputed to terrorize people, attacking their enemies, clawing them and disemboweling them as real leopards would do.

FURTHER READING:
Keel, John A. *Strange Mutants*. New York: Global Communications, 1984.

Lestat de Lioncourt (Tom Cruise) in Interview with the Vampire *(Author's collection)*

Lestat de Lioncourt   VAMPIRE character created by ANNE RICE in her Vampire Chronicles. Lestat de Lioncourt reinvents the vampire as a glamorous, seductive, philosophical, and even godlike creature, endowed with supernatural powers and abilities, well-dressed and sophisticated, who can live in the world of humans and can see his own reflection in a MIRROR. The success of Rice's vampire novels has had more influence on fictional vampires than any other writer since BRAM STOKER.

Lestat makes his debut in Rice's first novel, INTERVIEW WITH THE VAMPIRE (1976), narrated by Louis de Pointe du Lac. Lestat is the narrator and central figure of THE VAMPIRE LESTAT (1985), THE QUEEN OF THE DAMNED (1988), THE TALE OF THE BODY THIEF (1992), MEMNOCH THE DEVIL (1995), and of the final novel, BLOOD CANTICLE (2003). The Chronicles trace the immortal life and spiritual maturation of Lestat as he wrestles with the morality of his existence and the great questions of good and evil.

Rice's husband, Stan, was the inspiration for Lestat.

Lestat was a mortal in 17th-century France and was born the seventh son of an impoverished marquis. Four of his brothers died. At age 12, Lestat decided to join a monastery but was forbidden to do so by his father.

One day Lestat went out to hunt wolves and nearly was killed by a pack of eight of them. His bravery earned him the friendship of Nicolas, the son of a local merchant. Lestat and Nicolas went to Paris, where Lestat gained fame as an actor. A vampire, Magnus, forcefully made Lestat a vampire and then destroyed himself.

Lestat comes to terms with his new life and soon makes his dying mother, Gabrielle, and Nicolas into vampires. He battles a Paris coven led by the vampire Armand.

The novels recount his wanderings, activities, introspection, and philosophizing. Lestat meets and makes into vampires Louis and their child companion, Claudia. He finds the source of vampires, the ancients Akasha and Enkil, and reawakens Akasha from centuries of torpor. He goes into the earth from 1929 to 1984 and emerges to become a rock star. He breaks a vampire taboo by publishing information about vampires. He overcomes the need to drink BLOOD in order to survive, and yet he remains a vampire. He defeats Akasha and experiences body switching with a mortal. He makes a voluntary decision to reclaim his body and return to the life of a vampire. He meets the Devil and is taken on tours of heaven and hell, and he drinks the blood of Christ.

In the final novel of the Vampire Chronicles, *Blood Canticle*, Lestat falls in love with a mortal woman, Rowan Mayfair, of the dynastic family of witches in Rice's novel *The Witching Hour* (1990). At Blackwood Farm, he realizes he has outlived himself, and he surrenders some of his power to conform to the world of mortals.

Rice described Lestat as a "man of action," someone unwilling to be defeated no matter what happened to him. He is strong and unapologetic for his actions—the kind of vampire she would want to be if given the opportunity.

The model established by Lestat and other vampires in Rice's novels has dominated vampire-themed fiction. Lestat is far more humanlike than COUNT DRACULA, and is more alluring than terrifying.

FURTHER READING:
Ramsland, Katherine. *The Vampire Companion: The Official Guide to Anne Rice's* The Vampire Chronicles. New York: Ballantine Books, 1993.
Rice, Anne. *The Vampire Lestat.* New York: Alfred A. Knopf, 1985.
———. *Interview with the Vampire.* New York: Alfred A. Knopf, 1976.

leyak In Balinese lore, a sorcerer who has the ability to shape-shift (see SHAPE-SHIFTING) into a vampiric demon, causing death and destruction. While the sorcerer sleeps, the *leyak* flies in the night skies in the forms of a mysterious light, a monkey, or a bird. It withers crops, kills people, and causes calamities and misfortunes. If the *leyak* is destroyed, its human form dies instantly along with it.

lhiannan-shee In the fairy folklore of the Isle of Man, a vampiric spirit who appears as an irresistibly beautiful woman. The *lhiannan-shee* attaches herself to a man and draws off his life force, thus ruining him body and soul.

The Irish version, the *leanan-sidhe,* is an opposite, a life-giving spirit that inspires poets and musicians.

liderc In Hungarian lore, a supernatural entity with associations to the VAMPIRE, witch, WEREWOLF, MORA, INCUBUS, and SUCCUBUS. The *liderc* can be of human or demonic origins, and can take on an animal form.

One type of *liderc*, the *mit-make*, is a helping spirit similar to the FAMILIAR of a witch. The *mit-make* likes to lives in a house and perform endless chores. It takes the form of a chicken without feathers, appearing on its own or else hatched from an egg that is carried in the armpit. The *mit-make* can shape-shift (see SHAPE-SHIFTING) to human form.

The helping *liderc* literally helps its master to death. It works so fast and efficiently that it pesters its master for more and more. If not given sufficient work, it destroys its master. Once in a house, it is extremely difficult to dislodge. The only way to prevent it from becoming destructive is to give it impossible tasks, like carrying WATER or sand in a sieve. In some cases, the *liderc* can be stuffed into a hole in a tree trunk.

Other *liderc* are dark and demonic and create nightmares (see OLD HAG). A dead person who becomes a *liderc* lives as a night vampire.

The *liderc* also has sexual associations, supported by the belief that the double of another creature can be summoned by intense desire. *Liderc* lovers are really devil lovers whose intense and unrelenting affections cause their victims to waste away. They like to prey upon people whose lovers or spouses have been absent too long or who have died.

The incubus/succubus *liderc* comes down the chimney in the form of a flame or star. When it shape-shifts to human form, it has one leg like a goose, which gives away its true identity. Its entry can be prevented by taking a trousers belt or cord and securing the bedroom door with it. If a *liderc* has already gained entry to a house, it can be banished by hiding its human boot.

FURTHER READING:
Mack, Carol K., and Dinah Mack. *A Field Guide to Demons, Fairies, Fallen Angels, and Other Subversive Spirits.* New York: Henry Holt/Owl Books, 1998.
Pocs, Eva. *Between the Living and the Dead.* Szilvia Redey and Michael Webb, trans. Budapest: Central European University Press, 1999.

Lilith A winged, long-haired female demon of the night who vampirizes newborn children and seduces sleeping men—especially the newly married—in order to produce demon sons. She is accompanied by a horde of SUCCUBI demons, and she uses tens of thousands of names to disguise herself. Her powers are greatest during the waning MOON. In the late 17th century, she was described as a screech owl blind by day, who sucked the breasts or navels of young children, or the dugs of goats.

Lilith entered Jewish demonology from Babylonian and perhaps Sumerian sources, and then also was adopted into Christian and Islamic lore. In Islamic lore, she is the mother of the *djinn*, a type of demon.

Lilith originally was human. She was the first woman to have sexual relations with Adam, but left him when he refused to treat her as an equal. Adam complained to God, who sent three angels (in some Christian versions, three saints) to return her to Adam. She refused, and God began destroying 100 of her demon offspring every day. She retaliated by attacking women in childbirth and newborn infants.

Another version of her story says that she joined Adam after he and Eve were cast out of Paradise. The two produced demon sons who filled the world. Yet another story tells that Lilith became the bride of the angel Samael, who is equated with Satan.

Lilith can be warded off with magical amulets bearing the names of angels and local patron saints, and by saying one of her many names. Men who have nocturnal emissions have been seduced by Lilith during the night and must say incantations to prevent the offspring from becoming demons.

See also TLAHUELPUCHI.

FURTHER READING:
Guiley, Rosemary Ellen. *The Encyclopedia of Witches and Witchcraft*. 2d ed. New York: Facts On File, 1999.

living vampires   Persons who are born VAMPIRES or who become vampires while alive. According to folklore, living vampires are malevolent, evil people, such as certain VAMPIRE SORCERERS AND WITCHES who prey upon other living people through magic, the EVIL EYE, and PSYCHIC ATTACK.

Living Vampires in Folklore
According to lore, certain people are born fated to be vampires. They are born with oddities such as the CAUL, teeth already in, or a spine deformity that resembles a tail. In Romanian lore, if a pregnant woman does not eat SALT, her child will be a living vampire. The seventh child of seven children who are all the same sex will be a vampire. Various folk remedies exist for neutralizing the vampire power so that such persons will not go about casting the evil eye during their lifetime, and will not become the walking dead. Precautions are taken again when they do die (see BURIAL CUSTOMS).

If certain persons are thus fated to be vampires, they will become one whether they wish it or not. When they sleep, the soul comes out of their mouths in the form of a fly. If the body is turned so that the head is placed where the feet were, the vampire will die.

Living vampires generally are born and not "made." In Romanian lore, there is a class of female vampires who are not born so, but are taught to be vampires by real living vampires. They are helped by St. Andrew. Priests conceal from them the time of St. Andrew's Eve. These half-vampires become dead vampires when they die.

In Romanian lore, living vampires can always be identified by the fact that they fight with the tongues of hemp brakes, a trestlelike table or stand used by peasants for crushing hemp. The tongues should never be left in the brakes, because vampires will take them and fight with them until sparks fly. They also use them for flying.

Living Vampires Modeled on Fiction
Since the 19th century, the fictional vampire has created a new vampire myth of an undead creature who is powerful, exotic, alluring, and mysterious—a romantic antihero. This new myth inspires fans of the genre to want to become living vampires, and to seek out ways to accomplish that. ANNE RICE's vampires are "made" through an exchange of BLOOD; they live immortal lives in their own bodies, frozen in time at the moment of their "making"; they are incredibly beautiful. No ugly demons or ghoulish

REVENANTS, these literary vampires are creatures so exquisite and perfect they could pass for angels in appearance—a comparison often made by Rice.

Rice's books, plus the similar emphasis of numerous other authors who have followed her model, have led many vampire fans to think of vampires as edgy, independent outsiders to be admired and emulated. Vampire fan clubs, night clubs, Web sites, chat rooms, and role-playing games attract people who want to participate in a vampire lifestyle.

There are innumerable types, descriptions, and definitions of living vampires, many of whom spell the word with a *y*—*vampyre*—to distinguish themselves from the vampires of folklore and fiction. Many are under 30 years of age. Some claim they were born into vampire clans, while other say they were "made" by a vampyre. Some say they are "vampirelike," in that they have attributes of vampires (usually drawn from fiction) but they are not immortal or undead. Some also participate in other underground cultures, such as Goths, blood fetishism, and sadomasochism and domination-bondage sexual fantasies. Some are gay (Rice's books have a substantial gay following).

Many vampyres feel they have never fit into mainstream society. From early in childhood, they had considered themselves to be "outsiders." Many express feelings of being misunderstood or underestimated by others. The fictional vampire offers a way to escape to an exotic life, or build a self-image. Most vampyres are immersed in vampire fiction and films.

Some say that they had come from unhappy home environments where they had suffered psychological abuse, sometimes sexual abuse, and sometimes physical abuse that may have made them taste their own blood at a very young age. It is possible that dissociation is a factor in at least some vampire escape fantasies.

A vampyre candidate enters the subculture by seeking out other vampyres, perhaps in a nightclub, school, coven, or internet chat room. He or she may be "made" or initiated in rituals involving a small exchange of blood and sometimes sex.

Once convinced he or she has become a vampyre, the initiate may undergo changes, which probably are induced by autosuggestion but nonetheless are seen as proof of the transformation into living vampire. Changes can include a preference for nocturnal hours, an aversion and sensitivity to SUNLIGHT, an allergy to GARLIC, and an acquired taste for blood. Some believe they actually change physically; they "know" they have acquired supernormal strength or abilities, or the physical nature of their bodies was no longer entirely human. Some say their DNA has changed. They rarely seek any medical corroboration.

Vampyres often reinforce their new lifestyle by dressing in costume for socializing in clubs or with other vampyres, and by getting fitted with dental fangs. Some have permanent fangs implanted.

Many vampyres are ambivalent about maintaining a blood-drinking lifestyle, and some feel that living vampires do not need to subsist on blood. Some say they like blood, but they drink it only rarely or occasionally. Those who try to drink blood in substantial quantities usually become ill. Most consume small amounts—a few drops licked from a cut, or perhaps a little wineglass-full—at periodic intervals. Fear of AIDS and other diseases curb blood-drinking habits.

Extreme fringes of the vampyre subculture engage in frequent cutting and blood drinking. Some claim to have witnessed or participated in blood sacrifices and even vampire murders.

The fantasy of being a vampyre offers control in a world perceived as rapidly going out of control, due to global politics, war, crime, economic downturn, environmental crises, and more. The fantasy living vampire is untouched by the ravages of the world and is always in control.

See also CLINICAL VAMPIRISM; GAMES.

FURTHER READING:

Dresser, Norine. *American Vampires: Fans, Victims, Practitioners.* New York: W. W. Norton, 1989.

Guiley, Rosemary Ellen, with J. B. Macabre. *The Complete Vampire Companion.* New York: Macmillan, 1994.

Guiley, Rosemary Ellen. *Vampires Among Us.* New York: Pocket Books, 1991.

Murgoci, Agnes. "The Vampire in Roumania," in *The Vampire: A Casebook,* Alan Dundes, ed. Madison: University of Wisconsin Press, 1998.

Guinn, Jeff, with Andy Grieser. *Something in the Blood: The Underground of Today's Vampires.* Arlington, Texas: Summit Publishing, 1996.

Page, Carol. *Bloodlust: Conversations with Real Vampires.* New York: HarperCollins, 1991.

Ramsland, Katherine. *Piercing the Darkness: Undercover with Vampires in America Today.* New York: HarperPrism/HarperCollins, 1998.

Livonia Werewolves   A mass hysteria of LYCANTHROPY in northern Europe during the Inquisition. The Livonia area (now part of the Baltic Republics of Estonia and Latvia) was rife with superstitions and fears of WEREWOLVES. During the 1600s—the peak of the Inquisition's witch hunts—31 people in Livonia were brought to trial on charges of damage to animals, property, and people while running amok as werewolves.

According to lore, werewolves made night marches by the thousands in annual rites after Christmas. For 12 days, the people were transformed into wolves. While their human bodies lay in trance, the werewolves were beaten with chains or IRON rods by the devil and were forced to attack flocks of animals.

Casper Peucer, a Protestant physician, described the reported events in his *Commentarius de Praecipibus Divinationum Generibus* (1560):

At Christmas a boy lame of a leg goes round the countryside summoning the Devil's followers, who are countless, to a general conclave. Whoever remains behind, or goes

A gathering of werewolves, by Maurice Sand

reluctantly, is scourged by another with an iron whip till the blood flows, and his traces are left in blood. The human form vanishes, and the whole multitude become wolves. Many thousands assemble. Foremost goes the leader armed with an iron whip, and the troop follow, firmly convinced in their imagination that they are transformed into wolves. They fall upon herds of cattle and flocks of sheep, but they have no power to slay me. When they come to a river, the leader smites the water with his scourge and it divides, leaving a dry path through the midst, by which the pack go. The transformation lasts twelve days, at the expiration of which period the wolf skin vanishes, and the human form reappears.

The parting of the water was considered by demonologists to be a mockery of the biblical parting of the Red Sea for the exodus of the Israelites from Egypt.

In another case described by OLAUS MAGNUS, the wife of a Livonian lord publicly doubted the existence of werewolves. One of her servant boys promptly disappeared into a cellar and returned as a wolf. Dogs chased him into the woods and bit out one of his eyes. The next day he reappeared in human form with one eye missing. The sympathetic link of physical wounds between human and wolf forms is common in werewolf lore.

See also THEISS OF LIVONIA.

FURTHER READING:

Otten, Charlotte F., ed. *A Lycanthropy Reader: Werewolves in Western Culture.* New York: Dorset Press, 1989.

Robbins, Rossell Hope. *The Encyclopedia of Witchcraft & Demonology.* New York: Bonanza Books, 1981.

Summers, Montague. *The Werewolf.* New York: Bell Publishing, 1966.

lobishomen   In Portuguese lore, a type of WEREWOLF. *Lobishomen* also appear in South American folklore.

lobizon   In South American lore, a WEREWOLF or WERE-DOG that walks upright on hind legs. The *lobizon* is especially strong in Argentina, as well as parts of Brazil, Paraguay, and Uruguay.

The creature has been described as being short in stature, like an "enormous monkey," according to a junkyard owner who had a nighttime visit by one. It has sharp claws; large, hanging doglike ears; legs like those of a child; and a tail. It is covered in long, dark hair. Like the BEAST OF BRAY ROAD, it has an evil and chilling stare.

The *lobizon* has been reported to attack domestic dogs and menace humans, even coming into houses. According to a report from northern Argentina, a *lobizon* that entered a house was beaten and clubbed by the residents until it appeared to be dead. But when they dragged it outside, it sprang up as though uninjured and ran away.

In Argentinian lore, the seventh son is destined to be a *lobizon,* and will make his transformation at midnight on the nights of a full MOON—especially if it falls on a Friday—and then return to his normal human state at dawn. Juan Domingo Peron, Argentina's famous president, decreed that all seventh sons must be baptized.

Some of the *lobizon* reports have been associated with UFO activity.

See also *CHUPACABRA; EXTRATERRESTRIALS.*

FURTHER READING:
"Crying Wolf in Argentina." *Fortean Times,* September 2000, p. 6.

London After Midnight (1927)   First major American vampire film, directed by TOD BROWNING and starring LON CHANEY in his only VAMPIRE role, a character patterned after *The Cabinet of Dr. Caligari.* The screenplay was written by Waldemar Young, based on Browning's short story "The Hypnotist." The story title initially served as the title of the movie.

A silent film, *London After Midnight* probably was filmed to capitalize on the success of the stage play of *DRACULA.* It debuted to a mixed critical reaction but an enthusiastic popular audience. Its success made it the biggest-grossing of the 10 films Chaney did with Browning, earning a gross of more than $1 million and a net of $540,000. It was Chaney's 44th film.

Chaney plays the two lead roles: Edward C. Burke, a suave professor and inspector of Scotland Yard; and the "Man with the Beaver Hat," the "vampire" who haunts a house with a young vampire woman, Luna (originally Lunette), the "Bat Girl" (Edna Tichenor). As the vampire, Chaney sports a saw-toothed, bug-eyed leering death grin, disheveled hair poking from beneath his huge beaver stovepipe hat, and crouched stance. He wears a black cape that opens into BAT wings when he raises his arms.

The plot of the movie is convoluted. A country gentleman, Roger Balfour (Claude King), is found shot to death in his home by his butler (Percy Williams). Balfour leaves behind a SUICIDE note, but Professor Burke, called to the scene, suspects a murder. The mystery is not solved, and

The "vampire" (Lon Chaney) spreads his batwing cape to frighten a maid in London After Midnight. *(Author's collection)*

Balfour's house is vacated. Weird noises and ghostly shadows are seen there, and the house is believed to be haunted.

Burke concocts a scheme to unmask the murderer by staging a grand charade in which he and hired actors will masquerade as vampires and the dead man.

Five years elapse. Then suddenly the neighboring household of Sir James Hamlin (Henry B. Walthall) becomes fearful as the Balfour house is taken over by two sinister figures who are believed to be vampires: the Man with the Beaver Hat and the Bat Girl.

Hamlin's servants are horrified to see two monsters frolicking in Balfour's house and about the grounds: the Man with the Beaver Hat (Chaney) and the Bat Girl. Miss Smithson the maid (Polly Moran) cries out, "Honest, Sir James . . . They're dead people from the grave! Vampyrs is what they are!"

Hamlin calls Burke back on the scene. Strange events take place. Balfour's grave is found violated and his body missing. He is later seen alive inside his mansion. Unbeknown to others, the "dead man" is really a double made up to look like Balfour.

Hamlin discourages Burke from bringing in the police. Terrifying things happen. Balfour's daughter, Lucille (Marceline Day), is stalked by the "vampires," and is especially menaced by the female vampire. There is no actual biting or BLOOD drinking, however, since the vampires are a charade. The Man with the Beaver Hat menaces the maid, who swears he entered her room as a mist and then flew out the window.

Armadillos are seen scurrying about the haunted mansion's grounds—a touch that Browning used again in his 1931 film version of *Dracula*. The armadillos—weirdly out of place in the English countryside—were intended to add to the macabre atmosphere.

Burke tells the frightened household that an antidote against the vampires is a wreath of tuberoses with a knife or sword of sharp steel placed across it. These are positioned around the house, but the vampires demolish them and gain access. Burke uses hypnosis to draw out Roger's murderer. His theory is that when hypnotized and given the right circumstances, the murderer will reenact his crime. Burke hypnotizes Arthur Hibbs (Conrad Nagel), Balfour's nephew and the love interest of Lucille, and secretly eliminates him as a suspect.

Burke next sets the stage against Hamlin and traps him into reenacting the shooting. Apparently, Balfour had informed him that he was making him executor of his estate and the guardian of Lucille. Hamlin told Balfour he intended to marry Lucille, but Balfour said he would forbid it. Enraged, Hamlin left and then returned to Balfour's study to force him to write a suicide note, and then shot him.

Once the murder is solved, Burke reveals the charade. He is really an inspector for Scotland Yard. The hired actors pack up and leave.

London After Midnight was remade in 1935 as MARK OF THE VAMPIRE starring BELA LUGOSI. With the passage of the silent film era, the Chaney version became a "lost film" like other silent movies. In 1966 the only known print was believed to be destroyed in a vault fire in Hollywood, where the copy was last known to be stored.

Publicity stills survived, though many key scenes were missing. In 2002 Turner Classic Movies commissioned Rick Schmidlin to re-create the film by piecing together about 200 photographs. The stills were enlarged and were combined with dialogue and scene descriptions on intertitle cards and a score by Robert Israel. The 45-minute re-creation premiered on Halloween night 2003 to commemorate the 75th anniversary of the original film.

FURTHER READING:
Riley, Philip J. *London After Midnight*. New York: Cornwall Books, 1985.
Skal, David J., and Elias Savada. *Dark Carnival: The Secret World of Tod Browning, Hollywood's Master of the Macabre*. New York: Anchor/Doubleday, 1995.

loogaroo West Indies VAMPIRE, probably of African origin. The *loogaroo* is an old woman who has made a pact with the Devil and must supply him with large quantities of warm BLOOD. She shape-shifts (see SHAPE-SHIFTING) by first removing her own skin and becoming a blob of light. The *loogaroo* likes to suck human blood. Her name bears a strong resemblance to the French term for WEREWOLF, loup-garou. If the *loogaroo* is injured while in her shape-shifted form, she will, like the werewolf, show her wound when she changes back to human form.

Lorca, Mr. Alleged LIVING VAMPIRE in Germany. On October 25, 1974, a man known as "Mr. Lorca" was arrested in Germany for a vampirelike attack upon a man. According to news reports, Mr. Lorca was an odd man who ate only raw meat and slept in a COFFIN by day. He was active at night. His neighbors said he read occult books, and that he insisted on being called "Count."

One night Mr. Lorca reportedly lured to his home a drunkard, promising him food and shelter. Once there, he bit the man on the neck. The man fainted, and Mr. Lorca thought he was dead. He went to sleep in his coffin. But the man revived, escaped, and went to police. When the authorities arrived, they found Mr. Lorca still asleep in the coffin, with BLOOD on his lips. They arrested him.

FURTHER READING:
Perkowski, Jan L. *The Darkling: A Treatise on Slavic Vampirism*. Columbus, Ohio: Slavica Publishers, 1989.

Lord Ruthven Vampire antihero of THE VAMPYRE by JOHN POLIDORI, the first vampire story to be published in English, appearing in 1819 in *New Monthly Magazine*. Lord Ruthven established a model for the fictional vampire.

Polidori, who briefly served as physician to LORD BYRON, based his story on the ideas of his employer. He modeled Lord Ruthven (pronounced "rivven") upon Byron. The character's name was taken from the name for Byron in *Glenarvon*, a roman à clef by Byron's lover, Caroline Lamb, in which she satirizes Byron.

Lord Ruthven is a handsome, charismatic and mysterious rake who has a chilling, soulless appearance, but fascinates all who meet him, especially women:

> . . . a cold grey eye, which, fixing upon the object's face, did not seem to penetrate, and at one glance to pierce through to the inward workings of the heart, but fell upon the cheek with a leaden ray that weighed upon the skin it could not pass . . . In spite of the deadly hue, which never gained a warmer tint, either from the blush of modesty, or from the strong emotion of passion, though its form and outline were beautiful, many of the female hunters of notoriety attempted to win his attentions.

Ruthven gambles, seduces women, and duels. He is both immoral and amoral, ruining the virtues, reputations, and lives of others, and not caring about the consequences to them. He is sadistic in his delight of destroying others. Even his money is tainted, for those who accept it are cursed and sink into lives of crime or poverty and misery. There is the element of the psychic vampire about him, for others who come into contact with him lose their vitality, respectability, health, or wealth; they are in some significant way diminished, and as they are diminished, Ruthven grows in vitality.

Ruthven's traveling companion, Aubrey, feels inferior to him, perhaps mirroring Polidori's feelings of inferiority in the shadow of Lord Byron. As Aubrey becomes better acquainted with Ruthven, he is repelled by Ruthven's lack of moral character. Similarly, Polidori may have been repelled by Byron's self-absorbed behavior. Aubrey severs his connection to Ruthven, which may reflect a course of action Polidori wished he had taken with Byron. In reality, Byron ended his relationship with Polidori.

After Lord Ruthven is killed by bandits while traveling in Greece, Aubrey unwittingly helps him to reanimate as a vampire by setting his corpse under the rays of the MOON. Ruthven returns to England to continue his rakish ways. He succeeds in fatally seducing Aubrey's sister, and Aubrey goes insane.

FURTHER READING:
Senf, Carol A. *The Vampire in 19th-Century English Literature.* Bowling Green, Ohio: Bowling Green State University Popular Press, 1988.
Stuart, Roxana. *Stage Blood: Vampires of the 19th-Century Stage.* Bowling Green, Ohio: Bowling Green State University Popular Press, 1994.
Twitchell, James B. *The Living Dead: A Study of the Vampire in Romantic Literature.* Durham, N.C.: Duke University Press, 1981.

Lord's Prayer   The most familiar prayer in Christianity, and a protection against vampires, INCUBI and SUCCUBI, and all evil spirits and ghosts. The prayer, taught by Jesus in the New Testament, acts as an amulet when written or recited, according to lore. A common belief from about the 16th to early 18th centuries was that a true witch was incapable of reciting the Lord's Prayer from start to finish. The reasoning was that the prayer, or any passage from the Bible, was offensive to the devil, who would not permit his disciple to repeat it.

Lost Boys, The (1987)   Warner Bros. film, directed by Joel Schumacher, about a band of Peter Pan–like teenage vampires.

Kiefer Sutherland stars as David, the leader of the pack of youths who live in the fictional town of Santa Carla, California, known as the murder capital of the world. They idolize rock singer Jim Morrison as their icon of alienation and go about looking for trouble and attacking people. Like Peter Pan, they fly—and they never grow up.

The Emerson family, consisting of mother, Lucy (Dianne Wiest), Grandpa (Barnard Hughes), and two sons, Michael (Jason Patric) and Sam (Corey Haim), moves to Santa Clara. Soon Sam, the younger boy, is approached by two strange boys who are secret VAMPIRE HUNTERS, Edgar (Corey Feldman) and Alex (Jamison Newlander). They

give him a comic entitled "Vampires Everywhere" and say it may help to save Sam's life.

The adult "father" of the vampires, Max (Edward Hermann), decides the boys could benefit from the influence of a mother. He contrives a plot to ensnare Lucy in this role by bringing her sons into the group.

Michael is invited to join the pack and is tricked into drinking BLOOD, which turns him into a half-vampire. Sam discovers his dark secret and enlists the help of Edgar and Alex. They resolve to determine if their mother's new boyfriend, Max, is really the head of the coven of vampire boys. The vampire hunters arm themselves with GARLIC-treated holy WATER, which they have made in a bathtub and which they use to fill water guns.

In a grand finale of screeching and flying around the vampires' lair, the coven and Max are destroyed and Michael is freed of his curse.

FURTHER READING:
Silver, Alain, and James Ursini. *The Vampire Film: From Nosferatu to Interview with the Vampire.* 3d ed. New York: Limelight Editions, 1997.

louleerou   In French lore, a WEREWOLF. The *louleerou* is a certain kind of man, especially a bastard, who must transform into a diabolical beast at the full MOON.

According to lore, the transformation always takes place at night. In a fit, the lycanthrope dashes out a window and plunges into a well. He emerges with a goatskin that the devil has given him, and dons it. Transformed, he runs about the countryside on all fours, attacking and devouring dogs that he finds. At dawn he takes off his goatskin and returns home. Often the *louleerou* is sick from the dogs he has eaten, and vomits undigested paws.

If killed or wounded while in the *louleerou* state, the lycanthrope will return instantly to his human form at the first spilling of his BLOOD. Thus recognized, he brings great shame upon his family.

FURTHER READING:
Baring-Gould, Sabine. *The Book of Werewolves.* London: Smith, Elder & Co., 1865.

loup-garou   French term for WEREWOLF or "wolf-man." The term *loup-garou* may have come from the French "Loup, gardez-vous," which means "Wolf, watch out."

In the bayou lore of Louisiana, the loups-garous gather in the bayou for wild dances and celebrations. Each werewolf owns an airplane-size BAT that it uses for transportation. The loups-garous fly around invading people's homes. They drop down chimneys and bite sleeping persons. The victims are transformed into werewolves.

One remedy against the bayou loup-garou is similar to one employed against VAMPIRES: keeping it busy counting. When a colander or sifter is hung outside a house, the loup-garou will have to stop and count all the holes before it can enter. (See SEEDS.)

Other remedies against the loup-garou are SALT and frogs. If salt touches a loup-garou, it will start to burn, and the creature will throw off its wolf skin and resume human form. The werewolf is afraid of frogs and will flee if one is thrown at it.

FURTHER READING:
Mack, Carol K., and Dinah Mack. *A Field Guide to Demons, Fairies, Fallen Angels, and Other Subversive Spirits.* New York: Henry Holt/Owl Books, 1998.

lovage   Parsleylike herb with antivampire properties. In Romanian lore, rubbing a CORPSE with GARLIC and lovage will prevent it from becoming a *STRIGOI*.

Lovecraft, H. P.   See ARTS AND ENTERTAINMENT; LUMLEY, BRIAN.

luck   See CAUL.

ludverc   In Hungarian lore, a malevolent REVENANT that has characteristics associated with the VAMPIRE. The *ludverc* may have been borrowed from the vampire lore of TRANSYLVANIA.

The *ludverc* is a burning shaft of light or a star that flies about and enters homes through the chimney. Inside, it shape-shifts (see SHAPE-SHIFTING) to the form of a dead marriage partner—male or female—and sleeps with the surviving spouse, causing the person to become exhausted and pale. The *ludverc* can be exorcized by magical means.

Lugosi, Bela (1882–1956)   Hungarian actor who became synonymous with the character of COUNT DRACULA in the 1931 film version of BRAM STOKER's novel *DRACULA*. Despite the success of the movie and his fame as a VAMPIRE, Lugosi's career never succeeded according to his dreams.

Bela Lugosi was born Bela Ferenc Dezco Blasko in Lugos, Hungary. His father was a baker and the son of a farmer, and died when Lugosi was a teenager. In his 20s Bela changed his named to Lugossy and then to Lugosi.

Lugosi worked as a locksmith and then entered acting. He joined the Franz Joseph Theatre of Temesvar, landing supporting roles in classical plays and roles in operettas. He moved to Budapest in 1911 and took acting lessons at the Rkoski Szidi Acting School. Between 1913 and 1916 he performed dozens of roles, albeit small ones, in romantic roles and comedy. While acting, he joined the 43rd Royal Hungarian Infantry in 1914 and served in Serbia and Russia. After being wounded in 1916, he left the armed forces and returned to work at the National Theatre.

Bela Lugosi backstage on the set of Tod Browning's Dracula *(Courtesy Vampire Empire Archives)*

In 1917 Lugosi married the first of his five wives, Ilona Szmik. The same year, he made his first film, *A Leopard*, which has been lost. The Hungarian government was overthrown in 1918, and Lugosi participated in organizing actors under the new regime. But when that collapsed a year later, he had to flee, going first to Vienna and then to Berlin. He appeared in one of the films directed by F. W. MURNAU, *Der Januskopf*, another film now lost.

Ilona divorced him, and Lugosi went to New York in 1921 to seek fame and fortune there, even though he knew no English. He never really learned English at any time during the rest of his life, but memorized his lines phonetically.

Lugosi found work in film and on Broadway. He got his big break onstage in 1927 in the original Broadway production of *Dracula*, stepping into the lead when British actor Raymond Huntley turned it down. Lugosi became an American citizen in 1930.

He was not the actor of choice for the TOD BROWNING film production of *Dracula*. The role of Count Dracula would have gone to LON CHANEY, but the actor was in the last stages of terminal cancer and died in 1930. Lugosi lobbied for the role but trailed behind five other actors who were considered ahead of him. He finally secured it, but settled for pay of $3,500, a low sum even then. His failure to negotiate a better contract impaired his earning ability in Hollywood for the rest of his life.

Lugosi impressed fellow cast members as a mysterious fellow who said little to others but hello when he arrived and good-bye when he left. His lack of social interaction probably was due to his poor command of English. He would stand in front of a full-length MIRROR and practice his line, "I am . . . Dracula."

The movie *Dracula* made him a star. Audiences were riveted by his silky, heavily accented voice and his mesmerizing presence. But though the movie made a handsome profit for Universal Studios, it failed to vault Lugosi into the financial stratosphere of superstardom. He found himself typecast in the horror genre. He attempted to break free of the typecasting, but never succeeded. One prize he kept: Universal's Dracula ring, a heavy silver ring with a BAT's crest on it.

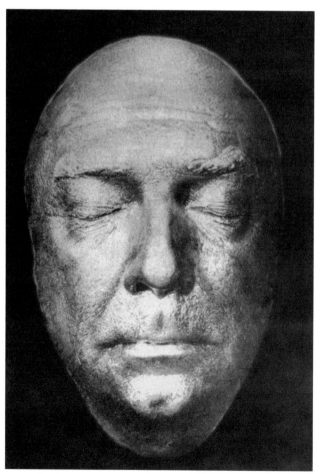

Death mask of Bela Lugosi (Courtesy Vampire Empire Archives)

Offered the role of Frankenstein's monster in the 1931 film *Frankenstein,* he turned it down, and it went to Boris Karloff. *Frankenstein* outperformed *Dracula* both at the box office and with critics, and established Karloff as Hollywood's leading horror star. Lugosi and Karloff starred together in several subsequent horror films, including *The Black Cat* (1934), *The Invisible Ray* (1936), *Black Friday* (1940), and *Son of Frankenstein* (1939). A bit of rivalry existed between them.

In 1935 HAMMER FILMS hired him to come to London to make *Mystery of the Mary Celeste,* based on the true story of a commercial ship of the same name that set sail in 1872 from New York bound for Genoa and a month later was found floating aimlessly at sea without a soul aboard and no sign of violence. The film, however, was tacky, according to critics.

Lugosi went on to appear in more than 100 films, mostly in roles of vampires, monsters, WEREWOLVES, GHOULS, and mad scientists. His other notable vampire films were MARK OF THE VAMPIRE (1935), *The Return of the Vampire* (1943) and *ABBOTT AND COSTELLO MEET FRANKENSTEIN* (1948), in which he played the role of Dracula for the second and only other time in his career. His career then slid into mediocrity, and he struggled to recapture the glamour of his Dracula fame. But Lugosi was essentially finished as a star, and never worked again for a major studio.

In 1951 he made what would be his final attempt at a comeback by traveling to Britain to appear in the stage production, *Dracula—The Vampire Play.* His hope was for a smashing West End tour, followed by a movie in England, a triumphant return to America for a revival of *Dracula* on Broadway, and then a remake of the black-and-white movie in Technicolor. He conceived of a showy arrival in Britain, concealing himself in full Dracula regalia inside a COFFIN. When customs opened the coffin, he planned to spring out for a photo opportunity. However, he was told that the British would not appreciate this publicity stunt, and he was persuaded to abandon the idea.

Lore has it that the tour was a dismal failure, closing prematurely and stranding Lugosi and his wife, Lillian, without sufficient funds to make their way back to America. Only after his appearance in a low-budget movie, *Old Mother Riley Meets the Vampire* (titled *Vampire Over London* in America), did he and his wife raise enough cash to go home.

In actuality, the play ran successfully for 24 weeks in the provinces and garnered excellent reviews. However, it did not open in London's West End, much to the keen disappointment of Lugosi. Nor did it make much money on its average box office takes. Lugosi eventually lacked the stamina to continue touring and asked for the tour to come to an end. Touring had taken a great toll on his health, which had been damaged by years of heavy drinking as well as his injuries and afflictions. He took injections of methadone (which Lillian passed off as insulin), and performed despite severe pain from sciata, old war injuries, and ulcers.

The tour ended on October 13, 1951, in Portsmouth. It was the last time Lugosi ever took the cape to play Dracula, a role he had performed onstage hundreds of times. After returning to the United States in December 1951, Lugosi struggled to make ends meet with small parts in Hollywood. His next role was in *Bela Lugosi Meets a Brooklyn Gorilla*. He had a difficult time remembering his lines.

In 1952 Lugosi met 28-year-old Edward D. Wood Jr., later called by film critics "the worst director of all time." Wood cast Lugosi in *Glen or Glenda,* a film based on Wood's own transvestism. Lugosi received $1,000 for one day of work. Still, he and Lillian could not make ends meet.

In 1953 Lillian left him, after weaning him off methadone. Devastated, Lugosi begged her to return, to no avail. Headlines in the United States trumpeted "Wife Divorces Dracula," but the news rated no mention in British press.

Lugosi struggled on with bit parts. Wood tried to help him, with some small success, most notably the launching of *The Bela Lugosi Revue,* a comedy show at the Silver Slipper nightclub in Las Vegas. The show was a hit; Lugosi ad-libbed, sang, and played musical instruments.

In April 21, 1955, Lugosi became the first Hollywood actor to admit an addiction to narcotics, and he committed himself to a county hospital. He said that shooting pains in his legs had driven him to morphine many years earlier. He had discovered methadone 17 years earlier in England and had smuggled some home. He relied on methadone or demerol. Lillian had gotten him off drugs, but he had returned to his habit after her departure.

Every day while he was in the hospital, Lugosi received morale-boosting letters signed "A Dash of Hope." After his release on August 3, he tracked down the letter writer, a woman named Hope Lininger, 36. They married on August 24. Lugosi resumed heavy drinking.

By then Lugosi was in the twilight of his life as well as his career. He had a nonspeaking bit part in *The Black Sleep*. He shot footage for Wood's *The Vampire Tomb*. Two days into the shooting, Hope found him dead in bed, on August 16, 1956. He was 73.

Lugosi was buried in one of the black capes he wore as the count. He had not requested this, but his family delivered the costume to the mortuary. Lugosi was buried in the Holy Cross Cemetery in Culver City, California, next to Bing Crosby and near Rita Hayworth.

Wood failed to get funding for *The Vampire Tomb,* but later incorporated the Lugosi footage into *Plan 9 from Outer Space,* released in 1959. Thrashed by critics and labeled the worst film of all time, *Plan 9* nonetheless went on to attract a large cult following; undoubtedly Lugosi's presence helped. The remaining scenes unfinished by Lugosi were done by a younger, taller actor who kept his cape pulled over his face.

Ed Wood (1994), a biographical film directed by Tim Burton and starring Johnny Depp as Wood, features Martin Landau as Lugosi. Landau won an Academy Award for best supporting actor.

Bela Lugosi as Dracula on the set of Tod Browning's Dracula (Author's collection)

FURTHER READING:
Skal, David J., ed. *Vampires: Encounters with the Undead.* New York: Black Dog & Leventhal, 2001.
———. *Hollywood Gothic: The Tangled Web of* Dracula *from Novel to Stage to Screen.* New York: W. W. Norton, 1990.
Stritto, Frank Dello and Andi Brooks. *Vampire Over London: Bela Lugosi in Britain.* Los Angeles: Cult Movies Press, 2001.
Stuart, Roxana. *Stage Blood: Vampires of the 19th-Century Stage.* Bowling Green, Ohio: Bowling Green State University Popular Press, 1994.

Lumley, Brian (1937–) English fantasy, science fiction, and horror novelist and creator of the Necroscope series about VAMPIRES and other supernatural creatures in a parallel world. Brian Lumley has written more than 40 novels, plus 10 volumes of short stories.

Lumley was born on December 2, 1937, in Horden, a colliery village in County Durham in northeast England. The son of a miner, he aspired to be writer. He began his working life in his mid-teens as a wood-cutting machinist. At age 21 he was drafted into service with the British Army, serving for 12 years. He was assigned duty as a military policemen and for a time was stationed in Berlin. In the mid-1970s he was the Royal Military Police Quartermaster of Edinburgh Castle in Scotland.

Lumley's writing career sparked in Berlin while doing a tedious tour of duty on the night desk at a checkpoint control center in the midst of the cold war. He passed time reading horror novels, especially the works of H. P. Lovecraft. After completing his first two of three short stories, he contacted Arkham House publisher August Derleth, whose main interest was to keep alive the works of Lovecraft. Within a year Lumley was putting together a horror collection for Arkham House.

After leaving the military, Lumley worked as a security guard in London and then moved to Devon with the intent of becoming a full-time writer.

His many short stories have a clearly defined Lovecraftian lilt. His early tales of psychic detective Titus Crowe contain monsters that would be at home in Lovecraft's Cthulhu Mythos. His Necroscope vampire books hold truer to Lovecraft's unspeakable creations than to BRAM STOKER's suave COUNT DRACULA.

Lumley left the army to become a full-time writer in the early 1980s.

His works have included such series as the *Psychomech* trilogy, a fantasy/science fiction combination that begins when a wealthy industrialist wants a new body for his immortal, and immoral, mind, and the Dreamlands series in which the victim of a road accident goes adventuring in the land of dreams. There are six Titus Crowe novels and three Primal Lands novels.

Among his other books are the apocalyptic *Demogorgon; The House of Doors* and *The House of Doors: Second Visit* (also released as *Maze of Worlds*), which follows the fortunes of a group of humans trapped in a machine that contains many worlds; and *Fruiting Bodies and Other Fungi*, a short story collection headed by his 1988 British Fantasy Award winner.

Lumley's best-known series, *Necroscope,* began in 1986 and ended in 2002 with volume 13. The hero is Harry Keogh, the Necroscope, the only person known to be able to hear and talk directly to the dead. Keogh becomes so skilled in "deadspeak" that the British Secret Service recruits him into the E-Branch, its paranormal unit. Keogh learns how to travel instantly between places and times via the mathematics of the Möbius Continuum. In his many adventures, Keogh becomes involved in the parallel world of Sunside/Starside, a planet ravaged by the remnant of a deteriorated black hole and divided into two sides. It is inhabited by GYPSIES (Szgany), desert-dwelling mystics (Thyre), SHAPE-SHIFTING vampire lords called WAMPHYRI, thralls, hags, "cartilage creatures," trogs, and various hideous living/undead "constructs" formed in vats of human and vampire fluids. Keogh and other psychic agents are VAMPIRE HUNTERS. Eventually, Keogh is bested

by the vampires and in the afterlife becomes a Wamphyr himself. The Necroscope mantle passes to a successor, Jake Cutter. Keogh telepathically communicates with Cutter. The 13 novels weave numerous subplots. The Necroscope books are

- *Necroscope* (1986): As a boy Harry Keogh knows he is different because he can talk to the dead as easily as the living. He becomes the Necroscope, the only person known to have such ability, and works for the British Secret Service's paranormal unit, the mysterious E-Branch. He and his Russian counterpart, Boris Dragosini, make contact with a vampire who has been buried in Romania and who lusts for freedom and revenge.
- *Necroscope 2: Wamphyri!* (1988): Keogh, dead, continues to search for a new body. He believes the war with the vampires ended in the destruction of Boris Dragosani, but an army of vampires is being assembled by Yulian Bodescu to destroy the earth.
- *Necroscope 3: The Source* (1989): Soviet scientists accidentally open a portal to the realm of the Wamphyri, unleashing a new horror upon the earth. A war against the Wamphyri rages as the vampires organize a mass invasion. Keogh searches for his missing wife and son.
- *Necroscope 4: Deadspeak* (1990): Keogh works with a multinational team of vampire hunters and goes to TRANSYLVANIA. He faces his foe, the master vampire Janos Ferenczy, and fights him for his love, Sandra. Keogh loses his powers.
- *Necroscope 5: Deadspeak* (1991): Keogh regains his powers. He must find a murderer and also battle a vampire seed placed within him by Faethor Ferenczy, the father of all vampires.
- *Blood Brothers* (1992): In this first of three books in a side series about the Vampire World, where vampirism is the norm and subjugation by vampires is part of life, the late Keogh has passed his torch to his twin sons, Nestor and Nathan. The sons are under the illusion that their father was a Gypsy, and all vampires have been destroyed. Vampire warriors from Starside attack their settlement on Sunside, and they are separated—Nathan is taken to Starside, where he evolves into the darker of the two.
- *The Last Aerie* (1993): Nestor, Wamphyri lord on Starside, plots to destroy his twin brother, Nathan, on Sunside. He throws Nathan into a gate of hell, which becomes a gate to earth. On earth Nathan is pursued by an evil Russian psychic who wants access to his powers. Nathan is aided by the British E-Branch, who teach him about his powers.
- *Bloodwars* (1994): Nestor sends Nathan through an interworld gate to earth, where the British E-Branch sends him to help the Szgany gypsies in their territorial "bloodwars." A rogue Russian E-Branch agent plans to seize control of Sunside/Starside and earth.

- *Necroscope: The Lost Years* (1996): In contemporary Europe, the inexperienced Keogh has vanquished Dragosani and has learned how to travel through space and time. His wife and infant son disappear. Keogh becomes caught in the middle of a struggle between two vicious vampires.
- *Necroscope: Resurgence The Lost Years: Volume II* (1996): Radu Lykan, the last of the original EXTRA-TERRESTRIAL invaders and first of all WEREWOLVES, suffers from the plague and seeks to insert his mind into Keogh's mind. Keogh is aided by one of Radu's female accomplices who falls in love with him, as well as dead historical figures such as Nostradamus, Harry Houdini, and Franz Anton Mesmer.
- *Necroscope: Invaders* (2000): The first volume of an offshoot trilogy returns to the present and introduces Jake Cutter, the successor to Keogh. His mind is taken over by the consciousness of Keogh, who foresees a future conflict between Cutter and a trio of destructive vampires: Nephran Malinari, Lady Vavara, and Lord Szwart. Cutter knows nothing of the alternate universe. He ultimately confronts Malinari in the Australian mountains.
- *Necroscope: Defilers* (2001): Cutter tracks down the Sicilian mobsters who killed his girlfriend, and deals with a dead vampire, Korath, who is stuck inside his head.
- *Necroscope: Avengers* (2002): In the conclusion to the Necroscope series, Malinari and the vampires Lady Vavara and Lord Szwart are at large and attempt to seed the world with virulent vampire fungi. Cutter still wrestles with his own vampire taint.

After the end of the series, Lumley published *Harry Keogh: Necroscope and Other Heroes!* (2003), a collection of short stories.

Lumley lives in Devon, England, with his wife, Dorothy, a literary agent.

FURTHER READING:
Brian Lumley Web site. URL:http://www.brianlumley.com. Downloaded on December 2, 2003.
Gilbert, John, "Brian Lumley: A Portrait," in *The Complete Vampire Companion* by Rosemary Ellen Guiley with J. B. Macabre. New York: Macmillan, 1994.
Lumley, Brian, and Stanley Wiater, eds. *The Brian Lumley Companion.* New York: TOR Books, 2002.

Lupercalia   Ancient Roman festival dedicated to the fertility god Lupercus, held on the 15th of February, the last month of the year. Origins of the festival were attributed to the mythical twin founders of Rome, Romulus and Remus, and also to the culture hero Evander. Most likely, the festival predates Rome.

The festival celebrated the arrival of Lupercus, personified by a wolf, to the cave on the Palatine where the she-wolf suckled and raised the abandoned infants Romulus and Remus. The Luperci, the priests of Lupercus, sacrificed goats and a dog and smeared the BLOOD on the foreheads of two noble youths. The priests wiped off the blood with wool dipped in milk while the youths laughed loudly. The priests ate. They cut up the goatskins and dressed themselves in pieces of them. They made other pieces of goatskin into whips. The goatskin-clad priests ran around the Palatine, whipping everyone they encountered. Women who were whipped were believed to become more fertile and to bear children more easily.

The festival also cleansed the land for the new year. The name of the month of February takes its name from the Latin term *februare,* "to cleanse."

FURTHER READING:
Leach, Maria, ed., and Jerome Fried, assoc. ed. *Funk & Wagnalls Standard Dictionary of Folklore, Mythology, and Legend.* San Francisco: Harper & Row, 1984.

Lust for a Vampire   See HAMMER FILMS.

lycanthropy   In medical literature, a clinical disorder in which a person believes himself to be transformed into a wolf, and acts accordingly. The term *lycanthropy* comes from *lycanthrope,* the Greek term for "man-wolf."

The words *lycanthropia* and *lycanthropus* made their first appearance in the English language in 1584 in the anti-witch-hunting book *The Discoverie of Witchcraft* by REGINALD SCOT. During the Inquisition, lycanthropy and werewolfism were used almost interchangeably. *Lycanthropy* now generally refers to the medical condition and not to mythical, magical, or demonic SHAPE-SHIFTING (see also WEREWOLF). It is linked to schizophrenia, multiple personality disorder, bipolar disorder, drug abuse, CLINICAL VAMPIRISM, mental retardation, necrophilia, and other psychological disorders.

The dominant features of lycanthropic behavior are

- profound alienation from self and society
- obsession with things demonic
- frequenting of CEMETERIES and other lonely places
- a secret process or ritual of supposed transformation from human form to wolf form
- belief that one actually grows fur, fangs, paws, and so on
- an insatiable lust for BLOOD
- wolflike behavior, including howling, running on all fours, gnawing objects, attacking people and animals with the intent to kill, biting and tearing at flesh, and the devouring of raw flesh, including human
- hypersexual activity, including bestiality
- supposed resumption of human form
- post-exhaustion, confusion, and depression
- impaired mental functioning

Despite myths of magical shape-shifting and wolf clans, lycanthropy has been recognized as a medical disorder since the second century. The Greek physician Galen (born ca. A.D. 130) considered it to be a melancholic disease with delirium. The Roman Marcellus of Side (ca. A.D. 161) described its symptoms. The Greek physician Paul of Aegina (625–690), who based his writings on those of Marcellus, was the first to link lycanthropy to melancholia. The symptoms of lycanthropes reported by Paul are

> . . . they are pale, their vision feeble, their eyes dry, tongue very dry, and the flow of the saliva stopped; but they are thirsty, and their legs have incurable ulcerations from frequent falls.

The prescribed remedies of ancient times were a form of medical exorcism aimed at driving the affliction out of the body: massive bloodletting to the point of fainting, a diet of "wholesome food," and baths of sweet water and milk-whey. The patient was purged with various agents, including toxic herbs. Rubbing the nostrils with opium prior to sleep also was prescribed—a remedy that probably exacerbated the condition rather than alleviated it.

During the Inquisition, lycanthropy was linked to demonic influences. Most demonologists considered it to be an illusion, the product of insanity or disease caused by the devil. Some believed that people made actual transformations into wolves with the help of demons. Coinciding with the witch hunts were regional hysterias over wolves that ravaged the countryside, killing people and animals. Many peasants believed man-eating wolves to be werewolves. Some high-profile werewolf trials involved confessions of witchcraft as well as lycanthropy. Descriptions of some of the accused, such as JEAN GRENIER, reveal them to be probable sufferers of the medical disorder.

Despite the writings of demonologists, some authorities of the 16th and 17th centuries considered lycanthropy to be madness alone, without the aid of enchantment or the devil. Among those of this opinion were Scot, the demonologist Johann Weyer, the French physician Jean Nynauld, and the Oxford cleric Robert Burton.

After the end of the Inquisition, lycanthropy was considered madness, insanity, hysteria, melancholy, and delusion well into the 19th century. With the emergence of the field of psychology, lycanthropy nearly disappeared from medical literature. Between 1873 and 1975, only one case was mentioned. Carl G. Jung briefly referred to a case resembling lycanthropy (or zoanthropy, referring to animals in general) in 1928 in an essay on how children are sensitive to the unconscious dynamics of their parents. In that particular case, the mother suffered insanity and would crawl around on all fours grunting like a pig, barking like a dog, and growling like a bear. The children had nightmares of her as a witch or dangerous animal.

In the mid-1970s cases of lycanthropy and zoanthropy were recorded in medical literature, along with an increase in diagnoses of multiple personality disorders. It

is doubtful the lycanthropy disappeared, but probably was diagnosed as another condition, such as paranoia or hysteria.

In psychology, lycanthropy may be related to the "beast within," a dissociated part of the psyche that separates humans from baser instincts and animalistic behavior. In Jungian terms, this is part of the Shadow, a hidden, primitive, and repressed personality that may go back to humanity's earliest ancestors. In cases of lycanthropy, this hidden side finds expression.

Treatment for lycanthropy includes antidepressants, neuroleptics and other medications, and psychotherapy. Some patients experience partial or complete remission.

See also PORPHYRIA.

FURTHER READING:
Noll, Richard. *Vampires, Werewolves and Demons*. New York: Brunner/Mazel, 1992.
Otten, Charlotte F., ed. *A Lycanthropy Reader: Werewolves in Western Culture*. New York: Dorset Press, 1989.

Lycaon   Mythical king of Arcadia, Greece, who became a WEREWOLF as divine punishment. The term *lycaon* means "deluding wolf." Lycaon was son of Pelasgus and the father of Callisto and 50 sons.

The story of King Lycaon appears in different works, among them Ovid's *Metamorphoses* and Vergil's *Georgics*. The myth may be related to a cannibalism practice that was part of the cult of Jupiter Lycaeus. According to the cult, a person who ate human flesh was transformed into a wolf and spent eight to 10 years in the wild. The werewolf could then resume human form, but only if it consumed no more human flesh.

According to Ovid, Jupiter was upset over the murder of Julius Caesar and the increasing wickedness of the human race. He descended from Mount Olympus and took on the form of a man, roaming about to check the state of affairs. At nightfall he entered the home of King Lycaon, an "inhospitable tyrant," and revealed himself as a god. The people bowed down to worship him, but Lycaon laughed at them. He proposed an infallible test to determine if Jupiter was god or man.

Lycaon intended to steal upon Jupiter and kill him while he was asleep. But first he took a hostage sent to him by the Molossian people and slit his throat. He cooked the man's limbs, boiling some and roasting some. He set the human flesh out on his banquet table for the god.

Enraged, Jupiter destroyed the household with avenging flames. Lycaon escaped into the countryside with his life, but not free of the wrath of Jupiter, who caused him to become a wolf. According to Ovid:

> There he uttered howling noises, and his attempts to speak were all in vain. His clothes changed into bristling hairs, his arms to legs, and he became a wolf. His own

savage nature showed in his rabid jaws, and he now directed against the flocks his innate lust for killing. He had a mania, even yet, for shedding blood. But, though he was a wolf, he retained some traces of his original shape. The greyness of his hair was the same, his face showed the same violence, his eyes gleamed as before, and he presented the same picture of ferocity.

Jupiter resolved to destroy the entire human race and replace them with an entirely new stock of men "of miraculous origin."

There are different versions of the myth:

- Lycaon's evil sons killed one brother, Nyctimus, and made a soup of him. They offered the soup to Jupiter, who had disguised himself as a poor laborer. Outraged, Jupiter killed the evil sons with a lightning bolt, restored Nyctimus to life, and turned Lycaon into a wolf. Lycaon suffered a ravenous thirst for blood and went out slaughtering flocks of animals.
- Lycaon himself offered Nyctimus's flesh to Jupiter to test whether he really was a god. Disgusted, Jupiter destroyed the earth with a flood. Only two people survived: Deucalion and his wife, Pyrrha.
- In a variant of the second version, Lycaon, a priest of Jupiter Lycaeus, survived the flood, but all his children were killed.

FURTHER READING:
Mercatante, Anthony S. *Encyclopedia of World Mythology and Legend.* Frenchs Forest, Australia: Child & Associates, 1988.
Otten, Charlotte F., ed. *A Lycanthropy Reader: Werewolves in Western Culture.* New York: Dorset Press, 1989.

Magnus, Olaus (17th c.)   Latinized name of Olaf Magnusson, the archbishop of Trondheim, Germany, who was known for his writings on WEREWOLVES.

In his work *A Compendius History of the Goths, Swedes, & Vandals, and Other Northern Nations* (1658), Magnus contends that werewolves especially plagued Prussia, Latvia, and Lithuania, and also Switzerland, France, Italy, and Germany. He divided werewolves into three types:

- men who imagine themselves to be wolves and who attack livestock
- men who dream they attack cattle as wolves, while the real attacks are carried out by wolves under the direction of the devil
- men who imagine they are wolves, but their ravages are done by the devil in the form of a wolf

Magnus stated that werewolves believed they transformed themselves into beasts by donning a wolf's skin and uttering magical incantations:

> The reason of this metamorphosis, that is exceeding contrary to nature, is given by one skilled in this witchcraft, by drinking to one in a cup of Ale, and by mumbling certain words at the same time, so that he who is to be admitted into that unlawful Society do accept it . . . Then when he pleaseth he may change his humane form, into the form of a Wolf entirely, going into some private Cellar, or secret Wood. Again, he can after some time put off the same shape he took upon him, and resume the form he had before at his pleasure.

Magnus wrote about wild werewolf gatherings:

> On the feast of the Nativity of Christ, at night, such a multitude of wolves transformed from men gather together in a certain spot, arranged among themselves, and then spread to rage with wondrous ferocity against human beings, and those animals which are not wild, that the natives of these regions suffer more detriment from these, than they do from true wolves; for when a human habitation has been detected by them isolated in the woods, they besiege it with atrocity, striving to break in the doors, and in the event of their doing so, they devour the human beings, and every animal which is found within. They burst into the beer cellars, and there they empty the tuns of beer or mead, and pile up the casks one above another in the middle of the cellar, thus showing their difference from natural and genuine wolves.

Magnus also wrote that devils were so commonplace in Scandinavia that people had learned not to pay much attention to them. The devils worked in the mines, cleaned stables, and fed livestock. They would not trouble people if they were not bothered. Magnus said that devils are excellent navigators, and unwary sea captains might sell their souls to them in exchange for safety at sea.

See also *BERSERKIR*; LIVONIA WEREWOLVES.

195

FURTHER READING:

Seligmann, Kurt. *The Mirror of Magic: A History of Magic in the Western World.* New York: Pantheon Books, 1948.

Sidky, H. *Witchcraft, Lycanthropy, Drugs and Disease: An Anthropological Study of the European Witch-Hunts.* New York: Peter Lang, 1997.

Summers, Montague. *The Werewolf.* New York: Bell Publishing, 1966.

Malleus Maleficarum   See SHAPE-SHIFTING.

mara   See MORA.

Maréchal de Retz   See GILLES DE LAVAL.

Marius   See LESTAT DE LIONCOURT; RICE, ANNE.

Mark of the Vampire (1935)   Director TOD BROWNING's sound remake of his silent 1927 original LONDON AFTER MIDNIGHT. In *Mark of the Vampire*, BELA LUGOSI reprises the role of the VAMPIRE played by LON CHANEY. While Chaney also plays the role of Professor Burke, who is really a Scotland Yard inspector, Lugosi plays only the vampire. The role of Inspector Neumann is played by Lionel Atwill. Professor Zelin is played by Lionel Barrymore. Carroll Borland is Luna the Bat Girl.

Mark of the Vampire is regarded by some film critics as inferior to the original, despite Browning's lavishing more atmosphere on the sound version. Borland's Luna has more depth than the character played by Edna Tichenor, but neither Lugosi nor Barrymore succeed in conveying the freakish horror that Chaney unleashes as the leering vampire. Both films have the contrived ending of the vampires being a charade to draw out a murderer.

FURTHER READING:

Skal, David J., and Elias Savada. *Dark Carnival: The Secret World of Tod Browning, Hollywood's Master of the Macabre.* New York: Anchor/Doubleday, 1995.

Marster, James   See BUFFY THE VAMPIRE SLAYER.

Marusia   Russian folktale about a girl, Marusia, who suffers at the hands of an UPIR, a VAMPIRE. The story is a variation of the Slavic tale THE GIRL AND THE VAMPIRE.

Marusia lives in a village in a "certain kingdom," the beautiful daughter of an old man and woman. At a celebration on the holiday of St. Andrew, Marusia meets a strange young man who is well dressed and neat, with a fine complexion. He is invited to join the party and brings out a purse full of wine, nuts and gingerbread, which he gives to all the girls present. He dances with Marusia and likes her the best.

At the end of the party, the stranger invites Marusia out for a walk and proposes marriage to her. He tells her he is a merchant's clerk. She agrees and goes home to tell her mother the good news. Her mother advises her to take a ball of thread, and next time she meets and parts from the man, to tie it around one of his buttons. Then she will be able to follow the thread and see where he lives.

Count Mora (Bela Lugosi) and Luna (Carroll Borland) in Tod Browning's Mark of the Vampire *(Author's collection)*

Marusia does this. When she follows the thread, it leads her a long way to the church, the gates of which are closed. She gets a ladder and climbs into the church through a window. There, to her horror, she sees her young man, who is bent over a CORPSE laid out for a funeral and is eating it. (See GHOUL.) In her haste to escape, she makes a noise.

Marusia does not tell her mother what she has seen. The next evening, she goes to a party. The young man shows up and presses her to go for a walk with him. He questions her about being in the church and whether she saw what he was doing, but she denies it. He tells her that her father will die on the morrow.

In the morning, Marusia's father is found dead, and is put in a COFFIN. In the evening, she joins friends, and once again meets the young man. He asks her the same questions, and once again she denies them. He says her mother will die on the morrow.

The next morning, Marusia's mother is found dead. Marusia weeps all day and then goes to be with friends. She meets the young man again. He asks her the same questions, and she denies them. He says she herself will die the following night.

Marusia consults her wise old grandmother, who is blind, and confesses everything. The grandmother tells her to instruct the priest that when she dies, a HOLE is to be dug under the door sill and her corpse is to be carried out of the house through the HOLE. (See BURIAL CUSTOMS; DOPPELSAUGER.) She is to be buried at a CROSSROADS.

Marusia does so. She buys a coffin and dies. The priest follows her instructions.

Soon after her burial, a barin, the son of a boyar, goes past her grave and sees a beautiful flower growing on it. He takes the flower home and plants it in a pot on a windowsill. It flourishes. One night a servant discovers that the flower transforms into a beautiful young maiden at the stroke of midnight.

The barin falls in love with her and marries her. She agrees on the condition that for four years they do not go to church.

Two years later, they have a son and are very happy. But neighbors gossip that Marusia is an infidel because she does not go to church. Insulted, the barin decides they will attend Sunday Mass.

Inside the church, Marusia sees the *upir* sitting on a sill; he is invisible to her husband. The vampire asks her the same questions. She denies them. He says her husband and son will die on the morrow. Marusia dashes from church and goes straight to her grandmother. The old woman gives her a vial of holy WATER and a vial of "the water of life" and tells her what to do with them.

The next day, Marusia's husband and son are found dead. The vampire comes to Marusia and asks her the same questions. This time, she tells the truth. She then casts the holy water on the *upir* and he turns instantly to dust. She sprinkles the bodies of her husband and son with the water of life, and they are restored to life. They all live happily ever after.

The morals of this folktale are to be wary of strangers (a warning especially for girls), and to always tell the truth.

FURTHER READING:
Perkowski, Jan L. *The Darkling: A Treatise on Slavic Vampirism.* Columbus, Ohio: Slavica Publishers, 1989.

Mathers, Samuel Liddell MacGregor (1854–1918)

Leading English occultist and a founder of the Hermetic Order of the Golden Dawn magical order. Samuel Liddell MacGregor Mathers was a skilled magician and engaged in a famous battle of PSYCHIC ATTACK with ALEISTER CROWLEY.

Born in Hackney, London, on January 8, 1854, Mathers had an intense interest in the occult in childhood. He became a Freemason in 1877, followed by membership in the Rosicrucians. In 1888 he and fellow Rosicrucians William Wynn Westcott and William Robert Woodman founded the Golden Dawn in London. His magical career was marred by poverty and being taken in by charlatans.

Mathers sponsored Crowley for membership in the Golden Dawn in 1898, but Crowley immediately was at odds with Mathers and thought he himself should be the head of the organization. Crowley declared war against Mathers. They both were soon expelled from the order, which infuriated Mathers. He went to Paris and established a competing lodge. He launched psychic warfare against Crowley in 1900, after preparing himself for six months with magical procedures and rites in order to create a vampiric THOUGHT-FORM.

According to fellow occultist DION FORTUNE, Mathers probably employed the power of Mars in creating the psychic vampire. Her description of such a ceremony follows:

All the occultist's magical instruments would be made of iron and his rod of power would be a naked sword. Upon the altar he would place five lights, five being the number of Mars. Upon his breast would be the symbol of Mars engraved on a steel pentagon. On his left hand would be a ruby ring. He would burn sulphur and saltpeter in his thurigible.

Then he would call upon the demonic aspect of the fifth Sephira [of the Kabbalistic Tree of Life], Geburah, the sphere of Mars. He would invoke the arch-devil of the Fifth Infernal Habitation. Having performed this mighty invocation, he would then offer himself upon the altar as the channel for the manifestation of the Force . . .

The story goes that Mathers then entered a trance state and concentrated his will into the psychic vampire, which rose up from his solar plexus. He ordered it to attack Crowley. However, he committed a grievous error to do the sending himself. In magic, apprentices are often used to do the sending, for if anything goes amiss and the magic boomerangs, it will be the apprentice who suffers and not the master magician.

Crowley, who was of superior magical skill, took the thought-form, made it nastier, and sent it back to attack

Mathers. This warfare supposedly went on for years and was chronicled by journalists around the world.

Mathers's health declined as the attacks continued. When Mathers succumbed in 1918, his widow blamed his death on Crowley's psychic vampirism. Prior to his death, Mathers once described the awful nature of the thought-form vampire:

> Only the upper portions of its body were visible when it would appear. Obviously female, it had narrow breasts protruding through some kind of dark raiment. Below the waist nothing existed. The curious eyes were deep-socketed, and glowed faintly with an intense coral-colored luminosity. The head was flat, set low between white, blubbery shoulders, as though it were cut off just below those fearful "eyes." Like tiny useless flippers, the arms seemed almost vestigial. They were like unformed limbs, still in the foetal stage.
>
> But the thing didn't need arms. Its terrifying weapon was an extraordinarily long, coated gray tongue. Tube-like and hollow, it bore a small orbicular hole at its tip, and that lascivious tongue kept darting snake-like in and out of a circular, lipless mouth. Always trying to catch me off guard it would suddenly strike at me, like a greedy missile, attempting to suck out my auric vitality.
>
> Perhaps the being's most terrifying feature was its absolutely loathsome habit of trying to cuddle up like a purring cat, rubbing its half-materialized form against me, all the while alert, hoping to find a gap in my defenses. And when it was sometimes successful—I was not always prepared nor strong enough to maintain the magical barriers—it would pierce my aura with that wicked tongue right down to my naked skin, causing a most painful sensation. This was followed by a total enervation of my body and spirit for a week or more. A listless, dread experience.

Individuals who knew Crowley believed him to be quite capable of manipulating such an insidious vampire.

FURTHER READING:
Fortune, Dion. *Psychic Self-Defence.* York Beach, Me.: Samuel Weiser, 1957. First published, 1939.
Hillyer, Vincent. *Vampires.* Los Banos, Calif.: Loose Change Publications, 1988.

Matheson, Richard Burton (1926–)   American novelist and screenwriter whose prolific and best-selling career has had a considerable impact on horror, science fiction, and fantasy genres with his visionary themes in short stories and novels. Richard Matheson has been called the "father of modern horror and fantasy," and his work has been cited as an inspiration by many authors, among them Stephen King, Dean Koontz, and Ray Bradbury.

Matheson's best-known VAMPIRE novel is I AM LEGEND (1954), considered a horror classic and still in print. He worked with producer and director DAN CURTIS on several projects, including the 1973 made-for-television film *Dra-cula,* starring Jack Palance (see DRACULA FILMS), and also wrote numerous scripts for television and film.

Matheson was born on February 26, 1926, in New Jersey. He started writing at age eight. In school he studied journalism. He served in the armed forces in World War II.

Matheson began his professional writing career with short stories, publishing his first, "Born of Man and Woman," in 1950. The same title was used for his first book, a collection of his stories, published in 1954. His first vampire story was "Drink My Red Blood," published in 1951. Other vampire-themed stories of note are "BLOOD SON" (1951), "The Funeral" (1955) and "No Such Thing As a Vampire" (1959). His major work on vampires is his novel I Am Legend, which treats vampirism as a bacteria-caused disease, and it became the first major contemporary novel to portray vampires as rational beings without the stigma of evil.

One of Matheson's biggest breaks came with the film adaptation of his 1956 novel, *The Incredible Shrinking Man,* for which he wrote the screenplay. He began working with director Roger Corman on a series of Edgar Allan Poe films starring Vincent Price: *The Fall of the House of Usher* (1960), *The Pit and the Pendulum* (1961), and *The Raven* (1963).

I Am Legend was filmed twice, in 1964 as *The Last Man On Earth* starring Vincent Price, and in 1971 as *The Omega Man* starring Charleton Heston.

During the late 1950s Matheson began working with Rod Serling on *The Twilight Zone,* scripting 14 episodes, including some of the show's most memorable. For example, "Nightmare at 20,000 Feet" stars William Shatner (in his pre–Star Trek days) as an airline passenger who is the only person aboard a storm-tossed plane to see a gremlin on the wing attacking the plane's engines.

Matheson began working with Curtis in 1971, writing the screenplays for the telemovie *The Night Stalker,* which became the television series KOLCHAK, THE NIGHT STALKER, and for the telemovie's sequel, *The Night Strangler.* Curtis produced *Trilogy of Terror,* a telemovie that features one of Matheson's short stories, "Prey," about a woman terrorized by a doll.

Matheson wrote the script for Steven Spielberg's first mainstream directing project, *Duel* (1971), starring Dennis Weaver, about a man in a car terrorized for unknown reasons by the driver of a tanker truck. He also has written scripts for western television shows.

Matheson has explored metaphysical territory in his novels *Somewhere in Time* (1975), filmed in 1980 starring Christopher Reeve and Jane Seymour in a time-traveling love story; and *What Dreams May Come* (1979), filmed in 1998 starring Robin Williams as a man who is killed in an auto accident and must adjust to life after death.

Matheson's spiritual and metaphysical ideas are presented in his nonfiction book, *The Path* (1993) and in *Reality* (1999), a CD recording.

Matheson has lived and worked in California since 1951. He has written more than 20 novels and 100 short stories. Nineteen of his screenplays have been filmed, and more than 55 television scripts have been filmed. Among his numerous awards are the World Fantasy Convention's Lifetime Achievement Award; the Horror Writers of America's BRAM STOKER Award for Life Achievement; the Science Fiction and Fantasy Writers of America's Hugo Award: the Mystery Writers of America's Edgar Allan Poe Award; and the Writer's Guild Award.

FURTHER READING:
Brejla, Terry. *The Devils of His Own Creation: The Life and Works of Richard Matheson.* Lincoln Neb.: iUniverse/Writer's Club Press, 2003.
Carroll, David. "Richard Matheson: Father and Son." From *Tabula Rasa #5,* 1995. Available online. URL: http://www.tabula-rasa.info/Dark Ages/Richard Matheson.html. Downloaded on January 15, 2003.

McNally, Raymond T. (1931–2002)

VAMPIRE scholar and author, best known for his work on VLAD TEPES, called the "historical" COUNT DRACULA.

Raymond T. McNally was born on May 15, 1931, in Cleveland, Ohio. After graduating from Fordham University, he became an instructor at John Carroll University in Cleveland. In 1958 he went to Boston College in Chestnut Hill, Massachusetts, where he eventually became director of its Slavic and East European Center. He spent a year in Leningrad (now St. Petersburg) in 1961 as an exchange scholar. In 1970 he achieved full professor status at Boston College. He was awarded a doctorate in Russian and East European History by the Free University of Berlin.

By the time he started teaching, McNally had long been a fan of *DRACULA* by BRAM STOKER and of horror films; one of his favorites was *NOSFERATU,* the 1922 silent film starring MAX SCHRECK. He wondered about the historical basis for Stoker's novel.

At Boston College, McNally met Romanian scholar RADU R. FLORESCU, and learned about Vlad Tepes. With Florescu's encouragement, he studied Romanian, and then visited Romania itself. McNally entered into a long partnership with Florescu involving collaboration on several books. In 1969 they participated in an exploration of the ruins of CASTLE DRACULA (see CASTLE POENARI), which they chronicled in their first book together, *In Search of Dracula* (1972), a best-seller. In undertaking the research, they worked with a team of Romanians and Americans.

That was followed in 1973 by a second book, *Dracula: A Biography of Vlad the Impaler, 1431–1476;* the two books became the basis for a film documentary, *In Search of Dracula* (1976), starring CHRISTOPHER LEE. McNally and Florescu collaborated on three more books: *The Essential "Dracula": A Completely Illustrated and Annotated Edition of Bram Stoker's Classic Novel* (1979); *Dracula, Prince of Many Faces: His Life and Times* (1989); and *In Search of Dr. Jekyll and Mr. Hyde* (2000).

On his own, McNally wrote *A Clutch of Vampires: Those Being among the Best from History and Literature* (1974), a compilation of essays, stories, and excerpts; and *Dracula Was a Woman: In Search of the Blood Countess of Transylvania* (1983), a biography of Countess ELIZABETH BATHÓRY. His essay, "An Historical Appraisal of the Image of Vlad Tepes and Contemporary Romanian Folklore," was published in 1991. In 1997 McNally issued a new annotated version of *Dracula* entitled *Dracula: Truth and Terror* on CD-ROM.

Much of McNally's research was funded by three Fulbright grants. Well traveled, he was fluent in French, German, Romanian, Russian, and Greek.

McNally's critics contended that he capitalized on a most tenuous connection between the fictional Count Dracula and Vlad Tepes. Though Tepes had committed bloody atrocities, he was not associated with vampire lore; he was known as "Dracula" ("son of the devil"), a name Bram Stoker borrowed for his vampire villain.

McNally witnessed a genuine vampire staking in Romania, where folklore superstitions and customs survived into modern times in rural areas. In 1969 he was passing through the village of Rodna near the BORGO PASS. He noticed a burial taking place in a village CEMETERY and stopped to watch. The bystanders told him the dead was a girl who had committed SUICIDE, and the villagers were afraid she would return as a vampire. To prevent this from happening, they plunged a STAKE through her heart.

McNally enjoyed great popularity and loved a touch of showmanship in his numerous lectures and presentations. He often wore a cape and swept it about like BELA LUGOSI in the 1931 film *Dracula.* Unlike Lugosi, he was not buried in his cape.

McNally died in October 2002 at age 71 of complications from cancer, in Brighton, Massachusetts.

He was survived by his wife, Carol, and two sons, three daughters, and several grandchildren.

FURTHER READING:
Long, Tom. "Raymond T. McNally, 71, Professor, author and Dracula historian," *Boston Globe,* Oct. 5, 2002. Available online at http://www.cesnur.org/2002/dracula/mcnally.htm. Downloaded on July 31, 2003.
McNally, Raymond T. *Dracula Was a Woman: In Search of the Blood Countess of Transylvania.* New York: McGraw-Hill, 1983.
———. *A Clutch of Vampires.* New York: Bell Publishing, 1984.
McNally, Raymond T., and Radu Florescu. *In Search of Dracula: a true history of Dracula and vampire legends.* Greenwich, Conn.: New York Graphic Society, 1972.
———. *Dracula: A Biography of Vlad the Impaler 1431–1476.* New York: Hawthorn Books, 1973.

Melrose Abbey Vampire (12th c.)

English vampiric REVENANT case recorded by WILLIAM OF NEWBURGH from oral accounts related to him by clerics.

The VAMPIRE (a term not in the English language in the 12th century) was a chaplain who attended a high-ranking lady. During life, the chaplain ignored his vows and lived as a layman. He spent so much time hunting with horse and hounds that he earned the nickname Hundeprest, or Dog Priest. Though of low repute, when he died he was buried in the Abbey of Melrose.

For several nights after his burial, the chaplain rose from his grave and tried to force his way into the cloister, but the holiness of the monks repulsed him. He was forced to wander elsewhere, and began appearing at the bedside of the lady whom he had served. He terrified her by shrieking and groaning. After several nights of this, the lady appealed to a senior monk at the abbey for special prayers on her behalf. The monk promised a remedy would be found.

The monk gathered three other brothers and went to the chaplain's grave for an all-night vigil, taking weapons with them. During the night it became quite cold, and three of the brothers went off to warm themselves by a fire. The senior monk remained alone at the graveside. At that point, the ghostly chaplain rose up in fury. Wrote William:

> . . . as the horrible creature rushed at him with the most hideous yell, he firmly stood his ground, dealing it a terrible blow with a battle-axe which he held in his hand. When the deadman received this wound he groaned aloud with a terrible hollow noise, and swiftly turning he fled away no less quickly than he had appeared.

The monk pursued him, and the specter retreated back into his grave, which opened to receive him and then quickly closed so that even the ground appeared undisturbed.

The next day, the four brothers dug up the CORPSE. It was marked with the wound. A huge quantity of black BLOOD had flowed out, seeming to swamp the entire tomb. The brothers carried the corpse beyond the bounds of the monastery and burned it, allowing the ASHES to scatter on the wind. Thus was the end of the trouble.

FURTHER READING:
Glut, Donald. *True Vampires of History.* New York: HC Publishers, 1971.

Memnoch the Devil (1995)   The fifth novel in ANNE RICE's Vampire Chronicles features her lead VAMPIRE, LESTAT DE LIONCOURT, in a debate with the Devil.

In New York City, Lestat stalks a cocaine dealer and smuggler of religious art. He kills the man, and then becomes interested in his daughter. A shadowy figure stalks Lestat—Memnoch the Devil. Memnoch reveals himself and invites Lestat to join him in hell. He takes the vampire on a tour of heaven and hell so that he can decide which side he wants to join. He learns about creation and hears the Devil's side of the fall and his views of God as a cruel being.

There are long debates about good and evil, and sin and redemption. Lestat is shown the crucifixion and drinks the BLOOD of Jesus while he is dying on the cross. He also talks with God.

Because of its theological content, *Memnoch the Devil* is one of Rice's most controversial books. Like THE TALE OF THE BODY THIEF (1992), Rice intended for this book to be the last in the Vampire Chronicles, ending it with Lestat going insane. Lestat and other vampires were continued in subsequent novels.

FURTHER READING:
Rice, Anne. *Memnoch the Devil.* New York: Alfred A. Knopf, 1995.

Merionethshire Werewolf   A 19th-century werewolf case from Wales, recorded by MONTAGUE SUMMERS in his book *The Werewolf.*

According to Summers, the case is probably the same as one described by J. Wentworth Day in the magazine *The Passing Show,* dated July 9, 1932. Summers's description is florid. The characteristics of the case, and the manner in which the werewolf is experienced, bear a similarity to the CROGLIN GRANGE VAMPIRE, an English case recorded in 1871. Both cases may have fictionalized elements.

The werewolf incident reportedly occurred in the 1880s on the shores of a remote lake in the hills of Merionethshire, Wales. An unnamed Oxford professor and his wife took a cottage on the lakeshore for a summer so that the professor could pursue his passion of fishing. They entertained a guest while staying there.

One day while rowing out into the lake, the professor discovered near the shoreline a skull that appeared to be that of a very large dog. He took it back to the cottage and left it on a kitchen shelf.

That evening, his wife was alone in the cottage. She heard a snuffling and scratching at the kitchen door that sounded like that of a dog. She went to bar the door:

> As she moved something drew her attention to the window, and there she saw glaring at her through the diamond panes the head of a huge creature, half animal, half human. The cruel panting jaws were gaping wide and showed keen white teeth; the great furry paws clasped the sill like hands; the red eyes gleamed hideously; it was the gaze of a man, horribly intensive, horribly intelligent. Half-fainting with fear she ran through to the front door and shot the bolt. A moment after she heard heavy breathing outside and the latch rattled menacingly. The minutes that followed were full of acutest suspense, and now and again a low snarl would be heard at the door or window, and a sound as though the creature was endeavoring to force its entrance. At last the voices of her husband and his friend, come back from their ramble, sounded in the little garden; and as they knocked, finding the door fast, she was but able to open ere she fell in a swoon at their feet.

Evidently the men had neither seen nor heard anything unusual. After the wife relayed what had happened, the men sat up all night, armed with sticks and a gun:

> The hours passed slowly, until when all was darkest and most lonely the soft thud of cushioned paws was heard on the gravel outside, and nails scratched at the kitchen window. To their horror in a stale phosphorescent light they

saw the hideous mask of a wolf with the eyes of a man glaring through the glass, eyes that were red with hellish rage. Snatching the gun they rushed to the door, but it had seen their movement and was away in a moment. As they issued from the house a shadowy undefined shape slipped through the open gate, and in the stars they could just see a huge animal making towards the lake into which it disappeared silently, nor did a ruffle cross the surface of the water.

The next morning, the professor rowed out into the lake and threw the skull as far as possible into the water. The werewolf was not seen again.

The case is similar to haunting and ghost lore that exists around the world, that the dead do not like to have their burial grounds and remains disturbed. Was the "werewolf" an angry ghost that wanted to repossess his own skull? Summers offers no opinion. In Welsh folklore, many of the lakes, especially in hilly, remote areas, are haunted, usually by fairies.

The HEBRIDES WEREWOLF is another example of a phantom werewolf looking for its missing bones.

A modern case from psychical research has some parallels to both the Merionethshire case and the similar one in the Hebrides off the coast of Scotland:

A deceased man professing to be named "Runolf Runolfsson" began speaking through one of Iceland's most famous mediums, Halfsteinn Bjornsson, in 1937. The "drop-in communicator," so-called because he spontaneously "dropped in" during the medium's sittings, said he was looking for his leg. In 1879 he had gotten drunk and died by drowning when he passed on out the shore during an incoming tide. He was 52. His body was taken out on the tide, but was washed back in January 1880, ravaged by animals and birds as well as the elements. The remains were buried, but a thighbone was still missing.

Historical records verified the existence of Runolfsson. In 1940 a thighbone was discovered interred in the wall of a house. No one was certain that it belonged to the dead man, but it was properly buried, and Runolfsson said he was happy. He did not disappear, but remained a "drop-in" with Bjornsson for years.

FURTHER READING:
Guiley, Rosemary Ellen. *The Encyclopedia of Ghosts and Spirits.* 2d ed. New York: Facts On File, 2000.
Summers, Montague. *The Werewolf.* New York: Bell Publishing, 1966.

metempsychosis   See SHAPE-SHIFTING.

Miller, Elizabeth (1939–)   Canadian scholar of Gothic literature and an expert on BRAM STOKER'S *DRACULA* (1897).

Elizabeth Miller was born in 1939 in St. John's, Newfoundland, Canada. She earned a doctorate at Memorial

Dracula expert Elizabeth Ann Miller (Courtesy Elizabeth Ann Miller)

University in Newfoundland and joined the faculty in the English department there, advancing to full professor. She retired and moved to Toronto, devoting herself full time to a range of scholarly activities related to *Dracula* and vampires.

Miller's interest in *Dracula* resulted from her academic interest in British romantic poets, such as Lord Byron—the subject of her master's thesis—and Percy Bysshe Shelley. That led her to Mary Shelley's *Frankenstein*—her second-most-important area of expertise—and then to JOHN POLIDORI, Byron's physician, who wrote THE VAMPYRE (1819), the first English vampire story. From there, Miller went on to *Dracula*, which she describes as "one of the most influential books ever written."

Miller's research and expertise have made her one of the world's leading *Dracula* scholars, and arguably the most featured and quoted in the media. She has lectured and presented papers at conferences, congresses, and symposia around the world. She is the author of several books, of which the best-known is *Dracula: Sense & Nonsense* (2000), which discusses errors in other books about Stoker and *Dracula*. *Dracula: Sense and Nonsense* received the 2000 Children of the Night Award for best book from the DRACULA SOCIETY in England.

Miller founded the Canadian chapter of the Romanian-based TRANSYLVANIAN SOCIETY OF DRACULA, which made her a baroness in 1995 at the World Dracula Conference in Romania. She is editor of the annual *Journal of Dracula Studies*, the only scholarly journal of its kind, which she founded in 1999. She has served as president of the Lord Ruthven Assembly, a scholarly organization interested in vampires. She was among the organizers of Dracula 97: A Centennial Celebration, held in Los Angeles, which commemorated the 100th anniversary of the publication of *Dracula*.

Miller's *Dracula*-related interests extend to vampires in folklore, literature in general, and popular culture. She does not believe in supernatural vampires or other supernatural creatures.

Miller's other books are

Reflections on Dracula: Ten Essays (1997), a collection of essays, with a contribution from another scholarly expert, Margaret L. Carter.

Dracula: The Shade and the Shadow (1998), an anthology edited by Miller of papers presented at Dracula 97.

Dracula (2001), a coffee table book published in English, German, and French.

A Dracula Handbook, published in English and Romanian.

FURTHER READING:
Elizabeth Miller's Dracula's Homepage Web site. URL: http://www.ucs.mun.ca/~emiller/miller.htm.
Miller, Elizabeth. *Reflections in Dracula: Ten Essays*. White Rock, B.C.: Transylvania Press, Inc., 1997.
———. *Dracula: Sense & Nonsense*. Westcliff-on-Sea, England: Desert Island Books, 2000.
———. *Dracula*. New York: Parkstone Press, 2001.
Miller, Elizabeth, ed. *Dracula: The Shade and the Shadow*. Westcliff-on-Sea, Essex, England: Desert Island Books, 1998.

Miller, Linda Lael   See ARTS AND ENTERTAINMENT.

millet   See SEEDS.

mills   In Balkan Slavic lore, a favorite abode of VAMPIRES and other evil spirits. A GYPSY folktale tells of a rich man who owned a mill that was infested with a vampire. The vampire kept eating his men, making one disappear each night. The mill owner had a difficult time finding people to work for him, despite his willingness to pay good wages.

Finally, a man came to him and asked to be paid "as much as a man's head is worth," and he would sleep in the mill. The rich man agreed. The man went to the mill and placed a wooden trunk on his bed and covered it up to look like a sleeping man. He hid in the attic to wait for the vampire.

The vampire arrived. He had a long beard like a clergyman. When he discovered the trunk, he lamented that he would have to remain hungry. He stayed until the COCK crowed at dawn, and then left. The man followed the vampire to discover its hiding place. Then he went to the mill owner, told him everything, and immediately died of fright. The mill owner had the vampire pierced through his forehead, and the vampire never appeared again.

FURTHER READING:
Vukanovic, Professor T. P. "The Vampire," in *The Vampire of the Slavs* by Jan L. Perkowski. Cambridge, Mass.: Slavica Publishers, 1976.

mirrors   In folklore, a soul stealer. A widespread folk belief calls for turning over the mirrors in a house when someone dies. If dead people sees themselves in a mirror, their souls will become lost or have no rest, or they will become vampires.

The power of mirrors to suck out souls is illustrated in the Greek myth of Narcissus, who sees his reflection in water and then pines and dies.

In Russian folklore, mirrors are the invention of the devil because they have the power to draw souls out of bodies. In other lore, seeing a CORPSE reflected in a mirror puts the living at risk for having one's soul carried off by the ghost of the dead. Seeing one's own reflection in a mirror in a room where someone has died means one's own impending death.

Folklore also holds that mirrors should be removed from a sickroom because the soul is more vulnerable in times of illness. It is considered unlucky for the sick to see their reflections, which puts them at risk of dying.

It is also considered unlucky to look into a mirror at night or by candlelight, for one will see ghosts, the devil, or a portent of one's own death. In Persian lore, ghosts may be seen in a mirror by standing in front of it and combing the hair without thinking, speaking, or moving.

Breaking a mirror is bad luck, for it damages the soul.

Mirrors and Vampires

The inability of VAMPIRES to cast a reflection in mirrors, and their desire to avoid them, is an invention of fiction. BRAM STOKER's vampire, COUNT DRACULA, avoids mirrors, calling them objects of human vanity. Jonathan Harker notices that there are no mirrors in the count's castle, and he accidentally observes that Dracula casts no reflection in his mirror while he shaves. The count, seeing Harker watching, breaks the mirror. Later in Stoker's novel, PROFESSOR ABRAHAM VAN HELSING forces unpleasant confrontation with the count by shoving a mirror in front of him; the vampire recoils violently.

Stoker was aware of superstitions about mirrors and adapted them to suit his fictional purposes. Dracula, as a soulless creature, also casts no SHADOW and cannot be painted or photographed; his likeness cannot be captured.

Dracula (Richard Roxburgh) casts no reflection in Van Helsing *(2004).* (Author's collection)

Stoker's fictional mirror lore dominated vampire fiction and film until the publications of ANNE RICE's influential vampire novels in the 1970s. Rice maintains that vampires must live in the same world as mortals, which means having reflections. Otherwise, in a modern world full of reflective surfaces, it would be difficult for vampires to remain unnoticed.

FURTHER READING:

Guiley, Rosemary Ellen. *Harper's Encyclopedia of Mystical and Paranormal Experience.* San Francisco: Harper San Francisco, 1991.

Opie, Iona, and Moira Tatem. *A Dictionary of Superstitions.* Oxford, U.K.: Oxford University Press, 1989.

Wolf, Leonard. *The Annotated Dracula.* New York: Clarkson N. Potter, 1975.

Miss Penelose   See "THE PARASITE."

mmbyu   In Indian lore, a VAMPIRE who frequents places where people have been executed. The *mmbyu* is attended by a retinue of demon servants.

moon   Ruling force of nature over WEREWOLVES and malevolent supernatural creatures of the night. The moon governs the night; thus, creatures of the night, including supernatural entities such as ghosts, demons, spirits, fairies, VAMPIRES, GHOULS, and the like, are the moon's children, thriving beneath its rays. Since ancient times, the moon has been associated with illusion and baleful, negative influences.

Insanity and the Moon

According to lore, the rays of the moon can induce seizures and insanity, giving rise to the terms *lunacy* and *moonstruck*. The 16th-century physician Paracelsus said that the moon had the "power to tear reason out of man's head by depriving him of humors and cerebral virtues." The moon, he added, was at its most powerful influence when it was full.

The Catholic Church attacked beliefs in the moon's power, but said that the real cause of madness was the devil acting on the moon. During the Inquisition of the late Middle Ages and Renaissance, church inquisitors allowed that celestial bodies could influence devils, who would in turn harass human beings. The *Malleus Maleficarum* (1486), the dominant inquisitors' handbook written by two Dominicans, Heinrich Kramer and James Sprenger, stated, "The stars can influence the devils themselves. [As proof of this] certain men who are called lunatics are molested by devils more at one time than at another; and the devils . . . would rather molest them at all times, unless they themselves were deeply affected by certain phases of the Moon."

Links between moon and madness took root in English law. Sir William Hale, who became chief justice of England, wrote in the 1600s, "The moon hath a great influence in all diseases of the brain . . . especially dementia; such persons commonly in the full and change of the moon, especially about the equinoxes and summer solstice, are usually at the height of their distemper."

The 18th-century English jurist Sir William Blackstone described a lunatic as someone who would "lose" or "enjoy" his reason, "depending on the changes of the moon." The British Lunacy Act of 1842 held that a lunatic was someone who was lucid during the two weeks prior to a full moon but who acted strange during the following 14 days. As late as 1940, an English soldier charged with murdering his comrade pleaded "moon madness" as his defense at Winchester Assizes. He said the madness overcame him each full moon.

Modern science does not support the link between lunar phases and insanity, but in folklore the belief persists.

Epilepsy and the Moon

According to lore, epileptic seizures are brought on and intensified by certain phases of the moon. In Greek mythology, Selene, goddess of the moon, punished those who had sinned against her by afflicting them with epileptic fits. Early medicine helped strengthen the belief in the link between the moon and madness. Roman physicians advanced the notion that the moonlight increased moisture in the air, causing brain seizures. Cures for epilepsy were tied to the moon, such as the plucking of peonies during phases of the moon and the use of powdered soapwort for three months at the time of the new moon. SILVER, because of its pale color, was thought to have a special kinship with the moon, and thus was prescribed in a variety of bizarre treatments, such as swallowing silver filings.

In the 18th century British surgeon Richard Mead stated that new and full moons brought on attacks of epilepsy among naval officers before battle. Medical literature also documented epileptic fits among the general population that occurred during these lunar phases.

Suicides and the Moon

Studies of a possible link between the moon and SUICIDE have various results. One study, conducted from 1964 to 1978 in Buffalo, New York, showed that more suicides took place around a full moon than at any other time. A study of 928 suicides in Cuyahoga County, Ohio, between 1972 and 1975 found that 120 people took their lives at a new moon—a figure about 43 percent higher than at other times of the year.

Other studies have found calls to suicide hotlines increase during different phases of the moon. Over a two-year period, the Suicide Prevention Center in Reno, Nevada, for example, recorded more calls for help when the moon was new or at the first quarter than at other times.

In separate studies in Melbourne, Australia, and Winnipeg, Canada, researchers found that women were more inclined to take their lives when the moon was at the first quarter.

In Eastern European folklore, suicide victims are doomed to become vampires.

Crime and the Moon

Popular belief holds that crime, accidents, and violence increase during the full moon. Psychologists Arnold Leiber and Carolyn Sherin reviewed 4,000 homicides that occurred between 1956 and 1970 in Miami and Cleveland. After completing the Miami study, Leiber wrote, "The results were astounding. Homicides in Dade County showed a striking correlation to the lunar phase cycle. Homicides peaked at the full moon." They peaked again, said Leiber, after a new moon. "Our results indicated that murders become more frequent with the increase in the moon's gravitational force."

The Cleveland results showed that the peaks in homicides occurred about three days after both the full and new moon. Leiber posited that the lag in the lunar effect was due to the different geographical location. He developed a controversial "biological tide" theory, published in *The Lunar Effect: Biological Tides and Human Emotions* (1978). Lieber stated that hormonal activity in the brain is affected by the gravitational pull of the sun and moon. Like the tides that occur at different times in different locations, so do people respond at different times to the effect of "biological tides." The biological high tides do not cause strange behavior, but makes it more likely to happen.

In subsequent years, other researchers have collected more evidence that ties violent human behavior to lunar phases. One of the most notorious murderers of the 20th century, New York's Son of Sam, killed five of his eight victims on nights when the moon was full or new.

Leiber's biological tide theory was attacked by many scientists who said that the studies were flawed. It was also pointed out that the moon's greatest gravitational influence is when it is closest to earth. By contrast, when the moon is full or new it is actually farthest away from the earth.

Werewolves and the Moon

The most fearsome supernatural creature, and the one most influenced by the moon, is the werewolf, a cursed human who undergoes a type of moon madness every month at the full of the moon, SHAPE-SHIFTING from human form to wolf form and going on a rampage of death and destruction. Not all werewolf lore is linked to the moon, but from ancient to modern times, there have been many cases of people who believed that they did in fact turn into wolves when the moon was full. Medical science describes this condition as LYCANTHROPY.

A modern case of lycanthropy concerns a "Mr. W.," documented in 1975 in the *Canadian Psychiatric Association Journal*. The subject was a 37-year-old Appalachian farmer. Shortly after his discharge from the U.S. Navy, Mr. W. began to show little interest in his farm chores or other any daily activities. He let his facial hair grow, making believe that it was fur. He slept in CEMETERIES and occasionally he would lie down on highways in front of approaching traffic. He howled at the moon. Mr. W.'s own explanation for his erratic behavior was that he had been transformed into a werewolf.

He was admitted to a psychiatric hospital, where doctors found that he was suffering from a chronic brain syndrome of undetermined origin, resulting in chronic undifferentiated schizophrenia. But doctors also concluded that the occurrence of his psychosis during the full moon—his moon madness—remained unexplained on an organic level.

Vampires and the Moon

The vampire has lunar associations both through eclipses and the werewolf in Slavic folklore: the *VUKODLAK* ("wolf's hair") is a Slavic vampire. The *VARCOLAC* is a Romanian eclipse demon associated with vampires, and which often takes the shape of a dog. In European lore, some vampires are believed to be able to shape-shift into wolves. According to one Eastern European superstition, werewolves become vampires when they die.

In Romanian lore, VAMPIRE SORCERERS AND WITCHES have their greatest power when the moon is full and are at their weakest when the moon is new. Other lore found throughout Eastern Europe holds that vampires who rise from the grave are weakest during the day and strongest at night (when, by inference, they are under the influence of the moon).

The first vampire story published in English, THE VAMPYRE by JOHN POLIDORI (1819), portrays the folklore belief in the supernatural relationship between vampires and the moon: The rays of the moon enable the vampire to resurrect himself.

BRAM STOKER borrowed upon folklore about the moon, vampires, and werewolves when he wrote his classic thriller, *DRACULA*, published in 1897. COUNT DRACULA has the power to shape-shift into BATS and wolves, and to command both animals and humans. Perhaps because of *Dracula* and other vampire popular fiction and films, it is thought by many that VAMPIRE BATS prefer to hunt on nights of the full moon. The opposite is the case, however. Vampire bats prefer to hunt when the light of the moon is absent or low, and thus cannot reveal their presence to their victims, usually animals.

Dracula and the Moon

Stoker made artful use of the moon as a backdrop to chilling action. His moonlit scenes in *Dracula* set a standard for vampire stories in both fiction and film: The moon is full, somewhere a wolf howls, and the vampire stalks its prey.

Dracula begins with the journey of British legal clerk Jonathan Harker to TRANSYLVANIA to arrange for Count Dracula (whom he does not know is a vampire) to purchase an estate in London. He travels by coach at night through the Carpathian Mountains to Dracula's castle. Along the way, Harker is spooked by natives who warn him not to travel at night. At the BORGO PASS, he leaves his coach and transfers to a coach sent for him by the count. Harker, in his diary, describes the harrowing, moonlit final leg of the journey:

At last there came a time when the driver went further afield than he had yet gone, and during his absence the horses began to tremble worse than ever and to snort and scream with fright. I could not see any cause for it, for the howling of the wolves had ceased altogether; but just then the moon, sailing through the black clouds, appeared behind the jagged crest of a beetling, pine-clad rock, and by its light I saw around us a ring of wolves, with white teeth and lolling red tongues, with long, sinewey limbs and shaggy hair. They were a hundred times more terrible in the grim silence which held them than even when they howled. For myself, I felt a sort of paralysis of fear. It is only when a man feels himself face to face with such horrors that he can understand their true import.

All at once the wolves began to howl as though the moonlight had had some peculiar effect on them. The horses jumped around and reared, and looked helplessly round with eyes that rolled in a painful way to see; but the living ring of terror encompassed them on every side, and they had perforce to remain with it. I called to the coachman to come, for it seemed to me that the only chance was to try to break out through the ring and to aid his approach. I shouted and beat the side of the caleche, hoping by the noise to scare the wolves from that side, so as to give him a chance of reaching the trap. How he came there, I know not, but I heard his voice raised in a tone of imperious command, and looking towards the sound, saw him stand in the roadway. As he swept his long arms, as though brushing aside some impalpable obstacle, the wolves fell back and back further still. Just then a heavy cloud passed across the face of the moon, so that we were again in darkness.

When I could see again the driver was climbing into the caleche, and the wolves had disappeared. This was all so strange and uncanny that a dreadful fear came upon me, and I was afraid to speak or move. The time seemed interminable as we swept on our way, now in almost complete darkness, for the rolling clouds obscured the moon.

We kept on ascending, with occasional periods of quick descent, but in the main always ascending. Suddenly I became conscious of the fact that the driver was in the act of pulling up the horses in the courtyard of a vast ruined castle, from whose tall black windows came no ray of light, and whose broken battlements allowed a jagged line against the moonlit sky.

At the castle, Harker meets the mysterious and ugly count, whose hairy palms are wolfish in appearance. It isn't long before the young clerk realizes he has become a prisoner of the castle. Strange things happen at night beneath the baleful rays of the moon. One night, Harker looks out from the window of his room and, to his horror, spies the count emerging from a window below and creeping like a lizard down the wall of the castle. "I thought it was some trick of the moonlight, some weird effect of shadow; but I kept looking and it could be no delusion," Harker writes in his diary.

The next night, Harker awakens to see brilliant moonlight streaming into his room. Framed in the light are three beautiful young women. He notices that though the moon is behind them, they cast no shadows on the floor. They have voluptuous red lips and their white teeth shine in the moonlight. The women are the count's vampire consorts, and they have come to drink Harker's BLOOD. But before they can do so, the count enters and forbids them to touch Harker.

Harker's nightmare imprisonment continues as he learns more about the count and the vampire women. He realizes that at some point the count intends to kill him, and his nights are filled with terror. One night Harker sits by his window, and suddenly notices little specks floating in the rays of the moonlight. They seem to be dust, and they whirl and collect in small shapes around him. In the valley below the castle, dogs begin to howl, and the howling seems to make the specks dance faster and take new shapes in the moonbeams, hypnotizing him with their movements.

> Quicker and quicker danced the dust, and the moonbeams seemed to quiver as they went by me into the mass of gloom beyond. More and more they gathered until they seemed to take dim phantom shapes. And then I started, broad awake and in full possession of my senses, and ran screaming from the place. The phantom shapes, which were becoming gradually materialized from the moonbeams, were those of the three ghostly women to whom I was doomed. I fled, and felt somewhat safer in my own room, where there was no moonlight and where the lamp was burning brightly.

Harker escapes the castle and returns to England. The count and his women travel by ship to England. Time and time again, Stoker uses the moon to create a half-lit, eerie world where fears take shape and the unthinkable becomes real. Mina Murray, Harker's fiancée and then bride, sees moonlight frame a great BAT wheeling across the sky. The moon shines high in the sky the night the wolf BERSICKER (Berserker) goes howling mad in the Zoological Gardens and escapes. Moonlight graces the sleeping faces of the count's victims and lights the cemetery where LUCY WESTENRA, Mina's friend and a victim-turned-vampire, stalks her own prey.

But when the count meets his grisly end by being stabbed, the action takes place in the dying rays of the sun.

FURTHER READING:

Guiley, Rosemary Ellen. *Moonscapes: A Celebration of Lunar Astronomy, Magic, Legend and Lore.* Englewood Cliffs, N.J.: Prentice-Hall, 1991.
Katzeff, Paul. *Full Moons.* Secaucus, N.J.: Citadel Press, 1981.

mora   A troublesome spirit universal in origin; its association with VAMPIRES is controversial among scholars. In Slavic lore, the *mora* behaves like the OLD HAG, causing nightmares and a wasting away of energy. If a *mora* falls in love with a victim, she drinks his BLOOD; otherwise she causes nightmares. In *Slavic Mythology,* Jan Machal states:

> It is the general belief that souls may pass into a Mora, a living being, either man or woman, whose soul goes out of the body at night-time, leaving it as if dead. Sometimes two souls are believed to be in such a body, one of which leaves it when asleep . . . The Mora, assuming various shapes, approaches the dwellings of men at night and tries to suffocate them . . . First she sends refreshing slumber to men and then, when they are asleep, she frightens them with terrible dreams, chokes them, and sucks their blood.

In some Slavic lore, a man can be a *mora;* if so, he has black, bushy EYEBROWS that meet.

Among the KASHUBS of Ontario, the *mora* has strong associations with the vampire. The *mora* is the wandering spirit of a dead or sleeping girl who has not been properly baptized. The spirit tries to suffocate its victims. If the victim awakens and tries to grab it, it materializes as an apple, a ball of wool, or a mass of hair, and then disappears. Protective measures against the *mora* call for swearing at it, filling the keyhole of the bedroom door—its point of entry—with wax, and pointing one's shoes away from the bed.

See also PROTECTION AGAINST VAMPIRES.

FURTHER READING:

Perkowski, Jan L. *The Darkling: A Treatise on Slavic Vampirism.* Columbus, Ohio: Slavica Publishers, 1989.

moroi   A Romanian VAMPIRE that is the returning dead. *Moroi* is used less often to describe vampires than the more prevalent term *STRIGOI. Moroi* may have entered Romanian through Slavic; it is found in MORA, the term for a female nightmare demon.

The *moroi* can shape-shift (see SHAPE-SHIFTING) into the forms of a man, dog, CAT, horse, sheep, toad, or any BLOOD-sucking insect. The *moroi* will kill cattle by drinking their blood, and will feed on his own relatives—preferably eating their hearts—trying to draw them into the grave.

When discovered in its grave, the *moroi* has long, freshly grown nails and blood streaming from its eyes, nose, ears, and mouth.

The *moroi* can be prevented by various remedies:

- Relatives who attend the burial should walk around the grave three times, and one of them should carry the candle last used by the deceased.
- Resin should be burned twice a week on Tuesday and SATURDAY nights.
- All of the clothes of the *moroi* should be burned.
- If the corpse of a suspected *moroi* is RED and ruddy, it should be stabbed in the heart with a needle, pin, or nail.

See also BURIAL CUSTOMS.

FURTHER READING:
Perkowski, Jan Lewis. "The Roumanian Folkloric Vampire," in *The Vampire: A Casebook*, Alan Dundes, ed. Madison: University of Wisconsin Press, 1998.

Morris, Quincey   See *DRACULA*.

moth   See BUTTERFLY.

Mothman   Mysterious human-like creature with bat wings that terrorized West Virginia in the mid-1960s. Sightings and activity were at a peak from 1966 to 1967 but continue to be reported today.

Mothman activity has indirect vampiric associations. No BLOOD-drinking attacks have been reported, but there was one incident in 1967 in which a UFO exhibited an intense interest in a Red Cross bloodmobile.

Sightings of Mothman began abruptly in mid-November 1966. On November 12, five men preparing a gravesite for a burial near Clendenin saw something that looked like a brown man with wings lift-off from the trees nearby. On November 14, glowing red eyes were reported in Salem, West Virginia. On the night of November 15, two married couples were driving late at night near Point Pleasant and reached on old abandoned TNT plant. They saw that the door to the plant seemed to have been ripped off its hinges. They saw a huge man-creature six to seven feet tall with hypnotic red eyes and wings folded on its back. Terrified, they sped off in their car. But the creature took flight and was able to keep up with them, even though they were traveling nearly 100 miles an hour. The creature suddenly broke off its pursuit and vanished.

With that, a rash of bizarre phenomena began, as well as numerous sightings of the creature, which was dubbed Mothman, after the cartoon character Batman.

Stainless steel Mothman unveiled at the 2003 Mothman Festival in Point Pleasant, West Virginia. Sculpture by Bob Roach of New Haven, West Virginia. Photo by Bruce Haines. (Courtesy Bruce Haines and the Pennsylvania Paranormal Society)

According to some early sightings, Mothman did not seem to have a head, but had eyes set near the tops of its shoulders. Some witnesses recalled seeing a head, but one without features. Some said the wings were not feathered, while others said the wings had small patches of feathers. Mothman shuffled on human-like legs and made a strange, high-pitched squeaking noise. The entity could take off straight up into the air without moving its wings. It flew as though gliding, without flapping its wings.

The creature chased cars driving near the Chief Cornstalk Hunting Grounds, the location of an abandoned World War II ammunition dump. Local wildlife authorities opined that people were seeing an owl or a sandhill crane, but witnesses insisted their descriptions were true.

Other mysterious phenomena included UFO activity, electrical and telephone disturbances, poltergeist phenomena, phantom dogs, other mysterious creatures, phantom people, and sinister "men in black," who are dark, cadaverous, mechanical-like men who harass UFO contactees and threaten them to keep silent. Numerous dogs disappeared and wild animals were found mutilated—activity that was linked to Mothman, though no one ever caught the creature in the act.

The supernatural activity attracted the attention of John A. Keel, a leading authority on UFOs and anomalies.

Keel traveled to West Virginia to investigate. According to Keel, at least 100 persons had sightings of Mothman. In his book *The Mothman Prophecies* (1975), Keel gives his first-person report of a bizarre incident where a UFO chases down a Red Cross bloodmobile loaded with blood:

> On the night of March 5 [1967], a Red Cross Bloodmobile was traveling along Route 2, which runs parallel to the Ohio River. Beau Shertzer, twenty-one, and a young nurse had been out all day collecting human blood and now they were heading back to Huntington, West Virginia, with a van filled with fresh blood. The road was dark and cold and there was very little traffic. As they moved along a particularly deserted stretch, there was a flash in the woods on a nearby hill and a large white glow appeared. It rose slowly into the air and flew straight for their vehicle.
>
> "My God! What is it?" the nurse cried.
>
> "I'm not going to stick around to find out," Shertzer answered, pushing his foot down on the gas.
>
> The object effortlessly swooped over the van and stayed with it. Shertzer rolled down his window and looked up. He was horrified to see some kind of arm or extension being lowered from the luminous thing cruising only a few feet above the Bloodmobile.
>
> "It's trying to get us!" the nurse yelled, watching another arm reach down her side. It looked as if the flying object was trying to wrap a pincers-like device around the vehicle. Shertzer poured on the horses but the object kept pace with them easily. Apparently they were saved by the sudden appearance of headlights from approaching traffic. As the other cars neared, the object retracted its arms and hastily flew off.
>
> Both young people rushed to the police in a state of hysteria. The incident was mentioned briefly on a radio newscast that night but was not picked up by the newspapers.
>
> In cases like this we have to ask: Did the UFO really intend to carry off the Bloodmobile? Or was it all a sham to "prove" the UFOs interest in blood. Later I tried to check to find out if any Bloodmobiles had actually vanished anywhere. The Red Cross thought I was a bit nuts.
>
> But I often found myself seriously wondering if we only hear about the people who get away!

The sightings and bizarre phenomena continued into 1967, but began to wane toward the end of the year. On December 15, 1967, a tragedy took place: the 700-foot Silver Bridge that crossed the Ohio River at Point Pleasant collapsed around 5 P.M., sending dozens of vehicles into the river. Forty-six people were killed; two bodies were never recovered. In addition, strange lights were seen in the sky, and people reported encounters with mysterious men. People linked the bridge collapse to Mothman, though no direct evidence ever could be found.

Keel opined that Point Pleasant was a "window" area, a place for periods of time another reality can bleed through to ours, where it, manifests as supernatural phenomena. Explanations put forward by others are toxic chemical spills or chemical experiments by companies or the military; a 200-year-old Native American curse on the town of Point Pleasant; a mutant strain of the sandhill crane; a creature summoned by occult ritual.

The curse is attributed to a Shawnee warrior chief, Cornstalk, whose forces were defeated in 1774 in an ambush by Virginia militiamen. According to lore, as Cornstalk lay dying he cursed the area for 200 years.

The description of Mothman is similar to other human-like, bat-winged creatures reported elsewhere, such as the COVENTRY STREET VAMPIRE.

In 2001, Sony Pictures released *The Mothman Prophecies,* based on Keel's book, starring Richard Gere as John Klein, based on Keel himself.

An annual Mothman Festival was started in 2002 in Point Pleasant.

See also EXTRATERRESTRIALS.

FURTHER READING:

Keel, John A. *The Mothman Prophecies.* New York: E. P. Dutton, 1975.

Taylor, Troy. "Mothman, the enigma of point pleasant." Available online. URL: http://www.prairieghosts.com/moth.html. Downloaded on August 2, 2003.

"The Mothman, the Legend of Point Pleasant, WV: History." Available online. URL: http://www.mothmanlives.com/mothmanhistory.html. Downloaded on April 23, 2004.

mullo   A GYPSY vampire. *Mullo* means the "living dead." *Mullos* are restless spirits of the dead who rise from the grave to avenge their deaths, wreak havoc upon those persons they disliked in life, and indulge in their insatiable sexual appetites. They strangle animals and humans for their BLOOD. They appear in human form, except that they have no bones, but leave them behind in their graves. Some of them have hair so long it touches the ground. Indian Gypsies see vampires with flaming yellow hair, flesh the color of congealed blood, and tusklike fangs.

Mullos return from the grave to have sex with their spouses, women or men they were never allowed to marry in life, or anyone they choose. They may be invisible to all but their lovers. *Mullos* may ask their lovers to marry them or come to the grave with them. They are so sexually insatiable that their human partners are likely to weaken and become ill from exhaustion. It is possible for a widow to become pregnant by her vampire husband. Among the Slavic Gypsies, the resulting child—which can only be male—is called a DHAMPIR.

Mullos can be destroyed in a variety of ways, according to lore. One can shout a Romanian curse, "God send you burst!" The vampire will oblige and will explode, leaving behind a puddle of blood. The vampire also can be struck in the stomach with an IRON needle or doused with holy WATER. It can be shot or knifed, preferably by a *dhampir.* It can be destroyed by black dogs, black COCKS, or white wolves. If the vampire's left sock is in one's possession, the sock can be filled with rocks or earth from the vampire's grave and tossed into running water. The vampire will wander off in search of its sock and will accidentally drown itself. The vampire's body also may be disinterred and staked, mutilated, doused with boiling oil, cut up, or burned.

Despite the Gypsy belief that the dead stay forever in their graves, the threat of a *mullo* is not unending. *Mullos* are believed to have limited lifespans of destruction, from 40 days after burial to three to five years, after which time they will sink back into their graves forever. Taking measures against them prior to their own demise depends upon the extent of their damage to the living.

FURTHER READING:

Trigg, Elwood B. *Gypsy Demons & Divinities*. Secaucus, N.J.: Citadel Press, 1973.

Munsters, The   American sitcom similar to THE ADDAMS FAMILY, about a family of strange supernatural people. *The Munsters* aired from 1964 to 1966 on the Columbia Broadcasting System (CBS).

The Munsters are an immigrant family from TRANSYLVANIA who live at 1313 Mockingbird Lane, a creepy, spider-filled mansion. Family members include Herman (Fred

The cast of The Munsters, *from left: Lilly Munster (Yvonne De Carlo), Grandpa (Al Lewis), Herman Munster (Fred Gwynne), Marilyn Was (Pat Priest), and Edward Wolfgang (Butch Patrick)* (Author's collection)

Gwynne), a Frankenstein-ish man who works at a funeral parlor; Lilly (Yvonne DeCarlo), his homemaker wife and a VAMPIRE; Grandpa (Al Lewis), a 378-year-old mad scientist who is the "real" COUNT DRACULA, quaffing strange potions and caring for a temperamental BAT named Igor; Edward Wolfgang (Butch Patrick), their son and a WEREWOLF; and Marilyn, their "horribly normal" niece, whom the family considers to be unlucky because of her normality. Marilyn was played first by Beverly Owen and then by Pat Priest.

The plots revolve around the family's eccentric habits and strange relatives. The vampire theme received more attention than in *The Addams Family*. The series lasted 70 episodes.

In 1988 MCA resurrected the series with *The Munsters Today*, featuring the same characters but played by different actors. The premise was that Grandpa (Howard Morton) had put the family into a long sleep with one of his potions. Though considered by critics as inferior to the original, the reprise ran for 70 episodes.

FURTHER READING:
Glut, Donald. *The Dracula Book*. Metuchen, N.J.: The Scarecrow Press, 1975.
"The Munsters." Available online. URL: http://timstvshowcase.com/munsters/html. Downloaded on December 27, 2003.
"The Munsters." Available online at TV Tome. URL: http://www.tvome.com/Munsters/ Downloaded on December 27, 2003.

Murnau, F. W. (1888–1931) German film director best-known for his direction of the 1922 silent film NOS-FERATU. Friedrich Wilhelm Murnau is credited with being the "inventor" of the vampire movie. He is regarded as one of the top-three German film directors of the 1920s, along with Fritz Lang and Ernst Lubitsch.

Murnau was born Friedrich Wilhelm Plumpe on December 28, 1888, in Bielefeld, North-Rhine-Westphalia, Germany. He attended the University of Heidelberg, where he studied art and literature history. During World War I, he served as a combat pilot. He was an imposing figure, well over six feet tall, and he was a closet homosexual.

After the war, Murnau entered the film industry, first as an assistant to theatrical producer Max Reinhardt. Reinhardt, a pioneer in the expressionist use of light, shadow, and spectacle, taught techniques to Murnau that he translated into his films, especially through his later pioneering use of the mobile camera. Murnau began making films in 1919 in Germany. His first was *Der Knabe in Blau (Blue Boy)*. Many of Murnau's early films were lost.

He was 32 years old when Prana-Film hired him to direct their only production, *Nosferatu*, a plagiarism of *DRACULA* by BRAM STOKER, starring MAX SCHRECK. Murnau shot *Nosferatu* on location in Wisborg, Germany, in the summer of 1921. He frequently improvised, as the finished product differs substantially from his own annotated script. The final film is a chilling, dream-like exploration of

horror. Stoker's widow, Florence, succeeded in getting a court order to have all copies destroyed, but some survived. Murnau never publicly discussed or commented on the legal tangle of *Nosferatu*.

Murnau directed 21 films during his career. In 1926 he went to work in Hollywood. His final film was *Tabu* (1931), which was censored for its inclusion of partial female nudity.

Murnau was killed in an auto accident in Santa Barbara, California, on March 11, 1931, shortly before the West Coast premiere of TOD BROWNING's authorized film *Dracula*.

Besides *Nosferatu*, two other of Murnau's films are considered masterpieces: *The Last Laugh* (1926), about a proud doorman's decline, and *Faust* (1926), an adaptation of Goethe's literary work.

FURTHER READING:
Maltin, Leonard. *Leonard Maltin's Movie Encyclopedia*. New York: Signet, 1994.
Skal, David J. *Hollywood Gothic: The Tangled Web of* Dracula *from Novel to Stage to Screen*. New York: W. W. Norton & Company, 1990.

murony In the lore of Wallachia, Romania, a SHAPE-SHIFTING VAMPIRE. The *murony* can assume many shapes, including CATS, dogs, mice, and even fleas.

mustard seeds See SEEDS.

mwere A Kashubian night demon who resembles the OLD HAG and MORA, suffocating and choking its victims. The *mwere*, or "succuba," attacks both men and women. It causes sleep disturbances and nightmares. Reportedly, most people in Kashubian society have an experience with a *mwere*.

The *mwere* is said to be the spirit of the unbaptized, especially children or girls who were not baptized before they died. They can come through keyholes and have forms like matted hair or balls of wool. If one awakens and attempts to grab it, it disappears. The *mwere* can be warded off by placing one's shoes beneath the bed with the toes facing out. (See PROTECTION AGAINST VAMPIRES.)

The *mwere* also will attack horses and make them sweat. The sweat materializes into objects and even other *mwere*. One anecdotal account tells of a man's horse who sweated an apple. The man bit the apple; the next day his face was bitten. In *folktales*, the *mwere* travel about on spinning wheels at night.

See also KASHUBS; SUCCUBUS.

Myiciura, Demitrious (d. 1973) Vampire-fearing man whose fear led to his death. Demitrious Myiciura was a

Polish immigrant living in Stoke-on-Trent, England. He had an obsessive fear of VAMPIRES and believed them to live in his neighborhood.

Myiciura sought to "vampire-proof" his room with various folk charms. He placed bowls of SALT and GARLIC mixed with his urine at entry points and outside his windows, stuffed garlic in his keyhole, and sprinkled salt and pepper on everything, including his bedding. He slept with a clove of garlic in his mouth, a bag of salt on the left of his head, and a bag of salt between his legs. One night in 1973 he swallowed the garlic in his sleep and choked to death. The investigating constable consulted *The Natural History of the Vampire* by Anthony Masters.

Myiciura's death was ruled accidental. He was 68 years old and had lived in England for 25 years.

See also PROTECTION AGAINST VAMPIRES.

FURTHER READING:
Perkowski, Jan L. *The Vampire of the Slavs.* Cambridge, Mass.: Slavica Publishers, 1976.

Myslata of Blau (14th c.)   Alleged VAMPIRE of Bohemia, also known as the Blau (Blow) Vampire. Myslata was a herdsman who lived in a village near Kadam, Bohemia. After his death, he appeared in public and called out the names of people he recognized. These people then died mysteriously within a few days.

Myslata's CORPSE was exhumed and staked in the heart. But the vampire appeared in a horrible form that night, suffocating several people to death and frightening others to death. He taunted the villagers and exclaimed that the STAKE would be useful in keeping off dogs. His body was exhumed again and given to an executioner, who pierced it with whitethorn stakes and burned it. The vampire complained and screamed throughout the entire ordeal.

An abbot named Neplach recorded a version of the story in a chronicle dated 1336:

> In Bohemia near Cadanus a league from a village called Blau a certain shepherd called Myslata died. Rising every night he made the rounds of the villages and spoke to people, terrifying and killing them. And while he was being impaled with a stake, he said, "They injured me severely, when they gave me a stick with which to defend myself from dogs." And when he was being exhumed for cremation, he had swelled like an ox and bellowed in a dreadful manner. And when he was placed in the fire, someone, seizing a stake, drove it in him and immediately blood burst forth as from a vessel. Moreover, when he was exhumed and placed on a vehicle, he drew in his feet as if alive, and when he was cremated, all the evil ceased, and before he was cremated, whomever he called by name at night died within eight days.

The case also was recorded in 1706 in *Magia Posthuma* by Charles Ferinand de Schertz.

FURTHER READING:
Perkowski, Jan L. *The Darkling: A Treatise on Slavic Vampirism.* Columbus, Ohio: Slavica Publishers, 1989.

nachzehrer   In Silesia and among the KASHUBS, a VAMPIRE who does not come in direct contact with its victims, but rather attacks them through sympathetic bewitchment. While in the grave, the *nachzehrer* first noisily eats its own clothing and flesh, which causes its nearest relatives to sicken and die. It can leave the grave and go to belfries, where it rings the bell. Whoever hears it will die. The *nachzehrer* also ties cow tails together. It sleeps with its left EYE open and one hand holding the thumb of the other hand.

nagasjatingarong   Indonesian VAMPIRE. In 1975 a *nagas-jatingarong* was blamed for the deaths of five husbands of a 25-year-old woman who lived in South Sumatra. All five husbands died of acute anemia within one month of their marriage to the woman. The woman's concerned parents consulted a local shaman, who determined that the woman was possessed by a *nagasjatingarong,* which had sucked the husbands' BLOOD.

neamma-parusha   In Indian lore, a vampiric spirit who wears a wreath of intestines about its head. The *neamma-parusha* tears the skulls of people and drinks their BLOOD through their brains.

nelapsi   Slovakian VAMPIRE. *Nelapsi* is an obscure term, possibly a local Eastern Slovakian reflex of the original Slavic term for vampire.

The *nelapsi* is able to vampirize and kill entire villages, including the livestock. It falls on its victims, suffocates them, and sucks their BLOOD. It can also kill with a single glance. (See EVIL EYE; MORA.)

The *nelapsi* is able to exist as a vampire because it has two hearts and thus two souls. There are telltale signs that reveal the vampire condition in a CORPSE: if the body has not become stiff, if it has two curls in its hair, if the face has not become pale, and if its eyes are open.

Numerous measures can be taken to prevent the *nelapsi*'s return from the grave. The corpse must be carried headfirst out of the house, and the COFFIN must be struck against the threshold and then placed in a special way in the grave. The corpse must be stabbed in the head or heart with an IRON wedge, a hat pin, or a STAKE made of HAWTHORN, BLACK THORN, or oak. The corpse's clothes, limbs, and hair must be nailed to the coffin. Poppy SEEDS or millet must be poured into the nose and mouth, and also into the coffin, the grave, the ground near the grave, and the road into the CEMETERY. Certain herbs, over which spells are said, are placed in the coffin; Christian objects may also be placed there. After burial, participants must carefully wash their hands, or purify them on a hot stove. (See BURIAL CUSTOMS.)

If these measures fail and the vampire returns from the grave, the corpse is exhumed and the preventative measures are repeated. The *nelapsi* will appear ruddy and will open its eyes, and fresh blood will flow when its heart is pierced.

FURTHER READING:
Perkowski, Jan L. *The Darkling: A Treatise on Slavic Vampirism.* Columbus, Ohio: Slavica Publishers, 1989.

New England Vampires   Cases of alleged VAMPIRES that occurred throughout the New England states in the 18th and 19th centuries, leading people to dig up CORPSES, mutilate them, burn the organs, and consume the ASHES, out of fears that the dead were afflicting the living with tuberculosis.

The cases shared common characteristics. Multiple family deaths had occurred due to consumption, which was blamed on one of the dead. The people involved were influenced by superstitions that if a person died of consumption, the corpse might literally feed on the living—usually family members—and cause the living to literally waste away as the corpse sucked off the nourishment. It was thought that consumption could be cured or prevented by digging up the body, removing the heart and/or other organs, such as the liver, burning them to ash and mixing them in medicine.

These "vampire" cases appeared in all states in New England: Connecticut, Rhode Island, Vermont, New Hampshire, Massachusetts, and Maine. Epidemics of consumption were common in New England in the 17th and 18th centuries; the highly contagious disease often ran through entire families one by one.

The most likely origins of these American beliefs were imported folklore and superstitions from Europe that colonists brought with them to the New World. Belief in the supernatural and magical remedies against it was strong among the New England colonists; illness could be caused by supernatural agents or by witchcraft. Some of the superstitions may have come from England, where European reports of vampires had enjoyed popularity. In addition, accounts of European vampires, including the burning of their corpses, were published in New England newspapers.

By the end of the 19th century, significant changes affected the "vampire" cases. In 1882 the tubercle bacillus was identified, thus advancing public understanding of contagious diseases and their treatments. In addition, there was a greater separation of religion, magic, and superstition. The MERCY BROWN case in 1892 in Exeter, Rhode Island, marked the last great vampire case of New England.

Rhode Island folklorist Michael E. Bell researched more than a dozen of these "vampire" cases. One—NELLIE VAUGHN—appears to be fictitious.

See also RACHEL HARRIS; FREDERICK RANSOM; RAY FAMILY VAMPIRES; ROSE FAMILY VAMPIRE; SPAULDING FAMILY VAMPIRES; SARAH TILLINGHAST; WALTON FAMILY CEMETERY; WOODSTOCK VAMPIRE; NANCY YOUNG.

FURTHER READING:
Bell, Michael E. *Food for the Dead: On the Trail of New England's Vampires.* New York: Carroll & Graf, 2001.

newlyweds   In Romanian lore, newlyweds are at special risk of being attacked by VAMPIRES, who will render them impotent or sterile. Preventive measures call for sprinkling the marital sheets with holy WATER, or sprinkling poppy SEEDS in front of a doorway, or leaving a tangled ball of yarn on a threshold. Holy water repels everything evil, and vampires must count seeds and untangle yarn before proceeding across a doorway.

See also LILITH.

nightmare   See OLD HAG.

Night of Dark Shadows   See DARK SHADOWS.

nosferatu   Mistaken term for "vampire" or "undead." *Nosferatu* has entered popular vampire lore via BRAM STOKER in *DRACULA* (1897) and F. W. MURNAU's film adaptation of his novel, *NOSFERATU* (1922). It has been described as a Romanian word for VAMPIRES, but *nosferatu* is not Romanian, nor is it found elsewhere in Eastern Europe.

Stoker apparently picked up the word from an article that was among his sources for *Dracula*: "Transylvania Superstitions" (1885) by Mme. EMILY DE LASZOWSKI GERARD. "More decidedly evil, however, is the vampire, or *nosferatu*, in whom every Roumenian [sic] peasant believes as firmly as he does in heaven or hell," Gerard wrote.

It is probable that Gerard garbled a term she heard during the time she spent living in TRANSYLVANIA. Some of the possibilities that have been put forward by contemporary researchers are these terms:

- *necuratul:* a Romanian term meaning "the Evil one"; "demon"; "the devil" or "diavol"
- *nesuferit:* a Romanian term meaning "unbearable"
- *nosophoros:* a Greek term meaning "plague carrier"

Stoker uses the term *nosferatu* twice in *Dracula*, both in the words of PROFESSOR ABRAHAM VAN HELSING, the vampire expert. The first reference is in Chapter 16, when Van Helsing explains to Arthur Holmwood about the Un-Dead, or "*nosferatu*, as they call it in Eastern Europe." The second reference is in Chapter 18, where Van Helsing makes his long and famous speech about the powers of vampires: "The *nosferatu* do not die like the bee when he sting once," he says, and he goes on to list the vampire's characteristics. (See COUNT DRACULA.)

Nosferatu might have sunk into obscurity as a term for vampire had it not been for Murnau's use of it as the title of his film. Denied film rights by Stoker's widow, he proceeded with an unauthorized version of *Dracula*, and therefore could not use Stoker's title. His film and its 1979 remake by Werner Herzog cemented *nosferatu* in the lexicon of popular vampire lore.

FURTHER READING:

Melton, J. Gordon. *The Vampire Book: the Encyclopedia of the Undead.* Rev. ed. Detroit: Visible Ink Press/Gale Research, 1999.

Miller, Elizabeth. *Dracula: Sense & Nonsense.* Westcliff-on-Sea, England: Desert Island Books, 2000.

Nosferatu   One of the most famous and acclaimed of VAMPIRE films, released in 1922 by the German company Prana-Film, directed by F. W. MURNAU and starring MAX SCHRECK as the vampire.

A silent film, *Nosferatu* tells the story of DRACULA with some variations. Scriptwriter Henrik Galeen changed the title, setting, and names of the principal characters, but it was still deemed a plagiarism of the novel by BRAM STOKER, and a court ordered all copies of it destroyed. Stoker's widow, Florence, relentlessly hunted down the copies, but did not succeed in seeing them all destroyed.

The expressionist film bears strong resemblances to elements in *The Golem* (1914 and 1920) and *The Cabinet of Dr. Caligari* (1919); it employs shadow, the occult, distortion, and extreme metaphor to explore an inner landscape. Unlike many of the vampire films made by others at later dates, *Nosferatu* is genuinely frightening. The full title of the film is *Nosferatu, Eine Symphonie des Grauens* (*Nosferatu, a Symphony of Horrors*).

Nosferatu is an adaptation of *Dracula,* using the main plot elements but changing names, locales, and other details. The vampire, GRAF ORLOCK, is more predatory monster than seductive human; he is a walking horror without a shred of attraction. The action is set in Bremen, Germany, instead of London, in the year 1838 (instead of 1893), a year of rampant plagues in that part of Germany. Waldemar Hutter, played by Gustav von Wangenheim, and his wife, Ellen, played by Greta Schroeder-Matray—Murnau's versions of Jonathan Harker and Mina Harker—are newlyweds and very happy. Ellen has a sympathetic, clairvoyant link with her husband, and frets about his safety when he goes away to visit the graf at the behest of his strange employer, Knock.

En route to the graf's castle, Hutter spends a night in a GYPSY inn and obtains a book about vampire superstitions. His business with the graf is real estate—Orlock intends to buy a house next to Hutter's home. Hutter delivers to Orlock a letter from Knock inscribed with strange symbols. The symbols are real ones from astrology and the Kabbalah. The detail is interesting, for Prana-Film cofounder Albin Grau was knowledgeable about occultism.

Hutter is uneasy around the graf. In addition to his creepy appearance, Orlock becomes visibly excited by the sight of Hutter's BLOOD when Hutter accidentally cuts himself. Orlock also shows a fascination for Ellen: When Hutter shows Orlock a portrait of her he says, "Is this your wife? What a lovely throat."

Hutter's unease is well founded. During the night, Hutter is attacked by the vampire in his bedroom. He tries to

Graf Orlock (Klaus Kinski) in Werner Herzog's remake of Nosferatu *(Author's collection)*

hide in his bed. Back home, his sleeping wife cries out his name, disturbing Orlock and causing him to withdraw.

The next day, Hutter discovers the graf sleeping in a rotting COFFIN in a crypt in the castle. He flees and watches horrified as Orlock awakens and loads a wagon for transporting his coffin-boxes of earth to Bremen via ship.

On board, Orlock stalks the crew. In one eerie scene, he rises up out of the ship's hold with a live white RAT on his arm. When the derelict ship arrives in the harbor, it releases a horde of plague-bearing rats into the city. The scene is one of the most chilling in the horror film genre.

Orlock becomes increasingly ratlike in appearance throughout the movie, sporting long, fanglike front teeth and long, clawlike fingernails. There is nothing erotic or seductive about him—he is pure horror, and he is unleashed upon the city.

Ellen reads the book of vampire superstitions brought home by Hutter. She learns that the vampire can be defeated only if a virtuous woman willingly allows him to spend an entire night with her, staying until dawn. She knowingly sacrifices herself to him in order to save the city.

Orlock spends a night with her, feasting on her blood. At dawn he is struck by the rays of the sun and dies by disintegration. Alas, Ellen lost too much blood, and dies.

Nosferatu was an ambitious first film for Prana-Film, founded in 1921, but it became the only film produced by the company. Prana-Film spent more money on promotion than on production, and mismanaged its money. Despite a good reception of the film in Germany and a few places elsewhere in Europe, *Nosferatu* had limited showings, and Prana-Film went into receivership.

Florence Stoker learned about the film shortly after its release when publicity materials were sent to her from Berlin. She was in dire financial straits and heavily dependent upon the meager income from *Dracula.* She had not yet attempted to sell film rights. Clearly *Nosferatu* was a copyright violation despite its cosmetic alterations. She immediately joined the British Incorporated Society of Authors and appealed to them for legal help.

Graf Orlock (Max Schreck) commands the rats in F. W. Murnau's Nosferatu. *(Author's collection)*

The society reluctantly responded, knowing the only reason why Stoker joined was to ask for their help. In addition, Prana-Film was already in receivership, and collecting any damages would be exceedingly difficult. A strong woman, Stoker nonetheless kept prodding the society to pursue the matter. Meanwhile, the receiver of Prana-Film's assets brazenly showed the film in other countries in Europe.

In March 1924 Stoker's case finally was heard by a German court. Stoker was asking the receiver for £5,000 in exchange for title to the film. The court ruled against the receiver, who decided to appeal. In February 1925 an appellate court upheld the verdict, but that, too, was subject to appeal.

Since money seemed unlikely, Stoker switched her tactics and pressed for destruction of all copies of the film, which she had never seen. In July 1925 the receiver agreed and also paid Stoker's legal fees for a German lawyer. The court ordered the destruction of the negative and prints, but never required any proof.

Stoker's peace of mind was short-lived. In October 1925 she discovered that a new organization in England, the Film Society, was planning a private screening of *Nosferatu* for its members. Adding insult to injury, the promotional literature credited *Dracula* to F. W. Murnau. Stoker once more appealed to the society of authors for help, and the society took up her cause again. The Film Society resisted, claiming that because they were a private organization that offered only private, not public, screenings, there was no copyright violation.

The authors' society tried to find the individual who had imported the film to England, but was unsuccessful. The man had tried to sell it to various theaters in London but could not, and so had offered it to the Film Society for free.

But the problems with *Nosferatu* did not end there. In 1928 the Film Society proceeded with a private screening of the film, claiming they had been given permission to do so by Universal Pictures, which had purchased the film rights. This was not true; Universal had leaked a false press release. Stoker threatened to sue.

In 1929 the Film Society turned its print of *Nosferatu* over to Stoker for destruction. But her attempts to legitimately sell film rights in Hollywood were jeopardized once again by the surfacing of new versions of *Nosferatu* in America. *Nosferatu the Vampire* had characters with yet different names, and was credited as being "inspired" by *Dracula*. The film was shown in New York City and Detroit. Reviews were lackluster. Most critics called it boring and soporific, a film that literally put its tiny audiences to sleep (critics in London had been equally negative).

In 1930 Universal legitimately purchased the film rights to *Dracula*, and obtained prints of *Nosferatu* for destruction. But *Nosferatu* refused to die, and, like the vampire of folklore who reanimates from the dead, it kept reappearing.

After Stoker's death in 1937, *Nosferatu* circulated more freely, although there was little interest in it. Critical acclaim for it was not forthcoming until after World War II. The film was "rediscovered" in condensed form for television in the 1960s and was re-released as a collector's film in 1972, under the title *Nosferatu the Vampire*.

Film critics and Dracula enthusiasts today are grateful that *Nosferatu* survived, for its artistic merit as an expressionist film and its contribution to the horror genre.

In 1979 Murnau's classic was remade by director Werner Herzog as *Nosferatu: Phantom der Nacht (Nosferatu: Phantom of the Night)*. Herzog wrote the script and produced the film as an homage to Murnau. Klaus Kinski is the vampire, and Isabelle Adjani is Lucy Harker (replacing the character of Ellen). The remake acknowledges *Dracula* as its source more than the Murnau film, but the new version compared poorly to the silent *Nosferatu* in the eyes of film critics, who disliked its ponderous tempo and less sinister vampire.

Nosferatu inspired several COMICS in the 1990s.

Graf Orlock is the first fictional vampire to die by exposure to SUNLIGHT—Stoker's COUNT DRACULA dies by stabbing. Destruction by sunlight became a much copied element in subsequent vampire films—including the first HAMMER FILMS vampire movie, *HORROR OF DRACULA* (1958), and also *SALEM'S LOT* (1980)—and literature.

FURTHER READING:
Skal, David J. *Hollywood Gothic: The Tangled Web of* Dracula *from Novel to Stage to Screen*. New York: W. W. Norton, 1990.
Silver, Alain, and James Ursini. *The Vampire Film: From* Nosferatu *to* Interview with the Vampire. 3d ed. New York: Limelight Editions, 1997.
Stuart, Roxana. *Stage Blood: Vampires of the 19th-Century Stage*. Bowling Green, Ohio: Bowling Green State University Popular Press, 1994.

nuckelavee   In Scottish lore, a skinless amphibian centaur whose VAMPIRE breath causes things to wither and die. The *nuckelavee* is part of the Fuath fairies, who have tails, manes, and webbed feet but have no noses. The *nuckelavee* has a human upper body on a horselike torso. It is the size of a small human but is several feet wide. Unlike its Fuath relatives, it has a piglike nose and snorts steam. Its one gigantic EYE is always bloodshot.

The breath of the *nuckelavee* sucks out the life force. Crops wither and people and animals die instantly. The *nuckelavee* causes droughts and epidemics, and makes livestock fall off cliffs into the sea. It lays waste at night by land, air, and sea.

The *nuckelavee* is repelled by fresh WATER and rain. Travelers should carry a bottle of water with them to ward off attacks. If pursued by a *nuckelavee*, one should cross a stream of running water; the monster will be unable to follow.

FURTHER READING:
Briggs, Katharine. *An Encyclopedia of Fairies*. New York: Pantheon Books, 1976.
Mack, Carol K., and Dinah Mack. *A Field Guide to Demons, Fairies, Fallen Angels, and Other Subversive Spirits*. New York: Henry Holt/Owl Books, 1998.

obayifo (obayifu)   In Ashanti lore, a vampiric witch, or sometimes a wizard, who sucks the BLOOD of children, causing them to pine and die. The *obayifo* also saps the vitality out of trees and crops, blighting them.

See also VAMPIRE SORCERERS AND WITCHES.

oborot   In Russian lore, a WEREWOLF. *Oborot* means "one transformed."

A person can magically transform himself into an *oborot*. First he must go into a forest and find a tree that has been cut down. He stabs the tree with a copper knife and walks around the tree, repeating an incantation:

> On the sea, on the ocean, on the island, on Bujan,
> On the empty pasture gleams the moon, on an ashstock lying
> In a green wood, in a gloomy vale.
> Toward the stock wandereth a shaggy wolf,
> Horned cattle seeking for his sharp white fangs;
> But the wolf enters not the forest,
> But the wolf dives not into the shadowy vale,
> Moon, moon, gold-horned moon,
> Check the flight of bullets, blunt the hunters' knives,
> Break the shepherds' cudgels,
> Cast wild fear upon all cattle,
> On men, on all creepings things,
> That they may not catch the grey wolf,
> That they may not rend his warm skin!
> My word is binding, more binding than sleep,
> More binding than the promise of a hero!

The person then springs over the tree three times. He will be transformed into a wolf, and can run off into the forest.

FURTHER READING:
Baring-Gould, Sabine. *The Book of Werewolves*. London: Smith, Elder & Co., 1865.

obur   In the lore of the Karachay, a SHAPE-SHIFTING witch or wizard. *Oburs* recognize each other.

Oburs possess the knowledge to make magical OINTMENTS. They take off all their clothing and smear their bodies with ointment, and then wallow in the ASHES on the edge of their fires. They mount brooms with whips in hand, run around the room in circles, and fly up the chimney in the form of cats. They enter the houses of victims via the chimneys after all members of the household have gone to sleep. They drink their BLOOD, especially of the children, and leave a black bruise at the wound. At dawn they return to their own homes, going back down the chimneys. They resume their normal human appearance.

Oburs can shape-shift into wolves and dogs as well. They also drink the blood of livestock that are out in pasture.

See also *TLAHUELPUCHI*; VAMPIRE SORCERERS AND WITCHES.

O'Donnell, Elliott (1872–1965)   Ghost-hunter, actor, and author of more than 50 books on ghosts and related occult lore, including one on WEREWOLVES. Most of Elliott

O'Donnell's books were nonfiction, though he did write occult fiction. Critics have contended that his fiction crept into his nonfiction.

O'Donnell was born in England to a family claiming lineage to famous Irish chieftains, including Niall of the Nine Hostages and Red Hugh, the latter of whom fought fiercely against the English in the 16th century. His family was reputed to have a banshee, a death omen spirit that wails before a member of the family dies.

At the age of five he had his first psychic experience: He saw an elemental spirit covered with spots inside a house.

O'Donnell was educated at Clifton College in Bristol, England, and the Queen's Service Academy in Dublin. He later said that as a young man he had nearly been strangled by a phantom while in Dublin.

After school, he went to the United States, where he worked on a ranch in Oregon and as a policeman in Chicago during the Railway Strike of 1894. He returned to England and worked as a schoolmaster while training for the theater. His first book, an occult novel, *For Satan's Sake,* was published in 1905. During World War I he served in the British Amry. After the war, he acted on stage and in film.

O'Donnell wrote other occult novels. He became an amateur ghost-hunter, investigating hauntings and collecting occult stories, which he chronicled in his nonfiction books. He also wrote numerous articles. His writings gained him great popularity on both sides of the Atlantic. He lectured often and made radio and television appearances in Britain and the United States.

O'Donnell said he believed in many of the things he wrote about, including ghosts and werewolves. In his book *Werwolves* [sic], he acknowledges that some cases of old were due to delusions, but werewolves did exist and still existed. He rejected the demonologists' central refutation of SHAPE-SHIFTING: that only God, the sole creator of everything, has the power to perform such a miracle. O'Donnell said:

> This property of lycanthropy, or metamorphosing into a beast, probably dates back to man's creation. It was, I am inclined to believe, conferred on man at his creation by Malevolent Forces that were antagonistic to man's progress; and that these Malevolent Forces had a large share in the creation of this universe is, to my mind, extremely probable . . . I cannot believe that the creation of man and the universe were due entirely to one Creator—there are assuredly too many inconsistencies in all we see around us to justify belief in only one Creative Force.

The Malevolent Forces created werewolves, and it originally was hereditary, O'Donnell wrote. But the condition migrated over time into the general populations. Not all werewolves may be human, either—some may be a sort of phantasmal elemental. He also said that after death, the wolf personality of a werewolf might remain earthbound and appear as a "lupine phantasm." O'Donnell himself had, in his ghost investigations in the British Isles, encountered entities that were half-human and half-beast, and might have been the earthbound spirits of werewolves.

Whether they are hereditary werewolves or acquire the ability of shape-shifting through magical means, werewolves can be identified by their telltale physical traits:

> Sometimes a werwolf [sic] may be told by the long, straight, slanting eyebrows, which meet in an angle over the nose; sometimes by the hands, the third finger of which is a trifle the longest; or by the fingernails, which are red, almond-shaped and curved; sometimes by the ears, which are set rather low, and far back on their heads; and sometimes by a noticeably long, swinging stride, which is strongly suggestive of some animal.

Although folklore links vampires to werewolves, O'Donnell saw them as two separate and very different entities. The werewolf is a hereditary condition among humans and also is a phantasm:

> It has an existence entirely separate from the vampire. The werwolf feeds on both the living and the dead, which it bites and mangles after the nature of all beasts of prey.

He stated this about vampires:

> A vampire is an Elemental that under certain conditions inhabits a dead body, whether human or otherwise; and, thus incarcerated, comes out of a grave at night to suck the blood of a living person. It never touches the dead . . .
>
> Vampirism is infectious; everyone who has been sucked by a vampire, on physical dissolution, becomes a vampire, and remains one until his corpse is destroyed in a certain prescribed manner. Lycanthropy is not infectious.

Vampires can be banished by exorcism but hereditary werewolves cannot be exorcized of their second and animal nature, he said.

Much closer to the werewolf in nature is the GHOUL:

> A ghoul is an Elemental that visits any place where human or animal remains have been interred. It digs them up and bites them, showing a keen liking for brains, which it sucks in the same manner as a vampire sucks blood.
>
> Ghouls either remain in spirit form or steal the bodies of living beings—living beings only—either human or animal. They can only do this when the spirit of the living person, during sleep (either natural or induced hypnotically), is separated from the material body; or, in other words, when the spirit is projected. The ghoul then pounces on the physical body, and, often refusing to restore it to its rightful owner, the latter is compelled to roam about as a phantasm for just so long a time as the ghoul chooses to inhabit the body it has stolen.

O'Donnell recounts numerous werewolf stories, some of them from historical accounts and some as reported to him by people he met.

He died on May 6, 1965, at age 93.

FURTHER READING:
O'Donnell, Elliott. *Werwolves*. New York: Longvue Press, 1965.

ogoljen   Czechoslovakian VAMPIRE. The *ogoljen* must be buried at a CROSSROADS in order to prevent it from returning to attack. Earth from its tomb must be placed in its navel.

ointments   Magical preparations said to enable SHAPE-SHIFTING to take place. Ointments and salves are reported in the records of werewolf cases, and also in European witchcraft trials. Witches said magical ointments enabled them to fly to witches' SABBATS as well as shape-shift.

Some individuals who claimed to change into wolf form said they did so when they rubbed an ointment all over their body. They said the ointments were given to them by a mysterious individual, either the devil or one of his representatives. The GANDILLON WEREWOLVES used an ointment to shape-shift into wolf and hare forms, and to attend witches' sabbats. JEAN GRENIER said a "black man of the forest" gave him his magical ointment. A similar story was told by the POLIGNY WEREWOLVES.

Among the many other cases involving ointments were three women near Neuchatel, France, who confessed in 1602 to using the devil's ointment to change themselves into wolves. They said they kidnapped a child, took him to a sabbat and ate him—except for his right hand, which God did not permit.

A key ingredient in such ointments was one or more hallucinogens, which probably gave the illusion of shape-shifting and flying. In werewolf cases, some ingredients may have facilitated the onset of wild and savage behavior. Some confessed werewolves said that their physical bodies were in trance during their transformation into beasts.

Hallucinogens might include solanum somniferum, aconite, henbane, nightshade, belladonna, opium, sium, and acorus vulgaris. These ingredients were macerated in alcohol and boiled in oil, or—as it was popularly believed—in the fat of little children who had been murdered for this purpose. Another belief held that BAT's BLOOD was added to the mix.

Henbane and nightshade were two readily available hallucinogenics. Active ingredients in henbane are hyoscyamine, atropine, and hyoscine, also known as scopolamine. Active ingredients in nightshade are hyoscyamine and atropine. Both henbane and nightshade were used in small doses since ancient times to relieve pain and induce sleep. But in higher and potentially toxic doses, both cause hallucinations, delusion, convulsions, madness, and strange dreams of transformation into beasts and of flying.

A recipe published in REGINALD SCOT's *Discoverie of Witchcraft* (1584) calls for sium, acarum vulgare (probably sweet flag), cinquefoil, bat's blood, oil, and solanum somniferum, combined with fat or lard. Witches vigorously rubbed the mixture into their skin "till they look red and be verie hot, so as the pores may be opened and their flesh soluble and loose."

Scot gave another recipe that called for the fat of young children to be boiled in water and combined with "eleoselinum" (probably hemlock), aconite, poplar leaves, and soot. Still another recipe called for aconite, poppy juice, fox glove, poplar leaves, and cinquefoil, in a base of beeswax, lanolin, and almond oil.

As early as the 15th century, most demonologists, including Scot, believed the effects of magical ointments to be imaginary and not real. In tests conducted by inquisitors and witch investigators, an accused witch rubbed herself down with her ointment and then fell into a deep sleep. Upon awakening, she insisted she had been transported through the air to a sabbat, when in fact she had been observed not moving for hours.

A contemporary researcher, Dr. Erich-Will Peuckert of the University of Göttingen, Germany, tested a medieval flying ointment recipe on himself and a colleague. The ingredients included deadly nightshade, thornapple, henbane, wild celery, and parsley in a base of hog's lard. The ointment caused the two men to fall into a trancelike sleep for 20 hours, during which each had nearly, identical, intense dreams of flying through the air to a mountaintop and participating in erotic orgies with monsters and demons. Upon awakening, the men had headaches and felt depressed, symptoms often described by witches and werewolves.

FURTHER READING:
Guiley, Rosemary Ellen. *The Encyclopedia of Witches and Witchcraft*. 2d ed. New York: Facts On File, 1999.
Otten, Charlotte F., ed. *A Lycanthropy Reader: Werewolves in Western Culture*. New York: Dorset Press, 1989.
Scot, Reginald. *The Discoverie of Witchcraft*. Yorkshire, England: E. P. Publishing, 1973.
Sidky, H. *Witchcraft, Lycanthropy, Drugs and Disease: An Anthropological Study of the European Witch-Hunts*. New York: Peter Lang, 1997.
Summers, Montague. *The Werewolf*. New York: Bell Publishing, 1966.

Olaus Magnus   See MAGNUS, OLAUS.

Old Hag   A nocturnal phenomenon involving nightmares, suffocation, paralysis, and supernatural smells, sounds, and apparitions. The Old Hag syndrome is blamed on VAMPIRES, restless ghosts, night terror demons, and witches. The syndrome has similarities to characteristics of poltergeists, and to the MARA, a demon that attacks humans at night and sexually assaults them.

The Old Hag syndrome has been recorded since ancient times. In folklore, hags are sometimes described as supernatural creatures which act on their own volition, or are directed to attack a person through magic. Hags also

A sleeper is menaced by a demonic night terror. (Author's collection)

are described as witches, sorcerers, and practitioners of magic who travel out of their bodies to attack other human beings in spirit form, riding their chests at night. The term *hag* is often used to refer to a witch, and to be "hagged" or "hag ridden" means to be assaulted by a witch in spirit form while asleep.

Victims may be sleeping at night or napping during the day. They almost always are sleeping on their backs. They may hear footsteps, feel and see a form and smell odors, or they may simply wake up suddenly feeling an invisible, crushing weight and paralysis, followed by sudden cessation of pressure and exhaustion. Regardless of the characteristics, the attacks are always terrifying.

In his book *The Terror That Comes in the Night* (1982), folklorist David J. Hufford estimates that about 15 percent of the general population worldwide suffer at least one hag attack during life. Some individuals suffer attacks several times a year. Rarely, individuals suffer frequent attacks over a limited period of time. Even rarer are those who suffer frequent and chronic attacks. Belief in the Old Hag, knowledge of the supernatural in general, and previous supernatural experiences do not seem to be factors in whether or not an individual has a hag attack.

No adequate explanation for the Old Hag has been put forward. Some cases have been attributed to sleep disorders and psychological conditions. The second-century Roman physician, Galen, attributed it to indigestion. Ernest Jones, an influential psychoanalyst of the Freudian school, equates hag attacks with nightmares in his monograph *On the Nightmare* (1931). Jones attributed nightmares to sexual repression. He notes that the term *nightmare* comes from the Anglo-Saxon terms *neaht* or *nicht* (night) and *mara* (INCUBUS or SUCCUBUS, literally "the crusher"). Up until the mid-17th century, the term *nightmare* was used to describe these types of nocturnal attacks. Jones also considers vampires and WEREWOLVES to be expressions of repressed sexuality as well.

Sexual repression may be a factor in some Old Hag cases, but cannot explain all cases. Sleep-related illnesses such as narcolepsy also may be a factor in some cases, but cannot account for all, or even a majority, of them.

Supernatural factors cannot be ruled out. As Hufford finds, the Old Hag syndrome has played a significant role in the development of various supernatural traditions, and the hag's relationship to cultural factors deserves more investigation.

Recorded cases of vampire attacks in Eastern Europe sometimes feature Old Hag characteristics. For example, a case cited by both MONTAGUE SUMMERS and occultist Dr. Franz Hartmann features, as Summers notes, "typical instances of vampirism" and strongly resembles the Old Hag encounter:

A miller at D—had a healthy servant-boy, who soon after entering his service began to fail. He acquired a ravenous appetite, but nevertheless grew daily more feeble and emaciated. Being interrogated, he at last confessed that a thing which he could not see, but which he could plainly feel, came to him every night about twelve o'clock and settled upon his chest, drawing all the life out of him, so that he became paralised [sic] for the time being, and neither could move nor cry out. Thereupon the miller agreed to share the bed with the boy, and made him promise that he should give a certain sign when the vampire arrived. This was done, and when the signal was made the miller putting out his hands grasped an invisible but very tangible substance that rested upon the boy's chest. He described it as apparently elliptical in shape, and to the touch feeling like gelatine [sic], properties which suggest an ectoplasmic formation. The thing writhed and fiercely struggled to escape, but he gripped it firmly and threw it on the fire. After that the boy recovered, and there was an end of these visits.

Similarly, the famous vampire cases of the BRESLAU VAMPIRE and JOHANNES CUNTIUS also involve Old Hag characteristics.

Hufford notes that BRAM STOKER probably was familiar with the characteristics of hag attacks and vampire folklore, as seen in this passage from DRACULA, in which Mina Harker describes a visitation by COUNT DRACULA:

There was in the room the same thin white mist that I had before noticed . . . I felt the same vague terror which had come to me before and the same sense of some presence . . . then indeed my heart sank within me: Beside the bed, as if he had stepped out of the mist—or rather as if the mist had turned into his figure, for it had entirely disappeared—stood a tall, thin man, all in black. I knew him at once from the description of the others. The waxen face; the high acquiline nose, on which the light fell in a thin white line; the parted red lips, with the sharp white teeth showing between; and the red eyes that I had seemed to see in the sunset on the windows of St. Mary's church at Whitby . . . For an instant my heart stood still, and I would have screamed out, only that I was paralyzed.

Hufford observes that Stoker is not "completely faithful" to folk vampire traditions, but that is almost always the case with fiction. Fiction must depart from fact in order to tell a good story. Nonetheless, Stoker's paralyzing vampire who appears at bedside portrays an authentic element of vampire lore.

Old Hag characteristic also appear in accounts of modern encounters with EXTRATERRESTRIALS.

See also MORA.

FURTHER READING:
Barber, Paul. *Vampires, Burial and Death: Folklore and Reality.* New Haven, Conn.: Yale University Press, 1988.
Hufford, David J. *The Terror That Comes in the Night: An Experience-Centered Study of Supernatural Assault Traditions.* Philadelphia: University of Pennsylvania Press, 1982.

opji   A Kashubian VAMPIRE. The *opji* (*wupji*) is the more dangerous of two types of vampires (see VJESCI), for his vampirism cannot be prevented. The *opji* is recognized at birth by the presence of one or two teeth.

See also KASHUBS.

Orlock   See GRAF ORLOCK.

Ornias   Vampiric, SHAPE-SHIFTING, soul-stealing demon controlled by the biblical King Solomon. According to the *Testament of Solomon,* an apochryphal text, Ornias is a fallen angel who lives in the constellation Aquarius. He strangles men born under the sign of Aquarius because they have passion for women born under the sign of Virgo. As a shape-shifter, he becomes a man who likes boys and causes them pain when he touches them; he turns into a heavenly, winged creature; and he takes the form of a lion.

According to lore, Ornias made his appearance during the construction of Solomon's Temple of Jerusalem. Every day at sunset, he came and took half the wages and food of the master workman's boy, who was Solomon's favorite. He sucked out the boy's soul through his right thumb. The boy wasted away. Questioned by Solomon, the boy revealed what the vampire demon was doing to him. Solomon asked God for help, and was given a magical ring from the archangel Michael that would enable him to quell demons.

Solomon gave the ring to the boy and told him to throw it at the demon's chest when he next appeared, and order him to go to Solomon. Ornias came as a flaming fire. When hit by the ring, he screamed and promised to give the boy all the GOLD and SILVER on earth if he would take the ring away and back to Solomon. But the boy delivered the demon to the king.

Solomon interrogated him. Ornias claimed he was descended from an archangel and had the gift of prophecy. He said demons fly up to heaven to eavesdrop on God. If they become exhausted, they plummet to earth as falling stars.

Solomon, with the help of the archangel Uriel, forced Ornias to cut stone from the quarry for the temple. Terrified by IRON, the demon begged for freedom, promising to call up other demons in return. When he was done with his work, he was delivered to the king Beelzebub, the Prince of Demons.

Further reading:
Guiley, Rosemary Ellen. *The Encyclopedia of Angels*. 2d ed. New York: Facts On File, 2003.
The Old Testament Pseudepigrapha. vols. 1 & 2. James H. Charlesworth, ed. New York: Doubleday, 1983; 1985.

otgiruru   In the lore of the Herero of southwestern Africa, angry ancestors who return from the grave to menace the living.

owenga   In Guinea lore, vengeful ancestors, evil spirits, or dead magicians who attack the living for their BLOOD. Spilled blood must be cleaned up in order not to attract the *owenga*. Anything stained with blood, such as clothing or objects, must be burned or thrown into the sea.

palis In Persian-Islamic lore, a vampiric demon that attacks victims at night and kills them by licking the soles of their feet until all their BLOOD has been sucked out. *Palis* means "foot licker." It is also used as the proper name of the demon.

The *palis* is not very intelligent. A popular folktale told in different versions describes how two camel drivers (or a caravan) discovered how to outwit the creature. When they lay down to sleep, they made sure the soles of their feet were touching the soles of another's feet. When the *palis* arrived, it could find no soles to lick. The demon cried out, "I have traveled a thousand valleys and thirty-three, but never met a man with two heads."

SALT is an effective repellent of the PALIS.

Paole, Arnod (Arnold) (d. 1732) VAMPIRE of Medvegia, Serbia, near Belgrade. Arnod Paole's case was documented by JOHANN FLUCKINGER, and received wide press in Europe.

Paole had been a soldier stationed in Greece and the Levant, where he learned about the local beliefs concerning vampires. While in Greece, he discovered that his company was staying near a site haunted by vampires. In Turkish Serbia, one night he believed he was attacked by a vampire. He went the next day to its grave and dispatched it. To prevent further trouble, he ate some of the earth of the grave, and smeared himself with the vampire's BLOOD.

His troubles did not end, however. In 1727 he returned home, but could not resume a normal life. He continued to feel weakened and depressed. He was pressured into marrying Mina, the daughter of a farmer who lived nearby. He told her about the vampire attack in Greece, and that he felt he had been cursed forever and was doomed to a premature death.

Soon thereafter, Paole fell off a hay wagon and broke his neck. He languished in bed for a few days and then died. About 20 to 30 days later, people complained that he had turned into a vampire and was attacking them and also livestock. Several persons stated they were being haunted by him, and afterward always felt "a state of extraordinary debility." Four persons died. The villagers were gripped by panic and began remaining indoors after dusk. Still, it was said, Paole could penetrate locked doors and barred windows.

Forty days after his death, Paole was dug up and was found to be in the vampire condition. His shirt, shroud, and COFFIN were blood-soaked. Here is MONTAGUE SUMMERS's description:

> It was seen that the corpse had moved to one side, and the jaws gaped wide open and the blub [sic] lips were moist with new blood which had trickled in a thin stream from the corner of the mouth. All unafraid the sexton caught the body and twisted it straight. "So," he cried, "You have not wiped your mouth since last night's work." Even the officers of the battlefield and the surgeons accustomed to the horrors of the dissecting room shuddered at so hideous a spectacle. It is recorded that the drummer boy swooned on the spot. Nerving themselves to their

awful work they inspected the remains more closely, and it was soon apparent that there lay before them the thing they dreaded—the vampire. He looked indeed, as if he had not been dead a day. On handling the corpse the scarfskin came off, and below there were new skin and new nails. Accordingly they scattered garlic over the remains and drove a stake through the body, which it is said gave a piercing shriek as the warm blood spouted out in a great crimson jet.

When this dreadful operation had been performed they proceeded to exhume the bodies of four others who had died in consequence of Arnold's attacks. The records give no details of the state in which these were found. They simply say that whitethorn stakes were driven through them and that they were all five burned. The ashes of all were replaced in consecrated ground.

The grotesque noises probably were caused by gases being forced up the throat by the violent compression of the chest cavity. (See VRESKET.) Four other corpses buried nearby were exhumed and staked with whitethorn as a precaution. Paole's CORPSE was burned and his ASHES were thrown into his grave.

Meanwhile, people who had eaten the livestock tainted by Paole also sickened and died. In three months, seven people sickened and died within two or three days.

Six years later, vampirism occurred again in the area, and several people died allegedly due to blood loss. This outbreak was blamed on three corpses. GYPSIES decapitated them and threw the heads and bodies into the river Morava.

See also STANA.

FURTHER READING:
Barber, Paul. *Vampires, Burial and Death: Folklore and Reality.* New Haven, Conn.: Yale University Press, 1988.
Perkowski, Jan L. *The Darkling: A Treatise on Slavic Vampirism.* Columbus, Ohio: Slavica Publishers, 1989.

Parasite, The   A novella by Sir Arthur Conan Doyle about a psychic VAMPIRE (see PSYCHIC ATTACK). Doyle, best known for his novels about detective Sherlock Holmes, was intensely interested in psychical research and the paranormal. *The Parasite* was written in 1894.

The psychic vampire is Miss Penelosa, a crippled old maid who becomes obsessed with a much younger college professor named Gilroy. Doyle describes Miss Penelosa as a small and frail creature "with a pale, peaky face, an insignificant presence and retiring manner." She requires a crutch to walk about. This appearance turns out to be misleading, to the destruction of Gilroy.

Miss Penelosa's vampiric powers are evidenced in her remarkable eyes. (See ERETICA; EYE.) She first attacks Gilroy's fiancée, mesmerizing her. Then she saps the professor's vitality, making him waste away and acquire dark, sunken eyes. To his horror, he realizes that he has fallen under her influence, and that she is a "monster parasite" who "creeps

into my form as the hermit crab creeps into the whelk's shell." He tries to resist, but whenever he is in her presence he becomes weaker still.

Gilroy shuts himself up in his bedroom and tosses the key out the window into the garden. He experiences some relief, but then he learns that Miss Penelosa has been ill at the same time, and her powers weaken whenever she is ill. He remains sequestered, but when she regains her strength and her powers, he is irresistibly pulled out.

When Gilroy next finds himself in Miss Penelosa's presence, he denounces her in a fury. This seems to break her hold on him, but once again the effect is only temporary. She visits the professor and warns him of the consequences in spurning her.

Gilroy's continued loathing incites Miss Penelosa to anger and a determination to destroy him. She persecutes him mercilessly. Gilroy is driven to confide his woes to a colleague, who prescribes traditional remedies of chloral and bromide. Gilroy does not believe these will help him, and he throws them into a gutter.

Miss Penelosa foments gossip about Gilroy and uses her powers to ruin his concentration during his lectures, causing him to babble nonsense. He becomes a laughing-stock and is suspended from his position.

Alone and in despair, Gilroy knows that no one will believe the truth about what has happened to him. He descends into madness, and robs a bank, assaults a friend, and nearly mutilates the face of his fiancée. His misery ends only when Miss Penelosa suddenly dies.

The Parasite is a dark story, for the protagonist has no effective defense against the vampire, who ensnares him in a spiderlike way. His only relief comes through her death due to outside circumstances.

See also ARTS AND ENTERTAINMENT.

FURTHER READING:
Auerbach, Nina. *Our Vampires, Ourselves.* Chicago: University of Chicago Press, 1995.
Perkowski, Jan L., ed. *The Vampire of the Slavs.* Cambridge, Mass.: Slavica Publishers, 1976.

pears   See THE VAMPIRE AND ST. MICHAEL.

pelesit   Demon who serves as a FAMILIAR to the Malaysian *polong* VAMPIRE. The *pelesit* is shaped like a cricket with a sharp tail. It bores into victims with its tail.

Pentsch Vampire   See JOHANNES CUNTIUS.

phi phu   Among the Shan tribe of Thailand, a spirit power that permanently resides within a person, transforming him or her into a witch or sorcerer who has, among many powers, the ability to shape-shift into were-animal form. The *phi phu* is passed down through family lines, but also is contagious. For example, if a person shares too many meals with a *phi phu*, the *phi phu* spirit will infect him. Marrying a person from outside the region will bring the *phi phu* into a family.

The *phi phu* also has the ability to send a human double to distant locations. The *phi phu* is considered to be unfortunate but not necessarily malevolent, as long as they conform to certain social expectations of behavior.

Once the *phi phu* comes into a person, it cannot be exorcized, save for one way: taking ordination as a Buddhist monk or nun.

See also SHAPE-SHIFTING.

FURTHER READING:
Tannenbaum, Nicholas. "Witches, Fortune, and Misfortune Among the Shan of Northwestern Thailand," in *Understanding Witchcraft and Sorcery in Southeast Asia*. C. W. Watson and Roy Ellen, eds. Honolulu: University of Hawaii Press, 1993.

pigs   In Wallachian lore, a favored shape-shifted form of a VAMPIRE. Killing a pig on the feast of St. Ignatius (October 17) and smearing its lard on one's body will prevent vampire attacks. If a CORPSE is smeared with the lard, it will prevent the corpse from becoming a vampire.

See also SHAPE-SHIFTING.

pijawica   Croatian VAMPIRE. The word *pijawica* comes from the root *pit*, "to drink." The name refers less to BLOOD-drinking than to alcoholism, which is associated with vampirism in Eastern European folklore. The *pijawica* can cut off its own head and hold it under one arm or between its legs.

pisaca   In Indian lore, a type of RAKASHA that is vampiric and ghoulish in nature. In Hindu mythology, the *pisaca* were created by the god Brahma from stray drops of the water used to create gods and humans.

The *pisaca* lives in water supplies and infects people with a fatal wasting illness when they drink the water. It also likes to lurk about CEMETERIES and eat CORPSES. In appearance, the *pisaca* looks like it is perpetually starving, for it is tall and gaunt and its ribs stick out. It goes about with its long hair sticking out, as though it has just been badly frightened.

Fire is the best way to repel a *pisaca*.

FURTHER READING:
Mack, Carol K., and Dinah Mack. *A Field Guide to Demons, Fairies, Fallen Angels, and Other Subversive Spirits*. New York: Henry Holt/Owl Books, 1998.

Pitt, Ingrid (1937–)   Actress famous for her roles in HAMMER FILMS productions, most notably her two VAMPIRE portrayals in *Countess Dracula* (1971) and *The Vampire Lovers* (1970). Called the "Queen of Horror," Ingrid Pitt has performed in more than two dozen films and numerous television roles. She is an author and also continues to make media and public appearances.

Pitt was born Natasha Petrovana on November 21, 1937, in Poland. At age five she was incarcerated in a Nazi concentration camp along with her family. She and her mother were separated from her father. They survived, and years after their release Pitt searched Europe, futilely looking for her father. She grew up in East Berlin, but managed to escape to the West. She changed her name to Ingrid Pitt and sought work as a model and actress.

Her first films were Spanish horror/science fiction productions, beginning in 1964 with *The Prehistoric Sound*. Her first major English-speaking film was *Where Eagles Dare* (1968), starring Clint Eastwood and Richard Burton. Pitt saw her future in action drama, but events took another course when she met James Carreras of Hammer Films at a cinema premiere party in London in November 1969. Complimenting her on *Where Eagles Dare*, Carreras said he might have three film roles for her.

Pitt's first film for Hammer was *The Vampire Lovers*, based on J. Sheridan Le Fanu's story "CARMILLA." Pitt starred as the vampire Countess Mircalla, who in the end is killed by staking by PETER CUSHING, who plays the General. With ample gore, sex, and lesbian scenes, *The Vampire Lovers* was a sensational hit that vaulted Pitt into stardom.

Pitt turned down other offers for vampire films, not wanting to be typecast. She accepted Hammer's *Countess Dracula* (1971), loosely based on the story of ELIZABETH BATHÓRY. As Countess Elisabeth Nadasdy, she bathes in the BLOOD of young girls in order to retain her own youthfulness.

Pitt played one other vampire role for Hammer, that of Carla Lynde in the spoof "The Cloak," part of the anthology *The House That Dripped Blood* (1971).

She played the role of the librarian in the cult hit *The Wicker Man* (1973). Her last film role was in *The Asylum* (2000).

Pitt lived for several years in Argentina, where she worked in her husband's production company, and befriended the Perons. She also lived with Native Americans in Colorado for a while.

She is the author of fiction and nonfiction. Her fiction includes a novel, *Cuckoo Run*, her very first book, about a female spy, and a novelization set in the Peron years in Argentina. Her nonfiction includes *Life's A Scream—The Autobiography of Ingrid Pitt* (1999); *The Ingrid Pitt Book of Murder, Torture, and Depravity* (2000), about famous murderers of history; and compilations of short stories in *The Bedside Companion for Vampire Lovers* (2000) and *The Bedside Companion for Ghosthunters* (2003).

Countess Elizabeth Nadasdy (Ingrid Pitt) in Countess Dracula, *based on Elizabeth Bathóry* (Author's collection)

Pitt writes several columns for magazines and makes appearances at fan conventions internationally. The Ingrid Pitt Fan Club holds an annual reunion in London.

FURTHER READING:
Pitt, Ingrid. *Life's A Scream—The Autobiography of Ingrid Pitt.* London: William Heinemann, 1999.
Pitt, Ingrid. "The Story of Hammer Films." Available online. URL: http://www.pittofhorror.com/hammer/htm. Downloaded on January 9, 2004.
Pitt of Horror Web site. URL: http://www.pittofhorror.com. Accessed on January 9, 2004.

Plogojowitz, Peter (d. 1725)   VAMPIRE case of Kisilova, Serbia. Peter Plogojowitz was a farmer who died in 1725 at age 62. Three days after his death, he appeared in his home at midnight and asked his son for food. His son complied, and the father appeared to eat it, and then left. Two nights later, the father appeared again and demanded food. This time, the terrified son refused, whereupon the father fixed him with a most threatening look. The next day, the son died. Within hours, five or six other persons in the village fell ill, suffering total exhaustion and a faintness, as though they lacked BLOOD. All said they had been visited in a dream by the dead Peter Plogojowitz, who seemed to glide into the room, catch them by the throat, bite them hard, and suck the blood out of the wounds. In less than a week, nine persons were dead. Plogojowitz's wife said he came to her in dreams and demanded his *opanki,* or shoes, be placed next to him in his COFFIN, because his bare feet were sore from walking about the cobblestoned streets at night.

The villagers resolved to open Plogojowitz's grave and prevailed upon their priest and the imperial provisor of the Gradisk District to grant their request and be present for the viewing. The provisor refused, but was informed by the villagers that they would leave the village out of fear that an evil spirit would destroy them all. The provisor acquiesced.

According to MONTAGUE SUMMERS, military officers opened the grave of the Plogojowitz and

... found him as though he were in a trance, gently breathing, his eyes wide open and glaring horribly, his complexion ruddy, the flesh plump and full. His hair and nails had grown, and when the scarfskin came off there appeared new and healthy cuticle. His mouth was all slobbered and stained with fresh blood. Thence they at once concluded it was he who must be the Vampire this molesting the district, and it was necessary at once to put a stop to his ravages in case he should affect the whole village. The executioner armed with a heavy mallet drove a sharp stake through his heart, during which the grave was deluged with the blood that gushed from the wound, his nose, ears and every orifice of the body. A big pyre of logs and brushwood having been built, the body was placed thereon. It was dry weather and the wood when kindled soon burned brightly the flames being fanned by a gentle breeze. In a very short time the body was reduced to ashes. No marks of vampirism being found upon the other bodies they were reburied with due precautions, garlic and whitethorn being placed in the coffins, and thenceforth the village was freed from any molestations.

Also burned were Plogojowitz's shoes.

Summers omits that one other telltale sign of vampirism was that Plogojowitz's corpse had an erection, not uncommon from natural bloating in decomposition, but during these times it was interpreted as a sign of the sexual activities of vampires.

See also ASHES; BURNING; CORPSES.

FURTHER READING:
Barber, Paul. *Vampires, Burial and Death: Folklore and Reality.* New Haven, Conn.: Yale University Press, 1988.
Calmet, Dom Augustin. *The Phantom World: Concerning Apparitions and Vampires.* Ware, England: Wordsworth Editions in association with the Folklore Society, 2001.
Summers, Montague. *The Vampire in Europe.* New York: E. P. Dutton, 1929.

Pniewo Vampire (d. 1870)   VAMPIRE case of a "Mrs. Gehrke," who caused her living relatives to become violently ill.

Mr. Gehrke was a forest keeper in Pniewo in the West Prussian district of Schwetz. His wife died in February 1870 and was buried in the Biechowo cemetery. Immediately afterward, Mr. Gehrke and the couple's children became severely ill. Mrs. Gehrke was suspected of being a vampire; according to local lore, vampires desire to be reunited with their family and their return from the grave makes the living ill and in danger of dying. Thus, the family will be reunited in death.

Four weeks after Mrs. Gehrke's burial, she was dug up at night by villagers and was seen to be in a vampire condition, with a ruddy face. Flaxseed (see SEEDS) and a fishing net were placed in the COFFIN to hold the CORPSE in place, but this was deemed by one observer—a wife of one of the group—to be insufficient. Consequently, Mrs. Gehrke's head was cut off with a spade and placed beneath her arm.

Mr. Gehrke, who had undergone an operation, quickly recovered. However, the VAMPIRE HUNTERS were convicted of grave desecration in district court.

See also BURIAL CUSTOMS.

FURTHER READING:
Perkowski, Jan L. *The Darkling: A Treatise on Slavic Vampirism.* Columbus, Ohio: Slavica Publishers, 1989.

Polidori, John George (1795–1821)   One-time physician of LORD BYRON and the author of the first vampire story published in English, the novella THE VAMPYRE.

John George Polidori was half Scottish and half Italian, and was fluent in Italian, French, and German. He earned his medical degree at age 19 from Edinburgh University, writing his dissertation on mesmerism and somnambulism. His real desire was to be writer, however. He joined a literary group; his particular interest was gothic novels.

By 1816 Byron was a pariah in polite society in England, due to his divorce, scandalous affair with Lady Caroline Lamb, various homosexual escapades, and outrageous behavior in general. He decided to exile himself for a time on the Continent, and hired Polidori to accompany him as his physician. Byron's publisher, John Murray, commissioned Polidori to keep a secret diary of Byron's activities.

Polidori was a miserable traveling companion, displaying moodiness, jealousy, and petty tantrums. He irritated Byron, who referred to him as "Polly-Dolly," and also complained to his publisher, "I was never much more disgusted with any human production than with the eternal nonsense, and tracasseries, and emptiness, and ill humor, and vanity of that young person."

In 1816 they arrived in Geneva, where Byron leased a villa on Lake Geneva. They were joined by the poet Percy Bysshe Shelley and his soon-to-be wife, Mary Wollstonecraft, and Mary's half sister, Claire Clairmont, who had previously been Byron's mistress and was pregnant by him (later bearing him a daughter, Allegra). The Shelley party took Maison Chappius, a few minutes' walk from Byron's villa.

Polidori immediately despised Shelley and Wollstonecraft, and attempted to goad Shelley into a duel over a boat race. Shelley and Wollstonecraft returned his dislike.

The parties engaged in seances and discussions of occult topics, including the ability of electricity—"galvanism"—to bring the dead back to life. They took drugs, including opium, laudanum, and ether; Shelley suffered hallucinations. One stormy evening the group read ghost stories and poems, and Byron challenged everyone to make up a story. Mary's idea eventually led her to write *Frankenstein.* Polidori's tale concerned a woman with a skull head who was punished for peeking through a keyhole, based on a fragment of a story that Byron had included at the end of his poem of Mazeppa. Mary ridiculed Polidori's story in her diary: "Poor Polidori had some terrible idea about a skull-headed lady, who was so punished for peeping through a keyhole—what to see I forget—something very shocking and wrong, of course . . ."

Byron's story concerned two friends traveling in Greece, one of whom died mysteriously, then reappeared very much alive in England, where he had an affair with his friend's sister. The story had vampiric elements.

Byron eventually lost his tolerance for Polidori and fired him. Returning to England, Polidori was desperate for money, and also hungered after the fame that he thought he deserved more than Byron.

Byron never pursued fleshing out his oral story or publishing it, but Polidori, who had kept substantial notes in his diary, did. He wrote his own version of the story over two or three idle mornings, borrowing heavily from his notes. Polidori's story lay unpublished until 1819, when he sold it for £30. It appeared as *The Vampyre,* part of "A Letter From Geneva, with Anecdotes of Lord Byron," in *New Monthly Magazine.* The novella was prefaced by a description of the storytelling evening. Polidori and Byron are referred to in the third person, indicating that the preface may have been written by the magazine's editor.

The article implied that Byron was the author of *The Vampyre,* which fueled its literary success, though initially more so on the Continent than in England. Byron was furious and declared, "I have a personal dislike to Vampires, and the little acquaintance I have with them would by no means induce me to reveal their secrets." In the ensuing flap, the magazine editor resigned, and Byron quickly sought publication of his own "FRAGMENT OF A STORY," without vampiric details.

Though soon revealed as the real author, Polidori had trouble staking his claim to fame. The public continued to believe that Byron had written *The Vampyre.* Even Johann Wolfgang von Goethe declared the story to be the best that Byron had ever written.

Polidori continued to lead a troubled life. He incurred heavy gambling losses that he could not pay off and suffered a severe loss of honor. Despondent, he died in August 1821 of a drug overdose.

The Vampyre remained the dominant influence on vampire stage productions until the publication of DRACULA by BRAM STOKER in 1897.

See also ARTS AND ENTERTAINMENT.

FURTHER READING:

Senf, Carol A. *The Vampire in 19th Century English Literature.* Bowling Green, Ohio: Bowling Green State University Popular Press, 1988.

Stuart, Roxana. *Stage Blood: Vampires of the 19th-Century Stage.* Bowling Green, Ohio: Bowling Green State University Popular Press, 1994.

Twitchell, James B. *The Living Dead: A Study of the Vampire in Romantic Literature.* Durham, N.C.: Duke University Press, 1981.

Poligny Werewolves (1521)   Werewolf trial in France. In December 1521 two men were charged with witchcraft and cannibalism and brought before the Inquisitor General for the diocese of Besancon, France. The accused were Pierre Burgot (also Bourgot), called Peter the Great because of his size, and Michel Verdun (also Verdung).

Partway into the trial, Burgot made a full confession. He said that 19 years earlier in Poligny, a terrible storm scattered his flock of sheep. He enlisted the help of others and went out in search of his lost sheep. Three black horsemen rode up to him and inquired about his troubles. One of the men promised three things: Burgot would find his lost sheep; he would be protected and would never have any more trouble; and he would be given money. He would have all of these things if he would pledge to serve only the man's master. Burgot agreed to meet the man again in four or five days.

Burgot did find all of his sheep, and he went to the meeting. He learned that the mysterious man was a servant of the devil. He swore allegiance to the devil and renounced Christianity. He kissed the man's left hand, which he described as "black and ice-cold as that of a corpse." He later learned the man's named was Moyset.

Burgot served the devil for two years. His flock was protected. But Burgot soon tired of this life and resumed attending church. He was approached by Michel Verdun and was persuaded to renew his compact with the devil on the promise of getting money. Verdun took him into the woods, where a ceremony was performed for transforming into WEREWOLVES. Burgot described it:

> In a wood near Chastel Charnon we met with many others whom I did not recognize; we danced, and each had in his or her hand a green taper with a blue flame. Still under the delusion that I should obtain money, Michel persuaded me to move with the greatest celerity, and in order to do this, after I had stripped myself, he smeared me with a salve, and I believed myself then to be transformed into a wolf. I was at first somewhat horrified at my four wolf's feet, and the fur with which I was covered all at once, but I found that I could now travel with the speed of the wind. This could not have taken place without the help of our powerful master, who was present during our excursion, though I did not perceive him till I had recovered my human form. Michel did the same as myself.
>
> When we had been one or two hours in this condition of metamorphosis, Michel smeared us again, and quick as thought we resumed our human forms. The salve was given us by our masters; to me it was given by Moyset, to Michel by his own master Guillemin.

Burgot insisted that, unlike the accounts given by other accused witches and werewolves, he felt no exhaustion after his shape-shifted adventures. He said that he and Verdun went out many times as wolves.

On one occasion, Burgot said he seized a boy of about six or seven years, intending to tear him to pieces and eat him. The boy screamed so loudly that Burgot was forced to retreat to his clothes and smear himself with OINTMENT in order to resume his human shape so that he could escape detection.

On another occasion, he and Verdun attacked and tore to pieces a woman who was gathering peas. They killed a man who attempted to rescue her.

They attacked, killed, and ate a girl of four, leaving only one arm. Verdun thought the flesh to be especially delicious.

They strangled another girl and drank her BLOOD.

In his human form, Burgot attacked a girl of nine who was weeding her garden. She begged for her life, but he snapped her neck, killing her. He attacked a goat and bit it in the throat, and then killed it with a knife.

Burgot told the inquisitor that he had to be naked in order to make the transformation into wolf, but Verdun could do it with his clothes on. Burgot could not explain what happened to his wolf hair when he shape-shifted back into human form; it just seemed to vanish.

Verdun corroborated all of Burgot's statements.

See also LYCANTHROPY; SHAPE-SHIFTING.

FURTHER READING:
Baring-Gould, Sabine. *The Book of Werewolves*. London: Smith, Elder & Co., 1865.

polong   Malaysian VAMPIRE in the shape of a tiny person, either male or female, and about the size of a thumbtack, with the ability to fly. A *polong* is made magically by collecting the BLOOD of a man who has been murdered. The blood is left in a bottle for two weeks, and magical incantations are said over it. The *polong* grows in the blood, and chirps when ready to emerge. Its human creator then must cut a finger daily for the *polong* to suck. The *polong* then can be dispatched to attack enemies by burrowing into them and making them sicken and die. It travels with its FAMILIAR, a *PELESIT*, a cricketlike demon with a sharp tail. The *pelesit* burrows its tail into the victim, making a tunnel by which the *polong* enters the body to suck blood. The bite becomes infected, and the victim goes insane and raves about CATS.

pontianak   Indonesian VISCERA SUCKER that is the spirit of a woman who dies in childbirth. The *pontianak's* favored prey are pregnant women. She kills both woman and fetus by stabbing the woman in the abdomen with her talons.

poppy seeds   See SEEDS.

porphyria   A rare congenital disease sometimes associated with CLINICAL VAMPIRISM and LYCANTHROPY. Porphyria is due to a recessive gene and affects men more than women. It has been reported more in Sweden and Switzerland than in other geographic areas.

In porphyria, the body has an inability to convert porphobilinogen to porphyrin in the bone marrow. Part of the hemoglobin goes into the urine rather than into the cells. The porphyrins reach toxic levels and affect the nervous system. The resulting conditions and symptoms are

- severe sensitivity to light
- reddish brown urine and teeth
- severe anemias, including haemolytic anemia
- pale and yellow, jaundiced skin
- ulcerated skin lesions
- progressive deformation of cartilage and bone, affecting especially the nose, ears, eyelids, and fingers
- in acute cases, nervous disorders such as hysteria, delirium, and manic-depression (bipolar disorder)

The symptoms are consistent with descriptions of WEREWOLVES in older literature, and with some people who exhibit a craving for BLOOD as seen in cases of clinical vampirism. However, porphyria is rare, and so is unlikely to provide an explanation for many cases of either lycanthropy or clinical vampirism.

Porphyria is known as "King George III's disease," after the English monarch (r. 1760–1820) who suffered from it. King George had dark red urine and suffered headaches, convulsions, and insomnia. He abruptly and inexplicably recovered, but 13 years later a relapse sent him into a stupor.

FURTHER READING:
Otten, Charlotte F., ed. *A Lycanthropy Reader: Werewolves in Western Culture*. New York: Dorset Press, 1989.
Ramsland, Katherine. *The Science of Vampires*. New York: Berkeley Boulevard Books, 2002.

Port Charles   Daytime soap opera featuring VAMPIRES, WEREWOLVES, and other supernatural beings.

Port Charles was spun off from the hugely successful *General Hospital* in 1997, and began its life as a hospital drama about first-year interns in the fictional town of Port Charles, somewhere in New York State. Ratings faltered, and so in 2001 the show changed its story line to "book" format and introduced a supernatural universe populated by vampires, werewolves, angels, and slayers among the mortals—a mix of *DARK SHADOWS*, BRAM STOKER, ANNE RICE and *BUFFY THE VAMPIRE SLAYER*.

In the story line "Tainted Love," Caleb Morley (Michael Easton) comes back to Port Charles. He hides his true identity as a vampire and goes by the name Stephen Clay, the lead of a popular rock band, the Stephen Clay Experience. Soon it is revealed that the entire band are vampires, as are their security guards. The reason why Caleb has returned is to regain his love, Livvie Locke (Kelly Monaco), who is now dominated by an alter ego, Tess.

"Tainted Love" did well, but its follow-up story line, "Tempted," did not, and the vampire story was dropped. A year later, vampires were reintroduced in a new story line,

"Naked Eyes," which led into "Surrender" and then other "books." Caleb and other vampires were back, and soon Port Charles was a hotbed of supernatural beings, so much so that mere mortals seemed pushed into the background. New vampires were made, including the resident villain, Joshua Temple (Ian Buchanan), who then plotted to overthrow Caleb and get rid of the slayers, Lucy Coe (Lynn Herring) and Rafe Kovich (Brian Gaskill). Joshua also had designs on Livvie, who did not return his affections. A healing springs was discovered that could "cure" vampirism. Caleb was cured, but not Joshua.

The audience, however, tired of the supernatural angle. Ratings fell and *Port Charles* was cancelled in September 2003.

What had once worked for *Dark Shadows* did not work in the long run for *Port Charles*. Producer DAN CURTIS had introduced the vampire BARNABAS COLLINS when *Dark Shadows* was on the brink of cancellation. The introduction of the supernatural not only saved the show but *made* the show. But *Port Charles* had a different heritage: It began as a hospital spin-off, not an original show, and its initial audience liked hospital drama. The audience apparently was willing to go along with vampires for a while, but not indefinitely, and an insufficient new audience of vampire fans did not materialize. Perhaps too much of its vampire lore copied Rice and *Buffy*. *Dark Shadows* had borrowed from numerous gothic literature sources, but the material was fresh to a television audience.

Port Charles represents a microcosm in the fictional vampire universe, and perhaps demonstrates what happens when vampires and other supernatural beings become too commonplace and open in society: The audience suffers from boredom. When vampires become just another eccentric relative or next-door neighbor, can interest, fear, and attraction be maintained? Given the direction of vampires in popular entertainment, the answer as yet is unknown.

FURTHER READING:
McAllister, Samantha. "Port Charles: Chronic Vampire Syndrome." Available online. URL: http://www.suite101.com/print_article.cfm/17159/100384. Downloaded on December 2, 2003.

Portugal Vampire   Living VAMPIRE case involving killing of a child. In September 1910 the bloodless corpse of a child was found in a field in Galazanna, Portugal. A man named Salvarrey was arrested and confessed to being a vampire.

Prest, Thomas Preskett   See *VARNEY THE VAMPIRE*.

pricolici   In Romanian lore, a VAMPIRE. The *pricolici* is the returning dead; it is also associated with the eclipse vampire, the *VARCOLAC*. The origin of *pricolici* is uncertain;

-lici has been related to the modern Greek term for "wolf." The earliest written reference to a Romanian *pricolici* came in a 1716 Latin manuscript about the history of Moldavia, in which the *pricolici* is equated with the French *loup-garou*, or WEREWOLF (see LOUP-GAROU).

As the vampiric returning dead, the *pricolici* feeds on its relatives. When exhumed, it is found in its grave lying facedown and with BLOOD on its lips. The blood must be fed to those who have been attacked by the *pricolici* so that they regain their health.

An infant who suckles after being weaned will become a *pricolici* after death and will torment his mother and relatives.

See also DOPPELSAUGER.

protection against vampires   Various folk lore precautions protect homes, individuals, and animals against VAMPIRE attacks. GARLIC is a chief means of protection. Garlic is rubbed around places where vampires enter a home—around the doors, the windows, and the chimney—as well as on livestock such as cows. Such precautions should especially be taken at times when vampires are believed to be the most active: St. Andrew's Eve, St. George's Eve, before Easter, and New Year's Eve.

In Romanian lore, on St. Andrew's Eve garlic is rubbed about, and all objects in the home are turned upside down. That way, vampires cannot ask the objects to open the door for them. All lamps should be kept turned off, and the occupants of the home should stay up all night and pray and tell stories. On St. George's Eve, people should turn their shirts inside out and put a knife or scythe under their head with the cutting edge turned outward while they sleep (see IRON). They should sleep reversed in bed, that is, with the head where the feet usually are. This prevents a vampire from finding them if it succeeds in getting in.

Another prescription found in Romanian lore holds that at any time, especially during the night, never answer someone until they call three times, for vampires can ask a question twice but never three times. If a person replies to a vampire, they then have the power to turn the victim's mouth askew, strike them dumb, cut off their foot, or even kill them.

CROSSES and holy WATER—influences added to vampire lore under Christianity—have the power to ward off vampires and purify spaces.

Other common remedies are

- saucers of nitric acid placed on tables in a home, but not in the bedroom
- incense burned for cleansing and protection of space
- the scattering of SEEDS and sand around thresholds and beds

Among some Slavic GYPSIES, sacrifices and appeasements are made to keep vampires at bay. Offerings of bread and cheese are taken in secret at night to the edge of another community, and vampires are called to come along and eat the food and not bother the people or animals of the village making the offering. Some Muslim Gypsies place offerings of halva, a prized sweet, in empty pots in their attics.

See also BURIAL CUSTOMS.

FURTHER READING:
Eaves, A. Osborne. "Modern Vampirism, in *The Vampire of the Slavs* by Jan L. Perkowski. Cambridge, Mass.: Slavica Publishers, 1976.

Murgoci, Agnes. "The Vampire in Roumania, in *The Vampire: A Casebook*, Alan Dundes, ed. Madison: University of Wisconsin Press, 1998.

Vukanovic, Professor T. P. "The Vampire," in *The Vampire of the Slavs* by Jan L. Perkowski. Cambridge, Mass.: Slavica Publishers, 1976.

psychic attack (psychic vampirism)   The draining of a person's energy and life force through magical or demonic attack. In magic and sorcery, certain individuals possess the skill to command demonic entities to attack and deplete other living things: humans, animals, and crops and plant life. The victim experiences a mysterious fatigue and exhaustion, troubling dreams and horrible nightmares, sexual assaults, and perhaps symptoms of the OLD HAG syndrome. Psychic attack also can be perpetrated by vampires, as attested in anecdotal accounts of attacks in the Eastern European vampire literature.

The English occultist DION FORTUNE is considered the leading authority on psychic attack. From her own experiences—first with a hostile boss and then with fellow occultists—she gained expert knowledge of how psychic attacks occur, their symptoms in unsuspecting victims, and how the attacks can be warded off or nullified. "I am of the opinion that psychic attacks are far commoner than is generally realized, even by occultists themselves," she states in her definitive work on psychic attack, *Psychic Self-Defence* (1930). She acknowledges that getting people to admit such attacks was not easy because of skepticism and fear of seeming to be mentally unbalanced.

According to Fortune, there are two types of psychic attack: by nonphysical entities and by human beings. The nonphysical entities may be acting on their own accord, or be directed to attack by a human being. These entities are said to be either demons commandeered by magic, or THOUGHT-FORMS, beings created by magic. Psychic attacks by human beings are said to be possible through formidable mental powers or traveling out-of-body in astral form. The weight on the chest of a sleeper, the primary symptom of a Old Hag attack, is considered by Fortune to be a symptom of psychic attack. The purposes of psychic attack are to weaken, debilitate, and destroy, to bend to the will of the attacker, or simply to draw off energy. In all cases, the victim ultimately is psychically vampirized due to a loss of life force. Exhaustion sets in, and in extreme cases, the victim falls seriously ill and may even die.

Most people normally are protected from falling victim to psychic attack because of the vitality of their own protective energy fields, and their inability to perceive the invisible forces of the Unseen. However, there are four conditions in which this protective veil can be rent, according to Fortune: 1) being in a place where occult forces are concentrated; 2) encountering people who are adept at handling these forces; 3) dabbling in the occult and getting out of depth; and 4) falling victim to certain pathological conditions.

Fortune stated that attack can occur at any time, but most attacks occur at night, and especially when the victim is sleeping, because those are times when psychic resistance is lowest. Phases of the MOON also are important: The waning moon and dark of the moon are considered to be the best times for the working of harmful magic.

Symptoms of an attack are varied and include unexplained behavior, disturbed dreams, the Old Hag syndrome, repulsive smells, exhaustion, confusion, dizziness, mental breakdown, illness, and the occurrence of poltergeist phenomena. In some cases, victims may show bruises or tiny bite marks, which may bleed. Fortune, who believed herself to be psychically attacked numerous times, awoke one morning with dried BLOOD on her pillow from a small puncture behind the angle of the jaw. She attributed the puncture to the presence of a girl who was a psychic vampire. Others in the girl's proximity reported the same puncture marks and blood.

Fortune's help was sought by many who feared they were victims of occult attack. One case she cites in *Psychic Self-Defence* is that of Mr. C. and his two wives, who were victimized by Miss X. As a young girl, Miss X. had been engaged to a man who, soon after the engagement was announced, developed consumption and died of a violent hemorrhage. A few years later, she became engaged again and the second fiancé also developed consumption. Although he, too, hemorrhaged, his illness was lingering, and he lived as an invalid for years. During his illness, Miss X. took a house, moved him in, and installed an aunt as chaperone. The aunt soon developed listlessness, and for days at a stretch would lie unconscious. However, no cause of her illness could be found.

During the tedium, Miss X. entertained herself by visiting Mr. and Mrs. C. She became infatuated with Mr. C., but her attentions went unrequited. Mrs. C. soon died of cancer of the womb. Much to the chagrin of Miss X., Mr. C. married another woman. The health of the second Mrs. C. began to decline. She suffered nightmares, epilepticlike fits, weakness, and fatigue. Eventually, she was diagnosed as having cancer of the womb. She, too, died.

At about the same time, Miss X.'s aunt and second fiancé also succumbed. Miss X. suffered a mental breakdown and was admitted to a nursing home in the country. In all likelihood, her vampirism finally turned on herself, Fortune believed.

Another modern example of psychic attack is reported in *The Psychology of Witchcraft* (1974) by Tom Ravensdale and James Morgan. It concerns a young woman and her husband who were offered accommodation by an older woman whom they knew slightly. Soon after moving in, the young woman began to feel uncomfortable by constant attention from the old landlady. She waited for the girl to come home from work every evening, and she would find a reason to visit the young woman when the husband was not present. She would fix the girl with an intense gaze. She seemed to emanate an unpleasant aura.

The young woman's energy declined, and her health deteriorated. As she suffered, the old woman blossomed with vigor and vitality. The girl's husband suggested a change of residence, but the girl declined and opted instead to stay longer at work. As soon as she decreased the time spent in the old woman's house, her condition improved— and the old woman's deteriorated. Within a week or two, the old woman was bedridden. Unfortunately, the girl took pity on her and took to caring for her. The old woman's health improved immediately, but the girl's health declined to the point where her husband sent her to a doctor. The doctor diagnosed her as anemic and overworked, and ordered her to rest and eat a better diet. She followed his instructions, but made no improvement. Instead, she steadily grew worse and suffered from complete exhaustion and severe headaches.

Then the husband noticed two small red patches on her throat. The marks didn't hurt and were of unknown cause, so they were ignored.

The old woman, meanwhile, had become so rejuvenated and youthful-looking that she decided to take a trip into the country to visit relatives. During her absence, the girl's health returned. She decided to consult a psychic. The psychic clairvoyantly saw the old woman as a psychic vampire surrounded by an aura of evil, and advised the girl and her husband to depart the house immediately. They lacked the funds to do so.

When the old woman returned, the girl's health once again declined. Now she was so weakened she was hospitalized. Her red marks returned, and now they bled. A Spiritualist friend visited and recommended that the girl wear a crucifix and a ring blessed by a priest, and have her room sealed with holy WATER. The terrified girl agreed. When these measures had been taken, she experienced an immediate and marked improvement in her condition.

The "vampire" in turn became furious and displayed an uncontrolled hatred toward the girl. But as the girl became stronger, the old woman weakened. At last the girl and her husband were able to move out. She made a complete recovery.

Not all cases of psychic vampirism are perpetrated by a calculating and malevolent individual. Some people seem to be unwitting energy vampires. Fortune, whose occult study was coupled with a study of psychoanalysis, found some clinic cases to be unusually exhausting. A nurse informed her that these same patients had an extraordinary capacity to absorb high voltages of electricity from the various therapy machines in use at the time.

Protection Against Psychic Attack
According to occult experts, protection against psychic attack and vampirism can be gained by picturing an ovoid shell of white mist surrounding one's body, becoming denser and denser with each outward breath. One should project with the will determination that evil forces will not be able to penetrate the shell. Form it in the morning and repeat at midday and whenever entering crowds or undesirable or threatening areas. Repeat at night prior to sleep.

When walking along streets, keep the hands closed to retain one's magnetic energies. On trains, buses, and so forth, sit with hands clasped and the left foot placed over the right. This closes the circuit of the body's electricity.

See also THE PARASITE.

FURTHER READING:
Eaves, A. Osborne. "Modern Vampirism, in *The Vampire of the Slavs* by Jan. L. Perkowski. Cambridge, Mass.: Slavica Publishers, 1976.
Fortune, Dion. *Psychic Self-Defence.* York Beach, Me.: Samuel Weiser, 1957. First published 1939.
Ravensdale, Tom, and James Morgan. *The Psychology of Witchcraft.* New York: Arco, 1974.

Qisaruatsiaq   In Inuit lore, a woman who shape-shifts into a wolf. Qisaruatsiaq has a wolf body and human head.
   See also SHAPE-SHIFTING.

Quarry, Robert (1925–)   Horror film star best known for his VAMPIRE count in the cult classics *COUNT YORGA* (1970) and *The Return of Count Yorga* (1971).

Robert Quarry was born in California and grew up in Santa Rosa. His father was a doctor. His grandmother introduced him to the theater. He acted in school and made his film debut at age 15 in Alfred Hitchcock's *Shadow of a Doubt*, which helped him start his career in film, television, and radio. At age 18 he joined the Army Combat Engineers. While serving in the army, he started a theatrical troupe. One of his productions was seen by President Franklin D. Roosevelt and his wife.

After the end of World War II, Quarry worked in television in New York City and struggled to get re-established in film. Though signed by two major studios—Metro-Goldwyn-Mayer and 20th Century Fox—his career languished. He acted onstage in productions around the country and did commercials. In 1963 he started a long-running role in the television series *Mr. Adams and Eve*.

In 1965 Quarry suffered cancer, from which he fully recovered. He landed some film roles, most notably with Paul Newman in *Winning* (from which his only scene was cut) and *WUSA*, in which he had a small part as a television station manager.

His fortunes changed in 1970, when he made *Count Yorga*, the first of three horror films that catapulted him into the spotlight. He did *The Return of Count Yorga* in 1971, followed by *The Deathmaster* (1972), in which biker teenagers meet horror at the hands of Quarry's Charles Manson–like vampire.

Quarry then starred in numerous horror films, usually playing villainous characters. In *Dr. Phibes Rises Again* (1974), he played opposite Vincent Price in the role of Biederbeck, a man who is obsessed with eternal life. Other acting roles are in action and disaster films, and in television shows.

In 1982 Quarry suffered severe injuries—broken knees, ribs, and a cheekbone—when he was mugged outside his apartment in North Hollywood. He was carrying only $22 on him. He credits his recovery to his positive attitude.

Quarry makes frequent appearances at fan conferences.

FURTHER READING:
"Robert Quarry." Available online. URL: http://www.tvtome.com. Downloaded on December 30, 2003.

quaxates   Mexican VAMPIRE who makes women weep before it bites them.

Quebec Werewolf   Creature that terrorized the Kamasouraska area in Quebec in the mid-18th century. No description is given of the beast, which might have been a large, marauding wolf. Hunts were organized against it. According to an article in the *Quebec Gazette* on December 2, 1764:

> We learn that a *Ware-Wolfe,* which has roamed throughout this Province for several Years, and done great Destruction in the District of Quebec, has received several considerable Attacks in the month of October last, by different Animals, which they had armed and incensed against this Monstre; and especially the 3rd of November following, he received such a furious Blow, from a small lean Beast, that it was thought they were entirely delivered from this fatal Animal, as it some Time after retired into its Hole, to the great Satisfaction of the Public. But they have just learn'd, as the most surest Misfortune, that this Beast is not entirely destroyed, but begins again to show itself, more furious than ever, and makes terrible Hovock wherever it goes.—*Beware then of the Wiles of this malicious Beast, and take good Care of falling into its Claws.*

There is no record how much longer the creature menaced the province, or its ultimate fate.

FURTHER READING:
Colombo, John Robert. *Mysterious Canada: Strange Sights, Extraordinary Events, and Peculiar Places.* Toronto: Doubleday, 1988.

Queen of the Damned, The (1988)   Third VAMPIRE novel by ANNE RICE, continuing the story of the vampire Lestat. Rice received an advance of $500,000 for the book.

In *The Queen of the Damned,* Rice pursues Lestat's theme of doing evil to accomplish ultimate good to its logical conclusion. The vampire queen, Akasha, destroys her mate, Enkil. She abducts Lestat to help her carry out her plans for a new world order: To rectify all the cruelty and injustice perpetrated by men over the centuries, particularly against women, Lestat will help her kill 99 percent of the men on earth. The surviving women will then exact peace and worship Akasha as their goddess of salvation.

Seduced by Akasha's beauty, Lestat begins the work on the island of Lykanos. He loves the bloodletting; he is, after all, a male vampire. Akasha justifies her actions by her power alone, claiming she is the Queen of Heaven. After meeting with his vampire friends, however, Lestat comes to realize that saving 1 percent of the men was Akasha's acknowledgment that women cannot perpetuate human-

Akasha (Aaliyah) in Queen of the Damned *(Author's collection)*

kind alone, and that possession of his male soul is her weak link. He sides with those morally opposed to Akasha's new order. The queen of the vampires is destroyed and humanity is saved.

FURTHER READING:
Holte, James Craig, ed. *The Fantastic Vampire: Studies in the Children of the Night, Selected Essays from the Eighteenth International Conference on the Fantastic in the Arts.* Westport, Conn.: Greenwood Press, 2002.
Ramsland, Katherine. *The Vampire Companion: The Official Guide to Anne Rice's* The Vampire Chronicles. New York: Ballantine Books, 1993.
Rice, Anne. *The Queen of the Damned.* New York: Alfred A. Knopf, 1988.

rain   In Romanian lore, rain falls from heaven when a LIVING VAMPIRE washes itself or wets its tail. During droughts, nobles ordered all their men to wash, in case one of them was a vampire. Certain vampires, such as VAMPIRE SORCERERS AND WITCHES, have power to control rain. In rarer cases, dead vampires are credited with causing rain.

Rakovic, Milos (d. 1836)   Serbian man suspected of being a VAMPIRE, who was dug up three times. Milos Rakovic died shortly after Easter in 1836 in the Serbian village of Svojdrug. By August he was suspected of being a vampire. Without informing the church authorities, who would disapprove, a group of villagers disinterred the CORPSE and examined it for signs of vampirism. The body was reburied. The priest was then informed, and the villagers and the priest returned to the grave and dug up the body a second time. The priest poured holy WATER on him and the body was reburied. This still did not end the vampire attacks, and so three days later, villagers returned to the grave a third time and dug up the body. This time, the corpse was shot through and was decapitated. The remains were reburied.

The case demonstrates failure of Christian remedies to end the vampire attacks. The attacks ceased only after traditional methods were employed.

FURTHER READING:
Fine, John V. A., Jr. "In Defense of Vampires, in *The Vampire: A Casebook,* Alan Dundes, ed. Madison: University of Wisconsin Press, 1998.

rakshasa (raksasa)   In Indian lore, a type of vampiric demon that operates at night, especially during the dark and new MOONS. *Rakshasa* means "destroyer. They are considered to be evil and hostile to mankind. Like the Greek birth demons, the rakshasa attacks the vulnerable, especially children and women at their weddings. They also attack men while they eat and drink, entering their bodies and driving them insane.

Rakshasas usually appear as gigantic, misshapen humans with fiery eyes and abnormally long tongues. Their bodies are covered with coarse, bristling hair. They have yellow or flaming RED matted hair and beards, horns, huge bellies, slits for eyes, and odd numbers of limbs, such as one arm and leg or three arms and legs. They may have a single EYE. They wear a wreath of entrails. If not black, they are yellow, green or BLUE. Sometimes they have animal heads. They can shape-shift (see SHAPE-SHIFTING) into dogs, eagles, vultures, owls, and cuckoos, and can masquerade as dwarves, husbands, and lovers.

Rakshasas can enter into a person through the mouth when one is eating or drinking. Women who are pregnant are especially vulnerable.

Rakshasas have disgusting habits, such as eating human flesh and drinking human BLOOD from the skull; eating food which has been sneezed upon, walked upon, or soiled by insects; and eating CORPSES. They also roam around forests, looking for animals to eat, always trying to satisfy an insatiable hunger. They have the power to reanimate corpses, and will take possession of an unwary man through his food, causing madness or illness. One touched by a rakshasa dies.

Rakshasas especially haunt jungles, wooded areas, and forests. Their powers increase with nightfall. When they walk about, they howl and cast their eyes from side to side as they search for prey to satisfy their bloodlust. They also like to haunt places of worship and to disrupt the prayer there.

A remedy against rakshasas calls for a ritual of eating rice pudding or porridge boiled over a bird's nest. The smell will placate the demon.

Despite their formidable evil powers, rakshasas, like many demonic beings, are reputed to be dimwitted. The ease with which rakshasas can be outwitted is demonstrated in stories in the *Pantschatantra, Mahabarata,* and *Katha Sarit Sagara* works of myth and lore.

According to one version in the *Pantschatantra,* a rakshasa that haunted a certain wood one day came upon a Brahmin, jumped on his shoulders, demanding to be carried. The Brahmin, fearful of the rakshasa, obeyed. But as he traveled along, he noticed that the demon's feet were as delicate as the stems of a lotus. The Brahmin asked the rakshaha why his feet were so weak and delicate. The rakshasa answered that he never walked nor touched the earth with his feet, and he had made a vow not do so.

Soon they arrived at a pond. The rakshasa ordered the Brahmin to wait while he bathed and prayed to the gods. The Brahmin was certain that when the demon finished, he would tear the man to pieces and eat him. He suddenly realized that if he ran away, the rakshasa could not pursue him because of his vow never to walk. So the Brahmin dashed off and escaped. The rakshasa could do nothing because he was afraid to break his vow.

See also *PISACA.*

FURTHER READING:
Baring-Gould, Sabine. *The Book of Werewolves.* London: Smith, Elder & Co., 1865.
Guiley, Rosemary Ellen. *The Encyclopedia of Ghosts and Spirits.* 2d ed. New York: Facts On File, 2000.
Mack, Carol K., and Dinah Mack. *A Field Guide to Demons, Fairies, Fallen Angels, and Other Subversive Spirits.* New York: Henry Holt/Owl Books, 1998.

ramanga   In the lore of Madagascar, a living VAMPIRE of sorts who served royalty. The *ramanga* drank the spilled BLOOD and ate the fingernail parings of their noble masters so that these would not fall into the hands of evil sorcerers.

Ransom, Frederick (d. 1817)   Alleged VAMPIRE case of Vermont. Frederick Ransom, of South Woodstock, Vermont, was a student at Dartmouth College when he contracted tuberculosis and died on February 14, 1817, at age 20. A belief had been handed down through the family that members had an inherited tendency to die of consumption before age 30. After Frederick's death, his father had his CORPSE exhumed and his heart cut out and burned in a blacksmith's forge in the hopes that this remedy would prevent others in the family from becoming ill due to the baleful influence of the dead.

Unfortunately, the measure was unsuccessful, for tuberculosis claimed the lives of Frederick's mother in 1821, a sister in 1828, and two brothers in 1830 and 1832. A younger brother, Daniel, did not fall ill, and lived into his 80s. Although only three years old at the time of Frederick's death, Daniel preserved family recollections of the events and left a written memoir.

See also NEW ENGLAND VAMPIRES.

FURTHER READING:
Bell, Michael E. *Food for the Dead: On the Trail of New England's Vampires.* New York: Carroll & Graf, 2001.

rats   Animals controlled by COUNT DRACULA, and part of his plague of evil upon humanity.

In BRAM STOKER's novel *DRACULA* (1897), Count Dracula grants his insane disciple R. M. RENFIELD a vision of his new order. Renfield describes it:

> . . . a dark mass spread over the grass, coming on like the shape of a flame of fire; and then he [Dracula] moved the mist to the right and left, and I could see that there were thousands of rats with their eyes blazing red—like his, only smaller.

Later in the novel, the protaganists, who have now become VAMPIRE HUNTERS—Jonathan Harker, PROFESSOR ABRAHAM VAN HELSING, Quincy P. Morris, Dr. John Seward, and Arthur Holmwood—go to the count's house, Carfax Abbey, to ascertain how many boxes of earth remain there. The count had brought 50 with him from TRANSYLVANIA. Holmwood fears the place may be full of rats and takes with him a whistle that will summon his terriers.

At the abbey, they find only 29 boxes left. Holmwood and Harker think they see a vision of the count's gloating evil face, with his RED eyes and red lips. Suddenly, the place becomes alive with rats swarming in the shadows. Holmwood leaps to action and blows his whistle, and three terriers come running.

But in a matter of moments, the numbers of rats increases dramatically. Harker describes the scene:

> They seemed to swarm over the place all at once, till the lamplight, shining on their moving dark bodies and glittering, baleful eyes, made the place look like a bank of earth set with fireflies. The dogs dashed on, but at the threshold suddenly stopped and snarled, and then, simultaneously lifting their noses, began to howl in the most lugubrious fashion. The rats were multiplying in thousands, and we moved out.

The dogs reorganize, and suddenly the rats vanish en masse. With them goes the feeling of an "evil presence."

Rats abound in F. W. MURNAU's film *NOSFERATU* (1922), an unauthorized adaptation of *Dracula.* Rats crawl over the

CORPSE-like form of the vampire, GRAF ORLOCK, as he journeys by ship from his native land to Bremen, Germany. There he unleashes hordes of plague-bearing rats upon the city, and they stream out from the ship as messengers of death. In Werner Herzog's 1979 remake of *Nosferatu*, the rat scene was filmed using sterile white laboratory rats.

Ray Family Vampires (1854)   Alleged vampires of Jewett City, Connecticut. Vampirism was suspected following the tuberculosis deaths of several members of the Henry B. Ray family of Jewett City, near Griswold, Connecticut, between 1845 and 1854. The first to die was the second oldest son, Lemuel Billings Ray, in March 1845, at age 24. Four years later, the father, Henry B., died. He was followed in 1851 by son Elisha H., 26.

According to a news report in the *Norwich Weekly Courier* in June 1854, another son (unnamed) was stricken with the same disease, and it was decided to dig up the two dead brothers and burn them to stop their vampiric effect upon the living family members.

The stricken son was probably Henry Nelson, born in 1819; his date of death is unknown, and it is possible that he survived his tuberculosis. Another surviving son, James Leonard, died in 1854.

MONTAGUE SUMMERS reports the father's name as Horace Ray, the name that appeared in the *Norwich Weekly Courier.* No records exist of a Horace Ray in Jewett City; however, the details of the case match the circumstances of the Henry B. Ray family.

See also NEW ENGLAND VAMPIRES.

FURTHER READING:
Bell, Michael E. *Food for the Dead: On the Trail of New England's Vampires.* New York: Carroll & Graf, 2001.

red   Color that protects against VAMPIRES, evil spirits, and forces. Red ribbons and amulets are worn by people and animals to protect against the EVIL EYE, bewitchment, and attacks by malevolent forces such as demons and vampires.

In Slavic lore, a telltale sign of vampirism is the red appearance of a CORPSE, which suggests the vampire has been feasting on the BLOOD of the living. The mouth especially will be red, as will be the face and head. Anecdotal accounts describe the corpse as "red as red" or "red as a vampire." Colloquial expressions among the Slavs refer to the redness of vampires in terms of someone being angry: "he was as red as a vampire."

Modern Romanian farm horses wear long red-colored yarn earlocks as a protection against misfortune and evil.
(Photo by R. E. Guiley)

In *DRACULA* (1897) by BRAM STOKER, the vampire COUNT DRACULA has notably red eyes as his vampire nature becomes increasingly apparent. Stoker also emphasized the count's red, blood-gorged lips.

See also BLUE.

Redcap   Fairy with BLOOD hat. Redcap is one of the most malignant and vampirelike goblins of the folklore of the border counties between England and Scotland. He lives in various old and ruined castles and peel towers, where he takes delight in wreaking evil upon unwitting visitors. He keeps his cap dyed red from human blood.

One description of Redcap is as follows:

> . . . a short thickset old man, with long prominent teeth, skinny fingers armed with talons like eagles, large eyes of a fiery red color, hair streaming down his shoulders, iron boots, a pikestaff in his left hand, and a red cap on his head.

If one encounters Redcap, it is useless to try to resist him by brute human strength. He can be repelled, however, by making the sign of the CROSS or reciting biblical scripture. Redcap will shriek and disappear, leaving one of his long teeth behind him.

Lord Soulis of Hermitage Castle in Scotland reputedly had a Redcap as a FAMILIAR. In European lore, Redcaps have a milder nature and are more like the helpful household brownies, who clean and do chores.

FURTHER READING:
Briggs, Katharine. *An Encyclopedia of Fairies.* New York: Pantheon Books, 1976.

Rémy, Nicholas (1530–1616)   French lawyer, demonologist, and witch-hunter who claimed to have sent 900 witches to their deaths over a 10-year period in Lorraine. Nicholas Rémy believed in SABBATS, pacts with the devil, and other evil acts of witches, including SHAPE-SHIFTING into beasts such as wolves. Rémy is best known for his book *Demonolatry,* which became a leading handbook for witch-hunters.

Rémy was born in Charmes to a family of distinguished lawyers. He studied law at the University of Toulouse and practiced in Paris from 1563 to 1570, when he was appointed lieutenant general of Vosges, filling a vacancy created by his retiring uncle. In 1575 he was appointed secretary to Duke Charles III of Lorraine. Rémy also was an historian and poet, and wrote several works on history.

As a youth, Rémy had witnessed the trials of witches. In 1582 he took up his own personal crusade against witches after a tragic incident that convinced him his son was bewitched to death. Rémy refused a beggar woman, and several days later his oldest son died. Rémy successfully prosecuted her for casting a fatal spell on his son. Like his contemporary JEAN BODIN, Rémy believed that witches should suffer and be burned as punishment.

In 1592 Rémy retired to the countryside to escape the plague. There he compiled *Demonolatry,* which was published in 1595 in Lyons. The book includes notes and details from his many trials.

Rémy writes that nearly all of the accused witches he tried confessed to being able to shape-shift into animal form in order to move about secretly. Some changed into wolves to wreak havoc and take revenge. Besides testimony at trials, he also heard stories of shape-shifting from people he considered to be credible sources.

He cites the 1581 trial of a shepherd, Petrone of Armentières:

> Petrone . . . was so moved with hatred or envy against the herdsmen of neighboring flocks, he used to utter certain words by which he was changed into a wolf; and being in such disguise, safe from all suspicion of ill doing, he would then fall upon and rend in pieces every beast of the herd that he could find.

Another case Rémy mentions concerns a woman from Thiecourt who had been given shape-shifting power by a demon:

> She had contracted an immoderate hatred of a shepherd of that village, and, wishing by any means to produce his heavy punishment, sprang in the form of a wolf upon his sheep as they were grazing. But he ran up and threw an axe at her and wounded her in the thigh, so that she was disabled and was forced to take refuge behind the nearest bush, where she was found by the pursuing shepherd, binding her wounds with strips torn from her clothing to staunch the blood which was flowing freely. On this evidence she was taken up, confessed everything as I have related it, and paid the penalty for her crimes in the fire.

Rémy agreed with other leading demonologists that no demon has the power to confer shape-shifting ability, and the human soul cannot enter into animal forms. However, so many accused witches were so adamant that they could shape-shift that their stories could not be entirely without warrant. He considered the possibility that shape-shifting was merely an illusion created by the devil:

> The Demon can so confuse the imagination of a man that he believes himself to be changed; and then the man behaves and conducts himself not as a man, but as the beast which he fancies himself to be . . .
>
> Secondly, these illusions can be caused extrinsically, when the Demon causes an actual object to assume the apparent shape which suits his purpose at the time, and so deludes a man's senses into the belief that an object can be changed into a different form.

Thus, the devil can make people think they themselves are transformed, and he can cause others to falsely see a transformed shape.

But Rémy's final conclusion is that these accounts do have a basis in fact, and that "these things are actually what they appear to be," made possible by demonic influence. Everything that is not natural is due to the devil, who can make witches take on animallike attributes and powers:

But there is another far stronger argument which might appear to prove the actuality of these transformations. It is not only the external physical shape that appears to be changed; the witch is also endowed with all the natural qualities and powers of the animal into which she is seemingly changed. For she acquires fleetness of foot; bodily strength; ravenous ferocity; the lust of howling; the faculty of breaking into places, and of silent movement; and other such animal characteristics, which are far beyond human strength or ability. For it is a matter of daily experience that Satan does actually so empower them. Thus they can easily kill even the biggest cattle in the fields, and even devour raw flesh, when they descend upon them as swiftly as any wolf or ferocious beast; and they enter locked houses at night like cats; and in every way imitate the nature and habits of the animals whose shape and appearance they assume. Now this cannot be explained away as a mere glamor or prestige by which our senses are deceived in the manner already set forth; for they leave behind them concrete traces of their activities.

Thus, according to Rémy, shape-shifting has a weird reality of both illusion and fact.

Rémy's claim of sending 900 witches to their deaths cannot be corroborated by existing records; he cites only 128 cases himself in his book. Nevertheless, *Demonolatry* was an immediate success and was reprinted eight times, including two German translations. Its popularity overshadowed the dominant witch-hunting handbook, the *Malleus Maleficarum,* in some parts of Europe.

FURTHER READING:

Guiley, Rosemary Ellen. *The Encyclopedia of Witches and Witchcraft.* 2d ed. New York: Facts On File, 1999.

Otten, Charlotte F., ed. *A Lycanthropy Reader: Werewolves in Western Culture.* New York: Dorset Press, 1989.

Rémy, Nicolas. *Demonolatry.* Secaucus, N.J.: University Books, 1974.

Renfield, R. M.   Character in BRAM STOKER's novel *DRACULA* (1897) who believes he must consume BLOOD in order to live.

R. M. Renfield is a 59-year-old psychotic confined to a mental asylum run by Dr. John Seward in the London area. Seward describes him as a suffering from "homicidal and religious mania" and "monomania." The latter was a common diagnosis of the times that later was replaced by "hysteria." Renfield has a "sanguine temperament; great physical strength; morbidly excitable; periods of gloom ending in some fixed idea which I cannot make out," writes Seward in his diary.

Renfield manages to escape his cell from time to time and wind up at Carfax Abbey, an abandoned estate next to

R. M. Renfield (Dwight Frye) with Professor Abraham Van Helsing (Edward Van Sloan) in Tod Browning's Dracula *(Author's collection)*

the asylum that is purchased by COUNT DRACULA. After the count arrives in London, he vampirizes Renfield and places him under his domination and influence. He sends fat flies, moths, and spiders to Renfield to eat.

Renfield becomes obsessed with consuming the life force of insects in order to boost his own vitality. He keeps a written record of the numbers he consumes. Soon this is not sufficient, and he begs Seward for a kitten. Seward refuses, and so Renfield captures a bird and eats it raw. He vomits up feathers, to the disgust of his attendant.

Renfield's condition progressively worsens. One night he escapes his cell and attacks Seward in his study. Wielding a dinner knife, he slashes Seward's left wrist, and blood flows onto the carpet. Seward writes:

When the attendants rushed in, and we turned our attention to him, his employment positively sickened me. He was lying on his belly on the floor licking up, like a dog, the blood which had fallen from my wounded wrist. He was easily secured, and, to my surprise, went with the attendants quite placidly, simply repeating over and over again: "The blood is the life! The blood is the life!"

Renfield turns on Dracula and is killed by him. After the count kills Lucy Westenra, he vampirizes Mina Harker, and Renfield does not like what the vampire has done. One night Dracula appears to Renfield in his cell and shows him a vision of multitudes of RATS. He says that Renfield can have unlimited rats if he will fall down and worship Dracula. Renfield agrees and opens the window to let the vampire in.

But the next day nothing arrives, not even a blow-fly. Renfield becomes angry. Then he is visited by Mina, and sees signs that Dracula has been drinking her blood. He decides to stop the vampire. When Dracula comes to Renfield that night, in the form of a mist, Renfield attempts to attack him and futilely grabs at the mist. Dracula gives him a fatal beating and then leaves as mist. Found by attendants, Renfield is able to relate what happened to PROFESSOR ABRAHAM VAN HELSING and Seward as he is dying. His actual death takes place offstage.

FURTHER READING:
Stoker, Bram. *Dracula.* New York: Grosset & Dunlap, 1931.

Renfield's syndrome   See CLINICAL VAMPIRISM.

revenant   The returning dead. The belief that the dead have the ability to return to the world of the living is ancient and universal.

Both humans and animals can be revenants. They can manifest as filmy ghosts or in forms that appear to be solid and alive. A VAMPIRE is a type of revenant. In Irish lore, revenants include living CORPSES, bodies that revive in order to briefly partake of their own funerals.

Reasons why revenants leave their graves are

- Their corpses were not handled properly.
- Their corpses were passed over by certain kinds of animals prior to burial.
- Their burial was not done properly.
- They were not buried at all.
- They are jealous of the living.
- Their soul is not at rest due to sin or unfinished business.
- They have been cursed by a witch or sorcerer.
- They died suddenly and violently or by SUICIDE.
- They were killed by a vampire.

Some revenants are benign and do not return to the living once remedial measures or exorcisms are performed. Some haunt certain locales as ghosts. Vampires, tormented souls, and those cursed by magical spells are seen as dangerous to the living and will attack people and animals and damage property. However, even these revenants can be laid to rest with the proper measures.

See also BURIAL CUSTOMS.

Rhode Island Vampires   See NEW ENGLAND VAMPIRES.

Rice, Anne (1941–)   Novelist famous for her VAMPIRES, and creator of a series called the Vampire Chronicles, which follow the life and adventures of the vampire LESTAT DE LIONCOURT, as well as other characters. Anne Rice has influenced the treatment of vampires in literature—as well as the public perception of vampires—more than any writer since BRAM STOKER.

Rice was born Howard Allen Frances O'Brien on October 4, 1941, in New Orleans, the second of four girls of Howard and Katherine O'Brien. She called herself Anne when she started first grade, and the name stuck. As a child, Rice made up stories and was fascinated by the paranormal world of ghosts, voodoo, and magic in New Orleans. She also loved the Catholic faith of her parents—but by her teens was doubting and rejecting its teachings.

Rice's earliest, and perhaps strongest, influence was her mother, Katherine. Katherine's Irish father had died an alcoholic, and Katherine resolved to be good and pure to compensate. She was very devout and expected the children to be good Catholics. On the other hand, Katherine had very modern ideas about child rearing, allowing the children great freedom. She encouraged their specialness whenever she could, allowing them to dress the way they wanted, or to skip school. She expected them to be perfect geniuses. Although such a background was liberating for a female, Rice often felt that she and her sisters were different, when what she wanted was to fit in.

Katherine could not cope with her husband's long absence during World War II, nor his long workday when he returned. She hated being alone, especially in the dark. Katherine began drinking, finally dying from alcoholism when Rice was 15. After Katherine's death, Howard moved his family to Richardson, Texas, a suburb of Dallas. Rice met Stan Rice, her future husband, in a high school journalism class. It was love at first sight for her, but not for Stan.

Rice rebelled at the double standards for women in the 1950s, and by her first year at Texas Women's University had completely lost faith in Catholicism as well. She transferred to North Texas State University in Denton her sophomore year, but at the end of six weeks left with her roommate for San Francisco. Meanwhile, by the time Stan realized he missed Rice, she had already left for California. They corresponded for a year, then married on October 14, 1961, when Rice was 20. They returned to San Francisco in 1962, where they lived in Haight Ashbury and took their bachelors' degrees from San Francisco State University: his in creative writing, hers in political science.

Living in San Francisco's Haight Ashbury district in the 1960s was a heady experience. Both Rice and Stan were attracted to poets and artists, and they rubbed elbows with nearly everyone who passed through. Stan became a celebrated poet. The couple gave huge parties, experimented with drugs, and drank. Rice found drugs scary, especially marijuana and LSD, but Stan believed in the drugs' mind-expanding capacities.

On September 21, 1966, Rice gave birth to their first child, Michele. Family was very important to both Rice and Stan, and they adored their beautiful blond little girl. Like her mother before her, Rice included Michele in all their activities, exposing her to adult ideas and situations. Their lives seemed to be going very well; Stan's poetry was receiving recognition, and Rice's short stories and books were starting to generate some interest. She began a master's program in creative writing at San Francisco State.

By late 1970, their world shattered. Michele was diagnosed with leukemia. Both tried to maintain normalcy—Rice finished her master's degree—yet they argued over whether to fight the disease to the last minute or let Michele enjoy life while she had it. Rice began drinking more heavily. On August 5, 1972, Michele died.

In the overwhelming grief and guilt that followed, Rice and Stan drew apart. Rice spoke of her early Catholic training with bitter longing and began exploring theories of the afterlife. Rice's drinking grew worse.

After a three-week stay alone with Stan's parents, Rice returned to San Francisco and took a job. But she hated it and asked Stan whether she should try writing full time. He encouraged her, and she began typing at night while Stan slept. During this period Rice suffered from Guillain-Barré syndrome, which gave her polio symptoms in her hands, feet, face, legs, and respiratory system.

Back in 1969, Rice had written a short story called "Interview with the Vampire," and she resurrected it in 1973 as the basis for her first book. It also became a vehicle for the healing of her grief over Michele.

The revised story concerns a reluctant vampire, Louis de Pointe du Lac, who tells his story to a reporter about how he was made a vampire by Lestat De Lioncourt, and the experiences he shared with Lestat and other vampires. Set in 1791 in Louisiana and Europe, the story is lush, erotic, and alluring, and casts vampires in an entirely new light in fiction: that of sympathetic heroes who constantly wrestle with issues of good and evil. One of the key characters is a child vampire, Claudia, made by Lestat, a symbol of Michele. In the initial version, Claudia lives at the end.

Rice finished the book in a feverish five weeks. Publishers rejected it initially, and overcome with a backlash of grief from Michele's death, Rice decided that she was poisoning the book and everything she touched. Obsessive-compulsive behavior caused her to constantly check locks and doors and to wash her hands incessantly.

Rice underwent therapy, but didn't completely lose her compulsions until after attending a writers' conference at Squaw Valley in August 1974. There she met agent Phyllis Seidel. By October, Seidel had sold the manuscript to Alfred A. Knopf for a $12,000 advance for hardcover rights, at a time when $2,000 was a more typical advance. The editor wanted some minor changes, but Rice was delighted.

Ten weeks later, Rice's minor changes had completely revised the story. Claudia is killed in the end, which psychologically buries Michele as well. Instead of the young radio interviewer escaping with his life and the tapes, he begs Louis to grant him immortality. INTERVIEW WITH THE VAMPIRE was published in 1976. It received 75 mixed reviews—far more than a usual first novel—and earned the Rices $750,000 for paperback rights and $150,000 for movie rights.

In 1977, only a year after *Interview with the Vampire*, Rice discovered she was pregnant. Both she and Stan worried about the birth, but it had been five years since Michele's death. Rice stopped drinking during the pregnancy, and Christopher Travis was born on March 11, 1978. One other important event occurred that year. Rice and Stan realized that their drinking had turned dangerous, leading to blackouts. Rice feared becoming an alcoholic like her mother, grandfather, and great-grandfather. So on May 31, 1978, they quit drinking completely.

Although Rice felt she wasn't finished with vampires—and especially Lestat—as a subject, she was eager to try something else for her next project. Her second novel was an historical look at the free people of color—blacks who were not slaves—in New Orleans during the 1840s. Like the vampires, they were outsiders of both the black and white races and had their own community with its own set of rules. She called the book *The Feast of All Saints*, named for the Catholic holy day on November 2 when the faithful go to the cemeteries and place flowers on the graves of their loved ones. The book garnered a $150,000 advance and appeared in 1979. But reviews were mixed and sales were fewer—only 20,000 in hardcover—yielding $35,000 for the paperback rights. Chief complaints about the book were that it was too heavy and dense to read easily.

Rice then turned to a historical novel, *Cry to Heaven*, about two castrati in 18th-century Italy. Published in October 1982, this book also received mixed reviews.

Stung by the criticism, Rice moved to contemporary fiction. Writing under the pseudonym A. N. Roquelaure (*roquelaure* means "cloak" in French), she produced a series of pornographic novels about the further adventures of Sleeping Beauty after her awakening by the prince: *The Claiming of Sleeping Beauty* (1983), *Beauty's Punishment* (1984), and *Beauty's Release* (1985). Using yet another pseudonym, Anne Rampling, Rice wrote *Exit to Eden* (1985), which deals with sexual pleasure and sadomasochism, and *Belinda* (1986).

In 1985, Rice's second vampire novel, THE VAMPIRE LESTAT, was published in October. The book landed on *The New York Times* best-seller list within two weeks and stayed there for seven. Knopf sent Rice on a thirteen-week promotional tour, an event which both excited and terrified her. *The Vampire Lestat* established the Vampire Chronicles, Rice's novels about the lives of Lestat and other vampires.

Before finishing her third vampire novel, THE QUEEN OF THE DAMNED (1988), Rice gave into her homesickness for New Orleans. The Rices bought a second house there in 1988 and moved permanently in 1989 to a Greek Revival mansion in the city's Garden District.

The fourth book in the Vampire Chronicles, THE TALE OF THE BODY THIEF, was published in 1992 and enjoyed a long stay on best-seller lists. The story is told by Lestat, who describes his attempt to commit SUICIDE in the sun, followed by his fascination with a mortal who has perfected the art of stealing bodies, and who offers Lestat the chance to once again enjoy life in a mortal body. Lestat takes it, then regrets it, but getting his own body back proves to be difficult.

In MEMNOCH THE DEVIL (1995), Rice picked up the story of Lestat again in what would become one of her most controversial novels. Lestat goes on a tour of heaven and hell with Memnoch the Devil, with whom he engages in lengthy debates about good and evil, sin and salvation. Lestat even drinks the BLOOD of Christ on the cross and talks with God.

Rice focused on other vampires in *Pandora* (1998), *Armand* (1998), *Vittorio the Vampire* (1999), and *Blood and Gold* (2001). *Pandora* features the story of Pandora, first introduced in *The Vampire Lestat,* the love of Marius.

Armand delves into the personal story of the Botticelli-beautiful Armand, the 17-year-old vampire made by Marius who makes his first appearance in *Interview with the Vampire* as the leader of the Paris coven of vampires that operates the Theater of the Vampires. The story begins in the aftermath of *Memnoch the Devil,* when Armand and other vampires gather around Lestat lying in a cathedral, either dead or in a coma. Armand tells his story of abduction as a child in Kiev, and his sale to a Venetian artist, who turns out to be Marius, the master vampire, and his 500 years of adventures.

Vittorio the Vampire introduces the vampires Vittorio and Ursula in a vampire version of *Romeo and Juliet.* In 15th-century Florence, the well-educated Vittorio enjoys a courtly life. One night his family is attacked by vampires and all are killed, save for Vittorio, who is saved by the vampire Ursula to be her lover. Vittorio seeks revenge for the slaughter of his family.

Blood and Gold tells the story of Marius, once a Roman senator, who was made a vampire by Druids. He is forced to become the keeper of the Divine Parents of all vampires, Akasha and Enkil. Marius is mentor to Lestat and maker of numerous vampires.

Rice delved into witches, creating the Mayfair dynasty of wealthy witches in *The Witching Hour* (1990). Rice used her own house as the setting. The hero of *The Witching Hour,* Michael Curry, carries Rice's great-grandfather's family name, and the large Mayfair family mirrors Rice's love of family and connectedness. Through Michael's impressions and memories of New Orleans, Rice relates lovingly her New Orleans girlhood and the effect the city had upon her.

Merrick (2000) is about Merrick Mayfair, a mixed-blood voodoo witch descended from the Mayfairs, who is a stu-dent of the Talamasca, the secret organization that for centuries has compiled data on the occult. Louis, Lestat, and the ghost of the child vampire Claudia are part of the plot.

Blackwood Farm (2002) features characters from the vampire and witch novels. It introduces Quinn Blackwood, the heir to Blackwood Farm, who becomes a vampire and who is haunted by his own vampiric doppelganger, Goblin. (See DOPPELSAUGER.) Blackwood seeks out Lestat for help.

BLOOD CANTICLE (2003) again mingles the witches and vampires, picking up at the end of *Blackwood Farm*. It was written during a devastating crisis—Stan's fatal illness. In August 2002, he was diagnosed with a cancerous brain tumor. His condition deteriorated rapidly, and he died on December 9 the same year. Rice finished *Blood Canticle* just weeks before he died. She dedicated the book to him.

Other books by Rice are

- *The Mummy of Ramses the Damned* (1989): The Egyptian pharaoh Ramses II, an immortal, reawakens in London in 1914. Ramses reawakens his old love, Cleopatra, and makes her an immortal, too.
- *Servant of the Bones* (1996): Azriel is a Babylonian Jew who is sacrificed, and his body is boiled down to the bones. A necromancer curses him to be bound to his bones, and he becomes the Servant of the Bones, at the mercy of whoever possesses his casket. He is evoked by a dangerous cult leader in modern times in New York City. The plot concerns his efforts to use his free will to defeat the evil cult leader.
- *Lasher* (1993): The demon Lasher from *The Witching Hour* haunts and pursues Rowan Mayfair and their strange child who is able to walk and talk and possess knowledge from birth.
- *Taltos* (1994): Ashlar is a seven-foot-tall taltos, the offspring of witches who possess an extra chromosome. The taltoses possess superhuman intelligence and strength and an extraordinary sex drive. Ashlar is descended from the Mayfair witches. Part of the plot concerns corrupt members of the Talamasca, who seek to kidnap and crossbreed taltoses.
- *Violin* (1997): The story tells of the love affair between a woman, Triana, who is haunted by the ghost of Stefan, a Russian aristocrat and violinist.
- *The Master of Rampling Gate* (2002): Originally a short story published in 1984 in *Redbook,* a sister and brother inherit a mansion haunted by a mysterious presence.

Rice continues to live in the New Orleans area. With the publication of *Blood Canticle,* Rice announced that it marked the end of the Vampire Chronicles, and that she would write no more about vampires or the damned. Her career would take a new turn. She acknowledged, however, that Lestat was a difficult character to end and held open the possibility of being drawn back to him again.

Although numerous novelists owe a debt to Rice for their own vampire characters, Rice said she has seldom read other vampire novels, and with the end of her Vampire Chronicles probably never would do so. Nor did she watch popular vampire-themed television shows such as *ANGEL* and *BUFFY THE VAMPIRE SLAYER*. The latter she termed "very amusing."

FURTHER READING:

Anne Rice Web site: URL: http://www.annerice.com. Accessed on November 29, 2003.

Auerbach, Nina. *Our Vampires, Ourselves.* Chicago: University of Chicago Press, 1995.

Austin, Joanne P. "Anne Rice: Giving the Vampire a Conscious," in *The Complete Vampire Companion* by Rosemary Ellen Guiley with J. B. Macabre. New York: Macmillan, 1994.

Holte, James Craig, ed. *The Fantastic Vampire: Studies in the Children of the Night, Selected Essays from the Eighteenth International Conference on the Fantastic in the Arts.* Westport, Conn.: Greenwood Press, 2002.

"Q&A with Anne Rice About *Blood Canticle.*" Available online. URL: http://www.randomhouse.com/features/annerice/interview03.html. Downloaded on December 21, 2003.

Ramsland, Katherine. *The Vampire Companion: The Official Guide to Anne Rice's* The Vampire Chronicles. New York: Ballantine Books, 1993.

———. *Prism of the Night: A Biography of Anne Rice.* New York: Dutton, 1991.

Rice, Anne. *Blood Canticle.* New York: Alfred A. Knopf, 2003.

———. *Blackwood Farm.* New York: Alfred A. Knopf, 2002.

———. *The Master of Rampling Gate.* New York: Alfred A. Knopf, 2002.

———. *Blood and Gold.* New York: Alfred A. Knopf, 2001.

———. *Merrick.* New York: Alfred A. Knopf, 2000.

———. *Vittorio the Vampire.* New York: Alfred A. Knopf, 1999.

———. *Armand.* New York: Alfred A. Knopf, 1998.

———. *Pandora.* New York: Alfred A. Knopf, 1998.

———. *Violin.* New York: Alfred A. Knopf, 1997.

———. *Servant of the Bones.* New York: Alfred A. Knopf, 1996.

———. *Memnoch the Devil.* New York: Alfred A. Knopf, 1995.

———. *Taltos.* New York: Alfred A. Knopf, 1994.

———. *Lasher.* New York: Alfred A. Knopf, 1993.

———. *The Tale of the Body Thief.* New York: Alfred A. Knopf, 1992.

———. *The Witching Hour.* New York: Alfred A. Knopf, 1990.

———. *The Mummy of Ramses the Damned.* New York: Alfred A. Knopf, 1989.

———. *The Queen of the Damned.* New York: Alfred A. Knopf, 1988.

———. *The Vampire Lestat.* New York: Alfred A. Knopf, 1985.

———. *Interview with the Vampire.* New York: Alfred A. Knopf, 1976.

Riley, Michael. *Conversations with Anne Rice: An Intimate, Enlightening Portrait of Her Life and Work.* New York: Ballantine, 1996.

Riva, James P., II (1958–) Convicted "vampire" murderer. On April 10, 1980, 22-year-old James P. Riva assaulted his invalid grandmother, Carmen Lopez, 74, of Marshfield, Massachusetts. He beat her, stabbed her, and then shot her in the heart with GOLD-painted bullets, and tried to drink BLOOD from her wounds. Then he doused her body with a gas-line antifreeze and set it afire. Riva claimed he was instructed to commit the crime by "the voices."

From early childhood, Riva had demonstrated an obsession with blood, drawing pictures of human body parts and hypodermic needles oozing blood. By the time he was an adolescent, he was fascinated with VAMPIRES. He used drugs, and became convinced that aliens had planted a transmitter in his head to control his body. He had two short stays in a mental hospital, and then his family became so frightened by his bizarre behavior that his mother went to court to get him out.

Riva wound up in Florida, where, he said, he met some bad vampires, including a 2,000-year-old who had given him some blood. He was afraid of them, and finally came home. He began killing and abusing animals for their blood, and was committed again to a hospital. Some time after he was released into the custody of his father (his parents were by then divorced), Riva murdered his paternal grandmother. He believed that she was using an icepick on him at night while he slept in order to take his blood to prolong her life.

In his trial, Riva's mother testified as to his long history of mental disturbances. She said he confessed the murder to her when she visited him at the Plymouth County House of Correction two months after the crime. She testified that Riva told her he had been a vampire for four years. Voices told him he had to be a vampire and had to drink blood. He said he had been talking with the devil for a long time.

He also told his mother that he argued with the voice against killing his grandmother, but felt he would die if he didn't. He was told to use gold-painted bullets because they would find their mark.

Medical records from 1978–81 showed that Riva had suffered hallucinations, that he believed that most people were vampires, and that he heard voice telling him to take the blood of others, or he would die.

The defense brought in four psychiatrists, three of whom diagnosed him as a paranoid schizophrenic, while the fourth diagnosed him as a manic depressive with delusional mania. The prosecution's rebuttal psychiatrist said Riva was "aware of wrongdoing" and was "criminally responsible" for his actions. All of the psychiatrists said Riva had told them that a vampire instructed him in 1978 to kill a cat, operate on it, and drink its blood.

On October 30, 1981, a jury found Riva guilty of second-degree murder and arson, as well as guilty of assault and battery on the police officer. He was sentenced to life in prison in Walpole State Prison, Massachusetts, with 19 to 20 years concurrently for the arson. He is eligible for parole after 15 years. He appealed his conviction, but in 1984 the Massachusetts Appeals Court upheld it.

FURTHER READING:
Guiley, Rosemary Ellen, with J. B. Macabre. *The Complete Vampire Companion*. New York: Macmillan, 1994.
"James P. Riva: The Schizophrenic Vampire." Available online. URL: http://www.sacrosanctum.org/research/riva.html. Downloaded on Apr. 23, 2004.

Romulus and Remus   See LUPERCALIA.

Rose Family Vampire **(1874)**   Alleged VAMPIRE of Rhode Island. According to 19th-century news reports and oral lore, William G. Rose, a native of Exeter, Rhode Island, dug up the body of his daughter in 1874 and burned the heart because he feared she had become a vampire and was draining the vitality of his members of his family. The name of the daughter is uncertain, but it probably was Ruth Ellen, born in 1859, who died on May 12, 1874, probably of consumption.

Some reports say the Roses lived in Peace Dale, Rhode Island, though no records exist that they did. Ruth Ellen was the daughter of William Rose and his first wife, who died in 1863. His second wife, Mary, was a great granddaughter of Stukeley Tillinghast, the father of SARAH TILLINGHAST. Rose may have been one of the persons who counseled George Brown to disinter the bodies of his daughter MERCY BROWN and her siblings on fears of vampirism.

William and Mary Rose are buried in South Kingstown. The gravesite of Ruth Ellen is unknown.

See also NEW ENGLAND VAMPIRES.

FURTHER READING:
Bell, Michael E. *Food for the Dead: On the Trail of New England's Vampires*. New York: Carroll & Graf, 2001.

roses   See WILD ROSES.

Roulet, Jacques **(1598)**   The "Werewolf of Angers." Thirty-five-year-old Jacques Roulet was a beggar tried and convicted of being a WEREWOLF in Angers, France.

In 1598 some men out in a remote area near Caude heard screaming and came upon two wolves tearing up the mangled and bloody freshly killed CORPSE of a boy. The wolves fled into the brush, and the men pursued them. Just as they lost the tracks, they found a half-naked man crouching in the thicket. He had long hair and beard, his hands were stained with BLOOD, and his teeth were literally chattering in fear. The man had long, clawlike fingernails that were filled with the fresh blood and gore of human flesh.

The man, Jacques Roulet, confessed that he had smothered the boy to death, but said he had been prevented from eating him by the arrival of the men.

Roulet lived as a beggar, going from house to house with fellow beggars, his brother Jean and his cousin Julian. Roulet had been given lodging in a nearby village, but had been missing for eight days.

At his trial, Roulet testified that he transformed himself into a wolf with the help of an OINTMENT given him by his parents. He did not know the ingredients in the ointment. He said the two wolves seen with the corpse of the boy were Jean and Julian, who also possessed the ability to take on wolf shapes. Roulet accurately described the boy who had been murdered, and the place and date. He accurately described the boy's father, who was the first to arrive when the boy screamed.

In prison, Roulet behaved like a madman. On his first day, he drank a pail of water and thereafter refused to eat or drink.

His parents testified at court and seemed to be normal, respectable folk. They provided evidence proving that Jean and Julian had been in distant locations on the day of the boy's murder.

Roulet said at his trial that he had killed and eaten other children, and also had attended witches' SABBATS. He used his teeth to kill the boy. His feet and hands became wolf's paws, but his head remained human.

The court sentenced Roulet to death, but he appealed the sentence to the Parliament in Paris. He impressed the Parliament as more of a poor idiot than an evil creature, and so his sentence was commuted to two years' imprisonment in an insane asylum, during which he was to receive religious instruction.

See also LYCANTHROPY; SHAPE-SHIFTING.

FURTHER READING:
Baring-Gould, Sabine. *The Book of Werewolves*. London: Smith, Elder & Co., 1865.
Robbins, Rossell Hope. *The Encyclopedia of Witchcraft & Demonology*. New York: Bonanza Books, 1981.
Sidky, H. *Witchcraft, Lycanthropy, Drugs and Disease: An Anthropological Study of the European Witch-Hunts*. New York: Peter Lang, 1997.

Ruthven   See LORD RUTHVEN.

ruvanush   In the lore of GYPSIES, a WEREWOLF. *Ruvanush* is a Romany term for "wolf-man," from *ruv* "wolf" and *manush* "man."

A *ruvanush* can be created by vampiric witches who suck the BLOOD of men born during the waxing MOON. A victim becomes a fierce werewolf by night. Even after resuming his human form at dawn, the *ruvanush* can consume only raw flesh and blood.

A witch can also be a *ruvanush,* as illustrated in the account of a 19th-century case of a poor Hungarian Gypsy fiddler named Kropan, who lived with his wife in Toresz in northern Hungary. Kropan became aware that his wife was slipping out of the house at night. He suspected her of carrying on an affair, and so he secretly watched her. She would wait until she thought he was asleep and then leave. But she was not out dallying with a lover. To Kropan's horror, she would return at dawn in the form of a wolf and change back into her human shape. She brought with her livestock she had killed, which she proceeded to cook for her husband.

Kropan said nothing. His earnings barely bought them bread, so he was grateful for the selection of fine meats, including lamb, beef, pork, and chicken. The couple had so much meat that he started selling it in a nearby town and grew rich in profits. He opened an inn that sold inexpensive dishes and attracted even more business.

Eventually, the wolfish ravages of the wife aroused suspicion among the villagers. Exposed, both Kropan and his wife were exorcized by a priest. When sprinkled with holy WATER, the wife shrieked as though she had been plunged into boiling oil. She disappeared. The angry mob turned on Kropan and killed him. Two peasants held to be the ringleaders of the murder were convicted and imprisoned for six years. They were released in 1881.

FURTHER READING:
Summers, Montague. *The Werewolf.* New York: Bell Publishing, 1966.

Rymer, James Malcolm (1804–1884)

Scottish author of at least most of the anonymous "penny dreadful" VARNEY THE VAMPIRE (1847).

Rymer, an ex-civil engineer, desired a literary career, and in 1842 he was editor of the esteemed *Queen's Magazine.* He wrote and published an article heaping ridicule on "penny dreadfuls," serial novels that sold for a penny for each installment and were cheap entertainment for the working classes. He characterized that audience as ignorant "animals" who were enthralled by superstition and fear:

If an author wishes to become popular—that is, to be read by the majority—he should, ere he begins to write, study well the animals for whom he is about to cater . . . But, it may be said, How then are we to account for the taste which maintained for so long for works of terror and blood? Most easily. It is the privilege of the ignorant and the weak to love superstition. The only strong mental sensation they are capable of is *fear* . . . There are millions of minds that have no resource between vapid sentimentality, and the ridiculous spectra of the nursery.

However, Rymer wrote penny dreadfuls himself, anonymously, as well as other popular fiction under pseudonyms. He discovered that he was very good at writing the lurid fiction he said he despised. He could manipulate the clichés that characterized such works and contributed to their popularity.

Rymer wrote two penny dreadfuls for *Lloyd's Penny Weekly Miscellany: Varney* and *Ada the Betrayed* (1847). Both were among Lloyd's best sellers for up to 15 years after publication. He spent the rest of his career writing penny dreadfuls and popular fiction, for Lloyd's until 1853, for John Dicks from 1853 to 1857, for *Reynolds' Miscellany* from 1858 to 1864, and for *London Miscellany* in 1866. The penny dreadful market became aimed primarily at children in the 1850s.

Rymer also wrote a novel, *The Black Monk* (1841). Two of his pseudonyms were Malcolm J. Merry and Malcolm J. Errym. Both last names are anagrams of Rymer.

For a long time credit for *Varney* was given to Thomas Preskett Prest, the author of *Sweeney Todd,* another highly successful penny dreadful. But in 1963, Louis James, who inherited some of Rymer's scrapbooks, established that Rymer was the true author of at least a majority of the work.

FURTHER READING:
Frayling, Christopher. *Vampyres: Lord Byron to Count Dracula.* London: Faber and Faber, 1991.
Haining, Peter, and Peter Tremayne. *The Undead: The Legend of Bram Stoker and Dracula.* London: Constable, 1997.

sabbatarians Persons born on SATURDAY who have special powers against ghosts, VAMPIRES, and spirits. Sabbatarians are able to see vampires day and night. If a vampire sees them, it must immediately flee head over heels.

Twins are especially powerful sabbatarians. They may be accompanied by their spectral dogs, who are a kind of fetch, or double. Gypsy sabbatarian twins wear their underwear inside out, especially effective against vampires.

A Greek case reports that a sabbatarian lured a VYRKO-LAKAS into a barn and forced him to count millet SEEDS. While the vampire was distracted, the sabbatarian attacked him and nailed him to the wall.

See also GYPSIES.

FURTHER READING:
Perkowski, Jan L. *The Darkling: A Treatise on Slavic Vampirism.* Columbus, Ohio: Slavica Publishers, 1989.

sabbats Frenzied secret gatherings of witches that featured cannibalism, lewd behavior, devil worship, spellcasting, and SHAPE-SHIFTING. Belief in sabbats prevailed during the witch hunts of the Inquisition, especially in Europe, despite the lack of real evidence of them. Most likely, the witches' sabbat was a fabrication of the witch-hunters, who tortured accused witches into making the desired confessions.

The sabbat first figured in a witch trial in Toulouse in 1335 and quickly became established as an accepted practice of witches. Witch-hunters such as JEAN BODIN wrote descriptions of sabbats. They claimed that the gatherings took place at night in remote locations, such as mountains, caves, and deep forest areas, at times coinciding with old pagan festivals tied to seasonal rites. To get to a sabbat, witches rubbed themselves with magical OINTMENTS and flew through the air on broomsticks or poles or astride the backs of demons that had shape-shifted into animals. The witches themselves sometimes shape-shifted into animals, including ravening wolves who devoured, roasted and boiled infants at the rites. The witches danced, paid homage to the devil, and engaged in sexual acts with demons.

FURTHER READING:
Guiley, Rosemary Ellen. *The Encyclopedia of Witches and Witchcraft.* 2d ed. New York: Facts On File, 1999.

Saberhagen, Fred (1930–) American science fiction and fantasy novelist whose work blends myth and science. Fred Saberhagen's books about VAMPIRES expand on COUNT DRACULA and VLAD TEPES. Creative and clever, his work has established him as one of the leading authors of vampire novels.

Saberhagen was born Frederick Thomas Saberhagen in Chicago and grew up there. Prior to becoming a full-time writer, he served in the U.S. Air Force, worked as a civilian electronics technician, and wrote science and technology articles for *Encyclopedia Britannica.* He began writing in 1962. His first novel, *The Golden People,* was published in 1964.

Saberhagen was well established as a leading science fiction and fantasy writer when he turned to vampires in the mid-1970s. In reading BRAM STOKER'S DRACULA (1897), he realized that the count is seldom onstage himself, but becomes known only through the eyes of the other principal characters. He was inspired to write a story in which the count could speak for himself. The result was *The Dracula Tape,* published in 1975, the first of a series of vampire novels. *The Dracula Tape* offers Count Dracula's viewpoint of events described in *Dracula.* The count claims he is not the monster that others portray him to be.

Dracula's story is on a mysterious tape found in modern times in the possession of Arthur and Janet Harker of Exeter, England. Arthur is the great-grandson of Mina Harker, wife of Jonathan Harker and one of Count Dracula's victims. The Harkers are forced to abandon their car in a heavy snowstorm in January, and they walk to a hospital where they are admitted and treated for exhaustion. Rescue workers find the tape in their car. The Harkers profess no knowledge of it and dismiss it as a joke.

Dracula, who prefers to be called "Vlad," says that Mina Harker was his greatest love, and that the events described by the main characters in *Dracula* were not quite accurate. The taped interview was conducted by the descendant of Mina, Arthur, and his wife.

The Dracula Tape preceded by one year the publication of ANNE RICE'S INTERVIEW WITH THE VAMPIRE, in which a vampire tells his story to a reporter who tapes it. Unlike Rice's vampire Louis de Pointe du Lac, Saberhagen's Vlad has no regrets about being a vampire, and is not in anguish over good versus evil.

The Dracula Tape was voted the best vampire novel featuring Dracula at Dracula 97: A Centennial Celebration, by attendees of the international conference held in Los Angeles to commemorate the 100th anniversary of the publication of *Dracula.*

Saberhagen then teamed Count Dracula and Arthur Conan Doyle's detective, Sherlock Holmes, in *The Holmes-Dracula File* (1978). Dracula—Holmes's vampire cousin— is key to solving serial killings in which CORPSES are left bloodless, and to tracking down criminals who are threatening to unleash thousands of plague-infested RATS on London. The villain proves to be Dr. John Seward, the character created by Stoker who runs the insane asylum near London.

In *An Old Friend of the Family* (1979), Dracula is summoned to modern-day Chicago by Judy Southerland. There he discovers a secret plot against him perpetrated by Morgan, a female vampire who resents his influence upon other vampires. Dracula bests her and decides to live in the United States.

In *Thorn* (1980), Dracula changes his name to Thorn. He hunts down modern art thieves, the chief of whom turns out to be a renegade princess he once hunted 500 years earlier in his mortal incarnation as Vlad Tepes.

Dominion (1982) sees Dracula changing his name once again, to Talisman. The plot involves Nimue, the Lady of the Lake, who is working against Dracula in favor of the master magician Falerin. Merlin comes to Dracula's aid.

In *A Matter of Taste* (1990), Dracula is Matthew Maule, the uncle of the Southerland family of Chicago. Other vampires plot to kill him, and he is poisoned to near death. As part of the plot, Dracula relates his origins as a vampire.

A Question of Time (1992) has Dracula as Mr. Strangeways, working with detective Joe Keough to locate the missing great-niece of Edgar Tyrrell, a sculptor and a vampire.

Seance for a Vampire (1994) returns to Victorian England for another Holmes-Dracula adventure. The story is narrated by both Dr. Watson—Holmes's right-hand man—and Dracula. A wealthy aristocrat, Ambrose Altamount, is approached by two shady mediums who offer to communicate with his dead daughter, Louisa. Confident it is a hoax, Altamount contacts Holmes and arranges to expose the mediums. Louisa manifests—but she is a vampire. One of the mediums is killed, and Holmes goes missing. Watson enlists Dracula's help.

In *A Sharpness on the Neck* (1996), the story starts in 1792, when Philip Radcliffe, the bastard son of Benjamin Franklin, saves Prince Vlad Dracula from the guillotine in France. Vlad is grateful, but his brother Radu vows to persecute Radcliffe and his descendants. In 1996 Dracula, masquerading as Mr. Graves, kidnaps the present Philip Radcliffe and his wife, June, while they are on their honeymoon. He is trying to protect them from Radu, but they fear for their lives. Saberhagen mixes in a variety of historical figures, among them Napoleon, Robespierre, and the Marquis de Sade.

Vlad Tapes (2000), reissues *Old Friend of the Family* and *Thorn* together as Book I and Book II.

In *A Coldness in the Blood* (2002), Matthew Maule competes against other vampires in a search for the Philosopher's Stone in Montana.

In addition to his vampire novels, Saberhagen has continued to write science fiction and fantasy. Among his other well-known creations are the berserkers, established in short stories in 1967, a race of violent self-programming and self-replicating robots.

Director Francis Ford Coppola chose Saberhagen and screenwriter James V. Hart to coauthor the novelization of Coppola's film treatment of *Dracula,* titled BRAM STOKER'S DRACULA (1992). Hart wrote the screenplay.

Saberhagen and his wife, Joan Spicci, live in Albuquerque, New Mexico.

FURTHER READING:
Fred Saberhagen Web site: URL: http://www.berserker.com. Downloaded on December 16, 2003.
Saberhagen, Fred. *The Dracula Tape.* New York: TOR Books, 1975.
———. *The Holmes-Dracula File.* New York: TOR Books, 1978.
———. *An Old Friend of the Family.* New York: TOR Books, 1979.

———. *Thorn*. New York: TOR Books, 1980.
———. *Dominion*. New York: TOR Books, 1982.
———. *A Matter of Taste*. New York: TOR Books, 1990.
———. *A Question of Time*. New York: TOR Books, 1992.
———. *Seance for a Vampire*. New York: TOR Books, 1994.
———. *A Sharpness on the Neck*. New York: TOR Books, 1996.
———. *A Coldness in the Blood*. New York: TOR Books, 2002.

Saint-Germain   Fictional vampire hero created by author CHELSEA QUINN YARBRO, based on the historical figure of the comte de Saint-Germain, who lived in Europe in the 18th century. The fictional count, Prinz Francesco Ragoczy da San Germano, stars in Yarbro's enduring and most popular series of novels.

The real Saint-Germain was an astute politician and somewhat of a mysterious figure. In occult lore, he has been credited with living for thousands of years and incarnating as some of history's most influential persons.

In researching real vampires and the post-Dracula vampire in fiction, Yarbro wanted to create a vampire who could genuinely exist in the world of human beings without being suspect. She thought the real count to be an ideal vehicle for her vampire hero: a mysterious, cultured, sophisticated man who moved with ease in the courts and highest circles of society.

The Occult History of the Historical Saint-Germain
Saint-Germain is considered by some to be an Ascended Master and the greatest adept since Jesus Christ. As part of the Great White Brotherhood of adepts, he protects the wisdom of the ages, only revealing it and himself to those he completely trusts.

According to occult lore, Saint-Germain had numerous illustrious incarnations, including the prophet Samuel; Joseph, the father of Jesus; St. Alban; Proclus; Merlin the wizard; Roger Bacon; Christopher Columbus; and Sir Francis Bacon. After these lives, he incarnated as the historical comte de Saint-Germain. He was said to be the third son of Prince Ferenc Rakoczy II of Hungary (Transylvania). At the time of his first appearance in Europe in 1743, he was taken to be in his mid-forties.

He was not particularly handsome, of medium height, with small hands and feet and extraordinary eyes. He dressed exceptionally well—usually in black and white—and wore diamonds on every finger. He had odd habits, such as rarely eating in public. He never drank wine, which must have been quite a feat at the court of France.

The comte supposedly was fluent and literate in Greek, Latin, Sanskrit, Arabic, Chinese, French, German, English, Italian, Portuguese, and Spanish, and was said to speak these languages without an accent. He collected fine art and jewels, played violin and harpsichord, painted, and displayed keen scientific knowledge. He was a canny statesman, traveling Europe for both Frederick the Great of Prussia and Louis XV of France.

Many critics called the comte a spy, and there is little doubt that he was working for Frederick at the same time he represented Louis XV. Ministers to Louis finally called Saint-Germain's bluff when he attempted to negotiate a peace between England and France without consulting anyone. Henry Walpole wrote that the comte lived and worked in London for a few years, eventually arrested as a Jacobite in 1743. In 1762, he supposedly helped put Catherine the Great on the Russian throne. Through prophecy, the comte tried to warn Louis XVI and Marie Antoinette of the coming revolution, but his pleadings went unheeded. Even after his death, ca. 1785–86, the comte allegedly appeared to members of the French court to warn them of the royal family's death and destruction.

The comte reportedly was a student of the occult, including the alchemical arts, and he led others to believe that he was far older than he appeared, saying that he had lived for thousands of years thanks to the Elixir of Life. He reportedly knew the secret of transmuting base metal into gold.

The comte probably died in 1786, but legend holds that he has been seen since then, even into modern times.

Saint-Germain the Fictional Vampire
Beginning with the first Saint-Germain novel, *Hotel Transylvania* (1978), Yarbro gradually divulged details about the comte's life over the course of her many novels about him. He was born 4,000 years ago in TRANSYLVANIA to a society that recognized a vampire god. He was initiated into the priesthood serving this god. A rival clan kidnapped, enslaved, and then executed him. However, they failed to cut off his head or burn his body, and thus he survived. Yarbro's novels detail his many adventures throughout time and history.

Saint-Germain's appearance is the same as descriptions given of the 18th-century man. He is enigmatic, wealthy, sophisticated, and cultured. A passionate man, he is able to engage in limited sexual encounters without actual copulation. His biting and drinking BLOOD remains the central erotic experience for himself and his victims and lovers. Some of the female characters become his devoted lovers. In addition to being passionate, he is also compassionate. But though he experiences human emotions, he tries not to embroil himself in the affairs of others. He has honor and strives not to lie. When he cannot be straightforward, he prefers to omit or skirt information rather than lie outright. He is able to walk about in SUNLIGHT because of small amounts of his native soil that fill the hollow heels of his shoes.

FURTHER READING:
DeRose, Christopher. "Chelsea Quinn Yarbro created one of fantasy's most famous vampires." Available online. URL: http://www.scifi.com/sfw/issue321/interview.html. Downloaded on December 21, 2003.
Guiley, Rosemary Ellen. *Harper's Encyclopedia of Mystical and Paranormal Experience*. San Francisco: Harper San Francisco, 1991.

Yarbro, Chelsea Quinn. *Hotel Transylvania.* New York: St. Martin's, 1978.

———. "From Dracula to Saint-Germain." Available online. URL: http://www.stealthpress.com/store/authors/Chelsea_Quinn_Yarbro/essay.asp?mscssid=D.htm. Downloaded on December 21, 2003.

———. "Researching Saint-Germain." Available online. URL: http://www.twbookmark.com/authorslounge/articles/2002/August/article15600.html. Downloaded on December 21, 2003.

St. Osyth Witches   See KEMPE, URSULA.

'Salem's Lot (1975)   VAMPIRE novel by best-selling horror author Stephen King. *'Salem's Lot* was King's second novel, following *Carrie* (1974), and is considered to be one of his best, and one of the best vampire novels overall. The vampire, Kurt Barlow, is patterned after COUNT DRACULA. The idea for the novel came in a conversation King had about what would happen if Dracula found his way to contemporary America. King has described the creative process as like a game of racquetball: *'Salem's Lot* was the ball and Dracula was the wall. The ball existed in the 20th century, but the wall was a product of the 19th century. He decided that the sexual undercurrent so powerful in BRAM STOKER's Victorian novel might have "run out of gas" by present times. The monster Barlow evokes fear and terror: He is evil through and through. Like Dracula, he has a fearsome presence, with RED lurid eyes that are "like the furnace doors to hell." His consumption of BLOOD revivifies him and makes him appear younger. And, like Dracula, his appearances are few, adding to the aura of mystery and terror that surrounds him.

In the story, Barlow, a foreigner, purchases the dilapidated Marsten House in Jerusalem's Lot, a small town in Maine, from Larry Crockett, a shady real estate agent who cannot resist the millions Barlow offers him. The town is anything but the idyllic stereotype of small-town America: It is not safe, secure, or tranquil. It seethes with secrets, alienation, and disaffection below its superficial surface. Even before the arrival of the vampires, it has been dying spiritually. The arrival of Barlow speeds up the town's death momentum. He quietly moves in and starts turning citizens into vampires, creating an army of the Undead. Slowly the vampires begin to take over the town, and fear reigns after dusk as packs of vampires roam about. Barlow has a RENFIELD-like assistant, R. T. Straker, who is more of a consciously evil person rather than a malleable lunatic. King hints that Straker may be supernatural, but ultimately he dies a human death. Straker commands truckers, who are the modern-day GYPSIES who serve the Master Vampire. He is far more capable and cunning than Renfield.

Dracula preys upon young women, but Barlow preys upon everyone. His chief victims are children. Civil authorities are useless, and so a group of citizens band together as the VAMPIRE HUNTERS:

- Ben Mears, a 30-year-old writer who has come back to the town to face old childhood nightmares
- Matt Burke, Ben's old high school teacher of literature, who is knowledgeable about folklore, and who is the first to openly question what is happening in the town
- Mark Petrie, a boy of 11 who is knowledgeable about vampires in popular culture
- Jimmy Cody, a doctor who is called to examine the bodies of some of the victims
- Father Callahan, a flawed priest

Initially, a young woman named Susan Norton, a romantic interest of Ben's, is part of the group, but she falls prey to Barlow and becomes a vampire herself.

Ben combines characteristics of Stoker's characters Jonathan Harker and Arthur Holmwood. He is reminiscent of Dr. John Seward. Cody refers to Matt as "Van Helsing," likening him to PROFESSOR ABRAHAM VAN HELSING, the chief vampire hunter of *Dracula,* but Van Helsing really is dispersed among the three men, Mark, Matt, and Ben. Matt withdraws from the actual killing, leaving that task to Ben and Mark.

The vampire hunters turn to DRACULA to learn what they must do to fight the vampires. They get holy WATER from a local Catholic church; they make STAKES out of firewood; and they make CROSSES from tongue depressors. In addition to battling the evil without, they must confront their own inner demons, and learn the importance of faith and ritual.

Ben and Mark are forced to overcome their fears and confront the wily and elusive "Master Vampire" in his lair. Ben must save the soul of Susan by driving a stake through her heart. Mark succumbs to Barlow's evil gaze when his COFFIN is opened. Ben stakes Barlow, who dies dramatically in his coffin with his skin disappearing and his fleshless skull thrashing about on his satin pillow.

But unlike the tidy ending of *Dracula,* in which all the monsters—Dracula and his three vampire brides—are destroyed, and Jonathan, Mina, and their son live in peace and security, *'Salem's Lot* ends on a note of uncertainty. Barlow the Master Vampire has been destroyed, but his vampire creations live on. The terror is not over.

Ben and Mark become like father and son. For a year after their ordeal, they wander about the country, psychologically scarred, and eventually go to Mexico. But they cannot forget that back in Jerusalem's Lot, vampires without a master are still roaming about. They go back and light a fire of purification that will destroy the town and the vampires. The implication is that a new and better town will rise up like a phoenix from the ASHES.

'Salem's Lot was adapted into a two-part miniseries for television in 1979, directed by Toby Hooper. It starred David Soul as Ben Mears, James Mason as Richard Straker in a role more prominent than the Straker character in the novel, Lance Kerwin as Mark Petrie, Bonnie Bedelia as Susan Norton, and Reggie Nalder as Mr. Barlow. Nalder's appearance departs from King's description of the vampire,

evoking MAX SCHRECK in his *NOSFERATU* role with his bald head, pale skin, and protruding RATlike fangs. He does not speak; rather, his words are conveyed to others by Straker.

A Return to Salem's Lot was released as a film in 1987. Directed by Larry Cohen, it features different characters and stars Michael Moriarty and Samuel Fuller. A new television adaptation aired in 2004, starring Rob Lowe as Ben Mears, Donald Sutherland as Richard Straker, and Rutger Hauer as Mr. Barlow.

FURTHER READING:
King, Stephen. *'Salem's Lot*. New York: Doubleday, 1975.
———. *Danse Macabre*. New York: Dodd, Mead, 1983.
Miller, Elizabeth. *Reflections on Dracula: Ten Essays*. White Rock, B.C.: Transylvania Press, 1997.
Silver, Alain, and James Ursini. *The Vampire Film: From Nosferatu to Interview with the Vampire*. 3d ed. New York: Limelight Editions, 1997.
Waller, Gregory A. *The Living and the Undead*. Urbana: University of Illinois Press, 1986.

salt   In folklore, a protective agent against VAMPIRES, witches, and all evil spirits. The power of salt is attributed to its purity in whiteness, its vital importance to life and health, and its ability to preserve, all of which are contrary to the corrupting, decaying influences of evil.

Salt placed in a newborn baby's cradle will ward off vampiric demons (see LILITH; *TLAHUELPUCHI*) until the infant can be given the protection of baptism. Salt carried on a person, especially at night, protects one against the evil entities that prowl about after dark. Salt thrown over the left shoulder ensures good luck and blinds any evil beings who always lurk about on the left. At death, salt is sprinkled in a COFFIN to help protect the soul from demons during its transition from earth to the afterlife. Salt sprinkled across a threshold or around a bed will ward off evil entities. Salt also protects against the EVIL EYE.

In Romanian lore, if a pregnant woman does not eat salt, her child will be a vampire.

salves   See OINTMENTS.

sampiro   VAMPIRE in Albanian lore. The *sampiro* stalks its victims while wearing heeled shoes and a shroud.

Sarbanovac Vampires (1839)   Serbian case of VAMPIRE grave exhumations, leading to convictions and punishment of those who dug up graves.

In 1839 villagers in the Serbian community of Sarbanovac concluded that nine persons who died had turned into vampires and were strangling women, men, children, and animals. The villagers turned to their priest for help, but were forbidden to undertake any traditional—and

pagan—remedies. When the priest was called out of town, the villagers took matters into their own hands. Led by a man named Novak Mikov, who agreed to serve as chief VAMPIRE HUNTER for a fee, a group of men dug up eight bodies. The hearts were cut out, cooked in boiling wine, and replaced in the CORPSES, which were reburied. A ninth body of a woman was disinterred but found not to be in a "vampire condition" and so was reburied intact.

When the grave desecrations were discovered, church officials turned the matter over to the secular court. Novak and Radovan Petrov, who played a leading role in the desecrations, were found guilty of digging up vampires and were sentenced to seven days in jail and 30 strokes of the cane.

The case is an example of the efforts made by the Christian Church in Europe to discourage vampire superstitions. Many villagers were convicted of grave desecration and corpse mutilation. Punishments usually were fines, jail terms, whipping, and required attendance at Mass. In some villages, priests were more sympathetic, and assisted villagers by praying over bodies that were exhumed, and cleansing them and the graves with holy WATER.

FURTHER READING:
Fine, John V. A., Jr. "In Defense of Vampires," in *The Vampire: A Casebook*, Alan Dundes, ed. Madison: University of Wisconsin Press, 1998.

sarkomenos   Ghoulish vampire of Crete and Rhodes. The name *sarkomenos* means "the fleshy one."

The Satanic Rites of Dracula   See HAMMER FILMS.

Saturday   The best day of the week for killing VAMPIRES. In Greek and European lore, Saturday is the time during the week that vampires must sleep in their graves or tombs, and thus can be found and dispatched.

In European lore, persons born on Saturday can see ghosts, spirits, and vampires, and possess powers against them. In Romania, Saturday children are destined to grow up dirty.

In other lore, Saturday is held to be an unlucky and unstable day for many activities, such as certain kinds of labor, housework, and planting of crops.

See also SABBATARIANS.

Scars of Dracula   See HAMMER FILMS.

Scholomance   In *DRACULA* (1897) by BRAM STOKER, a supernatural academy where COUNT DRACULA was schooled as an apprentice of the devil.

Stoker picked up this bit of lore in his research on TRANSYLVANIA from an article, "Transylvania Superstitions"

(1885) by Mme. EMILY DE LASZOWSKI GERARD, an English-woman who had lived in Transylvania. According to Gerard, the Scholomance is located in the mountains south of Hermannstadt (now Sibiu), where frequent thunderstorms occur. There the devil teaches "all the secrets of nature, the language of animals, and all imaginable magic spells and charms." Only 10 students are accepted at a time, and when the studies are done the devil keeps one of the 10 as payment. The apprentice is mounted on a dragon and becomes the devil's aide-de-camp.

Scholomance is not found in Romanian folklore, and it is possible that Gerard garbled another term she heard, as she probably did with the word *NOSFERATU*. It has been suggested that Gerard misunderstood the term *Solomanari*, who were said to have a magical arts school called "The School of the Dragon" somewhere in the center of the earth in a magic afterworld.

In *Dracula*, PROFESSOR ABRAHAM VAN HELSING relates that his friend Arminius informed him that Dracula's family—"the Draculas"—"were a great and noble race," but some of their scions dealt with the devil and learned his secrets in the Scholomance. In life Count Dracula was "a wonderful man" who was a statesman, soldier, and alchemist. Fearless and extremely intelligent, he "dared even to attend the Scholomance, and there was no branch of knowledge of his time that he did not essay."

FURTHER READING:
Miller, Elizabeth. *Dracula: Sense & Nonsense*. Westcliff-on-Sea, England: Desert Island Books, 2000.
Stoker, Bram. *Dracula*. New York: Grosset & Dunlap, 1931.

Schreck, Max (1879–1936)   German actor best known for his portrayal of the vampire GRAF ORLOCK in the 1922 silent film, *NOSFERATU*. *Schreck* means "terror" in German, an appropriate name—and real, not a pseudonym—given his most memorable role.

Max Schreck worked on the German stage for producer Max Reinhardt, who also employed F. W. MURNAU, who

Graf Orlock (Max Schreck) sails into Bremen aboard the death ship in F. W. Murnau's Nosferatu. (Author's collection)

became the director for *Nosferatu*. As Orlock, Schreck personifies reanimated death itself. His moves his cadaverously thin body in halting jerks. Dark makeup accentuates his hypnotic but dead eyes. Putty elongates his pointed ears and clawlike fingers. He has long, rodentlike fangs, and he controls plague-bearing RATS.

Schreck starred in numerous other films following *Nosferatu*, but none made him as famous as the pirated version of *DRACULA*. Ironically, his fame came posthumously; because of the years of legal entanglements over copyright violation, *Nosferatu* never received the attention it deserved until years after Schreck's death.

The horrible monster Schreck so aptly created was reprised in 1979 by Klaus Kinski in Werner's Herzog's version of *Nosferatu*, and inspired other vampires, such as the ratlike vampire Mr. Barlow in Steven King's novel *'SALEM'S LOT*, portrayed in the 1987 film adaptation, *'Salem's Lot*, by actor Reggie Nalder; and Radu, the vampire in *SUBSPECIES* (but who looks more like a Romanian *voivode* than a rodentlike walking dead). None come close to evoking the horror, dread, and terror embodied so well in Schreck's original.

FURTHER READING:
Silver, Alain, and James Ursini. *The Vampire Film: From Nosferatu to Interview with the Vampire*. 3d ed. New York: Limelight Editions, 1997.
Skal, David J. *Hollywood Gothic: The Tangled Web of Dracula from Novel to Stage to Screen*. New York: W. W. Norton, 1990.

Scot, Reginald (ca. 1538–1599) Skeptic who argued against prevailing superstitions of witchcraft and who was the first writer to use the terms *lycanthropia* and *lycanthropus* in the English language. In 1584 Reginald Scot self-published *The Discoverie of Witchcraft*, in which he refuted many of the beliefs concerning the power of witches, including their alleged SHAPE-SHIFTING ability into WEREWOLVES. He denounced the persecution of accused witches as the "extreme and intolerable tyranny" of the Inquisition.

Unlike other demonologists of his time who were scholars, philosophers, theologians, or professionals in law and medicine, Scot was a country gentleman who left Oxford without earning a degree. He was drawn to the subject of witchcraft because of his personal outrage at the torture and execution of people he considered to be innocent of any wrongdoing.

In composing *Discoverie*, Scot drew upon his knowledge of superstition in rural life, the law and literature, and ancient medical theories. He also drew upon the writings of numerous scholars, theologians, and experts in various fields, even those who disagreed with his own views. He was heavily influenced by the writings of Johann Weyer, a German physician who opposed the witch hunts.

Scot sharply criticized the Catholic Church for its views on demons, magic, and witchcraft. He especially refuted the "absurd" claims made by JEAN BODIN, one of the pro-witchcraft demonologists favored by the Church.

Scot's book became a classic in witchcraft literature, covering a wide range of subjects, including—besides witchcraft and LYCANTHROPY—ghosts, possession, charms, omens, divination, fairies, spells, magic, witchcraft, and the practices of the devil.

Scot defined four basic categories of witches, including those who confessed to lycanthropy:

1. the falsely accused innocent
2. the deluded and crazy who convinced themselves they were in a pact with Satan
3. the true, malevolent witch who harmed by poisoning, but not by supernatural power
4. impostors who collected fees for false spells, cures, and prophecies

Scot doubted the physical reality of the devil and thus any power the devil might have to cause human beings to transform into wolves or other animals. He dismissed the claims of people who said they turned into ravaging wolves as suffering from delusions and mental instability: the disease *Lupina melancholia* or *Lupina insania*. The claims that witches ate human flesh and drank BLOOD were incredible and preposterous. He stated that anyone who believed that a person could be transformed into any creature or shape by any other agency than God, the creator, was "without all doubt . . . an infidel, and worse than a pagan."

Scot also maintained that the manifestations of spirits were delusions due to mental disturbances in the beholder, and that the INCUBUS was a natural disease.

Scot was a major force in the skepticism about witchcraft that persisted in England. *Discoverie* was well received by the clergy in England, but King James I detested it and ordered copies of it burned. The king, an ardent believer in witchcraft, wrote his own refutation, *Daemonology*.

FURTHER READING:
Guiley, Rosemary Ellen. *The Encyclopedia of Witches and Witchcraft*. 2d ed. New York: Facts On File, 1999.
Otten, Charlotte F., ed. *A Lycanthropy Reader: Werewolves in Western Culture*. New York: Dorset Press, 1989.
Scot, Reginald. *The Discoverie of Witchcraft*. Yorkshire, England: E. P. Publishing, 1973.

seeds Protection against vampires. Small seeds, such as poppy, flax, mustard, and millet, represent delaying units of time, and are poured into COFFINS and sprinkled about gravesites. According to lore, vampires must pick up or eat every seed individually before they can leave the grave or attack the living; in some lore, such as among the KASHUBS, the vampires can pick up only one seed a year. Seeds also are scattered across thresholds and around beds to prevent vampires from entering a room or attacking a victim during sleep.

In the Ukrainian folktale of THE VAMPIRE AND ST. MICHAEL, pears and nuts serve the same function.

See also BURIAL CUSTOMS; PROTECTION AGAINST VAMPIRES.

Selby, David   Actor best known for his portrayal of QUENTIN COLLINS in the long-running gothic soap DARK SHADOWS.

David Selby was born in Morgantown, West Virginia. He grew up there and earned his bachelor's degree and master's degree at West Virginia University. He earned his doctorate at Southern Illinois University.

Selby started his acting career onstage in 1966 in West Virginia, and by 1967 was acting onstage in New York City.

He joined the cast of *Dark Shadows* in 1968, debuting in episode 646 as the ghost of Quentin Collins. He appeared in 305 episodes, with his final appearance coming in episode 1,230 near the end of the series. Tall, dark, and handsome with a sonorous voice, he created an appropriate brooding personality for his tortured character, who endured the curse of a werewolf for part of the show.

Following the end of *Dark Shadows* in 1971, Selby continued acting in television, film, and radio roles. He starred in two *Dark Shadows* movies, *House of Dark Shadows* (1971) and *Night of Dark Shadows* (1972). He had major roles in other series, most notably that of Richard Channing in *Falcon Crest* (1982–90), and also Michael Tyrone in *Flamingo Road* (1982) and Xavier Trout in *Soldier of Fortune* (1997–99). He made numerous guest appearances on other television shows, and performed roles in films and made-for-television movies.

In 2003 Selby reprised his role of Quentin Collins and appeared with other members of the *Dark Shadows* cast in *Return to Collinwood*, a radio play written by his son, Jamison Selby (b. 1969). The play debuted at the 2003 *Dark Shadows* Festival in Brooklyn, New York.

Selby has written three plays: *Where's Nova Scotia?*, which had a staged reading in 1998; *Lincoln and James (aka Better Angels)*, in which Selby played the role of Abraham Lincoln in performances in New York City, Washington, D.C., and Charleston, West Virginia, in 1997–99; and *Final Assault*, directed by Jamison and performed in Charleston in 2003. Selby also has written three books, including two collections of his poetry, *My Mother's Autumn* (2000) and *Happenstance* (2001), and *In and out of the Shadows* (1999), a book of career photos and poems.

Selby and his wife have three children and live in the Los Angeles area.

FURTHER READING:
David Selby Web site. URL: http://www.davidselby.com. Accessed on December 17, 2003.

seventh child   In Romanian lore, if a family has seven children of the same sex, the seventh child will be born with a TAIL and will be a VAMPIRE.

Seward, John   See DRACULA.

shadow   The shape of the soul; the animating principle within a person. In Romanian folklore, a person's shadow can be secured in order to strengthen a building. However, the person then becomes a vampire after death. In the lore of Slavic Muslim GYPSIES, VAMPIRES are a dead person's shadow. In Romanian lore, a dead man will become a vampire if the shadow of a living man falls over him.

In magic, a shadow is an astral THOUGHT-FORM that can be directed by a magician in a PSYCHIC ATTACK.

COUNT DRACULA, created by BRAM STOKER, is a soulless creature who is unable to cast a shadow; he also casts no reflections in MIRRORS and cannot be painted or photographed. All the lighting in Castle Dracula is arranged so that there are no shadows that will expose the count's vampire nature.

Shadow of the Vampire **(2000)**   Film about the making of F. W. MURNAU's NOSFERATU. The premise of *Shadow of the Vampire* is that Murnau made a devil's pact to have a real vampire play the role of GRAF ORLOCK. The film was directed by E. Elias Merhige.

The ambitious Murnau (John Malkovich) pursues his plans to make a film of BRAM STOKER's DRACULA, despite the refusal of his widow, Florence Stoker, to grant him film rights. Murnau and Albin Grau (Udo Kier), the producer and art director, change the setting, character names, and plot elements, thinking they can skirt copyright issues. Murnau lets it be known that he has hired an unknown professional character actor, MAX SCHRECK (Willem Dafoe), to play the role of the vampire Orlock. No one has heard of him.

Murnau is determined to make the most realistic vampire film ever made. He tells the crew that during the entire shooting, Schreck will always appear in full makeup and costume and be in his role. They are not to bother him. The shooting of all scenes with Schreck will be done only at night.

The shooting takes place on location in Czechoslovakia. A local woman begs them to put up CROSSES to protect themselves, but she is dismissed as foolish by Murnau.

Schreck makes a creepy entrance and casts a pall over the actors and crew with his inhuman appearance and bizarre behavior, but they carry on. In one scene, Schreck catches a BAT and tears it to pieces, sucking its BLOOD. The crew accept this as Schreck's odd habit of "staying in character."

Schreck cannot resist sneaking off to attack the crew for their blood. First he vampirizes the camera man to the point where he must be sent to a mental hospital. Gustav von Wangenheim (Eddie Izzard), who plays Waldemar Hutter, the Jonathan Harker character, sees one of Schreck's attacks on the man. Others also are attacked.

Murnau must leave the set to find another cameraman. He strikes a secret bargain with Schreck that if he controls himself during Murnau's absence, Schreck will be allowed to drink the blood of Greta Schroeder-Matray (Catherine McCormack), the morphine-addicted actress who is playing the role of Ellen Hutter, the Mina Harker character. Schreck agrees.

Greta goes into hysterics when, during the shooting of one scene, she sees that Schreck casts no reflection in a MIRROR. Despite this oddity, the shooting continues. Murnau returns with a new cameraman.

Murnau never offers an explanation to his employees for Schreck's horrors. The crew simply must put up with Schreck. The filming progresses to the final scene in which the script calls for Orlock to drink the blood of Ellen. She tricks him in her sacrifice, and he is destroyed by the rays of morning SUNLIGHT. She dies from the loss of too much blood.

Greta is groggy on morphine as the shooting begins. Schreck loses control and savagely bites her for real. He drains her blood and then—in a parody of the sleepiness that follows sexual orgasm—falls asleep on top of her. But Murnau has tricked the vampire, and has the room sealed off.

Schreck awakens and knows he has been betrayed. He implies there will be consequences of this betrayal. Fritz Wagner (Cary Elwes), the replacement cameraman, attempts to shoot Schreck, but several bullets have no effect. Schreck goes berserk and attacks Wagner and Grau, killing them. Murnau keeps the camera rolling, but he is not pleased. He orders the vampire to return to his original mark and follow the script. Others outside force open the entrance to the set and sunlight streams in. The vampire dies and disintegrates.

Dafoe is a convincing copy of Schreck's appearance and some of his mannerisms, and Malkovich bears a striking resemblance to Murnau. Genuine scenes from *Nosferatu* are mixed into *Shadow*, but the movie does not evoke the intense horror of the original.

shape-shifting (metamorphosis)

shape-shifting (metamorphosis) The transformation from one body into another, such as humans into the bodies of animals and birds. A human who transforms into an animal becomes a were-animal. Witches, sorcerers, and other magically empowered persons are said to have shape-shifting power at will. Gods and demons have shape-shifting ability and can take on human form.

Shape-shifting in Myth, Magic, and Sorcery

Beliefs about shape-shifting are ancient and involve both gods and humans. Myths tell of humans turned into beasts as punishment. The sorceress Circe turned Ulysses's men into swine, and Jupiter transformed LYCAON into a wolf. The myths recorded by Homer, Virgil, Ovid, Herodotus, Petronius, and other classical writers feature many examples of shape-shifting. One of the best-known classical tales is the *Golden Ass* by Apuleius, in which the protagonist uses a magic OINTMENT and turns himself into an ass.

David Kessler (David Naughton) shape-shifts into a werewolf in An American Werewolf in London. *(Author's collection)*

Shape-shifting is prominent in Norse, Scandinavian, and Teutonic mythologies. In the *Volsunga Saga*, Sigmund and Sinfjotli are transformed into wolves when they put on wolf-skins they stole from the king's sons. Deep in the forest, they come upon a house in which two of the king's sons are sleeping. The sons are skilled in witchcraft, as evidenced by their wolf-skins hanging above them. According to the story:

> Sigmund and Sinfjotli got into the habits, and could not get out of them again, and the nature of the original beasts came over them, and they howled as wolves—they learned both of them to howl. Now they went into the forest, and each took his own course; they made the agreement together that they should try their strength against as many as seven men, but not more, and that he who was ware of strife should utter his wolf's howl.

Sinfjotli comes upon 11 men in the forest and kills them all. When Sigmund learns this, and that Sinfjotli did not howl for help, he attacks Sinfjotli in a wolfish rage and bites through his throat.

In another tale in the saga, Bjorn, the son of King Hring, is punished by the queen. She strikes him with a wolf-skin glove and curses him to become a "rabid and grim wild bear" that will eat nothing but his father's sheep. The unfortunate Bjorn is hunted down by the king's men, who do not know his true identity, and is killed. The queen has him cooked up for a feast.

In folktales, wicked sorcerers and witches turned people into frogs or other creatures, who had to wait for the right person to come along and break the evil spell.

In werewolf lore, shape-shifting may be involuntary, such as at the full MOON, or may be for certain periods of time, such as the LIVONIA WEREWOLVES who spent 12 days every Christmas as wolves. Involuntary shape-shifting can also be the result of a curse made by a sorcerer or witch, or the result of being attacked by a sorcerer vampire or werewolf. (See RUVANUSH; WILLIAM OF PALERNE.)

According to traditions, the ability to shape-shift can be acquired through witchcraft, magical training, or endowment by a master. Magical ointments containing hallucinogens, magical GIRDLES or belts, dancing, drumming, and incantations may be part of the transformation process. As portrayed in myths, the donning of animal skins imparts the powers and characteristics of an animal (see BERSERKIR). In Navajo tradition, witches become WEREWOLVES and were-animals by donning animal skins, which enables them to travel about at night at great speed. (See SKINWALKERS.)

In Nordic and Icelandic lore, certain men were called EIGI EINHAMIR ("not of one skin") and had the ability to assume a second shape of an animal. The transformation was accompanied by extraordinary powers, and the man took on the behavior of the animal whose shape he assumed.

In cultures where shamanic practices are strong, the ability to shape-shift is accepted as a skill necessary for shamanic tasks, which include journeying to other realms and dealing with spirits. Shamans can take the form of their guardian animal spirits or power animals from whom they derive magical powers.

A sorcerer or witch might shape-shift to a were-animal, such as a werewolf, to do evil and lay waste to enemies by drinking their BLOOD and tearing them to pieces. Witch were-animals also attack and eat people without provocation, as part of their bestial nature. Widespread superstitions hold that were-animal witches meet in caves at night, where they initiate new members, plan ritual killings-at-a-distance, practice necrophilia with the CORPSES of women, and eat their victims.

In parts of Southeast Asia, it is believed that the witchcraft/were-animal spirit resides within a person—often passed down through heredity—and can be transmitted to others through contagion. A person who lives close to a witch can contract the "witch spirit" without the direct action or intent of the witch.

The animal shape taken varies by geography and usually is one common to an area. In parts of Europe where wolves once were common and posed an ongoing danger to farm animals and people, the wolf was the predator of choice of the sorcerer/witch. In Russia, the bear also is common as a were-animal. Elsewhere, were-animals are serpents, leopards, tigers, panthers, jackals, coyotes, owls, foxes, crocodiles, lions, sharks, and other feared creatures. Of all were-animals, the wolf elicits the most universal fear, and is the most dangerous of were-animals.

In Western magic lore, the magician ALEISTER CROWLEY was reputed to have the power to shape-shift others. He was supposed to have once turned the poet Victor Neuburg into a camel.

Shape-shifting in Western Witchcraft

During the witch trials of the Inquisition—the peak of which occurred in the 16th and 17th centuries—European demonologists debated whether shape-shifting could be conferred by the devil and his demons, or was merely a demonically inspired illusion. Some demonologists such as JEAN BODIN and Joseph Glanvill accepted shape-shifting, or metamorphosis, as fact. Most others, such as HENRI BOGUET, NICHOLAS RÉMY, and FRANCESCO MARIA GUAZZO, denounced it as fallacy. They cited the authoritative statements made in the early fifth century by St. Augustine and echoed in the 13th century by St. Thomas Aquinas.

Augustine said that metamorphosis is miraculous and the devil has no miracle-making power; thus metamorphosis is nothing but an illusion created by the devil and demons. In *The City of God*, Augustine wrote:

> It is very generally believed that by certain witches' spells and the power of the Devil men may be changed into wolves . . . but they do not lose their human reason and understanding, nor are their minds made the intelligence of a mere beast. Now this must be understood in this way: namely, that the Devil creates no new nature, but that he is able to make something appear to be which in reality is not. For by no spell nor evil power can the mind, nay, not even the body corporeally, be changed into the material limbs and features of any animal . . . but a man is fantastically and by illusion metamorphosed into an animal, albeit he to himself seems to be a quadruped.

In 906 the *Canon Episcopi*, one of the most important ecclesiastical documents of the Middle Ages, was put forward. When it was made public by Regino of Prum, Abbot of Treves, it was presented as an ancient authority dating back to the fourth century. Whatever its true origins, it was incorporated by Gratian into his *Concordance of Discordant Canons* around 1140 and became entrenched in the highest canonical law.

The *Canon Episcopi* upheld the Augustinian view and influenced demonologists well into the 17th century. Flying through the air and metamorphosing into animals were foolish illusions:

> Whoever therefore believes that anything can be made, or that any creature can be changed to better or to worse or be transformed into another species or similitude, except

by the Creator himself who made everything and through whom all things were made, is beyond doubt an infidel.

The *Malleus Maleficarum,* the first leading inquisitor's guide (1484), conformed to the canon's position. Such illusions, said the Dominican authors Heinrich Kramer and James Sprenger, were the result of God punishing some nation for sin. They cited verses from Leviticus 26, "If you do not obey my commandments, I will send the beasts of the field against you, who shall consume you and your flocks," and Deuteronomy 32, "I will also send the teeth of the beasts upon them." As to man-eating wolves, Kramer and Sprenger said they were not werewolves but true wolves possessed by demons. If a person thought himself turned into a wolf, it was the result of a witch's illusory spell.

Most other witch-hunting guides followed suit. Meanwhile, those who believed in the reality of shape-shifting had to find ways around Augustine and the *Canon Episcopi.* Some demonologists, such as Rémy and Guazzo, were inventive in their ways that the devil could create the illusions of shape-shifting while leaving behind physical evidence, such as the sympathetic wounds displayed by werewolves.

In colonial America, the Puritan preacher and witch-hunter Increase Mather called the notion of metamorphosis "fabulous." In *An Essay for the Recording of Illustrious Providences* (1684), Mather stated:

> But it is beyond the power of all the Devils in Hell to cause such a transformation; they can no more do it than they can be Authors of a true Miracle . . . Though I deny not but that the Devil may so impose upon the imagination of Witches so as to make them believe that they are transmuted into Beasts.

Mather recounts a story of a woman who was imprisoned on suspicion of witchcraft, and claimed to be able to transform herself into a wolf. The magistrate promised not to have her executed, in case she would turn into a wolf before him. The witch rubbed her head, neck, and armpits with an ointment and fell into a deep sleep for three hours. She could not be roused by "noises or blows." When she awakened, she claimed that she had turned into a wolf, gone a few miles away, and killed a sheep and a cow. The magistrate investigated and discovered that a sheep and cow in the location described by the witch had indeed been killed. It was evident that the Devil "did that mischief," and that the witch had merely experienced the dreams and delusions created by Satan.

Nonetheless, most witchcraft trials depended on testimony involving shape-shifting. Witnesses claimed that accused witches had appeared before them or tormented them in some nonhuman shape. For example, in 1663, Jane Milburne of Newcastle, England, did not invite Dorothy Strangers to her wedding supper. Consequently, Milburne alleged, Strangers transformed herself into a CAT and appeared with several other mysterious cats to plague Milburne.

Witches confessed themselves to shape-shifting, often after being tortured. In 1649 John Palmer of St. Albans, England, confessed that he had metamorphosed into a toad in order to torment a young man with whom he had had a quarrel. As a toad, Palmer waited for the man in a road. The man kicked the toad. Palmer then complained about a sore shin, and bewitched his victim.

Guazzo tells a similar story about a man who angered a barmaid. He refused to pay his full bill, knowing that she had doubled the amount he actually owed. He later came upon a huge and ugly toad, which his traveling companions sliced in the throat with a sword. The barmaid took to her bed with the same wound.

Shape-shifting made it possible to gain easy entry into a household in order to cast an evil spell upon an unsuspecting person, and also to escape pursuit. In 1547 it was reported that a witch brought before inquisitors in Navarre, France, was able to smuggle along her magic ointment. She rubbed herself down and turned into a screen owl, and escaped certain death.

Witches also confessed to shape-shifting in order to travel to their SABBATS. The most common forms were he-goat, wolf, CAT, dog, cow, hare, owl, and BAT, achieved after the application of an ointment that put them into trance.

Isobel Gowdie, a Scottish woman who voluntarily confessed to witchcraft in 1662, said she and her sister witches used incantations to transform themselves into hares, cats, crows, and other animals. Sometimes they were bitten by hunting dogs.

As late as 1664, arguments in favor of actual shape-shifting were still being put forward. The English physician Dr. William Drage contended that spirits do indeed have the power to metamorphose bodies. Eventually, as the witch trials came to an end, such views gave way to the position that LYCANTHROPY is a pathological condition and not a demonic or magical one.

See also ZUGARRAMURDI WITCHES.

FURTHER READING:

Baring-Gould, Sabine. *The Book of Werewolves.* London: Smith, Elder & Co., 1865.

Guazzo, Francesco-Maria. *Compendium Maleficarum.* Secaucus, N.J.: University Books, 1974.

Guiley, Rosemary Ellen. *The Encyclopedia of Witches and Witchcraft.* 2d ed. New York: Facts On File, 1999.

Otten, Charlotte F., ed. *A Lycanthropy Reader: Werewolves in Western Culture.* New York: Dorset Press, 1989.

Rémy, Nicolas. *Demonolatry.* Secaucus, N.J.: University Books, 1974.

Summers, Montague. *The Werewolf.* New York: Bell Publishing, 1966.

Watson, C. W., and Roy Ellen, eds. *Understanding Witchcraft and Sorcery in Southeast Asia.* Honolulu: University of Hawaii Press, 1993.

shroud   See BURIAL CUSTOMS.

signs of vampirism   See CORPSES.

silver   Precious metal with protective powers against negative influences and everything evil. Silver has been used since ancient times for amulets against the supernatural. Silver also has always been associated with the MOON.

Silver nails in a COFFIN prevent the spirit of the corpse from escaping. Silver amulets repel evil spirits from persons, houses, and buildings. In the folklore of parts of France, couples who are going to be married encircle themselves in a silver chain in order to avoid being bewitched en route to the church.

Silver bullets are believed to have the power to destroy kill VAMPIRES, WEREWOLVES, sorcerers, witches, giants, and persons who lead charmed lives. When FAMILIARS are wounded or killed with a silver bullet, their masters are wounded or killed in the same fashion. Silver also protects against the EVIL EYE. Silver nails in a coffin prevent a vampire or restless ghost from escaping its grave.

skinwalkers   In Navajo lore, witches and sorcerers who have the ability to shape-shift (see SHAPE-SHIFTING) into wolves, coyotes, and other animals and birds, and thus "walk" in their skins. The Navajo term for skinwalker witches is *yenaldlooshi*. Skinwalking is part of Witchery Way, the more general practice of witchcraft. According to myth, Witchery Way was started underground by First Man, First Woman, and Coyote, and then brought above ground and disseminated.

Both men and women can become witches, though men are more numerous. One becomes a witch through initiation, which involves killing a family member, usually a brother or sister. Witches use their magical skills to increase their wealth, sometimes by robbing graves and sometimes by causing illness. When the victim seeks healing, the witch splits the fee with the healer. Witches also are believed to injure and kill others out of anger, envy, spite, and revenge.

The lore of skinwalkers and Witchery Way is similar to the beliefs held about witches in European lore.

Witches are active primarily at night. When they don the skins of wolves or coyotes (other animals named to a lesser degree are bears, desert foxes, crows, and owls), they have the ability to travel at great speed. They are often invisible to humans, but they leave tracks larger than those of the real animals. If the tracks are followed, they often lead back to the home of the witch.

Skinwalkers are said to gather in caves at night to initiate new members, plan their evil activities, kill people at a distance through magic, have sex with female CORPSES, and practice cannibalism. The Chief Witch is an old man. The skinwalkers was sometimes said to eat coyotes and owls, and ground-up blue lizard. They are naked—even in winter—save for beaded jewelry and ceremonial paint, and

they sit in circles or run around on all fours. Their bows are made of human shinbones. They draw sandpaintings of their victims and then spit, urinate, or defecate on the images. They sing and howl like wolves and coyotes.

Skinwalkers use various herbal concoctions to sicken and poison people. They are also said to grind up the flesh of infants for some of their poisons, especially a powder that paralyzes victims when touched anywhere on the body. This is reminiscent of the paralyzing powders used to create zombies in Vodoun magical lore. Skinwalkers can cause wasting illnesses at a distance by using the name of the victim in a spell, or by taking bits of a victim's hair or nail parings and saying spells over them.

Skinwalkers make their poisons from the skin whorls cut off fingers and feet of victims. They especially like to poison twins because it is "interesting."

They crawl on top of hogans and throw their poisons and bad medicines down the smoke holes.

Other lore about skinwalkers:

- It is very bad luck to cross the tracks of a skinwalker in front of them—one must step over them.
- If a skinwalker is shot or wounded while in animal skin, it bears the same wound when transformed back into human shape.
- If a skinwalker is captured and the news is broadcast, the witch will die within a year.
- Horses smell skinwalkers at night and will jump.
- Skinwalkers can be distinguished from real animals because their TAILS hang down and move constantly, their ears move up and down constantly, and their eyes are slits through their masks.
- One must shoot a skinwalker through the neck, because then the bullet will pierce the real head of the witch. A bullet aimed at the body will pass harmlessly through the hide.
- The gall of an eagle is the best remedy against the poison of a skinwalker. Other remedies are the gall of a bear or mountain lion.
- Sweats will help cure fear of skinwalkers.

In *Navaho Witchcraft* (1944), anthropologist Clyde Kluckhorn includes numerous personal anecdotes recorded about skinwalkers and other witches and sorcerers, including the following:

A man said his grandfather's brother was a skinwalker who always acted strangely. People around him sickened and died. One night the grandfather followed him. The skinwalker went to the graves of twins and dug them up, taking out some of their brains. Then he cut off the whorls of their fingers and toes. Then he robbed the grave of a rich man. The skinwalker then went to a cave where other skinwalker coyotes and wolves were disappearing into a hole in the canyon wall. The grandfather spied on them and saw 20 skinwalkers with their hides off, around a fire. They had made a sandpainting of a wealthy man. Using bows made of human shin bones, they shot turquoise beads into it while they sang. They spit, urinated and defecated on the sandpainting.

Soon the rich man died, and the skinwalker was hanging around girls. The grandfather decided to kill him. At the first opportunity, he called the skinwalker close to him and shot him with an arrow through one eye. He said, "That the present I have for the witches."

FURTHER READING:
Kluckhorn, Clyde. *Navaho Witchcraft.* Cambridge, Mass.: Harvard University Press, 1944.

Slain's Castle   See CASTLE DRACULA.

sneezing   In Romanian lore, sneezing empowers a VAMPIRE unless a blessing is uttered immediately. One should always say "long life" or "good health" when someone sneezes in order to prevent a fatal bewitchment from a vampire who is a witch or wizard (see VAMPIRE SORCERERS AND WITCHES).

There are numerous and widespread folk beliefs that the soul is vulnerable after a sneeze, for the soul leaves the body through the mouth during certain times, especially during sleep and at death. Sneezing creates an opportunity for the devil or some other evil agency to enter into the body and take possession of it, or to bewitch or kill the sneezer.

In the Romanian folktale *The Thief and the Vampire,* a thief and a vampire are partners in crime. One evening the vampire decides he will go to the house of a man named Ion to bewitch Ion's son. The thief tells him to go elsewhere, for he has plans to go to the same house to steal some oxen. They argue and then decide they will both go to the house of Ion. Once there, the vampire goes to the door and the thief goes to the window. Then they hear the son sneeze inside. Immediately the thief says, "Long life." The blessing takes away the vampire's power. He is able to make the boy's nose bleed, but cannot kill him. The thief goes to the parents and tells them he has rescued their son from a vampire. In gratitude, they give him the very oxen he intended to steal.

In another Romanian folktale that is a variation of the above tale, a young nobleman prepares to go on a journey by horse. A thief is hiding, waiting to steal the horse. The thief spies a vampire hiding under the window of the house, waiting to put a spell on the noble. The noble sneezes, and the thief says, "Good health." The vampire is unable to put a fatal spell on the noble. He is so angry to be thwarted that he bursts. People gather at the commotion, and the thief shows them the burst body of the dead vampire. The parents of the noble are so grateful that their son was saved that they give the thief the very horse he intended to steal.

FURTHER READING:
Murgoci, Agnes. "The Vampire in Roumania," in *The Vampire: A Casebook,* Alan Dundes, ed. Madison: University of Wisconsin Press, 1998.

Snow Woman   In Japanese lore, a female demon with vampiric characteristics. Snow Woman likes to marry a man and then sap his strength, killing him. She also appears to travelers who have become exhausted in snowstorms. They fall into her welcoming embrace and then die.

sorcerers   See VAMPIRE SORCERERS AND WITCHES.

soucouyant   In Trinidad lore, a blood-sucking shapeshifter (see SHAPE-SHIFTING) who belongs to the class of evil spirits known as jumbies. The *soucouyant* is an old woman who sheds her skin at night, hiding it under the stone mortar she uses for grinding food. She turns herself into a ball of fire and enters the homes of victims through a crack or keyhole. She drinks the BLOOD of sleeping people.

Soucouyants can be neutralized by visiting their homes while they are out of their skins, finding their hidden skins and sprinkling them with hot pepper. The *soucouyants* will burn to death when they put their skins back on. One can also stop *soucouyants* from attacking by the remedy of scattering rice or flour in front of the doorway. This forces the *soucouyants* to stop and count all the grains. They will not be able to do so before dawn comes, and they lose their power.

Soucouyants are blamed for the wounds inflicted by VAMPIRE BATS.

Spaulding Family Vampires (18th c.)   Consumption deaths in Vermont believed associated with vampirism. Multiple tuberculosis deaths in the family of Lieutenant Leonard Spaulding of Dummerston, Vermont, near Manchester led to antivampire remedies of CORPSE disinterment, mutilation, and cremation. The case was described in the *Vermont Historical Magazine* in 1884; some important details are missing.

Over a period of 16 years, nine members of the Spaulding family died of consumption. All of the family members were hale and hearty, but once stricken with consumption, they deteriorated quickly to their deaths. The first to die was daughter Mary in 1782, at age 20. Leonard, the father, died in 1788. Leonard, Jr., died in 1792. Twins Timothy and John died in 1793. The last to die was son Josiah in December 1798, at age 27. Three daughters survived.

According to the magazine account, after "six or seven" members of the family had died, an unnamed daughter was taken ill with consumption and was expected to die. Apparently there was much talk among family and friends about the circumstances surrounding all of the deaths:

Among the superstitions of those days, we find it was said that a vine or root of some kind grew from coffin to coffin, of those of one family, who died of consumption, and were buried side by side; and when the growing vine had reached the coffin of the last one buried, another one of the family would die; the only way to destroy the influence or effect, was to break the vine; take up the body of the last one buried and burn the vitals, which would be an effectual remedy: Accordingly, the body of the last one buried was dug up and the vitals taken out and burned, and the daughter, it is affirmed, got well and lived many years. The act, doubtless, raised her mind from a state of despondency to hopefullness [sic].

It is not known whose body was disinterred; the most likely were Leonard, Jr., who died in 1792, or one of the twins, John, who died in 1793.

Grave plants and vines appear in various folklore traditions, but are not associated strongly with vampires. Twining grave plants united lovers after death, as in the tale of *Tristan and Isolde*. The type of plant growing on a grave is believed to indicate the state or fate of the soul, for some of the essence of the dead is transferred into the plant. For example, in Christianized German folklore, slain heathens cause BLACKTHORN to grow, while Christians produce white flowering plants. In French lore, nettles and thorns indicate the soul is damned; if they are mixed with other plants, the soul is in purgatory. The *Vermont Historical Magazine* does not elaborate on the type of vine growing on the Spaulding family graves.

See also NEW ENGLAND VAMPIRES.

FURTHER READING:
Bell, Michael E. *Food for the Dead: On the Trail of New England's Vampires*. New York: Carroll & Graf, 2001.

Spike   See BUFFY THE VAMPIRE SLAYER.

spittle   In folklore, a protective agent against evil entities and forces, including VAMPIRES and the effects of the EVIL EYE. Spittle represents the soul, and to spit it out is an offering to the gods for luck and protection. According to custom, spitting should be done immediately when one senses supernatural danger, or when one enters an area believed to be haunted or dangerous. Spittle also is used in magical spells to increase their effectiveness.

stake   A favored means of containing and destroying VAMPIRES. In European lore, a vampire is riveted into the grave by piercing its CORPSE with a stake, preferably fash-

A stake through the heart kills vampire Carolyn Stoddard (Nancy Barrett) in House of Dark Shadows. *(Author's collection)*

ioned from a thorn wood such as HAWTHORN, or another wood considered to be holy, such as ASPEN. Oak and juniper also are used.

The stake traditionally is driven through the heart, but is also plunged into the belly or the back between the shoulder blades. Witnesses to vampire destructions took care not to be splattered by the corpse's BLOOD, for they believed they would fall ill and die, or go insane, if they were touched by it. Sometimes a hide was placed over the corpse to contain blood spatters. Anecdotal accounts from Europe tell of vampire corpses shrieking and moaning when staked, probably due to the forced expulsion of natural gases. (See VRESKET.)

An anecdotal account from Serbia tells of a man from the village of Mihaljevci, whose head was crushed when he fell off a wagon. Eight days after his funeral, he returned as a vampire and slept with his neighbor's wife. She became pregnant and had to tell others and the village priest what had happened to her. In the daytime, the priest and villagers opened the grave and found the corpse on its stomach. They drove a hawthorn stake through his head. His skull exploded like a cannon, and a large flame issued from it. The priest gave the dead man his final benediction. The vampire never returned, but the woman gave birth to the child, who did not live long.

Among some Serbs, staking contained a vampire but did not destroy it; BURNING the corpse was necessary to destroy the vampire.

In film and fiction, staking destroys vampires, who scream, writhe, and disintegrate upon being pierced.

FURTHER READING:
Barber, Paul. *Vampires, Burial and Death: Folklore and Reality.* New Haven, Conn.: Yale University Press, 1988.
Krauss, Frederic S. "South Slavic Countermeasures against Vampires," in *The Vampire: A Casebook.* Alan Dundes, ed. Madison: University of Wisconsin Press, 1998.

Stana (18th c.)   Haglike VAMPIRE case reported in the 1730s in the Serbian village of Medvegia (Meduegna), as a result of the ARNOD PAOLE vampire case. According to the records of investigating medical officers, a woman named Stana (also recorded as Stanacka or Stanicka) "lay down to sleep fifteen days ago, fresh and healthy, but at midnight started up out of her sleep with a terrible cry, fearful and trembling, and complained that she had been throttled by the son of a Haiduk by the name of Milloe (Milloc or Milove), who had died nine weeks earlier, whereupon she had experienced a great pain in the chest and became worse by the hour, until finally she died on the third day."

In MONTAGUE SUMMERS's account of the case, as given in *The Vampire in Europe*, Stana confessed on her deathbed that she had "anointed herself in the blood of a vampire to liberate herself from his persecutions." Her baby died, too. Summers wrote that when vampire hunters dug up the woman's body, they found it untouched by decomposition.

When it was opened the chest was found to be full of fresh blood, the viscera had all the appearance of sound health. The skin and nails of both hands and feet were loose and came off, but underneath was a clean new skin and nails.

The body of her baby also was exhumed, but had been so savaged by wolves that too little was left of it to determine if vampirism was present. The body of Milloe was dug up after the 16-year-old boy had lain in the grave for 90 days. Said Summers, "It was rosy and flabber, wholly in the Vampire condition."

FURTHER READING:
Perkowski, Jan L. *The Darkling: A Treatise on Slavic Vampirism.* Columbus, Ohio: Slavica Publishers, 1989.
Summers, Montague. *The Vampire in Europe.* New York: E. P. Dutton, 1929.

Stoker, Bram (1847–1912)   Author of the most famous VAMPIRE novel in literature, DRACULA (1897), who almost single-handedly inspired an entire industry of vampire fiction, film, drama, and entertainment.

Unlike many other authors of celebrated novels, Bram Stoker lived a simple, conventional life. He was better known for his work as actor Henry Irving's theater manager than for his literary efforts, even in his own time. By the later half of the 20th century, few people could even say who created the evil COUNT DRACULA. The count had a life of his own, but the man who gave birth had been nearly forgotten. Today Stoker is one of the most written about and celebrated authors of horror fiction.

Bram, or Abraham, was the third child of Abraham and Charlotte Stoker, born on November 8, 1947, in Clontarf, Ireland. The elder Stoker was a civil servant; his mother was an ambitious promoter for her five sons, though neglectful of Bram's two sisters. By his own account, Stoker's childhood was marred by long periods of illness to the point of threatening his life. He never defined this illness or gave specific details of it, and in later years modified his account of the severity of his sickness. Whatever his early health, he grew up to be a vigorous man who kept a furious work pace through most of his adult life.

By age 16, Stoker already had begun "scribbling." He entered Trinity College at Dublin University in November 1864, throwing himself into athletics and philosophical debate, a claim that scholars have not been able to verify. He loved theater and literature, particularly Walt Whitman's controversial *Leaves of Grass.* Stoker's tastes ran to the macabre early on, perhaps fostered by his mother's harrowing tales of the Irish cholera epidemic of 1832.

Upon graduation in 1870, he followed his father into civil service at Dublin Castle, a monotonous career. Nights were spent at the theater. Incensed at the lack of quality dramatic criticism in the Dublin papers, he began writing dramatic reviews for the *Dublin Mail* in November 1871.

He was so confident of his opinions and the need for such a column that he wrote without pay.

Stoker's first book was the dry *Duties of Clerks of Petty Sessions in Ireland* (1879). His father encouraged young Stoker's career at Dublin Castle, warning him that the theater could be dangerous to his pension.

But he persisted. In 1876 the English actor Henry Irving returned to Dublin in *Hamlet*. Stoker had been thrilled with Irving's realistic portrayals years earlier and flattered him in his theater reviews. Irving invited Stoker to dinner, and the two men discovered they shared many views. After dinner, Irving's recitation of *The Dream of Eugene Aram* left Stoker hysterical, and Irving, also overcome with emotion, presented him with a signed photograph.

For the next two years, the men corresponded regularly and saw each other whenever their work permitted. By September 1878, Irving had purchased the Lyceum Theater in London and asked Stoker to be his acting manager. Stoker immediately resigned his position at Dublin Castle.

The other major event in 1878 was Stoker's marriage to Florence Anne Lemon Balcombe. She was a great beauty and 11 years Stoker's junior. Florence's other major suitor

A portrait of Bram Stoker (Courtesy Vampire Empire Archives)

was Oscar Wilde, who was a homosexual and probably pursued her out of convention. The two men remained rivals only a short time; Florence and Stoker were married on December 4, and left five days later to join Henry Irving in Birmingham. The Stokers' only child, a son, Noel, was born a year later on December 29, 1879.

Joining Irving was really a second marriage. Stoker threw himself into the management of Irving's theater and affairs. So many details had to be acknowledged: remodeling the building, hiring actors, establishing the repertory, covering the enormous debts already accumulating. Stoker rarely wrote fewer than 50 letters a day. The theater's grand reopening on December 30, 1878, was a great success, and even critics gave Stoker credit. From that first night onward, Stoker always stood in evening dress in the vestibule, greeting theatergoers and watching from the wings. He worshiped Irving as a god, and everything was done to make the actor's endeavors triumphant and effortless.

Playing Ophelia to Irving's Hamlet in that opening production was the famous actress Ellen Terry. She appeared with Irving's company for more than 20 years, and Stoker found her radiant, beautiful, and full of life. She referred to Stoker as her "mama" and to herself as his "dutiful daughter." The three of them—Irving, Stoker, and Terry—*were* the Lyceum in the late 19th century.

As Irving's star ascended, so did the Stoker's place in society; Florence reigned over dinner with all of London's elite from their home at 27 Cheyne Walk along the river in Chelsea. They entertained Alfred, Lord Tennyson; J. McNeill Whistler; Sir Edward Burne-Jones; Mark Twain; author Hall Caine; and W. S. Gilbert. Oscar Wilde also frequented Florence's salon.

The Stokers sold 27 Cheyne Walk three years later. On September 14, 1882, Stoker dove into the river to save a man trying to commit SUICIDE. After a five-minute struggle, Stoker and the unidentified man were brought aboard the riverboat *Twilight*, and Stoker took him to his home. Stoker's brother, Dr. George Stoker, was unable to revive him, and Florence never got over finding a CORPSE in the dining room. Stoker received the Bronze Medal of the Royal Humane Society for his heroism, but Florence would not stay in the house. She may also have been rebelling against Stoker's overwhelming devotion to Irving at her expense.

In the fall of 1883, Irving began his first American tour, carefully orchestrated and promoted by his faithful Stoker. Irving was received enthusiastically and continued to tour America until his retirement in 1904. Stoker lovingly attended to every detail and immersed himself in Americana while touring with the company. He was particularly taken with the beautiful homes, tramps, inexpensive real estate, America's lack of class consciousness and airs, the comfort of the middle classes, crime and punishment, the exaltation of American women, and the ease of the upper-class club life.

In addition to serving Irving, Stoker studied for the bar and passed his exams in 1890. He wrote several books and magazine articles, including a children's book, *Under the*

Sunset (1882), a collection of strange stories probably unsuitable for small listeners. Stoker traveled with the company, often without Florence or Noel, and maintained a schedule that few others could endure. Stoker also arranged opening-night galas and banquets, late-night intimate suppers, and all-night discussions over brandy about drama and the arts.

In 1891 Stoker entered into a risky business venture with the publisher William Heinemann to launch *The English Library*, a series of works by prominent British authors. The venture failed after a few years, and Stoker was thrown back on the Lyceum as his primary financial source. Money was a constant worry to him, for Florence spent lavishly and entertained in high style. Stoker could ill afford to pursue the career he desired as a literary writer. But even if money had not been an issue, Stoker probably would not have left Irving out of sheer loyalty.

Even while keeping a heavy work schedule for the theater, Stoker wrote on the side, mostly short stories. Despite his literary aspirations, his fiction gravitated to the occult. In 1886 he published his third nonfiction book, *A Glimpse of America*, based on his tour. His first novel, *The Snake's Pass*, was published in 1890, a year in which he also may have begun notes for *Dracula*, according to earliest known records. Set in Western Ireland, *The Snake's Pass* features Arthur Severn, a wealthy young Englishman who becomes embroiled in a legend of lost treasure in a mountain bog.

Stoker's travels served his craft. On holiday in 1892, Stoker came upon the small fishing village of Boscastle on the west coast of Cornwall. The sea squeezed through the rocks there with incredible power, and the locale became Pencastle in Stoker's short story *The Coming of Abel Behenna*. Exhibiting Stoker's interest in the macabre, the story tells of two fishermen in love with the same girl. One of the suitors dies, and his CORPSE washes ashore on the day of the other's wedding during a wild storm. Corpses and violent storms also figure in *The Watter's Mou'* (1895), a gothic tale of a coast guardsman in love with a fisherman's daughter, whose father's debts have pushed him into smuggling. Her father is lost at sea, and when the daughter drowns trying to save him, the young guard jumps in after her. Their corpses are washed ashore, joined together in an embrace. *The Watter's Mou'* appeared as a companion volume to Sir Arthur Conan Doyle's story "THE PARASITE."

As a setting for Stoker's works, Boscastle was surpassed by the town of Cruden Bay, a tiny fishing village below the ruins of Slain's Castle in Scotland that Stoker discovered in 1893. He used Cruden Bay in *The Watter's Mou'*, and again in a story called *Crooked Sands* (1897). More important, Cruden Bay was the place where Stoker felt most at ease, spending his holidays there yearly. During the summers of 1895 and 1896, Stoker strode the beaches, developing the plot for his vampire novel. It has been suggested that Slain's Castle served as the model for CASTLE DRACULA in *Dracula*. Stoker's extant notes do not verify this, but given the time he spent there, he may have drawn inspiration from the setting.

Stoker envisioned his boss, Henry Irving, as the best actor suited to play Count Dracula onstage. (Author's collection)

Stoker's horror stories played upon the reader's every fear. One of his best is *The Squaw* (1894), in which a young couple travel to Nuremberg Castle and are joined by an American eager to see the torture chamber, specifically the Iron Virgin. From high on a parapet, the American idly drops a pebble down and inadvertently hits a kitten playing with its mother, killing it. The tourists proceed to the torture chamber, where the American insists on standing inside the Iron Virgin to imagine the full effect. The custodian, holding the torture machine's rope, is attacked by the vengeful mother cat. He drops the rope, and the American is impaled.

Dracula was published in 1897 to mixed critical reviews. However, matters with Irving and the Lyceum eclipsed the novel's debut and all other concerns. The theater company was falling on hard times. In December 1896 Irving fell on a dark stairway at the theater and was unable to perform for 10 weeks, precipitating financial losses for the company. In February 1898 the storage warehouse for the theater burned down, losing over £30,000 worth of equipment, props, and costumes. Just that year, Irving had instructed Stoker to drop insurance coverage from £10,000 to £600 to cut expenses. The losses were devastating.

Irving withdrew completely, leaving Stoker to handle the business and the actors. The actor bitterly resented the loss, as well as the failure of his most recent production and competition from other theaters. Struggling to go on, he became ill with pneumonia and pleurisy, losing another seven weeks. Overcome with the worry of it all, Irving agreed to an offer from a syndicate called the Lyceum Theater Company to buy the Lyceum, much to Stoker's dismay.

By 1902 the syndicate was in arrears and Irving was without a theater in which to perform. He made tours at home and abroad, including a farewell to America tour in 1904, but his health was severely weakened. Nevertheless, lack of funds necessitated his constant working. By October 1905 Irving was near collapse. On the 13th he died in the lobby of his hotel following a performance of *Becket*.

Irving's death left Stoker completely bereft emotionally. In addition, Irving left no bequest for him out of his estate of nearly £21,000. Stoker's own financial difficulties had caused him to continue writing furiously, and with his theater career now irrevocably finished, he set himself a goal of a book a year.

Ten books came after *Dracula,* including a two-volume work, *Personal Reminisces of Henry Irving* (1906). Most of the rest were fiction. His book income was not sufficient for a livelihood, and he also did journalistic work for newspapers and magazines.

Stoker took up the cause of censorship of lewd fiction. His own fiction either emphasized horror or romance, with the heroines good and pure beyond belief. Stoker always claimed the highest regard for what he called "the fair sex," yet his supposedly chaste love scenes were loaded with sexual imagery. The descriptions of vampires licking their lips and writhing are erotic and sensual. Yet Stoker wrote scathing reviews in magazines against sex in literature, calling it "unclean" and an "abomination."

With all his output, Stoker achieved little fame and even less money in his lifetime. In his last years, his royalties hovered around £80 pounds a year, and his letters to friends were filled with comments on worries about money and health. He had suffered two strokes, in 1906 and 1909, which left his gait and eyesight permanently impaired. He needed a magnifying glass to write, which must have created quite a strain. In addition, Stoker developed gout and Bright's disease, a kidney ailment that causes blood poisoning. He spent long periods in bed, with Florence attending him as nurse.

In 1911 lack of money forced the Stokers to move from Chelsea, where they had lived for 30 years, to a cheaper residence in Pimlico. Stoker began work on his last novel, *The Lair of the White Worm,* which he finished in three months and was published the same year. Based on an ancient British legend that giant serpents or worms once dominated the landscape, its plot is confusing. It contains sexual imagery and hallucinations, causing critics in the future to wonder if Stoker had been influenced by the medications he was taking for his Bright's disease.

According to the story, a wealthy young Australian, Adam Salton, returns to his ancestral home to meet Lady Arabella March, an odd woman dressed in white who repels snakes. In truth, Lady Arabella is the dreaded great white worm, a 200-foot antediluvian leftover that feeds on innocents, similar to the vampires, in order to survive. She tries to lure Salton's fiancée down her slimy cave hole hidden in her grand home. Salton destroys her in a dynamite explosion that yields shreds of her human body, worms, and horrible stinking vermin for days.

With the completion of *Lair,* Stoker ran out of energy to create new works. He revised earlier works with plans to collect them into an anthology.

Stoker died quietly in bed at home at 26 George's Square on April 20, 1912, at age 64. He left an inheritance of £4,664 to Florence, the equivalent of about $20,000. The obituary that appeared in *The London Times* noted his devotion to Irving and briefly commented that Stoker was the master of lurid and creepy fiction. He was cremated and buried at Golder's Green, north of London.

In 1975 Daniel Farson, a great-nephew of Stoker's, created a controversy in his biography with his assertion that Stoker had died of tertiary syphilis, not exhaustion or kidney failure. Farson said that Stoker's search for the ideal woman came from sexual frustration with Florence, and that he had turned to prostitutes, thus contracting syphilis. By 1897, Farson said, Stoker and Florence had not had sexual relations for about 20 years.

Stoker's death certificate read, "Locomotor Ataxy 6 Months, Granular Contracted Kidney. Exhaustion." Farson consulted a doctor who told him that "locomotor ataxy" was a euphemism for tertiary syphilis commonly used in Victorian times, and referred to the inability to coordinate movement that characterized the last stages of the disease.

Syphilis is highly unlikely, and has been solidly refuted by Stoker scholars. There is no evidence that Stoker led that kind of lifestyle, nor did he exhibit any other symptoms common to late-stage syphilis. There is no verification of the Stokers' sexual relations.

Another controversial theory put forward in 1995 about Stoker was that he suffered sexual abuse in childhood at the hands of his father—hence his vague "illness" that required him to be bedridden for long periods of time—and his repressed memories were expressed in the sexual undercurrents of *Dracula.* Author Daniel Lapin, a clinical analyst, based his theory on an interpretation of the novel. There is no evidence in any of Stoker's personal papers, letters, or notes that abuse occurred in his family life.

Stoker's Legacy

The widow Florence did her best to make the most financially out of Stoker's writings, but the only property that made money was *Dracula.* A year after Stoker's death, she had his private papers, including his research and working notes for *Dracula,* sold at auction at Sotheby's. In 1914 she published *Dracula's Guest—And Other Weird Stories,* a collection of stories written early in Stoker's career. She said that prior to his death Stoker intended to publish three collections of short stories, and this was the first. She said DRACULA'S GUEST was originally a chapter of *Dracula* that had been cut from the novel, but the exact origins of the story have been debated by scholars since publication.

Florence licensed dramatic rights to *Dracula* to HAMILTON DEANE. She refused film rights to F. W. MURNAU, who went ahead with the plagiarized 1922 silent film NOSFERATU. Florence finally licensed film rights to Universal Pictures, who signed BELA LUGOSI to play the Count in TOD BROWNING's 1931 production.

Florence died on May 25, 1937, of colon cancer at age 78.

Dracula, the book that failed to earn either Stoker or his wife riches in their lifetimes, went on to spawn one of the most commercially successful subgenres of horror in fiction and film. But while the count and the novel became famous, Stoker himself slipped into obscurity. In the 1950s journalist Harry Ludlam began seven years of research to uncover the details of Stoker's life and career. The task proved more difficult than he first thought, for Stoker the man had been nearly forgotten, even in Ireland. Ludlam's biography, the first on Stoker, was published in 1962. Since then, Stoker has been the subject of numerous books, both popular and academic, as scholars and fans alike have analyzed the creative mind behind the greatest of all vampire novels. Researchers have pored over his writings and details of his life, speculating on his thoughts and motivations.

The Lair of the White Worm, though not so well known as *Dracula,* became Stoker's second most popular work, a cult favorite. It was made into a film by director Ken Russell in 1988, starring Hugh Grant. *The Jewel of Seven Stars* (1903), about an Egyptian mummy and a curse, became the basis of the film *Blood from the Mummy's Tomb* (1971), starring Andrew Keir and Valerie Leon. The film was remade in 1980 as *The Awakening* starring Charlton Heston and Susannah York.

Dracula was Stoker's only vampire novel. Lady Arabella March in *Lair* is vampirelike, as is another of Stoker's female characters, a princess who masquerades as a vampire, in *The Lady of the Shroud* (1909). *Dracula's Guest* features an offstage Count Dracula and a vampire and a vampire countess in the form of a BLOOD-drinking wolf.

Stoker's Interest in the Occult

Stoker's early interest in the macabre, fueled by his mother's cholera tales, continued throughout his life. During his lifetime, there was a great deal of public interest in spiritual, occult, and magical topics. Spiritualism and the physical effects of mediums were attracting people to seances. The Society of Psychical Research was founded in 1882 to establish scientific inquiry. Theosophy and magi-

The urn containing Bram Stoker's ashes (Courtesy Vampire Empire Archives)

cal orders such as the Hermetic Order of the Golden Dawn were in bloom.

Stoker was a thorough researcher. For *Dracula* alone, he consulted numerous sources for the background of history, geography, folklore, and myth (see DRACULA; GERARD, EMILY DE LASZKOWSKI; TRANSYLVANIA).

Stoker's own Irish heritage was a rich source of the supernatural. Stoker's childhood friend, author Hall Caine (see HOMMY-BEG) was knowledgeable about their native lore. Stoker traveled in circles whose members participated in psychical and occult research and activities. Lady Constance Wilde, Oscar Wilde's mother, knew a great deal of Irish folklore and was involved in both spiritualism and theosophy. Stoker attended at least one lecture at the Society for Psychical Research, given by founding member F. W. H. Myers on Sigmund Freud's including KING VIKRAM AND THE VAMPIRE. Stoker had friends who were members of the Golden Dawn. Among them was Pamela Colman Smith, who illustrated A. E. Waite's Tarot deck and drew the illustrations for the first edition of *The Lair of the White Worm.*

In her biography of Stoker, Barbara Belford posits that *Dracula* itself is a kind of Tarot journey symbolic of a gnostic quest. Jonathan Harker is The Fool; PROFESSOR ABRAHAM VAN HELSING is The Magician; Mina Harker is The Empress; Dr. John Seward is The Hermit; Lucy Westenra and her fiancé, Arthur Holmwood (Lord Godalming), are The Lovers; and Quincey Morris is The Hanged Man.

Stoker's Books

The following is a list of Stoker's nonfiction and fiction books, and their original year of issue. Nonfiction works are noted with an *N.* Only four of the full-length fictional works deal with the supernatural—*Dracula, The Jewel of Seven Stars, The Lady of the Shroud,* and *Lair of the White Worm:*

- *The Duties of Clerks of Petty Sessions of Ireland* (1879) N
- *Under the Sunset* (1881) N
- *A Glimpse of America* (1886) N
- *The Snake's Pass* (1890)
- *The Watter's Mou'* (1895)
- *The Shoulder of Shasta* (1895)
- *Dracula* (1897)
- *Miss Betty* (1898)
- *The Mystery of the Sea* (1902)
- *The Jewel of Seven Stars* (1903)
- *The Man* (1905)
- *Personal Reminisces of Henry Irving,* two volumes (1906) N
- *Lady Althyne* (1908)
- *Snowbound: the Record of a Theatrical Touring Party* (1908) N
- *The Lady of the Shroud* (1909)
- *Famous Imposters* (1910) N
- *The Lair of the White Worm* (1911)
- *Dracula's Guest—And Other Weird Stories* (1914)

FURTHER READING:
Auerbach, Nina, and David J. Skal, eds. *Dracula.* New York: W. W. Norton Co., 1997.
Belford, Barbara. *Bram Stoker: A Biography of the Author of Dracula.* New York: Alfred A. Knopf, 1996.
Farson, Daniel. *The Man Who Wrote Dracula: A Biography of Bram Stoker.* London: Michael Joseph, 1975.
Haining, Peter, and Peter Tremayne. *The Undead: The Legend of Bram Stoker and Dracula.* London: Constable, 1997.
Lapin, Daniel. *The Vampire, Dracula and Incest.* San Francisco: Gargoyle Publishers, 1995.
Leatherdale, Clive. *Dracula: The Novel and the Legend.* Wellingborough, Northamptonshire: The Aquarian Press, 1985.
Ludlam, Harry. *My Quest for Bram Stoker.* New York: Dracula Press, 2000.
———. *A Biography of Dracula: True Life Story of Bram Stoker.* London: W. Foulsham, 1962.

Stoker, Florence   See NOSFERATU; BRAM STOKER.

striges   In Greco-Roman lore, females who could shape-shift (see SHAPE-SHIFTING) into voracious birds of prey—usually the owl—and, like LAMIAE, feast upon the BLOOD and flesh of children. *Strix* (singular) is Latin for "screech owl." Striges are particularly fond of livers and internal organs. They fly at night, and no locks or barriers can keep them out.

The Roman poet Ovid said striges use their beaks to pick out a child's milk-fed bowels. He proposed three the-ories as to the origin of striges: they were born that way; they were enchanted; they were hags who had been put under a spell.

The Roman satirist Petronius said striges were wise women of the night who possessed the power to overthrow the natural order of things.

After the fall of the Roman Empire, striges became low Latin for *witch.* As Christianity spread, the striges, along with other pagan spirits, became associated with demonolatry. The Synod of Rome in 743 outlawed offerings to such spirits. In 744 a "List of Superstitions" drawn up at the Council of Leptinnes renounced "all the works of the demon . . . and all evil beings that are like them." Various laws were passed forbidding belief in striges and other pagan spirits, such as one in Saxony in 789, which punished such belief with execution.

By the Middle Ages, striges were believed to be servants of Satan and his demons. They were said to be women witches who practiced sorcery and flew through the air. They could turn themselves into blood-drinking birds with huge talons, misshapen heads, and breasts full of poisonous milk. They preyed upon unprotected sleeping men and children. With men, they turned into women, had sexual intercourse, then drank the men's blood. (See SUCCUBUS.) To children, they offered their poisonous milk.

The striges' association with screech owls gave rise to the term *owl-blasted,* a synonym for a wasting-away spell cast upon a man. *Owl-blasted* remained in popular use in Britain through the 16th century.

FURTHER READING:
Guiley, Rosemary Ellen. *The Encyclopedia of Witches and Witchcraft.* 2d ed. New York: Facts On File, 1999.

strigoi   A Romanian term for a male VAMPIRE, almost exclusively applied to the restless returning dead. *Strigoi* comes from the Latin term *strix* (plural STRIGES). The strigoi can shape-shift (see SHAPE-SHIFTING) into the form of a flying mammal, and is especially active on the feast days of St. George and St. Andrew. *Strigoi* are not inherently evil, but they are feared for their appearance bodes ill, and they are omens of sickness and misfortune.

Dead Strigoi
In Romanian lore, people who died unforgiven by their parents are in danger of becoming *strigoi.* In such cases, the CORPSE is exhumed while a priest reads from the Gospels. The body is cremated, and the ASHES are thrown to the winds. The *strigoi* will never return.

Unmarried people are at a high risk of becoming *strigoi.* Their corpses should be stabbed through the heart with a sickle, which will protect family members from being killed by the vampire.

Corpses walked over by CATS will become *strigoi.* To get rid of them, bury a bottle of wine near the grave, and six weeks later dig it up and drink the wine with relatives. Whoever drinks the wine will be protected against the *strigoi*, who will not return.

A person who is filled with pain and regret will turn into a cat or dog after death and return as a *strigoi* to torment his relatives. Piercing the body of the *strigoi* with a needle will prevent it from leaving the grave, as will placing a candle, coin, or towel in the hand of the corpse. Walking around the grave with burning hemp will cause the *strigoi* to become helpless.

One remedy against the *strigoi* is to bury a bottle of whiskey with the corpse; the *strigoi* will drink it and not return home.

A GYPSY remedy for killing a *strigoi* is as follows:

Dig up the vampire corpse, remove its heart, and cut the organ in two. Drive a nail into the forehead, place a clove of GARLIC under the tongue, and smear the body with the fat of a PIG killed on St. Ignatius's day. Turn the body face-down in the COFFIN.

A Romanian anecdote recorded in 1932 tells of a man who became a *strigoi* after death, and tormented the women in the household where he lived. The police went to his grave and dug him up, finding the corpse ruddy and bloated. Attempts to impale him with a pitchfork through the stomach failed when the skin mysteriously could not be pierced. A soldier who tried to hit the corpse with his rifle hit himself instead. A wise woman was summoned, who did magical incantations over the corpse while being alone with it. She then struck it in the stomach with a knife.

Living Strigoi

When applied to the living, *strigoi* refers to a witch or wizard (see VAMPIRE SORCERERS AND WITCHES). Living *strigoi* who perform magical work-for-hire are held in good regard.

A folk practice for protecting newborn children against attacks by *strigoi* call for tossing a stone behind one while saying, "This into the jaws of the *strigoi*."

A Romanian folktale tells of a *strigoi* who turned into a handsome young man. A young girl fell in love with him, and they were married. The *strigoi* at first refused to have a religious wedding, but the girl and her parents insisted, and so he agreed. As they left the church after the ceremony, he looked at his bride and bared his teeth. Frightened, she told her mother, who assured her that he showed his teeth because he loved her. But when the parents came to visit them, the couple could not be found. They had locked themselves in their house. Through a window, people could see the *strigoi* sucking the BLOOD of his wife. The villagers shot him through the window.

FURTHER READING:
Perkowski, Jan Lewis. "The Roumanian Folkloric Vampire," in *The Vampire: A Casebook*, Alan Dundes, ed. Madison: University of Wisconsin Press, 1998.

strigoica (strigoaica)   A Romanian term for a female VAMPIRE, either dead or living. A living *strigoica* is a SHAPE-SHIFTING vampire witch (see VAMPIRE SORCERERS AND WITCHES). The *strigoica* takes power from people and animals while living, and then turns into a vampire after death. The *strigoica* is especially noted for taking the power of cows by sucking all their milk so they have none to give.

A Romanian folk story tells about a *strigoica* who had no cow of her own. She kept a wooden cow in her attic and milked it day and night, taking the milk of the cows of others and bringing it to her wooden cow.

Another Romanian tale with Christian elements emphasizes the spiritual punishments that await the *strigoica*. A *strigoica* went to confession and told the priest she had taken the power of other people's cows. He told her to take butter from the milk and anoint a tree in the forest with it. After three days, she was to go back to the tree to see what happened. She did so, and discovered that all manner of serpents and horrible creatures were in the butter. The priest told her that these creatures would suck her BLOOD in the next world because she had taken power from everything in this world.

In another Romanian anecdote, the activities of a *strigoica* and the remedies employed against her are described:

The notary of the town of Vintere had a servant who was accused of taking milk from cows. He denied it and to prove his innocence he took off all his clothes and hid one night to see who was the guilty person.

He saw a *strigoica* who came as a dog and sucked the milk from the cows. He jammed his pitchfork into the dog and it fled, and when it got back to the house, it died.

The priest of the village heard what had happened and called the servant to him. He told him to go and buy new clothes and to pay the first price asked. He told him also to bury the dead witch without a casket and to watch over the body for three nights.

The servant hired another man to help him. The first night the witch came out of the grave, but he hid behind the church CROSS, and she didn't find him. She looked and looked until three in the morning, when she returned to the grave, weeping for not having found him.

The second night, two witches came out and looked and looked, and discovered him, but by then it was three o'clock and they had to go back to the grave.

He fled to his house and now he is married with children.

In the above story, there are associations with WEREWOLF lore: If a werewolf is wounded, the wound is present on the person when he or she shape-shifts out of animal form. If a werewolf is mortally wounded, the person will die.

An interesting variation of vampire lore is the forced return to the grave at 3 A.M. rather than at dawn at COCK crow.

FURTHER READING:

Murgoci, Agnes. "The Vampire in Roumania," in *The Vampire: A Casebook*, Alan Dundes, ed. Madison: University of Wisconsin Press, 1998.

Senn, Harry A. *Werewolf and Vampire in Romania.* New York: Columbia University Press, 1982.

Stubb, Peter **(d. 1589)**   German man accused of being a murdering sorcerer and WEREWOLF. Peter Stubb (also given as Stubbe, Stube, and Stumpf, and as Stubbe Peeter), of Bedbur, Germany, gained notoriety for making a lurid confession. An illustrated account of his trial and grisly execution is at the Lambeth Palace Library in London.

According to Stubb's confession, he had practiced the "wicked arts" from the age of 12. He had from early childhood had an evil bent, and began dabbling in magic, sorcery, and necromancy. The devil gave him a magic GIRDLE (belt) that enabled him to change into a wolf, and promised him that in exchange for wreaking evil in animal form, he would be protected from danger. When Stubb put on the girdle, he was:

. . . transformed into the likeness of a greedy, devouring wolf, strong and mighty, with eyes great and large, which in the night sparkled like brands of fire; a mouth great and wide, with most sharp and cruel teeth; a huge body and mighty paws.

By taking the belt off, he returned to the shape of a man.

Stubb spent the next 25 years stalking victims, both human and animal, as a werewolf. He would walk about the areas of Bedbur, Collin, and Cperadt as a nicely dressed man, looking for victims. When he could catch them unawares, he changed into a wolf and attacked and murdered them. He sexually assaulted maidens before tearing them apart.

Stubb terrorized the countryside at night, attacking children, women, men, lambs, sheep, and goats. He was an "insatiable bloodsucker," taking great pleasure in killing. He killed lambs, kids, and other livestock, devouring them raw and bloody.

Over the course of a few years, Stubb murdered 13 young children and two pregnant women. He tore the fetuses out of the women's wombs and "ate their hearts panting hot and raw," which he said were "dainty morsels."

Stubb also confessed to an insatiable sexual appetite. He committed incest with his daughter, Beell (Bell), who had a child by him. He carried on sexual escapades with various mistresses, including a "gossip," Katherine Trompin. Still

Scenes from the life, capture, torture and execution of the werewolf Peter Stubb (Author's collection)

his lust remained unsated, so the devil sent him a SUCCUBUS in the form of an angellike, beautiful woman.

Meanwhile, the townspeople did not suspect him. When the limbs and body parts of adults and children were found in the fields, it was believed that a savage wolf was responsible. Stubb finally was exposed when hunters chased him down in wolf form, and he slipped off his belt and was recognized.

Stubb was arrested and brought to trial at Bedbur. He was put on the rack. Fearing the torture, he quickly made a confession. A search was made for his magical girdle, but it was never found. It was assumed that the devil had spirited the evidence away.

Stubb named Bell and Trompin as accessories to some of his murders. The two women were arraigned. All three were found guilty on October 28, 1589, and were condemned to death. The sentences were carried out on October 31:

> Stubbe Peeter as principal malefactor, was judged first to have his body laid on a wheel, and with red hot burning pincers in ten places to have the flesh pulled off from the bones, after that, his legs and arms to be broken with a wooden axe or hatchet, afterward to have his head struck from his body, then to have his carcass burned to ashes.
>
> Also his daughter and his gossip were judged to be burned quick to ashes, the same time and day with the carcass of the aforesaid Stubbe Peeter.

After the executions, the magistrates of Bedbur constructed a warning to others. The wheel on which Stubb was broken was placed on a high sharpened pole and above it was fastened a likeness of a wolf in wooden frame. Sixteen yard-long pieces of wood, representing the 16 known victims of Stubb, were hung on the wheel. Stubb's head was stuck onto the pole.

FURTHER READING:
Otten, Charlotte F., ed. *A Lycanthropy Reader: Werewolves in Western Culture.* New York: Dorset Press, 1989.

Styria   The original setting for *DRACULA* (1897) by BRAM STOKER. Styria appears in Stoker's notes for his novel, dated 1890, seven years before the book was published. COUNT DRACULA's castle was placed in Styria, an area of Germany. Stoker may have been influenced by "CARMILLA" by Sheridan Le Fanu, which is set in Styria.

Stoker's plot notes called for the solicitor's clerk (Jonathan Harker) to travel from England to Munich, where he visits the Munich Dead House, and then travels by train from Munich to Styria.

Stoker later changed the setting to TRANSYLVANIA, probably after reading the lore of the place reported by EMILY DE LASZKOWSKI GERARD.

succubus   A female demon who seduces men, especially while they sleep. Folklore beliefs about VAMPIRES hold that they are sexually insatiable. Female vampires reportedly behave like succubi, returning from the grave to sexually attack their spouses, lovers, family, and acquaintances.

The succubus, along with its male counterpart, the INCUBUS, appears in ancient mythologies. Succubi can appear in the flesh as beautiful, voluptuous women, most commonly, who visit men in their sleep—especially those who sleep alone—and their sexual activities cause erotic dreams and nocturnal emissions.

By medieval times, succubi were believed to be agents of the devil, who continually tempted men to commit sexual sins, sometimes by promising them immortality in return. Succubi appeared often in the records of witchcraft trials. Men accused of witchcraft usually were tortured until they confessed having sex with demons, among other demonic crimes. In 1468 in Bologna, Italy, a man was executed for allegedly running a brothel of succubi.

See also LILITH; *MULLO*; OLD HAG.

FURTHER READING:
Guiley, Rosemary Ellen. *The Encyclopedia of Witches and Witchcraft.* 2d ed. New York: Facts On File, 1999.

suicide   The taking of one's own life puts one at risk for becoming a VAMPIRE. Suicide is considered a sin, an affront to God, for in it a person assumes godlike powers of deciding on life or death. Traditionally, suicides cannot be buried in hallowed ground. In Romanian lore, the CORPSES of suicides should be dug up immediately and put into running WATER to prevent them from becoming vampires.

In *DRACULA*, COUNT DRACULA takes refuge in the grave of "the lammiter," a suicide victim in WHITBY, ENGLAND.

See also BRESLAU VAMPIRE.

Summers, Montague (b. 1880)   Priest who believed in VAMPIRES, WEREWOLVES, and witches, and compiled accounts of their infernal activities.

Montague Summers was born Alphonsus Joseph-Mary Augustus Montague Summers on April 10, 1880, in Clifton, near Bristol, England, to a wealthy family. He was raised an Anglican, but later converted to Catholicism. He graduated from Cliton College and Trinity College, Oxford, and from Lichfield Theological College, earning both bachelor and master of arts degrees by 1906. He became a curate in the diocese of Bitton near Bristol, but left after a scandal involving choir boys.

In 1909 Summers left the Church of England and entered the Roman Catholic Church and became a priest. From 1911 to 1926 he supplemented an inheritance from his father by teaching at various schools and collected information for books on literature, drama, witchcraft, vampires, and werewolves. His first book on the supernatural, *The History of Witchcraft and Demonology,* appeared in 1926 and became a best seller in England. In his later years, Summers lived and studied at Oxford, where he worked at the Bodleian Library, and pored over the thousands of books he had collected. His peers considered him an odd man, and rumor circulated that while living abroad on the Continent for a period, he had become involved in occult and black magic practices. The rumors were never substantiated.

Summers devoted most of his time to an intense study of witchcraft, which he felt had been neglected by serious English history writers. He published a second book on the subject, *The Geography of Witchcraft,* in 1927. Summers acknowledged that he had "a complete belief in the supernatural, and hence in witchcraft," which prompted at least one reviewer of *Geography* to comment that he "is amusing us at our expense." Reviewers greeted Summers's other supernatural works with the same skepticism. His books on vampires and werewolves were blasted by critics as filled with unsubstantiated old wives' tales: *The Vampire: His Kith and Kin* (1928); *The Vampire in Europe* (1929); and *The Werewolf* (1933). In these books, he attempts to trace the traditions to their earliest inceptions, and to examine the folklore and superstitious practices that arose around them.

Montague Summers (Courtesy Vampire Empire Archives)

Summers opined that vampires do exist. "Cases of vampirism may be said to be in our time a rare occult phenomenon," he wrote in *The Vampire in Europe.* "Yet whether we are justified in supposing that they are less frequent to-day than in past centuries I am far from certain. One thing is plain—not that they do not occur but that they are carefully hushed up and stifled."

Criticisms of Summers are justified, especially in the hindsight of modern times. However, Summers's compilations of accounts have served scholars well.

FURTHER READING:
Guiley, Rosemary Ellen, with J. B. Macabre. *The Complete Vampire Companion.* New York: Macmillan, 1994.
Guiley, Rosemary Ellen. *The Encyclopedia of Witches and Witchcraft.* 2d ed. New York: Facts On File, 1999.
Summers, Montague. *The Vampire: His Kith and Kin.* New Hyde Park, N.Y.: University Books, 1960. First published 1928.
———. *The Vampire in Europe.* New York: E. P. Dutton, 1929.

sunlight   A detriment to VAMPIRES. In European lore, vampires are night creatures rising from their graves at midnight to wander about and attack the living. Some anecdotal reports, however, tell of vampires being out during the day to cause mischief. In Serbian lore, vampires have no power or strength during the day, but get their power at night from the devil.

There is no precedence in vampire folklore that vampires are actually destroyed by sunlight; this device has been popularized in film and fiction.

BRAM STOKER'S COUNT DRACULA sleeps in his COFFIN by day, though on occasion he appears out in public during the day. When he is out in daylight, his powers are reduced.

Stoker's Dracula dies by knife and not by exposure to the sun. In the final scene, Dracula is in his coffin being taken by GYPSIES back to his home in TRANSYLVANIA. His English pursuers catch up, fight off the Gypsies, and kill the vampire with knives: Jonathan Harker slashes his throat with a kukri knife and Quincey Morris plunges his bowie knife into the count's heart. The vampire instantly crumbles to dust.

The first vampire to die by sunlight is GRAF ORLOCK in the silent film *NOSFERATU* (1922), directed by F. W. MURNAU. Orlock spends the night with his irresistible victim, Nina, and is struck by the sun's rays in the morning. He disintegrates.

Death by sunlight appears in the endings of remakes of *DRACULA,* and became the favored means of vampire destruction in other films. In *Horror of Dracula,* the 1958 HAMMER FILMS remake of *Dracula,* PROFESSOR ABRAHAM VAN HELSING (PETER CUSHING) pulls open curtains to fatally expose Dracula (CHRISTOPHER LEE) to the sun. The 1979 version of *Dracula,* directed by John Badham and starring Frank Langella as the count, shows the vampire dying an agonizing, smoking death when he is struck by rays of the sun. As Dracula, Langella notes that he "must fight the dawn to live." Francis Ford Coppola's 1992 remake *BRAM*

Graf Orlock (Max Schreck) dies in the dawning sun in F. W. Murnau's Nosferatu. *(Author's collection)*

STOKER'S DRACULA, restores the count's original ability to move about in daylight—but with reduced powers.

Aversion to sunlight and its lethal effect on vampires appears in many vampire novels. ANNE RICE does not follow the fictional tradition, which gives her vampires greater range of power and activity in the world of mortals.

See also MOON.

FURTHER READING:
Miller, Elizabeth. *Reflections on Dracula: Ten Essays.* White Rock, B.C.: Transylvania Press, 1997.

Swiatek (19th c.)   Beggar of Austrian Galicia who confessed to cannibalism and behaved like the BERSERKIR. Swiatek lived in Polomyja, a Jewish hamlet of eight hovels and a tavern. The residents were woodcutters and maize farmers who eked out a miserable living. Swiatek supported his wife, 16-year-old daughter, and five-year-old son chiefly by begging. Occasionally he sold beads and small ornaments. Other residents resented the fact that he did not work, but relied on their charity.

In the mid-1840s, children began disappearing. One Sunday Swiatek was invited to a home for a meal. The couple had several children, including a little girl who attracted his attention. Swiatek gave her a ring and said he had found it under a big fir tree near the churchyard. There were dozens more rings there, he said, and he taught the girl a charm for discovering them. The girl and the other children ran off to search for the rings. Swiatek departed from the house. The little girl was never seen again.

Soon other children disappeared from the woods. Among them were a boy out playing with friends, a servant girl who had been sent on an errand, and a boy sent to fetch water from a fountain. The villagers blamed these and other disappearances on ravenous wolves, and hunts were mounted against the creatures.

In May 1849 ducks went missing from the property of the innkeeper at Polomyja. He immediately suspected Swiatek. The innkeeper marched to Swiatek's hut to confront him. He smelled meat roasting and was certain it was his ducks. He threw open the door and throttled the beggar. To his horror, a girl's head rolled out from beneath Swiatek's clothing.

Swiatek and his family were arrested, and their hut was searched. Villagers found the mutilated remains of a girl. Her legs and thighs were in a vat, partially raw, stewed, and roasted. Her heart, liver, and entrails, all cleaned and dressed, were in a chest. A bowl full of fresh BLOOD was under the oven.

En route to the magistrate, Swiatek acted like a madman, struggling wildly and flinging himself on the ground. He gulped down gobs of dirt in apparent attempts to choke himself to death.

Once subdued, Swiatek confessed to killing and eating six persons, even though the clothing of 14 children had been found at his hut. His own children testified that he had killed many more.

Swiatek said that his cannibalism had begun in 1846, when a tavern had burned down with the owner in it.

Swiatek poked through the ruins and came upon the half-roasted CORPSE. His hunger was so great that he was seized with the uncontrollable desire to eat it, and he devoured it with relish. It tasted so good that he knew he would have to eat human flesh again. He had periodically murdered and eaten children, and had even fattened himself in the process.

The beggar was taken to prison. Villagers were so outraged that officials feared they would storm the prison and rend him limb from limb. But Swiatek never went to trial. On his first night in jail, he hanged himself from the bars of his window.

FURTHER READING:
Baring-Gould, Sabine. *The Book of Werewolves*. London: Smith, Elder & Co., 1865.

tail In Slavic lore, anyone born with a tail—a bony protuberance at the end of the spine—is a VAMPIRE. Such a vampire has magical powers, such as the power over RAIN, and when he washes and wets his tail, rain will fall.

See also VAMPIRE SORCERERS AND WITCHES.

talamaur In Melanesian lore, the soul of a dead person that sustains itself by vampirizing the last sparks of strength of the dying and just-dead.

Tale of the Body Thief, The (1992) Novel by ANNE RICE, fourth in her Vampire Chronicles, in which the VAMPIRE LESTAT DE LIONCOURT attempts SUICIDE and then suffers a body switch with a mortal man.

World- and vampire-weary, Lestat tries to destroy himself by flying into the sun, but fails. Ironically, he is strengthened in the process.

A mysterious man, James Raglan, contacts Lestat and claims he has the ability to switch bodies. He offers to trade bodies with Lestat, promising it will be temporary. Lestat, desiring to experience again what it is like to be mortal, agrees. After the switch, Lestat realizes he prefers his vampire form, but Raglan decides to keep Lestat's body. He disappears.

Most of the plot concerns Lestat's international adventures as he seeks to reclaim his body. He appeals to his fledgling, Louis, and his mentor, Marius, for help, but they refuse him. He then turns to David Talbot, the head of the Talamasca, a secret order that collects data and artifacts relating to the occult. Talbot agrees.

Lestat reclaims his own body, but Raglan switches with Talbot. Talbot is pleased at trading in his 74-year-old body for a younger model. He accepts Lestat's offer of the Dark Gift—the transformation into vampire.

The Tale of the Body Thief is about selling one's soul to the devil and the lengths one will go to do that, according to Rice. She intended *Tale* to be the fourth and final volume of the Vampire Chronicles, but went on to write more books in the series.

FURTHER READING:
Ramsland, Katherine. *The Vampire Companion: The Official Guide to Anne Rice's* The Vampire Chronicles. New York: Ballantine Books, 1993.
Rice, Anne. *The Tale of the Body Thief.* New York: Alfred A. Knopf, 1992.

tanggal Indonesian sorceress who detaches her head and bowels from her body and flies about at night looking for human prey. The *tanggal* uses her large ears or lungs to fly.

Taste the Blood of Dracula See HAMMER FILMS.

tengu Japanese VAMPIRE demon in the shape of a man with a bird's wings and beak.

275

tetlachiwike   See TLAHUELPUCHI.

Thags yang   In Tibetan lore, a demon who assumes either tiger form or human form and tears victims to pieces. The Thags yang prowls about the outskirts of villages and preys upon unprotected travelers.

In her book *Magic and Mystery in Tibet*, Alexandra David-Neel relates a story told to her about a Thags yang. The storyteller was an old man, a lama. Many years earlier, he and his younger brother, Lodo, had left their monastery to follow a wandering ascetic. Part of their magical training from him involved overcoming fear of demons.

The ascetic ordered Lodo to go to a place known to be haunted by a Thags yang and tie himself by the neck to a tree there. He was to imagine that he was a cow intended for sacrifice to the demon. He was to low like a cow and experience the anguish of a cow about to be devoured. He was to do this for three consecutive days and nights.

However, when Lodo did not return by the fifth day, the ascetic told Lodo's brother that he had had a strange dream, and to go and fetch his brother from the tree.

When the brother arrived at the woods, he was horrified to find Lodo's mangled and partially devoured, bloody CORPSE. Part of it was still tied to the tree, and pieces of it were scattered about. He collected the pieces and hurried back to the ascetic. When he returned, he found the ascetic had hastily departed, taking all of his books and religious tools, and his traveling stick.

David-Neel was inclined to think that a panther or leopard had been attracted to Lodo's lowing and had killed him. But the lama said that the Thags yang had attacked and devoured his poor brother. It was strange that the ascetic had never taught Lodo the magical incantations that would have protected him from the demon. Therefore, it was likely that the ascetic himself had been the Thags yang, shape-shifted into human form in order to attract a victim. He was not able to kill Lodo while in human form, and so set a trap for him where the demon could attack in his tiger form. Then he escaped.

See also SHAPE-SHIFTING.

FURTHER READING:
David-Neel, Alexandra. *Magic and Mystery in Tibet*. New York: Dover Publications, 1971.

Thief and the Vampire, The   See SNEEZING.

Thiess of Livonia (1692)   WEREWOLF case in the Baltic area of northern Europe, where werewolf superstitions were strong. The case has characteristics of the *benandanti* of northern Italy, a pagan cult of men who went out of body at certain times of the year to fight witches in order to ensure good crops. In the Livonian case, the WEREWOLVES were men who left their bodies and in spirit assumed the shapes of wolves and descended into the underworld and battled the witches. The case was tried in 1692 in Jurgensburg, and involved an 80-year-old man named Thiess.

Thiess freely confessed to being a werewolf. He testified that his nose had been broken by a man named Skeistan, a witch who was dead at the time he struck Thiess. His story of how it happened was this: Skeistan and other witches prevented crops from growing by carrying SEED grain into hell. Thiess was a werewolf, who, with other werewolves, attempted to protect the crops by descending into hell and fighting with the witches to recover what was stolen. Three times a year, on the nights of St. Lucia, Pentecost, and St. John (seasonal changes), the battles took place. If the werewolves delayed their descent, the witches barred the gates of hell, and the crops and livestock, even the fish catch, suffered. The werewolves carried iron bars as weapons, and the witches carried broom handles. Skeistan had broken Thiess's nose with a broom handle wrapped in a horse's tail.

Asked what happened to werewolves at death, Thiess replied that they were buried like ordinary folk, and their souls went to heaven. The judges were shocked by this heresy, as well as notion that werewolves fought on the side of good against witches. Thiess insisted that the werewolves were the "hounds of God" who served mankind, preventing the devil from carrying off the abundance of the earth. If not for them, everyone would suffer. He said werewolves in Germany and Russia likewise fought the witches in their own hells.

Thiess refused to confess that he had signed a pact with the devil, despite the efforts of the judges. Even the parish priest, summoned to chastise him for his evil ways, failed to sway Thiess. The old man angrily said he was a better man than the priest, and he was neither the first, nor would he be the last, werewolf to fight the witches.

Thiess received a surprisingly light sentence, in light of the hysteria against both witches and werewolves. The judges sentenced him to 10 lashes for acts of idolatry and superstitious beliefs.

See also LIVONIA WEREWOLVES; SHAPE-SHIFTING.

FURTHER READING:
Guiley, Rosemary Ellen. *The Encyclopedia of Witches and Witchcraft*. 2d ed. New York: Facts On File, 1999.

Thornton Heath Poltergeist   English poltergeist haunting with VAMPIRE elements. In 1938 an outbreak of dramatic and bizarre poltergeist phenomena began occurring in the Forbes household at Thornton Heath. The poltergeist activity was centered on Pat Forbes, the mistress of Thornton Heath. The activity began abruptly and without apparent cause. Objects flew about the house, dropped from ceilings, and materialized from thin air. Glasses shattered. Pungent smells of violets and rotting flesh permeated the air. The phenomena escalated in frequency and strangeness until Mrs. Forbes reported the horror of being visited and attacked by an invisible vampire at night.

The case attracted the attention of the media, which resulted in a lengthy investigation by Nandor Fodor, a Hungarian lawyer and journalist who turned psychical researcher and, later, psychologist. Fodor's theories about psychological causes of some outbreaks of poltergeist activity were ahead of his time. He concluded that Mrs. Forbes was suffering from "poltergeist psychosis," an episodic mental disturbance of schizophrenic character. This, combined with Mrs. Forbes's unconscious mind, was responsible for the activities finally determined to be fraudulent.

The theory of the causes of Mrs. Forbes's experiences, including her encounters with a vampire, was so novel at the time that it was rejected by the psychical research establishment, and Fodor was so roundly criticized that he was moved to sue one publication for libel. Fodor was unable to tell the full story until 1945, when, as Director of Research of the International Institute for Psychical Research, he gave a lecture at the Association for the Advancement of Psychotherapy, published in the *Journal of Clinical Psychopathology*. Fodor then chronicled the case in his book, *On the Trail of the Poltergeist* (1958). Eventually he was vindicated.

The disturbances at Thornton Heath, the home of the Forbeses, began on February 19, 1938. Fodor was on the scene by February 24. His investigation lasted several months. During that time, Mrs. Forbes emerged as a medium who seemed capable of producing apports, or objects materialized through the air supposedly with the help of spirits. She also said she had the ability to travel out-of-body and visit people at distant locations. She said she had more than one control. (A control is an entity who claims to be a spirit of the dead who communicates through a medium and organizes other entities to do the same.) Mrs. Forbes also seemed to suffer a great deal of emotional and physical trauma during this time, showing burns, welts, and marks upon her body, which seemed to appear without physical cause, and enormous swelling of tissues for no apparent reason. On several occasions, she said she felt she was attacked by a spirit tiger, which raked her flesh and left long red claw marks.

The vampire came to visit her on the night of May 18, 1938. On the morning of May 19 Fodor telephoned Mrs. Forbes and found her so shaken that she said she feared she was going mad. She was, wrote Fodor, suffering from "sheer horror," and was unable to speak to her husband, George, about what had happened to her during the night. Her experience, said Fodor, "read like a page from Bram Stoker's *Dracula*," but nonetheless seemed excruciatingly real and terrifying. He stated:

She awoke feeling something like a human body lying beside her on top of the cover; something cold and hard which she took to be a head was touching her neck. She was unable to move. After a few seconds the thing left her with a flapping of bird's wings. Then she must have fallen asleep, and in the morning she awoke limp and bloodless. She pricked herself and drew no blood. There were two punctures with clots of blood on her neck.

With a Dr. Wills, Fodor examined Mrs. Forbes's neck. They found two irregular and fairly deep punctures behind the sternal mastoid muscle, about one-eighth inch apart. The skin was red and swollen and showed scratch marks around the punctures.

According to Mrs. Forbes's own account, she retired the previous night at about 10:15 P.M. As she reached the right-hand side of the bed, she heard the fluttering of a bird and noticed that the air was disturbed and vibrating. It occurred to her that a "thing" was present and that it might come again. After her husband came to bed, she fell into a heavy, unnatural sleep, as though knocked out by chloroform. She reported:

It may have been around midnight that I woke with the sensation that there was something ghastly on my left-hand side (which is away from my husband), on top of the cover. It felt like a human body. Pressing against my neck was something cold and hard, about the size of a man's head. I could not move, I could not shout, I was frozen with fear. I felt myself getting weaker and weaker, sinking. I felt like this when I lost a lot of blood after an operation.

Asked to elaborate, Mrs. Forbes said that as she started to feel weak, she felt the "thing" pressing into her neck. She had the impression of something biting her, but could not distinctly feel lips or teeth. The body of the "thing" lay still, like a dead weight, and felt "cold and nasty," she said. There was no pain, only a tingling sensation in her neck like the pins and needles felt when circulation has been cut off to an extremity. A smell of rotten meat permeated the air. When Mrs. Forbes recovered from her paralysis and was able to move, the thing left her suddenly, swishing through the air with a flapping noise like beating wings as it headed toward the window.

Upon awakening, Mrs. Forbes tasted BLOOD in her mouth and noticed her neck was sore. She felt her neck and discovered the two little lumps. There was no blood on her pillow. She felt extremely cold, and her hands and face looked deathly white to her. Even a neighbor noticed her paleness.

Mrs. Forbes also recalled that three weeks earlier, she had had a nightmare about being bitten on the neck, and in the morning had found tiny red marks upon it.

On May 20 Mrs. Forbes went into trance and Fodor asked one of her spirit controls, "Bremba," for an explanation of the bites. Bremba replied that Mrs. Forbes's soul had been cast out of her body, which was now possessed by the spirit of a young Indian girl. Mrs. Forbes's soul was returning in the form of a bird in order to take its sustenance from her body's blood in order to survive. If the bird was killed, Bremba said, the Indian girl would be forced to leave Mrs. Forbes's body, and her own soul could return.

Later, Mrs. Forbes told Fodor that she had an unaccountable desire to bite her husband on the neck, and she did so.

Toward the end of his investigation, Fodor concluded that most, but not all, of the phenomena manifested in the

Forbes house had natural explanations and were caused by psychological conditions within Mrs. Forbes. The spirit controls were secondary personalities, and most of the apports were staged by Mrs. Forbes. Fodor believed the "vampire attack" was a fantasy carried to its extreme by self-mutilation. He said Mrs. Forbes had subconsciously caused other physical trauma to herself, including the scratches and burns.

The psychological causes of these phenomena stretched back deep into Mrs. Forbes's childhood. Fodor peeled back layer by layer of her past. She had suffered a great deal of traumatic childhood illness and had had frightening hallucinatory experiences and visions of ghosts. Her childhood home seemed to be haunted by a ghost who cleaned the windows and polished the mirrors whenever they became the tiniest bit smudged. By her teen years, she had a strong desire to run away from everything, and by age 17 had run off to get married against her father's wishes. Her second child died in infancy—another severe shock—and in her 20s she suffered from hysterical blindness, coma, a debilitating kidney ailment, cancer of the breast, and alienation from her husband. She expressed a bizarre attraction to CEMETERIES.

While all of these things were contributing factors, the key factor remained missing. At last, in a free association test, in which Mrs. Forbes responded to words given by Fodor with the first thoughts that entered her mind, repressed memories of a childhood rape in the woods surfaced.

Fodor theorized that as a child Mrs. Forbes suppressed the horror of the rape by cutting off a part of herself—part of her was dead. She had essentially experienced a sort of psychic lobotomy, in which part of the mental system was torn off and left free-floating like a disembodied entity, but capable of personality development on its own. The window- and mirror-polishing ghost was the first manifestation of Mrs. Forbes's pent-up psychic energies. The energies were stirred again on her wedding night, which brought the rape horror closer to the surface of her consciousness and resulted in an unconscious desire to retaliate against her husband for what Fodor termed "the burdens of her soul." To retaliate, she turned on herself.

Fodor unfortunately was not allowed to conclude his investigation and see Mrs. Forbes to a resolution. His tracing of psychic phenomena to a sexual neurosis outraged the Council of the International Institute for Psychical Research, under whose auspices he was working. In the ensuing storm of controversy, Fodor was dismissed from his post as research officer for the institute, and the institute's chairman, J. Arthur Findlay, resigned in protest over Fodor's conclusions on the case. Fodor sued a spiritualist newspaper for libel and won two of his four claims in 1939. He then moved to New York, where he became a successful psychoanalyst. Some 20 years later, he still held his conclusions about the Thornton Heath case valid. The case has become one of the classics in psychical research, and psychological factors are now routinely considered in similar cases of apparent paranormal phenomena.

See also OLD HAG.

FURTHER READING:
Fodor, Nandor. *On the Trail of the Poltergeist.* New York: Citadel Press, 1958.

thought-form   In occultism, a nonphysical entity created by thought that exists in either the mental plane or astral plane. Vampire thought-forms can be created by magic for the purposes of PSYCHIC ATTACK.

The principle behind thought-forms is that every thought generates vibrations in the mental body of the aura and assumes a floating form and colors. The power of the thought-form and its viability depend on the nature and intensity of the thought and the skill of the person creating it. Thought-forms radiate out and attract sympathetic essences, thus forming the basis of the occult Law of Attraction, which holds that one attracts on the physical plane what one thinks on the mental plane. Thoughts which are low in nature, such as anger, hate, lust, greed, etc., create thought-forms that are dense in color and form. Thoughts of a more spiritual nature generate forms that have greater purity, clarity, and refinement.

Some thought-forms occur spontaneously. "Group minds" are formed whenever a group of persons concentrates on the same thoughts, ideas, or goals, such as a team of employees or a crowd of demonstrators. To some extent, the group-mind possesses the group, as witnessed in the psychic bonding and power that coalesces in crowds, and in the synergy of a close-knit working group. When the group disperses, the group-mind usually loses power.

Thought-forms can be directed against individuals. However, if the sender is not skilled, the thought-forms may return and attack them instead. ALEISTER CROWLEY, in his psychic warfare with SAMUEL LIDDELL MACGREGOR MATHERS, reportedly seized a vampire thought-form sent to him and returned it to Mathers to attack him.

Vampire thought-forms deplete energy, often without the victim realizing what is happening. Writing in *Aurora,* a British occult periodical, in July, 1973, David Edwards, an authority on magical operations, observes, "The vampire of occult attack is a deliberately created ghoul. In essence this is a thought form vitalized as an artificial elemental. But it is charged with one direction, 'Destroy!'" Edwards states that the victim often does not realize what is going on; he might just feel a bit run down. In the end, however, sudden death may be the final result.

Similarly, the modern magical theorist Kenneth Grant has remarked on the dark astral entity he refers to as the "shadow." He notes, "If the shadow is strongly developed and is under the control of a black magician, it can be projected into the aura of sleeping people and obsess them with sexual fantasies that can drive them to madness and suicide.

It is then withdrawn by the vampire who despatched it and he nourishes himself on the energy which the shadow has 'collected.'" Grant adds that the magician who collects energy in this way may greatly extend his normal life span.

One particular case of a vampire thought-form is related in an article that appeared in a theosophical magazine, *The Word*, in 1905. "The Voodoo Vampire" by James H. Connelly tells the story of an African-American musician named Alonzo from New Orleans who was performing at clubs in New York. One night in the city he saw a man that he believed had stolen the woman he loved. Seeking revenge, Alonzo went to a well-known Voodoo priestess by the name of Mama Mokele. In appearance, she looked to be less that 30 years old, but people in their 80s claimed she looked the same when they were young.

Taking a tablespoon of BLOOD from the little finger of Alonzo's left hand, she muttered something over the cut, which quickly healed. She told him to come back the following night at midnight. When he did, she gave him a small box, which she said contained a spirit form (or astral element) in the image of a BAT. His own blood had helped to create it. He was to slip the box into the coat pocket of the man he hated. Once that man opened it, the "bat of death" would crave fresh blood and eventually kill him.

The man who was targeted, John A., found the box in his coat pocket and opened it. In it he could see what looked like a stain of blood. He didn't think much of it, but that night he had dreams of drowning. In the morning he found a bleeding wound by his right jugular vein and felt so weak he had to return to bed. That night, wounds appeared on his hands, and he saw a bat darting away from one of them.

On the third night, the man's doctor and servant saw the materialized bat flying in his bedroom. The creature was promptly beaten to the ground and stomped on, at which point it burst like "a huge capsule of blood." Alonzo, the vengeful musician, was found dead the next morning, apparently having burst a blood vessel.

The duration of a thought-form, its strength, and the distance it can travel depend on the strength and clarity of the original thought. Thought-forms are said to have the capability to assume their own energy and appear to be intelligent and independent. Equally intense thought can disperse them, or, they can simply disintegrate when their purpose is finished. Some may last years. It is believed that some particularly powerful thought-forms can go out of control or turn on their creators. Mathers apparently was afflicted with the vampire thought-form for the remainder of his life, and his widow blamed his death on the drain upon his health.

FURTHER READING:

Guiley, Rosemary Ellen. *Harper's Encyclopedia of Mystical and Paranormal Experience*. San Francisco: Harper San Francisco, 1991.

Riccardo, Martin V. "Living Vampires, Magic and Psychic Attack," in *The Complete Vampire Companion* by Rosemary Ellen Guiley with J. B. Macabre. New York: Macmillan, 1994.

Tillinghast, Sarah (d. 1796)   Alleged VAMPIRE of South County, Rhode Island. Sarah Tillinghast was the oldest child of a well-to-do orchard farmer of pears and apples named Stuckley (also given as Stukelely), nicknamed Snuffy because of the tobacco color of his coat.

Stuckley and his wife, Honour, had 14 children, most of whom worked in the orchards. One night during the harvest season in 1796, Stuckley began to suffer a horrible and recurring nightmare, in which he would witness half of his orchard wither and die before his eyes. According to lore, his account of the dream, which he relayed to his wife, was recorded as follows:

> I was working among the trees, when I heard our daughter Sarah calling to me. As I turned to look for her, a cold wind picked up, blowing the leaves all around me, so that I was nearly blinded. When the wind died down, I looked to find Sarah, but she was nowhere in sight. I turned back to the trees to continue working, and saw that the leaves had all turned brown, and the fruit was rotting on the branches. A smell of decay washed over me, and I was nearly ill. Stepping back, I saw that fully half of the orchard was dead!

The repeating nightmare so disturbed Stuckley that he consulted his pastor, who opined that he was only worried about his harvest.

The harvest was good, but later on in the winter, Sarah became ill and died; the doctor attributed the cause of death to tuberculosis. Then five more children sickened and died, one by one, of the same wasting illness. The first to go were James, the youngest, followed by Andris, 14, and Ruth, the second oldest after Sarah, and then Mary. In 1798 Hannah died and Ezra became ill. Hannah, 26, did not live at home, but was married and lived in West Greenwich. She visited often at the Stuckley farm.

Stuckley was convinced that his dream was a prophecy of tragedy. The deaths were made even more ominous when the children complained that the dead Sarah visited them at night and sat upon them, causing great pain and misery. (See OLD HAG.) Even Honour complained of nocturnal visits from Sarah, and then fell ill. Stuckley consulted his neighbors, and learned from Jeremiah Dandridge about the returning dead and how to put them to rest.

The six children then were dug up. Five were in stages of decomposition, but Sarah was incorrupt, and her wooden casket was intact. She exhibited what witnesses believed were the classic signs of vampirism: Her eyes were open and fixed, her hair and nails seemed to have grown, and there was evidence that fresh BLOOD still flowed in her veins. Horrified, Stuckley cut out her heart and burned it on a rock.

Ezra died, but Honour recovered and was no longer bothered by nighttime visits of her dead daughter. The rest of the family remained untouched by disease and death.

The Tillinghast family cemetery is in the township of Exeter. The exact location of Sarah's reburial is not known, but perhaps may be one of several unmarked graves nearby.

FURTHER READING:
Bell, Michael E. *Food for the Dead: On the Trail of New England's Vampires*. New York: Carroll & Graf, 2001.
Rondina, Christopher. *Vampire Legends of Rhode Island*. North Attleborough, Mass.: Covered Bridge Press, 1997.

tin-tin   In the lore of Ecuador, a vampiric demon. The *tin-tin* whistles to adolescent girls on moonlit nights to lure them to him. He then carries them off to his cave and seduces or rapes them, impregnating them.

See also BLACKMAN.

tlahuelpuchi   In the lore of rural Tlaxcala, Mexico, a vampire witch (see VAMPIRE SORCERERS AND WITCHES) who can assume animal form, and who sucks the BLOOD of infants, causing them to die. The *tlahuelpuchi* is not a demon, but a SHAPE-SHIFTING person with supernatural powers. It epitomizes everything that is horrible, evil, and hateful. It can be either male or female, but usually is female; the female is considered to be the more blood-thirsty and evil of the two. At least 100 legends exist about it. The *tlahuelpuchi* provides a supernatural explanation for sudden infant death syndrome, or crib death, and helps to alleviate guilt over the death.

Origins and Characteristics

According to lore, *tlahuelpuchis* are born into their fate; they cannot transmit or teach their powers to others. They are independent agents of evil, but will do the bidding of higher evil forces, such as the devil. For example, they will act as intermediaries (in animal form) in transactions involving selling of the soul to the devil and making pacts with the devil. *Tlahuelpuchis* are more powerful than *nahuales*, a trickster type of supernatural agent.

When a *tlahuelpuchi* is born, it cannot be distinguished from an ordinary infant. Differences do not emerge until puberty, at which point their supernatural powers such as shape-shifting suddenly manifest. For females, this often occurs with the onset of the menses. When the powers manifest, the *tlahuelpuchis* of both sexes begin to have a lifelong, uncontrollable urge to drink human BLOOD, especially that of infants. This causes a great deal of unhappiness and shame to their families, who go to great lengths to cover up their secret in order to avoid being stigmatized and ostracized by the community.

Tlahuelpuchis cannot attack members of their own families, unless they reveal their secret. Although *tlahuelpuchis* cannot transmit their powers to others of their own volition, if they are killed, their powers go into the killer. Hence, family members are reluctant accomplices of sorts.

The *tlahuelpuchis* can shape-shift to numerous animal forms, among them turkey, donkey, dog, CAT, duck, buzzard, crow, ant, and flea. Their preferred forms are fowls, with turkey being the most favored of all. When shape-shifted, they are limited to the abilities of that particular creature, and cannot make it perform in magical ways—with one exception: they can make turkeys fly. When in animal form, they give off a luminescence or phosphorescence that is a telltale sign of their identity.

They prowl about at night—especially between the hours of midnight and four A.M.—but will operate during the day if their blood craving is extreme. *Tlahuelpuchis* are not out every night, but only when they experience their uncontrollable blood cravings, which ranges from one to four times a month. They are more active during rainy and cold weather.

Though they will drink the blood of any human, they overwhelmingly prefer the blood of infants between the ages of three and 10 months, because it is tastier and more invigorating. According to lore, the blood of younger infants is not so palatable to them. The *tlahuepulchis* have a keen sense of smell and can detect the presence of infants inside a home; thus they identify their best targets.

They steal into a home as a mist, sometimes luminous, that seeps under doors and windowsills, or through keyholes, or they crawl in as an insect. Once inside, they shape-shift into a turkey or buzzard, and hypnotize the occupants into a deep sleep so that they can carry out their attacks.

Tlahuelpuchis can recognize one another in both their human and their shape-shifted forms. However, they do not bond together in any social structure, but remain mostly solitary. They are jealous and aggressive toward their own kind, and protect their territories. Poaching on another's territory may result in a fight (in human form) to the death. They do share a common pact not to harm one another's primary family. They also share news of outside danger with one another.

Blood-Sucking Attacks and Remedies

Most *tlahuelpuchi* attacks are made on sleeping infants at night, followed by sleeping or resting infants during the day. The victims are not removed from the home. Occasionally, *tlahuelpuchis* will attack children and adults during the day, hypnotizing them to lure them away from their homes. The bodies are left in ravines and wooded areas.

The *tlahuelpuchi* prefers to suck the blood from the back of an infant's neck, but may take it from the sides of the neck or the cheeks. However, it cannot take blood from the chest or the lower body. Children may be attacked as well. The *tlahuelpuchi* rarely attacks firstborn infants, and even more rarely will attack two infants in a row in the same family.

The relatives of a victim may experience malaise—nausea or headaches—or disturbed sleep on the night of the attack. Sometimes family and neighbors say after the fact that they saw the witch flying through the air in the form of a luminosity or ball of fire, or sitting outside a window, or coming into a house. Almost anything unusual, such as the odd behavior of pets or animals, is considered evidence of the presence of a *tlahuelpuchi*.

The dead infants are discovered either in their cribs or on the floor or even out in the courtyard; doors usually are found ajar or open—a telltale sign that a *tlahuelpuchi* has struck. The bodies have bruises and purple and yellow spots; the faces and necks are purple, and sometimes the bodies have scratch marks. Occasionally there may be dried blood around the mouth. The *tlahuelpuchi* also sometimes leaves marks upon the victim's mother in the form of bruises on one breast, but never both breasts.

Neighbors must be notified immediately so that they can take steps to ward off more attacks on their own children. A victim's CORPSE must be cleaned immediately and placed in a simple wooden COFFIN on top of a table in the main room, with lighted candles at the head and feet. Underneath the table, an oblique CROSS of pinewood ASHES is made; pinewood is believed to be especially powerful for warding off evil and for cleansing the environment tainted by a *tlahuelpuchi*. Neighbors handle these activities, for families cannot handle their own dead.

A *tezitlazc*, a helpful sorcerer and healer, is called in to perform ritual cleansings of the corpse, mother, and space where the death took place. A representative cleansing, witnessed by family and friends, is done in the following manner:

The coffin is removed from the table and the table is taken away from the pine cross. The body of the infant is placed on top of the cross, with the head resting on the intersection of the arms. An incense burner is placed at the foot of the cross. The *tezitlazc* takes the incense burner and walks around the cross three times clockwise and three times counterclockwise, reciting litanies in Nahuatl and invoking the protection of local saints. He places the incense burner back at the foot of the cross. He takes a bundle of herbs and roots, including capulin branches, ocoxoxhiti leaves, and century roots, and brushes the body of the infant from feet to head and hand to hand three times, invoking for the infant the protection of Our Lord, the Holy Virgin, and a local patron saint. The corpse is then returned to the coffin, and the table is placed back over the cross.

The mother is made to stand against a wall with her arms spread in the form of a cross. The *tezitlazc* brushes her with the same cleansing brush three times from feet to head and from hand to hand, but in complete silence. The mother bares her breasts, which the *tezitlazc* brushes with zoapatl leaves. She kisses the foot of the oblique cross. The *tezitlazc* cleanses the entire room where the infant died by brushing the floor, walls, ceilings, doors, and windows. He recites litanies and prayers in Nahuatl while he does so. He buries the cleansing brush in a hole that he previously dug outside the house while praying in Nahuatl and facing north.

The *tezitlazc* may also instruct the mother to rub her breasts on something touched by the *tlahuelpuchi*, such as the floor.

The *tezitlazc* is likely to be needed later as well, to help alleviate the ensuing symptoms of grieving and psychological stress, such as seizures, headaches, nausea and vomiting, depression, and excessive weeping. These also are blamed on the *tlahuelpuchi* as the secondary results of the attack.

Funeral rites for victims of *tlahuelpuchis* are conducted in complete silence, save for a commendation of the soul of the infant when a cross is planted at the foot of the tomb. The pinewood ashes of the oblique cross are buried. The dead infant is to be completely forgotten, as though he or she never existed. The tomb is not visited, nor are flowers placed upon it, nor is the infant remembered at the family altar on All Saints Day and All Souls Day.

Preventative measures against the *tlahuelpuchi* include the use of GARLIC, onions, metals, and even pieces of tortilla, which have a similar function as sand and SEEDS. Infants can be protected with SILVER medals, pins, an open pair of scissors near the crib, metal crosses, and MIRRORS.

Cases of *tlahuelpuchi* attacks have been recorded in modern times, with some being identified, tried, and executed. While almost every extended Tlaxacalan family suffers multiple bloodsuckings over the course of generations, the accusations of bloodsucking witchcraft that result in trial and execution historically have not been common, and have declined considerably since the late 19th and early 20th centuries. The last known execution of a *tlahuelpuchi*, a woman, occurred in 1973.

Other Forms of Attacks

In addition to sucking the blood of infants, *tlahuelpuchis* can exercise evil powers over adults who are their enemies or who have offended them in some way. They can hypnotize sleeping victims and make them go to high places and jump to their deaths. They can injure and kill domestic and farm animals, and can ruin crops. There are no ways to protect against the destruction of one's animals and crops.

Adults can prevent *tlahuelpuchis* from taking control of them by several ways: wearing raw garlic in one's scapular or rubbing the scapular periodically with garlic; pinning undergarments with safety pins in the form of a cross; wearing a blessed cross or St. Christopher's medal; attaching a pin or needle to the inside of one's hat.

Killing Tlahuelpuchis

Tlahuelpuchis almost always are killed in their animal forms, for that is when they are most likely to be detected. Confrontation with one in its human form is rare. There are three principal ways to immobilize one, in the order of preference:

- take one's pants off, turn one leg inside out and throw the pants at the vampire
- knot three corners of a white handkerchief, wrap it around a stone, and throw it to the *tlahuelphuchi*
- take off one's hat, throw it on the ground, and drive a knife or machete through it

If any of these touch the *tlahuelpuchi* or fall within 10 meters, it will be immediately immobilized and can be clubbed or stoned to death. Directly touching a *tlahuelpuchi* is considered unclean. The body is retrieved by other *tlahuelpuchis* and returned to its home, where family members bury it in secret.

The vampire killers must be ritually cleansed with a brushing of capulin branches. Some people are particularly adept at killing *tlahuelpuchis* and acquire a good reputation for it.

If a *tlahuelpuchi* is killed in human form—by immobilization and clubbing or stoning—the corpse is symbolically killed again by the destruction of the sense organs: The eyes are torn out of their sockets, all the fingers are cut off, and the ears, nose, tongue, and lips are severed.

FURTHER READING:
Nutini, Hugo G., and John M. Roberts. *Bloodsucking Witchcraft: An Epistemological Study of Anthropomorphic Supernaturalism in Rural Tlaxcala.* Tucson, Ariz.: University of Tucson Press, 1993.

Tomb of Dracula, The   One of the most successful vampire comic books, along with VAMPIRELLA. *The Tomb of Dracula* made its debut in Marvel Comics in 1972, one year after a revised Comics Code lifted its 18-year-old ban on vampire characters in comics. It ran until 1979 for a total of 70 issues, plus six issues of a black-and-white magazine version.

Billed during the peak of its popularity as "Comicdom's Number 1 Fear Magazine," *The Tomb of Dracula* enjoyed huge sales and a longer run than any other comic book centered on the career of a villain. The artist for each issue was Gene Colan, a veteran who had already demonstrated a considerable talent for terror in *Creepy*. Colan had developed a moody, dramatic style with a strong emphasis on lighting and shadows, which he realized would find a perfect vehicle in a vampire epic. He lobbied for the job, which proved to be a highlight of his career.

The earliest issues of *The Tomb of Dracula* were written by Gerry Conway, Archie Goodwin, and Gardner Fox, but after a few issues the series was taken over by Marv Wolfman, who carried it on till the end. Wolfman, who claimed to be unfamiliar with any version of Dracula except the one in the original novel, employed a strategy similar to the one BRAM STOKER had originally used. Dracula was a powerful presence brooding over the narrative, and his entrances were impressive, but this appearances were cleverly rationed, and in some issues he barely bothered to drop in. Wolfman's story, which continued from month to month, gained much of its momentum from the human characters who interacted in the course of their battle against a bloodthirsty antagonist.

Wolfman's heroes included descendants of Stoker's creations, notably Quincy Harker—spelled "Quincey" by Stoker—the baby born at the end of the novel. In the comic, Quincy survives into the late 20th century as an elderly VAMPIRE HUNTER confined to a wheelchair. He is killed fighting Dracula, and so is the beautiful young Rachel Van Helsing, a descendant of Stoker's PROFESSOR ABRAHAM VAN HELSING. Rachel is transformed into a vampire and then demands her own destruction. Both Quincy and Rachel believe their sacrifices lay Dracula to rest at last, but his ability to resurrect himself gives him the last laugh.

Eventually sales declined and Marvel's Dracula was supplanted by other characters in the comic who came into their own, such as Blade, Hannibal King, and Frank Drake, who became *The Nightstakers,* a team of vampire and demon hunters. In *Dr. Strange,* another Marvel comic featuring the exploits of the world's most powerful wizard, Dr. Strange uses an incantation called the Montesi Formula to eradicate all vampires in the known universe, or at least Marvel's universe.

In the 1990s special editions of *Tomb* were issued, created by Wolfman, Colman, and Al Williamson.

FURTHER READING:
Daniels, Les. "It Seems to Be Our Vampire Friend Again: The Undead in Comic Books," in *The Complete Vampire Companion* by Rosemary Ellen Guiley with J. B. Macabre. New York: Macmillan, 1994.

Tomic, Paja (d. 1923)   Bosnian VAMPIRE. Paja Tomic, an old peasant in the village of Tupanari, died in 1923. A few days later, his wife, Cvija, complained that her dead husband was a vampire and appeared in the house every night, running through it and scaring all of the occupants. Some villagers believed her, and others did not. This went on for a month, and eventually Cvija's sons, Stevo and Krsto, also became aware of the vampire.

The sons called the entire village together to discuss what measures should be taken. Everyone agreed that the vampire should be destroyed. A group led by the sons went to the CEMETERY and dug up Tomic's CORPSE. They pierced it with a STAKE made of HAWTHORN, and burned the body to ASHES, which they dispersed. A few remaining charred bones were thrown back into the grave.

FURTHER READING:
Cajkanovic, Veselin. "The Killing of a Vampires," in *The Vampire: A Casebook.* Alan Dundes, ed. Madison: University of Wisconsin Press, 1998.

tool vampires   See GYPSIES.

tow   Herb used against vampires. In Romanian lore, tow is strewn on the grave of a VAMPIRE and then set on fire, so that the vampire will be singed.

Transylvania   Area in southeastern Europe that comprises about one-third of modern-day Romania. *Transylvania* means "the land beyond the forest." Little was known about it even in the times of BRAM STOKER, but he made it famous in his novel DRACULA (1897) as the homeland of the vampire COUNT DRACULA.

Transylvania achieved a measure of historical importance in the 11th century, when it was brought under Hungarian rule. Most of it was part of Hungary until 1920. Hungarian descendants of Attila the Hun settled in Transylvania, also with Rhinelanders (Saxons). Romanian, German, and Hungarian influences remain. For centuries, Transylvania and its neighbor to the south, Wallachia, served as buffer zones and war zones between the Christian West and the Muslim East. (See VLAD TEPES.)

Modern Transylvania encompasses 39,000 square miles with a population of about 7 million people. It is a contrast between rural Old World and the modern, cosmopolitan city. There are medieval towns and cities that retain much of their historical atmosphere. Rolling pastoral hills and broad flat plains are ringed by the stunning, heavily forested Carpathian Mountains. In the countryside, old folkways live on.

Romania has folk beliefs in the reanimated dead (STRIGOI) but has never figured as prominently in vampire folklore as other regions in Europe. The word *vampire* is of Serbian origin, not Romanian, and most of the early

Large wooden crucifixes with angels, erected for the blessings of divine protection, are a common sight in rural Transylvania. (Photo by R. E. Guiley)

accounts of vampires took place elsewhere, such as Serbia, Silesia, Moravia, Poland, and Hungary.

Dracula put Transylvania on the vampire map with Westerners. Stoker was not the first author to use it as a setting for eerie, supernatural, and mysterious stories, however. Alexandre Dumas (*père*) wrote about a vampire in the Carpathians in *Les Mille et un Fantômes* (1849). *The Mysterious Stranger,* an anonymous story published in 1860, features a Transylvanian vampire count. Jules Verne's *The Castle of the Carpathians* (1892) mentions supernatural beliefs in this region, including vampires.

According to notes he made in 1890, Stoker originally intended to set *Dracula* in Styria, Austria, (the same setting chosen by J. Sheridan Le Fanu for his story "CARMILLA"). However, in 1892 he changed the setting to Transylvania. The reasons that prompted the change are not clear, but Stoker's research notes show that he consulted several sources on Transylvanian geography, history, and folklore, including travelogues of contemporary English Victorians. Sources cited in Stoker's research notes were

- *Round About the Carpathians* (1878) by Andrew F. Crosse
- *On the Track of the Crescent* (1885) by Major E. C. Johnson
- *An Account of the Principalities of Wallachia and Moldavia* (1820) by William Wilkinson, which mentions the name Dracula as the voivode of Wallachia
- *Transylvania* (1865) by Charles Boner
- "Transylvania Superstitions" (1885) by Emily de Laszowski Gerard, later incorporated into her book *The Land Beyond the Forest* (1888)

Gerard's article—there is no evidence that Stoker consulted her book as well—provided key information on superstitions, folk customs, and religious customs. Among those used by Stoker were superstitions surrounding St. George's Day (the 23rd of April, or May 6 by the modern Western calendar). On this night, witches are said to hold their SABBATS, and all the buried treasures in the earth begin to burn and give off a bluish flame, thus making auspicious conditions for treasure hunting. Other superstitions Stoker made use of can be found in the following excerpts from Gerard's work:

> Transylvania might well be termed the land of superstition, for nowhere else does this curious crooked plant of delusion flourish as persistently and in such bewildering variety. It would almost seem as though the whole species of demons, pixies, witches, and hobgoblins, driven from the rest of Europe by the wand of science, had taken refuge within this mountain rampart, well aware that here they would find secure lurking places . . .
>
> The spirit of evil (or, not to put too fine a point upon it, the devil) plays a conspicuous part in the Roumenian [sic] code of superstition, and such designations as the Gregynia Drakuluj (devil's garden), the Gania Drakuluj

(devil's mountain), Yadu Drakuluj (devil's hell or abyss), &c. & c., which we frequently find attached to rocks caverns, or heights, attest the fact that these people believe themselves to be surrounded on all sides by a whole legion of evil spirits . . .

. . . I may as well here mention the *scholomance,* or school supposed to exist somewhere in the heart of the mountains, and where all the secrets of nature, the language of animals, and all imaginable magic spells and charms are taught by the devil in person. Only ten scholars are admitted at a time, and when the course of learning has expired and nine of them are released to return to their homes, the tenth scholar is detained by the devil as payment, and mounted upon an *Ismeju* (dragon) he becomes henceforth the devil's aide-de-camp, and assist him in "making the weather," that is to say, preparing the thunderbolts. . . .

Ravaging diseases, like the pest, cholera, &c., are attributed to a spirit called the *dschuma,* to whom is sometimes given the shape of a fierce virgin, sometimes that of a toothless old hag. . . .

Pomanas, or funeral feasts, are repeated after a fortnight, six weeks, and on each anniversary for the next seven years; also whenever the defunct has appeared in dream to any member of the family, this likewise calls for another *Pomana;* and when these conditions are not exactly complied with, the soul thus neglected is apt to wander complaining about the earth, and cannot find rest. These restless spirits, called *strigoi,* are not malicious, but their appearance bodes no good, and may be regarded as omens of sickness or misfortune.

More decidedly evil, however, is the vampire, or *nosferatu,* in whom every Roumenian [sic] peasant believes as firmly as he does in heaven or hell. There are two sorts of vampires—living and dead. The living vampire is in general the illegitimate offspring of two illegitimate persons, but even a flawless pedigree will not ensure anyone against the intrusion of a vampire into his family vault, since every person killed by a *nosferatu* becomes likewise a vampire after death, and will continue to suck the blood of other innocent people till the spirit has been exorcized, either by opening the grave of the person suspected and driving a stake through the corpse, or firing a pistol shot into the coffin. In very obstinate cases it is further recommended to cut off the head and replace it in the coffin with the mouth filled with garlic, or to extract the heart and burn it, strewing ashes over the grave. . . .

First cousin to the vampire, the long-exploded werewolf of the Germans is here to be found, lingering yet under the name of the *Prikolitsch.* [See PRICOLICI.] Sometimes it is a dog instead of a wolf, whose form a man has taken either voluntarily or as penance for his sins. . . .

Dracula begins and ends in Transylvania, and chapters 1 through 4 and part of 27 are set there. Stoker never visited

Transylvania himself, but his descriptions of it evoked the appropriate mysterious and wild atmosphere for the native home of a terrible monster. Stoker had been to Switzerland and Austria, but never farther east than Vienna. The alpine scenery in those countries could have inspired his descriptions of BORGO PASS and the terrain around CASTLE DRACULA. When an American journalist made an issue out of his lack of personal knowledge of Transylvanian terrain, Stoker replied, "Trees are trees, mountains are, generally speaking, mountains, not matter in what country you find them, and one description may be made to answer for all," thus reinforcing an old adage among novelists: Never let the facts stand in the way of a good story.

FURTHER READING:
Belford, Barbara. *Bram Stoker: A Biography of the Author of Dracula.* New York: Alfred A. Knopf, 1996.
Frayling, Christopher. *Vampyres: Lord Byron to Count Dracula.* London: Faber and Faber, 1991.
Gerard, Emily de Laszkowski. *The Land Beyond the Forest: Facts, Figures and Fancies from Transylvania.* Edinburgh and London: William Blackwood and Sons, 1888.
Miller, Elizabeth. *Dracula: Sense & Nonsense.* Westcliff-on-Sea, England: Desert Island Books, 2000.
Miller, Elizabeth. "Welcome to Transylvania!" Available online. URL: http://www.ucs.mun.ca/~emiller/Trans.htm. Downloaded on December 20, 2003.
Pascu, Stefan. *A History of Transylvania.* New York: Dorset Press, 1990.
Taylor, Jeffrey. "Transylvania Today." Available online. URL: http://www.theatlantic.com/issues/97jun/transyl.htm. Downloaded on December 27, 2003.

Transylvanian Society of Dracula Romanian organization founded in the early 1990s to promote studies of Romanian history and folklore especially related to VLAD TEPES, as well as studies of VAMPIRE folklore in other countries.

The Transylvanian Society of Dracula has established chapters in other countries, among them the United States, Canada, Japan, and Italy. It has sponsored or cosponsored (with the VAMPIRE EMPIRE and the Ghost Club of London) international activities, including the world Dracula congresses in 1995 and 2003 in Romania, and 1997 in Los Angeles, as well as an annual symposium in May that commemorates the journey of Jonathan Harker to CASTLE DRACULA, as depicted in BRAM STOKER's novel *DRACULA.*

The president and one of the founders of the society is Nicolae Padararu, formerly with the Romanian Ministry of Tourism. Padararu leads Dracula-themed tours in Romania.

Twins of Evil See HAMMER FILMS.

Uahti In the lore of the Tukano Indians of the Amazon, hairy demons who have VAMPIRE traits. The Uahti are small in stature with huge bellies and toeless feet and are covered with hair. They live in the rain forest and in the water. Sometimes they are described as having huge penises. They prey upon both adolescent girls and men, and sexually ravish them. The presence of the Uahti is also announced by flurries of BATS, especially large VAMPIRE BATS.

upier Polish variant name for VAMPIRE. The *upier*, a male, lies incorrupt in its grave with a ruddy face. Its head, eyes, mouth, and tongue may move. It eats its winding sheet and parts of its body for sustenance (see CORPSES). When it rises from the grave, the *upier* goes past CROSSROADS and houses, revealing himself to the living. It attacks people and tries to suffocate them. (See MORA.)

A female vampire is a *upierzyca* ("feathered one"), whose body is covered with down or feathers, and who is very light and agile. The association with feathers comes from the Polish word for feathers, *pierze*.

upior (upiorz) A Polish variant name for VAMPIRE. In some accounts, the *upior* has no fangs but has a sting under the tongue. It is active from noon to midnight, and is sometimes seen riding about on a horse. The *upior* has the power to dry up dew. It can be destroyed only by BURNING. When burned, the body bursts, giving rise to hun-dreds of small, disgusting animals such as maggots and RATS. If any of these creatures escape, the *upior*'s spirit escapes as well and will return to seek revenge.

See also VAMPIRE SORCERERS AND WITCHES.

upir VAMPIRE in Russian and Ukranian lore. In early Russian history, the term *upir* was used as a personal proper name and a name of place. It also was associated with "gods" who were the spirits of the unsatisfied dead (see REVENANT). From the 11th century, *upir* was used to refer to vampires. The term later was supplanted by ERETIK, which was extended from heretics to vampires.

The *Mercure Galent* of 1693 and 1694 gives a vivid description of the *upir*:

They make their appearance from noon to midnight, and come and suck the blood of living men or animals in such abundance that sometimes it flows from them at the nose, and principally at the ears, and sometimes the corpse swims in its own blood oozed out into its coffin. It is said that the vampire has a sort of hunger, which makes him eat the linen which envelops him. This reviving being, or *oupire*, comes out of his grave, or a demon in his likeness, goes by night to embrace and hug violently his near relations or his friends, and sucks their blood so much as to weaken and attenuate them, and at last cause their death. This persecution does not stop at a single person, it extends to the last person of the family, if the course be not interrupted by cutting off the head or opening the heart of the ghost, whose corpse is found in his coffin, yielding, flexible, swollen and rubicund, although he may have been dead some time. There proceeds from his body a great quantity of blood, which some mix up with flour to make bread of; and that bread eaten in the usual manner protects them from being tormented by the spirit, which returns no more.

A Russian folktale about a BLOOD-drinking stranger describes the characteristics of the *upir.* In the tale, a peasant rides through a field past a CEMETERY after dark. He is overtaken by a stranger dressed in a RED shirt and a sheepskin coat, who asks for a ride. When they arrive at the village, they find house after house with CROSSES on their gates. The stranger complains that the gates are locked. At last they reach a house that has only a giant, 18-pound padlock on the gates and no cross. The gates open by themselves, and the peasant and stranger enter the house. There they find an old man and a boy sitting on a bench. The stranger grabs a bucket, puts it behind the boy, and stabs him in the back. He catches the blood in the bucket, and when the bucket is full, he drinks the blood. The stranger does the same thing to the old man.

By then it is dawn, and the stranger tells the peasant, "Let's go to my place." In an instant the two are back in the cemetery. The *upir* tries to grab the peasant, but a COCK crows and the *upir* disappears.

The next day, the old man and boy are found dead. The villagers seek out the grave of the *upir* and open it to find the vampire lying in a pool of fresh blood. They take an ASPEN STAKE and impale him.

A case involving a *upir* in the Ukraine describes an entity that is more like a MORA than a blood-drinking vampire. According to the first-person testimony, six men went out to guard a cattle run. They heard a snicker along the stockade fence and saw a man whom they identified as a *upir.* At first only two of the four men actually saw him. The *upir* chased the horses, neighing like a horse. Later, the other four men spotted the vampire. The men said the *upir* can take the shape of a man, horse, or dog. When one goes fishing, one must give the *upir* some of his catch; the *upir* can fill up an entire cart. One must never speak to a *upir.*

See also MARUSIA.

FURTHER READING:
Calmet, Dom Augustin. *The Phantom World: Concerning Apparitions and Vampires.* Ware, England: Wordsworth Editions in association with the Folklore Society, 2001.

Oinas, Felix J. *Essays on Russian Folklore and Mythology.* Columbus, Ohio: Slavica Publishers, 1984.
Perkowski, Jan L. *The Darkling: A Treatise on Slavic Vampirism.* Columbus, Ohio: Slavica Publishers, 1989.

upor   Byleorussian variant name for the UPIR, a VAMPIRE. A Byelorussian folktale recorded in the 1890s tells how a *upor* carries a girl off to the grave.

A girl and a boy vow to marry each other, no matter what. The girl pledges that if she marries anyone else, the devil can take her. But a year later she proves to be fickle and decides to marry another man who is richer and more handsome.

On the evening of the wedding, a *upor* in the form of the jilted boy comes to the girl's cottage and tells her to follow him, for he has something to tell her. He takes her up with him onto a saddled horse and they ride off. He says, "A *upor* is flying (rushing), the moon is shining. Are you afraid or not?" She says she is not afraid. They ride farther, and the *upor* poses the same question. Again she says no. They come to some graves, one of which is open. The *upor* tells her to get down into the open grave. He reminds her of her pledge that the devil could take her if she married anyone else. He reveals himself as a devil. He unscrews her head and takes it down into the grave and into the ground.

FURTHER READING:
Perkowski, Jan L. *The Darkling: A Treatise on Slavic Vampirism.* Columbus, Ohio: Slavica Publishers, 1989.

ut   In Indian lore, a restless vampirelike entity who cannot stay in its grave because of improper burial, or because in life he never sired a son.

uvengwa   In West Africa lore, the restless spirit of a dead person that manages to resurrect itself from the grave and wander about. The *uvengwa* shape-shifts into many forms, seldom appearing as it did in human life. Most often it is white with one large cyclops-like EYE in the center of its forehead, and webbed feet. Though feared, the *uvengwa* does not vampirize victims.

See also SHAPE-SHIFTING.

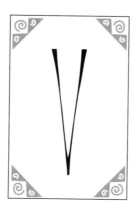

vampire A supernatural entity, REVENANT or supernaturally endowed person who attacks living things, weakening and possibly destroying them. The vampire has no single definition, but represents types of entities and people. In Western lore, the vampire is primarily the returning dead who drain the life force (BLOOD) of the living. Other types of vampires exist. Wide varieties of vampiric or vampirelike entities are found in lore and mythologies around the world.

Possibly the most inclusive definition of vampires is put forth by folklorist Jan L. Perkowski:

> . . . a being which derives sustenance from a victim, who is weakened by the experience. The sustenance may be physical or emotional in nature.

This definition encompasses the returning dead, LIVING VAMPIRES, psychic vampirism (see PSYCHIC ATTACK), CLINICAL VAMPIRISM, and VAMPIRE SORCERERS AND WITCHES.

A 19th-century definition of vampires, given by the Century Dictionary and reported in the *Providence Journal* of Rhode Island on March 21, 1892, presents beliefs about vampires:

> A kind of spectral being or ghost still possessing a human body, which, according to a superstition existing among the Slavic and other races of the lower Danube, leaves the grave during the night and maintains a semblance of life by sucking the warm blood of men and women while they are asleep. Dead wizards, werewolves, heretics and other outcasts became vampires, and anyone killed by a

vampire. On the discovery of a vampire's grave, the body, which is supposed to be found fresh and ruddy, must be disinterred, thrust through with a white thorn stake, and burned in order to render it harmless.

In the early 20th century, MONTAGUE SUMMERS gave this description of the vampire:

> The vampire has a body, and it is his own body. He is neither dead nor alive; but living in death. He is an abnormality; the androgyne in the phantom world; a pariah among friends.

Vampires originate in Slavic lore; however, some scholars hold that they originate in classical lore. Vampires have a strong presence in the folklore of Greece and where Slavic influence has reached in Europe, Russia, and Scandinavia. In its earliest forms, vampires are related to eclipse demons (see VARCOLAC) and to WEREWOLVES (see VLOKOSLAK and VYRKOLAKA). Later they became associated primarily with the returning dead. A vampire returned to the world of the living to take away life through wasting illnesses and a draining of blood.

Vampires are associated with contagious illnesses and plagues, crop blights and droughts. They embody fears of death and the consequences of improper burial (see BURIAL CUSTOMS), sudden death, and lives of sin and crime. The European vampire became contaminated with the lore of other wasting entities, such as the nightmare demon (see OLD HAG and *MORA*), the poltergeist and the INCUBUS and SUCCUBUS. Characteristics of the vampire

A demonic-looking vampire hovers by a victim in The Vampire-Beast Craves Blood. *(Author's collection)*

include poltergeist disturbances, unpleasant dreams, and sexual assaults during sleep. Vampires can shape-shift into animals, most often CATS, dogs, sheep, wolves, snakes, birds, and horses. BATS are not prevalent in European vampire lore, but have been popularized in fiction and film.

Vampires also are types of living people who possess supernatural powers. Traditionally, these have been individuals born with a marked physical trait, or who are sorcerers or witches. In contemporary times, due to the influences of popular literature and films, vampires are seen as supernaturally powerful people who are initiated into vampirism by choice or by attack by a vampire. Shared blood-drinking has a strong erotic appeal.

Appearance of the Term Vampire

The word *vampire* made its first appearance in French literature and correspondence in the late 17th century. The French publication *Mercure Galant* reported vampire cases in 1693 and 1694 in Poland and Russia. The term also was used in 1737 in *Lettres Juives*. In 1746 DOM AUGUSTINE CALMET made the word *vampire* a household term in France with the publication of his *Dissertations sur les apparitions et sur les revenants et les vampires*.

A cognate of *vampire*—the Polish term UPIOR—was published in German in scholarly literature in 1721, and in the media in newspaper accounts in 1725. JOHANN FLUCKINGER's reports of vampires in Medvegia appeared in 1732, and was translated into English.

The first use of *vampire* in German belles lettres appeared in 1748 in the poem "Der Vampyr" by August Ossenfelder, and most notably was used by Goethe in 1779 in "Die Braut von Cornith."

In England, WILLIAM OF NEWBURGH described cases of "blood-sucking" revenants in the 12th century. In 1679, in a work by Paul Ricaut (Rycaut), *State of the Greek and Armenian Churches*, Ricault describes the phenomenon of vampires but does not name them:

> . . . a pretended demon, said to delight in sucking human blood, and to animate the bodies of dead persons, which when dug up, are said to be found florid and full of blood.

By 1688 the term *vampire* evidently was known in England. In *Observations of the Revolution of 1688, vampires* is used to describe business practices.

The term was used in the anonymous work *Travels of 3 English Gentlemen from Venice to Hamburg, Being the*

Grand Tour of Germany in the Year 1734, which was published in 1810. *Travels* gives the first English explanation of vampires in some detail, quoting a paragraph from John Heinrich Zopfius's *Dissertatio de Vampiris Seruiensibus* (1733):

> These Vampyres are supposed to be the bodies of deceased persons, animated by evil spirits, which come out of the graves, in the night time, suck the blood of many of the living, and thereby destroy them. Such a notion will, probably, be looked upon as fabulous and exploded, by many people in England; however, it is not only countenanced by Baron Valvasor, and many Carnioleze noblemen, gentlemen, etc., as we were informed, but likewise actually embraced by some writers of good authority. M. Jo. Henr. Zopfius, director of the Gymnasium of Essen, a person of great erudition, has published a dissertation upon them, which is extremely learned and curious, from whence we shall beg leave to transcribe the following paragraph: "The Vampyres, which come out of the graves in the night-time, rush upon people sleeping in their beds, suck out all their blood, and destroy them. They attack men, women, and children, sparing neither age nor sex. The people attacked by them complain of suffocation, and a great interception of spirits, [exhaustion] after which, they soon expire. Some of them, asked at the point of death, what is the matter with them, say they suffer in the manner just related from people lately dead, or rather the specters of those people; upon which their bodies, from the description given of them, by the sick person, being dug out of the graves, appear in all parts, as the nostrils, cheeks, breast, mouth, etc. turgid and full of blood. Their countenances are fresh and ruddy; and their nails, as well as hair, very much grown. And, though they have been much longer dead than many other bodies, which are perfectly putrefied, not the least mark of corruption is visible upon them. Those who are destroyed by them, after their death, become Vampyres; so that, to prevent so spreading an evil, it is found requisite to drive a stake through the dead body, from whence, on this occasion, the blood flows as if the person was alive. Sometimes the body is dug out of the grave and burnt to ashes; upon which, all disturbances cease. The Hungarians call these specters Pamgri, and the Serbians Vampyres; but the etymon, or reason of these names, is not known . . ."

Zopfius's description was cited in many subsequent English works on vampires, including the writings of Summers.

From the early 19th century, the term and concept of vampires was firmly established in English literature and the popular press. In 1819 the first English story about vampires, THE VAMPYRE, was published and became an immediate success in England and Europe. Much of its success was due to the insinuation that LORD BYRON authored it; it was written by his one-time physician, JOHN POLIDORI, who plagiarized an oral story told by Byron. More works on vampires followed.

Vampire lore was imported to the American colonies and was especially prominent in New England areas ravaged by tuberculosis epidemics. (See NEW ENGLAND VAMPIRES.)

Etymology of Vampire
The origin of the word *vampire* has been debated by scholars ever since it made its first appearance in Western literature and media. Turkish, Hungarian, Greek, and Slavic sources have been put forward. Scholarly opinions on the origins of the word fall into four general groups:

- The first group is oriented around the opinion of Franz Miklosich, a late 19th-century Austrian linguist, who stated *vampire* and the Slavic terms UPIOR, *uper,* and *upyr* all derive from *uber,* a Turkish term for "witch." Montague Summers was among those who relied on Miklosich as an authority.
- The second group subscribes to the theory of a classical origin of the word. Summers also suggested that the Greek word for "to drink" is the origin of *vampire.*
- The third group, which includes most contemporary scholars, favors a Slavic origin with the Serbian word *bamiiup* as the root noun. Other possibilities put forward are the Serbo-Croatian verb *pirati* ("to blow") and the Lithuanian verb *wempti* ("to drink"). Still another theory put forward is that *bamiiup* is only a borrowing from an earlier Greek term.
- The fourth group includes some contemporary English and American writers who hold that *vampire* is a recent term of Hungarian origin. RAYMOND T. MCNALLY opined that the Hungarian word *vampir* was the source of *vampire.* However, *vampir* postdates the first appearance of the word *vampire* in the West by more than a century.

Types of Vampires
Vampires can be categorized as follows:

- folkloric vampires
- living vampires
- literary vampires
- psychic vampires
- psychotic vampires

Folkloric vampires include a wide spectrum of revenants and demonic beings, who have supernatural powers and characteristics and drain the vitality or blood from the living. Examples are the returning dead who died of plague, drowning, murder, SUICIDE, or unnatural or suddenly violent causes, or who died as a result of being killed by an active vampire; and corpses who become possessed by demonic or evil spirits. In Serbian lore, honest people cannot become vampires, unless a bird or animal flies or walks over their corpse. The soul is in the bones only as long as a person is alive.

The returning dead are the most common type of vampire. They come out at night, especially midnight, and must return to their graves by the crowing of the COCK at dawn. They do not come out on SATURDAY, when they must remain in their graves. They enter homes through keyholes and under doorsills and windowsills.

Living vampires are people who act as vampires while alive. Traditionally, they are certain supernaturally empowered people, such as witches and sorcerers, who drink blood or cause wasting illnesses and deaths, and crop blights. Living vampires also are people destined to become vampires after death, such as those born with the CAUL or born with a TAIL (protuberance at the end of the spine) or one or two teeth.

In contemporary times, living vampires are individuals who believe themselves to be vampires, more or less in accordance with popular fictional vampires and vampire motifs. Such individuals consider themselves "made" vampires after a blood-drinking and exchange ritual with an individual who is believed to already be a vampire. Many call themselves "vampyres" to differentiate themselves from fictional vampires.

Literary vampires are created in fiction, poetry, film, and the arts. They are based on folkloric vampires, but have many characteristics that have been invented by their creators.

Psychic vampires are living persons who either deliberately or unwittingly drain the energy and vitality of other people. Deliberate psychic vampirism can be accomplished through magic and ill intent. In the broadest sense, any act that drains another person can be considered a form of psychic vampirism, such as gift-giving that is intended to create a sense of obligation, and individuals who constantly ask for service and favors.

Psychotic vampires are people who commit blood crimes, such as mutilating or killing others and drinking their blood. Some of these individuals are declared criminally insane.

Prevention and Destruction of Vampires

Slavic customs call for various methods of preventing and destroying vampires. The most prudent approach is to bury a body properly, as described in BURIAL CUSTOMS. If a person is feared to become a vampire, such as the victim of an untimely death, a suicide or a criminal, preventative measures are taken at the time of burial. These include mutilating and staking the CORPSE and filling the COFFIN with various materials designed to keep the spirit from escaping the grave (see SEEDS).

If a spirit has escaped the grave and is attacking the living as a vampire, the grave of the vampire is opened and the corpse is staked, mutilated, weighed down with stones, dismembered, or burned to ASHES. If the identity of the vampire is unknown, a hunt must be undertaken to discover which corpse is in a "vampire condition," that is, incorrupt and exuding fresh-appearing blood from the orifices. In earlier times, VAMPIRE HUNTERS, individuals endowed with the supernatural ability to detect and destroy vampires, were employed to search out and eradi-

cate the culprit. (See DHAMPIR.) If a vampire hunter was not available, villagers undertook their own searches, by digging up the graves of the most likely suspects, or by employing various methods such as the use of WHITE HORSES to detect the right graves.

Among some Muslim Slavic GYPSIES, vampires can be destroyed by certain animals, chiefly the wolf, followed by a dog that has "four eyes," or two marks resembling eyes over each eye. In some cases, the dog must be black and the wolf must be white. Among other Gypsies, the wolf is the only creature that can strangle a vampire, but dogs and horses can sense one.

Contemporary popular fiction and film hold that SUNLIGHT and CROSSES destroy vampires. There is no folklore tradition for vampires being destroyed by exposure to sunlight, and many anecdotal cases in the folklore literature report vampires active in daylight hours. The origins of the destructive power of sunlight are found in the 1922 silent film *NOSFERATU*, directed by F. W. MURNAU.

The power of the cross over vampires—as well as over evil entities in general—is a Christian influence imposed upon a pagan folklore tradition. The Christian Church was opposed to the vampire cults it encountered in pagan Europe and sought either to suppress them altogether by forbidding vampire practices (see LASTOVO ISLAND VAMPIRES) or subordinate them to the power of the church by requiring priests to officiate.

Magical spells and exorcism are performed against psychic vampirism.

Vampirelike Entities

All mythologies have predatory, vampirelike entities that prey upon the living, sometimes with fatal consequences. Some are demons, while others are the restless spirits of the dead. Some are sexually rapacious, while others like to drink blood or cause illnesses and misfortune. Some are cannibalistic in nature (see GHOUL). One significant type of vampirelike being is the childbirth demon that preys upon infants and women who have just given birth (see LILITH; *TLAHUELPUCHI*). Many vampirelike entities have SHAPE-SHIFTING ability, such as demons who can masquerade as people and animals, and people who are half-human, half-animal or half-human, half-demon.

Vampire and St. Michael, The   Ukrainian folktale about how a young man is aided by an icon of the archangel St. Michael in the quelling of a VAMPIRE.

According to the tale, two men, one rich and one poor, were neighbors in a village. The poor man went to the rich man to beg for loan of a SILVER ruble. The rich man asked for surety, but the poor man had none. He pointed to an icon of St. Michael in the rich man's home and said that God and the angel would be his surety. The icon spoke to the rich man and told him to give the poor man the ruble, and that God would repay him.

Though blessings of good crops and good fortune were bestowed upon the rich man, he still wanted his ruble repaid. But the poor man died without doing so. In anger, the rich man took the icon and began beating it, gouging out its eyes and trampling it in the mud. A young man of about 20 who was passing by asked him to stop and said he would buy the icon for a silver ruble. The youth begged a ruble from his father and took possession of the icon. He cleaned and washed it and took good care of it.

The youth had three rich uncles who were shipping merchants. The youth persuaded them to allow him to sail on one of their ships, and he offered to make lathes and boards to take with him as goods to sell. He sailed to a distant czardom, where the reigning czar had an only daughter, the czarevna. One day the daughter went bathing in the river without first crossing herself, and she became possessed by an unclean spirit. She fell seriously ill and no one could cure her. She died.

People prayed over her body to try to exorcize the unclean spirit from it, but to no avail. Everyone who spent the night reading prayers for the dead over her CORPSE was found reduced to bones in the morning. The czar ordered all merchants who were passing through the country to spend a night reading the prayers. One by one, the merchants were killed by the vampire. When the time came for the uncles to be called, they asked the youth to go in their place. He refused at first, but was told by the icon of St. Michael to comply and to not be frightened. The angel instructed him to stand in the middle of the church, fenced by his laths and boards, and to have a basket of pears. When the vampire girl rushed him, he was to scatter the pears. The vampire would be required to pick them all up, a task which would take until the crowing of the COCK at dawn.

The youth followed the angel's instructions. He stood inside his protection and read. In the dead of night, the vampire czarevna rose out of her coffin with a mighty noise and attacked him, but could not get past the laths and boards. The youth threw the pears around the church, and she spent the rest of the night picking them up.

The next night he stood in for the second uncle. At midnight the vampire rose out of her coffin with a noise and fury that shook the entire church. He used a basket of nuts to distract her until dawn.

Before the third night, St. Michael told the youth to take the icon with him, and to sprinkle himself with holy WATER and incense himself. When the vampire left her coffin, he was to jump in it. He was not to allow her back in until she said, "My consort!"

The youth did as instructed and scattered consecrated poppy SEEDS all about him. In the middle of the night, the vampire rose up out of her coffin in a great tempest. The church shook and the holy images fell off the walls. The altar candelabra fell down. The vampire foamed at the mouth in fury as she attempted to attack the youth inside his laths and boards. The youth dashed to her coffin and jumped inside, taking the icon of St. Michael with him.

The vampire begged him to come out, but he did not budge, and kept praying to God.

At the first cock crow, the vampire finally shouted, "Alas! Come down, come down, my consort!"

When the villagers arrived at the church later in the morning, prepared to remove the bones of the youth, they found the youth and the girl on their knees praying. The czar, joyous, had his daughter baptized again and sprinkled with holy WATER, and the unclean spirit at last departed her. In gratitude, he gave the youth half his power and kingdom. The youth left with his uncles when they sailed home.

Meanwhile, the czarevna grew sad living alone with her father. One night the czar had a dream in which he was told that the daughter was in love with the youth and grieved his absence. He sent for the youth, who came back with the same boards and laths. When the wood was split open, out fell precious jewels. The czar gave his daughter to the youth in marriage, and they all lived happily together.

The story demonstrates the power of Christianity against the forces of evil. It shows the consequences of failure to follow religious rules: The daughter becomes possessed after failing to cross herself before bathing in a river, the dwelling place of unclean spirits. The story also shows how faith in God is rewarded: the rich man who is rewarded with bounty (and then throws his blessings away); and the youth who has faith in the instructions of the angel. The power of sacred image is also underscored in the talking icon of Michael.

FURTHER READING:
Perkowski, Jan. L. *The Vampire of the Slavs.* Cambridge, Mass.: Slavica Publishers, 1976.

vampire bats   Bats that subsist on the BLOOD of animals and also humans. A vampire bat can drink the equivalent of a wineglass of blood in about 20 minutes.

The term *vampire bat* was applied to blood-drinking bats of South America observed by European conquistadores when they arrived in the 16th century. The vampire bat dates to pre-Columbian times and was known through Central and South America. Bat gods were worshiped: The Aztecs had a bat god named Tzincacan, and the Maya worshiped Zotz, the god of death and twilight, and Camazotz, a vampire bat god. The vampire bat was unknown in Europe until Cortez and the Spanish conquistadores visited the New World and named it after the vampire of European lore.

In 1890 Charles Darwin was the first European to witness a vampire bat drawing blood. In the 1930s the vampire bat was identified as the carrier of paralytic rabies in Trinidad.

There are three species of blood-drinking bats. *Diaemus youngi* and *Diphylla ecaudata* feed primarily on bird blood. *Desmodus rotundis* will attack animals and humans. All three

The vampire bat (Author's collection)

species live in Central and South America. Fossil records show that thousands of years ago vampire bats lived in a much broader area, into Cuba and parts of North America.

It is popularly believed that vampire bats are huge and ugly, but that is far from the case. *Desmodus rotundis* is about the size of a mouse—approximately four inches in length—and has a wingspan of up to 14 inches. It is quite agile, and can run, hop, and walk on all fours. It has razor-sharp, scooplike incisors that hold the skin of prey and pierce it. The bat does not suck the wound, but scoops out a small chunk of flesh, called a divot, and then laps the blood that wells into the wound with its long tongue, much as a dog or cat laps water. The tongue has two grooves on the underside that create a strawlike effect; the bat can lap at the rate of four darts of the tongue per second. Saliva full of anticoagulants runs down the top of the tongue and into the wound, to keep blood flowing. If the wound flows freely, the vampire bat's lips never touch the flesh. If the blood is scant, the vampire bat licks the wound.

A vampire bat needs only about two tablespoonful of blood a day, which represents about 60 percent of its body weight. However, a single bat is capable of drinking much more: about 10 centiliters of blood, the amount held in a moderate-size wineglass. When sated with blood, the bat's body swells and becomes almost spherical in shape. If it repeatedly attacks the same animal, it will go to the site of the old wound to continue feeding. Animals who are repeatedly attacked by multiple vampire bats can be killed through gradual loss of blood. Each bat usually feeds on only one victim per night. Bats occasionally miss a meal

due to unsuccessful hunts, but they cannot survive two nights without eating. Vampire bats can survive up to 20 years in the wild.

Vampire bats prefer animals but will attack humans, usually on the extremities, such as the toes or nose. When near the victims, the bats do not flap their wings but approach with wings tightly tucked and thumbs extended to serve as forelegs, moving carefully in a very slow, silent, and light stalk. The bats have a heat sensor on their nose to detect where blood flows close to the skin. If the victim has fur, the vampire bat will use its razor-sharp teeth to clip it away, much like a barber shears a customer.

The bites are often painless, and sleeping victims are not aware they are being bitten. The bats can feed undisturbed. If an animal becomes restless and moves about, they can cling and quickly move crablike around the body.

It takes a bat about 20 to 25 minutes to drink enough blood for a meal. Within about two minutes of starting a feed, the bat begins urinating plasma, which has no nutritive value to the bat. Getting rid of the heavy plasma quickly is important for a fast getaway at the end.

When done, the bats open their wings and use their long thumbs to thrust upward. They silently and rapidly fly away, returning to their roost. They rest hanging upside down while they digest their meal.

Vampire bats roost in hollows, including caves, trees, and buildings. When surprised, they run like rodents along the vertical walls and look for crevices in which to hide. This behavior may have inspired BRAM STOKER's description of COUNT DRACULA's climbing down the sheer vertical walls of his castle.

Contrary to vampire lore in popular fiction, vampire bats do not like to hunt on nights of the full MOON, because they are more easily seen and avoided by the prey.

FURTHER READING:
Ditmars, Raymond L., and Arthur M. Greenhall. "The Vampire Bat: A Presentation of Undescribed Habits and a Review of Its History," in *The Vampire of the Slavs* by Jan L. Perkowski. Cambridge, Mass.: Slavica Publishers, 1976.
Fenton, M. Brock. *Bats*. Rev. ed. New York: Facts On File/Checkmark Books, 2001.
Wolf, Leonard. *Dracula: The Connoisseur's Guide*. New York: Broadway Books, 1997.

vampire bread   See BLOOD; *UPIR*.

vampire breath   See *NUCKELAVEE*; *YUKI-ONNA*.

Vampire Chronicles   See LESTAT DE LIONCOURT; RICE, ANNE.

Vampire Circus   See HAMMER FILMS.

Vampire Day   Holiday designated for celebrating vampires and vampire-related events. Vampire days usually are set as one-time events by local communities and organizations.

The city of São Paulo, Brazil, declared a Vampire Day on August 13, 2002, to help promote a city-wide BLOOD drive and to indirectly benefit a television soap opera, *Kiss of the Vampire*. The campaign was started by actress and author Mariliz Marins, daughter of the B-movie horror film maker Jose Mojica Marins, better known as "Coffin Joe." Mariliz created the character Lizvamp, who also served as the campaign's poster girl.

A onetime Vampire Day in Los Banos, California, was observed on November 4, 1988, to honor the publication of *Vampires* by resident VINCENT HILLYER. The entire community participated in vampire-themed promotions and events, creating a post-Halloween carnival mood. Costumed revelers, dressed in black capes, luminous plastic fangs, and gory makeup, filled the streets to dance and drink GARLIC wine and Bloody Marys.

A hair salon offered the special of the day, the "Vampire Cut." An apparel shop had costumed figures dressed like the monsters of horror films lined up before their doors. Strands of garlic were strung across storefronts.

A local evangelical cult objected to the celebration, screaming to the news media that "the author of this book is bringing vampires into our community to feed upon the local populace!" Cult members telephoned city hall, threatening to damage the building and start riots in the streets. They sent a message to the local mortuary that they would burn the place down if it participated in the holiday. The local newspaper sided with the cult. Fear of violence forced city officials to cancel the promised appearance of an out-of-town "vampire" and his coffin and hearse. Other celebrity appearances were canceled when the protestors assembled on the main street, shouting biblical verses and chasing celebrants dressed in vampire costumes.

For years rumors of a "Dracula's Curse" circulated, because various opponents of Vampire Day allegedly suffered misfortunes later.

FURTHER READING:
Guiley, Rosemary Ellen, with J. B. Macabre. *The Complete Vampire Companion*. New York: Macmillan, 1994.

Vampire Empire   The largest vampire and horror organization in the world, based in New York City and founded by JEANNE KEYES YOUNGSON as the COUNT DRACULA FAN CLUB in 1965. From 1974 to 1984 the club maintained a second headquarters in England. The club's name was changed to the Vampire Empire in 2000.

The Vampire Empire is dedicated to BRAM STOKER, his sanguinary count and the Romanian voivode VLAD TEPES, as well as other horror personalities and subjects. The Vampire Empire encourages study and research of vampires and related topics.

The organization has the following divisions:

- the Vampire Empire Research Library, a collection of books, journals, articles, and materials on vampirism, lycanthropy, horror, and related topics
- Dracula Press, a publisher of nonfiction and fiction books
- the Vampire Bookshop, a mail-order seller of Dracula Press titles
- the Golem Group, dedicated to the study of the Jewish golem in legend and lore
- the Lugosi Legacy, dedicated to BELA LUGOSI
- Dwight Frye Remembered, dedicated to actor DWIGHT FRYE, who played the character RENFIELD in the 1931 DRACULA film
- Vampires in the Media, concerned with film and stage productions
- Supernatural Spirits, which studies fairy lore and the spirit and zombie lore of Vodoun and the West Indies
- The Werewolf in Fact, Fiction, and Fantasy, a collection of werewolf and lycanthropy resources
- the Monster Menage, about monsters and mysterious creatures
- the Tepes Alliance, dedicated to Vlad Tepes and the research of RAYMOND T. MCNALLY
- Special Interest Division, concerned with other topics of interest to members
- Friends of the Library, which includes individuals who donate books and research materials
- the Halloween Connection, devoted to Halloween history, lore, and activities.

The Vampire Empire has the following associate organizations:

- the International Society for the Study of Ghosts and Apparitions, founded in 1985 by Youngson
- Vampire Studies, founded in 1977 by Martin V. Riccardo as the Vampire Studies Society, and publisher of *The Journal of Vampirism* from 1977 to 1979
- Dracula World Enterprises, directed by Shelley Leigh-Hunt, which tracks vampire club activities and maintains a horror stamp collection
- the International Frankenstein Society, founded by Youngson in 1980
- Jane Oz's Vault of Vampire Vageries, dedicated to collecting vampire cartoons and humor, directed by Jane Oz in collaboration with Kevin Welles
- the Vampire Information Exchange, founded in 1978 by Eric S. Held as a correspondence club, and, with the Vampire Empire, cosponsors a Vampire Pen Pal Network
- the Draculean Circle, a private, by-invitation-only organization run by and for the alumni of the University of Cincinnati, which holds various Stoker-related events

- American Friends of Henry Irving, founded in 1980 in Cambridge, England, as the Fans of Irving by Youngson and Professor G. R. I. Thompson. Friends of Irving sponsored discussion forums. It ceased to exist in England in 1985 and was reorganized as the American Friends of Henry Irving in 1999 in the United States
- the Bram Stoker Memorial Association, which maintains an archive of works on and by Stoker and Irving, and about the Lyceum Theatre.

The Vampire Empire publishes a quarterly newsletter. Its Worldwide Vampire Census surveys modern LIVING VAMPIRES.

From 1990 to 1999 the organization maintained a DRACULA MUSEUM, the only Dracula organization to do so.

FURTHER READING:
Guiley, Rosemary Ellen. *Vampires Among Us.* New York: Pocket Books, 1991.
"The Vampire Empire." Available online. URL: http://www.benecke.com/vampire.html. Downloaded on August 1, 2003.

vampire eye   See *ERETICA*; KASHUBS.

vampire fraud   Pretending to be a VAMPIRE for personal gain or to hide secrets. Cases of vampire fraud, documented in Europe, capitalize on indigenous fear of vampires.

In the former Yugoslavia, living persons impersonated vampires to defraud others and play tricks. During times of hunger, people dressed as vampires—with shrouds over their shoulders—would be seen lurking about MILLS and granaries. Young people traveled about in gangs, dressed in cloaks and impersonating vampires, and vandalized villages.

The most common vampire fraud was a cover for illicit love affairs. Women engaged in affairs who became pregnant passed off their children as the offspring of "vampire husbands." Villagers often were too frightened to ask questions or investigate. Widespread superstition held that vampires were sexually insatiable and returned from the grave to have sex with their spouses or even others.

One such case in Baja, Serbia (now in Hungary), involved a man who donned a white shroud threaded with bells, a white cap and socks, and paid nighttime visits to a widow who had recently lost her husband. The vampire made his first appearance two nights after the husband died. The vampire frightened people and rode on them as if they were donkeys. On most nights he was seen at midnight around the home where the widow lived. When he arrived, everyone in the household was so frightened that they fled, leaving just the young widow alone in her bed. After his visit, the vampire would depart with much bell ringing, clanking, loud cries, and rattling to imitate noises associated with the walking dead.

After about three months of this vampire, three brave youths got suspicious and decided to try to capture it. With the permission of the household head and his wife—the widow's in-laws with whom she lived—they hid behind the kitchen door, each armed with heavy rope. The widow had no knowledge of their plan. At midnight the vampire, attired in his white shroud, cap, and socks, arrived with much noise, scaring off the occupants of the home. As soon as he lay down beside the widow, the youths jumped out and grabbed him. The vampire struggled, moaned, and scratched, but was unable to break free. He was revealed to be the widow's neighbor, a man very much alive.

The youths took him to the village hall. The next day, the "vampire" and the widow were taken to the courthouse and interrogated. The two confessed to poisoning the husband. They had wanted to carry on an affair, but had no place to do so. They got rid of the husband and then conceived of the scheme for the man to disguise himself as a vampire, who could be passed off as the widow's dead vampire husband.

The pair were taken to the county seat and interrogated again. The court sentenced them to death: the vampire by hanging and the widow by beheading beneath the gallows. The sentences were carried out.

In Jan L. Perkowski's *The Vampire of the Slavs*, Professor T. P. Vukanovic writes that his own uncle masqueraded as a vampire during the Balkan Wars of 1912–13. The uncle, a farmer, draped himself in a white shirt and white sheet and went round the villages for sexual liaisons with young women, introducing himself as a vampire. One night in the village of Zagradje, peasants chased him with guns and dogs, nearly killing him. Thus ended his career as a vampire.

Vampire fraud also offered a cover for theft, as illustrated in a case among Slavic Muslim GYPSIES after World War I (1914–18). Vampires began to injure people and damage property, chiefly by hurling stones down from rooftops at night and causing people to flee their homes. The vampires moved from village to village and eluded the police. One night the abbot of the monastery of Decani—a rather corpulent man—managed to climb atop the roofs and catch several very live Gypsy men in the act of throwing stones. While they created this distracting disturbance, women and children were stealing goods from inside the houses and stealing crops from the fields. The police were summoned and the "vampire attacks" were ended.

FURTHER READING:
Fine, John V. A., Jr. "In Defense of Vampires," in *The Vampire: A Casebook*, Alan Dundes, ed. Madison: University of Wisconsin Press, 1998.
Oinas, Felix. "East European Vampires," in *The Vampire: A Casebook*, Alan Dundes, ed. Madison: University of Wisconsin Press, 1998.
Vukanovic, Professor T. P. "The Vampire," in *The Vampire of the Slavs* by Jan L. Perkowski. Cambridge, Mass.: Slavica Publishers, 1976.

vampire hunters   Individuals empowered, chosen, hired, or forced to hunt VAMPIRES and destroy them. In European lore, certain individuals, always male, are born destined to be vampire hunters (see DHAMPIR). They possess supernatural abilities, such as the clairvoyance necessary to see vampires, as well as the knowledge and skills necessary to track and destroy them. Such skills were highly valued, and vampire hunters commanded handsome fees of money, food, livestock, and goods.

The Hunting

In cases recorded in Europe, vampire hunters often had to hunt for an unknown vampire. They would be summoned, if a village was suffering a plague of illness, wasting deaths, crop failures, or other misfortunes, all of which were suspect as vampire-caused. Sometimes the vampire would be known or suspected, but oftentimes the hunter had to search for the right CORPSE. The *dhampir* would make a great show of looking for the vampire. In some areas, a priest had to accompany a vampire hunter or be present when a grave was opened, in order to say the correct prayers.

Traditional vampire hunters employed a variety of techniques:

- Scattering ASHES or SALT on and around suspected graves. The vampire will leave telltale footprints as he exits and enters the grave.
- Using a horse—either uniformly white or black, depending on prevailing beliefs—and leading it around the graves. Horses are sensitive to spirits and the supernatural, and will not step over the grave of a vampire. The best vampire-detecting horses are ones that have never stumbled. In some areas, virgin boys were put atop the horses in the belief that the purity in both boy and horse will recoil in horror at the evil of the vampire. (See BLACK HORSE; WHITE HORSE.)
- Using a dog to sense the grave of a vampire. The dog must be black and have "four eyes," that is, two marks resembling eyes over each eye.
- Using a white wolf to find the vampire. The wolf is capable of destroying the vampire as well, and accomplishes this by strangulation.
- Looking for an eerie, bluish flame in CEMETERIES at night. In European folklore, the blue glow is the soul, and a wandering blueish light indicates a soul out of its grave.
- Looking for graves with HOLES over them—exit points for vampires—or graves that are sunken or have crooked CROSSES or tombstones. All of these indicate that a vampire is dwelling underneath.
- Searching on SATURDAY, the only day of the week that vampires are forced to remain in their graves.

Once found, the vampire was dispatched by staking, decapitation, mutilation of the body, BURNING, and by placing various objects in the COFFIN. If such measures failed to stop the attacks on the living, more aggressive measures

Peter Vincent (Roddy McDowall) is a vampire hunter in Fright Night Part 2. *(Author's collection)*

were taken. For example, a corpse that had been staked might be burned and its ashes scattered. Or, the vampire hunter would keep searching for another vampire corpse. In some cases, numerous graves had to be dug up (see LASTOVO ISLAND VAMPIRES).

See also BURIAL CUSTOMS; CORPSES; PROTECTION AGAINST VAMPIRES.

Fictional Vampire Hunters

BRAM STOKER set a fictional model for vampire hunters in the character of PROFESSOR ABRAHAM VAN HELSING, a mature, wise and studied man who informs the other characters in *DRACULA* (1897) about vampires and tells them how they must hunt and destroy them. The crucifix-and-host, stake-and-hammer-toting vampire hunter dominated fictional vampire hunting and even spilled into real life in such cases as the vampire scare in London, the HIGHGATE VAMPIRE.

Van Helsing has been joined by younger and more dynamic vampire hunters, such as the tough men in John

Steakley's novel *Vampires,* who are professionals for hire, and female professionals such as the tough-but-sexy Anita Blake, created by LAURELL K. HAMILTON. Popular vampire hunters destined by birth are Buffy the Vampire Slayer, who is the "Chosen One," and the disembodied Harry Keogh of BRIAN LUMLEY's *Necroscope* series. Many fictional plots involve characters forced by circumstance to become vampire hunters, such as Ben Mears and his accomplices in Stephen King's *'SALEM'S LOT* (1975). Most notable of reluctant vampire hunters are teens, such as in *FRIGHT NIGHT* (1985 and 1988) and *THE LOST BOYS* (1987).

The standard tools of vampire hunting—crosses, STAKES, and hammers—are still part of the trade, but have been joined by such novelties as holy WATER in water guns. Exposing vampires to SUNLIGHT has been a tool since introduced in the 1922 film *NOSFERATU.*

FURTHER READING:
Guiley, Rosemary Ellen, with J. B. Macabre. *The Complete Vampire Companion.* New York: Macmillan, 1994.
Vukanovic, Professor T. P. "The Vampire," in *The Vampire of the Slavs* by Jan L. Perkowski. Cambridge, Mass.: Slavica Publishers, 1976.

Vampire Lestat, The (1985)   Second vampire novel by ANNE RICE, continuing the story of Lestat, the central character in *INTERVIEW WITH THE VAMPIRE.* The success of *The Vampire Lestat,* published in 1985, established the Vampire Chronicles for Rice, a series of books about vampires.

The Vampire Lestat opens in 1984 with Lestat awakened by a rock band after lying in the ground since 1929. He adapts to the mid-1980s immediately, becoming a rock star himself. (Rice found rock musicians outrageous, independent, and outsiders—an excellent vehicle for vampires.) Lestat rides a Harley motorcycle, listens to his Walkman radio, and discovers movies on video. He is appalled with the evils around him and decides that he must try to rationalize his basically evil nature by trying to show evil to others. He uses rock music to repudiate evil through art.

Lestat also finds Louis's interview tapes—the material for *Interview*—and thinks Louis has not told the complete story, especially from Lestat's point of view. He resolves to set the record straight with his own autobiography. He tells of his young manhood in prerevolutionary France and of his search for goodness and purity. His fame as an actor in Paris attracts Magnus, a vampire who forcefully transforms Lestat with the Dark Gift. Magnus immediately abandons Lestat by committing SUICIDE. Lestat makes his mother, Gabrielle, and his friend Nicolas into vampires.

Lestat goes off in search of a mentor he has learned about from the Paris vampire leader, Armand. He finds this mentor vampire, Marius, who tells him about the origins of vampirism in ancient Egypt. Lestat finds Enkil and Akasha, the Adam and Eve of all vampires. When they were alive, Akasha and Enkil were murdered by flesh eaters, and an evil spirit, Amel, entered Akasha through her wounds, and vampirism was born. Akasha and Enkil exchange blood and become deities demanding blood sacrifice. The vampires they create feed their blood needs through their own drinking, until the pair no longer need blood to survive. They are now so old and powerful they are like the stone statues of gods.

Lestat awakens Akasha, and she lets him drink her BLOOD, which gives him new powers. They share each other's blood until Enkil rouses and forces them apart. Marius sends Lestat away for his protection.

Lestat goes to New Orleans, where he meets Louis de Pointe du Lac and makes him, and then meets and makes the child vampire, Claudia. He gives a different perspective on the life the three shared than did Louis in *Interview.* His story is published, and vampires are angered at having their existence exposed.

The novel ends with Lestat's rock concert, in which he sings that mythic evils like vampires are irrelevant for the late 20th century; war and hunger are the demons to eradicate. His aim is to goad all the evil vampires into appearing against him so that he can fight them and truly bring goodness into the world. The final scene is a cliff-hanger—Akasha kidnaps Lestat—paving the way for the third book in the Vampire Chronicles, *QUEEN OF THE DAMNED.*

FURTHER READING:
Ramsland, Katherine. *The Vampire Companion: The Official Guide to Anne Rice's* The Vampire Chronicles. New York: Ballantine Books, 1993.
Rice, Anne. *The Vampire Lestat.* New York: Alfred A. Knopf, 1985.

Vampirella   Comic book series about a sexy female VAMPIRE by the same name. *Vampirella* debuted in 1969 from Warren Publications and was the first regularly scheduled comic book to include vampires in its title.

Publisher James Warren took credit for the idea of *Vampirella,* which was inspired by Jean-Claude Forest's *Barbarella,* a sexy French comic strip with a science fiction theme; a young Jane Fonda played the title role in the 1967 film version. Warren wanted an attractive female character to star in a horror comic and ended up with a totally sympathetic vampire years before such characters became commonplace in fiction. As presented to the public, she is wearing a scanty red costume on the cover of *Vampirella* 1. The striking cover illustration was the work of Frank Frazetta, whose powerful paintings had been one of the chief attractions of the earlier Warren comic books.

In the first issue, Vampirella's debut was a humorous space opera scripted by Forrest J. Ackerman, editor of *Famous Monsters of Filmland,* who coined the term *sci-fi,* and drawn by Tom Sutton. She was depicted as a native of Drakulon, a world whose ecology is based on hemoglobin rather than water. She drinks and bathes in BLOOD, exhales carbon monoxide, and cracks bad jokes. When Drakulon suffers a drought and begins to die, she gets a ride on a spaceship bound for Earth and escapes. She vampirizes the crew to sustain herself.

Within a few issues, her story took on a much more serious tone. Sutton toned down the more cartoonish aspects of his artwork, Archie Goodwin took over the writing, and Vampirella became a heroic figure, fighting off the forces of uncanny evil while fleeing from human enemies who fail to comprehend her basically virtuous character. She may live on blood, but somehow she never seems to kill anyone who doesn't deserve it.

With her magical powers, skintight costume, and endless battles against oppression, Vampirella became a supernatural superhero and enjoyed an extraordinarily long run. Along with other "Illustrated Tales To Bewitch and Bedevil You," her adventures appeared in 112 issues of *Vampirella,* from 1969 to 1983.

Vampirella underwent many a metamorphosis over the years. Among the writers were T. Casey Brennan, Steve Engelhart, and Bill DuBay. Perhaps the most notable artist was Spaniard Jose Gonzalez, whose European style suggested fashion illustration as much as comic book technique. A supporting cast evolved, including the father-and-son team of Conrad and Adam Van Helsing, who were descendants of PROFESSOR ABRAHAM VAN HELSING, the VAMPIRE HUNTER created by BRAM STOKER for *DRACULA* (1897).

COUNT DRACULA became a character in some of Vampirella's adventures. Later, the count was given his own series in the pages of *Vampirella,* with scripts by Gerry Boudreau and drawings by Esteban Maroto.

In the late 1980s, Harris Comics published issue 113 and then published reissues of some of the originals. New issues were produced in the 1990s, among them miniseries such as *Vengeance of Vampirella,* which ran from 1994–1996. *Vengeance* was written by Tom Sniegoski and illustrated by a number of artists. A made-for-television movie was made in 1996, with Talisa Soto as Vampirella, and rock star Roger Daltry as Vlad, a cult leader on Vampirella's home planet.

FURTHER READING:
Daniels, Les. "It Seems to Be Our Vampire Friend Again: The Undead in Comic Books," in *The Complete Vampire Companion* by Rosemary Ellen Guiley with J. B. Macabre. New York: Macmillan, 1994.

Vampire Lovers, The   See HAMMER FILMS.

Vampire of Nuremberg   See HOFFMAN, KUNO.

vampire sorcerers and witches   Persons who are sorcerers, witches, or wizards, especially of an evil nature, during life and thus are a type of LIVING VAMPIRE. Vampire sorcerers and witches cast the EVIL EYE and bewitch people

"Vampire Magician," from The Vampire Tarot *by Robert Michael Place* (Courtesy Robert Michael Place)

and animals with malevolent spells. Upon death, some become undead vampires and leave their graves at night to fatally suck the BLOOD of the living.

European Lore
In Romanian lore, vampire sorcerers and witches can shape-shift (see SHAPE-SHIFTING) into dogs, CATS, and horses in order to frighten people. They can bewitch others to death. Female vampires are dry in the body and RED in the face before and after death. When they go out to work their evil, they leave their homes through their chimneys and return exhausted and in rags. Male vampires are bald, and after death they grow a TAIL and hooves.

In Russian lore, living sorcerers have the power to take over the body of a person who is dying or who has died, and become a type of vampire called the *ERESTUN.*

Vampire sorcerers and witches can come out in the daytime all year round. Their power is greatest at the full MOON and weakest at the new moon. They meet with dead vampires and teach them magical incantations and spells, and decide on their programs of evil. The living vampires walk about the boundaries of villages, taking "power" from things, such as certain animals, bread, and bees. When the power is taken, the animals do not perform their natural functions: Hens do not lay eggs, cows do not give milk, bees do not make honey. A female vampire who has power over bread steals the taste from the bread of other women and puts it into her own bread. Some living vampires have power over RAIN and can prevent it from falling and nourishing crops.

Besides taking power for themselves, living vampires can take power for others who pay them. They can take beauty away from women and give it to another, and they can take love away. They can take milk away from a nursing mother.

"Vampire High Priestess," from The Vampire Tarot *by Robert Michael Place* (Courtesy Robert Michael Place)

Vampire sorcerers and witches are especially active on St. Andrew's Eve and St. George's Eve, and the period in between; also before Easter and at the last day of the year. During such periods, precautions should be taken by placing GARLIC about to prevent them from entering.

A Russian folktale describes how a vampire sorcerer operated, and how he was bested by a soldier. A soldier set off on leave to go home. En route he stopped to visit a miller who was a friend. They had a good visit, and as night descended, the miller urged the soldier to stay with him because a dreadful sorcerer had died recently and was rising from his grave at night to attack the soldier's village. The soldier declined because he wanted to get home as soon as possible.

The road led past the cemetery. There the soldier found the sorcerer sitting beside a campfire, stitching his boots. The sorcerer invited the soldier to accompany him to a wedding. When they arrived at the wedding, they were given food and drink.

The sorcerer drank until he became angry. He chased away all the wedding guests and put the bride and groom to sleep. He took out a pin and pricked their arms and collected their blood in two vials. He and the soldier left.

On the way back to the cemetery, the sorcerer said that he took the blood so that the couple would die. Tomorrow no one would be able to awaken them. Only he knew how to revive them. Questioned by the soldier, the sorcerer explained that the remedy was slitting the heels of the couple and pouring their blood back into the wounds. He had the blood of the groom in his right pocket and the blood of the bride in his left.

The sorcerer kept boasting that he could do whatever he wanted. The soldier asked if there was any way he could be stopped. Yes, said the sorcerer; he could be stopped if he were cremated in a bonfire of a hundred cartloads of ASPEN wood. However, his belly would split open in the fire and vipers, worms, maggots, and vermin crawl out, and magpies and crows would fly out. All would have to be captured and thrown back into the fire. If so much as a single maggot escaped, the sorcerer would escape, too.

After confessing his secrets, the sorcerer declared that he would have to kill the soldier. They engaged in a fierce battle that went on a long time, and the soldier thought all was lost. Then dawn came and the COCK crowed, and the sorcerer fell lifeless. The soldier took the vials of blood and returned to the wedding cottage.

There he found everyone in sorrow and anguish over the deaths of the bride and groom. He restored them to life and was handsomely rewarded. Then he instructed the peasants to gather 100 cartloads of aspen wood and make a bonfire. They dug the sorcerer from his grave and burned him in the fire, taking care to catch and burn all the creatures and vermin that escaped from his belly. The soldier scattered the ASHES to the wind.

From then on, peace and happiness reigned in the village. The soldier returned to his duty with his fortune, served out his term, and then retired and lived happily ever after.

Native American Lore

Although Native American lore does not include European-style vampires, there are legends that parallel European vampires and vampire sorcerers and witches. For example, in Cherokee lore there are old witches and wizards who live off the livers of the dead. When a person falls ill, the witches and wizards shape-shift into invisible forms and gather around the bedside, tormenting the person until he is dead. After the person is buried, they dig up his body and feast on the liver. In this manner, they gain strength and lengthen their own lives as many days as they stole from the dead person.

An Abenaki folktale tells of an old male witch who is comparable to an undead vampire. The witch died and was buried in a tree in a grove used as a burial place. Later in the winter, an Indian man and his wife decided to camp in the grove for a night, and built their campfire. After supper, the wife looked up and saw dark things hanging in the trees. Her husband said they were the dead of long ago. The wife felt uneasy and said they should stay awake all night. The husband ignored her and went to sleep.

Soon the fire went out. The wife heard a gnawing sound, like an animal chewing on a bone. She was too frightened to move, but stayed awake all night. In the morning, she tried to wake her husband, but found he was dead. His left side had been gnawed away, and his heart was gone. Terrified, she ran away. She came upon a lodge and spilled out her story, but the people suspected her of murdering her husband. They all went to the scene, where they found the husband's body, and the dead witch hanging overhead in the tree. They took the witch down and unwrapped it from its burial shroud. Its mouth and face were covered with fresh blood.

FURTHER READING:

Bell, Michael E. *Food for the Dead: On the Trail of New England's Vampires.* New York: Carroll & Graf, 2001.

Murgoci, Agnes. "The Vampire in Roumania," in *The Vampire: A Casebook,* Alan Dundes, ed. Madison: University of Wisconsin Press, 1998.

Perkowski, Jan L. *The Darkling: A Treatise on Slavic Vampirism.* Columbus, Ohio: Slavica Publishers, 1989.

Vampire: The Masquerade   See GAMES.

Vampyr **(1932)**   German VAMPIRE film by Danish director Carl Theodor Dreyer. *Vampyr,* Dreyer's first sound film, has a surreal, dreamlike atmosphere. In fact, much of the key action takes place within dreams. Dreyer employs a SHADOW that moves independently, a device later used by Francis Ford Coppola to great effect in *BRAM STOKER'S DRACULA. Vampyr* has fallen into obscurity but remains a noteworthy contribution to the vampire film genre.

Vampyr is based on a novel by J. Sheridan Le Fanu, *In A Glass Darkly,* about a man who vacations in a town that he discovers is under the control of a vampire. It also is reminiscent of Le Fanu's "CARMILLA," about a female vampire who preys upon other young females. Dreyer was less interested in the story line than in evocative visuals and atmosphere, and at times the film is confusing. Nonetheless, Dreyer evokes more horror using light, shadow, and imagination than many modern filmmakers manage to create with a host of multimillion-dollar special effects.

Dreyer cowrote the screenplay with Christen Jul. Dreyer preferred not to work with professional actors, and selected most of the cast for *Vampyr* from people he met at random on the streets of Paris. The lead role of Allan Gray is played by Julian West, a count who agreed to finance the film in exchange for the role. The film was shot entirely on location at a deteriorated castle outside of Paris.

The opening of the film explains that Allan Gray's studies of devil worship and vampires have "made him into a dreamer, for whom the boundary between the real and the unreal become dim." He takes "aimless journeys." On one of these, a fishing trip, he arrives at a lonely inn in the village of Courtempierre, where a room mysteriously has already been reserved for him. He is spooked by a disfigured man and locks his door. Later, he falls into a restless sleep.

Gray is awakened when a strange man (Maurice Schultz) enters his supposedly locked room and tells him "she" must not die. The man gives him a package marked with the instructions that it is to be opened after the man's death, and then leaves.

Wondering who "she" is, Gray gets up and goes out to investigate. He follows the shadow of a one-legged man, which takes him to the man himself, and to more mysterious shadows and people. He eventually arrives at a secluded manor home, which is owned by the strange man who visited him in his room. The man has two daughters, Gisele (Rena Mandel) and Leone (Sybille Schmitz), the latter of whom suffers feverish nightmares about BLOOD. The lord of the manor is shot in his home by a shadowy assailant—who seems to be the one-legged man—and dies. The family asks Gray to stay with them, and he agrees.

Gray opens the package and finds a book, *The History of Vampires* by Paul Bonnard. The book says that vampires are demons, and they rise at the full MOON to suck the blood of children and young people in order to prolong their own life "in the land of the shadows."

Leone is found wandering about a CEMETERY at night, being preyed upon by an older woman (Henriette Gerard). Gisele and Gray rescue her.

Gray continues reading the mysterious book. A servant (Albert Braz) also reads it. The book says that vampires are under the aegis of the Prince of Evil, and their victims become vampires. Vampires try to drive their victims to SUICIDE. The vampires are aided by the shadows of executed criminals. The book also gives instructions for killing vampires by driving a metal bar into their hearts. In addition, it says that a foul epidemic in Courtempierre many years before claimed 11 victims, and was rumored to be caused by a vampire, identified as Marguerite Chopin,

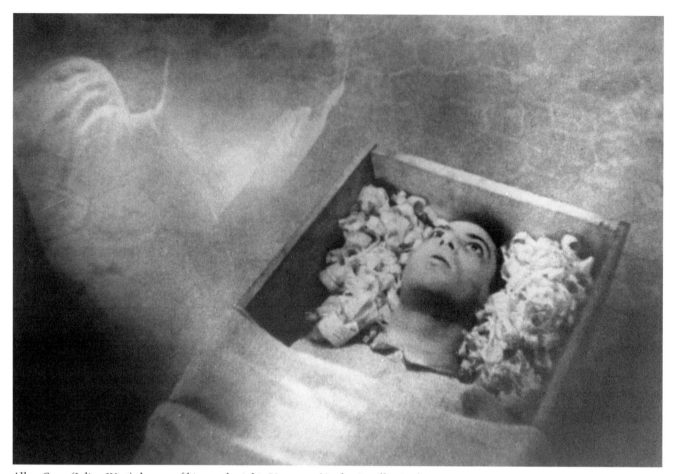

Allan Gray (Julian West) dreams of his own burial in Vampyr. (Author's collection)

who was buried in the village churchyard. During her life, she had been a "monster in a human body" and had died without remorse. The Church refused her.

A doctor (Jan Hieronimko) comes to attend to Leone. Gray gives her a transfusion of his own blood. During the transfusion, Gray dreams the truth that Leone is being vampirized. He struggles with the doctor, who flees. Gray follows him and finds his lair, where Gisele is tied up and in a swoon. He also finds a partially-finished COFFIN covered with a shroud. Pulling it back, he sees himself inside, his eyes open.

The doctor and an assistant arrive, and Gray hides under a trapdoor in the floor. The assistant fits the coffin with a windowed lid that leaves exposed Gray's staring face. The coffin is carried through the streets to the cemetery; the camera provides the perspective of seeing things from the vantage point of Gray inside the coffin.

Gray wakes up in the cemetery. He and the servant from the manor house find the crypt grave of the old woman vampire. The servant stabs her in the heart with an IRON pole, and Gray hammers it in. Her body turns into a skeleton.

Back home in bed, Leone is instantly healed. A tempest arises, and the doctor's one-legged assistant is killed. Gray frees Leone, and they leave on a boat. The doctor seeks refuge in the manor house, but is buried by dirt piled on him by a giant wheel.

Vampyre, The   The first VAMPIRE story published in English, a novella written by JOHN POLIDORI, physician to LORD BYRON. *The Vampyre* appeared in England's *New Monthly Magazine* in April 1819.

Polidori borrowed heavily from an oral story he heard Lord Byron tell one night during a trip in Europe. The story originally was published with the implication that Byron wrote it, and it and was hailed by critics and quickly translated into French and German. Byron was furious. Polidori revealed himself as the true author.

The Vampyre draws upon a folklore belief that a vampire CORPSE can be repeatedly revived under the rays of the MOON. Polidori also made use of the Greek lore that one becomes a vampire as punishment for a heinous crime committed in life and is doomed to prey upon those whom he loved the most while upon the earth.

The vampire antihero is the mysterious but suave and seductive LORD RUTHVEN, whom Polidori modeled upon Lord Byron. Ruthven (pronounced "rivven") was taken from a satire of Byron, *Glenarvon,* written by Byron's lover,

Lady Caroline Lamb. There may have been a real-life association as well: Lord Grey de Ruthyn had tried to seduce Byron when he was young.

The character of Lord Ruthven is "a man entirely absorbed in himself." It is likely that Polidori based Ruthven's friend, Aubrey, upon himself. The character of Aubrey is naive and trusting, a man who cultivates "more his imagination than his judgment."

Lord Ruthven is introduced to society in London and attracts the interest of a young rich man, Aubrey, an orphan, to whom Ruthven is attracted. Together they travel about the Continent. However, they part company in Rome when Aubrey learns of his companion's immoral nature and is repulsed by his shallowness.

In Greece, Aubrey falls in love with a peasant girl named Ianthe, who tells him terrifying legends about the "vampyre . . . forced every year, by feeding upon the life of a lovely female victim to prolong his existence for the ensuing months." Aubrey recognizes Lord Ruthven as having the same characteristics.

One night Aubrey defies the warning of locals and travels through a dark wood during a violent storm. He hears fiendish laughter and a woman's screams, and investigates. Entering a hovel, he is attacked by something that seems superhuman in force and is rendered unconscious. When he awakens, he is horrified to find Ianthe has been murdered—her badly mutilated body is covered with BLOOD and there are teeth marks on her throat. A strange-looking, bloody, dagger is nearby.

The news of Ianthe's gruesome murder causes her parents to die of grief and shock. Aubrey remains ill and bedridden. Ruthven arrives on the scene, coming from Athens, and he nurses Aubrey back to health.

Ruthven and Aubrey resume their travels together in Greece. Out in the remote countryside, they are beset by bandits, and Lord Ruthven is mortally wounded by gunshot. For two days he lingers. He makes Aubrey swear not to reveal his death back in England for a year and a day. Ruthven further orders the robbers to expose his corpse to the "first cold ray of the moon" on a mountaintop. They do so. The following night, Aubrey discovers that the corpse has mysteriously vanished, and he assumes the robbers stole it for the clothing. He finds the bloodstained sheath of the dagger found near Ianthe's body.

Aubrey returns to England, where he is astonished to see Lord Ruthven at a fashionable party. Ruthven reminds him of his oath to keep quiet about his death in Greece. Distraught, Aubrey's mental health begins to suffer. He sees vampires everywhere and then is confined to bed with brain fever.

Meanwhile, Aubrey's sister announces her engagement to the earl of Marsden. She shows a miniature portrait of the earl to Aubrey. He is astonished to see that it is Lord Ruthven. He flies into a rage, is judged insane, and is confined. He confronts Ruthven, but again is reminded of his oath. Aubrey bursts a blood vessel in apoplexy and lapses into incoherence. On midnight of the day before the wedding—the time when Aubrey's oath of silence is over—Aubrey is dying. He informs his guardians of his secret and urges them to save his sister. The story ends: "The guardians hastened to protect Miss Aubrey; but when they arrived, it was too late. Lord Ruthven had disappeared, and Aubrey's sister had glutted the thirst of a VAMPYRE!"

The Vampyre caused a sensation in Europe and reined as the dominant influence on literature and drama until the publication of DRACULA by BRAM STOKER in 1897. In its wake, novels, stories, and plays about Lord Ruthven and other vampires then flooded the marketplace. Charles Nodier's novel, *Lord Ruthven ou les vampires* (1820), was revised as a play entitled *The Vampire; or, The Bride of the Isles*. It was translated into several languages and toured Europe and North America for years to come. The Irish playwright Dion Boucicault wrote his play *The Vampire* based on the story. The vampire, Alan Raby, "dies" during the reign of Charles II. He is finally brought to his demise when he is shot with a charmed bullet.

Adaptations of *The Vampyre* appeared on a regular basis until the middle of the century. The last noteworthy performance, Alexandre Dumas père's play *Le Vampire*, opened at the Ambrigue-Comique in 1851.

It is difficult to gauge what the impact of *The Vampyre* might have been if it had first been published under Polidori's name. Certainly the name of Byron guaranteed it wide attention.

The Vampyre established important elements of vampire fiction that became more embedded in subsequent creations of other authors, such as Stoker and J. Sheridan Le Fanu. The notable elements that became embedded in the literary vampire are

- The vampire is the reanimated dead.
- The vampire is not a creature of the past, but lives in present society, passing undetected among his victims.
- The vampire is not a peasant, but is a wealthy aristocrat who has the freedom to travel.
- The vampire is brooding, mysterious, dark, and fatally seductive—but is amoral in that he cares not about the destruction and ruination of others.
- The vampire does not attack simply for food; there is an erotic element between the vampire and his victim. The erotic and libertine elements are given more emphasis than any need for blood.
- The vampire exerts a psychic vampirism on his victims as well as blood vampirism.
- The vampire has a supernatural relationship with the moon.

See also PSYCHIC ATTACK.

FURTHER READING:
Haining, Peter, and Peter Tremayne. *The Undead: The Legend of Bram Stoker and Dracula*. London: Constable, 1997.

Senf, Carol A. *The Vampire in 19th Century English Literature.* Bowling Green, Ohio: Bowling Green State University Popular Press, 1988.

Stuart, Roxana. *Stage Blood: Vampires of the 19th-Century Stage.* Bowling Green, Ohio: Bowling Green State University Popular Press, 1994.

Twitchell, James B. *The Living Dead: A Study of the Vampire in Romantic Literature.* Durham, N.C.: Duke University Press, 1981.

vampyres   See LIVING VAMPIRES.

Vampyrotouthis infernalis   Deep ocean mollusk so named because of its fierce appearance. *Vampyrotouthis infernalis* means "vampire of hell." The mollusk is not a supernatural creature, but is a distant relative of the octopus. It measures a mere two inches, but has RED eyes measuring an inch in diameter. Its mouth is ringed with sharp white teeth, and its black body has numerous glowing lights on it. It has 10 tentacles. Little is known about its life cycle.

FURTHER READING:
Keel, John A. *Strange Mutants.* New York: Global Communications, 1984.

Van Helsing (2004)   A Universal Studios release in which monster hunter Gabriel Van Helsing takes on the most famous monsters of the supernatural realm. Written and directed by Stephen Sommers of *The Mummy* and *The Mummy Returns* fame, *Van Helsing* stars Hugh Jackman as a 19th-century hero who is not a mere VAMPIRE HUNTER but a warrior against all evil. The original BRAM STOKER character of PROFESSOR ABRAHAM VAN HELSING is the inspiration for a reinvented vampire hunter, a Van Helsing meets Indiana Jones meets James Bond action hero.

Gabriel Van Helsing is a man who cannot remember his past. He has been cursed to fight evil. A secret society made up of representatives of all the world's religions sends him to TRANSYLVANIA to hunt and destroy Count Vladislaus Dracula (Richard Roxburgh). There Van Helsing meets Anna Valerious (Kate Beckinsale), who is intent on ridding her family of a WEREWOLF curse, which can be accomplished only by the demise of the vampire. Anna's brother

Richard Roxburgh as Dracula in Van Helsing *(2004)* (Author's collection)

Dracula (Richard Roxburgh) and his vampire brides in Van Helsing *(2004).* (Author's collection)

Velkan (Will Kemp) has been bitten by a werewolf and has become the Wolf Man, who transforms into a rampaging werewolf every full MOON. At first, Valerious disdains Van Helsing's help, but the two become allies and then are powerfully drawn to one another.

Van Helsing and Valerious meet up with Dr. Victor Frankenstein (Samuel West) and face a host of villains, among them Frankenstein's monster (Shuler Hensley); Frankenstein's evil assistant, Igor (Kevin J. O'Connor); Dr. Jekyll (Stephen H. Fisher) and Mr. Hyde (Robbie Coltrane); and Dracula's three brides, Aleera (Elena Anaya), Verona (Silvia Colloca) and Marishka (Josie Maran). Dracula, Frankenstein, and the Wolf Man are the primary villains. Dracula, banished by the secret society to an ice castle in 1462, was given 15-foot wings by the devil. He holds the key to Van Helsing's past.

Van Helsing's right hand man is Carl (David Weham), a mad scientist who works for the secret society. In a role similar to the Q character in the James Bond movies, Carl invents state-of-the-art weaponry to fight the deadliest forces of evil. Among his creations are an explosive called glycerin 48, an automatic crossbow, and a switchblade-like SILVER stake. Automatic guns shoot silver nitrate bullets. Van Helsing also borrows from the Eastern martial arts in employing *tojo* blades.

The women in the film are molded as updated tough-but-sexy characters. Valerious and the brides of Dracula are formidable fighters, yet ultra-seductive as well. The brides are more significant players than in earlier DRACULA FILMS. They compete among themselves for Dracula's attention, but when he focuses on claiming Valerious, they join forces to try to eliminate her.

Action is set in London, Paris, Rome, and Transylvania.

FURTHER READING:
Van Helsing Web site. URL:http://www.valhelsing.net. Accessed April 26, 2004.

Van Helsing, Professor Abraham   The VAMPIRE expert and chief VAMPIRE HUNTER in BRAM STOKER's novel *DRACULA* (1897). Professor Abraham Van Helsing established the mold for generations of fictional vampire hunters and experts on the occult.

Professor Abraham Van Helsing (Edward Van Sloan) uses a crucifix against Count Dracula (Bela Lugosi) in Tod Browning's Dracula. (Author's collection)

In *Dracula*, Van Helsing is a friend of Dr. John Seward's, and lives in Amsterdam. Seward summons him when he becomes worried about the mysterious malady and neck wounds suffered by Lucy Westenra. She is under attack by COUNT DRACULA, but no one yet realizes this. Seward describes the professor as an expert on obscure diseases, a metaphysician, a philosopher, and "one of the more advanced scientists of his day." He is a skilled hypnotist.

Upon his arrival and examination of Lucy, Van Helsing becomes very concerned, but he shares little of his thoughts and even less of his knowledge with the other principal characters. He decrees that Lucy is in need of BLOOD. He orders her to wear garlands of GARLIC at night and to keep her doors and windows festooned with it. He offers no explanations why, other than that garlic is "medicinal." Even after Lucy dies, he still keeps the others in the dark, saying only that her soul is not at peace. He mentions VAMPIRE BATS to Seward, but does not follow up with an explanation. It is not until he takes the men to see Lucy in her vampire condition in her tomb—deep into the story—that Van Helsing finally opens up and delivers a long mono-

logue on vampires. He then organizes and orchestrates the hunt for Dracula.

One of Van Helsing's most significant remarks about vampires is, "The power of the vampire is that people do not believe he exists." This statement explains one of the many reasons why vampires continue to fuel fascination and interest. Numerous plots of vampire novels and films turn on this disbelief, which enables vampires to exist and prey in the world. Then "rational" characters are plunged into profound shock—and fear and terror—when disbelief is forced to become belief.

Stoker left no extant notes about his exact inspiration for the character of Van Helsing. *Dracula* scholars have speculated that he based Van Helsing on Arminius Vambery, a Hungarian professor he met in London. Van Helsing has a friend back in Amsterdam named "Arminius." Scholars also point to Van Helsing's first name, Abraham, which is the same as the first names of Stoker and his father, concluding that Stoker must have identified personally with Van Helsing. Other possibilities put forward are Helsingor, the Danish name for Hamlet's castle; Dr. Hesselius of J.

Sheridan Le Fanu's "CARMILLA" (1872), and Van Helmont, an alchemist mentioned in a text Stoker consulted in his research, *On Superstitions Connected with the History and Nature of Medicine and Surgery* (1844) by T. J. Pettigrew.

According to Stoker's notes, he originally had three characters that became combined into Van Helsing. One of them was a German professor named Max Windschoeffel, possibly based on a real German professor of religion and mythology, Max Muller.

FURTHER READING:
Miller, Elizabeth. *Dracula: Sense and Nonsense.* Westcliff-on-Sea, England: Desert Island Books, 2000.
Miller, Elizabeth. "Van Helsing." Available online at Dracula's Homepage. URL: http://www.ucs.mun.ca/~emiller/VHelsing. htm. Downloaded on January 7, 2004.

varcolac (vircolac)   In Romanian lore, an eclipse demon sometimes associated with VAMPIRES. The term *varcolac* is borrowed from Southern Slavic, probably Bulgarian, and refers to an evil spirit that eats the sun and MOON, thus causing eclipses. *Varcolaci* are described as dogs, always two in number; animals smaller than dogs; dragons, animals with many mouths that suck like octopi; or spirits.

Various explanations are given for their origins and activities:

- They are the souls of unbaptized children or the children of unmarried parents, who are cursed by God.
- They rise up during the making of maize porridge if one makes the mistake of putting the porridge stick in the fire.
- They rise up if one sweeps dust out of the house at sunset in the direction of the sun.
- They rise up from the air of heaven if women spin at night, especially at midnight, without a candle and if they cast spells as they spin. One should never spin by moonlight, for *varcolaci* will fasten themselves to the thread and go up it to eat the moon and cover it with BLOOD, and eat the sun. Their power lasts as long as the thread is not broken, and they can go wherever they wish. If the thread breaks, they go to another part of the sky.
- They are recognized by their pale faces and dry skin, and by the deep, deathlike sleep they fall into whenever they send their spirits out through their mouths to eat the sun or moon. If they are roused or moved during their sleep, they die, for their returning spirit will not be able to find the mouth out of which they issued.

During an eclipse, people traditionally beat on shovels and other IRON tools, fired guns, and rang church bells to frighten away the *varcolaci*. In the end, the moon triumphs over the *varcolaci* with its superior strength, for if the moon truly were to be eaten, the world would come to an end. One belief holds that God orders the *varcolaci* to eat the moon in order to convince people to repent.

The *varcolaci* also are called PRICOLICI.

FURTHER READING:
Murgoci, Agnes. "The Vampire in Roumania," in *The Vampire: A Casebook*, Alan Dundes, ed. Madison: University of Wisconsin Press, 1998.
Perkowski, Jan L. *The Darkling: A Treatise on Slavic Vampirism.* Columbus, Ohio: Slavica Publishers, 1989.

Varney the Vampire; or the Feast of Blood   First VAMPIRE novel published in the English language, in 1847. *Varney the Vampire; or the Feast of Blood* began in the mid-1840s as an anonymously written serial novel called a "penny dreadful" or "penny blood." Penny dreadfuls were serial tales published for the working class masses as cheap entertainment. *Varney the Vampire* was so successful that the 220 installments were published as a novel of nearly 900 pages in 1847.

Credit for *Varney the Vampire* was given by MONTAGUE SUMMERS and others to Thomas Preskett Prest, "The Prince of Lurid Shockers" and author of *Sweeney Todd.* But in 1963 scrapbooks of the Scottish writer JAMES MALCOLM RYMER established him as the author of at least most of *Varney.* Given the nature of penny dreadfuls and their frequency, it was not unusual for more than one writer to work on any given series.

Rymer borrowed from Shakespeare and from JOHN POLIDORI's THE VAMPYRE, originally published in 1819 and turned into a penny illustrated format in 1840. Like LORD RUTHVEN in *The Vampyre, Varney* features an aristocratic vampire, though not so charming. Sir Francis Varney preys upon the wealthy Bannerworth family. Varney is out not only for their BLOOD but also for their family home as well. In fact, much of his evil as a parasite centers on his lust for money. He discovers that—alas!—he really *is* a vampire.

The poor quality of the writing—there is ample purple prose—and inconsistencies in the plot are offset by unrelenting action and a vivid portrait of the vampire. Varney is hideous and ugly: he is tall and gaunt, with a white, bloodless face, fierce eyes that shine like polished tin, long fangs, and long nails that appear to hang from the ends of his fingers. In a series of repetitive adventures, he attacks women and transforms some of them into vampires. Eventually, he comes to regret his actions. He commits SUICIDE several times but—like Lord Ruthven—is always revived by the light of the MOON. He haunts Ratford Abbey and preys upon maidens. Finally, he is overcome with disgust at the horror of his life and destroys himself for good by throwing himself into the crater of Mount Vesuvius.

Varney the Vampire is one of the most important early vampire tales, and some of the incidents in it were copied in subsequent works. BRAM STOKER probably was familiar with at least some of it, but experts disagree about what influence it may have had on his creation of DRACULA (1897).

FURTHER READING:
Carter, Margaret L. "From Villain to Hero," in *The Complete Vampire Companion* by Rosemary Ellen Guiley with J. B. Macabre. New York: Macmillan, 1994.
Frayling, Christopher. *Vampyres: Lord Byron to Count Dracula.* London: Faber and Faber, 1991.
Senf, Carol A. *The Vampire in 19th Century English Literature.* Bowling Green, Ohio: Bowling Green State University Popular Press, 1988.

Vaughn, Nellie (d. 1889)   Alleged VAMPIRE case of Rhode Island. Nellie Vaughn was a real person, but the story about her being a vampire is fictitious, and in part is a confusion with lore about MERCY BROWN.

Nellie L. Vaughn was the daughter of George B. and Ellen Vaughn of West Greenwich, Rhode Island. At age 19, she contracted pneumonia and died on March 31, 1889. She was buried in the Plain Meeting House Baptist Church CEMETERY. The circumstances surrounding her death were not the same as the consumption deaths in other cases related to fears of a vampirelike wasting away. Her body was not exhumed; nor did other members of her family die of consumption. There are no accounts, oral or written, of Vaughn being a "vampire."

The first published reference to Nellie Vaughn appeared in 1977 in the *Westerly Sun* newspaper in Rhode Island and associated her with being a vampire. The article said her grave was sunken and continued to sink, and no vegetation would grow around it, despite the best efforts of caretakers. The headstone read, "I am waiting and watching for you." (In European vampire lore, a sunken grave is a sign of vampirism.)

As a result, curiosity seekers, mostly teenagers, began visiting the cemetery where Nellie was buried. Vandalism increased dramatically. By 1982 members of the church adjacent to the cemetery were out of patience with the continuing vandalism to the cemetery and the church. Tombstones were always overturned. Vaughn's tombstone was ripped out, chipped, and stolen. Attempts were made to dig up her grave. Flowers were taken off other graves and placed on her grave. Some people even left coins on the grave—which were picked up later by others.

The source of the vampire attribution was by this time said to be an unnamed high school teacher at Coventry High School—said in some versions to be a man and in other versions to be a woman—who told the students there was a vampire buried in this cemetery, a girl who had died at age 19. Students went to the cemetery, found Vaughn's grave, and assumed she was the vampire. Some versions of this story said the teacher was talking about Mercy Brown, but students mistook Vaughn's grave for that of Brown.

As plausible as that core story sounds, there is no evidence of any basis in fact to it; it appears to be urban legend, the kind of story that springs up to explain events. There is no record of the identity of the teacher. No one ever seems to know the name, but credits the story from a "friend of a friend."

Another addition to the legend were reports that Vaughn haunted her grave. Curiosity seekers reported seeing her ghost and hearing it say, "I am perfectly pleasant." The ghost sometimes was said to scratch the faces of those who disagreed. This addition to the legend seems to attempt to rectify the earlier false legend of Nellie Vaughn being a vampire: She returns from the grave to defend herself.

The inscription on Vaughn's headstone, "I am waiting and watching for you," likewise has nothing to do with a mysterious and ominous death. The inscription was not uncommon at the time of Vaughn's death, and was used for those who died young and thus await a reunion with their family members in heaven.

In 1993 someone dug up a COFFIN at the Plain Meeting House cemetery and opened it, exposing the recently buried CORPSE of an older man. Apparently the VAMPIRE HUNTERS were looking for Vaughn's grave, which was unmarked—the headstone had been removed to a safe place in an effort to stop further vandalism of it. The corpse of the man was found with a can of beer in one hand and a pack of cigarettes in the other.

Although the vampire legend of Nellie Vaughn has been debunked, it still persists and is reiterated in stories about the NEW ENGLAND VAMPIRES.

FURTHER READING:
Bell, Michael E. *Food for the Dead: On the Trail of New England's Vampires.* New York: Carroll & Graf, 2001.

vegetable vampires   See GYPSIES.

Verdun, Michel   See POLIGNY WEREWOLVES.

Vermont Vampires   See NEW ENGLAND VAMPIRES.

Verzeni, Vincenzo (19th c.)   Italian man convicted for murder and CORPSE mutilation in 1871. Vincenzo Verzeni drank human BLOOD. He was sentenced to life in prison. His teeth were so sharp and strong that authorities feared he would gnaw through the steel cell bars, and so he was placed in a specially reinforced cell.

vetala   In Indian lore, a type of GHOULS or VAMPIRES that lurk about CEMETERIES and reanimate the dead. The *vetala* is demonic in appearance, with a human body, the hands and feet of which are turned backward. The *vetala* lives in stones scattered about the hills; in Decca, it guards villages and lives in RED-painted stones. Its eerie singing is often reported heard in cemeteries. It enjoys playing nasty tricks upon the living.

A type of *vetala* is an OLD HAG who sucks the BLOOD of sleeping women who have gone to bed drunk.

vieschtitsa   In Slavic lore, a SUCCUBUS who copulates with VAMPIRES who are living men seized with a BLOODlust. The *vieschtitsa* has wings of flame and swoops down upon men in their sleep. The demon also takes on the form of a hyena and drags children off into the woods.

vilkodlak   Medieval term in Bohemia for WEREWOLF.

viscera sucker   In Philippine and Malaysian lore, a vampiric demon that has the form of a human torso. Viscera suckers fly about at night and attack people to suck out their entrails and body fluids. They suck out the fetuses of pregnant women.

See also LILITH; *TLAHUELPUCHI*.

***vjesci* (*vieszcy*)**   A Kashub vampire. The *vjesci* is identified at birth by the presence of the CAUL. Its vampirism can be prevented by the reduction of the caul to ASHES, and fed to the child in a drink at age seven. Another telltale sign of the *vjesci* is that its left EYE remains open after death.

The *vjesci* sucks the BLOOD sleeping victims, who are found dead the next morning with a small wound on the left side of the breast, exactly over the heart.

See also KASHUBS.

vjiesce   A Slovincian term for a VAMPIRE. Slovincian, a Slavic language, died out after World War II. *Vjiesce* is similar to the Kashubian *vjesci* or *vieszcy*. It comes from the Slavic root *ved-io-*, which means "knowledge," and is also applied in cognates in other Slavic languages to sorcerers, witches, warlocks, and soothsayers.

A *vjiesce* case recording in folk literature tells of an unnamed man from Zelazo—formerly in West Prussia and now in Poland—who was known to be a vampire while alive. When he died, he was buried in the Gardno church CEMETERY. Soon thereafter, he was seen walking about in daylight, going through fields and yards and into cottages. In order to stop him, villagers went to his grave at midnight, dug him up, and cut off his head. The wanderings then stopped.

FURTHER READING:
Perkowski, Jan L. *The Darkling: A Treatise on Slavic Vampirism.* Columbus, Ohio: Slavica Publishers, 1989.

Vlad Tepes (1431–1476)   Voivode (prince or ruler) of Wallachia, a province south of Transylvania and now part of Romania, and namesake of BRAM STOKER's vampire, COUNT DRACULA. Vlad Tepes means "Vlad the Impaler," a name earned because of Vlad's impalement of his enemies upon STAKES and spikes.

It is a popular misconception that Vlad Tepes is the "historical Dracula." Vlad's sole connection to the fictional character is in his name. He was often called "Dracula." His father, Vlad II, was known as Dracul, or devil. *Dracula* means "son of Dracul," or "son of the devil." Vlad committed his many and atrocities against his enemies and subjects alike.

Vlad has no association with folkloric vampirism. Modern accounts say he drank the BLOOD of his enemies on at least one occasion, but no evidence exists to support this. Even so, such a practice in warfare symbolizes the total conquering and absorption of the enemy and has no connection to vampires. Despite the lack of historical evidence of Vlad drinking blood, a woodcut shows him dining while surrounded by victims impaled on stakes—his favorite means of punishment.

Vlad's principality of Wallachia came into existence in the late 13th and 14th centuries, and was the first Romanian state to form. The first ruler was Basarab I (r. 1310–52), who was followed by his son Nicolae Alexandru (r. 1352–64). The capital was established in Curtea de Arges, where a fortress was built at a strategic point overlooking the Arges River (see CASTLE POENARI). The Wallachian society was organized as a feudal system, with a ruling class of landed aristocracy called boyars beneath the voivode.

Vlad's father, Vlad II Dracul ("Vlad the Devil"), came to power in 1443 after his brother, Vlad I, died of illnesss without an heir. Vlad II held the throne by force. Wallachia was—and had been for some time—under constant threat by invading Turks from the expanding Ottoman Empire. There were ongoing battles and fighting, including clashes of the Crusades.

In 1447 Vlad II was killed, and his sons Vlad III and Radu fled to the Ottoman court. In less than a year, Vlad III invaded Wallachia with Ottoman support, and briefly seized control. He next came to power from 1456 to 1462. The details of his return to power are not known.

During this second reign, the capital of Wallachia was in Targoviste, where Vlad established a residence. The boyars were increasing their wealth and influence, and Vlad reportedly committed atrocities against them to keep them in check. One source, the Byzantine chronicler Laonic Chalkondyles, stated that Vlad killed 20,000 men, women, and children in a short period of time.

On another occasion, he is said to have invited boyars to a feast. When it was over, he quizzed them one by one on how many princes there were in Wallachia. The correct answer was seven. No one gave the correct answer, and so all 500 of them were impaled on stakes. One Easter he invited citizens and their families to a feast. At its conclusion, he had the old ones impaled around the city and marched off the younger ones—including children—to be forced laborers building Castle Poenari.

If Vlad suspected anyone of treason, he had them and their families tortured and impaled. Thousands and

Vlad Tepes dines while his victims die by impalement on stakes. (Author's collection)

thousands of people were supposedly impaled. According to German stories, he also had churches and villages burned, and he ruined crops. He locked people into rooms and burned them. He forced people to dig their own graves and then had them beheaded at graveside. He boiled people alive in a cauldron, forcing them to put their heads through holes in the lid so that they could not move. He boiled to death a Tartar thief and forced other Tartars to eat him. He impaled women holding their nursing infants, and when the mothers died, he cut off their breasts and stuffed the infants inside them.

He did not save his wrath for his enemies alone. He ordered his mistress's stomach be split open to prove her pregnancy. He had the turbans of visiting ambassadors nailed to their heads when they did not remove them in his presence, and he burned a whole group of beggars alive at a sumptuous feast, justifying his actions as eliminating a source of pestilence. When a boyar complained of the screams and stench from the impaled Turks, Vlad had him impaled also—on a higher stake, above the scene.

The list of atrocities goes on. While some of these accounts may be exaggerated, Vlad nonetheless acquired a reputation of extreme ruthlessness and cruelty that undoubtedly was justified.

In 1462 Vlad was ousted and his brother, Radu cel Frumos, was installed on the throne. Vlad was imprisoned in Hungary for 13 years. He bargained a release in 1475 and made plans to take the throne for a third time. He was successful in 1476. But his third reign was short-lived. About a month into it, Ottomans invaded and Vlad was killed.

Different accounts of his death are given. He was allegedly shot to death with arrows in battle. Or, he was assassinated by a Turk in the forest near Snagov, and was beheaded and his head staked in Constantinople. The monks of the monastery at Snagov took pity and buried his remains on the monastery ground. Another legend has it that Vlad and his wife were trapped at Castle Poenari when the invading forces arrived. Vlad's wife threw herself off the side into the river far below. Vlad supposedly escaped through secret tunnels. This story line opened Francis Ford Coppola's film BRAM STOKER'S DRACULA (1992).

If Vlad was buried at Snagov, the location of his grave remains a mystery.

Stoker and Vlad Dracula

Stoker came across the name Dracula in *An Account of the Principalities of Wallachia and Moldavia* (1820) by William Wilkinson, one of several sources he consulted. His original name for his vampire was Count Wamphyr, using one of the Eastern European terms for *vampire*. He liked the meaning of Dracula—"devil"—and substituted the name. From then on his vampire was called Count Dracula. Stoker also incorporated some of the Wallachian lore and history in Wilkinson's account into his novel. There is no evidence that Stoker had any detailed knowledge of Vlad's life, acts, or characteristics. Thus constitutes the connection between the historical man and the fictional vampire.

Some scholars have concluded that Dracula is based on Vlad from a remark made by the character PROFESSOR ABRAHAM VAN HELSING, in which he says that Dracula "must, indeed, have been that Voivode Dracula who won his name against the Turks . . . If it be so, then was he no common man; for in that time, and for centuries after, he was spoken of as the cleverest and most cunning, as well as the bravest of the sons of the 'land beyond the forest.'"

Despite the thin connection to Stoker, Vlad Tepes continues to be heavily promoted as the "historical Dracula." Books, both nonfiction and fiction, and films—such as Coppola's—reinforce the association, and in Romania, an entire portion of the tourist industry depends on it. Vlad Tepes—one of many provincial princes in the history of the region, and one who could not even hold onto his own power—has become the most recognizable face of the nation.

See also TRANSYLVANIA.

FURTHER READING:

Florescu, Radu R., and Raymond T. McNally. *Dracula: Prince of Many Faces: His Life and Times.* Boston: Little, Brown, 1989.

Miller, Elizabeth. *Reflections on Dracula: Ten Essays.* White Rock, B.C.: Transylvania Press, Inc., 1997.

———. *Dracula: Sense and Nonsense.* Westcliff-on-Sea, England: Desert Island Books, 2000.

McNally, Raymond T., and Radu Florescu. *Dracula: A Biography of Vlad the Impaler 1431–1476.* New York: Hawthorn Books, 1973.

Treptow, Kurt W. *Vlad III Dracula: The Life and Times of the Historical Dracula.* Oxford, U.K.: The Center for Romanian Studies, 2000.

vlokolak In West Slavic lore, a WEREWOLF. A folktale tells about a *vlokolak* who has nine daughters, and grows weary of supporting them all. He goes out into the forest to chop wood. His daughters come one by one, starting with the oldest, to bring him food. He throws them into a pit, kills them, and roasts their heads.

The youngest—and most beautiful—daughter knows he is a werewolf. She is the last to arrive and inquires about her sisters. He leads her to the pit and tells her to undress, for she is about to die. The girl asks her father to turn around while she undresses. She seizes the moment and pushes him into the pit, but he climbs out and chases her, howling in rage. She throws her kerchief behind her and says he cannot catch her until he tears the kerchief to pieces, unravels them, spins them, weaves them, and stitches them anew. This the werewolf does in half an hour. The chase resumes. The girl casts off her skirt, dress, vest, and blouse, and the werewolf does the same to them as he did to the kerchief. Finally, the girl hides herself in a small haystack. The werewolf tears all the haystacks up but cannot find his daughter. He goes away howling in a furious rage.

Three days later, a king comes along, hunting in the forest. His dog finds the girl, and the king marries her. Her one condition is that no beggar ever be allowed to spend the night in their castle. They have two sons and are very happy.

Several years later, the werewolf comes to the castle disguised as a beggar and convinces the staff to let him inside to sleep under a broom. In the middle of the night, he slits the throats of the sons with his daughter's knife, which he lays upon them. He escapes.

The king drives away his wife, but lets her bind the necks of his sons. She wanders until she finds a hermit, who directs her to a lizard who has a curative herb in its mouth. With this she restores the dead sons to life. The king takes her back.

Once again the werewolf comes to the castle and tries to get in for the night. He is recognized by the servants and taken before the king. The werewolf confesses to slaying the sons. The king has the werewolf bound to a wagon and pushed over a cliff into the sea. The werewolf breaks his neck and perishes. The king, his wife, and sons live happily ever after.

FURTHER READING:
Perkowski, Jan L. *The Darkling: A Treatise on Slavic Vampirism.* Columbus, Ohio: Slavica Publishers, 1989.

vlokoslak A Serbian VAMPIRE. The *vlokoslak* appears as a person wearing white clothes, but sometimes assumes the shape of horses and sheep. (See SHAPE-SHIFTING.) It can be active both day and night. The *vlokoslak* eats its victims as well as drinks their BLOOD. It can be killed by cutting off its toes, or by driving a nail through its neck.

The term *vlokoslak* is also applied to WEREWOLVES. They like to hold gatherings in winter. They meet in the woods and hang their wolfskins on trees. If anyone finds the skins and burns them, the werewolves will be disenchanted.

Volsunga Saga See SHAPE-SHIFTING.

vresket Croatian term for the peculiar sound made by VAMPIRE CORPSES. The *vresket* apparently is the noise made by corpses when they are exhumed and perhaps prodded or poked. According to lore, only vampire corpses make this sound. The noises most likely are made by gases escaping the corpse, and thus account for the sounds described in various cases as moaning, shrieking, and groaning, especially when a corpse is impaled.

See also LASTOVO ISLAND VAMPIRES; ARNOD PAOLE.

vukodlak A Serbo-Croatian term for a type of VAMPIRE. The name *vukodlak* means "wolf's hair," and most often refers to a male. The *vukodlak* has been associated with WEREWOLVES in the English sense of the word, which some scholars say is not accurate.

In its earliest form, the *vukodlak* was associated with eclipses as an eater of the sun and MOON (see VARCOLAC). The earliest description of a *vukodlak* dates to a Serbian account of 1262, which states, "the pursuers of the clouds were called *vukodlaci* by the peasants. If the moon or the sun is extinguished, they say that the *vukodlaci* have devoured the moon or the sun. But all this is fables and lies."

Bulgarian and Macedonian folklore texts describe the *vukodlak* as an imaginary evil spirit incarnated from the CORPSE of a murdered person. In other lore, a child born feet first or with teeth will become a *vukodlak*. A man can become a *vukodlak* by being transformed by a sorcerer through magical power, especially when he is on his way to his wedding. If so transformed, he will run about the village in the form of a wolf, casting plaintive looks about for help, but he will remain in wolf form until the spell is undone by the same sorcerer who cast it.

The *vukodlak* sleeps in the grave with its EYE open. Its hair and nails grow to excessive lengths. When the moon is full, it leaves the grave and attacks men to drink their BLOOD.

In other lore, the *vukodlak* is created 40 days after death by the entry into the corpse by a demonic spirit, which reanimates the body. When it rises up out of the grave in human form, its body is covered with thick hair. The *vukodlak* leaves its grave to drink human blood and to have sexual relations with his former wife or girlfriends, or young widows. If a child is born of such a union, he is said to have no bones and a body like jelly.

In Serbian lore, the *vukodlak* is most active in the winter, between Christmas and Spasovdan, a moveable feast about 40 days after Easter.

FURTHER READING:

Fine, John V. A., Jr. "In Defense of Vampires," in *The Vampire: A Casebook,* Alan Dundes, ed. Madison: University of Wisconsin Press, 1998.

Machal, Jan. "Slavic Mythology," in *The Vampire of the Slavs,* Jan L. Perkowski, ed. Cambridge, Mass.: Slavica Publishers, 1976.

Perkowski, Jan L. *The Darkling: A Treatise on Slavic Vampirism.* Columbus, Ohio: Slavica Publishers, 1989.

Summers, Montague. *The Vampire in Europe.* New York: E. P. Dutton, 1929.

vyrkolaka   Greek VAMPIRE. The term *vyrkolakoi* (plural) refers to REVENANTS in general, persons whose souls are lost and thus are consigned to ghostly wanderings. The *vyrkolaka* that is a true vampire is a person whose body and soul are taken over by a demon between death and burial, so that the CORPSE becomes reanimated, leaves the grave, and drinks the BLOOD of its own kin by going up their noses, causing a wasting away of health even to death.

The *vyrkolaka* also preys upon other humans and animals for their blood and tears out their livers. It sleeps in its grave with its EYES open, and especially likes to wander about when the MOON is shining brightly. The *vyrkolaka* can assume any guise, human, or animal.

In folklore beliefs, there are numerous factors that create *vyrkolakoi*. These factors fall into two general classes, unabsolved sin and ritual neglect of the dead by the living. There is overlap among the factors that create lost souls (wandering but harmless revenants) and dangerous vampires:

- persons who are not given proper burials
- violent and sudden death, especially drowning and unavenged murder
- people who commit SUICIDE
- children conceived or born on a great church festival
- stillborn children
- those who die under a curse, especially that of a parent or a curse called on one's self
- excommunicated persons
- those who die unbaptized or apostate
- immoral behavior, especially lying and drunkenness
- the practice of sorcery and evil
- those who have eaten sheep killed by wolves
- those whose bodies are passed over by animals, especially CATS
- those whose bodies were left unguarded between death and burial
- thieves, especially those who steal from schools and churches

"Vampire Hermit," from The Vampire Tarot *by Robert Michael Place.* (Courtesy Robert Michael Place)

In some areas of Greece, the lack of corruption of a corpse is not immediately taken as a sign of vampirism, for it is believed that a vampire reveals itself 40 days after death, or not at all. A telltale sign of its presence is a grave with a HOLE (see FINDING VAMPIRES).

To destroy a *vyrkolaka,* the corpse is exorcized by a priest sometime between SATURDAY evening and Sunday morning, when the vampire must stay in its grave. The priest performs the exorcism at the gravesite while boiling oil and vinegar are poured into the hole. These measures extinguish the demonic-possessed soul, which goes into neither heaven nor hell, but into oblivion. But if the vampire trouble persists, the exorcism is repeated. Or, the body is dug up again and cut into pieces.

A *vyrkolaka* case told in oral lore in the village of Ambeli involved a dead woman whose corpse was inadvertently passed over by a child. The child was immediately handed back over, but the damage could not be undone. The woman became a *vyrkolaka* and terrorized her husband and children. A hole was discovered at her grave. The exorcism had to be performed on three Saturdays before peace was established.

The Greek Island of Santorini was for centuries reputed as a place rife with *vyrkolakoi*. The reputation might be due to the island's volcanic soil, which preserves the dead perhaps too well. It might also be due to the Greek tradition of removing suspected vampire corpses to distant islands in the belief that vampires could not travel over water. Santorini, one of the southernmost of the Greek Cyclades Islands and a popular vacation place, supposedly became a favorite dumping ground. MONTAGUE SUMMERS claimed that around 1906 he was shown a suspected vampire cadaver being prepared for exorcism in a Santorini church.

The term *vyrkolaka* is also applied to WEREWOLVES, people who fall into cataleptic trances, assume the form of wolves and go out on bloodlust hunts. After returning to human form, the werewolf is exhausted. After death, it becomes a vampire. The *vyrkolaka* can assume dog or hyena form as well as wolf. It frequents battlefields where it sucks the dying breaths out of fallen soldiers.

People who are dark and savage-looking or have misshapen limbs are called *vyrkolaka*, and are believed to have the power to run in wolf form.

FURTHER READING:
Baring-Gould, Sabine. *The Book of Werewolves*. London: Smith, Elder & Co., 1865.
Du Boulay, Juliette. "The Greek Vampire: A Study of Cyclic Symbolism in Marriage and Death," in *The Vampire: A Casebook*, Alan Dundes, ed. Madison: University of Wisconsin Press, 1998.
Summers, Montague. *The Vampire in Europe*. New York: E. P. Dutton, 1929.

Walton Family Cemetery Connecticut burial grounds showing evidence of the New England vampire superstitions related to consumption deaths.

In 1990 a gravel pit excavation in the town of Griswold, Connecticut, exposed two human skulls from an old abandoned family CEMETERY. A subsequent archaeological investigation revealed that 29 persons had been buried there. The six adult males, eight adult females, and 15 children and infants were members of the Walton family.

The original Waltons, Nathaniel and Margaret, had moved from Boston to Griswold in 1690 to establish a farm. Their family cemetery, a piece of land measuring only about 50 by 60 feet, was established in 1757 on land purchased from a neighbor. It was active until the early 1800s, when the family moved to Ohio. The cemetery was used by another, unidentified family until about 1830, when it was abandoned. The uninscribed fieldstone markers deteriorated and vanished.

Some of the children buried together may have died in measles or smallpox epidemics, which swept the area in 1759 and 1790, respectively.

Only one set of remains, the complete skeleton of an adult male, showed signs of having died of tuberculosis. The lid of his COFFIN was inscribed in tacks "JB-55," probably his initials and his age at death. He was buried sometime between 1800 and 1840, and had been exhumed after burial. His skull and femora were found in a "skull and crossbones" position on top of his ribs and vertebrae, which were in disarray. Researchers hypothesized that sev-

eral years after JB's death, another family member contracted tuberculosis, and JB's body was disinterred. The soft tissue had probably decomposed, however, and there were no heart and liver to burn, the traditional remedy. As an alternative, JB's bones were purposefully arranged, perhaps in an effort to prevent him from leaving the grave and thus stopping the progress of the disease.

Similarly, decapitation or placing a skull underneath an arm were common postmortem measures in Europe agains vampirism.

See also NEW ENGLAND VAMPIRES.

FURTHER READING:
Bell, Michael E. *Food for the Dead: On the Trail of New England's Vampires*. New York: Carroll & Graf, 2001.
Sledzik, Paul S. and Nicholas Ballantoni. "Bioarchaeological and Biocultural Evidence for the New England Vampire Folk Belief," from *The American Journal of Physical Anthropology*, no. 94, 1994. Available online at the National Museum of Health and Medicine Web site. URL:http://nmhm.washingtondc.museum/collections/anatomical/articles/vampire.html. Downloaded on August 16, 2003.

Wamphyri VAMPIRE lords created by author BRIAN LUMLEY in his 13-volume series of Necroscope novels. The Wamphyri live in a parallel universe on a divided world called Sunside/Starside.

A prolific author, Lumley developed a complex reality for his vampires and the humans who hunt them, including Harry Keogh, the man known as the Necroscope, because of his ability to talk directly to the dead. In creating the Wamphyri, Lumley did not try to improve on BRAM STOKER's COUNT DRACULA, as he noted in an interview:

Given all the flowery passages, given all the waffle, take them away from the basic idea of *Dracula* and you've got a story which is hard to beat. I didn't set out to beat it when I wrote *Necroscope* [the first in the Wamphyri series]. I felt that Stoker had a good idea here, he made his characters very, very, real indeed, and I wanted my characters in *Necroscope* to be real with unreal powers and yet come across with believability.

Lumley took the vampire from its European romantic roots, made it strong and attractive despite its physical ugliness and provided it with a reason for existence. According to Lumley:

The way I saw the Wamphyri was that vampirism had started on a parallel world. By means of a gate, certain of them had come through to Earth and started vampirism—this could be 2,000, 3,000 years ago.

On the other side of the gate they are all-powerful. They come from a world which is split by the Barrier Mountains: on one side is Starside, their night side, and the other, Sunside. When the sun goes down, the vampires come across the mountains. They can't during sun-up because it would have the same effect our sun has on them—a chemical effect. The fact is that some people, albinos for example, have a hard time in sunlight. But, there is that in the vampire make-up which deepens the effect: they will literally evaporate. Their fats steam away, they become less coherent, they fall to pieces, they turn black, they char. Anybody who doubts that sort of effect only has to hold a magnifying glass over a piece of paper in the sunlight and see what happens. That effect on the Wamphyri is magnified.

Lumley discloses the existence of the parallel world in book three of the Necroscope series, *The Source*, and builds hints toward the central revelation. The GYPSY races of our world are, for instance, forever traveling because of survival instincts their ancestors picked up in the home world of the Wamphyri:

There, a day is a week in our terms: the night lasts three days. It restricts the Wamphyri's moves: they can't go into Sunside for four of our days at a stretch, which gives the Sunsider humans plenty of time to move on. They daren't stay in one spot too long, lest the vampires find them too easily come nightfall. That's why the humans have become Travellers.

The Wamphyri have little in common with Count Dracula. They share a feudal instinct, but their powers appear to be greater than those exhibited by Bram Stoker's count, and their capacity for evil is more evident:

A human being is to a vampire as a coconut is to a South Sea islander, useful in many ways: on their world, they refashion people to provide their fliers [their main mode of transport], refashion men for their warriors; in their aeries on Starside, the stairways are made of bone or cartilage. The awnings which carry their sigils are flayed skin, vampirized first to give it strength.

But on earth the Wamphyri face challenges:

The vampires, used to these long nights in which they were masters, have now come to a world where the nights are so much shorter. Also, there are far more human beings than there were Travellers, and we're years more advanced. We have atomic weapons, shot guns, silver and sciences that the Travellers lost after a holocaust in their world. So the vampire is very much more susceptible to death in this world.

Apart from varying levels of strength and evil, Lumley's creatures are still familiar vampire monsters:

I don't see my vampires as being different from the ones we all know. I see mine as having a reason for being which they didn't have before. We've always known what they do, but there's been no reason for these damn things. And, one thing that's always puzzled me: we've known there were quite a few of these guys, so why hasn't the plague proliferated, spread abroad? I've tried to supply an answer; because anonymity guarantees longevity, they can't become too apparent. Unlike on Starside, here on Earth people are going to come looking for them during the daylight.

Lumley's vampire is seductive to both men and women who want immortality, until they learn the dreadful price—more dreadful than fear of losing one's soul or of having to dig out of a COFFIN.

We all wish we had these powers. We all know what we would do and what we would be. Alas, we're wrong. That's us thinking as human beings. But once we become a vampire, he's the one that takes over.

My Wamphyri are two creatures: the human and the vampire within him. While the human thinks it's guiding its own destiny, the vampire is really guiding its destiny and causing it to do the things it wants. The horror of it is that we aren't in control.

The lack of control and the feelings of what it is like to be a vampire are explored to only a small extent in Stoker's novel. Lumley narrates large portions of the novels through the vampires' EYES, showing the slow process of vampiric metamorphosis.

Mankind has already worked out its greatest fears. We already know the things which frighten us. We are frightened of diseases: like vampirism and lycanthropy. These are serious, hurting, diseases. We also hate having something in us which has a grip on us. We can't bear to think that somebody else is in control.

We like something of the old tradition in our books because they are the basic fears we've all held ever since the caveman woke up in the morning and gave a sigh of relief that nothing had ventured into his cave the night before.

The "vampire within" is perhaps the greatest monster of all. Keogh is plagued by such an invasion, and in the end, becomes a Wamphyri himself. The prey bests the hunter. The vampire species survives.

FURTHER READING:
Gilbert, John, "Wamphyri: Vampires for Modern Times," in *The Complete Vampire Companion* by Rosemary Ellen Guiley with J. B. Macabre. New York: Macmillan, 1994.
Lumley, Brian, and Stanley Wiater, eds. *The Brian Lumley Companion.* New York: TOR Books, 2002.

Washington, D.C., Vampires   According to lore, VAMPIRES once prowled America's capital, Washington, D.C. The fantastical stories—probably an early kind of urban legend—circulated several years after publication of BRAM STOKER's novel *DRACULA* in 1897.

One story tells about a girl from a well-respected family who fell in love with a European prince in the 1850s. She met him at an embassy party and was immediately entranced by his stunning good looks and his piercing black eyes. He romanced her and beguiled her and her family. One night under a full MOON, he secretly drained her BLOOD, and her pale CORPSE was found the next morning, in a clearing a few miles from her home. Her long hair hid the vampire's fang marks on her neck. The prince mysteriously disappeared.

The girl was buried in a white lace dress that was to have been her wedding gown. She was laid to rest in her family vault, only to rise herself as a vampire. People began to whisper about a white-clad girl or woman whose face was hideously distorted by wolflike fangs.

In 1923 a writer for the *Washington Post,* Gorman Hendricks, published a long account of the vampire girl's alleged terrorizing. A woodcutter, en route home one night, saw her specter float through the sealed vault door. He told others, but no one believed him. And then one day, he was found dead, drained of blood, with fang marks on his neck.

The woodcutter's death started a panic, and people began protecting their homes and themselves with bunches of GARLIC. Armed guards were posted at the girl's burial vault.

She did not appear again until the eve of St. George, during a thunderstorm. The guards heard the sound of squeaking hinges and saw a ghostly figure glide out and disappear into the nearby woods. The guards fled.

The next morning, a group of citizens inspected the vault and found that a huge stone slab that had been placed over the coffin had been moved. The girl was in the COFFIN, her bloodred lips parted by wolflike fangs. The terrified people had the presence of mind to replace the slab, but they did nothing else—certainly nothing "traditional," such as driving a STAKE through her heart.

The vampire specter continued to haunt the area. One male witness described it as floating through trees near the vault, emitting a maniacal laugh, and smelling like a charnel house. He died a week later.

Meanwhile, the girl's distressed family moved away. No one would buy their house, and it and the burial vault fell into ruin. The hauntings apparently ended with Hendricks's story.

FURTHER READING:
Guiley, Rosemary Ellen, with J. B. Macabre. *The Complete Vampire Companion.* New York: Macmillan, 1994.

water   In folklore, the element that defeats the forces of evil. Witches, ghosts, and evil spirits cannot cross running water, a symbol of life.

Water has ancient associations with the pure and holy and is regarded to have cleansing and healing powers. In European lore, VAMPIRES can be destroyed by luring them to running water, for if they enter it, they will drown.

Holy water blessed by a priest is used in procedures for destroying vampires in their graves and cleansing the grave sites. When sprinkled around houses, it repels evil forces and prevents them from entering.

In WEREWOLF lore, bathing in running water enables a werewolf to change back into human form. Some confessed werewolves said they rolled in dewy grass. Since some used magical OINTMENTS with hallucinogenic properties to accomplish their SHAPE-SHIFTING, the bathing may have had the practical effect of removing the ointment and thus its effects.

In *DRACULA* (1897) by BRAM STOKER, vampires cannot cross running water except at slack or flood tides.

wawkalak   In White Russian lore, a WEREWOLF cursed by the devil. The *wawkalak* is a man who incurs the wrath of the devil and is punished by being transformed into a wolf and sent among his relations. The *wawkalak* is recognized by his family, who feeds him and takes care of him. He has a gentle disposition and wreaks no havoc and even displays his affection by licking the hands of his benefactors. But the *wawkalak* is doomed to be driven from village to village by his own need for change.

Stories of the *wawkalak* illustrate the dangers of angering the devil.

weredogs   Persons who transform themselves into dogs. This SHAPE-SHIFTING ability is called *"kuanthropy"* or *"cyanthropy,"* which derives from *cyanthrope,* or *man-dog.*

A Native American legend tells about weredogs who became tribal ancestors. According to the story, an Indian took up residence along the shores of the Great Bear Lake. He had a female dog who was pregnant. It gave birth to eight puppies. Whenever the Indian man went out to fish, he tied up the puppies in his tent to prevent them from straying. Upon his return, he would hear childish laughter and talking coming from his tent, but when he entered it, he would find only the puppies.

One day he pretended to go away to fish, but hid near the tent. When he heard the children's voices, he rushed into the tent and found beautiful children there laughing and playing. They had dog-skins by their sides.

He took the dog-skins and threw them on the fire. The children were stuck in their human form, and they became the ancestors of the "dog-rib nation."

See also BURNING.

FURTHER READING:
Baring-Gould, Sabine. *The Book of Were-Wolves*. London: Smith, Elder & Co., 1865.

werewolf   A human being who turns into a wolf and later resumes human form. During their episodes as wolves, werewolves savagely attack, kill, and devour animals and people. The word "werewolf," or "man-wolf," was first recorded in Old English the 11th century in the Ecclesiastical Ordinances of King Cnut (1017–1037). It was sometimes used to refer to outlaws.

Werewolf lore has existed since antiquity. Early humans may have established strong bonds with wolves—from whom dogs evolved—and there is evidence of various animal cults, in which humans acquired animal powers by donning their skins. The *BERSERKIR* and *EIGI EINHAMIR* are examples of later animal cults. Early humans may also have practiced cannibalism. In the earliest religions, gods and goddesses had animal attributes. In ancient Egypt, the images of gods were as were-animals: human bodies with animal heads.

Legends and myths of human transformation into wolves—one of the most feared of all animals—are thousands of years old. The wolf is prominent in Greek stories and in Norse, Scandinavian, Icelandic, and Teutonic lore (see SHAPE-SHIFTING). In some legends, the werewolf is a person born under that curse, who cannot prevent himself from his hellish metamorphosis, which happens on nights of the full MOON. The person, usually a man, but also a woman or a child, acquires the shape of a wolf and all its attributes, and roams about the countryside attacking and eating victims. In other tales, the werewolf is a witch who accomplishes the transformation by magical means or with the aid of DEMONS.

In most tales, the werewolf is wounded, and the wound sympathetically carries over to the human form and reveals the identity of the werewolf. The sympathetic wound appeared as evidence later in witch trials. (See AUVERGNE WEREWOLF; *FEAST OF TRIMALCHIO*.)

Werewolf superstitions may have some basis in lingering practices of primitive cannibalism. As others became more civilized, those who still liked to eat human flesh were increasingly ostracized and demonized.

Werewolf beliefs were particularly strong in parts of Europe where wolves were common and presented dangers. Superstitions and fears of wolves ran high in the Baltic regions (Livonia, Latvia, and Lithuania), France, Germany, Switzerland, and even parts of Spain. Plague epidemics that decimated local populations enabled wolves to flourish. As they lost natural prey to hunters, they turned to livestock, pets, and even humans, though attacks on humans are rare. France was particularly plagued with wolf terrors, the greatest of which was the BEAST OF GEVAUDAN. In England, wolves were exterminated by the 16th century, and so fear of wolves—and consequently stories of werewolves—are less common than in other parts of Europe.

Werewolf sightings and encounters continue into modern times, and mingle with reports of other mysterious creatures such as Bigfoot, *CHUPACABRAS*, DOGMEN, and the Skunk Ape, as well as with reports of UFO activity (see EXTRATERRESTRIALS). The BEAST OF BRAY ROAD has had numerous sightings and close encounters in Wisconsin.

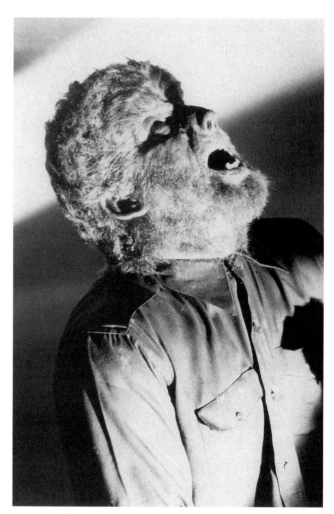

A werewolf howls at the moon (Lon Chaney Jr. in The Wolfman*) (Author's collection)*

Werewolves and Ghosts

Whether the werewolves actually live in the physical world or are part of some parallel world that occasionally and temporarily becomes accessible has been debated by researchers. Some encounters seem more like ghosts, suggesting a parallel world or dimension.

ELLIOTT O'DONNELL recorded a case of an apparent werewolf phantom, told to him by the young woman who had the experience. Jean St. Denis was staying at a small farm in Merionethshire, Wales. She would go to the railway station platform to do her sketching. One evening at dusk as she was packing up her equipment, she noticed an odd and indistinct figure sitting on a truck nearby. The figure seemed to be staring at her. At the same time, she became acutely aware that the station was deserted, save for her and the figure, whom she took to be a man. She asked it the time, but it gave no response. St. Denis quickly finished packing and departed. She had to walk to the farm alone in the growing darkness.

Along the way, she realized she was being followed. Looking over her shoulder, she could see the strange figure behind her. With the loneliest and darkest stretch of road ahead of her, she decided to confront it. She was horrified to see that her pursuer was part man and part wolf. It had a naked, gray, man-like body and a hideous wolf's head with blazing eyes. When she turned her flashlight into its face, it pulled back and put its paw-like hands in front of its eyes. The figure then faded completely away, like a ghost.

O'Donnell relates another werewolf "ghost" case from the Valley of the Doones in Exmoor. A woman walking home alone late one night suddenly saw in front of her a tall gray man with a wolf's head, stalking a terrified rabbit that was frozen still. Just as the werewolf seemed ready to spring, a stag burst out of the brush and startled it, and the figure abruptly vanished.

More recently, the British parapsychologist Robin Furman reported a phantom werewolf encounter in his home in Grimsby, England. When his daughter complained of a strange, apparitional figure watching her from her bedroom door, Furman switched rooms with her. Once in the room, he felt that he was not alone, and then noticed the figure of a tall wolf-headed man looking in through the doorway. The form faded and then disappeared. Furman felt no hostility or evilness from the figure, but thought that it was more looking at him out of curiosity. The figure was never seen again.

Phantom werewolves angrily looking for their missing bones have been reported, as in the HEBRIDES WEREWOLF and MERIONETHSHIRE WEREWOLF cases. A demonic phantom werewolf manifested in conjunction with the discovery of the stone HEXHAM HEADS in Northumberland, England in 1972.

Werewolves and Witchcraft

In the 15th and 16th centuries, the Inquisition was at its peak. Werewolves, like witches, were seen as servants of the devil, and trials of accused witch werewolves increased.

Werewolf (David Naughton) in An American Werewolf in London *(Author's collection)*

The cases were characterized by murder and cannibalism. In Europe people accused of shape-shifting and other acts of witchcraft were burned. In the Pyrenees alone, some 200 men and women "werewolves" were sent to their deaths.

Demonologists accepted werewolves, but most believed them to be delusional with the aid of the devil, or simply delusional. King James I of England (King James VI of Scotland) wrote in his *Demonology* (1597) that werewolves, or "ManWoolfes," were not people under the influence of the devil, but suffered from delusions and melancholia, and imitated wolf behavior.

Some accused werewolves clearly were mentally unstable and deranged people (see GRENIER, JEAN and ROULET, JACQUES). In 1541, a deranged farmer in Pavia who murdered several persons was arrested as a werewolf. One of his claims upheld a popular superstition, that werewolves have their wolf pelts on the inside of their human skins. To verify this, the authorities cut off all his limbs. They found no wolf pelt, of course. They accused, now innocent, unfortunately died several days later.

In many cultures, witches, sorcerers and other magically empowered individuals are able to shift into the forms of wolves or other animals. As werewolves or were-animals, they are able to move with great speed, become invisible, and use supernatural powers to attack and kill enemies. (See SKINWALKERS.)

Types of Werewolves

In lore there are two general types of werewolves: involuntary and voluntary.

The involuntary werewolf is a person cursed, perhaps because of a sin. The curse might last a few years or a lifetime. For example, an Armenian folk belief holds that a

Werewolf monster in The Howling *(Author's collection)*

sinful woman is condemned to be a werewolf for seven years. A demon appears to her and commands her to don a wolf skin. When she does so, she assumes the nature of a wolf, devouring her children and then strangers, wandering about at night to wreak havoc and returning to human form in the morning.

The voluntary werewolf is a person who likes to eat human flesh and acquires magical skills that enable transformation into wolf form at will. The transformation is accomplished in various ways:

- By completely disrobing
- By donning a GIRDLE or belt made of wolf skin or human skin
- By rubbing the body with magical OINTMENT
- By drinking rain water out of a wolf's FOOTPRINTS
- By reciting magical incantations
- By being aided by the devil or his demons

In MONTAGUE SUMMER's collection of werewolf lore in the British Isles, a self-described werewolf named Calcevayra related that he did his transformations on nights of the full moon. He would go to a distant location, strip off all his clothes and hide them beneath a rock or in a thornbush, and then roll to and fro in the sand until he "rose up in the form of a wolf, raging with a wolf's fierce appetites." Calcevayra also said that wolves always run with their mouths open because it helps their speed. If their jaws are closed, they cannot easily unclench their teeth.

Characteristics of both types the werewolf are

- An insatiable desire for the raw flesh and BLOOD of animals and humans
- Insatiable sexual lusts
- Wolfish behavior, such as howling and running about on all fours
- Savage attacks on animals and people
- Exhaustion after werewolf episodes end

In addition, there are lycanthropes, sufferers of LYCANTHROPY, which medicine recognizes as a mental and nervous disorder. Lycanthropes exhibit the same characteristics as the werewolves of lore.

Werewolves and Vampires
In Slavic lore, the werewolf is closely related to the vampire; the name of the Serbo-Croatian *VUKODLAK* vampire means "wolf's hair." *VLOKOSLAK*, a Serbian term, and *VYRKOLAKA*, a Greek term, are among the names that are applied to either a vampire or a werewolf. Many European superstitions about vampires hold that they can shape-shift into various animal forms besides wolves.

In Greek and Serbian lore, werewolves are doomed to become vampires after death.

See also FORTUNE, DION; MAGNUS, OLAUS.

FURTHER READING:
Baring-Gould, Sabine. *The Book of Werewolves*. London: Smith, Elder & Co., 1865.
Downes, Jonathan, and Richard Freeman. "Shug Monkeys and Werewolves: The Search for Dog-Headed Men," in *Fortean Studies Vol. 5*, Steve Moore, ed. London: John Brown Publishing, 1998.
Noll, Richard. *Vampires, Werewolves and Demons*. New York: Brunner/Mazel, 1992.
O'Donnell, Elliott. *Great Ghost Stories*. London: Foulsham & Co., 1983.
Otten, Charlotte F., ed. *A Lycanthropy Reader: Werewolves in Western Culture*. New York: Dorset Press, 1989.
Sidky, H. *Witchcraft, Lycanthropy, Drugs and Disease: An Anthropological Study of the European Witch-Hunts*. New York: Peter Lang, 1997.
Spence, Lewis. *Legends and Romances of Brittany*. Mineola, N.Y.: Dover Publications, 1997.
Summers, Montague. *The Werewolf*. New York: Bell Publishing, 1966.

Werewolf, The (1913)   First film about a WEREWOLF, produced by Bison Films of Canada. *The Werewolf*, a silent black-and-white film, features a Navajo Witch Woman who transforms her daughter into a wolf to attack and kill invading white settlers. The transformation depicts an actual wolf.

Werewolf of Angers   See ROULET, JACQUES.

Werewolf of London, The (1935)   First major and full-length WEREWOLF film, directed by Stuart Walker. Dr. Wilfred Glendon (Henry Hull) is an English botanist who goes to Tibet to search for the *Marifasa lupina,* or moon poppy, a rare flower that exists only in Tibet and blooms in the light of the MOON. Glendon is successful, but he is bitten by a strange creature. Back in London, he discovers to his horror that he transforms into a werewolf during the next full moon. He goes out on a rampage and kills a woman.

Glendon is visited by a mysterious Asian man, Yogami (Warner Oland), who explains to Glendon what has happened to him: He was bitten by a werewolf and is doomed himself to become a werewolf every full moon. There is only one known antidote—the flower that Glendon found in Tibet.

Glendon is powerless against his curse, despite his best efforts. London falls under savage attack. But there now seem to be *two* werewolves preying upon the city. The second werewolf turns out to be Yogami, who wants the cure in Glendon's possession. The two fight, and Yogami is killed.

Glenton tries to take the antidote, but instead attacks his own wife (Valerie Hobson). The police arrive and fatally shoot him. As Glendon dies, he changes back into his human form.

The werewolf makeup for Hull is minimal compared to the heavy, hairy makeup used for LON CHANEY JR. in *THE WOLF MAN* (1941).

Werewolf of Paris, The (1933)   Novel by Guy Endore, based on the true and grisly story of SARGEANT FRANÇOIS BERTRAND, a French soldier who in 1848 and 1849 dug up bodies buried at Père-Lachaise Cemetery in Paris, mutilated them and even ate parts of them.

The Werewolf of Paris became the basis of HAMMER FILMS' *The Curse of the Werewolf* (1961), starring Oliver Reed.

Werewolf: The Apocalypse   See GAMES.

Westenra, Lucy   See *DRACULA.*

Weyland, Edward   Fictional VAMPIRE created by author SUZY MCKEE CHARNAS. Edward Weyland is a solitary vampire as a species of one who has no inkling of his origins. An anthropologist by profession, he debuts in Charnas's novel *The Vampire Tapestry* (1980). Weyland is not and never was human. He has survived for thousands of years by withdrawing into suspended animation, the "long sleep," whenever life in the current place and time becomes too hazardous. Throughout the novel Weyland is referred to, and refers to himself, as an animal—a lynx, a tiger, a hawk. In the opening episode, "The Ancient Mind at Work," Weyland delivers a lecture in which he explores how nature would design a vampire, toying with his audience by detailing his own characteristics as the perfect predator. He has no longings about what it was like to be mortal, has no love of mortals, and has no lust for human bodies. Human beings are simply a source of food.

Charnas's stated objective in writing the story was to deromanticize the vampire, to present the nonsupernatural vampire as a superbly adapted beast of prey, equal or superior to humans in intelligence, but with "the inner emotional life of the average house cat."

Weyland is the object of sexual fascination. Female readers consider him as attractive as certain female characters within the novel do, despite Weyland's own contempt for pop culture vampires who "mix up dinner with sex" and his scornful remark, "Would you mate with livestock?" He does not engage in sex, though, to maintain his human facade. In one case, he shares genuine communion in an erotic encounter with the psychologist Floria Landauer, who discovers his secret. But Weyland's sexual appeal is understated. According to critic Margaret L. Carter, central to Charnas's strategy in making Weyland attractive is the way she contrasts his predation to the far worse things people do to one another. Weyland seldom kills, except when driven to the act in self-defense. Most of his victims are none the worse for the small amount of BLOOD he takes. In contrast to the destructive ambitions of human predators, Weyland says, "I wish only to satisfy my appetite in peace." Landauer, the psychologist, reflects on the contrast between Weyland and some of her human patients, who have done far more damage to their fellow beings.

Charnas portrays the vampire as vulnerable, helpless and the object of persecution. In the novel's second episode, "The Land of Lost Content," Weyland is shot by a would-be vampire killer. Near death, he becomes the prisoner of an opportunistic New Yorker who cooperates with a fanatical Satanist cult leader in putting the vampire on exhibition to a select audience of paying customers. The cultist plans to use Weyland as the centerpiece in a May Eve ceremony, with the vampire's death as the climax. Confined, humiliated, and finally starved in preparation for the rite, Weyland is both less dangerous and less evil than the Satanist who wants to exploit him.

In *The Vampire Tapestry,* the vampire interacts with one person whom he treats as an exception to his general rule of considering everyone else his prey—Landauer, whom he originally plans to use as a tool for keeping his professorship, but to whom he eventually reveals his true nature. Part of the appeal of Weyland's vulnerability is connected with his (at first reluctant) act of reaching out to a human being. Against his will, he finds that the more he reveals himself to Landauer, the more real she becomes to him, and is no longer simply a potential food source. When she begins to know him, she perceives that "beneath your various facades your true self . . . wants, needs to be honored as real and valuable through acceptance by another. I try to be that other." She wishes neither to destroy, use, nor reform him, but simply to understand him. The allure of the vampire as alien is the allure of the Other. The reader is fascinated with getting to know a mind that is almost human, yet not human, a mind that gives a fresh, skewed viewpoint on human life and its limitations.

In the end, Weyland sees the dangers of emotions and intimacy, and he decides to withdraw from humanity and return to one of his long slumbers. Charnas says that his story is "the tragedy of a being with human potentiality who lacks the courage to make the final step into becoming a human being—the step from relying on instinct to taking chances on trust—and whose forgotten history is a long series of such retreats, repeated again and again and again."

FURTHER READING:

Carter, Margaret L. "From Villain to Hero," in *The Complete Vampire Companion* by Rosemary Ellen Guiley with J. B. Macabre. New York: Macmillan, 1994.

Charnas, Suzy McKee. "Scarlet Ribbons." Available online. URL: http://suzymckeecharnas.com. Downloaded on December 21, 2003.

Whitby, England   Town in Yorkshire, England, where BRAM STOKER set three chapters of his novel DRACULA. Of all the settings Bram Stoker used in *Dracula*, few are more vivid and memorable than Whitby, located at the mouth of the River Esk on a bend in the coastline in northern Yorkshire, facing out to the North Sea. It is an ancient Anglo-Saxon fishing port that still retains some of the mysterious aura that appealed to Stoker in the late 19th century.

The Town

Whitby was settled in the fifth or sixth century C.E. and has a narrow harbor flanked by two high cliffs, East Cliff and West Cliff. The town is perhaps best known as a holiday destination and as a setting for *Dracula*. It has other claims to fame. Captain James Cook once worked there as a young merchant seaman. Whitby is home to the best jet in the world, mined out of the local cliffs since Roman times. Jet is a semiprecious stone of fossilized resinous driftwood, pressured between layers of shale during the Jurassic period. Queen Victoria wore it as a symbol of mourning.

The majestic ruins of Whitby Abbey sit on East Cliff. The abbey was founded by St. Hilda, who came to Whitby from Northumbria in 657. The abbey earned its place in

Allen Gittens, founder of the Vampyre Society, on the 199 steps leading to the ruins of St. Mary's Church, Whitby, England (Photo by R. E. Guiley)

church history by being chosen as the site of the synod of 664, at which the Celtic and Roman Catholic Churches agreed on the date for the observance of Easter. It was destroyed by the Danes in 867 and lay in ruins until the Normans arrived and built a monastery there. The place prospered until dissolved by Henry VIII in 1539. It fell into disrepair, and in World War I was damaged by shelling from a German battle cruiser. St. Hilda's ghost—a "lady in white"—inhabits the ruins, and is said to appear on stormy nights to guide seamen to safety. This story may have inspired the abbey ruins scene in *Dracula,* in which the deceased Lucy Westenra, as a woman in white in the ruins, is seen by Mina Harker.

Also on East Cliff and near the ruins is the Parish Church of St. Mary. The church was built between 1100 and 1125 by Abbot William de Percy with some of the abbey stones. The church has some interesting tombstones, which were inspected in detail by Stoker. The church has no electricity.

St. Mary's Church, Whitby, England (Photo by R. E. Guiley)

Stoker's Visit to Whitby

Stoker visited Whitby in 1890, after he had begun keeping notes for the novel that was to become *Dracula*. He was looking for a good place for a family holiday with his wife and son, and a friend had recommended Whitby. Stoker was enchanted, and he and his family spent three weeks there, enjoying the sea air. They took apartments at Mrs. Veazey's house at 6 Royal Crescent, a row of elegant houses on the West Cliff. Three ladies from Hertford, Isabel and Marjorie Smith and their friend Miss Stokes, also stayed at the crescent. It has been speculated that the two girls became models for the characters Lucy Westenra and Mina Harker, but Stoker left no clues to that in his notes.

Stoker liked the brooding ambience of Whitby, and especially the foreboding atmosphere of the abbey ruins. He made a discovery here that proved to be crucial for his novel. In the town's library, he found a book entitled *An Account of the Principalities of Wallachia and Moldavia* by William Wilkinson, published in 1820. The book mentioned the historical figure of Vlad Dracula (VLAD TEPES). Stoker had been considering naming his vampire count with the Hungarian term for vampire, Wampyr, but he changed his mind to use the more alluring Dracula, for its association with "devil." "Count Dracula" proved to be a wise choice, being far more evocative and mysterious than

"Count Wampyr." Dracula aficionados consider Whitby to be the "birthplace of Dracula."

Chapters six through eight of *Dracula* take place in Whitby. Mina arrives in Whitby to join Lucy and her family for a holiday. She is concerned about her fiancé, Jonathan Harker, who has gone to do business in TRANSYL- VANIA, and has since been ominously silent. Mina manages to enjoy outings with Lucy. They meet an old seaman, Mr. Swales (Stoker took the last name from a Whitby tombstone), who regales them with tales of the supernatural while they sit in the churchyard of the ruins of Whitby Abbey on the East Cliff. Lucy's favorite seat there, she learns, sits at the grave of a SUICIDE victim.

But their holiday is soon marred. The ill-fated Russian ship *Demeter,* bearing the caskets of earth containing the count and his vampire brides, crashes into Whitby's harbor. The captain is dead, lashed to the wheel with a crucifix clutched in his hands. A huge dog is seen leaping from the wreckage. Lucy begins to suffer restless nights. Two days later, Mr. Swales is found dead of a broken neck at the "suicide's seat" in the abbey ruins.

Lucy seems under a mysterious spell. She begins sleepwalking, and her energy diminishes. One night, Mina awakens to find Lucy gone. Looking out from the West Cliff to the ruins of Whitby Abbey and the churchyard of

The harbor of Whitby, England (Author's collection)

St. Mary's Church across the harbor, Mina spies the white-dressed figure of Lucy half-reclining on the suicide's seat. She dashes out and as she gets nearer, sees a sinister, dark figure bending over her friend. She cannot tell if it is man or beast. She cries out for Lucy, and the figure looks up. Mina sees RED EYES. Mina momentarily loses sight of them, and when she sees again, only Lucy is present. The rescue comes too late—Dracula's destruction of the beautiful Lucy has already been set in irrevocable motion.

Local lore has it that the *Demeter* incident may have been inspired by a genuine tragedy that occurred the summer that Stoker was in Whitby. A northbound ship smashed into a fishing coble, a type of boat descended from the Vikings' longship and unique to England's northeast coast. The men on the coble shouted frantically to ward off the oncoming ship, but strangely no one was on watch and the decks were deserted. The ship sailed on as though oblivious to the damage it had done to the coble. Several of the coble's crew were rescued, but two drowned.

More likely, the *Demeter* incident was more inspired by another real event: On October 24, 1885, a Russian schooner named *Dimitry* ran into the harbor in a strong gale and managed to avoid the rocks. Stoker made note of the incident in his research notes; it is thought that he changed the name to *Demeter* out of deference to the *Dim-*

itry crew. Stoker also made note of other shipwrecks told to him by local fishermen.

At night, numerous, squeaking little BATS flit about the town. It is not known if the Whitby bats gave Stoker the idea for Dracula's SHAPE-SHIFTING to bats, which are nearly absent from European vampire folklore. Stoker "extended" vampire folklore considerably to fit his story, and many of these extensions have formed their own pop culture vampire lore.

Another local phenomenon that may have been incorporated into the novel was the evening activity of pigeons: At twilight the birds perched on the window ledge of Stoker's room and tapped at their reflections in the glass. It is speculated that this became Dracula's tapping of Lucy's window with his long fingernails.

The Dracula Trail
Many of the landmarks Stoker put in his book can be visited and seen today on "The Dracula Trail," a self-guided tour for the curious available at the city's visitor's center.

The starting point, and perhaps the best vantage point on the West Cliff, is the Bram Stoker Memorial Seat. This small, Victorian-style seat was erected by the Scarborough Borough Council and the Dracula Society of London in April 1980 to commemorate the link between Stoker and

Whitby, and the inspiration he received there. The seat looks out to the East Cliff, and from it, one can see all the major landmarks in *Dracula*.

Right behind the seat is the famous Crescent, now called the East Crescent, a neighborhood built in the 1850s, and where Stoker stayed. In *Dracula*, this is where Mina and Lucy stay, and also where the count's lawyer lives, the man arranges for his importing to England his cargo of boxes of earth.

From this viewpoint, one can visualize Mina and Lucy as they admire evening sunsets. Far across the harbor is the West Cliff, with the graveyard of St. Mary's Church and the abbey ruins, where Mina spies the sinister form bending over Lucy. And, on a later occasion, Lucy and Mina see a dark figure sitting on their favorite churchyard seat, and two glowing points of light that Lucy comments are "his red eyes again."

It is possible to retrace the exact route taken by Mina on her mission of rescue that fateful night. It goes down the West Cliff, follows the river along a market pier, goes across an old wooden drawbridge, cuts through the cobblestoned and quaint Old Town, and leads to the worn 199 church stairs. In the book, Mina covers the ground in what seems like a very short time, yet the path is not that easy to negotiate, and the stairs alone require stamina.

In actuality, for Mina to see Lucy at night, even with the aid of moonlight, would have required exceptional eyesight. Mina's run from the West Cliff to the abbey would have taxed a marathon runner, let alone a Victorian lass who, in the custom of the time, did nothing strenuous. Mina would have had to scramble down the West Cliff, run along the market pier, dash across a wooden bridge, run to the base of the 199 stairs and leap up them, and finally run across a large expanse of ground before she could reach Lucy. The cobblestones would have hampered running. Even Mina's diary description of this event does not mitigate what would have been an unusual feat for a man, let alone a fragile young woman:

> The time and distance seemed endless, and my knees trembled and my breath came laboured as I toiled up the endless steps to the abbey. I must have gone fast, and yet it seemd to me as if my feet were weighted with lead, as though every joint in my body were rusty.

From the graveyard atop the East Cliff, the town of Whitby spreads out below in glory. Rows and rows of weathered tombstones jut at crazy angles. Coupled with the old church and the ancient ruins, they create a spooky atmosphere. The "suicide's seat" favored by Mina and Lucy cannot be found today, but there is no lack of interest. One can rest on seats scattered among the graves and spend hours contemplating this town frozen in time, as well as the classic tale of horror that unfolded here.

FURTHER READING:
Guiley, Rosemary Ellen, with J. B. Macabre. *The Complete Vampire Companion.* New York: Macmillan, 1994.
Miller, Elizabeth. *Reflections on Dracula: Ten Essays.* White Rock, B.C.: Transylvania Press, Inc., 1997.
————. *Dracula: Sense & Nonsense.* Westcliff-on-Sea, England: Desert Island Books, 2000.

white horse In Romanian lore, a VAMPIRE detector. White horses are unable to step over the grave of a vampire, or anything unholy. A white horse is led through a CEMETERY at night—sometimes ridden by a virginal boy—in order to locate the right grave for exhumation of the offending CORPSE.

A Romanian case from the early 20th century describes how a white horse was used to find the grave of a vampire witch who was causing illness. A Transylvanian peasant, Dimitriu Vaideanu, had married a woman in Vaguilesti and had settled there. They had many children. Then a mysterious malady began striking and killing the children. Seven died within a few months of their birth, and some of the older children died as well. The people in the village became concerned about a vampire being loose among them. They decided to take a white horse to the cemetery at night to see if it would pass over the graves of all of the wife's relatives.

The horse jumped over all the graves except for one: that of the wife's mother, Joana Marta, who in life had been renowned as a witch. When the horse reached Marta's grave, it stood still, neighing and snorting and beating the earth with its hooves.

On a night soon thereafter, Vaideanu and a son went out at night with candles to dig up the grave. According to a written description of the case:

> They were seized with horror at what they saw. There she was, sitting like a Turk, with long hair falling over her face, with her skin all red, and with finger nails frightfully long. They got together brushwood, shavings and bits of old crosses, they poured wine on her, they put in straw, and set fire to the whole Then they shoveled the earth back and went home.

These remedies evidently stopped the attacks and the deaths of the children.

See also BLACK STALLION; VAMPIRE SORCERERS AND WITCHES.

FURTHER READING:
Murgoci, Agnes. "The Vampire in Roumania," in *The Vampire: A Casebook*, Alan I. Dundes, ed. Madison: University of Wisconsin Press, 1998.

wild roses VAMPIRE deterrents. Roses and wild roses are associated with Christ, and thus in folklore have the power to repel or contain evil. Wild roses, especially their thorny stalks, are placed on a body in a COFFIN, or are bound around the coffin, or placed around the grave of a suspected vampire to prevent it from leaving the grave. In

Muslim Slavic GYPSY lore, a vampire can be killed by thrusting a sharp STAKE of wild rosewood through its belly at dusk. The stake must not show above the grave.

In DRACULA by BRAM STOKER, a long branch of wild rose must be placed in his coffin to prevent him from leaving it.

William of Newburgh (1136–1198)   Augustinian canon of Newburgh, England, who recorded local VAMPIRE or "blood-sucker" cases in his history of England.

William of Newburgh was born in Bridlington, in a remote part of Yorkshire. At an early age he entered the recently established Augustinian Priory in Newburgh, where he remained to the end of his life. He became a canon.

William is known for his work *Historia Rerum Anglicarum,* a historical and philosophical account of the history of England from 1066 to 1198. He apparently wrote this shortly before his death in 1198. William was critical of mythological approaches to history, such as executed by Geoffrey of Monmouth in his legends of King Arthur, which William dismissed as "impudent and shameless lies."

In his history, William states that he has heard so many stories of the restless dead that were he to include them all his book would be quite tedious to read. He decided to include a few cases reported to him by other clerics of undisputed repute, which he says will serve as a warning to readers—presumably about the consequences of a sinful life. He acknowledges that the facts are hard to believe that "the bodies of the dead may arise from their tombs and that vitalized by some supernatural power, they speed hither and thither, either greatly alarming or in some cases actually slaying the living, and when they return to the grave it seems to open to them of its own accord." He states that no similar cases can be found in old histories—an error probably due to his limited access to information.

William does not use the term *vampire,* which would not be introduced to the English language for several centuries. Rather, he uses the Latin term *sanguisuga,* for "bloodsuckers."

See also ALNWICK CASTLE VAMPIRE; BUCKINGHAMSHIRE VAMPIRE; MELROSE ABBEY VAMPIRE; REVENANT.

FURTHER READING:
Glut, Donald. *True Vampires of History.* New York: HC Publishers, 1971.

William Palerne   A 13th-century romance about a noble WEREWOLF. According to the tale, Alphonsus is the son of the king of Spain and the rightful heir to the throne. But his stepmother desires to see her own son inherit the throne, and she uses magical charms and OINTMENTS to transform Alphonsus into a werewolf.

The werewolf Alphonsus rescues the infant William, who is heir to the throne of Sicily, from a scheming and wicked uncle. He gives the baby to a cowherd to raise. When William becomes a boy, he tends cattle.

Years later, Alphonsus is out hunting with the emperor of Rome, and he brings him to the place where William is tending his herd. The emperor takes William home to raise with his daughter. The two fall in love, and years later they elope, disguised as white bears.

Alphonsus surreptitiously leads William and his wife to Sicily, and William regains the throne. Alphonsus returns to Spain and forces his stepmother to give him back his original form. This is accomplished with a ring tied with RED thread that he places around his neck. Alphonsus is hailed as the rightful heir, and he marries William's sister.

William of Palerne is similar to an earlier French romance, THE LAY OF THE WERE-WOLF, in that it concerns werewolves who becomes the victims of curses or act of evil, and who are noble in nature.

windigo (wendigo, wiendigo, witiko)   In North American Indian lore, a dangerous, cannibalistic GHOUL-like being. The Algonquian say the windigo roams about forests, devouring human beings. Hunters who become lost and are forced to eat human flesh become windigos. The Objibwa consider it an ice monster who can possess individuals and cause them to eat their own family members.

The windigo is a cadaverous, 15-foot-tall being in dazzling white, with a star in the middle of its forehead. It roams the forests, swamps, and prairies, using trees for snowshoes. It covers huge distances with each stride, and wherever it goes, blizzards follow. It emits a terrifying scream that paralyzes its victim. It rips out the vital organs and then plays with the skull. If necessary, it will eat one of its own kind.

The Ojibwa and Cree say that the windigo once was a normal human who has become a possessed cannibal. This possession can happen from being bitten by a windigo, by a sorcerer's curse, by magical rites, and even by dreaming of a windigo. An individual can elect to become a windigo by going into the forest and offering himself as a victim. If he is not eaten, he will be adopted by a windigo. He will become transformed into a sort of windigo, acquiring a heart of ice, a hairy body, a craving for human flesh, and demonic behavior.

The earliest recorded sightings of a windigo date to the 1600s by Jesuit missionaries in Canada. Sightings were reported in the 1700s. White settlers in Minnesota regarded the windigo of the Ojibwa as a death omen. Its appearance, in either day or night, was followed by a death in the family.

If one is attacked by a windigo, one should throw excrement at it, which will confuse it long enough to make an escape. Windigo possession can be averted by a shaman, or by killing the creature, cutting its body into pieces and BURNING them. SILVER bullets are considered to be effective.

FURTHER READING:
Mack, Carol K., and Dinah Mack. *A Field Guide to Demons, Fairies, Fallen Angels, and Other Subversive Spirits.* New York: Henry Holt/Owl Books, 1998.

winding sheet   See BURIAL CUSTOMS.

witchcraft   See LYCANTHROPY; SHAPE-SHIFTING; VAMPIRE SORCERERS AND WITCHES; WEREWOLVES.

Witchery Way   See SKINWALKERS.

Wolf (1994)   WEREWOLF film directed by Mike Nichols, starring Jack Nicholson as the werewolf and Michelle Pfeiffer as his romantic interest. *Wolf* is similar to THE WOLF MAN (1941) with some different plot elements. Will Randall (Nicholson) is an unassertive New York book editor. Driving one snowy night, he hits what seems to be a large animal. He gets out to inspect and discovers he has hit a wolf. The animal is not dead, for when he bends over, it bites him, thus infusing him with the werewolf curse. Whereas *The Wolf Man*'s Lawrence Talbot (LON CHANEY JR.) descends into utter despair over his curse, Randall is not entirely unhappy with his newfound powers. He fights another werewolf, played by James Spader, for Pfeiffer.

Wolfen, The (1978)   Novel by Whitley Streiber about a race of super WEREWOLVES. Two New York City detectives, George Wilson and Becky Neff, investigate a series of brutal murders and mysterious disappearances. They are attacked themselves, and through coincidences they discover that the crimes they are investigating have been committed by werewolves—a separate race that has been hidden from existence and discussed only in legends throughout history: the Wolfen. When the Wolfen realize the detectives are on to them, they retaliate. They are highly intelligent and superior to human beings, whom they consider weak and easy prey. They have their own rich cultural heritage. They can attack with such speed that if a person sees one, his or her throat has already been ripped to shreds. (Despite their intelligence and thought communication, however, the Wolfen commit the mistake of attacking the detectives in the beginning of the story and thus setting them on their trail.) Streiber weaves in plenty of werewolf lore and facts about the intelligence and social organization of wolves, and provides narrative from the perspective of the Wolfen. The major subplot deals with the relationship between Wilson and Neff: Neff is married but has problems at home, and Wilson—20 years her senior—is attracted to her.

The success of *The Wolfen* established Streiber as a leading horror writer. The novel was loosely adapted in a film, *Wolfen* (1981), directed by Michael Wadleigh and starring Gregory Hines, Albert Finney, Diane Venora, and Edward James Olmos. In the film, a detective and his criminal psychologist lover call in a wolf expert to track the Wolfen. The plot gets submerged in a subplot about the plight of Native American Indians.

FURTHER READING:
Streiber, Whitley. *The Wolfen.* New York: William Morrow, 1978.

Wolf Man, The (1941)   The first major WEREWOLF film, starring LON CHANEY JR. as the werewolf. Directed by George Waggoner, *The Wolf Man* was a commercial hit for Universal Pictures and established Chaney Jr. as a leading horror actor. BELA LUGOSI, whose fame was already on the decline, plays a minor role as a fortune-telling GYPSY.

The Wolf Man is especially significant for its establishment of fictional werewolf lore that became accepted as fact and was incorporated into other werewolf films and werewolf novels:

- The "sign" of the werewolf is a pentacle, and every werewolf bears this mark on his body.
- A werewolf clairvoyantly sees a pentacle in the palm of the person who will be his next victim.
- Wearing a SILVER pentacle can protect a person against a werewolf.
- Being bitten by a werewolf always dooms a person to become a werewolf.
- Transformation only takes place on nights of the full MOON.
- Werewolves wear their human clothing but not their shoes, and go about upright on their legs.
- Werewolves can only be killed with silver.

Larry Talbot (Chaney Jr.) comes home from America, where he has been studying, to Talbot Castle, his family estate in a Wales village. He is welcomed by his father, Sir John Talbot (Claude Rains). Soon after his arrival, he is attracted to Gwen Conliffe (Evelyn Ankers), the daughter of an antiques dealer. Larry meets her for the first time at the shop. She is a veritable fount of werewolf lore, talking about them as though they were common topics of conversation. She repeats a poem that is repeated several times in the film:

> Even the man who is pure at heart
> And says his prayers by night
> May become a wolf when the wolfbane blooms
> And the moon is clear and bright

Larry buys a present for his father: a walking stick that has a large silver wolf on its head. The wolf has the sign of the pentagram, and Gwen tells him it is a werewolf.

Larry takes Gwen and one of her girlfriends, Jennifer (Fay Helm) to see a Gypsy fortune-teller named Bela

Larry Talbot, the werewolf (Lon Chaney Jr.), menaces his girlfriend, Gwen Conliffe (Evelyn Ankers) in The Wolf Man (Author's collection)

(Lugosi) who has just arrived on the outskirts of town with his mother, Maleva (Maria Ouspenskaya). Bela reads for Jennifer while Larry and Gwen walk in the forest. Bela sees the pentagram on her palm and tells her to leave immediately. His secret is that he is a werewolf. Jennifer flees into the forest, but Bela transforms and attacks her as a wolf. Larry beats the creature off and kills it with the walking stick, but not before he is bitten. It is too late for Jennifer—she is dead.

Larry leaves the stick at the scene. Townspeople find the shoeless body of Bela. Larry insists he killed a wolf, not a man.

Thus infected with the bite of a werewolf, Larry becomes a werewolf himself at the next full moon. He attacks and kills a man working in the graveyard one night. The townspeople mount a hunt for the creature. Larry sees the pentagram in the palm of Gwen. Panicked,

he goes to his father and begs him for help, but Sir John thinks that he is suffering only from mental delusions. He ties Larry to a chair and then goes off to watch the hunt.

Larry escapes from the chair and becomes a werewolf. He attacks Gwen, but his father beats him to death with the wolf-crowned walking stick. Gwen, Sir John, and the others watch in horror as he dies and returns to his human form.

The Wolf Man was so popular that Universal Pictures employed Chaney Jr. to reprise his role as Larry Talbot in FRANKENSTEIN MEETS THE WOLF MAN (1943); *House of Frankenstein* (1944); *House of Dracula* (1945); and ABBOTT AND COSTELLO MEET FRANKENSTEIN (1948).

Woodstock Vampire (1830)   Famous case of an alleged VAMPIRE in Vermont. The main account of the case has so many fantastic details that the story may be heavily fictionalized.

The case of the Woodstock Vampire first appeared in print in 1889 in the *Journal of American Folklore.* The account was recorded 50 years after the actual event, based on the recollections of an anonymous "old lady" who claimed to have been an eyewitness.

According to the story, a man's brother died and was buried; six months later the living brother contracted consumption. The family had the dead brother exhumed and his CORPSE examined. The heart reputedly was "undecayed, and containing liquid blood." It was cut out and the body was reburied. The heart was taken to the center of Woodstock Green, where it was burned to ASHES in an IRON pot.

This version, simple and without names, conforms to similar cases of vampire fears documented in New England in the 18th and 19th centuries, when waves of tuberculosis took the lives of many families. Another vampire case had occurred in Woodstock in 1817 (see RANSOM, FREDERICK).

In 1890 the story was printed in Woodstock's weekly newspaper, the *Vermont Standard,* but with considerable embellishment to "fill in with further details what she [the old lady] has left incomplete."

According to the newspaper's version, the Woodstock Vampire event took place in June 1830, and involved the Corwin family, which was related to Thomas Corwin, an esteemed senator from Ohio. A Corwin brother died of tuberculosis, and a second brother then fell ill. Several prominent physicians were "clearly of the opinion that this was a case of assured vampirism," and all recommended exhumation of the body. There was some slight disagreement between two of the doctors as to whether the vampire—the dead brother—had begun his vampirism of the living brother while he himself was still alive, or had become a vampire after death.

The rest of the newspaper account reads like a horror novel:

> The boiling of the pot on Woodstock Green, spoken of by the old lady, was attended by a large concourse of people. There ceremonies were conducted by the selectmen, attended by some of the prominent citizens of the village then residing on the common . . . old men of renown, sound-minded fathers among the community, discreet careful men. The old lady has forgotten to state what was done with the pot and its ghastly collection of dust after the ceremonies were over. A hole ten feet square and fifteen feet deep was dug right in the center of the park where the fire had been built, the pot with the ashes was placed in the bottom, and then on top of that was laid a block of solid granite weighing seven tons, cut out of Knox ledge. The hole was then filled up with dirt, the blood of a bullock was sprinkled on the fresh earth, and the fathers then felt that vampirism was extinguished forever in Woodstock. Eight or ten years after these events

> some curious-minded persons made excavations in the Park, if by chance anything might be found of the pot. They dug down fifteen feet, but found nothing. Rock, pot, ashes and all had disappeared. They heard a roaring noise, however, as of some great conflagration, going on in the bowels of the earth, and a smell of sulphur began to fill the cavity, whereupon, in some alarm they hurried to the surface, filled up the hole again, and went their way. It is reported that considerable disturbance took place on the surface of the ground for several days, where the hole had been dug, some rumblings and shaking of the earth, and some smoke was emitted.

Although the account is no more bizarre than many of the accounts recorded from vampire disinterments in Europe, it nonetheless stands alone among documented cases in America. In New England, a few bodies were exhumed and their hearts or other organs removed and burned for medicine. But nowhere are there accounts of the BLOOD of a sacrificed bullock, roaring noises, sulphurous fumes, and hellish disturbances. In this case, four prominent doctors favored exhumation on grounds of vampirism; in the famous case of MERCY BROWN of Rhode Island, the doctor was highly skeptical. None of the doctors mentioned in the Woodstock case left any letters, articles or papers that would support the claims made in the newspaper story.

The article states that the Corwin brother suspected of being a vampire was buried in the Nathan Cushing cemetery. None of the surviving headstones bear that name, nor do the town records show any birth or death of a Corwin. The absence of these do not disprove the case altogether— the names may be errors, or the Corwin name a pseudonym. Perhaps the true story of the "Woodstock Vampire" remains unknown.

See also NEW ENGLAND VAMPIRES.

FURTHER READING:
Bell, Michael E. *Food for the Dead: On the Trail of New England's Vampires.* New York: Carroll & Graf, 2001.

wulver   In Shetland lore, a man with a wolf's head and a body covered with short brown hair. The *wulver* lives in caves on hillsides. It is harmless and even benevolent and will not bother humans unless bothered by them. The *wulver* likes to fish and does so by sitting for long hours on rocks in deep water. Such rocks are known as the "Wulver's Stane" (Wulver's Stone). If feeling generous, the *wulver* leaves some of his catch on windowsills as a gift for humans.

See also DOGMEN; WEREWOLVES.

FURTHER READING:
Briggs, Katharine. *An Encyclopedia of Fairies.* New York: Pantheon Books, 1976.

xiang shi (*ch'iang shih*)   In Chinese demonology, a VAM-PIRE created from the *po,* one of the two souls possessed by every human. Either the *po* or the *hun,* the higher soul, can remain with the CORPSE, but only the *po* has the power to become an evil spirit in the form of the *xiang shi.* The vampire, which has RED, staring eyes and long crooked talons, lives inside the corpse and keeps the host alive by preying on other corpses or living persons. It wreaks death and destruction. According to Chinese tradition, an unburied corpse is a great danger because it invites inhabitation by the evil spirits believed to be present everywhere at all times.

The *xiang shi* story has different versions. According to one *xiang shi* folktale, four travelers arrived late one night at an inn near Shangtung. There were no rooms available, but the travelers persuaded the innkeeper to find them any space where they could sleep. They were placed out in a little shack, where, unbeknown to them, lay the unburied corpse of the innkeeper's daughter-in-law, who had died earlier in the day. Her body was laid out on a plank behind a curtain.

Three of the travelers fell asleep immediately, but the fourth could not because he had a foreboding of danger. Presently, he saw a bony hand pull the curtain aside. The corpse, green and with glowing eyes, emerged and bent over the sleeping travelers, breathing the foul breath of death upon them. They died instantly. The fourth traveler managed to pretend to be asleep and held his breath while the *xiang shi* breathed on him, thus saving his life. When the monster returned to its plank, he ran out the door. The monster heard him and gave chase.

The man hid behind a willow tree, but the *xiang shi* found him. With a shriek, it lunged at him. He fainted from terror, an act that saved his life again, for the monster missed him and sank its claws so deep into the willow tree that it could not extricate itself. The next morning, others found the corpse, now no longer animated by spirits, and the man, who was still unconscious.

Yarbro, Chelsea Quinn (1942–) Prolific author of fantasy and horror novels, and creator of the SAINT-GERMAIN vampire series. Chelsea Quinn Yarbro has written more than 70 books and more than than 60 short stories. The Saint-Germain series has reached 16 novels.

Yarbro was born on September 15, 1942, in Berkeley, California. She became interested in the occult and paranormal as a youth and has remained a "skeptical occultist" throughout life through wide-ranging study. She read BRAM STOKER's DRACULA at age 14. She attended San Francisco State College from 1960 to 1963, where she took a class in folklore and myth that rekindled her interest in the vampire archetype. She wrote a comprehensive paper comparing worldwide cross-cultural vampire myths.

After college, Yarbro worked as a demographic cartographer. From 1969 to 1982 she was married to Donald Simpson; the marriage ended in divorce.

She sold her first piece of fiction, a short story, in 1968 to *If* magazine. In 1970 she became a full-time writer and served for two years as secretary of the Science Fiction Writers Association. She continued her study of the occult and even briefly worked as a Tarot card reader and palmist.

Still interested in vampires, Yarbro considered ways to give the vampire depth and interest. She concluded that the primary purpose of BLOOD-drinking was not nourishment—since vampires do not digest and eliminate in the same manner as humans—but to achieve an intimacy of the life force. The *act* of taking the blood is what nourishes the vampire. Religious symbols, such as the CROSS, cannot control a vampire, but a vampire can be killed by traditional means in lore, such as BURNING and staking the CORPSE and severing the head. (The fictional Saint-Germain says that ". . . perhaps one of those unpleasant new bullets, anything that breaks the spine will kill me.")

When Yarbro researched the real 18th-century historical figure of the Comte de St. Germain of Europe, she knew she had the ideal vehicle. The real count was a mysterious figure, wealthy, sophisticated, charming, cultured—and rumored to have discovered the alchemical secret of immortality. He lived during the reign of Louis XV, a lavish period in which there was much interest in the occult and interaction with foreigners. Women had limited autonomy. Yarbro created the fictional Saint-Germain by combining history and fantasy.

In 1971 Yarbro tried to sell a novel about her 4,000-year-old vampire hero, the nobleman Francesco Ragoczy da San Germano, but could find no interest. The novel eventually was sold to St. Martin's Press and was published in 1978. *Hotel Transylvania*, set in France in 1743, became an enduring classic and launched a continuing series, including spin-of books for other characters in the Saint-Germain novels.

In *Hotel Transylvania*, Saint-Germain is a mysterious man in the court of Louis XV, and so is his manservant, Roger. Madelaine de Montalia makes her society debut and falls in love with the count, not knowing he is a vampire. She is destined to become his great love. She is imperiled by a coven of devil worshipers, having been promised to

Chelsea Quinn Yarbro's Hôtel Transylvania *introduces the vampire* comte de Saint-Germain. *(Author's collection)*

them by her own father in a deal. Meanwhile, the count must deal with Saint Sebastien, an enemy of his for the past 30 years and who is leader of the coven. Saint-Germain reveals to Madelaine his dark secret and his long history of many lives and many names. He pledges that though he will leave her at times, he will always return to her and will never desert her.

Other Saint-Germain books are

- *The Palace* (1978): In Florence in 1490, Saint-Germain engages in a steamy affair with Estasia, cousin to Botticelli. His enemy is the monk Savonarola, obsessed with routing out and destroying all heretics.
- *Blood Games* (1979): The count is in Rome during the reign of Nero in the first century. The Roman senator Cornelius Justus Silias, has ruthless ambitions and is sadistically torturing his wife, Atta Olivia Clemens. Olivia is rescued by Saint-Germain and becomes a vampire and one of his other great loves. He battles the senator.

- *Path of the Eclipse* (1981): In 1216 the count is in a city in China but is forced to leave the city when the prevailing political climate against foreigners make life there uncomfortable. He goes to an outpost to help defend it against Mongol barbarians. The fortress falls and he goes to Tibet and meets an amazing Buddhist child in a monastery. Going on to India, Saint-Germain becomes involved in a cult worshiping the goddess Kali.
- *Tempting Fate* (1982): In 1917 the count is guardian to a Russian war orphan and travels with him in Europe. He has encounters with a tempting duchess, a corrupting widow, and his irresistible love, Madelaina de Montalia.
- *The St. Germain Chronicles* (1983): A compilation of short stories.
- *A Flame in Byzantium* (1987): Set in 545, the story is the first in a trilogy about Olivia. She is forced to flee Rome in the wake of war. In Constantinople she is regarded with suspicion, being wealthy and unmarried. General Belisarius becomes her patron, but her position is jeopardized when he falls out of favor with Emperor Justinian.
- *Crusader's Torch* (1988): Set in 1188, the second in a trilogy about Olivia as she strives to leave Tyre and return to Rome. She becomes involved with the Knights Templar and Knights Hospitaler.
- *A Candle for D'Artagnan* (1989): Set in 1637 in France during the reigns of Louis XIII and Louis XIV, this book concludes the trilogy about the vampire Atta Olivia Clemens. Olivia falls in love with Charles D'Artagnan of the king's musketeers and uncovers a plot of treachery.
- *Out of the House of Life* (1990): In 1825 Madelaine de Montalia, now a vampire, goes to Egypt to excavate ruins at Thebes to look for the House of Life. The count relates his early life in pharaonic Egypt.
- *Better in the Dark* (1993): Set in 937 in Upper Saxony, Germany, Saint-Germain is shipwrecked and washed ashore near a keep. He is found by Ranegonda, the princess of the keep, who becomes one of his great loves.
- *Darker Jewels* (1993): Set in 1582, Saint-Germain must deal with the ravages of the bloody and violent reign of Ivan the Terrible.
- *Mansions of Darkness* (1996): The count is in Peru in 1640, trying to keep a low profile while the Church persecutes the Inca for being pagans, but the local clergy consider him to be a practitioner of witchcraft. Saint-Germain's friendship with an Inca woman places him in double jeopardy.
- *Writ in Blood* (1997): Set in 1910–12, the count is in Europe on secret diplomatic missions as war tensions mount. He seeks to bring Russia, England, and Germany into an arms agreement in an effort to prevent war.

- *Blood Roses* (1998): Set in 1345, Saint-Germain endures the ravages of the Black Plague in France. He uses ancient Egyptian healing techniques to save lives. But his own resistance to the disease raises suspicions about him and places him in danger.
- *Communion Blood* (1999): In the 17th century, the count travels from TRANSYLVANIA to Rome to help a vampire friend, Niklos, in a legal dispute over the will of Olivia Atta Clemens, one of the count's lovers. Niklos was her servant. They must avoid arousing the suspicion of the Inquisition as to their true natures.
- *Come Twilight* (2000): Action spanning 500 years begins in seventh-century Spain, where Saint-Germain saves the life of Csimenae by—against his better judgment—turning her into a vampire. She becomes evil, and over the course of time the count must deal with her. She assembles a vampire army that preys upon religious pilgrims and invading Moors.
- *Night Blooming* (2002): In the eighth century, the emperor Charlemagne engages Saint-Germain to help the monks of Tours, France, in mapping territory outside the western fallen lands of the Roman Empire. The count becomes involved with a stigmatic albino, Gynethe Mehaut.
- *Midnight Harvest* (2003): The count is living well in the 1930s in Spain, but is forced to flee when civil war appears imminent. He goes to America, where he reunites with his lover Rowena Saxon, who is thinking of asking him to make her a vampire. He is secretly pursued by Cenere, an assassin.

Yarbro's other books are science fiction, fantasy, horror, and mystery. She writes under several pseudonyms, Quinn Fawcett (a collaboration with Bill Fawcett), Terry Nelson Bonner, and Vanessa Pryor. In the late 1970s, she wrote *Messages from Michael* and *More Messages from Michael*, nonfiction books about channeled messages from the archangel Michael, based on her experiences in a group involved in channeling.

Yarbro reads an average of 40 nonfiction books to research each novel, and also interviews experts about the time periods and subjects she intends to feature. Her novels are set against historical backdrops and feature authentic lore and details of the periods. The Hotel Transylvania in the novel by the same name is a real place, built in the reign of Louis III and named after Prinz Franz Leopold Ragoczy, who stayed there from 1713 to 1717.

Yarbro lives in her hometown of Berkeley.

FURTHER READING:
Chelsea Quinn Yarbro Web site. URL: http://www.chelsea quinnyarbro.com. Accessed on January 3, 2004.
Yarbro, Chelsea Quinn. *Hotel Transylvania*. New York: St. Martin's Press, 1978.
———. *The Palace*. New York: St. Martin's Press, 1978.
———. *Blood Games*. New York: St. Martin's Press, 1979.
———. *Path of the Eclipse*. New York: St. Martin's Press, 1981.
———. *Tempting Fate*. New York: St. Martin's Press, 1982.
———. *The St. Germain Chronicles*. New York: Pocket Books, 1983.
———. *A Flame in Byzantium*. New York: TOR Books, 1987.
———. *Crusader's Torch*. New York: TOR Books, 1988.
———. *A Candle for D'Artagnan*. New York: TOR Books, 1989.
———. *Out of the House of Life*. New York: Orb/TOR Books, 1990.
———. *Better in the Dark*. New York: TOR Books, 1993.
———. *Darker Jewels*. New York: TOR Books, 1993.
———. *Mansions of Darkness*. New York: TOR Books, 1996.
———. *Writ in Blood*. New York: TOR Books, 1997.
———. *Blood Roses*. New York: TOR Books, 1998.
———. *Communion Blood*. New York: TOR Books, 1999.
———. *Night Blooming*. New York: Warner Aspect, 2002.
———. *Midnight Harvest*. New York: Warner Aspect, 2003.

Yellow Cat   GYPSY tradition called Sari Kedi, which means "Yellow Cat," about a comely vampire maiden who has the power to shape-shift into a yellow CAT and victimize young men for their BLOOD. The true origins of the Yellow Cat legend are lost, but it is reminiscent of the legends of the dangerous Lorelei and the sirens, and of the "Strange Woman" in Proverbs. Essentially, it expresses the theme of man who is powerless in the face of the eternally feminine.

Traditionally, the Yellow Cat ballad is sung without accompaniment as a semi-recitative by a maiden about 15 years old or so. Ideally, she has waist-length, raven black hair and a green cat's eye glint to her EYES. The rendering of the ballad is entertainment done for profit. It is the Gypsy girl's specialty and designed to extract as much money as possible from the audience. In the light of the fire, her eyes blaze green, and she makes people look over their shoulders in fear that the Yellow Cat is creeping up silently behind, ready to pounce in lethal strike. On moonless nights pierced by howling winds and screeching owls, it is whispered that the girl who sings the ballad is truly the Yellow Cat herself, and young men should beware.

The ballad, recorded by Englishman W. V. Herbert in his book *By-paths in the Balkans* (1906) is as follows:

> The Yellow Cat on the hilltop stood,
>   With her eyes of glittering grey.
> She longed for a drink of purple blood,
>   For the noise and joys of the fray.
> And all ye good people, remember that:
> Beware, if you dare, of the Yellow Cat.
>
> The Yellow Cat is a maiden bold,
>   A maiden fair and frail;
> Her hair has the color of burnished gold;
>   'Twas pressed to her breast in the gale.
> And all ye good people, remember that;
> Beware, if your dare, of the Yellow Cat.

The Yellow Cat can purr and kiss,
 And sing a wonderful tune.
The Yellow Cat can scratch and hiss
 And bite and strike in the moon.
And all ye good people, remember that:
 Beware, if you dare, of the Yellow Cat.

The young man saw the yellow-haired maid,
 And heard her entrancing wail.
She purred and fawned and kissed and bade
 Him come to her home in the dale.
And all ye good people, remember that:
 Beware, if you dare, of the Yellow Cat.

She chanted divinely of earthly bliss,
 And heavenly joys ere long,
With a wile and a smile and a lying kiss,
 And the call and the thrall of her song.
And all ye good people remember that:
 Beware, if you dare, of the Yellow Cat.

They found the young man, white and stark,
 As the morn dawned in gold and in rose.
What are they whispering? what talking of?
 —Hark!
 "Tis he whom the she-devil chose."
And all ye good people, remember that:
 Beware, if you dare, of the Yellow Cat.

"What has felled him, sturdy and good?"
 "What smote him, passing fair?"
"What is become of his purple blood?"
 "What blanched his nut-brown hair"
Oh, all ye good people, just think of that:
 His blood quenched the thirst of the Yellow Cat.

yenaldlooshi   See SKINWALKERS.

Yorga   See *COUNT YORGA.*

Young, Nancy (1807–1827)   Alleged VAMPIRE of Foster, Rhode Island. Nancy Young was the second of eight children and the oldest daughter of Captain Levi Young and his wife, Anna. Captain Young retired from the military to a farm near the Connecticut border. When she grew up, Nancy assumed the accounting duties of the farm.

In 1827, at age 19, she fell ill with what at first was taken to be a cold, but probably was tuberculosis. She remained bedridden for a month, and then died on April 6 of "galloping consumption."

Prior to her death, Nancy's younger sister, Almira, fell ill with similar symptoms. Several other children also became sick.

While Almira was still alive, Captain Young had Nancy's CORPSE exhumed and burned on a pyre. The family members stood around it inhaling the smoke in the belief that it would cure those who were sick and would prevent the others from becoming sick.

Almira died on August 19, 1828, at age 17. Four other siblings also died of consumption: Olney, a son, on December 12, 1831, aged 29; Huldah, in August 1836, aged 23; Caleb, on May 8, 1843, aged 26; and Hiram, on February 17, 1854, aged 35. Two other sons and a daughter survived. See also NEW ENGLAND VAMPIRES.

FURTHER READING:
Bell, Michael E. *Food for the Dead: On the Trail of New England's Vampires.* New York: Carroll & Graf, 2001.
Rondina, Christopher. *Vampire Legends of Rhode Island.* North Attleborough, Mass.: Covered Bridge Press, 1997.

Youngson, Jeanne Keyes   American film producer, VAMPIRE researcher, author, and founder and president of the VAMPIRE EMPIRE, formerly known as the COUNT DRACULA FAN CLUB.

Jeanne Keyes Youngson was born in Syracuse, New York, and grew up in Sussex, New Jersey. She received her education at Franklin Junior College in Lugano, Switzerland, the Sorbonne in Paris, and New York University. She has taught extension courses in Cambridge and Oxford Universities in England.

In 1960 she married film producer Robert Youngson, who won two Academy Awards for *The World of Kids* and *This Mechanical Age.*

Jeanne Keyes Youngson among her vampire and monster museum collections (Photo by R. E. Guiley)

Youngson became interested in vampires in 1965, following a visit to Romania in which she learned about VLAD TEPES serving as an inspiration for the name of BRAM STOKER's fictional COUNT DRACULA. Stoker's novel had long fascinated Youngson, and she decided to form the Count Dracula Fan Club. The founding day was June 25, 1965; the club quickly attracted members. The club published two newsletters and an assortment of small books and pamphlets. Youngson established divisions of the club devoted to specialized interests about vampires, WERE-WOLVES, and horror characters and topics.

Robert Youngson, a diabetic, died unexpectedly in 1973 after suffering a diabetic coma. In 1974 Youngson moved to England and established a counterpart club headquarters, first in London and then in Cambridge. She divided her time between the United States and England. In 1984 she closed the English headquarters and returned to the United States to live. She resides in New York City, where she oversees the club's numerous activities and divisions. In 2000 the club name was changed to the Vampire Empire.

Youngson conducts research and assists research projects for books, films, and documentaries. She lectures and travels extensively.

FURTHER READING:
Guiley, Rosemary Ellen. *Vampires Among Us*. New York: Pocket Books, 1991.
Hillen, John Sean. *Digging for Dracula*. Dublin: Dracula Transylvania Club, 1997.
"The Vampire Empire." Available online. URL: http://www.benecke.com/vampire.html. Downloaded on August 1, 2003.

yuki-onna   In Japanese lore, a demon who appears as a maiden and whose VAMPIRE breath sucks the life force from her victims. *Yuki-onna* means "lady of the snow."

The *yuki-onna* appears as a beautiful maiden, dressed completely in white, whose breath is like frost. She also takes the form of white mist, which enables her to slip into homes via cracks and under doors. If seen, she may look like a white mist hovering over the body of her victim. She gives fatal kisses and breathes her killing mist into the victim.

The *yuki-onna* especially likes to attack travelers who are stuck in snowstorms. If a *yuki-onna* takes a liking to a man, she will become his wife, but he will always have the threat of death over him.

FURTHER READING:
Mack, Carol K., and Dinah Mack. *A Field Guide to Demons, Fairies, Fallen Angels, and Other Subversive Spirits*. New York: Henry Holt/Owl Books, 1998.

yuruga   In Prussian lore, a VAMPIRE who smells so bad it can be detected up to a mile away.

zoanthropy   See LYCANTHROPY.

Zugarramurdi witches (1610)   Witches in the Basque village of Zugarramurdi, some of whom were accused of vampiric behavior. The trials of the witches from June 10 to November 8, 1610, were an attempt by the Spanish Supreme Inquisition to stem public hysteria over witches and sorcerers. Six persons were executed by BURNING.

Zugarramurdi, a Navarre town on the borders of the Labour region, was steeped in superstition about witchcraft. Nearby was a large subterranean cave, cut through by a river called the Infernukeorreka, or "stream of Hell," where villagers believed witches gathered and practiced their abominations.

Inquisitor Don Juan Valle Alvarado spent several months gathering testimony, which cast suspicion of witchcraft crimes upon nearly 300 adults and also on some children. Testimony of wild diabolical activities was accepted without question. Alvarado determined that 40 of the suspects were guilty and had them arrested and taken to Logrono for trial before three judges.

According to the testimony given at the trials, the Zugarramurdi witches were organized in a hierarchy. At the top were senior sorcerers and witches, followed by sec-

ond-grade initiates who served as tutors of novices. First-grade initiates were responsible for making poisons and casting spells. Children were recruited. They all worshiped an ugly, gargoyle like devil.

The witches were accused of SHAPE-SHIFTING into animal forms; casting evil spells upon humans, animals, and crops; poisoning humans and animals; and vampirism and cannibalism.

They allegedly poisoned animals and murdered human beings by administering poisonous powder or OINTMENTS that caused people to become ill and die. Villagers claimed the witches stole children out of their beds at night, carried them off, and drank their BLOOD and ate them. Some cases of vampirism of adults were given at court.

Of the 40 accused witches, 18 confessed and begged for mercy. They were reconciled with the church. Six were burned at the stake. Five of the accused died during the trials; effigies of them were burned along with the six who were executed. The remaining 11 presumably were not convicted.

FURTHER READING:
Guiley, Rosemary Ellen. *The Encyclopedia of Witches and Witchcraft.* 2d ed. New York: Checkmark Books/Facts On File, 1999.

BIBLIOGRAPHY

Anderson, Robert G. *Faces, Forms, Films: The Artistry of Lon Chaney.* Cranbury, N.J.: A. S. Barnes, 1971.

Ashley, Leonard R. N. *The Complete Book of Vampires.* New York: Barricade Books, 1998.

Auerbach, Nina. *Our Vampires, Ourselves.* Chicago: University of Chicago Press, 1995.

Auerbach, Nina, and David J. Skal, eds. *Dracula.* New York: W. W. Norton, 1997.

Barber, Paul. *Vampires, Burial and Death: Folklore and Reality.* New Haven, Conn.: Yale University Press, 1988.

Baring-Gould, Sabine. *The Book of Werewolves.* London: Smith, Elder & Co., 1865.

Belford, Barbara. *Bram Stoker: A Biography of the Author of Dracula.* New York: Alfred A. Knopf, 1996.

Bell, Michael E. *Food for the Dead: On the Trail of New England's Vampires.* New York: Carroll & Graf, 2001.

Bettelheim, Bruno. *The Uses of Enchantment: The Meaning and Importance of Fairy Tales.* New York: Alfred A. Knopf, 1976.

Brejla, Terry. *The Devils of His Own Creation: The Life and Works of Richard Matheson.* Lincoln, Neb.: Universe.com/ Writer's Club Press, 2003.

Briggs, Katharine. *An Encyclopedia of Fairies.* New York: Pantheon Books, 1976.

Brite, Poppy Z. *Lost Souls.* New York: Asylum/Delacourte, 1992.

Brown, David E. *Vampiro: the Vampire Bat in Fact and Fantasy.* Silver City, N.M.: High-Lonesome Books, 1994.

Burton, Isabel, ed. *Captain Sir Richard F. Burton's King Vikram and the Vampire.* Rochester, Vt.: Park Street Press, 1992.

Calmet, Dom Augustin. *The Phantom World: Concerning Apparitions and Vampires.* Ware, England: Wordsmith Editions in association with the Folklore Society, 2001.

Carter, Margaret L., ed. *The Vampire in Literature: a critical bibliography.* Ann Arbor: UMI Research Press, 1989.

Child, Alice B., and Irvin L. Child. *Religion and Magic in the Life of Traditional Peoples.* Englewood Cliffs, N.J.: Prentice-Hall, 1993.

Clark, Jerome. *Encyclopedia of Strange and Unexplained Physical Phenomena.* Detroit: Gale Research, 1993.

Clark, Jerome. *Unexplained! 347 Sightings, Incredible Occurrences and Puzzling Physical Phenomena.* Detroit: Visible Ink, 1993.

Cluckhorn, Clyde. *Navajo Witchcraft.* Boston: Beacon Press, 1994.

Collins, Nancy A. *Sunglasses After Dark.* New York: New American Library, 1994.

———. *Midnight Blue: The Sonja Blue Collection.* Atlanta: White Wolf Publishing, 1995.

———. *A Dozen Black Roses.* Atlanta: White Wolf Publishing, 1997.

Colombo, John Robert. *Mysterious Canada: Strange Sights, Extraordinary Events, and Peculiar Places.* Toronto: Doubleday, 1988.

Copper, Basil. *The Vampire in Legend and Fact.* New York: Citadel Press, 1973.

Coppola, Francis Ford, and James V. Hart. *Bram Stoker's Dracula: The Film and the Legend.* New York: Newmarket Press, 1992.

Corrales, Scott. *Chupacabras and Other Mysteries.* Murfreesboro, Tenn.: Greenleaf Publications, 1997.

Cushing, Peter. *An Autobiography and Past Forgetting.* Midnight Marquee Press, 1999.

Daniels, Les. *Living in Fear: A History of Horror in the Mass Media.* New York: Charles Scribner's Sons, 1975.

David-Neel, Alexandra. *Magic and Mystery in Tibet.* New York: Dover Publications, 1971.

Deane, Hamilton, and John L. Balderston. *Dracula: The Vampire Play.* Garden City, N.Y.: Nelson Doubleday, 1971.

Del Vecchio, Deborah. *Peter Cushing: The Gentle Man of Horror and His 91 Films.* Jefferson, N.C.: McFarland, 1992.

Dresser, Norine. *American Vampires: Fans, Victims, Practitioners.* New York: W. W. Norton, 1989.

Dundes, Alan, ed. *The Vampire: A Casebook.* Madison: University of Wisconsin Press, 1998.

Elworthy, Frederick Thomas. *The Evil Eye: An Account of This Ancient and Widespread Superstition.* New York: OBC, 1989.

Evans-Pritchard, E. E. *Witchcraft, Oracles and Magic Among the Azande.* Oxford, U.K.: Oxford University Press, 1976.

Farson, Daniel. *The Man Who Wrote Dracula: A Biography of Bram Stoker.* London: Michael Joseph, 1975.

Feehan, Christine. *Dark Desire.* New York: Dorchester Publishing, 1999.

———. *Dark Prince.* New York: Dorchester Publishing, 1999.

———. *Dark Challenge.* New York: Dorchester Publishing, 2000.

———. *Dark Gold.* New York: Dorchester Publishing, 2000.

———. *Dark Magic.* New York: Dorchester Publishing, 2000.

———. *Dark Fire.* New York: Dorchester Publishing, 2001.

———. *Dark Guardian.* New York: Dorchester Publishing, 2002.

———. *Dark Legend.* New York: Dorchester Publishing, 2002.

———. *Dark Melody.* New York: Dorchester Publishing, 2003.

———. *Dark Symphony.* New York: Jove, 2003.

———. *Dark Destiny.* New York: Jove, 2004.

Fenton, M. Brock. *Bats* Rev. ed. New York: Checkmark Books/Facts On File, 2001.

Florescu, Radu R., and Raymond T. McNally. *Dracula: Prince of Many Faces: His Life and Times.* Boston: Little, Brown, 1989.

Fodor, Nandor. *On the Trail of the Poltergeist.* New York: Citadel Press, 1958.

———. *The Haunted Mind.* New York: Helix Press, 1959.

Fort, Charles. *The Complete Books of Charles Fort.* New York: Dover, 1974.

Fortune, Dion. *Psychic Self-Defence.* York Beach, Me.: Samuel Weiser, 1957. First published 1939.

Frayling, Christopher. *Vampyres: Lord Byron to Count Dracula.* London: Faber and Faber, 1991.

Frost, Brian J. *The Monster with a Thousand Faces: Guises of the Vampire in Myth and Literature.* Bowling Green, Ohio: Bowling Green State University Popular Press, 1989.

Garden, Nancy. *Vampires.* New York: Bantam Skylark, 1973.

Gerard, Emily de Laszkowski. *The Land Beyond the Forest: Facts, Figures and Fancies from Transylvania.* Edinburgh and London: William Blackwood and Sons, 1888.

Gladwell, Alicia, ed. *Blood and Roses: The Vampire in 19th Century Literature.* Rev. ed. Creation Books, 1999.

Glut, Donald. *True Vampires of History.* New York: HC Publishers, 1971.

———. *The Dracula Book.* Metuchen, N.J.: Scarecrow Press, 1975.

Godfrey, Linda S. *The Beast of Bray Road: Tailing Wisconsin's Werewolf.* Black Earth, Wisc.: Prairie Oak Press, 2003.

Gross, Edward, and Marc Shapiro. *The Vampire Interview Book: Conversations with the Undead.* New York: Image Publishing, 1991.

Guazzo, Francesco-Maria. *Compendium Maleficarum.* Secaucus, N.J.: University Books, 1974.

Guiley, Rosemary Ellen. *Harper's Encyclopedia of Mystical and Paranormal Experience.* San Francisco: Harper San Francisco, 1991.

———. *Moonscapes: A Celebration of Lunar Astronomy, Magic, Legend and Lore.* Englewood Cliffs, N.J.: Prentice-Hall, 1991.

———. *Vampires Among Us.* New York: Pocket Books, 1991.

———. *Dreamwork for the Soul: A Spiritual Guide to Dream Interpretation.* New York: Berkley Books, 1998.

———. *The Encyclopedia of Witches and Witchcraft.* 2d ed. New York: Facts On File, 1999.

———. *The Encyclopedia of Ghosts and Spirits.* 2d ed. New York: Facts On File, 2000.

———. "Vampires from Outer Space: An Exploration of Common Ground Shared by Vampires and Extraterrestrials Concerning Death and Immortality." Paper presented at the "Communication with the Beyond" colloquium in Sinaia, Romania, May 10–12, 2002, sponsored by the Transylvanian Society of Dracula, Bucharest; International Society for the Study of Ghosts and Apparitions, New York; and Ghost Club, London.

———. *The Encyclopedia of Angels.* 2d ed. New York: Facts On File, 2003.

Guiley, Rosemary Ellen, with J. B. Macabre. *The Complete Vampire Companion.* New York: Macmillan, 1994.

Guinn, Jeff, with Andy Grieser. *Something in the Blood: The Underground of Today's Vampires.* Arlington, Texas: Summit Publishing, 1996.

Haining, Peter. *The Dracula Centenary Book.* London: Souvenir Press, 1987.

———. *The Dracula Scrapbook.* London: Chancellor Press, 1992.

Haining, Peter and Peter Tremayne. *The Undead: The Legend of Bram Stoker and Dracula.* London: Constable, 1997.

Hamel, Frank. *Human Animals: Werewolves and Other Transformations.* London: William Rider and Son, 1915.

Hamilton, Laurell K. *Guilty Pleasures.* New York: Ace Books, 1993.

———. *The Laughing Corpse.* New York: Ace Books, 1994.

———. *Circus of the Damned.* New York: Ace Books, 1995.

———. *The Lunatic Café.* New York: Ace Books, 1996.

———. *Bloody Bones.* New York: Ace Books, 1996.

———. *The Killing Dance.* New York: Ace Books, 1997.

———. *Burnt Offerings.* New York: Ace Books, 1998.

————. *Blue Moon.* New York: Ace Books, 1998.

————. *Obsidian Butterfly.* New York: Berkley Books, 2000.

————. *Narcissus in Chains.* New York: Berkley Books, 2001.

————. *Cerulean Sins.* New York: Berkley Books, 2003.

Herbert, W. V. *By-Paths in the Balkans.* London: Chapman & Hall, 1906.

Heuvelmans, Bernard. *On the Track of Unknown Animals.* London: Kegan Paul, 1995.

Hill, Douglas. *The History of Ghosts, Vampires and Werewolves.* New York: Harper & Row, 1973.

Hillen, John Sean. *Digging for Dracula.* Dublin: Dracula Transylvania Club, 1997.

Hillyer, Vincent. *Vampires.* Los Banos, Calif.: Loose Change Publications, 1988.

Holder, Nancy, Jeff Mariotte and Maryelizabeth Hart. *Buffy the Vampire Slayer: The Watcher's Guide,* vol. 2. New York: Pocket Books, 2000.

Holte, James Craig, ed. *The Fantastic Vampire: Studies in the Children of the Night, Selected Essays from the Eighteenth International Conference on the Fantastic in the Arts.* Westport, Conn.: Greenwood Press, 2002.

Howe, Deborah, and James Howe. *Bunnicula: A Rabbit-Tale of Mystery.* New York: Atheneum, 1979.

Hoyt, Olga. *Lust for Blood: The Consuming Story of Vampires.* Briarcliff Manor, N.Y.: Stein and Day, 1984.

Hufford, David J. *The Terror That Comes in the Night: An Experience-Centered Study of Supernatural Assault Traditions.* Philadelphia: University of Pennsylvania Press, 1982.

Katzeff, Paul. *Full Moons.* Secaucus, N.J.: Citadel Press, 1981.

Kaveney, Roz, ed. *Reading the Vampire Slayer: An Unofficial Critical Companion to* Buffy *and* Angel. London: Tauris Parke Paperbacks, 2002.

Keel, John A. *The Mothman Prophecies.* New York: E. P. Dutton, 1975.

————. *Strange Mutants.* New York: Global Communications, 1984.

Kenyon, Sherrilyn. *Born of the Night.* New York: Pinnacle, 1996.

————. *Fantasy Lover.* New York: St. Martin's Press, 2002.

————. *Night Pleasures.* New York: St. Martin's Press, 2002.

————. *Dance with the Devil.* New York: St. Martin's Press, 2003.

————. *Night Embrace.* New York: St. Martin's Press, 2003.

————. *Kiss of the Night.* New York: St. Martin's Press, 2004.

————. *Night Play.* New York: St. Martin's Press, 2004.

King, Stephen. *'Salem's Lot.* New York: Doubleday, 1975.

————. *Danse Macabre.* New York: Dodd, Mead, 1983.

Kluckhorn, Clyde. *Navaho Witchcraft.* Cambridge, Mass.: Harvard University, 1944.

Krinard, Susan. *Prince of Wolves.* New York: Bantam, 1994.

————. *Prince of Dreams.* New York: Bantam, 1995.

————. *Prince of Shadows.* New York: Bantam, 1996.

————. *Touch of the Wolf.* New York: Bantam, 1999.

————. *Once a Wolf.* New York: Bantam, 2000.

————. *Secret of the Wolf.* New York: Berkley, 2001.

————. *The Forest Lord.* New York: Berkley, 2002.

————. *To Catch a Wolf.* New York: Berkley, 2003.

Lang, Andrew, ed. *The Green Fairy Book.* New York: Dover Publications, 1965.

————. *The Yellow Fairy Book.* New York: Dover Publications, 1966.

Lapin, Daniel. *The Vampire, Dracula and Incest.* San Francisco: Gargoyle Publishers, 1995.

Leach, Maria, ed., and Jerome Fried, assoc. ed. *Funk & Wagnalls Standard Dictionary of Folklore, Mythology, and Legend.* San Francisco: Harper & Row, 1984.

Leatherdale, Clive. *Dracula: The Novel and the Legend.* Wellingborough, Northamptonshire, U.K.: Aquarian Press, 1985.

Leatherdale, Clive. *The Origins of Dracula.* London: William Kimber, 1987.

Leatherdale, Clive, ed. *Bram Stoker's Dracula Unearthed.* Weston-on-Sea, Essex, England: Desert Island Books, 1998.

Lecouteaux, Claude. *Witches, Werewolves and Fairies: Shapeshifters and Astral Doubles in the Middle Ages.* Rochester, Vt.: Inner Traditions, 2003.

Lee, Christopher. *Tall, Dark and Gruesome: An Autobiography.* London: W. H. Allen, 1977. Rev. ed. London: Victor Gollancz, 1997.

————. *Lord of Misrule: The Autobiography of Christopher Lee.* London: Orion Books, 2003.

Lennig, Arthur. *The Count: The Life and Films of Bela "Dracula" Lugosi.* New York: Putnam's, 1974.

Lodge, Oliver. *Peasant Life in Jugoslavia.* London: Seely, Service, n.d.

London, Sondra. *True Vampires: Blood-Sucking Killers Past and Present.* Los Angeles: Feral House, 2004.

Ludlam, Harry. *A Biography of Dracula: True Life Story of Bram Stoker.* London: W. Foulsham, 1962.

Lumley, Brian, and Stanley Wiater, eds. *The Brian Lumley Companion.* New York: TOR Books, 2002.

MacKenzie, Andrew. *Dracula Country: Travels and Folk Beliefs in Romania.* London: Arthur Barker, 1977.

Mack, Carol K., and Dinah Mack. *A Field Guide to Demons, Fairies, Fallen Angels, and Other Subversive Spirits.* New York: Henry Holt/Owl Books, 1998.

Maltin, Leonard. *Leonard Maltin's Movie Encyclopedia.* New York: Signet, 1994.

Marrero, Robert. *Horrors of Hammer.* Key West, Florida: RGM Productions, 1984.

Masters, Anthony. *The Natural History of the Vampire.* New York: G. P. Putnam's, 1972.

Matheson, Richard. *I Am Legend.* New York: TOR Books, 1997.

McEwan, Graham. *Mystery Animals of Britain and Ireland.* London: Hale, 1986.

McNally, Raymond T. *Dracula Was a Woman: In Search of the Blood Countess of Transylvania.* New York: McGraw-Hill, 1983.

————. *A Clutch of Vampires.* New York: Bell Publishing, 1984.

McNally, Raymond T., and Radu Florescu. *In Search of Dracula: A True History of Dracula and Vampire Legends.* Greenwich, Conn.: New York Graphic Society, 1972.

———. *Dracula: A Biography of Vlad the Impaler 1431–1476.* New York: Hawthorn Books, 1973.

Melton, J. Gordon. *The Vampire Gallery: Who's Who of the Undead.* Detroit: Visible Ink Press/Gale Research, 1998.

———. *The Vampire Book: The Encyclopedia of the Undead.* Rev. ed. Detroit: Visible Ink Press/Gale Research, 1999.

Mercatante, Anthony S. *Encyclopedia of World Mythology and Legend.* Frenchs Forest, Australia: Child & Associates Publishing, 1988.

Michelet, Jules. *Satanism and Witchcraft.* Secaucus, N.J.: Citadel Press, 1939.

Middleton, John, ed. *Magic, Witchcraft, and Curing.* Austin: University of Texas Press, 1967.

Miller, Elizabeth. *Reflections on Dracula: Ten Essays.* White Rock, B.C.: Transylvania Press, Inc., 1997.

———, ed. *Dracula: The Shade and the Shadow.* Westcliff-on-Sea, Essex, England: Desert Island Books, 1998.

———. *Dracula: Sense & Nonsense.* Westcliff-on-Sea, England: Desert Island Books, 2000.

———. *Dracula.* New York: Parkstone Press, 2001.

Miller, Mark A., and Peter Cushing and Christopher Lee. *Christopher Lee and Peter Cushing and Horror Cinema: A Filmography of Their 22 Collaborations.* Jefferson, N.C.: McFarland, 1994.

Monter, E. William. *Witchcraft in France and Switzerland.* New York: Cornell University Press, 1976.

Moore, Steve, ed. *Fortean Studies,* vol. 5. London: John Brown Publishing, 1998.

Noll, Richard. *Vampires, Werewolves and Demons: Twentieth Century Reports in the Psychiatric Literature.* New York: Brunner/Mazel, 1992.

Nutini, Hugo G., and John M. Roberts. *Bloodsucking Witchcraft: An Epistemological Study of Anthropomorphic Supernaturalism in Rural Tlaxcala.* Tucson, Ariz.: University of Tucson Press, 1993.

O'Donnell, Elliott. *Werewolves.* New York: Longvue Press, 1965.

———. *Great Ghost Stories.* London: Foulsham & Co., 1983.

Oinas, Felix J. *Essays on Russian Folklore and Mythology.* Columbus, Ohio: Slavica Publishers, 1984.

Opie, Iona, and Moira Tatem. *A Dictionary of Superstitions.* Oxford, U.K.: Oxford University Press, 1989.

Otten, Charlotte F., ed. *A Lycanthrophy Reader: Werewolves in Western Culture.* New York: Dorset Press, 1989.

Page, Carol. *Bloodlust: Conversations with Real Vampires.* New York: HarperCollins, 1991.

Parrinder, Geoffrey. *Witchcraft European & African.* London: Faber and Faber, 1958.

Pascu, Stefan. *A History of Transylvania.* New York: Dorset Press, 1990.

Perkowski, Jan L. *The Darkling: A Treatise on Slavic Vampirism.* Columbus, Ohio: Slavica Publishers, 1989.

Perkowski, Jan L., ed. *The Vampire of the Slavs.* Cambridge, Mass.: Slavica Publishers, 1976.

Philostratus. *The Life of Apollonius of Tyana.* F. C. Conybeare, trans. London: Heinemann, 1912.

Pocs, Eva. *Between the Living and the Dead.* Szilvia Redey and Michael Webb, trans. Budapest: Central European University Press, 1999.

Pratt, Bob. *UFO Danger Zone: Terror and Death in Brazil—Where Next?* Madison, Wisc.: Horus House Press, 1996.

Radford, E., and M. A. Radford. *Encylopedia of Superstitions.* Edited and revised by Christina Hole. London: Book Club Associates, 1974.

Ramsland, Katherine. *Prism of the Night: A Biography of Anne Rice.* New York: Dutton, 1991.

———. *The Vampire Companion: The Official Guide to Anne Rice's The Vampire Chronicles.* New York: Ballantine Books, 1993.

———. *Piercing the Darkness: Undercover with Vampires in America Today.* New York: HarperPrism/HarperCollins, 1998.

———. *The Science of Vampires.* New York: Berkeley Boulevard Books, 2002.

Ravensdale, Tom, and James Morgan. *The Psychology of Witchcraft.* New York: Arco, 1974.

Rémy, Nicolas. *Demonolatry.* Secaucus, N.J.: University Books, 1974.

Rice, Anne. *Interview with the Vampire.* New York: Alfred A. Knopf, 1976.

———. *The Vampire Lestat.* New York: Alfred A. Knopf, 1985.

———. *The Queen of the Damned.* New York: Alfred A. Knopf, 1988.

———. *The Mummy or Ramses the Damned.* New York: Alfred A. Knopf, 1989.

———. *The Witching Hour.* New York: Alfred A. Knopf, 1990.

———. *The Tale of the Body Thief.* New York: Alfred A. Knopf, 1992.

———. *Lasher.* New York: Alfred A. Knopf, 1993.

———. *Taltos.* New York: Alfred A. Knopf, 1994.

———. *Memnoch the Devil.* New York: Alfred A. Knopf, 1995.

———. *Servant of the Bones.* New York: Alfred A. Knopf, 1996.

———. *Violin.* New York: Alfred A. Knopf, 1997.

———. *Armand.* New York: Alfred A. Knopf, 1998.

———. *Pandora.* New York: Alfred A. Knopf, 1998.

———. *Vittorio the Vampire.* New York: Alfred A. Knopf, 1999.

———. *Merrick.* New York: Alfred A. Knopf, 2000.

———. *Blood and Gold.* New York: Alfred A. Knopf, 2001.

———. *Blackwood Farm.* New York: Alfred A. Knopf, 2002.

———. *The Master of Rampling Gate.* New York: Alfred A. Knopf, 2002.

———. *Blood Canticle.* New York: Alfred A. Knopf, 2003.

Richardson, Alan. *Priestess: The Life and Magic of Dion Fortune.* Wellingborough, England: Aquarian Press, 1987.

Riley, Michael. *Conversations with Anne Rice: an Intimate, Enlightening Portrait of Her Life and Work.* New York: Ballantine Books, 1996.

Riley, Philip J. *London After Midnight.* New York: Cornwall Books, 1985.

Robbins, Rossell Hope. *The Encyclopedia of Witchcraft & Demonology.* New York: Bonanza Books, 1981.

Ronay, Gabriel. *The Truth About Dracula*. Briarcliff Manor, N.Y.: Stein and Day, 1972. First published 1972 as *The Dracula Myth*.

Rondina, Christopher. *Vampire Legends of Rhode Island*. North Attleborough, Mass.: Covered Bridge Press, 1997.

Roth, Phyllis A. *Bram Stoker*. Boston: Twayne, 1982.

Saberhagen, Fred. *The Dracula Tape*. New York: TOR Books, 1975.

———. *The Holmes-Dracula File*. New York: TOR Books, 1978.

———. *An Old Friend of the Family*. New York: TOR Books, 1979.

———. *Thorn*. New York: TOR Books, 1980.

———. *Dominion*. New York: TOR Books, 1982.

———. *A Matter of Taste*. New York: TOR Books, 1990.

———. *A Question of Time*. New York: TOR Books, 1992.

———. *Seance for a Vampire*. New York: TOR Books, 1994.

———. *A Sharpness on the Neck*. New York: TOR Books, 1996.

———. *A Coldness in the Blood*. New York: TOR Books, 2002.

Saletore, R. N. *Indian Witchcraft: A Study in Indian Occultism*. Atlantic Highlands, N.J.: Humanities Press, 1981.

Scot, Reginald. *The Discoverie of Witchcraft*. Yorkshire, England: E. P. Publishing, 1973.

Scott, Kathryn Leigh. *35th Anniversary Dark Shadows Memories*. Los Angeles: Pomegranate Press, 2001.

Scott, Kathryn Leigh, ed. *The Dark Shadows Companion 25th Anniversary Collection*. Los Angeles: Pomegranate Press, 1990.

Scott, Kathryn Leigh, and Jim Pierson, eds. *Dark Shadows Almanac: 30th Anniversary Tribute*. Los Angeles: Pomegranate Press, 1995.

———. *Dark Shadows Almanac Millennium Edition*. Los Angeles: Pomegranate Press, 2000.

Seligmann, Kurt. *The Mirror of Magic: A History of Magic in the Western World*. New York: Pantheon Books, 1948.

Senf, Carol A. *The Vampire in 19th Century English Literature*. Bowling Green, Ohio: Bowling Green State University Popular Press, 1988.

Senn, Harry A. *Were-Wolf and Vampire in Romania*. New York: Columbia University Press, 1982.

Shepard, Leslie, and Albert Power, eds. *Dracula: Celebrating 100 Years*. Dublin: Mentor Press, 1997.

Sidky, H. *Witchcraft, Lycanthropy, Drugs and Disease: An Anthropological Study of the European Witch-Hunts*. New York: Peter Lang, 1997.

Silver, Alain, and James Ursini. *The Vampire Film: From Nosferatu* to *Interview with the Vampire*. 3d ed. New York: Limelight Editions, 1997.

Skal, David J. *Hollywood Gothic: The Tangled Web of* Dracula *from Novel to Stage to Screen*. New York: W. W. Norton, 1990.

Skal, David J., ed. *Vampires: Encounters With the Undead*. New York: Black Dog & Leventhal, 2001.

Skal, David J., and Elias Savada. *Dark Carnival: The Secret World of Tod Browning, Hollywood's Master of the Macabre*. New York: Anchor/Doubleday, 1995.

Skipp, John, and Craig Spector. *Fright Night*. TOR Books, 1985.

Slemen, Thomas. *Strange But True: Mysterious and Bizarre People*. New York: Barnes & Noble Books, 1998.

South, James B., ed. *Buffy the Vampire Slayer and Philosophy: Fear and Trembling in Sunnydale*. Chicago: Open Court Publishing, 2003.

Spence, Lewis. *Legends and Romances of Brittany*. Mineola, N.Y.: Dover Publications, 1997.

Steiger, Brad. *The Werewolf Book: The Encyclopedia of Shape-Shifting Beings*. Detroit: Visible Ink Press/Gale Research, 1999.

Stoker, Bram. *Dracula*. New York: Grosset & Dunlap, 1931.

Streiber, Whitley. *The Wolfen*. New York: William Morrow, 1978.

———. *The Hunger*. New York: William Morrow, 1981.

Stritto, Frank Dello, and Andi Brooks. *Vampire Over London: Bela Lugosi in Britain*. Los Angeles: Cult Movies Press, 2001.

Stuart, Roxana. *Stage Blood: Vampires of the 19th-Century Stage*. Bowling Green, Ohio: Bowling Green State University Popular Press, 1994.

Stuart-Glennie, John S. *The Women of Turkey and their Folklore*. London: David Nutt, 1890.

Stutley, Margaret. *Ancient Indian Magic and Folklore: An Introduction*. Boulder, Colo.: Great Eastern, 1980.

Summers, Montague. *The Vampire: His Kith and Kin*. New Hyde Park, N.Y.: University Books, 1960. First published 1928.

———. *The Vampire in Europe*. New York: E. P. Dutton, 1929.

———. *The Werewolf*. New York: Bell Publishing, 1966.

Symonds, John, and Kenneth Grant, eds. *The Confessions of Aleister Crowley, an Autobiography*. London: Routledge & Kegan Paul, 1979.

Treptow, Kurt W. *Vlad III Dracula: The Life and Times of the Historical Dracula*. Oxford, U.K.: The Center for Romanian Studies, 2000.

Trigg, Elwood B. *Gypsy Demons & Divinities*. Secaucus, N.J.: Citadel Press, 1973.

Twitchell, James B. *The Living Dead: A Study of the Vampire in Romantic Literature*. Durham, N.C.: Duke University Press, 1981.

Underwood, Peter. *The Vampire's Bedside Companion*. London: Leslie Frewin, 1975.

Vallée, Jacques. *Passport to Magonia: From Folklore to Flying Saucers*. Chicago: Henry Regnery, 1969.

———. *Confrontations: A Scientist's Search for Alien Contact*. New York: Ballantine Books, 1990.

Volta, Ornella. *The Vampire*. London: Tandem, 1965.

Waller, Gregory A. *The Living and the Undead*. Urbana: University of Illinois Press, 1986.

Waring, Philippa. *A Dictionary of Omens and Superstitions*. London: BCA, 1995.

Watson, C. W., and Roy Ellen, eds. *Understanding Witchcraft and Sorcery in Southeast Asia*. Honolulu: University of Hawaii Press, 1993.

Wilcox, Rhonda V., and David Lavery, eds. *Fighting the Forces: What's at Stake in* Buffy the Vampire Slayer. Lanham, Md.: Rowman and Littlefield, 2002.

Wolf, Leonard. *A Dream of Dracula: In Search of the Living Dead.* Boston: Little, Brown, 1972.

———. *The Annotated Dracula.* New York: Clarkson N. Potter, 1975.

———. *Dracula: The Connoisseur's Guide.* New York: Broadway Books, 1997.

Wright, Dudley. *Vampires and Vampirism.* London: William Rider and Son, 1914.

Yarbro, Chelsea Quinn. *Hotel Transylvania.* New York: St. Martin's Press, 1978.

———. *The Palace.* New York: St. Martin's Press, 1978.

———. *Blood Games.* New York: St. Martin's Press, 1979.

———. *Path of the Eclipse.* New York: St. Martin's Press, 1981.

———. *Tempting Fate.* New York: St. Martin's Press, 1982.

———. *The St. Germain Chronicles.* New York: Pocket Books, 1983.

———. *A Flame in Byzantium.* New York: TOR Books, 1987.

———. *Crusader's Torch.* New York: TOR Books, 1988.

———. *A Candle for D'Artagnan.* New York: TOR Books, 1989.

———. *Out of the House of Life.* New York: Orb/TOR Books, 1990.

———. *Better in the Dark.* New York: TOR Books, 1993.

———. *Darker Jewels.* New York: TOR Books, 1993.

———. *Mansions of Darkness.* New York: TOR Books, 1996.

———. *Writ in Blood.* New York: TOR Books, 1997.

———. *Blood Roses.* New York: TOR Books, 1998.

———. *Communion Blood.* New York: TOR Books, 1999.

———. *Night Blooming.* New York: Warner Aspect, 2002.

———. *Midnight Harvest.* New York: Warner Aspect, 2003.

Yeffeth, Glenn, ed. *Seven Seasons of* Buffy. Dallas, Tex.: Benbella Books, 2003.

Youngson, Jeanne Keyes. *The Bizarre World of Vampires.* New York: Count Dracula Fan Club/Adams Press, 1996.

INDEX

Lumley, Brian, **189–91**
Lupercalia, **191**
Lust for a Vampire, 54, 151
lycanthropy, 26, 135, 140, 174, 183, **191–92**
Lycaon, **192–93**

M

Magic and Mystery in Tibet, 276
Magnus, Olaus, 183, **195–96**
Malleus Maleficarum, 259
Manor of the Devil, The. See Devil's Manor, The
Maréchal de Retz. *See* Gilles de Laval
Mark of the Vampire, 185, **196**
Marusia, **196–97**
Masquerade, The, 131–32
Mather, Increase, 259
Mathers, Samuel Liddell MacGregor, 126, **197–98**, 278
Matheson, Richard Burton, 29, **198–99**
McNally, Raymond T., 57, 60, 156, **199**
Melrose Abbey Vampire, **199–200**
Memnoch the Devil, 200, 244
Mercure Galent, 285–86
Merionethshire Werewolf, **200–201**
Metamorphoses, 192
metamorphosis. *See* shape-shifting
Miller, Elizabeth, **201–2**
mills, **202**
mirrors, 104, **202–3**
mmbyu, **203**
moon, **203–6**
mora, **206**
More, Henry, 91
Morgan, James, 234
moroi, **206–7**
Morte Darthur, Le, 7
moth. *See* butterfly
Mothman, **207–8**
mullo, **208–9**
Munsters, The, **209–10**
Murnau, F. W., **210**, 256–57
Music of the Night, The, 64
mwere, **210**
Myiciura, Demitrious, **210–11**
Myslata of Blau, **211**

N

nachzehrer, **213**
nagasjatingarong, **213**
Native American lore, 35, 315, 324
    Cherokee, 163
    Inuit, 2, 235
    Maya, 27
    Navajo, 260–61
    Tukano, 285
neamma-parusha, **213**
necrophagia, 68
necrophilia, 68
necrosadism, 68
nelapsi, **213–14**
New England Vampires, **214**
newlyweds, **214**
Night of Dark Shadows, 99–100
Noll, Richard, 68
nosferatu, **214–15**
Nosferatu (1922), 32, 214, **215–17**, 238–39, 252–53, 254–55, 256–57
Nosferatu (1979), 138, 214, 217, 239, 255
nuckelavee, **217**

O

obayifo (obayifu), **219**
oborot, **219**
obour. See krvopijac
obur, **219**
O'Donnell, Elliott, **219–21**, 317
ogoljen, **221**
ointments, **221**
Old Hag, 34, **221–23**
opji, **223**
Ornias, **223–24**
otgiruru, **224**
overlooking. *See* evil eye
Ovid, 192–93
owenga, **224**

P

Padararu, Nicolae, 284
palis, **225**
Paole, Arnod (Arnold), **225–26**
Parasite, The, **226**
pelesit, **226**
Pentsch Vampire. *See* Cuntius, Johannes

Perkowski, Jan L. *See The Vampire of the Slavs*
Peucer, Casper, 183
Phantom World, The, 51–52
phi phu, **226–27**
pigs, **227**
pijawica, **227**
pisacra, **227**
Pitt, Ingrid, **227–28**
Plogojowitz, Peter, **228–29**
Pniewo Vampire, **229**
Polidori, John George, 185, **229–30**
Poligyny Werewolves, **230–31**
poltergeist disturbances, 91, 154
    vampires and, 172–73, 276–78, 287–88
polong, **231**
pontianak, **231**
porphyria, **231**
Port Charles, **231–32**
Portugal Vampire, **232**
Prest, Thomas Prescott, 305
pricolici, **232**
protection against vampires, 27, 48–50, 68, 80, 89, 124, 133, 138, 142, 163, 186, 187, **232–33**, 239–40, 249, 253, 255–56, 262–63, 272–73, 282, 323–24
pseudo-vampirism, 13
psychic attack, 125–26, **233–34**
Psychic Self-Defence, 125–26
psychic vampirism, 12–13, 126, 290. *See also* psychic attack

Q

Qisaruatsiaq, **235**
Quarry, Robert, **235**
quaxates, **235**
Quebec Werewolf, **235–36**
Queen of the Damned, The, 236, 244

R

rain, **237**
Rakovic, Milos, **237**
raksasa. *See* rakshasa
rakshasa, **237–38**
ramanga, **238**
Ransom, Frederick, **238**
rats, **238–39**